Sir Martin Gilbert.

From his private collection

SIR HORACE RUMBOLD

Winston S. Churchill, Volume III, 1914–1916
  Main and document volumes
The Appeasers (with Richard Gott)
The European Powers 1900–1945
The Roots of Appeasement
Recent History Atlas, 1860–1960
British History Atlas
American History Atlas
Jewish History Atlas
First World War Atlas
Russian History Atlas

Editions of documents

Britain and Germany Between the Wars
Plough My Own Furrow, the Life of Lord Allen of Hurtwood
Servant of India: Diaries of the Viceroy's Private Secretary 1905–1910
Churchill (Spectrum Books)
Lloyd George (Spectrum Books)

For young readers

Winston Churchill (Clarendon Biography)
Winston Churchill (Jackdaw)
The Coming of War in 1939 (Jackdaw)
The Second World War

Editor
A Century of Conflict: Essays for A. J. P. Taylor

1   Sir Horace Rumbold in 1923.

Sir Horace Rumbold

Portrait of a Diplomat

1869–1941

by

Martin Gilbert

HEINEMANN : LONDON

William Heinemann Ltd
15 Queen St, Mayfair, London W1X 8BE

LONDON MELBOURNE TORONTO
JOHANNESBURG AUCKLAND

First published 1973
© Martin Gilbert 1973
434 29197 8

Printed and bound in Great Britain by
Richard Clay (The Chaucer Press) Ltd
Bungay, Suffolk

Contents

List of Photographs

Frontispiece

1 Sir Horace Rumbold when Ambassador to Berlin, 1928–33.

Section One

2 Rumbold with his father, Athens, 1887.

3 Rumbold in Cairo, 1900.

4 Rumbold's father and stepmother, Vienna, 1900.

5 Newspaper photograph of Rumbold and his bride, London, 1905.

6 Visit to a Shinto priest, Tokyo.

7 Rumbold and his family in Japan, 1912.

8 Rumbold's brother William.

9 Nevile Henderson, while at the Tokyo Embassy.

10 Facsimile of Rumbold's handwriting.

11 Facsimile of Rumbold's father's handwriting.

12 Rumbold's father on his 82nd birthday.

Section Two

13 Rumbold's son Tony in Berne.

14 The British Embassy, Berne, 1917.

List of Maps

Preface

Horace Rumbold entered the diplomatic service in 1891 and remained in it for more than forty years, until 1933. He served his apprenticeship during the last decade of Queen Victoria's reign, in Egypt, Spain and Austria-Hungary. On the eve of the First World War, in the absence of the British Ambassador, he was Chargé d'Affaires in Berlin, and was in a position of responsibility during the immediate crisis preceding the outbreak of war. During the war itself, while he was British Minister to Switzerland, he was involved not only in diplomacy but also in espionage and intrigue, and in the discussions for a negotiated peace with both Austria-Hungary and Turkey. He was British Minister in Warsaw in August 1920, when the Bolshevik army approached the city, determined to crush the newly independent Polish state. He was senior Allied High Commissioner in Constantinople during the Chanak crisis of 1922, and Ambassador to Germany when Hitler came to power in 1933. During the six years after his retirement he watched in Europe the realization of his fears and forecasts. In 1936 he served on the Royal Commission of Inquiry in Palestine, which recommended two separate states, one Arab, one Jewish.

Rumbold spent most of his life abroad. He had no patron among English politicians, and no friend in the Foreign Office to give him the postings he wanted. He advanced his career by his own efforts. Politically he was a Tory. But he acted abroad according to his day-by-day interpretation of events. He had strong prejudices, but they did not distort his professional advice. He never sought to curry favour with the Foreign Secretaries who were his masters. He spoke his mind without deceit, and took the initiative without hesitation when he felt action was needed.

Throughout his life, Rumbold's private correspondence was marked by caustic references to the foreigners with whom he had to deal. No nation escaped his scathing comments, or could compare, in his view, with his fellow-countrymen. 'An Englishman always has a better sense of fair play than a foreigner', he wrote. 'We are the linch-pin of the world's political structure'. In his work he was meticulous; his despatches were well-argued and informative. His powers of work were formidable. He was often involved in events of great tension and uncertainty. Writing to a friend while at Warsaw, he described himself as 'the stormy petrel of the diplomatic service'. In times of crisis he could not be ruffled or deflected from what he believed to be the correct course.

To look at, Rumbold gave many people the impression of blandness, even stupidity. But his intelligence was obvious from the advice which he gave, and in the numerous impressive reports which he sent to London. Writing about him in 1944, Harold Nicolson, who had served under him in Berlin, described the attributes which had struck him most:

His greatest diplomatic quality (apart from patience) was the gift of discernment. He was never a garrulous man nor did he seek to embody his conclusions in epigrams which might be repeated and do harm. He would listen unimpressed and unresponsive to the paradoxes of others, and there would be times when some brilliant conversationalist would pause in his discourse, wondering whether the Ambassador had really understood. Sir Horace always understood: he understood, not merely what was being said, and why it was being said, but exactly what relation even the most gifted sentence bore to reality. . . .

Rumbold's extreme value as an Ambassador and negotiator was based upon his utter reliability. The Government at home knew that in him they possessed an agent who would always accurately interpret instructions, or who, if he disagreed with their policy, would say so with moderation and good sense. The Governments to which he was accredited became aware that here was a man without prejudice or vanity, a man of complete integrity, a man whom they could trust to understand and report their point of view, a man whose every word was riveted in concrete.

Acknowledgements

In telling Sir Horace Rumbold's story I have drawn principally on two sets of archival sources, his own private collection of letters and documents, and the Foreign Office records, which contain the letters and telegrams which he sent to London between his appointment to Munich as Chargé d'Affaires in 1909 and his retirement from Berlin in 1933. I have supplemented these two sources with material from several private archives, and with discussions and correspondence with those who knew him, or served under him.

Many people have contributed generously to the content of this volume. I am grateful above all to Sir Anthony Rumbold, who put his family's archive at my disposal, answered my questions about his father's career, and gave me many personal recollections; and to Mrs Constantia Farmar, who gave me the benefit of many memories of her father, and of access to her mother's letters, and to her family photograph albums.

During the ten years in which I have been collecting material for this biography I received recollections and information from many of Rumbold's colleagues and contemporaries. I am particularly grateful to: Sir James Bowker; the late Timothy Breen; the Hon. Herbert Brooks; Victor Cavendish-Bentinck; the late Philip Conwell-Evans; Eliahu Elath; André François-Poncet; Sir John Hathorn Hall; Group-Captain Justin Herring; Joshua Iusman; Arthur Lourie; Sir Henry Mack; General Sir James Marshall-Cornwall; Sir John Martin; René Massigli; the late Sir Basil Newton; the late Sir Harold Nicolson; the late Sir Lancelot Oliphant; Joseph L. Reading; Lady Ryan; Douglas Reed; Lady Guy Salisbury-Jones; the late Frank Savery; Lord Strang; Christopher Sykes; Colonel Peter Thorne; and the late Alexander Wirth.

The principal archives on which I have drawn, other than those of Horace Rumbold himself and of the Foreign Office, were: the Churchill papers (private possession); the Cromer papers (Public Record Office); Geoffrey Dawson papers (letter quoted on p. 396, transcript provided by the late Sir Evelyn Wrench); the de Bunsen papers (private possession); the Farmar papers (private possession); the Halifax papers (Public Record

Office); the Hankey papers (Churchill College, Cambridge); the Nevile Henderson papers (Public Record Office); the Lothian papers (Scottish Record Office); the Sir John Martin papers (private possession); the Newton papers (private possession); the Harold Nicolson papers (private possession); the Oliphant papers (Public Record Office); the Weizmann papers (Weizmann archive), and the Henry Wilson papers (private possession). I have listed the archival sources in the appendix at the end of the volume; all other quotations come from the Rumbold papers.

For each person mentioned in the volume, I have included a biographical note. These notes appear on the first occasion a person is mentioned. Many individuals and institutions have given me access to material in their possession, which has enabled me to complete these notes. I should like to thank: Dr Beckmann, Geheimes Staatsarchiv (Preussischer Kulturbesitz), Berlin Dahlem; Timothy J. Benbow, Editor, Crockford's Clerical Dictionary; F. Birrer, Cultural and Information Section, Swiss Embassy, London; Dr Richard Blaas, Director des Haus-, Hof-, und Staatsarchivs, Vienna; W. G. Bridger, Superintendent Bournemouth Crematorium and North Cemetery; J. P. Brooke-Little, Richmond Herald of Arms; Miguel Angel Ochoa Brun, Secretary of Embassy, Ministry of Foreign Affairs, Madrid; Jean Bruno, Conservateur, Bibliothèque Nationale, Paris; L. W. Burnett, Army Records Centre, Hayes, Middlesex; A. D. Campbell, Reuters, London; Major C. R. Campbell, Australian Army Staff, Office of the High Commissioner for Australia, London; B. Cheeseman, Library and Records Department, Foreign and Commonwealth Office; Nicholas Heredia Coronado, Secretariat of the Civil Governor of Barcelona; Mrs M. A. Cousins, Library and Records Department, Foreign and Commonwealth Office, London; A. G. Davey, Army Records Centre, Hayes, Middlesex; V. Faekov, Soviet Embassy, London; Dr Fenzl, Ministerialrat, Bayerisches Staatsministerium des Innern, Munich; Dr Fleischer, Bundesarchiv (Militärarchiv), Freiburg-im-Breisgau; James B. Hastie; Miss Hawkins, Army Records Centre, Ministry of Defence; Frau von Hueck, Deutsches Adelsarchiv, Marburg; H. Kouyoumdjian; Commander G. M. A. James, RN, Naval Attaché, British Embassy, Ankara; W. R. Lancaster, Director, Australian War Memorial, Canberra; P. Lenain, Director, Institut Belge d'information et de documentation, Brussels; Anna-Lisa Littorin, The Library, The Swedish Institute, Stockholm; M. le Maire, Mairie de Cannes; H. von Nostitz, German Embassy, London; Umit Pamir, First Secretary, Turkish Embassy, London; D. S. Petrounakos, Director, Secretariat-General for Press and Information, Athens; Gordon Phillips, Archivist, *The Times*; Fritz Platten, Schweizerisches Sozialarchiv, Zurich; L. V. H. Rowley,

Library and Records Department, Foreign and Commonwealth Office, London; S. Sjöblom, Bureau of Personnel, Royal Ministry for Foreign Affairs, Stockholm; Patrick W. Montague Smith, Editor, *Debrett*; P. C. Soeters, Koninklijke Bibliotheek, The Hague; Sarkis Spencer-Kaye; Frank Stewart; Dorothea Tyrrell, Press and Information Office, Royal Greek Embassy, London; Vasco Valente, 3rd Secretary, Portuguese Embassy, London; Dr Weinandy, Auswärtiges Amt, Bonn; Sven Welander, Chief, Historical Collections' Section, United Nations Library (League of Nations Archives), Geneva; D. J. van Wijnen, Counsellor for Press Affairs and Information, Royal Netherlands Embassy, London; Major Cyril Wilson; Dr Winter, Direktor des Kriegsarchivs, Oster-reichisches Staatsarchiv, Vienna; and D. Xenos, Counsellor of Embassy, Royal Ministry for Foreign Affairs, Athens.

Further biographical information was provided in the latter stages of my work by Archivio Storico Diplomatico, Ministry of Foreign Affairs, Rome; D. L. Bacon, Chief, Army Reference Branch, St Louis, Missouri; J. Bax, Director, Public Relations, City of Rotterdam; C. Constantinescu, Cultural Attaché, Embassy of the Socialist Republic of Romania, London; Professor Dr Béla Czére, Museum of Communications, Budapest; M. Degros, Le Conservateur en Chef des Archives, Ministry of Foreign Affairs, Paris; María del Carmen Guzmán, Archivo Histórico Nacional, Madrid; Professor St Stefănescu, Academia de Ştiinţe Social Şi Politice, Bucharest; Hermann Weiss, Institut fur Zeitgeschichte, Munich; and Dr Hedwig Wolfram, Federal Ministry for Foreign Affairs, Vienna.

Finally I should like to thank those who read the book in typescript or proof, and whose suggestions were of particular value: Frank Ashton-Gwatkin; Nigel Viney and Sir John Wheeler-Bennett.

I am grateful to Mr T. A. Bicknell who drew four of the maps in this volume from my drafts, and to Sir John Martin, who gave me a copy of the map specially prepared for the Royal Commission to Palestine, printed on page 401.

During the course of my researches, I was helped by Kate Fleming, who tracked down many obscure facts and details; and by Susie Sacher, who examined the Foreign Office material at the Public Record Office, and made many valuable criticisms of style and content. I should also like to thank Sarah Graham, Wendy Lofts and Judy Holdsworth, who bore the brunt of the typing.

Youth

1869–1892

Horace Rumbold's ancestors had been in the public service for more than three centuries before his birth in 1869. Thomas Rumbold, a cavalier, had been taken prisoner by the Cromwellians after the battle of Naseby in 1645. His elder son William, who was also present at the battle, escaped, and served throughout the interregnum both as secretary to the secret royalist council and as Charles II's financial agent. He was rewarded for his loyalty by being made Controller of the Great Wardrobe, a profitable sinecure. Thomas Rumbold's younger son, Henry – from whom Horace Rumbold was descended – was for several years a wine merchant in southern Spain. While in Spain he passed valuable intelligence to the Madrid Government about the movements of the Cromwellian fleet. In 1660, as a reward for his services, he was appointed by Charles II British Consul at Cadiz. By his second marriage, to the daughter of a grandee of Spain, Henry Rumbold had a son William Rumbold, who served in the East Indian Civil Service. William Rumbold died in 1728; his son William also served in the East India Company, and his grandson Thomas entered the East Indian Civil Service in 1751, at the age of fifteen.

Thomas Rumbold brought both fame and notoriety to the family. In 1753 he transferred from the civil to the military service of the East India Company. He was present in the military operations at Trichinopoly in 1754, and two years later fought at the siege of Calcutta. In 1757 he served as aide-de-camp to Clive at the battle of Plassey. Severely wounded in the battle, he returned to the Civil Service of the Company, and in 1763 was appointed chief magistrate of Patna. Three years later he became a member of the Bengal Council. In 1770 he returned to England a rich man, and was elected to Parliament for New Shoreham in Dorset. Seven years later he returned to India as Governor of Madras. His work was arduous and its rewards uncertain. In 1778, after the capture of Pondicherry from the French, his power was formidable, and in the following year he was made a Baronet. Immediately on his return to England he had been elected MP for Shaftesbury, but was accused of corruption during the campaign, and the election was declared void. Subsequently, in 1781, he was elected to Parliament for Yarmouth, Isle of Wight. But within a year he had been accused by Parliament of military recklessness while in India, and of oppressive and corrupt dealings with the Indian landowners. The charges were eventually dismissed, but he was widely believed to have used his authority in India largely for personal gain. His daughter Elizabeth compiled a substantial volume in his defence – *A Vindication of the Character and Administration of Sir Thomas Rumbold* – which was published in 1868, only a year after her own death, but seventy-seven years after his, and too late to counteract the accumulated innuendoes and accusations which had become a part of later histories.

Sir Thomas Rumbold's eldest son, who fought as a subaltern at the siege of Pondicherry, and was subsequently a Member of Parliament for Melcombe Regis in Dorset, died at the early age of twenty-six. The Baronetcy therefore passed from Sir Thomas to his second son, George, who became the first diplomat in the Rumbold family. In 1803 he was sent as British Ambassador to the Hansa Towns and minister resident at Hamburg. In October 1804, on Napoleon's orders, he was seized by French troops and taken to Paris. The Prussians were outraged at Napoleon's action in spiriting away their British minister, and demanded his release, threatening to break off diplomatic relations with France if he was not set free at once. Sir George Rumbold, after one night in prison in Paris, was taken to Cherbourg, where he was transferred by a French cutter, under flag of truce, to a British frigate. Returning shortly afterwards to the Baltic, Sir George died of fever at Memel in 1807, at the age of forty-three. His son William, who succeeded him as 3rd Baronet, went to India, where he worked in the banking house of William Palmer and Company, whose principal business was in Hyderabad. In 1820 the banking house was charged, by the British Resident at Hyderabad, Sir Charles Metcalfe,[1] with dishonest dealings, and placed under an official ban. Three years later it was driven to bankruptcy. Sir William Rumbold spent the last six years of his life in a vain attempt to prove that the failure of the banking house arose, not through any financial impropriety, but because of arbitrary and illegal measures taken by the East India Company. He died, penniless, at the age of forty-six. Of his six sons, four succeeded in turn to the Baronetcy.

Sir William Rumbold's fourth son, Sir Horace Rumbold, was only four years old when his father died. He entered the Diplomatic Service in 1849, at the age of twenty. His early life was spent in Paris; most of his

---

[1] Sir Charles Metcalfe, 1785–1846. 2nd Baronet. Entered the Bengal Civil Service, 1800. Resident, Hyderabad, 1820–25. Civil Commissioner, Delhi, 1825–27. Provisional Governor-General of India, 1835–36. Lieutenant-Governor, North-West Provinces, 1836–38. Governor of Jamaica, 1839–42; of Canada, 1843–45. Created Baron, 1845.

relations by marriage were French.[1] In 1867 he himself married Caroline Harington, from a distinguished American family. Her father, George Harington, had been Assistant Secretary of the Treasury throughout the Civil War, and when the war was over had been appointed United States Ambassador at Berne. Caroline Harington's grandfather on her maternal side was Joshua Barney, a leading naval officer during the War of Independence, who had been taken prisoner by the British in 1777 and had been exchanged later in the year. Three years later, having seized several British ships and brought them as prizes into American ports, he had been captured again and taken to England but had escaped. In 1782, while in command of the warship *Hyder-Alley*, he captured a larger British warship, the *General Monck*. Shortly after the end of the war with Britain, Barney went to France, where, from 1796 to 1802 he served as a commodore with the French Navy, fighting once more against the British. In 1812, during the war between Britain and the United States, he was put in command of the special naval forces which tried, in vain, to prevent British troops sailing up the Potomac to Washington; but his defensive action during the British attack was highly commended. Barney had died in 1818, at the age of fifty-nine.

Sir Horace Rumbold's ties with England were few; four of his brothers died before he was fifty, three of them childless. Europe absorbed him; to his contemporaries he seemed the perfect cosmopolitan. He was sent to Turin in 1849, to Frankfurt in 1852, to Stuttgart in 1854, to Vienna in 1856, to Ragusa in 1858, to China in 1859, to Athens in 1862 and to St Petersburg in 1868. At St Petersburg, in the early hours of 5 February 1869, his eldest son, Horace Rumbold – the subject of this biography – was born. Within a minute of the boy's birth, Sir Horace later recorded, 'the admirable doctor who presided at it suddenly snatched him up and carried him to the washing-stand, where, pouring water into a glass, he took a gulp of it, and, to my horror, deliberately spat it into the wretched infant's face making it sneeze and sputter and give clear indications of a vitality which, as he afterwards explained to me, he at first almost feared wanting'.[2] After his son's birth, Sir Horace's diplomatic career continued on its varied course. From St Petersburg he was sent first to Constantinople,

[1] His sister Emily Rumbold was married to Comte Gaston de la Rochefoucauld. His aunt Emily Rumbold was married to Ferdinand, Baron de Delmar; his aunt Caroline Rumbold to Colonel Adolphe de St Clair. Another aunt, Maria Boothby, married, first Comte César de Choiseul, and second Prince Jules de Polignac, French Ambassador to London 1823–29 and Foreign Minister 1829–30. Among her children by her second marriage was a daughter Yolande, who married Sosthènes de Rochefoucauld, Duc de Doudeauville.

[2] Quoted in Sir Horace Rumbold's *Recollections of a Diplomatist* (London 1902), Vol. 2, p. 241. The doctor was Doctor Krassofski, of Polish extraction. He attended the birth of most members of the Russian Imperial family.

then to Santiago de Chile, Berne, Buenos Aires, Stockholm, Athens, The Hague and Vienna.

The young Horace Rumbold spent most of his early years abroad. But they were not easy ones. In 1872, when he was only three and a half, his mother, Caroline Rumbold, died; she was only twenty-five. After her death, Sir Horace, despite his constant travellings, made great efforts for his son, to whom he was devoted. Later he recalled with affection the times they were able to spend together. In Chile, when his son was seven, he took him to the foothills of the Andes to watch the sunrise, recalling in his memoirs how he drew his son's attention 'to the striking effect of the sun rising over the great chain of mountains, bidding him remember in after years that in his early childhood he had seen that wondrous spectacle'. Two years later, while Minister in Berne, he took his son to a high ridge in the Grindelwald to show him 'the very heart of the glorious mountain solitudes . . . face to face with the sublimest scene it is possible to conceive'. That same year, in London, father and son went to see the young boy's godfather and relative by marriage, Lord Rokeby,[1] who had fought in the Guards at Waterloo sixty-four years before, and had commanded a Brigade at the battle of Inkerman during the Crimean War. Sir Horace recalled in his memoirs how:

The boy squatted at his feet, and presently asked him to tell him something about Waterloo, at which battle he knew from me that his godfather had been present. Nothing loth, the dear old man then related how he had been drafted out from England at seventeen to his battalion of the Guards, and had joined it only a few days before the great battle. He then told us of the terrible fight round Hougoumont, where the Guards and Brunswickers had held out all through that never-ending June day against the repeated attacks of the enemy. It was a story to be remembered for life, as I said to my little fellow; for the boy-guardsman, whose baptism of fire was now described to him, had lived to command the brigade, and with it had likewise gone through the long anxious hours at Inkerman, when a few thousand English had successfully stood their ground against such fearful odds. . . .

While he was with his father, Rumbold had a German tutor; but his German lessons were fraught with unexpected problems. 'When I was a small boy', Rumbold wrote many years later to an American colleague, 'I had a personal experience, extending over several months, of the

---

[1] Henry Montagu, 6th Baron Rokeby, 1798–1883. Entered the Army as an Ensign, 3rd Regiment of Foot Guards (Scots Guards), 1814. Served at Waterloo. Lieutenant-Colonel commanding the Scots Guards, 1854. Major-General Commanding the Guards Brigade in the Crimea, 1855. Lieutenant-General, 1861; General, 1869. Retired from the Army, 1877.

brutality of a Prussian officer of the Guard. I have not forgotten it.' The officer not only taught Rumbold German; he also forced him to do military exercises in the courtyard of the Legation to which his father was then accredited.

In May 1879, before Sir Horace returned for the second time to South America as Minister to the Argentine, he placed his son at a preparatory school in England, Hawtrey's, at Slough, known as 'Little Eton'. Sir Horace continued upon his cosmopolitan course, leaving his son to imbibe, for six years, a thoroughly English education, first at Hawtrey's and then at Eton itself. His two younger sons, William,[1] born in 1870, and George,[2] born in 1871 also remained in England. From the age of seven Rumbold wrote regularly to his father; a correspondence which continued until his father's death in 1913. In September 1880 he and his two brothers met one of the leading statesmen of the time. 'Lord Granville[3] invited us to dinner twice last week', he wrote to his father, 'and gave each of us a present. He gave me a telescope and Willie a large box of tools and to Georgie a knife. . . . Georgie had better be careful with his knife or else he will cut himself.' In July 1881 Sir Horace married Mrs Louisa Caulfield, a widow of thirty-eight, by whom, three years later, he had a fourth son, Hugo.[4] After Hugo's death on 25 November 1932, 'a friend' wrote to *The Times*: 'He was essentially a Bohemian and a clubman, who was witty and amusing and always tried to pass on his zest of life to others. He served gaily and gallantly in the South African War and the Great War and he was artistic to his finger tips. A really gifted designer of scenery for theatre, he carried out several contracts in London. Later he took to film producing. He was indeed something of a dilettante and a dabbler in many pursuits. Had he been more of a "striker" he would have made more of a name for himself.'

[1] William Edwin Rumbold, 1870–1947. Educated at Wellington College and the Royal Military Academy, Woolwich. 2nd Lieutenant, Royal Artillery, 1891; Captain, 1899. Served in the Uganda Protectorate, 1899–1903. Major, 1911. Awarded both the French and Belgian Croix de Guerre during the First World War. Colonel, retired, 1921.

[2] George Rumbold, 1871–1951. Honorary Attaché, The Hague, 1892. Served as a Lieutenant in the Royal Navy during the First World War. Worked at the Air Ministry, 1939–45.

[3] Granville George Leveson-Gower, 2nd Earl Granville, 1815–91. Foreign Secretary, 1851–52. Leader of the Liberals in the House of Lords, 1855. In June 1859 Queen Victoria asked him to form a Government, but he was unable to do so. Colonial Secretary, 1868–70. Foreign Secretary, 1870–74 and 1880–85. Colonial Secretary, 1886.

[4] Hugh Cecil Levinge Rumbold, 1884–1932. Educated at Eton, 1897–1901. Served in the South African War as a 2nd Lieutenant, Rifle Brigade, 1901; Lieutenant, 1902. Resigned his Commission, 1904. Rejoined, 1914, as a 2nd Lieutenant, Grenadier Guards; Lieutenant, 1915. Wounded on the Western Front. Employed in the Ministry of Munitions, 1918. Retired on account of ill-health, 1919. Theatrical designer. He died in California.

The distance created by diplomacy did not diminish the family ties, and Rumbold was deeply fond of his stepmother, with whom he corresponded regularly until her death in 1940.

In 1883 Rumbold went to Eton, but he left two years later, when he was sixteen. On his departure in December 1885 his housemaster, Edward Lyttelton,[1] wrote to Sir Horace: 'Very often his Latin is bald and wooden but he has learnt how to find his own English which is very important, and to keep much clearer of bounders than before.' Rumbold went out to Athens, where his father was British Minister. In 1886, when he was seventeen, he set to work to index the manuscript volume of his father's correspondence for the previous four years. While at Athens, he also copied into a heavy leather-bound volume all his father's official letters and despatches from February 1886 to June 1887. After a short while studying at Lausanne, he went in June 1888, as an Honorary Attaché, to the British Legation at The Hague, to which his father had been transferred from Athens four months before. 'Your appointment', Rumbold was informed by the Foreign Office, 'will not entitle you to any pay or promotion in the diplomatic service.' Eighteen months later, having helped his father once more by copying out all his despatches in his small, clear handwriting, he returned to London where, in January 1890, he enrolled at Scones's tutorial establishment, in order to cram for the Foreign Office examination a year later. In the recollections, which he wrote several years afterwards,[2] Rumbold described how, at Scones, cramming also went on for the Indian Civil Service, 'and we used to see rather pallid youths wandering about in the lecture rooms at lunch time, consuming a modest lunch which they had brought in small, black bags'. The service in which his great-great-grandfather, Thomas Rumbold, had achieved such fame no longer held its lustre, although it could offer in the late nineteenth century a less precarious occupation than in his day.

In February 1890, while working for the Foreign Office examination Rumbold reached his twenty-first birthday. 'Shortly afterwards', he recalled, 'I became a Free-mason. . . . My non-masonic friends, hearing that I was going to be initiated had drawn dreadful pictures of what was going to happen to me. One wag suggested that I should have to ride the Piccadilly goat[3] naked round the table.' But, in the event, 'the initiation

[1] Edward Lyttelton, 1855–1942. 2nd son of the 4th Lord Lyttelton. Assistant Master, Eton, 1882. Headmaster of Haileybury, 1890–1905; of Eton, 1905–16. Author of several works on education, Christianity and birth control.

[2] Rumbold wrote these recollections while he was in Tokyo in 1911. They were never published.

[3] A goat which, in the early 1890s, wandered untended in the neighbourhood of the Duke of Cambridge's house in Piccadilly.

wasn't such a very formidable affair, after all, and I have since spent many a pleasant evening at the Lodge'.

In the autumn of 1890 Rumbold learned that he could sit the examination in the following June. There were to be thirteen candidates in all, competing for three attachéships. As winter approached, he recalled, 'I began cramming to the tune of ten hours a day.' All but one of the candidates was older than he was, some three and four years older. The examination lasted a week, with six hours of writing each day. Rumbold spent his twenty-second birthday waiting for the results. He doubted if he could take any of the first three places, and put his hopes on coming fourth, when, he felt, the Foreign Office might take pity on him as the son of a diplomat, and 'create' a vacancy for him. Then, four days after his birthday, he received a telegram to say that he had come top.[1]

Rumbold's father was not unduly excited by the spate of congratulatory letters which he received on his son's behalf. 'I suppose you're glad you have passed', he wrote; but at the same time he deprecated the idea of his son taking a holiday. Rumbold therefore went at once to begin work at the Foreign Office. He was put into the Eastern Department, under Francis Bertie.[2] Turkey, Greece, Persia, Egypt and the Balkan States were the countries with which he had to deal. But neither the exotic nature of the countries, nor the fact that he knew Greek politics well, could make the work interesting. Rumbold's tasks were arduous ones. He had to copy all incoming despatches in longhand, cipher outgoing telegrams and decipher incoming ones. His only glimpse of high policy was while circulating Confidential Prints to Cabinet Ministers. Rumbold had to ensure that the Ministers to whom the Print was sent returned both Print and pouches promptly. These special, locked pouches shuttled to and fro between the Foreign Office and the various ministries. Rumbold later recalled that the First Lord of the Treasury, A. J. Balfour,[3] was a 'great sinner' with his Print. 'We often could not get his pouches back', he wrote. 'At last we used to put a danger-signal, i.e. a slip of pink paper with the words *Pouches Nos. so and so not returned* on it into his pouch, and send it to him in lieu of print.' This stratagem was generally successful.

[1] Rumbold's best marks were for orthography (195 out of 200), German (460 out of 500) and French (424 out of 500); his worst for English Constitutional history (89 out of 200).

[2] Francis Leveson Bertie, 1844–1919. Entered the Foreign Office, from Eton, in 1863. Senior Clerk, 1889. Assistant Under-Secretary of State, 1894. Knighted, 1902. British Ambassador to Rome, 1903–4 and to Paris, 1905–18. Created Baron, 1915; Viscount, 1918. His First World War diary, *The Diary of Lord Bertie 1914–1918* was published in 1924.

[3] Arthur James Balfour, 1848–1930. Conservative MP, 1874–85, 1885–1906 and 1906–22. Leader of the House of Commons and First Lord of the Treasury, 1891–92 and 1895–1906. Prime Minister, 1902–5. First Lord of the Admiralty, 1915–16. Foreign Secretary, 1916–19. Lord President of the Council, 1919–22 and 1925–29. Created Earl, 1922.

Hours of work were long. Only the senior Foreign Office officials lunched tolerably, at the Travellers' Club in Pall Mall. Rumbold and his friends ate what he later recalled as 'very inferior' food in a basement room at the Foreign Office, below the level of the Horse Guards Parade. But Francis Bertie was a tolerant chief, and Rumbold managed, in his own words, to 'screw two months leave out of him' quite easily.

Sir Horace hoped that his son would be posted to Brussels, but Rumbold himself was anxious to go to the East. Having experienced Greece and Holland, he hankered after something more exotic. The 'Eastern Question' and its wide implications had awakened his interest. He was delighted therefore when he learned that the British Agent and Consul-General in Egypt, Sir Evelyn Baring,[1] had asked the Foreign Office for a Third Secretary, and that his own name had been put forward.

Rumbold spent the new year with his father at The Hague, before returning to London to await his posting to Cairo. Sir Horace was both depressed and angry. He waited in Holland for a better posting, but with every ambassadorial change he was passed over. His frequent, strident letters to Lord Salisbury,[2] in which he rehearsed his claims to advancement, went unanswered. His bitterness grew. The new year of 1892 was filled with rumours of impending diplomatic promotions. Sir Horace had set his heart on going to Madrid. But Henry Drummond Wolff,[3] the Minister in Bucharest, was reported to be equally eager for a posting to Spain.

As soon as Rumbold returned to London he reported fully to his father about the impending changes. It was clear that Drummond Wolff was in a strong position, the Foreign Office being anxious to console him 'in some way or other' for not having been appointed to Constantinople. A senior official confided to Rumbold that 'Wolff is a kind of barnacle and we can't get rid of him'. Rumbold was unable to give his father any cause for optimism. Lord Salisbury, he reported gloomily, 'bottles up his appointments and nobody knows anything until he chooses to divulge

[1] Evelyn Baring, 1841–1917. Entered the Army as a cadet, 1855. Served in the Ionian Islands, 1858–67, and in the Intelligence Division of the War Office, 1870–72. Private Secretary to the Viceroy of India, 1872–76. British Commissioner of the *Caisse de la Dette*, Egypt, 1877–80. Finance Member of the Viceroy's Council, India, 1880–83. Knighted, 1883. British Agent and Consul-General, Egypt, 1883–1907. Created Baron Cromer, 1899; Earl, 1901. In 1908 he published a two-volume work, *Modern Egypt*. Chairman of the Dardanelles Commission of Enquiry, 1916–17.

[2] Robert Arthur Talbot Gascoyne-Cecil, 1830–1903. Succeeded his father as 3rd Marquess of Salisbury, 1868. Three times Prime Minister: 1885–86, 1886–92 and 1895–1902.

[3] Henry Drummond Wolff, 1830–1908. Entered Foreign Office, 1846. Knighted, 1862. Conservative MP, 1874–85; a member of the 'Fourth Party'. Minister to Teheran, 1887–91; to Bucharest, 1891–92. Ambassador at Madrid, 1892–1900.

them'. Apparently Drummond Wolff had been sending a stream of telegrams from Bucharest pressing his claims. 'All points to this, therefore,' Rumbold reported sadly, 'that Wolff is your only rival for Madrid, but a formidable one.' The only consolation which the son could offer was that 'if you are passed over this time . . . the FO sympathise with you'. Two days later the blow fell – 'Wolff is going to Madrid' – and Rumbold could only seek to soothe his father by abusing Lord Salisbury, who, as well as being Prime Minister, was also Foreign Secretary: 'He has behaved like a brute to you and the whole service will howl at his latest job. I shall rejoice on the day he is ousted from the FO.'

Rumbold's own plans were now complete: he would go to Cairo at once, and would by the end of the year be drawing a salary of three hundred pounds, provided he could pass the Arabic exam, which he was confident of doing. On 15 January 1892 he left London for Egypt. Henceforth almost his whole career, a few months short of forty-one years, was to be spent abroad.

2

Cairo

1892–1895

Rumbold reached Egypt in January 1892. It was ten years since the British occupation had begun. During that time the efforts of the British Agent and Consul-General, Sir Evelyn Baring, had brought a measure of efficiency and routine to a formerly chaotic government. The Turks still held a nominal suzerainty; but the British occupation, originally intended as only a temporary one, was unlikely to be ended. British control of Egypt and the Suez Canal were essential if the sea route to India was to remain secure. At the same time, Sir Evelyn Baring, who had once been Private Secretary to a Viceroy of India, hoped to turn Egypt into a model of imperial rule, which even the British in India would envy.

The nominal ruler of Egypt was still the Egyptian Khedive, but since the British occupation the Khedive, Tewfik Pasha,[1] had accepted British advice in all matters of foreign policy and internal organization. He had his own Egyptian Prime Minister, a Cabinet and a Legislative Council. But everything that these Ministers did was scrutinized by the British Agency, which had its own administrative departments. The other European powers were also represented in Cairo, and retained certain powers over financial matters, but they, like the Khedive, accepted British control as the ultimate reality, backed as it was by an Army of Occupation of over 8,000 men, and a series of British Governments in London determined to control the political and economic destiny of Egypt.

To the south of Egypt, following the murder of General Gordon[2] at

---

[1] Mohammed Tewfik Pasha, 1852–92. Eldest son of the Khedive Ismail. His father, believing him to be stupid, neglected his education. For a few months in 1878 he was President of the Council of Ministers, during one of the crises which precipitated his father's deposition. Khedive of Egypt, 1879–92. On British insistence, he abandoned Egyptian sovereignty over the Sudan, 1884.

[2] Charles George Gordon, 1833–85. 2nd Lieutenant, Royal Engineers, 1852; served in the Crimean War at the siege of Sebastopol, 1854. Commanded the 'Ever Victorious Army' against the Taiping rebellion, China, 1863; henceforth known as 'Chinese Gordon'. Took service under the Khedive of Egypt, 1874; Governor-General of the Sudan, 1876–79. Left Egypt, 1879; returned, 1884, charged by the British Government with the evacuation of the Sudan, of which he was again appointed Governor-General. Murdered by Mahdists at the siege of Khartoum, January 26, 1885.

Khartoum in 1885, the Dervishes, religious fanatics, patriots and soldiers, controlled the Sudan. The loss of the Sudan irked Sir Evelyn Baring, whose ambition was to supervise the economy both of Egypt and the Sudan unfettered and unchallenged.

Rumbold arrived in Egypt shortly after the death of the Khedive, Tewfik Pasha. In his first letter to his father he reported 'that the Khedive had the "clap" when he died as also syphilitic tumours on the arm. How about the "model of domestic virtue" which the Times and other papers represented him as being?' Tewfik was, it appeared, treated by two doctors, enemies of one another. 'One injected morphine when his kidneys hadn't acted for 48 hours and he had congestion of the lungs. . . . The last bulletin the doctors issued about him stated that he was much better when, in reality, he had been unconscious for hours.'

Rumbold was immediately attracted to Egypt, 'quite delighted' as he wrote to his father, 'with the sun and warmth and general brightness'. He was quickly absorbed in the activity which Baring created all around him. He began Arabic lessons at once, intending to pass the Foreign Office examination within seven months. The official Annual Report had to be prepared, and involved much paperwork, 'a great grind' for junior officials. Within a month of his arrival Rumbold reported to his father that the Agency had already sent out sixty-eight telegrams that year to the Foreign Office and over a hundred elsewhere. As there were no secretaries and no typewriters, the junior officials had the tedious task of copying out all telegrams themselves, in longhand. But they were not entirely cut off from high policy. Baring confided in them frequently, and they understood his difficulties and aspirations. 'Never, apparently,' wrote Rumbold to his father, 'has French and Russian intrigue been more rife . . . they are doing their very best to put a spoke in our wheel.' The unexpected appearance of both the French and Russian fleets off Alexandria was intended to show their unity towards Egyptian affairs, and their disapproval of British dominance. But Baring, seldom at a loss for an effective riposte, telegraphed at once to Lord Salisbury for an English squadron, stronger than the combined Franco-Russian Fleet, to sail immediately for Egypt. 'Now that he has to be on the look out against French intrigues', Rumbold told his father, 'he is very happy.'

A crisis arose in February 1892 over the ownership of the Sinai Peninsula. No clear boundary existed between British Egypt and Turkish Palestine. The Turks were anxious to extend their control westwards across the desert to the Suez Canal. The Turkish Commissioner in Egypt, Mukhtar Pasha,[1] expressed the alarm of the Turkish Government at the

[1] Ghazi Ahmed Mukhtar Pasha, 1832–1919. Commanded the Turkish military mission to

arrival of a small colony of eight Jews, financed by a German philanthropist, who were trying to settle in Sinai, on the Gulf of Akaba. Rumbold
reported how, in Turkish eyes, this tiny band seemed to herald 'the return
of a kingdom of Jewland'.

Since 1882, the British had claimed the Sinai peninsula as part of
Egypt; but the Egyptian War Office had never delineated a frontier. Not
the long-considered demands of Imperial policy, but a small group of
determined Jews, forced official attention to focus on the inhospitable
wilderness that lay between two Empires. Sir Evelyn Baring was able, in
Rumbold's words, 'to pose as a protector of Egyptian interests' by insisting
on a formal frontier agreement which would put Sinai entirely under
British control. After three weeks of diplomatic activity in Cairo and
Constantinople, the line was drawn from El Arish to the head of the Gulf
of Akaba.[1]

Visitors from England abounded. Rumbold, being the most junior of
the Agency staff, was responsible for all social arrangements. On one
occasion he had to organize the visit of the Duchess of Cleveland.[2] When
she arrived Rumbold took her on a donkey to the bazaar, where he
discovered 'what a good hand she is at haggling over her purchases.
What's more', he told his father, 'she always get them cheap.' The culinary
life of the Agency was exotic. Later Rumbold recalled his first meal there,
served by Indians with white turbans and gold-embroidered breastplates.
The meal opened with reindeers' tongues and peach bitters. These were
followed by a prawn curry whose fame had spread far beyond the Nile
Delta. On one visit to Egypt the Prince of Wales[3] had telegraphed the
Agency from Port Said asking specially for the prawn curry to be included in the luncheon to which he had been invited. Rumbold found 'a
particularly fine green chartreuse' in the Agency cellar, and wrote in his
diary that although he had 'since been told that this is a deleterious liquid',
he had nevertheless taken to it so much that 'in about two years I had
finished the whole stock'.

During March there was, Rumbold wrote to his father, 'something on

---

the Yemen, 1870. Minister of Public Works at Constantinople, 1873. Commanded the
Turkish forces in Bosnia, 1876, winning twenty battles and losing none. Defeated by the
Russians in eastern Turkey, 1877. Turkish High Commissioner in Egypt, 1885–95.

[1] This British success had the reverse of its intended effect. Egypt, gaining its independence
in 1922, came into possession of Sinai. Britain, receiving a Mandate over Palestine in 1920,
had to make do with the restrictions she had imposed on Turkey.

[2] Lady Catherine Lucy Wilhelmina Stanhope, 1819–1901. Daughter of the 4th Earl of
Stanhope. She married, as her second husband, the 4th Duke of Cleveland in 1854.

[3] Albert Edward, 1841–1910. Eldest son of Queen Victoria. Prince of Wales until he
succeeded to the throne as Edward VII on January 22, 1901.

every day now – riding, parties, picnics'; after a mixed picnic of sixteen young people with only a single chaperone, Rumbold told his father that no incidents occurred to cause mothers any anxiety'. The season ended with the coming of the hot weather at the end of March and the return of Lady Baring[1] to England. The Agency at once became 'the abomination of desolation', wrote Rumbold. Only speculation about Honours and promotions kept people alive. 'Some of the ladies here would give their eyes to be called Lady.'

In 1892 Baring was made a peer, and decided to call himself Lord Cromer. Rumbold found rooms, took on a servant and rented a piano from Lady Cromer. 'I propose to pass my Arabic examination about the middle of July', he told his father, 'and can already talk a little and quite enough to tell my servant all I want done.' He actually passed in June; Colonel Wingate[2] being one of his examiners.

In July, Rumbold swam the Nile with Arthur Hardinge,[3] who was in charge of the Agency when Cromer went on leave. Bathing and riding filled the summer months, and he and Hardinge were 'devoured by bugs, sand-flies, mosquitoes and ants'. Hardinge, a Fellow of All Souls at the age of twenty-two, was considered one of the most brilliant men in the Foreign Service. 'Insignificant in appearance and untidy in dress', Rumbold described him in his diary. Hardinge had strange habits. When he had been appointed as Second Secretary to St Petersburg in 1888 he was said to have set off from London with no belongings except a toothbrush in a small black bag. 'He constantly wore an odd pair of socks or boots', Rumbold recorded, 'and, when in thought, would chew his handkerchief. When he was amused, which was pretty often, he would go into hyena-like peals of laughter.' One day an important document was missing, a letter from Balfour to Cromer. 'We hunted high and low for this document. It was eventually discovered in one of Hardinge's boots.'

[1] Ethel Errington, 1843–98. Daughter of Sir Rowland Errington, 11th Baronet. She married Baring in 1876.

[2] Francis Reginald Wingate, 1861–1953. Lieutenant, Royal Artillery, 1880; Captain, 1889. Governor of the Red Sea Littoral, 1894. Director of Military Intelligence during the reconquest of the Sudan, 1896–98. Knighted, 1898. Commanded the operations which resulted in the death of the Khalifa, 1899. Commander-in-Chief of the Forces of Egypt, and Governor-General of the Sudan, 1899–1916. General, 1913. High Commissioner, Egypt, 1917–19. Created Baronet, 1920. He published *Mahdism and the Egyptian Sudan* in 1899. One of his three sons was killed in action in 1918.

[3] Arthur Henry Hardinge, 1859–1933. Educated at Eton and Balliol College, Oxford. Entered the Foreign Office, 1880. Fellow of All Souls, 1881. Served in Madrid (1883), Petrograd (1888), Constantinople (1888), Bucharest (1890), Cairo (1891), Zanzibar (1894) and East Africa (1896). Knighted, 1897. Minister to Teheran, 1900–5; to Brussels, 1906–11; to Lisbon, 1911–13; Ambassador to Madrid, 1913–19. He published two volumes of memoirs, *A Diplomatist in Europe* (1927) and *A Diplomatist in the East* (1928).

Hardinge and Rumbold became good friends. 'His only defect from my point of view', wrote Rumbold in his diary, 'was the facility with which he wrote, and I was kept very busy copying out his drafts which were plentiful and of considerable length.'

Rumbold and Hardinge travelled together up the Nile. They visited the temples and tombs at Luxor. 'If I had been a very rich man', wrote Rumbold, 'I would have offered to spend large sums in clearing and restoring them.' In a particularly foul-smelling and bat-infested mortuary chamber Rumbold was amazed when Hardinge attempted to ask the guide, in his elementary Arabic, what he thought of the doctrine of the Trinity. At Wadi Halfa, the boundary between Egypt and the Sudan, they accompanied a military reconnaissance into the desert, riding for about ten miles into Dervish territory. 'The desert there is quite appalling in its desolation . . . a series of narrow valleys – almost at right angles – formed by black rocks.' Returning down the Nile they visited Abydos, where they were entertained by the local sheikh. 'The meal seemed unending and about every fifth dish was a sweet. Amongst other things a whole sheep was brought in.' Their host 'tore off pieces of the flesh with his fingers'. At Assiout their knowledge of Arabic was put to the test when a local official entered into a long religious discussion with them. 'His delight at finding we were free-masons was unbounded . . . we adjourned to a room upstairs where, after locking the doors, we held a meeting during which our host offered us a strange liquor to drink. All the proceedings were in Arabic.'

While in Cairo, Rumbold looked with contempt upon the foreign diplomats; representatives, he told his father, 'of Brazil and other shady countries. I never saw such swine in all my life.' The largest group were the French, whom he had found 'somewhat second-rate'. Their Chief was the French Consul-General, the Marquis de Reverseaux,[1] who had 'a shifty eye, was clever and, needless to say, an Anglophobe', and whose staff were 'beneath contempt – the Secretaries might have been taken from the magasins du Louvre'. The minor powers were represented 'by Syrian Jews who had bought Papal titles and lived at Alexandria'.

Rumbold found the consular corps 'scugs' and 'ruffians' and enjoyed giving his father thumb-nail sketches of them; 'many', he wrote, 'are not in the diplomatic service at all, some are swindlers and almost all very weird. We treat them very much *de haut en bas* and they have a wholesome respect for us accordingly.' Sir Horace reciprocated with news of a duel

[1] Jacques Marie Ferdinand Frédéric Guéau, Marquis de Reverseaux de Rouvray, 1845–1916. French Minister, Belgrade, 1884–91. Consul-General, Cairo, 1891–94. Ambassador, Madrid, 1894–97; Vienna, 1897–1905.

between a German and a Spanish diplomat at The Hague 'arising out of some high words at lawn tennis'. He went on to stress yet again his own claims for a posting to an Embassy preferably Vienna.[1] 'It is quite inconceivable that they should pass you over again', his son replied sympathetically. And in a later letter: 'it would be a cruel shame to pass over your head again'. Yet even the new Foreign Secretary, Lord Rosebery,[2] a friend of Sir Horace, could not persuade the Foreign Office to look with favour upon his claim, and in its next diplomatic shuffle gave him no promotion.

The new Liberal Government came into office at a time of crisis in Egypt. Tewfik Pasha's successor as Khedive, Abbas Hilmi,[3] had decided to try to assert his independence from Britain by dismissing his Prime Minister, Fahmi Pasha,[4] whom he considered too pro-English, and appointing in his place someone of whom Baring did not approve. 'A besotted old Turk of bad character', Rumbold described the new Prime Minister, Fakhri Pasha.[5] Unless Fakhri were dismissed at once, Rumbold told his father, 'English prestige will be ruined and the work of ten years undone.' Much of the strength of the British position in Egypt depended upon the Khedive accepting British guidance on all major political matters, but Rumbold realized that it was 'natural that a boy – coming as he did to the throne (such as it was) before he was of age – and surrounded by not overwise people – should wish to be "boss" in his own country'. He thought that the young Khedive might even put himself at the head of an 'Egypt for the Egyptians' movement, and seek to rid Egypt, not only of British but of all foreign influence. He was, he told his father, 'a d-d young fool, though plucky'.

[1] In 1900 there were British Ambassadors in only eight capitals: Vienna, Paris, Berlin, Rome, St Petersburg, Madrid, Constantinople and Washington. Before 1914 only one further Embassy was created, that of Tokyo, in 1905.

[2] Archibald Philip Primrose, 1847–1929. Succeeded his grandfather as 5th Earl of Rosebery, 1868. Secretary of State for Foreign Affairs, 1886 and 1892–94. Prime Minister 1894–95.

[3] Abbas Hilmi, 1874–1944. Eldest son of Tewfik Pasha. He succeeded to the Khedivate in 1892. In July 1914, while visiting Constantinople, he was shot and wounded. When Turkey entered the war in November 1914 the British refused to allow him to return to Egypt; he was deposed on December 19, 1914, in favour of his uncle. Lived in exile, chiefly in Switzerland, until his death. He died in Geneva. On July 16, 1917, Rumbold wrote to Ronald Graham about Abbas Hilmi: 'I do not suppose a more tortuous or untrustworthy person ever existed.'

[4] Mustafa Fahmi Pasha, 1874–1908. Prime Minister of Egypt, May 1891–January 1892. Lord Milner wrote of him, in his diary, that he was 'terribly weak and fears offending the Khedive too much to exercise control over him'. He also had a weakness for fine shirts, which he would send to England to be washed and ironed. His uncritical support of English policy led to his Government being described as the 'ministries of dummies'.

[5] Fakhri Pasha. Minister of Justice, 1890–91; Prime Minister for three days, January 15–18, 1892.

Cromer acted swiftly. Three days later the Khedive agreed to replace his Prime Minister by a former Prime Minister, Riaz Pasha,[1] of whom the British Agency approved. Cromer followed this up by asking Lord Rosebery to increase the size of the British Army of Occupation, already over 8,000 strong. The Liberals were in an embarrassing position. They had pledged themselves to bring the occupation of Egypt to an end. They looked with disfavour upon Cromer and his 'empire.' In the Cabinet a strong anti-imperialist group wished to refuse Cromer's request. But Rosebery himself was a convinced imperialist, and told Cromer that he would resign as Foreign Secretary if the Cabinet rejected the increase in the Army of Occupation. Cromer replied by saying that he too would resign, and return to England to raise the issue in the House of Lords. 'One afternoon', wrote Rumbold in his diary, 'we went back to the Agency after a game of tennis and found a cypher telegram awaiting us. It was to say that Lord Rosebery had carried the day against all his colleagues. . . . Lord Cromer and I decyphered this together.' The new troops soon arrived raising the total to over 10,000. 'When the Black Watch marched into Cairo with their kilts', Rumbold wrote, 'many natives thought they were the wives of the other British soldiers.'

In February 1893 Rumbold was promoted from Attaché to Third Secretary, and with his Arabic allowance of £100, now earned £400 a year. He was also elected to the Travellers' Club in Pall Mall – 'It is a very dull Club', wrote his father, 'so I hardly know whether you are to be congratulated.' In March he was at General Kitchener's[2] fancy-dress ball dressed as an Indian Rajah, with Cromer's cummerbund and Lady Cromer's jewels. In April he went on leave, after fifteen months in Egypt. While on leave he began to read for the international law exam, hoping further to augment his knowledge and his salary. On his return to Egypt Hardinge 'who seemed to know everything, took me in hand and coached me'. Rumbold passed, and his salary was raised to £500.

In August Rumbold and Hardinge went to Tantah, whose fair was

[1] Riaz Pasha. Prime Minister of Egypt, 1879–81. Minister of Justice and the Interior, 1882. Prime Minister for the second time, 1892–94. In 1897 he had been denounced in the mosques of Cairo as a friend of the Christians, and his life threatened by Muslim fanatics.

[2] Horatio Herbert Kitchener, 1850–1916. Entered Army, 1868. 2nd Lieutenant, Royal Engineers, 1871. Attached to the Palestine Exploration Fund, 1874–78. Surveyed Cyprus, 1878–82; the Sinai Peninsula, 1883. Governor-General, Eastern Sudan, 1886–88. Commander-in-Chief of the Egyptian Army, 1892–98. Knighted, 1894. Defeated the Dervishes at Omdurman, 1898. Created Baron Kitchener of Khartoum, 1898. Commander-in-Chief, South Africa, 1900–2. Created Viscount, 1902. Commander-in-Chief, India, 1902–9. Field-Marshal, 1909. A Member of the Committee of Imperial Defence, 1910. British Agent and Consul-General in Egypt, 1911–14. Created Earl, July 27, 1914. Secretary of State for War, August 5, 1914, until drowned at sea, June 5, 1916.

reputed to be as magnificent as that of the medieval Russian fair at Novgorod. Over three hundred thousand Muslims crowded into the city for the occasion. Rumbold later described the main procession in his diary:

The procession opened with men on horseback dressed like women – after whom came women dressed like men. Then there were several mounted men wearing the armour taken from the crusaders at Rosetta or Damietta. Presently appeared the great Sheikh of the Mosque wearing his ceremonial robes, on his head being a metal turban of such weight as to bow him down over his horse's neck. Men walked on each side of him propping up his arms. The close of the procession was the gigantic wooden figure of a man – stark naked standing on a flat cart drawn by horses. This figure had an enormous 'phallus' to the end of which a cord was attached which passed over the shoulder and the other of which was held by a native walking behind the cart. As the procession moved along the man lowered or raised the cord. Then came a man naked to the waist, with a bell tied on to him which rang as he walked. The central figure, i.e. the wooden image, was evidently a relic of phallic worship. Not long afterwards that particular portion of the procession was suppressed by the police and so we were glad to have seen it for the last time.

In September 1893 Rumbold was briefly in charge of the British Agency, while Cromer was in London and Hardinge away. But nothing eventful took place and no decisions had to be made. 'I kick my heels and do nothing except read novels', he told his father. In his diary he described a typical day: work all morning, lunch at the Turf Club, work or siesta after lunch, polo or tennis in the afternoon, fencing later, after which, 'we used to get a man to play on us with a hose', dinner at the Turf Club, and whist until midnight. 'Then to bed, dog tired but not to sleep', for, he wrote to his father, the mosquitoes found him a tasty morsel, and he spent his nights 'in scratching, sweating and swearing (forgive vulgarity of language).'

In April 1894 Rumbold took his second leave. While in London he began shorthand and typewriting lessons, but soon abandoned them. He was again angered by Rosebery's failure to promote his father: vacancies at Vienna and Rome went to others – 'you have been again baulked of the prize', he wrote on his return to Cairo. When Sir Frank Lascelles[1] was appointed Ambassador to St Petersburg Rumbold wrote: 'It is a d–d shame and a worthy ending to Lord Rosebery's dealings with yourself and the service before he left the Foreign Office.[2] The putting in

[1] Frank Cavendish Lascelles, 1841–1920. Entered the Diplomatic Service in 1861, twelve years after Sir Horace Rumbold. Minister in Teheran, 1891–94. Ambassador at St Petersburg, 1894–95. Knighted, 1896. Ambassador at Berlin, 1895–1908.
[2] Rosebery had left the Foreign Office in March 1894 to become Prime Minister.

of Durand[1] (in Persia) was also disgraceful seeing that so many men in the service would have done well there. What *are* we coming to?'

In November Rumbold joined Sir Herbert Kitchener, the Commander-in-Chief of the British forces in Egypt, on his tour of inspection to Suakin, an Egyptian port on the Red Sea and formerly the terminus of a busy caravan route to the two Sudanese cities of Berber and Khartoum. It was an isolated outpost in a forlorn spot, which had remained in British hands after the Dervishes had driven the British out of the Sudan.

For two days they steamed southwards. 'Played cards,' Rumbold recorded, 'read Gibbon and slept a great deal. . . . Put out a line to catch fish but didn't get any.' They reached Suakin at eight in the morning. Kitchener was greeted by a salute of thirteen guns and Rumbold, as Lord Cromer's representative, inspected the guard of honour. After a day visiting the prison and reviewing the troops, and a dinner made dismal because the garrison ice-making machine had broken down, Rumbold set off for Erkowit, a remote fortress forty-five miles inland from Suakin and 4,000 feet above sea-level. Pheasant shooting and a vain chase after gazelle made the excursion enjoyable, but the passes were high, the camels noisy at night and the water 'smelt of camels . . . even when mixed with whisky'. On his return to Suakin he played cricket, to make up the garrison team against a gunboat team, got cut by a cricket ball, and was glad to return to Cairo.

During the visit to Suakin Rumbold reflected on Kitchener's qualities. He had already seen much of him in Cairo, and this long journey together confirmed many of his opinions. He respected Kitchener's talent for finance and administration, but saw that he was 'brutal in his methods and would get the last ounce of work out of a man'. Cromer had once said to him, 'Kitchener is hardly human', and to Rumbold himself, Kitchener seemed 'quite devoid of emotions or sentiment'.

Returning to Cairo, Rumbold found 'the usual amount of shoddy heiresses on the look out for an officer . . .', and plenty of social chores, organizing charity shows and Agency entertainments, for the 'Cairo season' which had arrived once more. On 16 March 1894, a tired bowed figure struggled out of the desert from the Sudan into a British military outpost of Assuan. It was Rudolf Slatin,[2] an Austrian lieutenant who, in

[1] Henry Mortimer Durand, 1850–1924. Entered the Bengal Civil Service, 1873. Secretary to General Roberts during the Kabul Campaign, 1879. Foreign Secretary to the Government of India, 1884–94. Knighted, 1889. Minister to Teheran, 1894–1900. Ambassador to Madrid, 1900–3; to Washington, 1903–6. Unsuccessful Conservative candidate, 1910.

[2] Rudolf Carl Slatin Pasha, 1857–1932. Born in Austria. Went to Africa at the age of seventeen. Financial Inspector of the Sudan, 1879. Governor of Darfur, 1881. Surrendered to the Mahdi, 1883; escaped, 1894. Colonel, Egyptian Intelligence Department, 1895; on

1878, had left his regiment in Bosnia to join Gordon in the Sudan. He had become Financial Inspector of the Sudan, then Governor of the Province of Darfur. He had led an army against the Dervishes, but in vain. He surrendered, and was taken into captivity for eleven years. Later, when Gordon was killed, the Dervishes had brought his severed head into Slatin's cell. 'The blood rushed to my head', he later recalled in his memoirs, 'and my heart seemed to stop beating; but with a tremendous effort of self-control I gazed silently at this ghastly spectacle. His blue eyes were half-opened; the mouth perfectly natural; the hair of his head and his short whiskers were almost quite white.'

When Slatin reached Cairo he became the centre of all attention. Rumbold saw him at once when Wingate, who had worked for years to help his escape, brought him to the British Agency. 'His long captivity', Rumbold recalled, 'did not seem to have left any particular trace on him except that he was rather bowed – as if expecting to be struck.' In Cairo he became at once 'the lion of the day. Everybody tumbled over each other in their eagerness to entertain him', in Europe every court vied in receiving him with celebrations and honours. 'I used to chaff him', wrote Rumbold in 1910, 'that he got one star a year as regularly as clockwork. At a ball at Marlborough House in 1903 he was the most decorated man in the room.'[1]

Slatin's escape raised again the question of the reconquest of the Sudan in the minds of all who met him. 'I hankered after the Sudan', wrote Rumbold, 'and wondered whether I should ever get there. The mere name was anathema maranatha to "the Lord" – as Cromer used now to be called.'

Rumbold now began to worry about promotion. 'I have been here very nearly $3\frac{1}{2}$ years', he wrote to his father, 'and have always been at the bottom of the staff. My duties have been to copy, to do all the ADC work of the Agency and to arrange tennis for Lord Cromer. . . . You know that I have been here three summers almost alone and twice quite alone with the Chargé d'Affaires, that I really had a lot of work to do in the very hottest and dullest part of the year.' He now knew Egypt well: 'I do all I can to be in thorough touch with the spirit of the place.' As for his personal ambition, he wished to stay on in Cairo to become the senior Second

Kitchener's Staff, 1897-98. Knighted, 1900; Major-General, 1907. Created Baron of the Habsburg Empire, 1906, President of the Austrian Red Cross Aid to Prisoners of War, 1914-18. He published *Fire and Sword in the Sudan* in 1898.

[1] Of the British Orders, Slatin held, in 1903, the CB (1895), the MVO (1896) and the KCMG (1898). He later received the CVO (1904) and the KCVO (1908). He also held numerous foreign orders.

Secretary, to act as Chargé d'Affaires in Cromer's absence, and finally to succeed Arthur Hardinge, who had become Consul-General in Zanzibar. 'This may seem to you to be flying high but it is as well, I am sure, to have a definite aim for which to work.'

Rumbold asked his father to put in a good word for him when he was in London – 'I don't see why somebody shouldn't speak for me' – but it was to no avail. He reached London on leave in June, and learned much to his disappointment, that he was not to return to Cairo, but would be sent to Teheran instead. While in London, Rumbold received an ebullient letter from his father, on Windsor Castle notepaper, informing him of 'a very noteworthy change in high places as regards me . . . it is a real satisfaction to find oneself treated properly again, and both the Prince and Princess of Wales'[1] manner when we dined at Marlboro' House, as well as that of the Queen[2] herself to both of us yesterday was kindness itself.' Sir Horace did not conceal his excitement. 'It may almost seem silly to you that I should attach so much importance to all this, but to say the truth I have felt so crushed and sore for some time past now that I am much relieved at this change for the better, although I am not such a fool as to expect anything more substantial will come of it.' Nor did any promotion follow.

Rumbold was sad to be leaving Egypt. Working under Cromer had taught him a great deal, both of diplomacy and of men. 'One could not help being influenced', he later wrote, 'by Lord C's method of doing business. . . . He was punctiliously punctual'; and in this respect, he added, 'I have tried to imitate him.' In his recollections the young diplomat gave a pen sketch of his first 'chief':

He was devoted to children and very fond of music. Often have I heard him hammering out a Strauss waltz while waiting for dinner. He hated Wagner and modern operas whilst liking Verdi and the old Italian operas. He was very fond of shooting and fishing. Although he did not say much he hated being beaten at lawn-tennis or losing at whist and subsequently at bridge. He was not a very ideal partner at bridge. If things went well, all was right, but if they didn't, he was inclined to be snappy. He could be alarming when he chose, especially to British officials in the Egyptian service. But he was always charming with his

[1] Alexandra Caroline Mary Charlotte Louise Julia, 1844–1925. Daughter of Prince Christian of Schleswig-Holstein-Sonderburg-Glucksburg (later King of Denmark). Married Edward, Prince of Wales (later Edward VII), 1863. Queen consort, 1901–10. Founded the Queen Alexandra Imperial Military Nursing Service, 1902. A friend of Lord Kitchener, she placed herself at the head of the memorial appeal after his death in June 1916.

[2] Queen Victoria, whom Sir Horace had first met in 1860 at Balmoral, 'Dinner was got through quickly' he recorded of this occasion in his *Recollections of a Diplomat* (Vol. 2, p. 55), 'a rather startling effect being produced upon me at dessert by the entrance of her Majesty's piper, who marched round the table performing some wild tune. . . .'

own staff. He was accused of being rough in his manner with the Khedive. I do not believe this. I was only present at one interview on business between the two and on that occasion Lord C was as nice as he could be. Lord C knew and spoke French and Italian well. He knew German pretty well and had learnt a good deal of Turkish. . . . He knew no Arabic except the words 'Wallad, koora' (boy – the balls) which he used to shout out when playing tennis. He had practically taught himself ancient Greek – of which he was very fond. In fact he had, through his own exertions, become a classical scholar above the average. Altogether he was very versatile. He had an excellent memory and remembered what he read. He was devoted to Dickens and could have passed a very good examination on that author. . . . One could not help learning something from and being influenced by such a man.

3

Teheran

1895–1897

While on leave in London in the summer of 1895 Rumbold continued to work on his father's behalf, reporting to The Hague whatever news he could glean. In July it seemed that Sir Horace might have a chance of being sent as Ambassador to Germany, for Lady Ampthill[1] reported that Lord Salisbury 'really didn't know whom to send to Berlin', and that interest in the appointment had also been shown at Windsor, where Sir Horace now knew he was looked upon with favour. But he was again passed over.

Rumbold managed to spend three weeks with his father at The Hague, but it was a difficult time, for Sir Horace was extremely nervous about his future. When Rumbold returned to London he hastened to assure his father that 'it never enters into my head to look down either upon your position or your establishment at The Hague. If such were the case I should be a poor kind of fellow and deserve kicking.' As for the Foreign Office officials who kept his father from his ambition, 'the whole crew make me sick and I'm thankful that I shan't see the d–d humbugs for 2 years'.

Rumbold set off for Persia in the first week of September 1895. He travelled by train through Paris and Vienna to Constantinople, where he found, as he told his father, 'my pet aversion', the Third Secretary, William Max Müller[2] – 'a cad and a snob'.

From Constantinople, Rumbold travelled by ship across the Black Sea to Batum. Thence he took a train through the Caucasus to Baku. The journey was not a success. 'At the end of an hour a Russian officer got in and was soon snoring like a hog. . . . I could even hear it above the rattle of the train.' From Tiflis he had a compartment to himself, and was 'fairly comfortable all night though washing arrangements don't exist on these lines'. Baku made a poor impression, and the oil town which he

---

[1] Lady Emily Theresa Villiers, 1843–1927. 3rd daughter of the 4th Earl of Clarendon. She married the 1st Baron Ampthill (later British Ambassador in Berlin) in 1868, and was a Lady of the Bedchamber to Queen Victoria, 1885–1901.

[2] William Grenfell Max-Müller, 1867–1945. Entered Diplomatic Service, 1892. 3rd Secretary, Constantinople, 1892–94. After twenty-eight years as a diplomat, he was appointed Minister to Warsaw in succession to Rumbold in 1920. Knighted, 1922.

visited near by he found 'extraordinarily interesting but quite beastly. . . . The place is gloomy beyond words and every blessed thing is black.' From Baku he took a ship southwards through the Caspian – 'I was far too ill to care what we were doing or where we were'. He left the ship at the Persian town of Enzeli. Here, at so remote a spot, was a glimpse of civilization, for the Minister at Teheran, Sir Mortimer Durand, had sent a messenger to meet Rumbold, and to give him some 'champagne, wine and soup' for the difficult overland journey to the capital, which he reached almost a month after leaving London.

The British Legation at Teheran was a remote and frustrating place to be posted to for long. The contrast with Egypt was a stark one. At Cairo, Lord Cromer presided over an Agency whose immediate concern was the government of a country which, while officially only 'occupied' by Britain was in fact a part of the British Empire. The opinions and actions of the British officials directly affected the lives and future of the Egyptian people. But in Teheran British influence was minimal. Russia, with a common border and easy access, dominated the Shah[1] and his Court. Cossack troops under Russian officers kept order in the capital. A Russian veto prevented any railway building by British firms in the south. Nor did the British Government seek to challenge the Russian dominance, even though as Rumbold later wrote, 'the bogey of Russian designs on northern Persia and India was always present to our minds'.

Rumbold soon found that his colleagues in Teheran 'abused the place like poison'. He himself was surprised at the 'complete absence of society and especially of ladies . . .', the few women being 'very fiddleheaded'. In November a storm destroyed a bridge on the Batum-Baku railway line, along which Rumbold had travelled, and broke all telegraphic and carriage communications between Persia and Europe. The Legation found itself 'as completely cut off from the outside world as if we had been living in Uganda'.

There was little work to do in Teheran; Rumbold's time was taken up mostly by paperchases, tent-pegging, hare-coursing and duck-shooting. 'It is raining hard as I write', Rumbold complained to his father, 'and I long for an Egyptian sky.' A long letter from Lady Cromer added to his nostalgia for Egypt. Sir Horace was rather irritated by his son's frequent references to his former post, and by his desire to return there as soon as his two years in Persia were over. 'You must let me say', he wrote, 'that by that time you will have been a good five years at those distant Eastern

[1] Nasir-ud-Din, Shah of Persia from 1848 until his assassination on May 1, 1896. He made three visits to Europe; in 1889 he was received by Queen Victoria at Windsor and given the Order of the Garter.

posts, which in my humble opinion is an ample allowance.' He would then be nearly twenty-nine, 'high time', in his father's view, to go to 'some big European post', from the peripheral business of remote Legations 'into *la grande politique* which is only carried on at great European centres'.

Sir Horace had stern words to say about his son's way of life and his attitude to those around him:

I also think that in Egypt, as in Persia, you are thrown too much on your own countrymen. It is all very well, and no doubt pleasant, to endeavour to be a downright good Britisher, and to look down on those 'd-d foreigners', but, to become a successful diplomatist, you must allow for a little more cosmopolitism. . . . I confess this attitude of mind in you rather riles me & does not seem to me quite devoid of *pose*. Nor is it perhaps quite flattering to *me* whose bringing up & general career . . . have been so diametrically opposed to the ideal to which you seem to aspire.

Rumbold replied at once to his father's strictures. Everybody who had been even a short time in Egypt, he pointed out, 'hankers after it and longs to get back there'. He had never found an exception to that rule. And surely, he asked, 'you consider that the Egyptian question comes within the sphere of the "grand politique"?' At the Agency in Cairo there was 'every advantage – good pay, interesting work, great touch with home, very cosmopolitan'. 'You must remember', Rumbold continued, 'that posts like Cairo etc have taken the place of Florence and Turin and that the old order has given place to the new.' As for his father's principal complaint, it was, he insisted, unjustified: 'My liking for Eastern posts has no connection with a dislike of foreigners. I meet the latter wherever I go and it would only be a question of degree were I to be sent to Berlin or elsewhere. As a matter of fact I get on very well with foreigners and they with me and I have no dislike for them as such. . . . Of course I avoid a foreign bounder as I would an English one.' Rumbold conceded that he was not entirely free from bias: 'I admit that I do dislike the French as a whole and think they are a nation of apes and cads. I hope I may one day see them reduced by us to the level of a second-rate power.' He did, of course, consider his fellow Britons to be 'the salt of the earth', but this, he stressed, 'does *not* exclude the possibility of getting on well with foreigners'. As for his attitude being a pose, as his father had suggested, this was untrue: 'I am not in training to become a regular Britisher nor do I go about making allusions to d-d foreigners. If I did I admit it would be a "pose" but such is not the case. Having been brought up at a private and a public school in England has made me what it makes everybody else and my attitude of mind is no different to that of thousands of others who have had the same education as myself. We are English and that's all . . .'

Rumbold remained at Teheran for nearly two years. His xenophobia did not abate. 'The Persians are a beastly people', he wrote within three weeks of receiving his father's rebuke, 'and Teheran is a foul hole, the only decent corner being where our Legation stands.' He doubted whether his father could picture 'how utterly rotten the state of things is'. The central government was so weak 'that it is powerless to enforce its orders. . . . Highway robberies are very frequent and the guards which the authorities give travellers are just as likely to rob you as the tribesmen.' Lady Cromer, in a twelve-page letter, gave Rumbold a vivid account of social life in Cairo, and concluded: 'Teheran must be a deadly place & so ugly.' Even Sir Horace came soon to accept his son's pessimistic analysis of Persian affairs – 'we must be prepared, I fear', he wrote, 'to see it some day fall an easy prey to the Russians.'

News of Kitchener's impending expedition against the Dervishes made Rumbold wish 'more keenly than ever' to be in Cairo again. 'In the midst of it all', as he wrote to his father. He wrote nostalgically to his father of how he should like 'to be with my pals in the Sudan.[1] I am very fond of anything in the way of an expedition.'

On 3 September 1896, Slatin wrote to Rumbold from the Sudan describing the somewhat dispiriting progress of the expedition:

We have evil days behind us. In extreme heat the railway had to be built and the enemy driven out of Ferket. To this was added the Cholera epidemic; and the Nile, exceptionally, rose so slowly that only a few days ago was it possible to bring the steamers over the cataracts. In a land in which it has only rained once in the last 10 years, thunderstorms & sandstorms are the order of the day. A storm destroyed the railway along a 12 mile stretch, so that at the very moment when we wanted to begin our march forward we are being kept back to re-establish communications. A gale overthrew my tent and some minutes later a second one, the so-called 'Intelligence Office'. We endeavoured to save what could be saved. Nevertheless a part of the more or less valuable papers were carried off by the wind or destroyed by water. We let them go with a farewell tear – tears of anger because the work of many hours had been destroyed in a moment. My private diary I held, as a tender mother does her

---

[1] The campaign for the reconquest of the Sudan was inaugurated in June 1896 by the defeat of a Dervish force at Ferket. A year later, in August 1897, the advance up the Nile began with the capture of Abu Hamed and Berber. Kitchener advanced slowly and methodically, building a railway as he went. On September 2, 1898, with 25,000 British and Egyptian troops, he defeated a Dervish army of 50,000 at Omdurman; two days later he entered Khartoum. The whole campaign cost only 60 British and 160 Egyptian lives, while several thousand Dervish had been killed. The pacification of the Sudan continued until November 1899, when the Khalifa was killed by troops led by Sir Reginald Wingate.

child at the approach of danger, pressed to my breast; but in the morning I noticed to my horror that a great part of my records had become unreadable because of the rain. . . .

In Teheran Rumbold had to be content with snipe-shooting, chasing gazelle and billiards. There was also a great deal of tedious paperwork, for he had been appointed Acting Vice-Consul, which put him in charge of administering not only the British Legation, but also the three Consulates-General and the many telegraph establishments of the Indo-European Telegraph service. 'I shall have to keep an account of and answer for about £25,000–£30,000. . . . The work will, of course, tie me dreadfully by the leg.' He began to learn Persian, and, after five months could understand it 'quite easily', passing the exam early in April. He was presented to the Shah, who observed 'that he thought I was the sort of chap who could ride'. On the same occasion he met the Shah's third son, the Commander-in-Chief of the Army and Governor of Teheran, who 'looked what he is, an oily, dissolute beast – but he was civil enough'.

A month after this audience, the Shah was murdered. The European community feared riots and anarchy, but these were averted. By a tacit Anglo-Russian agreement the Shah's second son,[1] the Valiahd, who was Governor-General of the Azerbaijan province, succeeded him. All the Ministers and relatives of the dead Shah who were in Teheran at once collected, as Rumbold reported 'in the telegraph office attached to the palace, and from there telegraphed their loyalty and submission to the Valiahd who was in the telegraph office at Tabriz'. The murdered Shah's eldest son, the Zil-es-Sultan, whose low birth prevented him from succeeding to the throne, was apparently 'in a great funk'. He too telegraphed his submission, from Ispahan where he was Governor-General, and at the same time begged the British to protect him from the new Shah. 'We told him we would see he wasn't harmed', wrote Rumbold, 'but his business was to prevent rows and keep his province in order.' The Valiahd's half-brother, who a year previously had tried to poison him, 'sent an earnest appeal' for protection to the British Legation. Sir Mortimer Durand, who went to see him, found him in his garden, 'squatting on the ground', Rumbold wrote to his father, 'in the middle of a dusty path wearing a pair of light blue trousers entirely covered with dirt and some exceedingly pointed leather shoes. He was in an indescribable funk.' He beseeched Durand to let him become a British subject, but this was politely refused.

---

[1] Muzaffar-ud-Din, 1853–1906. As Shah he visited Europe twice; England in 1902. In 1906 he agreed to set up a National Assembly and a Court of Justice; he died a few days after opening the National Assembly.

The Russians, to whom he then turned, agreed to make him a 'Russian protected person'.

The new Shah set out slowly from Tabriz for Teheran, 600 miles away. In Teheran itself the British Bank helped reduce tension by paying the wages of the Shah's troops. The only disturbances were on the southern road from Teheran to the Persian Gulf, where nomad tribes looted all caravans, and seized three thousand pounds worth of belongings when they attacked the caravan of the new German Minister,[1] on his way to the capital to take up his appointment.

Rumbold's administrative duties made the summer of 1896 a weary one for him. 'The Consular Work', he told his father, 'is the devil's own business. It's without exception the dullest, most irritating and persistent work I have ever done in my life.' Dealing with Persians as much as he had to was, he added, 'enough to spoil the sweetest temper in the world, and mine is by no means that'. Further irritation was caused by the need to send all letters to Europe via Tabriz and Batum at 'the tender mercies of the Persians and Russians. . . . They are both equal swine.'

A brief escape from the Orient came with the 4th of June. There were four old Etonians in Teheran on that day, and short though Rumbold's stay at Eton had been, he remained all his life a passionate Etonian. The supper party was held in his rooms. 'We made a fearful row', he reported to his father, 'and wound up with a football match in the room which was destructive to limbs and property . . . 2 chairs, 10 glasses and a part of the fireplace were broken.' In this quiet life, he added, it was 'a great relief to let off steam by making a row occasionally'.

Rumbold's distaste for Persia was increased when, in June 1897, Persian tribesmen attacked, mutilated and murdered an Englishman in southern Persia. It was not the first incident of its kind, and yet, as before, the Shah's authority was insufficient to punish the offenders. 'Nothing has been done', Rumbold complained, 'and our prestige and influence down south have vanished.' Sir Mortimer Durand wanted to send a gunboat to Mohammerah to enforce punishment of the tribesmen and payment of an indemnity. Rumbold agreed with such a course. In his view, he told his father, it was essential to 'make it generally hot for these filthy Persians'. But the Foreign Office disagreed. 'They take no interest in Persia', Rumbold complained; 'They have too many irons in the fire.'[2]

[1] Karl Wilhelm Günther, Freiherr von Gärtner-Griebenow, 1856–98. Born in Berlin. German Minister to Persia from 1896 until his death. He died in Teheran.

[2] The murdered Englishman was E. Graves, Inspector of the English Telegraph line from Jask eastwards. When the Persian Government eventually tried to seize the murderers, a considerable revolt broke out in the tribal area, and the Shah was forced to despatch a military expedition to restore his authority. One of the murderers was caught, and hanged, in May 1898.

In July Rumbold was presented to the new Shah, and found him 'a strange mixture of magnificence and untidyness, wearing the very finest diamonds but an ill-fitting uniform, being unshaved and with dirty side-spring boots on . . . very characteristic of his country which is also a mixture of ruin and flashy appearance.' In September the Grand Vizier gave a dinner for the whole of the British Legation. 'I sat between the "Assayer of the Kingdom" and the "Commander of the Empire" – the latter a dull dog.' Other Persians at the dinner included 'the Trusted One of the Privacy', 'the Calculator of the Kingdom' and 'the Giver of Orders'. The Grand Vizier's butler sang 'exceedingly monotonous and very ugly music' until the Grand Vizier ordered him to stop. 'It doesn't do to be an exile in the East too long', Rumbold wrote to his father in November, 'and I have come round to your view of the matter.' The Persians, he concluded, 'are in reality the greatest beasts on the face of the earth', a view from which nothing could dislodge him.

Throughout his first year in Persia, Rumbold had watched anxiously as his father's prospects of an Embassy fluctuated from month to month. Sir Horace was sixty-eight. He was regarded in the Diplomatic Service as cantankerous and quarrelsome. For several years a story had circulated that he had insulted a Dutch ticket-collector at The Hague by forcing his way through the barrier while shouting out that he was the British Minister, and refusing to show his ticket. There were other, similar, stories, including one in which he was supposed to have come to blows with a Dutch court official. Sir Horace's rudeness had become a byword in diplomatic circles, where he was known as 'Sir Horrid Grumbles'.

In March 1897 Sir Horace received a message from Lord Rosebery containing 'a sort of apology' for having been influenced adversely by stories of his alleged misconduct four years before. But this apology by the former Liberal Prime Minister could not improve his position with the new Conservative administration. When, a month later, Sir Horace tried to find out what Lord Salisbury intended, he was unable to do so. 'Secretaries being without bowels of compassion as we all know.' A month later he wrote to his son: 'What hopes I had vanish more & more and day by day.' In June Eric Barrington[1] wrote encouragingly that 'there are several Embassies for which you would be excellently suited'; but Sir Horace was depressed by his long wait, and felt that his chances had become 'so slender now that they are hardly worth speaking of'. But on August 7,

---

[1] Bernard Eric Edward Barrington, 1847–1918. Younger son of the 6th Viscount Barrington. Entered Foreign Office, 1867. Private Secretary to Lord Salisbury, 1887–92 and 1895–1900; to Lord Lansdowne, 1900–5. Knighted, 1902. Assistant Under-Secretary of State for Foreign Affairs, 1906–7.

1897, he received a letter from Barrington to say that Lord Salisbury had asked him to inquire whether 'in the event of Vienna falling vacant I would accept the Embassy if offered to me'. This was the appointment Sir Horace had most desired. 'I have not only dispelled the cloud produced by the absurd, not to say calumnious stories spread about me', he wrote to his son, 'but am held to be a possibly useful and deserving servant scurvily treated.' Five years of unhappiness were at an end; Sir Horace was at last an Ambassador. Yet even then he was not entirely content. 'I left The Hague', he wrote in his memoirs, 'with very mixed feelings, for, great though was the sense of relief that I had at last, after no little tribulation, reached the topmost rung of the diplomatic ladder, I could not but feel that, at my age, the long desired promotion came almost too late.'

Even before the Vienna Embassy was finally settled Sir Horace had written to his son: 'If I do go to Vienna I shall put it to you strongly whether you would not somewhat curtail your time in Persia, and come and join me.' Rumbold was delighted with this suggestion. The remoteness of Persia vexed him, as did the constant Russian interference with the British Legation's mail and documents – 'I suppose these contain reflections on their own beastly country and people.' On one occasion Rumbold received a letter without its envelope, 'having evidently been read with interest by the post office officials *en route*'. But it was over a year before the Foreign Office would let him join his father in Vienna.

Life at the Legation in Teheran was often a strain. Sir Mortimer Durand had spent twenty years in India, during the last ten of which he was Foreign Secretary in the Viceroy's Council. The chaos of Persia irked him, and, as Rumbold saw, he 'fretted at his powerlessness'. Nor could Teheran provide him, or his wife,[1] with the social interest of Calcutta or Simla. 'We all lunched and dined with the Durands every day', wrote Rumbold. 'After dinner we generally played billiards. After a time, the inevitable happened. . . . We exhausted all topics of conversation.'

In March 1897 Teheran was filled with rumours that the Shah had died. 'People fled to their houses and the breadshops were shut', Rumbold reported. The rumour was soon found to be untrue. 'The spreader of false news', wrote Rumbold, 'was discovered and captured, a hole drilled in his nose and a ring passed through, and he was then led through the streets by a string attached to the ring. Such are the barbarous habits still prevailing here.'

Fifteen years later Rumbold set down his opinions of Persia in his recollections. 'It would be difficult', he wrote, 'to admire the Persian character. With few exceptions Persians are dirty, liars and thieves. They

[1] Ella Sandys. She married Mortimer Durand in 1875, and died in 1913.

were very conceited and rather traded on their past history. They were clever enough, had good manners on occasion, and were cheerful scoundrels. . . . The preoccupation of members of the official class was to squeeze as much money as they could out of the country. Governorships etc were sold to the highest bidder who recouped himself as best he could.' Most vexing of all for the diplomats, 'the servant class was very unsatisfactory but showed wonderful resource in lying'.

On October 14, shortly before Rumbold left Teheran, Charles Hardinge[1] wrote to Lord Salisbury of the 'ability and care' which Rumbold had shown in carrying out his duties, adding that 'his never failing tact and good humour have made him generally popular with the British and foreign communities'. Before he left, Rumbold sent on to Vienna by diplomatic bag '1 large silk carpet, 1 small ditto, 1 piece of Bokhara work, 1 piece of Italian silk and 3 silver photograph frames'. His route back was through southern Persia. At Ispahan he visited the Zil-es-Sultan, who asked him 'point blank' why Britain did not divide Persia with the Russians, a division which the Zil-es-Sultan felt to be inevitable. Rumbold managed to avoid a direct answer, but in his report of the journey which he wrote for the Under-Secretary of State for Foreign Affairs, George Curzon,[2] he made his position clear. There was, he told Curzon, no means whereby the existing Persian government could possibly improve by its own exertions. 'I cannot help thinking', he wrote, 'that a large proportion of the Persians of the south would not object to a substitution of our rule for that of their own countrymen', if only because 'they see money or business transactions between the English and themselves punctually and honestly carried out' and because they know 'that as a rule the English paid higher wages than the Persians.' Under British rule both peasants and workers would be able 'to keep a great portion of their earnings instead of – as now – those earnings being extorted from them almost in their entirety'.

Rumbold felt that a start could be made by a more direct British control

[1] Charles Hardinge, 1858–1944. A cousin of Rumbold's friend Arthur Hardinge. Entered Foreign Office, 1880. Knighted, 1904. Ambassador at Petrograd, 1904–6. Permanent Under-Secretary of State for Foreign Affairs, 1906–10. Created Baron Hardinge of Penshurst, 1910. Viceroy of India, 1910–16. Reappointed Permanent Under-Secretary of State for Foreign Affairs, 1916–20. Ambassador to Paris, 1920–23.

[2] George Nathaniel Curzon, 1859–1925. Conservative MP, 1886–98. Under-Secretary of State for India, 1891–92; for Foreign Affairs, 1892–98. Created Baron, 1898. Viceroy of India, 1898–1905. Created Earl, 1911. Lord Privy Seal, May 1915–December 1916. President of the Air Board, 1916. Lord President of the Council and Member of the War Cabinet, 1916–19. Secretary of State for Foreign Affairs, 1919–24. Created Marquess, 1921. Lord President of the Council, 1924–25. From 1889 to 1890 Curzon himself had travelled extensively throughout Persia, and in 1892 published *Persia and the Persian Question*.

of the Telegraph Line, which was the only safe communication between Teheran and the Persian Gulf and carried telegraphic messages from Britain to India. 'I am aware that there are good reasons for employing Armenians in certain telegraph stations', he wrote, 'but I can not help thinking that . . . it would be perfectly possible to employ English clerks. . . . There is no doubt they would command far greater influence.' Ideally, in his opinion, all the Telegraph officials ought to be corporals or sergeants in the Royal Engineers. They could become 'a great factor for the spread of our influence if properly directed'. Rumbold concluded his report on a pessimistic note:

It was depressing to my mind to pass through towns of historical interest hurrying to decay as fast as the fine Persian climate would allow. The climate alone is nowadays responsible for the preservation of any monuments remaining, no effort being made by the government or people to preserve buildings which should on the contrary be a source of pride to them.

The 'stationary state' in the history of a nation has been described as the most melancholy of all states but I cannot help thinking that it is even more melancholy to witness the utter decay of one of the oldest monarchies in the world. The future of Persia as an independent state is difficult to foresee for it is fairly evident that it cannot stand much longer by itself. With a ruling class in which it would be difficult to find a single member possessing an ounce of patriotism, and with a population apathetic to the fate of the country and resigned to oppression and exactions Persia must soon hasten to dissolution. If it does, it will at all events have been interesting to have lived in the country whilst it was yet independent, and instructive to have been able to compare the results of uncontrolled oriental despotism with those produced by an administration like that of England in Egypt.

4
Vienna
1897–1900

Rumbold served under his father as Second Secretary at the Embassy in Vienna for nearly three years, from the winter of 1897 until shortly after his father's retirement from the Diplomatic Service in the autumn of 1900. Being third in the hierarchy of Embassy officials, he had none of the responsibility which he had known for the previous three years as Head of Chancery at Teheran. But his work was no lighter, for he acted also as his father's private secretary, copying out by hand several hundred of his father's despatches. There was much to record; the continual quarrels between the Austrians and Hungarians, the breakdown of parliamentary government in Austria, the Emperor Franz-Josef's[1] increasing closeness to the Germany of Kaiser Wilhelm II,[2] the discontent of the Slavs, the growing pressure of Jews fleeing from Russia, the fear of anarchist plots. These introduced Rumbold, for the first time, to the intricacies of European diplomacy.

The social life of Vienna fascinated Rumbold as much as its politics. Stories about fellow diplomats abounded. Many of the scandals centred around the German Ambassador, Count Eulenburg.[3] He and the German Military Attaché Count Moltke,[4] would, Rumbold recalled, 'make music together by the hour'. Moltke's cheeks were painted, he had a mincing walk, and 'he obviously wore stays'. Later, when Moltke married, 'gossips asserted that his wife – indignant at the hours he spent with his chief – used to thrash him when he came back'. The Papal Nuncio, Monsignor Taliani,[5] was a figure of fun on account of his appetite. 'One night', Rumbold re-

[1] Franz-Josef, 1830–1916. Emperor of Austria from 1848; king of Hungary from 1867. His only son committed suicide in 1889; his wife was murdered in 1898.

[2] Wilhelm von Hohenzollern, 1859–1941. First cousin of George V. Succeeded his father as German Emperor 1888. Abdicated, November 1918. In exile in Holland after 1918.

[3] Philip zu Eulenburg und Hertefeld, Graf zu Sandels, 1847–1921. German Ambassador in Vienna, 1894–1902. A close personal friend of the Kaiser. Tried for homosexual offences, 1906, and banished from Court.

[4] Count August Karl Friedrich Detlef Kuno von Moltke, 1847–1923. 2nd Lieutenant, 1868. Wounded in the Franco-Prussian War, 1870. Major, 1890. Military Attaché, Vienna, 1893–99. Lieutenant-Colonel, 1897; Colonel, 1899; Lieutenant-General, 1914.

[5] Emidio Taliani, 1838–1907. Ordained, 1861. Papal Nuncio, Vienna, from 1896 until his death. Created Cardinal, 1903.

called, 'I dined at the Spanish Embassy – the dinner being at 7.30 p.m. Taliani was the principal guest and I noticed that he ate steadily through the menu – although it was a long one. One of his Secretaries was sitting next to me and I said to him: "what a fine appetite your chief has!" He replied in tones of admiration "yes, hasn't he? We have just come on from another dinner to some Bishops at 5 o'clock and my chief ate through that also".'

At a series of Court and Embassy balls Rumbold danced with the daughters of Princes and Counts. He hunted on their vast, scattered estates, in Austria, Hungary and Silesia. Hunting and horse-racing, bridge and poker, Court dances and lavish picnics filled his time. Each year, at the beginning of May, all the Embassies moved from Vienna to Pesth,[1] where, at the annual races, the Hungarians tried to impress the diplomatic corps with their superiority over the Germans of Austria. 'Hungarians are about the vainest people in Europe', Rumbold noted in his recollections. 'When one has realized this, as one quickly does, the way to their heart is easy. One has only to praise them and their town and hospitality and the trick is done.' After a month, the Embassies returned to Vienna, where early in June the Vienna Derby ended the social season, and the aristocrats dispersed for the rest of the summer to their estates.

In June 1898, the moment the Vienna Derby was over, Rumbold returned to England and took the four months leave to which he was entitled as a result of his service in Persia. But the long absences caused by a diplomatic career made friendships difficult to retain, and Rumbold did not find the summer in England as enjoyable as he had hoped. 'I am in the state of not knowing whom I know and whom I don't', he wrote to his father on June 15. 'An entirely fresh lot of young men and girls has appeared on the scene and it is rather a grind getting into it again.' During two days at Ascot, at several dances, at the Opera, and at Cowes during race week, he found it hard to find old friends or to make new ones. 'For every nice person I meet over here,' he informed his father, 'there are at least 2 snobs, which is a pity.'

While in England, Rumbold learned that an Italian anarchist had assassinated Franz-Josef's wife, the Empress Elizabeth.[2] 'Vermin like the Anarchists', he wrote to his father on September 12, 'should be destroyed

[1] The twin cities of Buda and Pesth (or Pest), on either side of the Danube, were incorporated into a single municipality in 1872, but continued to be known by their separate names. In 1900 the combined city had a population of 730,000, of whom over a quarter were Jews; a fact which also caused the city to be known as Judapest.

[2] Elizabeth Amelia Eugénie, 1837–98. Daughter of Duke Maximilian Joseph of Bavaria. She married the Emperor Franz-Josef in 1854. Her assassin was a twenty-five year old Italian anarchist, Luigi Lucheni.

without mercy wherever found for they are no better than stoats.' He was delighted with the news of Kitchener's victory over the Dervishes at Omdurman. 'I now hope we shall hoof the French out of Fashoda', he wrote; and when the French were forced to withdraw from the upper Nile he was much relieved. He saw France as Britain's principal rival in imperial affairs, and his distrust of French policy was intense. Nor did Frenchmen please him. 'I have come across few French diplomatists whom I like', he wrote ten years later, recalling his time at Vienna.

In October 1898 Rumbold returned from leave; in the spring of 1899 he went to Pesth to try to introduce polo to the Hungarians. Two games were soon arranged. He returned to Vienna at the end of the month for more dancing, poker and shooting. 'Nowadays I never get more than six hours in bed', he complained to his father, who was then on leave. The Russian Ambassador, Count Kapnist,[1] went with him trout fishing. 'He spent a considerable part of the time', Rumbold wrote to his father, 'in abusing the French and all their works and evidently hates them like poison.' In the autumn he went to Nathaniel Rothschild's[2] estate at Schillersdorf on the Austrian–Prussian border where, in five days' shooting, 10,000 pheasants were killed. 'I was the worst shot of the whole party', he recorded in his recollections of 1911. On one of the days, while he shot 30 pheasants, his neighbour shot 180.

It was on his return from a shoot near Vienna in October 1899 that Rumbold learned that war had broken out in South Africa. The atmosphere in Vienna changed at once. The rest of the diplomatic corps was sympathetic to the Boers. 'We had only 2 friends amongst nations,' Rumbold recalled in 1910; 'i.e. Denmark and Greece.' The Viennese newspapers were filled with anti-British feeling; this was particularly annoying, Rumbold recalled, because many of them 'are controlled by Jews who have peculiar reason to speak well of England where there is almost total absence of anti-Semitism. Nevertheless the Jews were unanimously hostile to us. . . .' With each Boer success during November and December 1899, anti-British feeling grew more strong. The pro-Boer sentiments of the Jewish-controlled Press were paralleled by equally pro-Boer feeling among the Viennese anti-Semites, led by the Burgomaster of Vienna, Dr Lueger.[3] Rumbold's father protested to the Austrian Govern-

---

[1] Peter Alexeevich Kapnist, 1839–1904. Entered the Ministry of Foreign Affairs, 1861. Served in Rome, Paris and The Hague. Ambassador to Vienna from 1895 until his death.

[2] Nathaniel Rothschild, 1836–1905. Born in Frankfurt, he played a leading part in the development of the Viennese branch of the Rothschild banking empire.

[3] Karl Lueger, 1844–1910. Appointed Mayor of Vienna, 1897. He installed efficient gas, electricity and tramway systems to the city. A vociferous anti-semite, his denunciations of the Jews had a strong influence on Adolf Hitler, who was then living in Vienna.

ment about Lueger's offensive language, for Lueger had turned to vilifying a Protestant Queen with the same venom which he used against the Jews and the 'Judaeo-Magyaren', as he used contemptuously to refer to the Hungarians.

'Many Bavarian artists,' Rumbold later recalled, 'taking as their text the struggle of the Tyrolese against French domination, compared the Boers with Hofer[1] and his gallant followers. This was legitimate if exaggerated, but there was no excuse for the filthy caricatures of the Queen and our Royal Family which were published in Paris, at Munich and at Leipzig, and scattered broadcast over Europe.' Anti-British postcards, printed in Germany, were sold throughout Austria, and every Boer victory made the delight of the Viennese at Britain's distress more evident. The new German Military Attaché in Vienna, von Bülow,[2] openly held the British up to ridicule; whenever he met someone from the British Embassy he would dwell at length, as if sympathizing, on the most recent British reverse. 'We all hated him', Rumbold recalled, 'and avoided him as much as possible.' But when Eulenburg, the German Ambassador, returned from a visit to Berlin in November 1899, he gave Rumbold's father a surprisingly sympathetic message from the Kaiser. Sir Horace at once passed on this unexpected support to Lord Salisbury in London:

> The Emperor spoke very severely of the attitude of those who seemed bent on producing ill-will between Germany and Great Britain. It showed utter want of sense and political judgment. The right policy for Germany was to keep on very cordial terms with Great Britain.
>
> My colleague, thereupon expatiating on this theme, observed, in proof of the folly of the press crusade against us, that no sane politician could desire to see serious reverses attend our arms in the very arduous campaign in which we were engaged. Any diminution of British Power and prestige would be regrettable in the interests of the general peace and equilibrium &, added Count Eulenburg, this view was, he knew, strongly held by the Emperor Francis Joseph. . . .

A month later Eulenburg went to see Rumbold's father again. Once more the evident German sympathy for Britain prompted the Ambassador to send Lord Salisbury a full report:

---

[1] Andreas Hofer, 1767–1810. Tyrolese patriot, he led the revolt against Bavarian rule in 1809, and for two months ruled the Tyrol in the name of the Emperor of Austria (August–September). In January 1810 he was captured by Italian troops and sent in chains to Mantua. He was shot, apparently on Napoleon's direct orders, on February 20, 1810.

[2] Karl Ulrich Stephan Wilhelm von Bülow, 1862–1914. A brother of Chancellor Bülow and of Major-General Adolf von Bülow. Second-Lieutenant, 1884; Captain, 1896. Military Attaché, Vienna, 1899–1901. Major, 1901; Colonel, 1909; Major-General, 1913. Commanded the 9th Cavalry Division, August 1, 1914; killed in action in Belgium, August 6.

He wished, he said, to assure me of his heartfelt sympathy in the adverse turn taken by our military operations in South Africa. He spoke in terms of the greatest admiration of the valour displayed by H.M. forces. He was shocked, he said, by the losses we had sustained and which he attributed to tactics ill-suited to the arms of precision of the enemy and to under-estimation of their fighting powers and resources. – He made no doubt of the final issue of the struggle, but would not pretend to conceal his impression that Great Britain was now going through a very serious ordeal. Our position, as perhaps the most leading civilized Power (Kultur-staat) was of such importance that all right-thinking and en-lightened persons could not but wish us well, while anxiously watching the course of the contest in which we were engaged. . . .

Sir Horace also reported that the Russian Ambassador, Count Kapnist, had likewise spoken sympathetically of Britain's difficulties; but these were the only two friendly comments. 'There is no concealing the fact', he telegraphed to Lord Salisbury on December 29, 'that public opinion in this Country, as expressed in a prejudiced and unprincipled press and in mostly ill-informed social circles, continues unfriendly towards us.'

Although Rumbold's social activities continued unabated, the atmos-phere was less relaxed, and he could not escape bad news from the war. During December 1899, while he was shooting with several Austrian friends in the Banat, on the southern frontier of the Habsburg Empire, the Manager of the Hungarian Railways[1] arrived to join the shoot, and brought news of the British defeat at Colenso. 'I felt very sick', Rumbold recalled, 'and went up to my room where I sat alone for some time. – The others were all as nice as they could be but I realised perfectly well that they were glad we had had a bad knock.' The Foreign Office decided not to use its telegraph facilities to keep its Ambassador informed of these defeats. To avoid the humiliation of learning the news accidentally, or while at some social function, the British Embassy arranged with *The Times* correspondent in Vienna, William Lavino,[2] to telephone the news to them from his head office. 'The effect upon me', Rumbold's father later wrote, 'of the distant muffled voice conveying this intelligence, word by word, was more sinister than I can express. . . .'

[1] Julius Ludvigh, 1841–1919. His father was the intimate friend of the Hungarian patriot Kossuth; after 1848 they lived in exile in Brussels. As a young engineer he built railways in Spain. Returned to Hungary, 1867. Manager of the Hungarian Railways, 1887–1910.

[2] William Lavino, 1846–1908. The son of Dutch parents who had become English by naturalization. Worked in a merchant's office in Antwerp from 1865; and in Paris in 1870, when he served with an ambulance unit during the siege. Entered journalism, 1874. Vienna correspondent of the *Daily Telegraph*, 1878–91. Vienna correspondent of *The Times*, 1892–1902. Paris correspondent of *The Times* from 1902 until his death. A strong advocate of Anglo-French and Anglo-Russian reconciliation.

At the beginning of 1900 Franz-Josef took a personal initiative in moderating anti-British feeling. On January 9, during a State Ball given at the Hofburg, he made a special point of speaking for some minutes about the war to Sir Horace, and, as the Ambassador reported to Lord Salisbury on the following day, had said 'with marked emphasis' that he was entirely on the English side. The Emperor's actual words were in French: 'Dans cette guerre,' he told Sir Horace 'je suis complètement Anglais.'

During 1900 the British began slowly to win the military advantage over the Boers. In Vienna, Rumbold found the social disapproval less acute. In July the British were able to take advantage of Franz-Josef's friendly attitude, and to give the Austrians an impressive demonstration of British power. The Mediterranean Squadron, commanded by Vice-Admiral Sir John Fisher,[1] visited Trieste and Fiume. Franz-Josef gave orders that on his arrival the British Admiral was to receive a guard of honour from a regiment of the Trieste garrison; 'a mark of distinction', Sir Horace informed Lord Salisbury on July 15, 'usually reserved for Crowned Heads'. For a week Sir John Fisher was fêted by the Austrians. Sir Horace was particularly pleased that the Admiral's visit appeared to act as a counter to the growing German influence at Vienna. Three days later he sent Lord Salisbury an account of the benefits gained by the visit:

. . . the splendid reception accorded to Sir John Fisher and his force may be looked upon as a significant rebuke to the tendencies which, under the influence of the Pan-germanic party in this Country, have lent so strangely Anglophobe a colouring to the reports given in the Vienna Press of the South African war and the dangers it entailed for our world-power and influence.

After their assiduous prophesying for months past of our approaching decline, and their gloating over our military disasters, it has been a rough shock to the leaders of the anti-English movement to witness the arrival in Austrian waters of a fleet so clearly symbolizing our unbroken power. . . .

Fear of German influence in Austria-Hungary, and a desire to show that the Boer War was not the beginning of the decline of British power, were subordinated throughout the spring and summer of 1900 by the threat to the Europeans besieged by the Chinese at their Legations in Peking. This created an atmosphere of increasing foreboding which briefly lessened European rivalries. Rumbold's father took a personal initiative in asking

[1] John Arbuthnot Fisher, 1841–1920. Known both as 'Jackie' and, because of his somewhat Oriental appearance, 'the old Malay'. Entered the Navy, 1854. Vice-Admiral Commanding the Mediterranean Squadron, 1899–1901. Admiral, 1901. Second Sea Lord, 1901–3. First Sea Lord, 1904–10. Admiral of the Fleet, 1905. Created Baron, 1909. Retired, 1911. Head of the Royal Commission on Fuel and Engines, 1912–14. Reappointed First Sea Lord, October 1914; resigned, May 1915.

the Japanese Minister at Vienna, Makino,[1] to press his Government to send a relief expedition to Peking without waiting for the other promised contingents from the European powers. The Japanese, afraid of European – and especially Russian and German – censure, held back until the other forces were ready. Sir Horace could do nothing to deflect them from their caution. 'Thus', his son later recalled, 'the jealousy and suspicions of some of the Powers nearly brought about a dreadful calamity.' Fortunately, the international force arrived in time to save the Europeans. Shortly before the expedition reached Peking, the *Daily Mail* had reported that the Legations had in fact fallen and that the Europeans had all been massacred. 'I often wondered', Rumbold later wrote, 'why some of the people concerned never brought an action against the *Mail* for moral and intellectual damages. The false news ought to have been a blow to the prestige of the paper.' Rumbold never lost his deep distrust of Press sensationalism.

Sir Horace retired from the Diplomatic Service in September 1900, having served for fifty-one years. Once his father had gone, Rumbold could see no attraction in remaining in Vienna. He longed to return to the East, and while on leave in London that summer was delighted when, at a chance meeting with Lord Cromer at dinner, Cromer asked him if he would like to return to Egypt. Rumbold agreed, and on the following day asked the Foreign Office to let him go. He was told that as soon as the new Ambassador to Austria-Hungary, Sir Francis Plunkett,[2] had settled in to his post, he could leave Vienna and go straight to Cairo. His father left Vienna on September 16; Rumbold remained with the new Ambassador for two and a half months. From Vienna he kept his father informed of social events, of more dances, and hunts. On November 3, he went to Pardubitz for two days at the races. There were dinner parties each evening and dances at the casino. 'I took a tender farewell of various fairies', he wrote to his father on November 7, 'and nearly wept.' He at once made plans to take a boat from Trieste to Alexandria. 'The town is in such a filthy state', he wrote to his father from Vienna on November 21, 'and the weather so dismal that I am quite glad to be going to the sun and warmth.'

On December 9 Rumbold left Vienna for a short holiday in Hungary. 'Mr Rumbold was a great favourite in Vienna society', Sir Francis

[1] Nobuaki Makino, 1862–1949. Educated in the United States, 1871–79. Japanese Minister in Vienna, 1900. Minister of Education, 1907; of Agriculture, 1911; of Foreign Affairs, 1913. Minister of the Imperial Household, 1920. Narrowly escaped assassination during the military revolt of 1936.

[2] Francis Richard Plunkett, 1835–1907. Youngest son of the 9th Earl of Fingall. Entered Diplomatic Service, 1855. Minister at Tokyo, 1883–87; at Stockholm, 1888–93; at Brussels, 1893–1900. Knighted, 1894. Ambassador at Vienna, 1900–5.

Plunkett wrote to the new Foreign Secretary, Lord Lansdowne,[1] later that day, 'where his departure is much regretted, and I feel it due to him that I should place on record my entire approval of his services during the few months I have been his Chief. His accurate knowledge of German and his steady application to his duties made him a peculiarly helpful member of this Embassy.'

On December 12, after two days' shooting at an estate near Lake Balaton, Rumbold sailed from Trieste, reaching Alexandria on December 15, and there took the train to Cairo that afternoon.

[1] Henry Charles Keith Petty-Fitzmaurice, 1845–1927. 5th Marquess of Lansdowne, 1856. Governor-General of Canada, 1883–88; Viceroy of India, 1888–93; Secretary of State for War, 1895–1901; Foreign Secretary, November 1900–December 1905. Minister without Portfolio, May 1915–December 1916. In 1917 he publicly advocated a negotiated peace with Germany. His second son was killed in action in France, October 30, 1914.

5

Cairo

1900–1907

The Egypt to which Rumbold returned as Second Secretary in December 1900 was ruled by Lord Cromer with absolute confidence and control. 'The Lord', whose authority had, since 1898, extended into the Sudan, was determined to make his administration a model of imperial rule. An influx of schoolmasters and bank clerks had replaced the earlier flow of soldiers and adventurers. Rumbold's first shock was to find, as he later recalled, that the once exclusive Turf Club 'was swamped by the above 2 categories of people and was no longer the Club I used to know. . . . It was soon clear to me that the Cairo of the early nineties had gone for good.' The new prosperity surprised him: the rich Egyptian landowners had developed all available cultivable land and the towns had expanded. But he was annoyed to find that the younger Egyptians, 'not having had a bad time themselves . . . saw no particular cause for gratitude towards the English who had mainly contributed to their present prosperity'. Although the South African War continued, Rumbold was disgusted to discover, as he wrote to his father on February 17, that the British residents in Cairo 'don't take much interest in the war and are quite ready to dance and otherwise amuse themselves. However,' he continued, 'dancing is strictly barred for the present, and quite rightly so. . . .' By day, racing and horse shows continued as before, so that, he added, 'nobody can complain'.

Rumbold's work involved all the activities of the British Agency. But he found it difficult at times to confide in his chief. The reason was that the Agency's Oriental Secretary, Harry Boyle,[1] had, since Lady Cromer's death in 1898, made himself indispensable to Cromer, and seemed to stand, Rumbold later recalled, 'between us and our Chief'. One of Boyle's chief defects, Rumbold went on, 'was his incapacity to repeat a story just as it was told him. He would either grossly exaggerate it or even, if it suited his purpose, actually invent details. He had become very Oriental. He loved power – and would not be particular in what he said – in order to keep it. We all used to wonder how much Lord Cromer believed of

[1] Harry Boyle, 1863–1937. Entered Consular Service, 1883. Oriental Secretary, Cairo, 1899–1909. Consul-General, Berlin, 1909–14. Employed in the Foreign Office, August 1915–October 1916; in the Intelligence Division, War Office, 1917.

what Boyle told him. No doubt he knew his man and discounted a large percentage of what he was told but when a man is constantly making unfavourable allusions to a third person – something will probably stick.' This unexpected barrier made Rumbold's six years in Egypt less rewarding than he had hoped.

Early in May Rumbold had a serious accident at polo. His horse fell under him, his helmet came off as he was thrown to the ground, and he landed on his bare head. He was knocked unconscious. 'One morning', he later recalled, 'I woke up in bed without any realization of how I had got there or of what had happened the previous evening . . . the game in which the accident occurred, as well as the game which preceded it, was completely blotted out from my memory.' Unaware of any serious damage, Rumbold went out to dine the next evening. On his way back he collapsed in the street. The doctor ordered three days in bed, and no more polo that spring. Two weeks later, when Lord Cromer asked him to join him in a game of tennis, he found that he was still too weak even to hit the ball over the net. Cromer sympathetically ordered him to go back to London on leave.

Before setting off on leave, Rumbold completed his first serious piece of work for Cromer, a report on British trade with Egypt between 1895 and 1900. In it, he commented tersely on the failure of many British firms to take advantage of Egyptian markets. He pointed out that whereas in certain items, such as saddlery, 'German competition has practically ceased', other foreign companies were still much in the ascendant. Austria-Hungary and France still supplied all the paper; Belgium, America, Germany and Austria-Hungary were competing successfully with British rolling-stock. One reason for British trading weakness, Rumbold asserted, was the inconvenience caused in Egypt by British weights and measures. He believed that the introduction of the metric system, and of a decimal currency, would greatly enhance Egypt's trading potential, and that certainly all weights and measures should be shown in metric as well as British units. 'Draughtsmen in the United Kingdom', he commented, 'should be equally at home in their own and the metrical system of measurement.' And he added with some acerbity: 'British firms do not seem to see the necessity for adapting themselves to altered conditions, but will spend a great deal of time in endeavouring to persuade a customer that he is wrong in requiring modifications of which he is the best judge.' As a final criticism of British business methods, he pointed out that: 'The British manufacturer is some way behind his Continental rival in the preparation and drawing of plans. German and Swiss houses send out drawings which are models of neatness and accuracy.' Cromer sent

Rumbold's report to Lord Lansdowne; it reached the Foreign Office in June 1901, and was published a month later as part of a series of Diplomatic and Consular reports presented by Lansdowne to both Houses of Parliament.

Rumbold left Cairo on May 24, reaching Vienna on May 30, and, after three days as the guest of Sir Francis Plunkett at the Embassy and watching the Vienna Derby, he reached London on June 4. He spent three months in England, relaxing, dancing, and seeing much of his father, who was finding retirement a considerable bore. Cromer himself returned to London during the early summer, and in August he received an Earldom. Shortly afterwards Rumbold called on Cromer to congratulate him. 'He was then staying', Rumbold later recalled, 'at a small hotel in Curzon Street. I asked the waiter whether the great man was at home; he said "yes" so I went up – knocked at the door and put my head in. Lord C who, I think, had one of the Suez Canal Directors with him, looked up, glared at me and said "what do you want?" I said meekly "I only came to congratulate you" upon which he said "that's allright – goodbye." Before I had shut the door he was deep in the conversation which I had interrupted. The whole interview had lasted perhaps 20 seconds. This sort of thing – though in a modified form – was calculated to annoy the ordinary person who did not know his man, but we who did were only amused by it.'

While on leave Rumbold played bridge for the first time. His partner was the First Lord of the Treasury, A. J. Balfour. A leading member of the Liberal Opposition, R. B. Haldane,[1] was one of their opponents. The game took place at a weekend country house party. Often during the weekend Rumbold found himself next to Lady Katharine Thynne,[2] who made a particularly poor impression upon him. Although he tried every subject he could think of, he found her difficult to talk to. 'Possibly it was my fault,' he recalled, 'but I had seen a good deal in my life and could tell her about some interesting things.' She did not respond to the varied experiences of the much travelled young diplomat of thirty-two, and he found her 'far from clever'. Much to his surprise, shortly after his return to Cairo in September he received a cypher telegram which read: 'Following from Lord Cromer:– I am engaged to Lady Katharine Thynne'.

After his marriage, Cromer returned to Cairo with his wife. Henceforth, Rumbold saw much of the new Lady Cromer, but he remained unimpressed. She was, he recalled, 'rather narrow-minded, very obstinate

[1] Richard Burdon Haldane, 1856–1928. Liberal MP, 1885–1911. Secretary of State for War, 1905–12. Created Viscount, 1911. Lord Chancellor, first under Asquith, 1912–15; then under Ramsay MacDonald, 1924.

[2] Lady Katherine Georgiana Louisa Thynne, 1865–1933. Daughter of the 4th Marquess of Bath. She married Lord Cromer on October 22, 1901, as his second wife.

and extraordinarily tactless, on occasion'. But his immediate reaction to the news had been one of relief. 'I am very glad for the old gentleman's sake', he wrote to his father on 29 September 1901. 'He will be ever so much happier and it will make everything much easier. Someone was badly wanted at the Agency to keep people together, for Cairo society, since Lady Cromer's death, has split up into absurd sets.' One result of Cromer's second marriage was that Boyle's influence declined, and Rumbold found it easier to win Cromer's attention, and confidence. 'The hours which Boyle could use to further or injure the interests of his friends or enemies were over', he wrote in his recollections.

There was little pressure of work during the autumn and winter of 1901. 'I have now entered on my duties as Manager of the Society for Prevention of Cruelty to Animals', he wrote to his father on November 10: 'It gives me something to do. Otherwise I have literally no work.' Even protecting ill-treated animals gave Rumbold an insight into Cromer's problem, for although, as he recalled, 'we have very complete powers over natives', the European dog-owners were sheltered from Agency scrutiny by their special status under the Capitulations of 1882. These European privileges, the most serious of which was in financial affairs, Cromer was determined to remove. Rumbold was not directly involved in the slow, patient process whereby Cromer persuaded the British Government to assert fuller powers over Egypt in return for giving France – Britain's principal rival at Cairo – special rights over Morocco. 'We of the staff', he recalled somewhat bitterly, 'had no experience, or means of acquiring experience, of our own although we learnt a certain amount from seeing Lord Cromer at work. . . . I have since often regretted, for many reasons, spending such a number of years at Cairo.' In an attempt to make himself useful, Rumbold decided to enlarge on his Trade report of the previous June, and to prepare a more voluminous study of Egypt's trade with foreign countries. Later he recalled: 'When I suggested writing this report to Lord Cromer, he said, indifferently, "allright" and seemed, if anything, rather surprised that any member of his staff should want to do work.'

Early in 1902 Rumbold took up polo again. In April he began to make plans for going on leave. 'I have literally no work to do now', he wrote to his father on April 20, 'and spend most of my time reading.' He returned to England in May. The end of the war in South Africa made London less gloomy than it had been the previous year, and Rumbold immersed himself in social life. At one dinner, he wrote to his father on June 26, he met a Belgian girl, 'calculated to knock most people out in the first round – happily I have remained calm'.

Rumbold was back in Egypt in time for the celebrations of Edward VII's Coronation. On Coronation Day, August 9, he went to Alexandria for three religious services, which he described in his recollections:

The first service was in the Greek Cathedral. The Metropolitan – supported by a large body of clergy in gorgeous robes, officiated and the Captains of the British ships in harbour with their staffs attended in full uniform. At the end of the service the Greek Archbishop, who had mounted the pulpit, called for 3 cheers for the King – the people in the Cathedral responding most vigorously. We English, unaccustomed to cheering in Church, were much taken aback and surprised. From the Greek Cathedral we went to the Jewish synagogue where there was a service in honour of the King. On this occasion the Chief Rabbi[1] had unveiled the inner sanctuary. He delivered a panegyric on the King which was translated, as he went along, by a young gentleman in a frock coat with a tall hat slightly at the back of his head. The Chief Rabbi, amongst other remarks, said that the Jews had peculiar reason to be grateful to King Edward.[2] From the Jewish synagogue we went to St Andrews where we had our own service.

Ten days after the Coronation ceremony, Rumbold reported to his father that the King's friend, the banker Sir Ernest Cassel,[3] was said to be trying to have Cromer removed from Egypt – and sent as Viceroy to India – in order to gain control of the finance of Egypt as soon as Cromer had abolished the international *Caisse de la Dette*. Cassel, Rumbold reported to his father on August 19, 'has got HM to back him by holding out promises of a share in the spoil. . . . I don't think – that if the facts were known – the British public would stand seeing Egypt being delivered into the hands of the Jews.' Cassel's alleged intrigue came to nothing. Cromer remained in Cairo, and made his plans for the ending of the international control of Egypt's finance.

During August Rumbold became concerned with the ravages of cholera. By the end of the month over 400 Egyptians were dying each day.

---

[1] Elijah Bekor Hazan, 1840–1908. Member of a distinguished rabbinical family. Born in Smyrna. Went to Jerusalem at the age of fifteen. Clerk of the Jerusalem congregation, 1866. Solicitor of Alms for Palestine, 1871. Rabbi of Tripoli, 1874–88. Chief Rabbi (or Grand Rabbi) of Alexandria, 1888–1908. In 1903 he presided over the orthodox rabbinical convention at Cracow. An advocate of the strictest orthodoxy, he denied the truth of the Copernican system.

[2] Edward VII's friendship with Jews was much commented on. On November 9, 1902, Rumbold wrote to his father: 'I wonder whether any of the chosen people will get any honours this birthday. Judging by the press HM spends almost his whole time with Hebrews.' In December 1902 Sir Ernest Cassel received the KCVO and was made a Privy Councillor.

[3] Ernest Joseph Cassel, 1852–1921. Of German birth and Jewish descent. Naturalized as a British subject, 1878. Financier and philanthropist. Instrumental in acquiring for Vickers the Barrow Naval and Shipbuilding Construction Company, and the Maxim Gun Company. Knighted, 1899. In 1909 the National Bank of Turkey was created under his auspices.

'The Sanitary people are putting disinfectants into the wells,' Rumbold wrote to his father towards the end of August, 'and the ignorant people are beginning to accuse them of poisoning the water. It is rather trying to have to deal with such folly.' Sir Horace wrote to say that no mention of cholera had appeared in the English papers. 'Their correspondents must have been squared by the Cairo hotel-keepers', Rumbold replied on September 2; '. . . 12,000 people have already gone to kingdom come.' A thousand people were dying each day. 'I am getting awfully bored with the cholera,' Rumbold wrote to his father on September 14, 'for nobody seems to be able to talk about anything else. . . . It has killed 20,000 people now.'

Rumbold was angered by news from England that the Secretary of State for War, St John Brodrick,[1] had invited the Germans to attend British manoeuvres; 'but what can one expect', he wrote to his father, 'from a set of rotters like the present Govt'. A month later, on October 12, he sent his father further reflections on Balfour's Conservative administration. 'I believe our Government or its authorities are absolutely incorrigible', he wrote, 'and that not even a great national disaster would convince them that everything is not for the best in the best of Administrations. All one can hope is that they are slowly but surely exasperating the public who will one day kick out the collection of prigs and four-letter men who compose the Cabinet.' At the end of October Lord Kitchener came to stay with Cromer at the Agency. 'I think he was very happy here,' Rumbold wrote to his father on November 2, 'because we none of us lionised him.' Kitchener gave Cromer a pessimistic account of the state of the British Army. 'He says', Rumbold wrote to his father, 'that not one of our generals – not excepting men like French[2] etc – is capable of meeting any of the trained Generals of the Continent,' and that above the rank of Captain 'intelligence is in inverse proportion to increase of rank'.

In November Rumbold's father published an article in the *National Review* warning of the dangers of the increasing German influence in Europe. Even in Cairo his article caused comment. 'There is a genuine hatred of the Germans among the soldiers here', Rumbold wrote on

[1] St John Brodrick, 1856–1942. Conservative MP, 1880–1906. Under-Secretary of State for War, 1895–98; for Foreign Affairs, 1898–1900. Secretary of State for War, 1900–3; for India, 1903–5. Succeeded his father as 9th Viscount Midleton, 1907. Created Earl, 1920.

[2] John Denton Pinkstone French, 1852 1925. Entered Navy, 1866. Transferred to Army, 1874. Lieutenant-General, commanding the Cavalry in South Africa, 1899–1902. Knighted, 1900. Chief of the Imperial General Staff, 1912–14. Field-Marshal, 1913. Commander-in-Chief of the British Expeditionary Force in France, August 1914–December 1915. Commander-in-chief, Home Forces, 1915–18. Created Viscount, 1916. Lord Lieutenant of Ireland, 1918–21. Created Earl of Ypres, 1922.

November 15, 'the more intelligent among whom have read the article with joy.' As a result of his experiences of German activities in Vienna, and the growing dominance of William II over Franz-Josef, Rumbold shared his father's fears. In a postscript he added: 'I am very glad you have made those Germans sit up so much.' But a few days later he wrote again, worried because the editor of the *National Review*, Leo Maxse,[1] had begun to give the article enormous publicity, which had even led to questions in the House of Commons. Rumbold warned his father not to write any further articles which Maxse 'might twist for his own purposes', and added that he had learned that the '*National Review* and *Spectator* is in reality inspired by Chirol[2] of *The Times*'. The affair continued to have repercussions for some weeks. Lansdowne wrote formally to Sir Horace rebuking him for the anti-German tone of his article. But Sir Horace was not without supporters. Lord Cromer, Rumbold wrote on September 11, 'is in entire agreement with your feelings as regards the Germans and recognises them as the enemy'.

The coming of winter saw a stream of visitors to Cairo, and Agency life centred around their entertainment. 'Cassel's little lot will be the first to arrive', Rumbold wrote to his father at the end of November, adding that the banker's group would include Winston Churchill,[3] who, Rumbold wrote, 'will probably tell us more about our own business than we know ourselves'. Joseph Chamberlain[4] and the Duke of Connaught[5] both arrived in the first week of December, and Rumbold's time was entirely taken up, as he wrote to his father on December 7, 'grinning like a dog and running about the city'. Lord Cromer took the Duke of Connaught to see the new dam at Assuan, and the excursion became a social event of great magnitude. Some of the guests, Rumbold reported to his father on

---

[1] Leo J. Maxse, 1864–1932. Bought the *National Review* in 1893; he edited it, and remained the largest shareholder, until his death.

[2] Valentine Chirol, 1852–1929. Director of the Foreign Department of *The Times*, 1899–1912. A member of the Royal Commission on Indian Public Services, 1912. Knighted, 1912. Author and publicist. He published his memoirs, *Fifty Years in a Changing World* in 1927. He wrote the article on Rumbold's father in the *Dictionary of National Biography*.

[3] Winston Leonard Spencer Churchill, 1874–1965. As a subaltern, and war correspondent, he fought in the Malakand Campaign, 1897; at Omdurman, 1898; and in South Africa, 1899–1901. Conservative MP, 1900–4; Liberal MP, 1904–22; Conservative MP, 1924–64. Entered the Cabinet, as President of the Board of Trade, 1908. Prime Minister, 1940–45 and 1951–55. Knight of the Garter, 1953.

[4] Joseph Chamberlain, 1836–1914. Liberal MP, 1876–85; Liberal Unionist MP, and leader of the Liberal Unionists, 1885–1914. Secretary of State for the Colonies, 1895–1903.

[5] Arthur William Patrick Albert, Duke of Connaught, 1850–1942. Third son of Queen Victoria. Entered the Army as a Lieutenant, Royal Engineers, 1868. Major-General Commanding the Brigade of Guards at the occupation of Alexandria, 1882. Field-Marshal, 1902. Inspector-General of the Forces, 1904–7. Governor-General of Canada, 1911–16.

December 17, gave their maids and valets champagne every night, 'and I noticed that the servants had a sleek and well-fed look about them produced by food and copious drinks'. During the journey Rumbold was attracted by one of the guests, Miss Beatrice Stuart-Wortley,[1] but, as he wrote to his father, 'although the conditions were perfect for philandering . . . i.e. moon, warm nights, etc, I must confess to my shame that I played "bridge" with Lord C and the other 2 men, leaving the ladies to amuse themselves as best they could.' In his recollections Rumbold explained – as he had not done to his father – that it was Cromer who had kept him from Miss Stuart-Wortley, telling him: 'You will stop and play bridge with us.' 'It seemed rather vandalism', Rumbold recalled, 'on such a fine evening.' During the visit to Assuan Rumbold was delighted to find that the Duke of Connaught sympathized with his father over the *National Review* article, reporting in his letter of December 17 that 'he is as anti-German as any other Englishman'.

During 1903 Rumbold began to think seriously of marriage. On January 17, three weeks before his thirty-fourth birthday, he wrote to his father: 'Diplomacy is devilish slow work unless one can collar a wife like Mrs Hardinge.'[2] On February 1, learning that his brother William was engaged, he wrote again: 'As regards any influence one may secure through one's wife, I believe that under the present regime marriage with a Jew's daughter – with a dash of foreign blood in her – would be the thing to do, unless one secured a phoenix like Mrs Hardinge.'

In February Rumbold visited Khartoum, staying for a week as the guest of the Governor-General of the Sudan, Sir Reginald Wingate, and going over the battlefield of Omdurman. One unexpected sight was the local Omdurman football team setting off to play the Khartoum eleven in a temperature of 100° F in the shade. The Omdurman team, he recalled, 'consisted of youths of 13 to 15 or so dressed in striped jerseys – shorts and boots of huge length for these natives have very long feet. The sight of this football eleven brought home to me more forcibly than anything else the change brought about by our conquest of the Soudan and the extraordinary progress made in 5 years.' To his father he wrote from Khartoum on February 18 of how he himself had played polo on a ground just outside the square where once the crowds had gathered to hear the Mahdi

---

[1] Beatrice Susan Theodosia Stuart-Wortley, born 1881. Daughter of the 1st Baron Stuart of Wortley. She married Captain James Cecil in 1906 (he died in 1936). She recalled seventy years later that Rumbold had wanted to marry her, and described him as 'nice, ugly and amusing'.

[2] Winifred Selina Sturt, 1868–1914. Daughter of the 1st Baron Alington. She married Charles Hardinge in 1890. Her courage in India, during the attempted assassination of her husband in 1912, led over three million Indian women to present her with a petition of congratulation.

and the Khalifa denounce the British and rally the faithful to do battle against them. But the main surprise of his visit was on the journey itself. At one point, he recalled, 'there was a stop of $\frac{1}{2}$ an hour to allow the passengers to have a bath. There was a row of large bath houses in the station and every passenger was allowed to use a bath-room for 10 minutes. There was hot and cold water ad lib. and we would lie down in the baths.'

Back in Cairo, Rumbold returned to his researches on Egyptian trade; work which involved, as he recalled, 'wading through masses of Custom House statistics'. But his life was far from strenuous. 'Up at 7 am,' he explained to his father on September 13, 'then a swim, after which we have breakfast and then read and write till lunch at 1 pm. Then a siesta and at 4 pm either polo, lawn tennis, a ride or a sail. Some man or other generally comes to dine and we go to bed at 10.30 pm. Sometimes I spend sleepless nights owing to the bites of some beastly insect or other.'

In 1904 the British position in Egypt was strengthened as Cromer had wished. As part of the Anglo-French Entente the internationally controlled *Caisse de la Dette* ceased to exercise any influence over Egyptian finance. Henceforth the surplus profits from government enterprises, such as the customs, went, not to foreign bondholders, but to the Egyptian revenue, where they could be used by the Government of Egypt for its various agricultural, industrial and educational schemes. 'Every service wanted a share in the spoil', Rumbold recalled. 'A few years soon showed how quickly this large fund went. There was an immense and costly irrigation system under consideration which alone would swallow up millions.' The political effects of the Anglo-French Entente were more lasting. In return for a dominant influence in Morocco, France gave up all her powers in Egypt by which she could hinder British influence on the Nile. 'Egypt breathed more freely', Rumbold recalled. The negotiations, as far as Egyptian matters were concerned, had been conducted directly between Cromer and Lansdowne. Rumbold busied himself with finishing his Report on the trade of Egypt, which, because it seemed to justify the imposition of tariffs, was taken up by the British Press as ammunition in the Free Trade controversy, then at its height. 'The principal papers took up the report and wrote leaders on it,' Rumbold recalled, 'each side twisting it so as to suit their own purposes.' He was much amused, having had no intention of entering into the controversy, and having expressed no strong preference either way. He was annoyed not to be thanked by the Foreign Office for the Report, which had involved him in three months' work. 'Possibly,' he recalled, 'my conclusions were not acceptable to the powers that be – for at that time many of the higher officials were tariff reformers.' On March 5 he wrote to his father that one of the commentators who had read an anti-tariff message into his Report, 'says that if ever Chamberlain becomes Prime Minister I shall be exiled to S. America'. Seven days later he wrote again; his Report, he had discovered, 'has even been used as an argument for strengthening the Chamberlainite case'. To his delight, the Report was circulated to all Government schools in Egypt in order to teach commercial geography. Another report which he did at the same time, for the Egyptian Society for the Prevention of Cruelty to Animals, was also distributed to all Cairo schools, having been translated into Arabic. 'So the young Egyptians', he wrote to his father on March 26, 'ought to know all about me.'

Rumbold's opinions were still at times dogmatic – 'I hate Jews', he wrote to his father on March 26, explaining why he did not intend to be introduced to a friend of his brother Hugo. But he was not uncritical of the dogmatic attitudes of others. Of the much debated 'yellow peril', he wrote on May 22: 'It is a good cry for the Germans and other Continental nations but it is not a serious danger.' The wave of assassinations throughout Russia no longer led him to repeating the fashionable denunciations of all anarchic acts. 'By establishing a reign of terror,' he wrote to his father on August 1, 'the Nihilists will bring about a modification of the present regime in Russia – and a good thing too.' He had no regard for the Tsarist regime. 'I suppose it would be difficult', he added, 'to find a more utterly rotten country.'

Throughout the autumn and winter of 1904, the imminent defeat of Russia by Japan dominated conversation both in Egypt and London. 'I admire the Japs', Rumbold wrote to his father on November 6, shortly after his return to Cairo, 'in proportion as I despise their enemies.' Although Britain's alliance with Japan, signed in 1902, did not commit Britain to intervene on Japan's behalf, Rumbold believed that, as he wrote to his father on November 19, 'it is quite on the cards that we shall have a war with Russia after all'. But, he asserted: 'They can't do anything to us. Our navy is fully prepared and of course we should wipe out the wretched remnant of their fleet. They would dash themselves against a stone wall in India – or rather in the attempt to get to India and they would complete their financial ruin and the ruin of their prestige.' If the Germans joined the Russians, 'so much the better', Rumbold wrote; 'Their navy is not nearly ready and we could smash up what there is of it. They can't get at us on land. A race hatred of Germany already exists in our country and,' he added, 'I think there is now a race-hatred of the Russians.'

At the end of 1904 Rumbold was promoted to First Secretary. In January 1905 he began, for the first time in his life, to keep a diary. This step coincided with an important development in his life. 'Engaged to

Miss Fane',[1] he telegraphed to his father from Cairo on January 15; and a brief entry in his diary for January 28 testifies to his delight at the change of the previous two weeks. 'Take Miss Fane for rides,' he noted, 'and have a very good time generally. Do not go much to the Chancery. There will be time for that afterwards.' Ethel Fane was the daughter of a diplomat, Sir Edmund Fane.[2] Her father had died in 1900 after forty-two years in the foreign service. Rumbold had known her for several years,[3] and she had come out to Egypt at the end of 1904. When Lady Fane heard that her daughter had become engaged to a diplomat she telegraphed, dissuading: 'Consider small means and foreign life.' But Ethel Fane was not deterred. On February 6 she returned to England: 'It was not considered proper by her uncle and aunt',[4] Rumbold noted in his diary, 'that I should travel down to Port Said with her, as I wanted to do, and so, not wishing to make myself disagreeable, I didn't insist.'

During May Rumbold was involved in his first independent discussion of Anglo-German relations. A German diplomatic mission to Abyssinia, headed by Count Rosen,[5] was passing through Cairo on its way back to Berlin. The aim of the mission had been to extend German influence in Abyssinia, and in particular to secure a German Director on the board of the Abyssinian Bank. Britain's approval for this was essential, for Cromer had the power to veto it. On May 2 Rumbold took Rosen to the pyramids, noting in his diary Rosen's warning: 'If you refuse this request it will make a deplorable impression, because it will only confirm our view that,

[1] Ethelred Constantia Fane, 1879–1964. She married Rumbold in July 1905. From 1916 to 1919 she was President of the Prisoners of War Bread Bureau in Berne, and of the British Legation Red Cross in Switzerland. She was created a Commander of the British Empire in 1920, in recognition of her war work.

[2] Edmund Douglas Veitch Fane, 1837–1900. Entered the Diplomatic Service, as an Attaché in Teheran, 1858. Minister at Constantinople, 1892–93; at Belgrade, 1893–98; at Copenhagen from 1898 until his death. Knighted, 1899. His home was at Boyton Manor, Heytesbury, in Wiltshire. In 1875 he married Constantia Wood, daughter of Major-General Robert Blucher Wood. Lady Fane died in 1940.

[3] Rumbold had, in fact, been present – aged ten – at his wife's christening, which had taken place in Berne when his father had been Minister, and her father was one of his staff.

[4] John Ramsay Slade, 1843–1913. 2nd Lieutenant, Royal Artillery, 1861; fought in the Afghan war, 1879–80 and in the Transvaal, 1881–82. Military Attaché, Rome, 1887–95. Major-General Commanding the British Troops in Egypt, 1903–5. Knighted, 1907. Gentleman Usher to King George V, 1910. In 1882 he married Janet Wood, daughter of Major-General Robert Blucher Wood.

[5] Friedrich Rosen, 1856–1935. Born in Leipzig. German orientalist; in 1887 he was awarded a doctorate in Persian and Hindustani. Author, translator and dramatist. Entered the Diplomatic Service, 1890. Consul, Jerusalem, 1900. Mission to Abyssinia, 1905. Minister in Tangier, 1907; in Bucharest, 1910; in Lisbon, 1912; at The Hague, 1923. Foreign Minister, 1921. He published his *Oriental Memories* in 1930. In June 1933 Hitler forced him to refuse most of his pension because he was a Jew, and had served in a 'Marxist' Government in 1921. He died in exile, in Peking.

wherever we are or whatever we propose, you are always trying to thwart us.' Rosen added: 'You have got so much in every quarter of the earth that you can well afford to grant us this request.' Rumbold saw Cromer on the following day and advised him to refuse Rosen's request. Cromer imposed his veto. That night Rumbold and Rosen dined alone together. Rosen was bitterly disappointed at the failure of his mission. After the meal the two men discussed Anglo-German relations. Rumbold noted in his diary:

To my surprise he served up to me all the stories of our intrigues etc at different times which may be found any day in any Anglophobe German newspaper. Amongst other things he asserted that all our Press was corrupt and venal and in the pay of Russia. I couldn't have believed that such a clever man could talk such rubbish. While he was talking – which he did with great intensity – he grew paler and paler – his eyes seemed to disappear and all I could see was his great Jew nose and thick red lips.

As we were talking so openly I said to him that it certainly was unfortunate that our two countries did not seem to hit it off very well at present, that the conduct of the German press during the S. African war had been largely responsible for this, that our people had got it into their heads that the Germans did not wish us well and that, once we got hold of an idea it was not easy for us to get rid of it again. We parted at midnight – on the best of terms. I can see that Rosen is a bitter Anglophobe. His hatred of us comes as much from jealousy as from anything else.

In June Rumbold returned to England on leave, going by boat from Port Said to Brindisi and thence by train. He was impatient to see his fiancée again. 'The train crawls through Italy,' he noted in his diary, 'stopping at a lot of unnecessary stations.' Back in England, he was introduced to Miss Fane's relations, took her to Hurlingham to see the final of the inter-regimental polo tournament, went to a garden party at Windsor and, on July 18, was married. 'Arrived in good time for the service,' he noted in his diary, 'feeling as cool as a cucumber. . . . The service went off well and there was a refreshing absence of tears.'

Rumbold did not have to return to Egypt until the end of August. He and his wife spent much of the time at Cowes. On August 8 he saw the French Fleet at anchor, noting scathingly in his diary: 'Their ships looked top-heavy – and are of different types. Their launches . . . looked rather dirty and badly kept.'

On August 31 Rumbold set off for Egypt, leaving his wife to follow as soon as possible. At Calais, a Parsee entered his compartment in which he was about to go to bed. Rumbold summoned the conductor. 'I told him', he noted in his diary, 'that I refused to share a compartment with a black gentleman. . . . Luckily the conductor was a man who had travelled up from Brindisi with me in June and whom I had tipped handsomely. He got me a compartment to myself. . . . The moral is that a good tip to sleeping car conductors is money well invested.' At Marseilles Rumbold went by boat to Port Said, reaching Cairo on September 5. There was not much work to be done. Swimming, polo, tennis and bridge filled up most of the day. Rumbold was troubled by the revived influence of Boyle who, as he noted in his diary on October 31, 'tries to usurp and often does usurp the duties of head of the chancery. He has access to Lord C at all times. . . . How Lady Cromer hates Boyle.'

On November 15 Ethel Rumbold arrived at Port Said. She was delighted to find how much her husband enjoyed the social activities of his post. 'Horace was splendid', she wrote to her mother after their first dinner party, 'and really arranged it all, ordered the food, told the servants what to do and saw about the whole thing, even to the correct spelling of the names.' She added that her husband 'makes an awfully good host, and doesn't fuss a bit like his father does!'

At the beginning of December, Curzon and his wife[1] passed through Cairo. After an unsuccessful attempt to limit Kitchener's powers as Commander-in-Chief, Curzon had finally resigned the Viceroyalty of India. The Rumbolds entertained the Curzons at lunch, and took them to the Bazaar. In his diary, Rumbold noted the sequel:

He said he wanted to buy some large carpets for his house in London but did not know exactly what measurement they should be. As it was time for him to go off to the station I kept on pressing him to leave the bazaar. His private Secretary[2] was evidently afraid of him and didn't like to urge him to go so he shoved all the hustling on to me. At last I prevailed on him to leave the bazaar. He said he would write and let me know which carpets he wanted. I don't know whether he expects me to remember all the carpets we looked at – I certainly shan't remember them. We said goodbye and then I rushed off to change and get down to the polo ground where I was to play in a match. They had been waiting more than $\frac{1}{2}$ an hour for me.

On December 5, following Balfour's resignation, the Liberal leader, Sir Henry Campbell-Bannerman,[3] became Prime Minister. On the following day the Agency nearly lost its Chief, for Campbell-Bannerman telegraphed

[1] Mary Victoria Leiter. The daughter of an American millionaire, Levi Ziegler Leiter of Chicago, she married Curzon in 1895, and died in 1906.

[2] Robert Nathan, 1868–1921. Entered the Indian Civil Service, 1888. Private Secretary to Lord Curzon, 1905. Commissioner in Dacca, 1907. Chief Secretary, Eastern Bengal and Assam, 1910–15. Knighted, 1919. Author of the *Official History of Plague in India*.

[3] Henry Campbell-Bannerman, 1836–1908. Liberal MP, 1868–1908. Liberal leader in the House of Commons, 1899. Prime Minister, December 1905 to April 1908.

to Cromer, offering him the post of Foreign Secretary. Cromer was much tempted to accept, and Rumbold believed that he ought to do so, 'for the good of the country', as he wrote in his diary on December 6. But, he added, 'Lord C is by no means well. His doctor is trying a new remedy for curing him of neuritis in the arm etc ie by injecting diptheric serum. This brought on fever and generally made the old man feel very uncomfortable.' On December 7 Cromer turned down the offer. 'Feel very sorry he should not be able to go to the FO', Rumbold noted that day in his diary. 'He would have enormously strengthened the Cabinet and both parties would have had implicit confidence in him. But he says he doesn't like some of the crew with whom he would have to work.' Three days later Sir Edward Grey[1] was appointed Foreign Secretary.

Cromer's illness was serious. Rumbold doubted the value of the doctor's treatment. 'You oughtn't anyhow to experiment on an oldish man', he noted in his diary on December 11. Cromer had to remain in bed. The Counsellor at the Agency, Findlay,[2] was in London on leave. The result was that Rumbold found himself temporarily in charge of the Agency's work, and was extremely busy. He worked for five hours each morning and four each afternoon; interviewing the Egyptian Ministers; seeking a means of quelling an outbreak of Muslim unrest in Alexandria, unrest which seemed to be fomented by the local Greek community; working at despatches from the Sudan and Abyssinia; discussing legal appointments; and calling on Cromer to report progress and receive his approval. His main task was to give instructions to strengthen the blockade of the upper Nile, in order to halt the growing Belgian expansion from the Congo. The aim of the various blockade measures which he advised was, he wrote in his diary, to 'see how unpleasant we can make it for the Belgians'. Rumbold gave instructions that goods travelling up the Nile for the Belgian territory in dispute would be taken off their ships and left at the quayside. Cromer supported these measures, which were then telegraphed to London, where Sir Edward Grey gave them his approval. But within three months the Liberal Government was suggesting a less bellicose approach, as Rumbold noted in his diary on March 7: 'Grey says that in the present state of affairs in Europe it is very desirable to avoid complications . . . which might easily result in exciting the feeling of

---

[1] Edward Grey, 1862–1933. 3rd Baronet, 1882. Liberal MP, 1885–1916. Under-Secretary of State for Foreign Affairs, 1892–95. Foreign Secretary, 1905–16. Created Viscount, 1916. He published his memoirs, *Twenty-Five Years 1892–1916* in 1925.

[2] Mansfeldt de Cardonnel Findlay, 1861–1932. Entered Diplomatic Service, 1885. Secretary of Legation, Cairo, 1901–4; Counsellor of Embassy, Cairo, 1904–7. Minister to Saxony and Saxe-Coburg Gotha, 1907–9. Minister to Bulgaria, 1909–11; to Norway, 1911–23. Knighted, 1916.

Belgium against this country.' The blockade was dropped, and negotiations opened for a compromise agreement.

Early in the new year Cromer recovered, Findlay returned from leave,
and Rumbold was irked to find himself once again a spectator of events
for which he was keen to be responsible. He was thirty-seven; his ambition was to succeed Findlay as Counsellor, and thereby to become
Cromer's principal assistant. He believed that there was much he could
do in a responsible position. His fears of Germany were increasing. During
1906 several events seemed to confirm them. On January 2 he noted in his
diary that Mukhtar Pasha, the Turkish Commissioner in Egypt, and a
strong believer in Turkey's ultimate return to sovereignty over Egypt, had
said to a French resident of Cairo: 'At Constantinople we have had more
than enough of the English and their domineering policy. With twelve
army corps ready in Syria, and the German army at our back, it would not
be difficult for us to turn them out of this country.' Rumbold commented
that in view of remarks like this it was not surprising 'that the natives
should think that Germany is at the back of the Turks'. The British Agency
had been alarmed for some months by a proposed branch line of the
Hedjaz railway which would give the Turks a railhead at Akaba, which
could much increase the power of any Turkish attack on Egypt. The
Hedjaz railway, Rumbold noted, was in the charge of German engineers;
the Akaba branch would likewise be in their control. British control in
India, and indeed in Egypt, had owed much to the building of railways.
Kitchener's reconquest of the Sudan had depended upon the railway
which he had built specially for that purpose. The news of German
engineers in the Turkish provinces south of Damascus seemed to indicate a
similar deliberate policy of expansion, to be followed by control. The
British Agency therefore took alarm when, in mid-January, the Turks
suddenly renewed their claims to the Sinai peninsula, which the Egyptian
War Office had administered since the boundary agreement of 1892, and
whose control by Britain was an essential protection to the Suez Canal
from Turkish attack. Cromer was determined to give the Turks no chance
to establish themselves at any point on the canal. It was believed in the
Agency, Rumbold noted on January 28, 'that the Germans are behind the
Turks in this matter'. He himself was not entirely certain of this. But
he was determined, as he noted three days later, to keep the Turks off the
canal. On February 14 Cromer sent a British cruiser, the *Diana*, to the
Gulf of Akaba, as a warning to the Turks that Britain did not intend to
give up its control of Sinai. On May 14, after many threats from Turkey,
and a firm response, first from Cromer and then from Grey, the Turks
accepted Britain's claim that the whole Sinai peninsula east of a line

drawn from Gaza to Akaba was under Egyptian control. But before the Turks gave way, the German question had been raised again. The Oriental Secretary at the German Agency in Egypt, Max von Oppenheim,[1] was reported to be, as Rumbold noted in his diary on March 8, 'in constant communication with Pan-Islamic agents both in Egypt and elsewhere', and to have inspired articles in the Egyptian newspapers to the effect that Islam was 'threatened with extinction by Europe', that England and France were at the head of the anti-Islamic movement, that the Sultan of Turkey[2] was 'the last hope of the faithful', and that Germany also was 'the friend of the Sultan' and a true supporter of the Muslim cause. Oppenheim, Rumbold noted, was 'a horrid intriguing little Jew', whose only object was to 'stir up ill-feeling' against British rule. He was believed to be in direct correspondence with the Kaiser. Rumbold interpreted Oppenheim's activities in Cairo, like Eulenberg's in Vienna, as proof that Germany intended to frustrate British influence when opportunity arose.

The Pan-Islamic Egyptians felt aggrieved that Germany had not intervened on Turkey's behalf over the Sinai dispute. 'Germany will lose prestige,' Rumbold noted in his diary on May 18, 'and a good thing too.'

In July Rumbold left Egypt for England. He was anxious to return. His wife had been in England since January awaiting the birth of their first child, and on May 1 he had learned of the birth of a daughter, Constantia.[3] He had been told the news just as he was about to play polo. 'Played the match and won it,' he noted in his diary that evening, 'and then rushed off to the telegraph station to wire congratulations.' Rumbold saw his daughter for the first time on July 20. 'She is a little pet', he noted in his diary. 'Hope she will keep her blue eyes and that they won't turn grey or grey-brown. . . . She has very dark hair already. She goes by the name of the "trout".'

For some months Rumbold had been worried about his future career. Cromer's illnesses, his more brusque manner, Lady Cromer's reluctance to give the Agency officials the family status which they had known earlier, Boyle's persistent influence; these all turned his thoughts to a new appoint-

[1] Max Adrian Simon Hubert, Freiherr von Oppenheim, 1860–1946. Born in Cologne, of Jewish origin. A member of the Frankfurt banking family of Oppenheim; himself a Catholic. Orientalist and explorer, he travelled widely through Syria, Mesopotamia, the Persian Gulf and Anatolia. His *Journey through the Syrian Desert and Mesopotamia to Mosul and Bagdad in 1893* was published by the Manchester Geographical Society in 1894. Oriental Secretary at the German Agency in Cairo, 1896–1903. Author of *Die Beduinen* (the fourth and final volume of which was published posthumously in two parts, in 1967 and 1968).

[2] Mehmed Reshad Effendi, 1844–1918. Succeeded his elder brother Abdul Hamid as Sultan, 1909. Known as Mehmed V. He had no influence on Turkish policy, which was controlled by the Young Turks.

[3] Constantia Dorothy Rumbold, born 1902. In 1944 she married Flight Lieutenant Hugh Farmar.

ment. While in London he pressed Sir Charles Hardinge, the Permanent Under-Secretary of State at the Foreign Office, to let him have a Chargé-ship at a Legation. But Hardinge asked him to go as First Secretary to Madrid. 'I said it was surely better,' he noted in his diary on July 18, 'to be first or cock of a small dung-hill than second on a large one'. Hardinge was not convinced. 'Finally,' Rumbold noted, 'he muttered something about my eventual promotion being prejudiced if I insisted on going to a Legation.' After discussing the problem both with his wife and Lord Cromer – who was also in London – Rumbold decided to accept Madrid if he were offered it. 'Everybody tells me it is a beastly place', he noted on July 23, 'and that they hate it.' He still hoped that he would be asked to succeed Findlay as Counsellor in Cairo. It was for this that he had been content to remain in Egypt for so long. For, if he became Cromer's immediate subordinate, he would have frequent opportunities of being acting British Agent during Cromer's long absences in London.

In October Rumbold and his wife returned to Egypt. Their return coincided with an important advance in Cromer's Egyptian policy, the appointment of the first Egyptian as a Minister in the Government. On October 26 Said Bey Zaghloul[1] was appointed Minister of Public Instruc-tion. On November 3 Cromer drafted a despatch to Grey in which he explained the reasons for Zaghloul's appointment:

... the freedom of thought and speech enjoyed by Egypt under the present regime, combined with the undoubted intellectual awakening which was taking place, had had the result of creating in the minds of educated Egyptians a strong desire to see the higher officers of the Administration filled, as far as possible, by men of true Egyptian origin, rather than by those of Turkish or Turco-Egyptian descent.

Such appointments, Rumbold felt, could not satisfy the growing demand among Egyptians for a greater say in their own affairs. On November 2 he wrote in his diary:

There isn't much future for the young Egyptian when one comes to think things over. The highest billets to which he can aspire are those of Minister, Mudir, Judge or Colonel of a Regiment. Of course there are some Under-Secretaryships and one or two high posts in the Army but these appointments – all told – are very limited. Not that the average gilded Egyptian youth is fit to be turned into a Minister or Mudir. He is a wretched specimen with a veneer of French civilisation – but with all the defects of the Egyptian and Frenchman

[1] Said Bey Zaghloul, 1860–1927. A Judge in the Native Court of Appeal, Cairo, 1893. Minister of Public Instruction, 1906; Minister of Justice, 1910. Appealed to the British to give Egypt its independence, 1918; arrested and deported to Malta, 1919. Deported to Aden, and then to the Seychelles, 1921. Interned in Gibraltar, 1922. Released by the British, 1923. Prime Minister of Egypt, 1924.

combined. Being idle and having plenty of money he easily becomes discontented and listens to those who tell him that, under our rule, he has nothing to look forward to. It is a difficult problem, and likely to become more so with the increase in the wealth of the native.

No decision had yet been made about Rumbold's future posting. He continued to believe that Cromer would ask him to succeed Findlay, whose departure for another post was imminent. But on November 3 he learned that he was not to succeed Findlay: the new Counsellor was to be Ronald Graham,[1] then serving at the Foreign Office, and a year his junior. Rumbold reacted immediately, recording in his diary:

Determined to speak to Lord C without loss of time. Went to see him at about 5 and found him playing bridge. I plunged in medias res. He was much embarrassed and kept his eyes steadily fixed on the cards. He never once looked me in the face. I did not let out that I knew that Graham was coming here but merely said that I had no wish to be passed over. He said 'I really can't recommend you for the post of Counsellor here; you haven't enough experience.' I said that I laid no claim to promotion on the spot but that I had been kept on at Cairo in the most unaccountable manner – unless it was to lead to something. He looked very uncomfortable and, seeing this, I got up to leave the room upon which he hastily said 'you need have no fear about your future; you're allright'. As I was going to Sakkarah next day I wrote him a letter in which, with reference to our conversation, I pointed out that 2 men in his confidence had told me some time ago that he destined me to succeed Findlay – that when I had enquired, before getting married, whether I was to stay on at Cairo, I had been strongly advised to do so by the Private Secretary in a letter which I had shown him, Lord C, at the time. That on the strength of that letter I had set up house only to be moved within a year. Finally, that I had been put to the maximum amount of inconvenience and expense. Am thoroughly disgusted at being let in all round by people whom I thought were my friends – C. Hardinge, Lord C & Findlay. Don't feel as if I could ever trust anybody again. To be passed over by a man with no experience of the place and younger than myself is very hard after nearly 10 years' service under Lord C. There is nothing to be done but to be philosophical but I shan't forget this experience in a hurry.

Rumbold's father was full of sympathy when he learned of this unfortunate interview. 'But the fact is', he wrote from Bournemouth on December 24, 'that our countrymen as a rule have little warmth of feeling about them & still less geniality.' Sir Horace was shocked at what he

[1] Ronald William Graham, 1870–1949. Entered Diplomatic Service, 1892. Counsellor of Embassy, Cairo, 1907–9. Adviser to the Egyptian Ministry of the Interior, 1910–16. Knighted, 1915. Assistant Under-Secretary, Foreign Office, 1916–19. Minister at The Hague, 1919–21. Ambassador to Rome, 1921–33. British Government Director, Suez Canal Company, 1939–45.

described as 'the thanklessness of your chief'. Earlier that year he had gone so far as to advise his son to give up diplomacy altogether, and to go into business instead, writing on March 3, from Rome, that the diplomatic profession was 'a rotten one at its best', and that his son would do better to look for the chance of 'some big financial business at home, which would be a far more solid basis than that of even a prosperous Diplomatic career'. But Rumbold, though vexed by the slow progress of his promotion, had no intention of abandoning his career. Early in December he learned that he was to be transferred to Madrid at the end of the year, with the rank of First Secretary, and as Head of Chancery. 'I know how fortunate I am in getting you to take charge of it. You will find it rather an Augean stable,' the Ambassador, Sir Maurice de Bunsen,[1] wrote on December 17.

Rumbold's final weeks in Cairo were marred by Cromer's coldness. Not having been invited to dine with Cromer on Christmas Day, he had gone instead to a hotel for the occasion. 'Feel rather sad,' he noted in his diary, 'that after nearly 10 years service under Lord C should eat my last Xmas dinner in Egypt with comparative strangers.' It was a melancholy ending to his Egyptian career. 'Time was,' he wrote in his diary on January 6, 'when I should have left Cairo with the deepest regret but I do not feel leaving so much now.' On the following day he said good-bye to Cromer. He recorded the farewell in his diary:

I was only in his room for a couple of minutes as I did not feel like spinning out the interview. Felt a queer feeling at being in a room – where I had seen him working for so many years – for the last time. 'Goodbye, Sir' I said and beat a hasty retreat. I knew that I had served him to the best of my power for the best part of 10 years. I have never asked him for anything and he has done nothing for me. I leave him owing him nothing. He is a great man – the greatest we have – and I shall not serve under his like again. He has the defects of greatness. Gratitude is not one of his strong points.

That afternoon Rumbold took the train to Port Said. From there, at five o'clock, he sailed away from Egypt. 'I wondered', he wrote in his diary that night, 'whether the future had anything so interesting in store. For the first and last time I had a deep feeling of regret at leaving a country which had practically become my second home.' On board the boat were the Irish Nationalist leader, John Redmond,[2] returning to England from

---

[1] Maurice William Ernest de Bunsen, 1852–1932. Entered Diplomatic Service, 1877. Secretary of Embassy, Constantinople, 1897–1902; Paris, 1902–5. Knighted, 1905. Minister at Lisbon, 1905. Ambassador in Madrid, 1906–13; in Vienna, 1913–14. Special Ambassador to the States of South America, 1918. Created Baronet, 1919.

[2] John Edward Redmond, 1851–1918. MP, 1881–1918. Chairman of the Irish Parliamentary Party at Westminster.

Egypt, and Ramsay MacDonald,[1] the Labour MP, who had been touring in Australia. 'Politics are avoided', Rumbold recorded in his diary. He disembarked at Gibraltar on January 15, lunched with the Governor,[2] who was a family friend, crossed to Algeciras and took the train from there to Madrid, reaching his new post on the morning of January 17. Rumbold was never again to serve in a single post for as long as he had served in Cairo, and he was often to look back on his years under Cromer as the high point of his early career, despite their frustrations. But he never came to accept Cromer's policy of giving Egyptians responsible posts in the administration. Within four years of leaving Cairo, on 12 June 1910, he wrote in his diary: 'They are playing with the idea that the Egyptians will be fit to govern themselves in the future. They *never* will, and the sooner that is realized the better.'

[1] James Ramsay MacDonald, 1866–1937. Labour MP, 1906–18, 1922–29 and 1929–31. Leader of the Labour Party, 1911–14. Prime Minister and Secretary of State for Foreign Affairs, January to November 1924. Prime Minister, 1929–35. National Labour MP, 1931–35. Lord President of the Council, 1935–37.
[2] Frederick William Edward Forestier Forestier-Walker, 1844–1910. Served in the Zulu War, 1879. Knighted, 1894. Lieutenant-General Commanding the Lines of Communication, South Africa, 1899–1901. Governor of Gibraltar, 1905–10.

6

Madrid

1907–1908

Rumbold was angered on reaching Madrid. 'There are considerable arrears of work', he wrote in his diary on January 18, 'which will take some time to clear off and the papers etc are in great confusion. This state of things is most discreditable to Acton[1] and George Young,[2] the former incumbents of the chancery. Had either of them been here when I arrived I should have made it my business to see that he cleared out the pig-stye.' Within a few days he noted that the Ambassador, Sir Maurice de Bunsen, was 'a charming chief', although his bitterness towards his predecessors still remained. The Youngs,[3] he wrote in his diary on January 22, had charged him 'an unconscionable sum for their furniture – a good deal of which is made out of packing cases. Much of it is filthy and only fit to be burnt. . . . It will be a lesson to me never to buy in the dark again.' To his father he wrote, five days later, his scorn undiminished: 'The bath didn't work, and the geyser would have blown up had we used it. . . . We have had to have the nursery disinfected, as it was used by a drunken maid. . . . The Youngs' wash-hand stands and other articles of furniture were so filthy that I am burning them for firewood (wood being expensive here).'

Rumbold was not impressed by the Spaniards. 'Their character', he noted in his diary on February 7, 'is thoroughly Oriental. They have the same objectionable characteristics as are to be found among the Easterns in addition to which there is an absurd pride and a want of discipline. Their pride has been their ruin, and their want of discipline seems to be a bar to stability of Government without which the country cannot hope to

---

[1] Richard Maximilian Dalberg-Acton, 1870–1924. Entered the Foreign Office, 1894. Succeeded his father as Baron Acton, 1902. 2nd Secretary, Madrid, 1906–7; The Hague, 1907. Chargé d'Affaires, Darmstadt, 1911–14. Consul-General, Zurich, 1917–19. Envoy to Finland and Lithuania, 1919–20.

[2] George Young, 1872–1952. Entered Diplomatic Service, 1896; Attaché, Madrid, 1904–6; First Secretary, Lisbon, 1914. Organized an Admiralty Intelligence Section, 1915. *Daily News* correspondent, Berlin, 1919. Professor of Portuguese at London University, 1919–22. Unsuccessful Labour candidate at the elections of 1923, 1924 and 1929. Succeeded his father as 4th Baronet, 1930. Among his many publications were *New Germany* (1920), *Diplomacy Old and New* (1921) and *Constantinople* (1925).

[3] In 1904 Young had married Jessie Helen Ilbert, the daughter of Sir Courtenay Ilbert, a former Legal Member of the Viceroy's Council in India, and for nearly twenty years (1902–21) Clerk of the House of Commons.

progress rapidly.'[1] Rumbold passed on these complaints to his father, who, for once, shared his son's prejudices. 'They are a played out people,' Sir Horace wrote from London on February 19, 'and though they at one time had a great part in history, were never really first-rate. I don't remember caring much for any of my Spanish colleagues.'

For two weeks in February, while the Ambassador went on leave to Gibraltar and Tangier, Rumbold was in charge of the Embassy. On February 9, after only three weeks in Madrid, he set down in his diary his reflections on the people with whom he would have to live for nearly two years. 'The more I see of the ordinary town Spaniard', he wrote, 'the less I like him. He is vain and full of pride, untruthful, dirty and inclined to idleness. He will "try it on" whenever he can safely do so. . . . One sees pretty faces in the streets but there is little real beauty in society.' Rumbold believed that the Spanish dislike of foreigners arose because 'they cannot help contrasting the position once occupied by their country in the world, with that which it occupies now'. He was surprised at how touchy Spaniards were if a foreigner criticized their country or its institutions. 'I begin to doubt whether Spain can ever have been a really great nation', he noted on February 12. Five days later he went to a bull-fight, which he found 'a brutalising sport' but he reflected that 'the people of every country require some form of amusement, failing which they will prob-ably drink too much. The Spaniards, whatever their faults, are not drunk-ards.' Rumbold's complaints continued. 'Servants in Spain', he wrote to his father on March 23, 'are the greatest swine unhung.'

During the first three months of 1907 France, already linked with Britain by the Anglo-French Entente of 1904, drew Spain into the orbit of the Entente by opening negotiations for an Anglo-Franco-Spanish agreement, designed to prevent any German settlement on the Moroccan coast. Rumbold's father saw danger in the increasing isolation of Germany which the agreement entailed, but Rumbold himself disagreed. 'I don't see what they can do to harm the rest of the world now', he wrote on March 31. 'They were so turbulent and uncertain that it was necessary to create a ring-fence round them and they have only themselves to thank.' Negotiations reached a climax at the beginning of April, when Edward VII met King Alfonso[2] of Spain off the Spanish port of Cartagena. After two

---

[1] Rumbold himself had Spanish blood in his veins. In 1663 his ancestor Henry Rumbold had married Francisca Maria, daughter of Brian I'Anson, and granddaughter of Sir Brian I'Anson, Bart, and Beatriz Rico.

[2] Leon Fernando Maria Isidro Pascual Antonio, 1886–1941. Posthumous son of King Alfonso XII of Spain, he was king at birth, as Alfonso XIII. Narrowly escaped death in a bomb incident in Paris, 1905; and again on his wedding day in Madrid, 1906. Fired at three times, but escaped unhurt, in Madrid, 1913. He abdicated in 1931.

days of discussions between the two sovereigns and their senior Foreign Office officials, the Anglo-Spanish aspects of the agreement were settled. 'Neither party', Rumbold wrote in his diary on April 8, 'wishes to frame an agreement in such words as to appear to be aimed at Germany.' Under the agreement, Britain and Spain agreed to maintain the *status quo* along the Mediterranean and Atlantic coasts of Morocco. Neither power would invite another foreign power to establish its sovereignty. A similar *status quo* agreement was signed between Spain and France. 'Of course the Germans will think it is aimed at them', Rumbold wrote in his diary on April 9. For his own part in the proceedings at Cartagena Rumbold was made a Member of the Victorian Order, which was given to him on April 9 on board the Royal Yacht *Victoria and Albert*. 'I accepted as solemnly as I could', he wrote in his diary that night, 'and signed the necessary papers. After all the chaff etc which I had indulged in about this decoration it really was rather comic that I should get it myself. I felt an ass.' At dinner that night Rumbold talked with Sir Charles Hardinge, whom he held responsible for his failure to be promoted in Cairo. 'He congratulated me on the MVO', Rumbold wrote in his diary, 'and I noticed that he had captured a fresh grand cordon. He is hung like a Christmas tree.'[1]

On April 14, having returned to Madrid, Rumbold sent his father a long account of the visit to Cartagena. Tea with Edward VII had included 'Eggs, sardines, every conceivable scone and cake – all were put away with ease'. Of his MVO he wrote, 'I have had my tongue in my cheek about it the whole time.' He also reported the unexpected news that Cromer had retired from Egypt: 'I suppose he has overworked himself. . . . I can't imagine Cairo or Egypt without him. I certainly never thought that I should practically see him out.' Two days later, Rumbold received a letter from Cromer himself. 'By the time this reaches you,' Cromer had written, 'you will know that my Egyptian career is over. I cannot stand the strain of the work any more, and I really think that, after nearly half a century of official work, I am entitled to a rest.'

Towards the end of April Rumbold left Madrid for a three-week tour of inspection of the British Consulates and Vice-Consulates in southern Spain. He visited Cordova, Malaga, Granada, Seville and Cadiz, discussing the problems of British trade, admiring the Moorish architecture,

---

[1] By April 1907 Sir Charles Hardinge had received the following decorations: KCMG (1904), KCVO (1904), GCMG (1905) and GCVO (1905). He was later made a GCB (1910) and created Baron (1910). He held eleven foreign orders, including the Grand Cross of the Spanish Order of Charles III. By the time of his death he was the most highly decorated Foreign Office official of his generation (as Viceroy of India he was to receive the GCSI and the GCIE).

and cursing the tourists, one group of whom he described in his diary on April 26 as 'an appalling collection – all Germans . . . they make the place hideous'. He had harsh words for most of the hotels and travel facilities. 'The Spanish mosquito nets', he wrote two days later, 'like so much else in Spain – are idiotic and inefficient arrangements, being slit down one side. Mosquitoes can get in with the greatest ease.' At Cadiz a dealer in a curiosity shop offered him a so-called Velasquez, for five pounds, 'but we did not close'. He found Cadiz 'a dead town', but was sorry to leave it, for, as he noted in his diary, one of his ancestors had been British consul there 'over $2\frac{1}{2}$ centuries ago'.[1] On returning to Madrid on May 6 he found that he had been given a Spanish decoration, the Order of Isabella the Catholic, noting in his diary: 'It is a pretty star, in gold with red and green enamel. Showed it to the child, who was delighted.' But a week later a curt note from Charles Hardinge to de Bunsen informed him that 'the King had refused me leave to accept and wear the Spanish decoration'. He did not mind, although he was 'sorry that the Spaniards, who have been very civil about it, should receive a slap in the face by having the decor- ation returned to them'. Later Rumbold met the Spanish Foreign Minister, Allendesalazar,[2] who looked 'deeply annoyed' about the rejected decor- ation, and said that King Alfonso himself 'was much put out'.

Of Rumbold's paperwork at this time two brief diary entries give a glimpse: 'May 11. Began a report on present day electoral methods in Spain. May 12. Finished my report on Spanish elections.' For recreation he took up polo again, playing three times a week. The rejection of the Spanish decoration continued to cause trouble; twice Hardinge wrote to de Bunsen to abuse Rumbold for accepting it, and declaring that Rumbold's conduct 'had been improper'. De Bunsen had stood up for Rumbold, but Hardinge insisted that he should be told of his 'irregular' conduct in accepting the Order. 'I consider Hardinge is a bully and a cad', Rumbold wrote to his father on May 15. 'It is a bad look out, for however well one may work etc it is comparatively easy for Hardinge to pick a quarrel with one and then make that an excuse for delaying one's promo- tion. He is trying to establish a sort of personal rule at the FO and I can't think what our Foreign Secretary is about. Little by little Hardinge will fill the more important posts with his gang and then the whole show will be under his thumb.' Sir Horace replied sympathetically that the affair con- firmed his own impression of Hardinge as 'an exceedingly over-bearing

[1] Thomas Rumbold, 1628–1706. Consul at Cadiz. He married Rafaela de los Cameros, widow of Richard Crocker. He was buried at San Lucar.

[2] Manuel Allendesalazar, 1856–1923. Entered the Spanish Parliament as a Conservative, 1894. Lord Mayor of Madrid. Minister of Finance, 1901. Minister of Public Instruction, 1902. Minister of Agriculture, 1903. Foreign Minister, 1907. Prime Minister, 1919 and 1921.

jack-in-office', but he advised his son: 'Don't distress yourself about the wretched occurrence, for it cannot possibly do you harm.'

In June Rumbold set off for another official tour, this time to inspect the three British Consulates in northern Spain, at Barcelona, Corunna and Bilbao. The Consul at Corunna, Charles Trayner,[1] had been at preparatory school with him. 'He looks horribly ill,' Rumbold noted in his diary on June 10, 'in fact he is a living skeleton and I did not recognize him at first. . . . A long spell of Guatemala has done the mischief.' From San Sebastian Rumbold sent the Ambassador his Report on the Consulates he had visited. 'One and all desired a change of post', he noted in his diary for June 21. 'The Consular inspection has been most instructive for one does not realize the difficulties with which the Consuls have to contend until one sees them at work.' He felt that the Consuls were all seriously underpaid, and in his Report, which was sent to the Foreign Office, strongly advised immediate increases in their salary. To Rumbold's surprise, his Report was well received, and most of his recommendations were acted upon.

From San Sebastian, Rumbold proceeded to England on leave. He was glad to have returned. 'Delighted to be back again in my own country', he noted in his diary on June 24. On his previous leave he had felt rather isolated and unnoticed; this time his wife persuaded him to put a notice in the *Morning Post* to say that they had returned to London. 'I did this rather unwillingly', Rumbold informed his father that same day; but it seemed to have its effect. 'Were much questioned about Spain', he wrote in his diary on June 26, after he had been to a polo match.

Rumbold was thirty-eight years old. He had been a member of the Diplomatic Corps for sixteen years. His hopes of becoming a Counsellor of Embassy in Cairo had been disappointed. He had little chance of being promoted to Counsellor in Madrid, where the post had only been filled a year earlier. He felt himself without a patron in the Foreign Office, where Charles Hardinge's hostility seemed to pose a barrier to his advancement, despite his father's frequent attempts at reassurance. He felt no sympathy for the Liberal Government, which had been in office for nearly a year and a half. He resented what he believed to be Grey's failure to rule the Foreign Office effectively. He was suspicious of the growing influence of the Liberal Party's radical wing, and of its Labour allies. Visiting the Foreign Office on June 27 he wrote bitterly in his diary: 'Gather that Charles

[1] Charles Hugh Maxwell Trayner, 1867–1908. Elder son of Lord Trayner, a judge. Entered the Consular Service as Vice-Consul, New York, 1893. Consul, Guatemala, 1897–1903. Consul for the Spanish Provinces of Galicia, the Asturias and Leon, resident at Corunna, 1903–8. He died in Corunna on February 25, 1908.

Hardinge and his wife are all powerful. He bears the same relation to our service that Fisher does to the Navy. Both have the King's ear. Think that C. Hardinge's rise has been too rapid. There are very few men in this world who can bear a sudden rise to power without having their heads turned and suffering from "swelled head". . . . Whilst I was in the Private Secretaries' room he came in and it seemed to me he looked uncomfortable when he saw me. I suppose he realised he had made an ass of himself about the Spanish decoration.' On the following day he went to the Foreign Office annual party. 'I never saw such a bear garden,' he wrote in his diary, 'nor such a collection of hideous, dowdy women. The labour party seemed to be in force, the men dressed in blue serge suits, their women-kind like maids out for a Sunday. . . . Will avoid these parties in future or as long as the present Government are in office.'

While on leave Rumbold spent much of his time watching polo. He was present at the Army finals between the 11th and 20th Hussars on July 6, when Lord Roberts[1] gave away the cup which, Rumbold recorded in his diary, 'was full of champagne'. The soldiers made him drink out of it, 'saying I was one of their oldest friends'. Ten days later he was annoyed to learn that he could not go to the Court Ball, as no diplomat below the rank of Counsellor of Embassy was being invited. 'This is all wrong in principle,' he wrote in his diary, 'the fact being that diplomatists among others are crowded out by an increasing horde of Jews and Americans.'

Rumbold puzzled over his future, and wrote to his Ambassador for advice. 'The modern system is indeed inscrutable,' de Bunsen replied from Madrid on July 10, 'but as I have myself been highly favoured under it I cannot complain. How this came about is a mystery to me, for I hardly know the Hardinges & certainly owe nothing to him. I think I am very happily placed in Spain which lies rather outside the whirlpool. Certainly it suits me very well & I am in no hurry to move on.' On July 21 de Bunsen wrote again: 'I trust all will come right for you, for no one better deserves rapid promotion.' On August 20, as Rumbold's leave was coming to an end, he noted disconsolately in his diary: 'It has occurred to me that 14 years ago – when I first became a 3rd Secretary I received a salary of £450 a year. My salary is now £500 a year . . . what an advantageous and brilliant service the diplomatic service is.'

The pleasures of Rumbold's leave grew upon him. So did his disenchantment with diplomacy. 'Came to the conclusion', he wrote in his

[1] Frederick Sleigh Roberts, 1932–1914. 2nd Lieutenant, Bengal Artillery, 1851; served during the Indian Mutiny. Commanded the Kabul Field Force, 1879–80. Commander-in-Chief, India, 1885–93; Ireland, 1895–99. Created Baron, 1892. Supreme Commander, South Africa, 1899–1900. Earl, 1901. Commander-in-Chief of the British Army, 1901–4. He published *Forty-One Years in India* in 1897.

diary on September 1, 'that I would leave the diplomatic service at once had I the wherewithal to live comfortably at home. Find that I dislike leaving England more and more each year, and go back to it with increasing pleasure. One only, presumably, lives once. Why, therefore, spend most of one's life abroad, however interesting this may be.' Two days later he had to leave London for Spain.

Much of Britain's diplomatic activity in Spain during the autumn of 1907 consisted in trying to persuade the Spaniards to support the French punitive measures in Morocco, where the murder of a French subject had led to a French military occupation of Casablanca. The Spanish were reluctant to become embroiled. Rumbold spent September decyphering telegrams about the incident, paraphrasing them for the Ambassador, and drafting the Ambassador's replies. His thoughts were elsewhere. He did not want to stay in Madrid unless, as he wrote to his father on September 8, it 'saved me from going out to the Far East'. He wanted to be sent to Rome, and asked his father to use his influence to that end. 'Rome is worth £1140 a year to the Counsellor', he wrote, and he added that he preferred the Italians to the Spaniards. 'Spain is an interesting country to see and travel about in', he had written to his father on August 23, 'but it isn't a white man's country as a residence. I call it the land of the dirty hidalgo.' Writing to his father from Madrid on October 13 Rumbold declared that he would accept anything 'to escape from Madrid. If I have to go far afield, which I should hate for obvious reasons, I am anxious to go to Japan.' Sir Horace passed on his son's reflections to Grey's Private Secretary, William Tyrrell,[1] and reported back that Tyrrell 'was very nice about the whole thing. I could see by his manner that you are well thought of. He said he was very glad indeed to know what were your wishes.' In his diary for October 29 Rumbold reflected caustically: 'The above is a typical Private Secretary's utterance, full of soft sawder and blarney. . . . Meanwhile my dislike of this place grows stronger every day and I am losing all interest in it.' Rumbold was offered no promotion and had to remain in Madrid for a further year. 'There is only one consolation in it all,' he wrote in his diary on November 7, 'and that is that I do not owe anything to anybody and that nobody so far has given me a helping hand in my career.'

Rumbold remained in Spain throughout 1908. His work involved sending the Foreign Office details of anarchist outrages in Barcelona,

[1] William George Tyrrell, 1866–1947. Entered the Foreign Office, 1889. Private Secretary to Sir Edward Grey, 1907–15. Knighted, 1913. Assistant Under-Secretary of State at the Foreign Office, 1919–25; Permanent Under-Secretary, 1925–28. Ambassador in Paris, 1928–34. Created Baron, 1929. President of the British Board of Film Censors, 1935–47. Two of his sons were killed in the First World War.

rumours of royal marriages, a précis on Spanish electoral laws, and trade statistics to the Board of Trade, which, Rumbold wrote in his diary on January 27, were 'always on us for reports on every conceivable question. They are the greatest bores in the world.' Spain's tariff policies gave Rumbold, now an ardent Free Trader, frequent examples of the follies of Protection which he sent back to London. 'Nobody will ever persuade me that protection is a good thing for people's pockets', he wrote to his father on April 18. 'It is, on the contrary, the invention of the devil. I have just drafted a despatch to the FO, giving a splendid example of the imbecility of protection. . . .' But attempts to influence opinion in London were infrequent. 'A large part of our work here', he noted in his diary on February 1, 'consists in getting British firms out of trouble caused by their own stupidity or carelessness.' He added as an afterthought: 'Wonder whether German firms are equally imbecile?'

For relaxation, Rumbold played bridge at the Austrian Embassy, made many visits to the Opera and a few to the Prado, was invited to Court Balls, and to 'a tiresome little dance' at the American Legation. 'We have been living in a whirl of gaiety here,' he wrote to his father on January 28, 'never in bed till past 2 a.m.'

On February 1 the King of Portugal[1] was assassinated in Lisbon. 'All decent minded men will rally to the monarchy', Rumbold noted in his diary on the following day. Anarchism, and its threat to monarchies, became a constant theme of discussion. When the King of Spain dined at the British Embassy at the beginning of March he told de Bunsen that he did not want to be like the Emperor of Russia,[2] 'who was practically a prisoner in one of his Palaces, but wished to be able to travel all over his dominions'. Alfonso himself had already survived five attempted assassinations, including a bomb which exploded in front of his carriage on the day of his wedding to Princess Ena of Battenberg.[3]

Rumbold continued to worry about his future, and about Hardinge's supremacy at the Foreign Office. 'Since his rise to power', Rumbold

---

[1] Don Carlos, 1863–1908. Succeeded to the throne on the death of his father in 1889. In May 1907 he suspended the constitution of Portugal and appointed a dictator, Senhor Franco, as Prime Minister. Carlos was assassinated in Lisbon, on February 1, 1908, together with his eldest son. He was succeeded by his only surviving son, Manoel, who abdicated in 1910. On October 6, 1910, Rumbold wrote in his diary: 'There is not much advantage in being King over a somewhat debased nation like the Portuguese.'

[2] Nicholas II, 1868–1918. Succeeded his father Alexander III as Tsar, 1894. Married Princess Alix of Hesse, a granddaughter of Queen Victoria, 1894. He abdicated in March 1917 and was murdered, together with his wife and children, at Ekaterinburg in July 1918.

[3] Princess Victoria-Eugenie, 1887–1969. Known as 'Ena'. A granddaughter of Queen Victoria and daughter of Prince Henry of Battenberg. She became a Roman Catholic on March 7, 1906, and married King Alfonso XIII of Spain on May 31, 1906.

wrote to his father on March 3, 'Hardinge has never troubled himself to be conciliatory. He has made many enemies where he could have made friends, and he doesn't seem to have grasped the fact that it pays to be civil to people and that it is a mistake to ride rough-shod over them . . . the duration of his influence and power largely depends on the King's favour. He has put his trust in Princes. I hope he may not regret it.' Rumbold believed that Grey was entirely dominated by Hardinge; 'this is why', he explained to his father, 'there is more uncertainty in our service than there has been for a long time past'.

In June Rumbold returned to England on leave. On June 26, the day following his arrival in London, he went to the Foreign Office, hoping to hear of a change of post, and perhaps of promotion. But, he recorded in his diary, 'they merely asked when I was going back to Madrid'. Two weeks later, on July 10, Hardinge asked him to call at the Foreign Office again. At last he learnt good news; he was to be promoted Counsellor by the end of the year, and would be sent to a new post. On July 14 he learned, from Tyrrell, that he was to be posted to Teheran. He did not want to return to Persia, nor did his wife want to go there. 'It is a bad place for women', he wrote in his diary. On July 16 Rumbold went to the Foreign Office and made his protest. Tyrrell, who was sympathetic, agreed not to send his name forward for royal approval. Rumbold said that he knew the Counsellorship in Tokyo would soon fall vacant, 'and that I would wait for that'. Tyrrell asked Rumbold to be patient, declaring that both Tokyo and promotion to Counsellor would only be a question of time, and asking him to return in the meantime to Spain. Rumbold agreed, but confided to his diary: 'Great bore having to go back to Spain when one knows one is going to be shifted.' He left London on September 1, reaching Madrid two days later. In England he had been struck by something he had not felt before, 'the apparently rooted conviction', as he had written in his diary on August 12, 'that the German is the enemy'. He ascribed this conviction 'to the behaviour of the Germans themselves, and to the campaign carried on by the Times, Daily Mail, National Review and Spectator'. He did not disapprove of the new attitude. 'If only this idea would impress itself on our Government,' he continued, 'perhaps they would bestir themselves about our defence forces. What we want is a General Staff at the Admiralty and a modified form of conscription.'[1]

Rumbold waited in Spain throughout September hoping to learn of his Tokyo posting. For two weeks he stayed at San Sebastian, sightseeing and doing routine work; then he moved to Madrid. He sold his furniture

---

[1] An Admiralty War Staff was set up (by Winston Churchill) in October 1911 but Conscription was not introduced until May 1916.

and gave notice to leave his flat on October 15. By October 10 no news of his transfer had yet arrived, and he wrote urgently to the Foreign Office asking when he could leave Madrid. On October 17, having persuaded his landlord to let him stay on longer, he received a letter from Theo Russell[1] at the Foreign Office that 'Tokyo may not be vacant for some time'. Tyrrell suggested that he stay on at Madrid, but if this really vexed him, as indeed it did, he might go for a few months to Munich, with the rank of Counsellor, until the Tokyo vacancy. On October 24 Rumbold abandoned the Madrid Embassy. 'Have decided to go down to Valencia', he wrote in his diary that day, 'and travel in the South of Spain until such time as the FO make up their minds what is to happen to me. I have finished my work here and have literally nothing more to do. Have just finished a précis of the Local Administration Bill, about the dullest bit of work I have ever had to do.' In November he and his wife went to Biarritz. 'We spent our time very pleasantly', he wrote in his diary on November 30, 'and wonder why we don't hear from the FO.' On December 9, after his return to Madrid, he received a telegram from Tyrrell, informing him that he was to go to Munich as Chargé d'Affairs in the New Year, and stay there for at least two months, until he could proceed to Tokyo. 'It will feel very strange', Rumbold wrote to his father on December 14, 'to be a cock on a small dunghill after being third on a large one for so many years.'

On December 13 Rumbold said his farewells in Madrid. De Bunsen had proved a more sympathetic, more communicative chief than Cromer, and gave him a friendly send off, saying that he wished he would stay on as Counsellor. 'There is no man in the service under whom I would rather serve', he wrote to his father on December 16. 'When we think of the difference in the goodbye we received from the de Bunsens,' he added, 'after under 2 years at Madrid, as compared to that of the Cromers, after nearly 10 years, the latter don't show up well.' But he was determined to put Madrid behind him as quickly as he could.

[1] Odo William Theophilus Villiers Russell, 1870–1951. 2nd son of the 1st Baron Ampthill. Entered the Diplomatic Service, 1892; 1st Secretary, 1905. Served at the Foreign Office, 1905–8, as Private Secretary to Sir Edward Grey. Counsellor of Embassy, Vienna, 1909–15. Diplomatic Secretary to the Foreign Secretary, London, 1915–19. Minister at Berne, 1919–22; at the Vatican, 1922–28; at The Hague, 1928–33. Knighted, 1923.

7

Munich

1909

Rumbold was Chargé d'Affaires at the British Legation in Munich – as Britain's representative to the Kingdoms of Bavaria and Württemberg – for two and a half months. It was his first diplomatic post in Germany, and his first period in sole charge of a diplomatic mission. It was during his time in Munich that he reached, on February 5, his fortieth birthday, and three days later he was promoted Counsellor, the advancement which he had wanted for several years. He had hankered after this responsibility throughout his two years in Spain, and was confident of his ability to interpret international events. Over the previous decade, while in Cairo and Madrid, he had read the selection of Embassy and Legation telegrams sent out by the Foreign Office – the Confidential Print. He had been concerned not only with the rivalries within the Foreign Office on which his letters to his father had dwelt so frequently, but also with the problems and developments of British foreign policy.

As Chargé d'Affaires at Munich, Rumbold would now have to contribute his own views to the Confidential Print. Although the principal work was done at the Berlin Embassy, Munich as capital of the Kingdom of Bavaria – and Stuttgart, the capital of the Kingdom of Württemberg – were both independent in the sphere of diplomatic representation, even though political power in Germany centred upon Prussia and was based on Berlin.

Rumbold's principal task while at Munich was to read through the south German Press and to report back to London on its general tone and implications. He had also to glean what political information he could from the Bavarian and Württemberg authorities, and from the other diplomats accredited to the Bavarian Court. He set to work at once reading the papers; his German was fluent, both for reading and conversation. In his diary for January 3 he noted that the leading Munich papers, the *Münchener Neueste*, was 'a most pestilential sheet, & hardly a day passes but that it contains some poisonous allusion to England'. Although it was only a Bavarian paper, Rumbold treated its opinions seriously, because, he noted on January 6, 'the Prussian Legation can control & inspire this paper to a considerable extent'. The principal Württemberg paper, the *Schwäbische*

Merkur, was, he decided, less offensive, but nevertheless 'not particularly friendly'. On January 5, after four days of diligent reading, Rumbold sent the Foreign Office his first despatch, a summary of the yearly review of the events of 1908 which had appeared in all the papers. 'The main point that these local papers make', he wrote in his diary that day, 'is that the combination of Germany & Austria with their population 105 millions & their armies of 5 millions is the best guarantee for the peace of Europe. In other words, tho' they don't say so they would commit almost any illegality & none of the other powers would feel inclined to tackle them.' Rumbold disliked the German Press' habit of constant harping on a combination of German strength and British duplicity, but he did not share the outspoken hostility towards Germany which, within the Foreign Office, was most marked in the memoranda and comments of Eyre Crowe,[1] who was said to be assuming an influence over Sir Edward Grey rivalled only by that of Hardinge and Tyrrell. 'Crowe is quite cracked about Germany', Rumbold had written to his father from Madrid on 9 November 1908.

On January 7 Rumbold had a private audience with the Regent of Bavaria, Prince Luitpold.[2] 'He is rather deaf but does not like people to shout at him, so I spoke slowly & clearly. We then drifted into German, & got on better. He asked about the King but I thought he meant the King of Spain & answered at cross purposes, but it didn't matter.' 'We had supper with the Royalties', he wrote in his diary on January 13; 'Each Royalty had a page behind their chairs. Everything very well done but glad to get to bed.'

While he was in Munich, Rumbold became convinced that the growing German Navy was intended as a threat to Britain, and he was prepared to say so. 'Had a long talk after dinner with Baron Soden',[3] he wrote in his diary on January 21; 'He and everyone else always ask me why we object to their having a fleet. They say they only require it to protect their commerce. I asked who is going to attack their commerce. He had no answer to this.' Three days earlier Rumbold set out his feelings in his diary. 'We shall never be on good terms with Germany', he wrote, 'as long as

---

[1] Eyre Crowe, 1864–1925. Entered the Foreign Office, 1885; Senior Clerk, 1906; Assistant Under-Secretary of State, 1912; Permanent Under-Secretary of State, 1920–25. Knighted, 1911. Both his mother and his wife were German.

[2] Luitpold, 1821–1912. Son of Ludwig I of Bavaria. From 1886 until his death he ruled as Regent, first for his nephew Ludwig II, then for Ludwig's brother Otto I.

[3] Julius von Soden, 1846–1921. Entered the Württemberg diplomatic service, 1872. Served in Bucharest, Algeria, Canton, Havana, Lima and St Petersburg. Governor of German East Africa, 1891–93. Head of the Cabinet Secretariat of the King of Württemberg, 1901–6.

this fleet question exists.' The real test of the German Government's intentions would come, he believed, 'when their present naval programme has been carried out i.e. whether they will propose a fresh large programme. If so it will be clearly meant against us.' On February 14, after Edward VII's visit to the Kaiser at Berlin, Rumbold noted in his diary, 'The fleet question doesn't seem to have been touched on, which is, perhaps, just as well', and he commented that the anti-British tone of the Bavarian Press had moderated during the visit. Writing to Sir Edward Grey on February 15 Rumbold noted that 'for fully a fortnight before the visit took place, there was a cessation of the articles – unfriendly to England – which had appeared almost daily in one organ or another of this part of Germany. It seemed almost as if a "mot d'ordre" had come from Berlin to exercise reserve in view of the impending visit.' Moderation was the exception, not the rule; a month earlier, on January 12, Rumbold had sent Sir Edward Grey a report on the Bavarian Press, in which he commented on 'the way in which the press of this country seizes on everything which it can work up for sensational purposes'. This was the view of 'one or two well-informed persons' to whom he had talked, two of whom had, a few years before, tried to produce a moderate paper, but had failed. The paper, Rumbold told Grey, 'was too respectable, and not sensational enough for the public. The German press was not, generally speaking, in the hands of gentlemen. Unfortunately it made public opinion and therefore had to be watched.'

At the end of February Rumbold went to Stuttgart, the capital of Württemberg, where he had several talks with the Minister-President, Dr von Weizäcker,[1] who complained that the increased naval expenditure of the Imperial Government in Berlin threatened to be a severe drain on the finance of the individual German states. 'He said that the expenditure of the Empire had grown in a manner which could not have been foreseen when that Empire was founded', Rumbold wrote in his diary on February 23; 'Finally he let slip the words "Drang nach der Nordsee" in part explanation of the increased expenditure.' This episode confirmed Rumbold's fears that the traditional German 'drang nach Osten' – the Drive towards the East – was being eclipsed by a new Drive towards the North Sea. On March 2, having returned to Munich, he wrote in his diary: 'It is quite clear that a forward naval policy would prove expensive and that then would come a time when large fleet construction programmes could no longer be paid for out of loans. The Germans have only got what they deserve.' But on March 11 he added, not without some hope: 'The money that the fleet is costing will soon begin to make

[1] Karl von Weizsäcker, 1853–1926. Minister-President of Württemberg, 1906–18.

Germans think a bit.' Two days later his Munich Chargéship came to an end.

Returning to London, Rumbold found Anglo-German naval rivalry the principal topic of conversation. In Parliament, the Prime Minister,[1] had just announced that the Germans were building warships much faster than the British Government had realized. There was a growing public demand for an increase in battleship building, and the Australian, New Zealand and Canadian Governments had each offered to build battleships to help maintain British naval supremacy. 'The Germans won't like this,' Rumbold wrote in his diary on March 21, 'as they didn't bargain to deal with the whole Empire. Any good done by the King's visit to Berlin is now undone. The *Observer* openly suggests "going for" the Germans now.' On March 31, after more than two weeks in London, he noted in his diary: 'The bugbear of Germany is larger than ever.'

Before leaving for Japan, Rumbold saw both Sir Edward Grey and Charles Hardinge at the Foreign Office. Grey asked him about the German Fleet, and he reported on the reluctance of Bavaria and Württemberg to bear the heavy expenditure involved. Hardinge told him, as he recorded in his diary on April 2, 'that the Germans were not to be trusted, and that the only way to make them stop building ships was to lay down two keels for one'. Rumbold did not disagree; his contact with German affairs had been brief, but it left a strong and foreboding impression on his mind.

On April 6, after saying good-bye to his father, Rumbold left London for the long voyage to Japan.

[1] Henry Herbert Asquith, 1852–1928. Liberal MP 1886–1918 and 1920–24. Prime Minister, 1908–16. Created Earl of Oxford and Asquith, 1925.

8

Tokyo

1909–1913

On 8 April 1909, Rumbold, his wife, and their two-year-old daughter sailed from Genoa on board the North German Lloyd passenger liner *Eitel Friedrich*[1] for the five-week voyage to Japan. On April 13 they reached Port Said. 'Seemed odd to me not going up to Cairo by the afternoon train', Rumbold wrote in his diary that evening. On April 18 they were at Aden, and five days later at Colombo, where Rumbold went ashore and spent some time with the agents of his family tea plantation, the Melford Estate.[2] 'Their returns were not satisfactory to me', he wrote in his diary on April 23, 'and I asked them to explain matters. But their explanations were not very clear or satisfactory to me.' There was no time to enquire further. The voyage continued. When the *Eitel Friedrich* reached Singapore, the passengers learned of Lloyd George's[3] budget. 'Supertax on incomes of over £5000', Rumbold noted – his own income was now £865 a year – 'increase in death duties, progressive tax on motors, tax on petrol, increased tax on whisky and tobacco. There will be general discontent with this budget.' Hong Kong was reached on May 5 and Shanghai on May 8, a month after leaving Genoa. 'Shanghai simply reeks of money', he wrote in his diary, 'and yet people complain that their trade is bad.'

On May 11 the *Eitel Friedrich* came in sight of the Japanese coast, and the passengers spent a day ashore at Nagasaki, 'supposed to be one of the prettiest harbours in Japan', Rumbold noted in his diary. On May 13 the

[1] On the outbreak of war the German Admiralty took over the *Eitel Friedrich*, armed her, and sent her into action against unarmed British merchant ships. She was active in the Pacific in 1914, then passed through the Panama Canal and attacked British merchantmen in the Caribbean. In April 1915 she sought refuge in the United States port of Newport News, where she was interned for the rest of the war.

[2] Originally a six-hundred acre coffee estate, bought for Rumbold's father in the 1830s by his guardian Lord Rivers. In the 1880s a leaf disease destroyed the coffee. After several costly and unsuccessful experiments, tea was planted. 'I am happy to think you will succeed to something worthwhile', Rumbold's father wrote to him on February 1, 1912. In the 1920s the estate prospered; on its profits Rumbold was able to buy his Rolls-Royce and his Berlin yacht. The estate was sold by Rumbold's son in 1947.

[3] David Lloyd George, 1863–1945. Liberal MP, 1890–1931. Chancellor of the Exchequer, 1908–15. Minister of Munitions, May 1915–July 1916. Secretary of State for War, July–December 1916. Prime Minister, December 1916–October 1922. Independent Liberal MP, 1931–45. Created Earl Lloyd-George of Dwyfor, 1945.

ship reached Kobe. The Consul-General, Henry Bonar,[1] took Rumbold around the town in a rickshaw, and then 'took me to the club and introduced me to the prominent Britishers at the inevitable "bar". No club seems complete without a "bar". Played bridge with considerably better players than myself and won 14 yen[2].' On May 14 the ship set off on the last lap of its journey, reaching Yokohama on the morning of May 15. 'Hall[3] the Consul-General, and Crowe[4] the Commercial Attaché came on board to meet us', Rumbold wrote in his diary; 'Likewise our headboy, cook and coachman. The former did not look very attractive in a black suit with an old pot-hat. Am told he is a great robber.' Hall, 'an oldish man, very deaf and rather blind', engaged Rumbold in a discussion of Positivism, 'a curious conversation on first landing at Yokohama'. After lunch with Crowe, Rumbold took the train to Tokyo, which was to be his home for almost exactly four years.

For seven years Britain's relations with Japan had been based upon the Anglo-Japanese alliance of 1902. This alliance had been made by Balfour's Conservative Government, primarily to offset the growing power of Russia in the Far East. Britain, temporarily caught up in the South African War, and worried both about the growth of Russian naval power off the China coast and about the threat of Russian overland expansion towards India, joined Japan in what was largely, for the British Cabinet, a necessary defensive measure. But since 1905 the nature of the relationship had changed. In that year Japan defeated Russia in the Far East, and Japanese influence was at once extended deep into Korea, Manchuria and Mongolia. From that moment, Japanese economic penetration of China flourished unchallenged. British policy had also taken an unexpected path when, in 1907, Britain and Russia settled their territorial disputes throughout Asia. Henceforth, Britain no longer feared Russia's activities in the Far East, for Russia, much weakened after its defeat by Japan, posed no threat to British interests.

By 1909 many Englishmen felt that the Anglo-Japanese alliance had lost

[1] Henry Alfred Constant Bonar, 1861–1935. Entered Japan Consular Service, 1880; Consul-General at Kobe, 1908–9; at Seoul (Korea), 1909–12.

[2] In 1909 the yen was worth 2 English shillings.

[3] John Carey Hall, 1844–1921. Student Interpreter, Japan, 1867. Acting Assistant Judge, Supreme Court for China and Japan (at Shanghai), 1888–89. Consul at Hakodate, 1889–90; at Nagasaki, 1890–92; at Yokohama, 1895–96; at Kobe, 1897–1902. Consul-General at Yokohama, 1903–14.

[4] Edward Thomas Frederick Crowe, 1877–1960. Entered the Consular Service, 1897, as a Student Interpreter, Japan. Commercial Attaché, Tokyo, 1906–18; Commercial Counsellor, Tokyo, 1918–25. Knighted, 1922. Comptroller-General, Department of Overseas Trade, London, 1928–37. President of the Royal Society of Arts, 1941–43. President of the Japan Association, 1951–52.

its value, and would serve merely to encourage the Japanese to continue their penetration of China, under the cover of British support, but with no compensating advantage for Britain. But these doubts did not affect the Foreign Office or the Admiralty, where the Anglo-Japanese alliance was still highly prized. Both Sir Edward Grey and Sir Charles Hardinge welcomed a strong Japan in the Far East, and believed that there was room enough on the China coast for several powers. The Admiralty believed that the friendship of Japan was an essential facet of British naval strategy. Since 1902 the battleship strength of the Royal Navy in Far Eastern waters had been halved; the North Sea had become the area of overriding British concern. The Admiralty therefore looked to Japan to maintain the naval balance against Germany in the Far East, and thus to uphold British interests. Support for Japan's own expansionist policies towards China seemed a small price to pay if, by maintaining the Anglo-Japanese alliance and encouraging Anglo-Japanese friendship, Britain could feel un-threatened east of India, in the South China Sea, and throughout the vast expanses of the Pacific.

When Rumbold reached Tokyo, he was a firm believer in the value of the Anglo-Japanese alliance, and the need to preserve and foster Anglo-Japanese friendship. On May 22 the Ambassador, Sir Claude Mac-Donald,[1] returned to England on leave, and Rumbold was in charge of the Embassy. That day he had a long conversation with Valentine Chirol, foreign editor of *The Times*, who, with Dr G. E. Morrison,[2] the paper's Peking correspondent, was visiting Japan to learn at first hand of Japanese policy towards China. 'He realizes that enthusiasm for the alliance is waning in England', Rumbold wrote in his diary on May 22, 'and is going to try, by means of the Times, to stop the "dry rot", as he calls it.' The German problem was uppermost in Rumbold's mind. On May 27 the British Naval Attaché, Captain Dundas,[3] told him that 'the only way to

---

[1] Claude Maxwell MacDonald, 1852–1915. Entered the Army, 1872. Major, 1882. War Office representative at the British Agency, Cairo, 1883–87. Consul-General, Zanzibar, 1887–88. Knighted, 1892. Minister to China, 1896–1900; he commanded the Legation Quarter during the siege of Peking, June–August 1900. Ambassador to Japan, 1900–12.

[2] George Ernest Morrison, 1862–1920. Born in Australia. Joined *The Times*, 1894; correspondent in Peking, 1897–1912. His despatches defending China against the Japanese were often modified in London. Political Adviser to the President of the Chinese Republic, 1912–19. An advocate of China's interest at the Paris Peace Conference, 1919.

[3] Charles Dundas of Dundas, 1859–1924. Entered Navy, 1874. Captain, 1901. Naval Attaché, Japan and China, 1908–10. Promoted Rear-Admiral, July 1910. Principal Naval Transport Officer, France, 1915–17. Vice-Admiral, 1916. Knighted, 1917. Admiral, 1919. Rumbold noted in his diary on July 23, 1910, after Dundas had become a Rear-Admiral: 'One of the reasons why Dundas is so pleased with his promotion is that he will get a higher grade Japanese decoration on leaving the country. There is no accounting for some people's ambition.' In 1910 Dundas received the Order of the Rising Sun, 2nd Class.

stop the Germans going on building is to lay down 2 keels for every one they lay down'. At dinner on May 28 the Japanese Minister of Marine, Saito,[1] told Rumbold provocatively that 'he didn't understand the German armaments. Against whom were they directed?' On the following day Rumbold dined with the Prime Minister, Katsura,[2] who was equally out-spoken. Their conversation was conducted in German, the only language they had in common. 'He also alluded to the German naval armaments', Rumbold wrote in his diary that evening, 'and said, with a smile, that they were perhaps directed against Japan. I said there were countries nearer to Germany than Japan. He said "as far as the Japanese Government and I are concerned, England can concentrate the whole of her Navy in home waters. *We* will look after the peace of the Far East".' Katsura added, as Rumbold wrote to Sir Edward Grey on May 30, 'that the alliance with England was a cardinal feature of Japan's policy'.

On May 31 Rumbold lunched with Chirol and Morrison. The two journalists had spent over two hours at the Japanese Foreign Office, and had spoken with a greater authority on eastern affairs than Rumbold could aspire to. Rumbold noted in his diary that Chirol, 'was all in favour of close cooperation with the Japanese in everything, and the Times would take that line'. But Chirol had also taken it upon himself to give the Japanese officials a word of warning. He had told them, Rumbold noted, 'that, as in everyday life the English and Japanese didn't come into contact with each other politically, but did so commercially, it was important that the Japanese should do nothing to impair the confidence of the English nation in Japan's financial and commercial integrity. Otherwise a feeling might be aroused in England which would make it difficult for any English Government to renew the alliance.' Rumbold made no comment on Chirol's caution. Morrison had also sounded a note of warning. On May 31 Rumbold informed Grey that Morrison feared that Japan's demands in China were 'rather exaggerated'.

On August 6 Rumbold received a letter from Sir Claude MacDonald, who was still in England. The Ambassador had been doing his utmost to halt the flagging support for Japan. 'I am working away', he wrote, 'in the

[1] Makoto Saito, 1858–1936. Second Lieutenant, Imperial Japanese Navy, 1882. Studied naval strategy in the United States. Participated in the Sino-Japanese and Russo-Japanese Wars. Vice-Minister of the Navy, 1898. Rear-Admiral, 1900; Admiral, 1912. Created Baron, 1907. Navy Minister, 1913–14. Governor-General of Korea, 1919–29. Created Viscount, 1925. Prime Minister and Foreign Minister, 1932–34. Resigned on account of the Army's increased voice in state affairs. Assassinated by young Army officers.

[2] Tano Katsura, 1847–1913. Deputy Minister of the Army, 1886–95. Created Viscount after the Sino-Japanese War of 1894–95. Minister of the Army, 1898–1901. Three times Prime Minister: first, 1901–6, after which he was created Marquis; second, 1908–11, after which he was created Prince; and third, 1912–13. He died in October 1913.

good cause of bringing the allies together! or rather making this side appreciate what useful friends they have on the other if only they will accept them.' But two months of working with the Japanese Foreign Office had raised doubts in Rumbold's mind. 'I am perfectly straight with them', he wrote in his diary on August 8, 'but feel that they are not equally straight with me. Am told that it is the nature of the beast. They are extraordinarily suspicious.' But the Japanese had reason for their suspicions. At the end of May, Sir Edward Grey had asked Rumbold to secure, on behalf of the First Lord of the Admiralty, Reginald McKenna,[1] full details about Japanese naval constructions, naval movements, harbour works, water supplies in Japanese ports, local defences, wireless installations and weapons practice 'including airships'. This information, Rumbold informed the British Consuls in Japan[2] on June 3, 'should be forwarded by safe opportunity only, i.e. by Foreign Office bag, by British ship or, if necessary, in cypher'.

During August a chance incident gave Rumbold an insight into Japanese thinking about Germany. Colin Davidson,[3] one of the British Embassy staff, was invited to a dinner at which he was the only non-Japanese. The dinner was a jovial one and there was much drinking of saké. At one point in the evening the conversation turned to Germany. 'They all broke out', Rumbold wrote in his diary on August 15, 'into abuse of the Germans and their ways, and drank "down with the German pigs! We know that they are our real enemies". . . . There was no diplomacy towards an ally in all this as they were beyond the diplomatic stage. It is what they really thought, and always are thinking.'

Throughout the autumn of 1909 Captain Dundas tried to obtain Rumbold's support for continued Anglo-Japanese naval manoeuvres. Rumbold feared the German reaction to such an event, but Dundas was persistent. On September 12 Dundas wrote to him: 'I am more and more convinced of the thorough friendship of the Japanese towards us and of the great importance of our alliance. If we broke off how would we like to

---

[1] Reginald McKenna, 1863–1943. Practised as a Barrister, 1887–95. Liberal MP, 1895–1918. He served in Asquith's Cabinet as First Lord of the Admiralty, 1908–11; Home Secretary, 1911–15 and Chancellor of the Exchequer, 1916. Chairman of the Midland Bank from 1919 until his death.

[2] There were British Consular officials at eight Japanese cities – Yokohama, Kobé, Nagasaki, Shimonoseki, Chemulpo, Osaka, Hakodate and Seoul (Korea).

[3] Colin John Davidson, 1878–1930. Entered the diplomatic service as a student interpreter in Siam, 1901. Transferred to Japan, 1903. Assistant in the Japanese Secretary's Office, Tokyo, 1908–11 and Private Secretary to Sir Claude MacDonald, 1909–11. Vice-Consul, Seoul, 1912–13; Yokohama, 1913–14. Interpreter with the British force operating against Tsingtau, September–November, 1914. 1st Secretary, Tokyo, 1923–27; Counsellor, 1927. Knighted, 1930. He died in Tokyo.

2 Rumbold and his father, Athens, 1887.

3   Rumbold in Cairo, 1900.

4   Rumbold's father and stepmother, 1900.

MR. HORACE MONTAGUE RUMBOLD AND MISS ETHELDREDA FANE, MARRIED AT HOLY TRIN[ITY] CHURCH, CHELSEA. (Photographed by Thomson, New Bond Street.)

5 The marriage took place on 18 July 1905.

6 Rumbold and his wife visit a Shinto priest in Japan.

7   Rumbold's summer house at Chusenji, outside Tokyo.
Left to right: Nanny, Tony, Ethel, Constantia and Horace Rumbold.

8 Rumbold's brother William.

9 Nevile Henderson, while serving in the Tokyo Embassy, 1909.

Ramleh,

September 6. 1892.

Dear Father,

Thanks for your letter and
cheque which reached me in safety 3 days
ago. — I was surprised to hear from you from
Marienbad as I didn't know you had any
need of a cure and thought that anyhow
you had given up watering-places as a bad
job

10/11 Part of a letter
from Rumbold to
his father, with
the reply.

The Hague
September 27. 1892

My dear Boy,

We returned from Marienbad
on Friday last after a cure which
has on the whole, I believe, done no
good. — They say that the full effects only
show themselves after a couple of months
but I have little doubt that our digestions
especially mine, will have benefited
by the waters. — The air of Marienbad
is excellent, it being 2000 feet above
the sea level & surrounded by beautiful
pine

On my 82nd Birthday

12   Rumbold's father in retirement, 2 July 1911.

see Japan allied to Germany or any other Power?' Rumbold was worried lest the Japanese would use the combined manoeuvres to gain important knowledge of naval techniques and give nothing positive in return.

When Sir Claude MacDonald returned from his leave at the end of September, Rumbold had more time for relaxation and travel. He attended wrestling matches, played cricket, went sailing and visited Kyoto. His views on British politics were unchanged. 'Personally I hope we shall soon have conscription,' he had written on August 6; 'nothing would be better for the loafers who abound at home.' He sympathized with the House of Lords in their approach to Lloyd George's budget. 'I don't think that England is ready for socialism just yet', was his diary comment on September 24. The rapid pace of inventions was also often in his mind. 'The last papers from home are full of Blériot's[1] flight across the Channel', he had written on September 8; '. . . the papers will have henceforth to devote ever increasing space to flying machines, dirigible balloons and such-like inventions, although, presumably, these machines won't go out so often in winter.' Six weeks later, on October 15, he noted that if the 'present rate of progress' continued, 'everybody will have his aeroplane – just as everybody who can afford it has his motor car'.

In November, Lord Kitchener arrived in the Far East on a visit to China and Japan. He had just reached the end of seven years as Commander-in-Chief of the forces in India, and had been promoted Field-Marshal on September 10. The Liberal Government found him a political embarrassment, and were anxious to keep him as far from Whitehall as possible. They therefore encouraged his visit to the Far East, although at the same time they specifically refused to allow him to accept any Japanese decorations. 'He seemed pleased to see me', Rumbold noted in his diary on November 2; 'He doesn't look a day older than when I saw him last, 7 years ago, on his way out to India. . . . The Japanese are flattered and delighted at his coming. They admire 2 Englishmen above all others i.e. Lord Cromer & Kitchener.' On November 9 Rumbold noted: 'Have been invited to 5 dinners and 2 lunches in honour of K. Of these entertainments 4 are à la Japonaise. I don't like Japanese food and the dinners bore me because they last such a time. . . . The great K departs on the 16th and we shall then have peace, I hope.'

Rumbold saw Kitchener every day during his visit. 'He is a curious mixture', he wrote in his diary on November 13, 'of the brutal soldier

<hr>

[1] Louis Blériot, 1872–1936. Aeroplane designer and constructor. On July 25, 1909, he flew from Calais to Dover, the first crossing of the Channel by a heavier than air machine. His flight won him the *Daily Mail* Thousand Pound Prize. Between 1909 and 1914 he built over 800 aeroplanes of 40 different types; in 1918 his works produced 18 aeroplanes a day.

and an enthusiastic collector of china, swords etc, always with an eye open to the main chance.' On Kitchener's last evening, at a special dance, over eighty geisha girls were provided for the entertainment of the Field-Marshal and the British diplomats. Rumbold described the scene in his diary:

They were mostly young geisha about 14 to 16 – all pretty and attractive. In fact we practically had the pick of the geisha from all over Tokyo – both Sir C and Davidson – who is an expert, saying that they had never seen such a good and large collection before. I soon had one geisha on my knee, my arm round a second whilst a third cuddled up against me. Henderson[1] was buried among them and Sir C had picked out two of the best for himself. My eyeglass seemed to amuse them no end. Unfortunately I could only tell them how pretty they were but that seemed to please them. K wouldn't have one on his knee and whenever Sir C saw him gently push one away he, Sir C, annexed her by way of making amends. K's staff played up well, Brooke[2] and FitzGerald[3] being very active. Every now and then the geisha left us to dance and play a kind of round game – like cotillion figures. They then would come back and plump down on one's knee again. Finally K's staff, Sir C and his staff rushed in and joined the geisha in a sort of game corresponding to 'here we go round the mulberry bush', while one of the geisha squatted on the floor and thumped the drum. The rest of the audience, i.e. 80 odd, including Hayashi[4] and a lot of other swells, stood up and cheered wildly. Finally, as a climax, the Ambassador squatted on the floor and whacked the drum for all he was worth. The company fairly roared. What would the great Hardinge have thought. We then broke up after one of the best evenings known in Tokyo.

Ethel Rumbold was not as impressed by Kitchener as were the Japanese. 'To me', she wrote to her mother on November 15,

[1] Nevile Meyrick Henderson, 1882–1942. Enter the Diplomatic Service, 1905. 3rd Secretary, Tokyo, 1909–11. Counsellor, Constantinople, 1921–24. Minister at Belgrade, 1929–35. Knighted, 1932. Ambassador at Buenos Aires, 1935–37; at Berlin, 1937–39. He published an account of his Berlin Embassy, *Failure of a Mission*, in 1940. His memoirs, *Water Under the Bridges*, were published after his death, in 1945.

[2] Victor Reginald Brooke, 1873–1914. Entered the Army, 1894; served in the Boer War, where he was wounded, and won the DSO; accompanied Sir Louis Dane's Mission to Kabul, 1904–5; Military Secretary to the Viceroy of India, 1907–14; killed in action on the Western Front, September 1, 1914. His brother (later Viscount Alanbrooke) was Chief of the Imperial General Staff, 1941–46, and created Field-Marshal in 1944.

[3] Oswald Arthur Gerald FitzGerald, 1875–1916. Lieutenant, Indian Army, 1897; Captain 1904. A member of Lord Kitchener's staff, 1904–16. Lieutenant-Colonel, August 1914. Personal Military Secretary to Kitchener, 1914–16. Drowned in HMS *Hampshire* while accompanying Kitchener to Russia.

[4] Gonsuke Hayashi, 1861–1939. Entered the Japanese Diplomatic Service, 1887. Served in the London Embassy, 1893–98. Minister at Seoul (Korea), 1899–1906; at Peking, 1906–8. Created Baron, 1907. Ambassador to Rome, 1908–16; to Peking, 1916–19; to London, 1920–25. Grand Master of Ceremonies in Tokyo from 1929 until his death.

he is most unattractive and unhuman, just like a big overpowering machine, and so common and underbred looking. He takes all he can and gives nothing in return, as Lady M[1] remarks, 'he would take a piece of sugar out of a bird's cage'! For instance he was presented with a sword worth £250 by one of these generals, and he said to Sir Claude 'Of course I will send him my photo when I get back to England.' I am glad to say Sir Claude rubbed it in well and said that would be impossible and he *must* send him a handsome present, at which K grunted and looked bored. Then he is always in a hurry to move on and gets up abruptly before an entertainment is over and says good-bye without hardly any polite phrases.

Kitchener left Japan on November 16. He had used his stay with some skill to augment his collection of Oriental wares. 'Hear that K has shipped 25 cases on board the P&O steamer at Yokohama,' Rumbold noted that day in his diary, 'containing £3000 worth of porcelain etc.'

By the end of November Rumbold was able to carry on conversations entirely in Japanese. He practised on every possible occasion. On November 16, meeting the distinguished General Nogi[2] at dinner, he noted in his diary, 'As Nogi talks nothing but Japanese I practised on him.' On December 3 he wrote to his father: 'I am working hard at Japanese and hope soon to be able to go up for the exam. It is an awful grind and I am bored to death with it now.' On New Year's Day, 1910, Rumbold passed his exam, and was granted an allowance of £100 a year.

Towards the end of 1909 two events had angered Rumbold considerably. The first was an American proposal to internationalize all railways being built in Manchuria. This was a direct threat to the rapidly expanding Japanese interests, among which railways were paramount. 'I hope we shall stick to the Japanese', Rumbold wrote in his diary on Christmas Day, 'and not encourage the Yankees in any way.' Two days later he commented that the Americans were 'upsetting the apple cart' in Manchuria, and that the Japanese 'are by no means pleased with the appearance of the Yankee on the scene'. Unsupported even by Russia, who while worried about Japan's influence in Manchuria had no desire to see it replaced by America's, the American proposal foundered, much to Rumbold's relief. Japan's desire to expand in Manchuria, he believed, was a legitimate one, and in no way conflicted with British interests. 'It is so easy for Americans to

[1] Ethel Armstrong. She married Sir Claude MacDonald (her second husband) in 1892. A Member of the Executive Committee of the Overseas Nursing Association, she was created a Dame of the British Empire in 1935. She died in 1941.

[2] Maresuke Nogi, 1849–1912. Commissioned as a Major when the army system was established in Japan, 1871. Served, as a Lieutenant General, in the Sino-Japanese War, 1894–95. Governor-General of Formosa, 1896. General, commanding the Japanese Third Army at the siege of Port Arthur, 1905; his two sons were both killed during the campaign. Created Count, and appointed President of the Peers' School, 1907. Member of the Imperial Military Council from 1907 until his death.

make proposals of this nature', he wrote on January 7, 'when they themselves have not spent a brass farthing or sacrificed a single life for the purpose of acquiring the 3 railways in question.'

Rumbold's second vexation was the political situation at home. 'The Liberals are very sick with the Lords,' he had written in his diary on December 2, 'with Lloyd George and his pal Winston showering abuse on them. What a pity the latter wasn't shot in S. Africa. The Conservatives will have to work very hard if they want to kick the present lot out.' Rumbold favoured reform of the Lords, to strengthen it. 'It is absurd nowadays', he wrote, 'that farceurs like Rosslyn[1] and similar creatures should have a voice in the affairs of the nation. All reform of the House of Lords should be directed to weeding out the black sheep and lame ducks and making it far more efficient. With increased efficiency would come increased strength which the Radicals wouldn't like. They hate a "drag" and the House of Lords will always tend to be a "drag" in the long run on hasty or ill considered legislation.' On December 31 Rumbold received a letter from Lord Cromer, written a month earlier, with further comments on the crisis. 'I do not believe', Cromer had written, 'there is nearly so strong a feeling against the Lords in the country as the Radicals make out.' Rumbold had already come to a forecast of his own, having written in his diary on December 1: 'I foresee that the Liberals will come in again because their present majority is so huge as to make it almost impossible for the other side to wipe it out. But the Liberal majority will be so reduced as to make it impossible for the present lot to do much harm. Should the Conservatives get in by a fluke – *their* majority will be so slight as to prevent them from carrying a tariff reform bill. Therefore, in either case, it looks as if we were in for a period of stale-mate as regards internal politics. This is always bad for foreign politics, but let's hope that the fleet will be kept up, whichever side wins.' The election was held between 14 January and 9 February 1910; the Liberals won 275 seats, the Conservatives 273, and the Liberal power to rule depended upon the 82 Irish Nationalist and 40 Labour MPs.[2] Nearly a year later, on 10 November 1910, Rumbold reflected on the election in a letter to his father. 'I expect', he wrote, 'that Lloyd George's vulgarity and violence disgusted a lot of moderate men, and caused a large turn over of votes.'

[1] James Francis Harry St Clair-Erskine, 1869–1939. Son of the 4th Earl of Rosslyn, whom he succeeded, as 5th Earl, in 1890. War Correspondent of the *Daily Mail* in South Africa, 1900; served as a Lieutenant, at the relief of Ladysmith. Secretary, unpaid, to the Secretary for Scotland, 1904. Major, King's Royal Rifle Corps, 1915–17.

[2] It had been the largest electorate to date in British history, over 6,667,404 people having cast their vote. Although a million more people voted than in 1906, the Liberal vote fell by over 100,000.

On 6 May 1910, Edward VII died in London. 'Newspaper corre-spondents are swarming round', Rumbold noted in his diary on May 7. 'One of them asked me for details of the King's home life. I pointed out that this was rather a large order and that I really couldn't oblige him. Went in to see the Ambassador later in the afternoon and found him with his legs up on his table, reading Punch.... We can do nothing until we get instructions from home.' On May 8 all the European papers printed in Japan, and one Japanese paper, were published with black borders. 'The trams', Rumbold noted in his diary, 'are flying British and Japanese flags draped in crêpe.' May 20, the day of the King's funeral, was observed throughout Japan as a day of mourning. The banks were shut, and flags flew at half-mast. For the memorial service in Tokyo, the Americans lent their Cathedral to the British. On the following day Rumbold was present at a Buddhist memorial service. 'Never before', he wrote in his diary, 'has a service of this kind been held in honour of a foreign sove-reign.' The Chaplain to the British Embassy[1] at once protested at a service designed, as he alleged, 'merely in order to extol Buddhism'. 'These missionaries,' Rumbold noted, ' – or most of them – are very narrow-minded.'

The Japanese Government hoped during 1910 to negotiate a commercial Treaty with Britain. The negotiations were much hindered by a series of new Japanese tariffs, announced early in the year, which were a blow to British traders. They were also, as Rumbold had pointed out both to the Japanese Foreign Minister, Komura,[2] and to Sir Edward Grey, less severe on German than on British trade. 'Japan will have to be careful what she does', he had written in his diary on March 10; 'She seems to me to make the mistake of thinking that she can treat political questions quite distinct from commercial ones.' Not only the new tariff, but such fraudulent imitation by Japanese firms of British trade marks, worsened commercial relations. Yet the Japanese intended to drive a hard bargain, believing that the British would go to extreme efforts not to lose the naval advantage

---

[1] Lionel Berners Cholmondeley, 1858–1944. Grandson of the 1st Baron Delamere. Ordained deacon, 1884 and priest, 1885. Chaplain to the Bishop of Japan, 1887–1922. Honorary Chaplain to the British Embassy, Tokyo, 1902–22. Vicar of Edge, in Gloucester-shire, 1922–31.

[2] Jutaro Komura, 1855–1911. Sent as a student to the United States by the Japanese Government, 1877. Returned to Japan to serve first in the Department of Justice and then in the Foreign Ministry. Successively Minister to Washington, St Petersburg and Peking. Foreign Minister, 1901–6. Created Baron, 1902. Conducted the peace negotiations at Portsmouth, USA, at the end of the Russo-Japanese War, 1905. Ambassador to London, 1906–8. Created Count, 1907. He was made an honorary Knight Grand Cross of both the Order of St Michael and St George (1905) and the Royal Victorian Order (1907). Foreign Minister for the second time, 1908–11. Created Marquis, 1911.

which the Anglo-Japanese alliance provided. Rumbold was angered by
the Japanese attitude. 'These little people here', he wrote in his diary on
March 29, 'evidently don't realize that they are not playing the game. It is
very shortsighted of them.'

During June Rumbold spoke bluntly to Komura about the danger of a
deterioration in Anglo-Japanese relations if the Japanese tariff were persisted in. In London, Grey told the Japanese Ambassador, Kato,[1] that, as
Rumbold recorded in his diary on July 2, 'the new Japanese tariff would
ruin a great part of British trade with Japan. In these circumstances we
would not conclude a Treaty. . . .' Rumbold commented, 'The Japanese
will be very sick', and added: 'I think people in England will be disappointed that the alliance has not had any effect in modifying the tariff
where we are concerned, but sentiment plays no part with these people,
after a certain point is passed. They are the Jews of the Far East and will
have their pound of flesh.'

Rumbold speculated continually about the Japanese character. He was
puzzled to find that, despite his previous confidence in delineating national
characteristics, those of the Japanese eluded him. As rumours grew of a
possible Japanese annexation of Korea, he commented in his diary, on
July 5: 'These people are going ahead very fast, some think too fast. We
can't understand why they can't be satisfied with the present state of
things in Corea where they have everything they can want.' Later that
month, on July 21, he noted in his diary the increasing popular talk of a
possible war between Japan and the United States: 'It would be interesting
to really get at the thoughts of the Japanese Government. Who knows
whether they have not got limitless ambitions.' His own analysis of the
war talk was pessimistic, in the long term. It reminded him, he wrote in
his diary, 'of the similar talk between us and Germany. In both cases,
people and papers assert that of course there is no possible reason for war
between the respective countries and that those countries are on perfectly
friendly terms. But the idea is there, and the more the papers go on declaring that it is absurd for the USA to think of fighting Japan – or vice
versa – the more people will think that there is something in it. No smoke
without fire.' The one factor for peace, he believed, was 'that Japan is so
hard up that she *can't* go to war and nobody would lend her any money
for the purpose'. 'There is some loose talk of war between the two countries', Rumbold had written in his diary on April 18, 'but the commercial

---

[1] Takaaki Kato, 1860–1926. After a brilliant career at University and in business, appointed
Director of the Taxation Bureau, Tokyo, 1891. Minister to London, 1894–99. Minister of
Foreign Affairs, 1900–1 and 1906. Ambassador to London, 1908–13. Created Baron, 1911.
Foreign Minister, 1913 and 1914–15. Created Viscount, 1916. Prime Minister, 1924–26.

interests at stake are too great and neither side dreams of war. I am told that the Japanese would walk round the Americans at the present moment and would have little difficulty in taking the Philippines.'

On 22 August 1910 Japan annexed Korea. 'Thus', wrote Rumbold in his diary on August 29, 'an independent country of about 13 million inhabitants disappears as a separate entity. Perhaps the most remarkable thing about it all is the ease and entire absence of fuss with which the annexation has been carried through. The Japanese are past masters in the art of choosing the right moment for their political coups.' He recalled the Japanese promises in 1905, after the Russo-Japanese War, to respect Korean independence. 'Japan', he wrote, 'now becomes a Continental Power and I wonder how that role will suit her. . . . The Japanese are like the Germans in the way they practise "real-politik".' Rumbold could see no immediate barrier to further Japanese expansion north of Korea, into Manchuria. But he added perceptively: 'What will happen, however, when China wakes up in earnest and can put an enormous and efficient army into the field? The day is not yet, but may be nearer than some people think.' The annexation of Korea prompted Rumbold to reflect on the morality of international affairs:

The end of an old kingdom, by absorption at the hands of a stronger Empire, is rather sad. At one end of the world an independent kingdom of some 13 million souls is quietly absorbed by another Empire, and at the other end of the world an opera comique Princelet – i.c. the Prince of Montenegro[1] blossoms into a King with much éclat. Only a few weeks ago Russia practically put an end to the autonomy of Finland and except for a few futile protests from our sentimental Radicals, nobody minded. It looks as if the most important events could be put through nowadays with as much ease as eating one's breakfast. In reality, however, only a really strong Power which knows its own mind can do these things. Moral, have your army and navy ready and know what you want.

In October the Americans asked the British to protest about the annexation of Korea, and to demand proper treatment there for all foreign nationals. 'But', Rumbold wrote in his diary on October 5, 'we are not going to pull the chestnuts out of the fire for the Yankees. That is a game they have constantly tried on in the Far East.' One result of the annexation of Korea was that the Japanese tariff was extended to cover the new territory. *The Times*, which, Rumbold noted in his diary on

---

[1] Nicholas (Nikita), 1841–1921. Succeeded as Prince of Montenegro after the assassination of his uncle, 1860. Declared war on the Turks, 1876; victorious, 1878. In 1896 his daughter Helena married the Crown Prince of Italy (later Victor Emmanuel III). Proclaimed himself King of Montenegro, 1910. Surrendered to the Austro-Hungarian army, January 1916, and fled to Italy. Deposed by the National Assembly of Montenegro, November 1918. In exile in Paris from 1918 until his death.

September 2, had always been 'the champion of the Anglo-Japanese alliance', commented tartly that 'we should have welcomed a little more regard to the views of an allied power which our constant regard for the Japanese view might have led us to expect'. Anti-Japanese feeling was also strong in the Royal Navy. Towards the end of September Rear-Admiral Winsloe[1] and his staff paid an official visit to Tokyo. 'Am told there is a decided anti-Japanese bias amongst the fleet', Rumbold wrote in his diary on September 23, 'and it is difficult to find the cause. One of the officers described it as "anti-men" feeling i.e. they do not like the idea of being allies of men who look so much like monkeys.'

Early in October, Rumbold sent the Foreign Office in London a detailed memorandum on Japanese socialism. 'The Authorities are harrying the Socialists indiscriminately', he wrote in his diary on October 1, '. . . and are adopting most repressive measures. They want to root them out, but it is doubtful whether they will succeed by these means.' He was still uncertain about the extent of Japanese overseas aspirations, and listened carefully to the opinions of others. In November he had two talks with Dudley Braham,[2] a special correspondent of *The Times* who had just spent four months in the Far East. 'Could see he has an anti-Japanese bias as a result of his travels in Manchuria and in China', Rumbold wrote in his diary on November 17; 'He says the J's are not behaving well in Manchuria and that it is at least on the cards that they will grab it some day.[3] He says that they are engaged in creating vested interests in the Yangstse region so as to have an excuse for coming in if there is a serious row with China.' On the following day Rumbold learned that the Japanese Admiralty had just placed an order with Vickers for a 27,000-ton battleship, to be delivered in thirty months.[4] 'This is a notable move on the part of our friends', Rumbold noted; 'They will get a first-class ship quicker than they could build her themselves, and at the same time they will have done something – a good deal – for British trade at a moment when they are

[1] Alfred Leigh Winsloe, 1852–1931. Entered Navy, 1865. Served in the Egyptian campaign of 1882. Captain and 4th Sea Lord, 1906–10. Knighted, 1909. Rear-Admiral Commanding the China Station, 1910–13. Retired, 1913.

[2] Dudley Disraeli Braham, 1875–1951. *The Times* correspondent in St Petersburg, 1901–3, and Constantinople, 1903–8; assistant to Chirol in the Imperial and Foreign department, 1908–10; Far East correspondent, 1910–12; Editor, *Sydney Daily Telegraph*, 1914–22; leader writer on *The Times*, 1929–45.

[3] The Japanese invaded Manchuria in 1931, and in 1934 set up the puppet state of Manchukuo. After the defeat of Japan in 1945 Manchuria was occupied by Russia; in 1949 it became part of the Chinese People's Republic.

[4] The battleship was the *Kongo*, ordered in November 1910. It was launched at Barrow in May 1912, and handed over to the Japanese in August 1913. It was of 27,500 tons, with eight 14-inch and sixteen 6-inch guns, as well as eight torpedo tubes. The three other ships of its class were built in Japan.

being freely accused of trying to kill that trade by means of their new tariff.' Rumbold could not decide what Japan intended. When, on November 20, MacDonald told him that he approved of the Japanese annexation of Korea, Rumbold wrote in his diary: 'his pro-Japanese bias comes in here, or, it would be more correct to say, that he seeks for the good of the Japanese where others seek the bad.'

During November Rumbold had begun to note the British Foreign Office's dislike of MacDonald's attitude. 'Our Government do not trust their man here to be sufficiently energetic in his language', he wrote in his diary on December 1, 'and think he looks at things too much from the Japanese point of view.' Rumbold was apprehensive about the future. 'If I had the renewal of the alliance', he wrote to Lord Cromer on December 17, 'I would not renew for more than 5 years, which would bring us to 1920. Events move too quickly nowadays for long term alliances.'

In his letter to Cromer, Rumbold turned to a British problem. 'I have often wondered', he wrote, 'why the police didn't use the hose on the suffragettes. They, the police, know that these scandalous women always demonstrate in the neighbourhood of Westminster and Downing Street. . . . I can't imagine anything which would take all the kick out of the suffragettes and their pals better than a stream of cold water. One doesn't want to physically hurt a lot of wretched women, but the hose would make them ridiculous without injuring them. After all, they have now become female hooligans, and deserve all they get.' Commenting on the Liberal victory in the second of the two elections of 1910 he wrote in his letter to Cromer: '. . . if the British elector likes to have his show run for him by a vulgar & violent creature like Lloyd George – helped by Redmond – I wish him joy, while pitying poor old England.'[1]

At the end of 1910, and during the early months of 1911, Rumbold thought seriously of transferring to a European Embassy. On December 21 he wrote in his diary that he had told Sir Claude MacDonald of his desire to try for a post in Europe. 'I said that one was always exposed to the danger of going to S America on promotion and that I did not want 2 distant posts running.' But on learning from his father that Sir Arthur Nicolson,[2] Hardinge's successor as Permanent Under-Secretary of State at the Foreign Office, was said to be promoting his favourites to the best

[1] At the General Election of December 1910 the Liberals and Conservatives both won 272 seats. The Liberals were therefore dependent for a majority upon the 82 Irish Nationalist MPs, led by Redmond. In return for Irish support, the Liberals brought in a Home Rule Bill for Ireland; but it never came into force on account of the outbreak of war.

[2] Arthur Nicolson, 1849–1928. Entered Foreign Office, 1870. Knighted, 1888. Succeeded his father as 11th Baronet, 1899. Ambassador at St Petersburg, 1905–10. Permanent Under-Secretary for Foreign Affairs, 1910–16. Created Baron Carnock, 1916.

diplomatic posts, he replied, on 14 January 1911, cursing favouritism, and adding: 'I fear the little man is also a snob which his predecessor was not. . . . 5 years in S America would do Nicolson, Lister,[1] O'Beirne,[2] Theo Russell et hoc genus omne a power of good and I only regret I can't send them there.' In February 1911 Rumbold decided to write direct to Tyrrell to ask if he could be appointed to the first Counsellorship that fell vacant in western Europe. On February 18 he wrote to his father: 'Tyrrell will have difficulty in refusing my request, which is natural and reasonable'. But Tyrrell did refuse, and Rumbold remained in Tokyo for a further two years.

On March 7 Ethel Rumbold gave birth to a son, whom they named Horace Anthony Claude.[3] 'He is a good specimen', Rumbold wrote to his father on the following day, 'and weighs just on 8 lbs. He has grey eyes, a determined chin and a smaller mouth than Baba's [his daughter] . . . we are both overjoyed, as we were most anxious for a boy.' That night Rumbold was a guest at an official dinner given by Katsura, the Prime Minister. 'The whole company,' he wrote to his father, 'foreign and Japanese, drank my health. . . . The Japanese Cabinet Ministers (among them the Prime and Foreign Ministers) and Vice Ministers . . . fairly mobbed me in their attempts to shake my hand. . . . These people attach special importance to the birth of a boy and they felt that such an event happening to me – whilst living in their country – reflected honour on themselves.' Rumbold was touched by the Japanese reaction. 'If I were more senior,' he continued, 'I believe they would be glad to have me as Ambassador – eventually – and I know my chief would strongly recommend it, for he has told me so. But all this is a dream and I doubt whether we shall ever come back here again.' He was convinced, he wrote to his father on May 14, that Tokyo had become 'one of the centres of the world, because Japan "is on the make" – just as Germany is'. But he did not want to stay on. 'It is not a good thing', he wrote to his father, 'to spend too long in the east. One loses one's sense of proportion.'

At the beginning of 1911 Rumbold asked the Ambassador if he could seek permission to attend the otherwise secret session of the Japanese court which was to try twenty-six anarchists on charges of attempting to

[1] Edgar Graham Lister, 1873–1956. Entered Foreign Office, 1899. Acting 3rd Secretary, Constantinople and Sofia, 1903–5 and Paris, 1905–6. Assistant Clerk, Foreign Office, 1907–13. Resigned from the Foreign Office, 1913; temporarily re-employed, 1915–19.

[2] Hugh James O'Beirne, 1867–1916. Entered the Diplomatic Service, 1892, as an Attaché at St Petersburg. 1st Secretary, Washington, 1905; Paris, 1905–6. Councillor of Embassy, St Petersburg, 1906–16. Drowned while accompanying Lord Kitchener to Russia.

[3] Horace Anthony Claude Rumbold, 1911– . Known as 'Tony'. He entered the Foreign Office, 1935, serving in various posts for thirty-five years. Ambassador in Bangkok, 1965–67; in Vienna, 1967–70. With his retirement in 1970, the three generations of Rumbolds completed an unbroken span of 121 years in the diplomatic service.

assassinate the Emperor.[1] MacDonald agreed, and the Japanese Government allowed Rumbold to be present in court throughout the trial. He was impressed by the apparent fairness of the proceedings, and took careful notes. On January 20 twelve of the anarchists were sentenced to be hanged. 'I am convinced', he wrote in his diary, 'that the sentence will not strike terror into the hearts of any other anarchists there may be about. When people lose their reverence for a man who has been looked up to as a semi-divine person, feelings of respect are apt to go down with a run.' A week later he recorded: 'The 12 Anarchists were hanged in the Tokyo prison yesterday – rather a holocaust.' Rumbold was told that in Japan it took fourteen minutes on average to hang a man. 'When Crippen[2] was executed,' he noted in his diary, 'only 60 seconds elapsed between the time the executioner entered his cell and the moment life was extinct. We do these things better in England.' So shocked was Rumbold at the method of execution that he asked Sir Claude MacDonald 'to use his influence to see that people are put out of the way more expeditiously and humanely', as he wrote in his diary on January 26. But he believed that the trial itself had been a fair one, and sent a full report to this effect to the Foreign Office.

When news of the sentences reached England there was an outcry among Labour MPs. Keir Hardie[3] asked the Government to protest against the trial being held in secret. In his reply, the Parliamentary Under-Secretary of State for Foreign Affairs, McKinnon Wood,[4] quoted from Rumbold's report, and stated that it was Rumbold's opinion that the trial had been conducted with dignity and fairness, and that the anarchists had been properly and indeed ably defended. 'He apparently referred to me by name', Rumbold noted in his diary on February 16; '– in fact the Government sheltered themselves behind me. . . .' But he was glad, as he wrote 'that my previsions were fully justified and that the action of this Embassy has been useful to our Government and enabled them to dispose of the Socialists and sentimental Radicals who always sympathise with the victim or the intended victim.'

[1] Mitsuhito (Meiji), 1852–1912. Emperor of Japan for forty-five years, from 1867 until his death on July 30, 1912.

[2] Crippen had been born in Michigan, USA, in 1861. He settled in London as a dentist, and as agent for 'Munyon's Remedies'. On January 31, 1910, he poisoned his wife, cut her up, burned her bones, and buried her flesh in the cellar. Then a young typist, Ethel Le Neve, came to live with him. After police became suspicious, he sailed on the *Laurentic* to Canada, but was arrested on landing. His trial opened in London on October 8, 1910; he was executed on November 23, 1910.

[3] James Keir Hardie, 1856–1915. Worked in the mines from the age of seven to the age of twenty-four. Labour MP, 1892–95 and 1900–15. Chairman, Independent Labour Party.

[4] Thomas McKinnon Wood, 1855–1927. Liberal MP, 1906–18. Parliamentary Under-Secretary of State at the Foreign Office, 1908–11; at the Treasury, 1911–12. Secretary for Scotland, 1912–16. Chancellor of the Duchy of Lancaster, 1916.

During the early months of 1911, on Japanese insistence, negotiations began in London between Grey and Kato to revise and strengthen the Anglo-Japanese alliance. Rumbold feared too great a British commitment to Japan. He had become convinced that Japan's ambition would extend not only to China, but even, if circumstances ever permitted it, to the Dutch East Indies. 'We ought so to conduct our policy', he wrote to his father on March 31, 'as not to get mixed up in any row these people may have with China.' But he had heard that the new King, George V,[1] was 'strong on the alliance', and he believed that Grey would support it. He was right. Grey shared the belief of Reginald McKenna, the First Lord of the Admiralty, that Britain needed Japan as a naval ally in the Far East. Rumbold did not accept this view, believing that the alliance had no more advantage for Britain. 'The J's are getting far more out of it than we are', he wrote to his father in his letter of March 31. Three months earlier he had drafted the foreign relations section of the Embassy's Annual Report, in which he had pointed out that 'the action of Japan in annexing Corea six and a half years after she had given a solemn assurance that she would "definitely guarantee the independence and integrity" of that country, will no doubt be borne in mind by Russia and other countries in considering Japanese assurances with regard to Manchuria and other subjects'. And in his diary on March 18 he had written: 'Japan has far more to gain from the alliance than we have. We don't want protection against Russia. The very argument used in our country in favour of the alliance i.e. that we are able to withdraw our ships from the Far East to Home Waters, is, to my mind, an argument against the Alliance for we ought not to neglect our interests in the Far East, which are enormous. We ought to keep a strong fleet out here – alliance or no alliance.'

Towards the end of March, Grey agreed to renew the alliance in a strengthened form. When the news reached Tokyo Rumbold was dismayed. 'Of course, these people are delighted', he noted in his diary on March 25; 'Grey seems to me to have acted hastily. The present Alliance treaty should have been allowed to run out. . . . The uncertainty as to the renewal of the Treaty of Alliance would have hung over the Japanese Government and put them on their best behaviour.'

The Tokyo Embassy made one attempt to change Grey's mind. On April 8 the Ambassador, Rumbold, and Hampden,[2] a senior Embassy

---

[1] George Frederick Ernest Albert, 1865–1936. Succeeded his father as King, 1910. On his accession Rumbold wrote in his diary, on May 31, 1910: 'Americans and Jews will not be in particular favour at the new court. They say the new King is a Tory.'

[2] Ernest Miles Hobart-Hampden, 1864–1949. Entered the Consular Service, China, 1888. Transferred to Japan, 1889. Vice-Consul, Yokohama, 1904. Japanese Secretary, British Embassy, Tokyo, 1909. First Secretary, Tokyo, 1916. Retired, 1919.

official, drafted a strong protest, urging that the alliance should not be renewed until the whole question could be re-examined. Rumbold noted in his diary: 'Sir C, Hampden and I have been making de la plus haute politique this morning as a result of which a long telegram has gone home which will somewhat startle the FO. Sir C has sounded a very necessary note of warning but it may be too late as our people seem to have committed themselves very far. Am thoroughly enjoying helping to pull the strings in a matter of the highest importance. We have the Alliance dinner[1] to-night at Komura's and our hosts would have been greatly surprised had they known of the morning's conference and its issue. . . .' But the Embassy's collective protest was in vain. Grey and Nicolson both minuted on the telegram their feeling that the Tokyo Embassy was judging the alliance too exclusively from the Far Eastern standpoint, and ignoring its European implications. On April 9 Grey telegraphed his reply. If renewal of the alliance were delayed for four years, he argued, 'Alliance would then have become unpopular, apprehension that it might not be renewed would have grown rapidly, and must have affected seriously both Japanese naval shipbuilding and our own in next few years.' These considerations, Grey declared, 'outweigh those urged by you on other side'. The Embassy protests were thus of no avail; Grey was not to be persuaded. On May 26 he explained his policy to a special meeting of the Committee of Imperial Defence in London, at which representatives of Canada and Australia were present. 'It is the Naval question', he told them, 'which underlies the whole of our European Foreign Policy, and more than the European Foreign Policy.'

Since MacDonald's departure on leave on April 1, Rumbold was Chargé d'Affaires for the second time. Grey therefore sent him a summary of the arguments he had used at the Committee of Imperial Defence, and informed him that the Dominion representatives 'had agreed so cordially to the extension of the alliance', that it should be proceeded with at once. Henceforth Rumbold had to act as Grey's emissary in Tokyo, and, on Grey's instructions, resolved each of the disputed points as they arose.

Negotiations continued throughout June and into July. The Japanese wanted a mutual pledge regarding Japan's Korean frontier and Britain's Indian frontier. Rumbold combated this clause, believing, as he wrote in his diary on July 5, that it would be 'infra dig. on our part to even appear to rely on an Asiatic Power for help in India'. The effect on Britain's Indian subjects, he felt, of a Japanese pledge to help defend Britain's imperial

---

[1] The Alliance dinner was an annual event in Tokyo, at which, to commemorate the signing of the Alliance in 1902, the Japanese Foreign Minister entertained the British Ambassador and several members of his staff.

frontiers, 'must be bad', for they would see reliance placed 'if only in an Agreement – on an Asiatic people. It is calculated to undermine their confidence in our Power'. Rumbold raised the matter with the Foreign Minister, Komura, who agreed, on July 6, not to include the clause in the revised draft. On July 13 the revised agreement was signed in London. Rumbold and his wife were having a brief holiday outside Tokyo when Grey's telegram announcing the signature arrived. 'Ethel and I', he wrote in his diary on July 14, 'decyphered this momentous telegram in our verandah after lunch. This is a grand thing for Japan for she knows where she is for the next ten years.' But the Japanese did not respond with much enthusiasm. Rumbold explained why in a letter to Grey on July 17. 'The thermometer stood at over 85° at 10 pm that evening', he wrote, 'and Japan has, moreover, had quite a surfeit of treaties of late. Indeed, the new treaties with Germany and Norway were issued as extras, and six arrangements, namely, the *modus vivendi* with Canada, Belgium, Denmark, Italy, Holland, and Switzerland, were published the same day as the extended alliance.' On July 17 yet another 'arrangement', the Anglo-Japanese Treaty of Commerce, was signed, allowing the Japanese to impose largely increased tariffs on British goods. 'People would say', Rumbold wrote in his diary on July 17, 'that we have given everything away without getting anything in return'. On July 30 Rumbold set down his conclusions in a despatch to London. He believed that the Japanese would not allow any alliance to tie down their hands, if they felt the need to seek new areas of expansion, or new allies. 'I think various circumstances will combine', he wrote in his diary that day, 'to throw Russia and Japan more closely together as time goes on.'

Rumbold's hopes of leaving Japan had received a setback on June 2 when he received a letter from Tyrrell – sent from London via the Trans-Siberian railway on April 3 – declaring that the Foreign Office were 'as yet unable to hold out any hope' of a transfer from Tokyo. On learning of various diplomatic promotions later in the month, Rumbold wrote despondently to his father on June 25: 'The present policy seems to be to fill the European Embassies with Counsellors far junior to any of us in the East. As far as I can see, there is nothing to prevent my being kept in exile until I am promoted to a Legation in S America – a fresh exile.' On July 1 he confided in his diary that he and his wife were 'thoroughly sick' of Tokyo. 'A period of nearly 10 months in the "compound"', he wrote, 'is enough for anybody's happiness and one feels very stale at the end of it.'

At the end of July Sir Claude MacDonald returned to Tokyo. 'I have now cleared up all my arrears of work,' Rumbold wrote to his father on

July 30, 'written my last drafts, and shall hand him an absolutely clean slate.' On August 1 he noted in his diary: 'Can now kick my heels a bit'. A month later he left Tokyo for a private journey to Korea and Manchuria. The Koreans, he noted in his diary in mid-September, 'are a much finer race than the Japanese, but all the "go" seems to have been knocked out of them. . . . Never have I seen so many able-bodied loafers about any-where as in the streets of Seoul. The men seemed so apathetic and so evidently disinclined to work. This is the result of centuries of a system of extortion and oppression which has taken away all incentive to work.' On September 19 he reached Mukden, and on September 23, after three days' sightseeing, took the train to Port Arthur, where he examined the principal sites of the siege during the Russo-Japanese War. On October 1 he was back in Tokyo, and planning his six months' leave, which was to begin at the end of the year. 'It is useless hanging on here', he wrote to his father on October 24, in answer to his father's report that, according to Sir Arthur Nicolson, there was 'no prospect of any moves in the near future'. He did not expect to return to Japan again, hoping that, once back in England, he would be transferred to a European capital. 'Now that the time is drawing near for us to leave this place,' he wrote to his father on November 2, 'I must confess I feel the very greatest regret. We shall never be better off than we have been here, and may be a great deal worse off in the future.' His letter continued:

I have got attached to our house and to the life. This seems odd to many of the foreigners who miss the life of an European capital with its theatres etc. Of course, one misses these things also at times, but there are many compensations, especially to those who, like ourselves, are somewhat domesticated and don't like being out night after night. I know quite well that I shall often wish myself back here – from the material point of view alone – for it is not everywhere one can get a cook – as good and as light handed as a French cook – for £26 a year. The bare thought of an English 'good plain cook' is enough to give one dyspepsia in advance. Cooking isn't in the nation, though let's hope we have other compensating advantages.

On November 8 Rumbold noted in his diary a bizarre incident which contrasted Europe with Japan. The Emperor had been going to manoeuvres by train, and there was a twenty minute delay at one of the stations *en route*. 'The stationmaster concerned', Rumbold wrote, 'promptly committed suicide, leaving a note of humble apology for having been (probably the innocent) cause of the delay. When one thinks of the Imperial person which, if it is not, at all events *looks* rather "gaga", one can't help wondering at the relic of an age, quite recent, when Emperors were looked on as divine.' On December 9 Rumbold sailed from Japan, not expecting to see it again. His wife and their two children sailed with him. On December 13 they reached Shanghai, and six days later Hong Kong, from where he went for a day to Canton. There were numerous signs of the recent revolution.[1] 'Every now and then', Rumbold wrote in his diary on December 20, 'we met bands of revolutionary soldiers, generally headed by a General dressed like a rat-catcher – all young men in soidisant European clothes.' While Rumbold was in Canton a fight broke out between revolutionaries and monarchists less than a mile from where he was sightseeing, and about fifty monarchists were killed. That night Rumbold returned to Hong Kong, and to his ship, which reached Singapore on Christmas Day. On December 29 the ship was at Penang. On board ship on December 31 – between Penang and Colombo – he noted in his diary: 'So closes a year which has been a very pleasant one throughout and has brought us what we wanted, namely a boy.'

Rumbold and his family reached Marseilles on 6 February 1912. For more than eight months, until September 1912, he remained on leave, first at Biarritz, then in England, then back at Biarritz again. Frequent letters from Sir Claude MacDonald kept him in touch with Japanese affairs. 'I miss you awfully', the Ambassador wrote on February 9, 'and the Ambassadorial machine creaks a bit at times.' MacDonald hoped Rumbold would return to Japan before the end of the year. Rumbold hoped otherwise; but early in May he learned that he was, in fact, to continue as Counsellor in Tokyo until at least the end of 1912. Towards the end of his leave he also learned, from Tyrrell, that there was no particular position in line for him after Tokyo, and that he would have to stay there at least until the spring of 1913. On August 15 he wrote despondently to his father: 'I have noticed that Japan is a difficult place to get away from. . . . Sometimes I think that nobody will ever go, but that all chiefs will indefinitely remain at their posts in a mummified position.'

In September 1912 Rumbold and his wife returned to Japan, taking a train from Ostend to Moscow, and crossing Russia by the Trans-Siberian railway. 'It was interesting going round the southern shore of Lake Baikal,' he wrote to his father on September 26; 'Gangs of convicts superintended by armed soldiers, were busy double-tracking the line.' From Vladivostok they went by ship to Japan. The journey began well, but suddenly the ship was caught in a typhoon, which Rumbold described in his letter:

At 9 p.m. the typhoon struck us and then the trouble began. Never do I wish to see another. There was no question of sleep, for it was all we could do to

[1] An anti-monarchical rebellion had broken out in China in September 1911. The Manchu Emperor abdicated in February 1912, and China became a Republic.

remain in our bunks. The wind was terrific – in fact it was one continuous roar. I have read about waves being mountains high but had not seen them until that night. Every now and again the foghorn went. Of course every man Jack of the crew and all the officers were on duty through the night. Our luggage was thrown about the cabin anywhere and anyhow – it was hopeless to keep anything in place. There were constant crashes of breaking crockery and glass. At 4 a.m. Ethel came into my cabin quite terrified and convinced that we were sending up distress rockets but it was only the chain of the sea anchor which the captain had thrown out to steady the ship – and which was banging against the side. My fear – which I didn't impart to Ethel – was that, as we were near the dangerous Japanese coast, we should be driven on to the rocks and then, of course, we should all have been done for. Ethel behaved very well, as did all the other passengers, some of whom never undressed. She and I squeezed into one berth – with our heads opposite one another – and so managed to remain in the bunk. Nobody thought of being sea-sick. At about 5 a.m. the ship gave a tremendous lurch down our side which seemed to be buried beneath the water. Simultaneously there was a hissing roar from the engine room which lasted several minutes and we all thought that the seas had broken right over the ship and swamped the engines. I must say I thought we were then in a parlous condition. Poor Ethel thought the end was at hand but luckily an officer came along and reassured us. I reconnoitred in the passage and round by the saloon twice in the early morning and found a group of pale stewards holding on to anything they could lay hands on. They couldn't tell me anything. At 7 a.m. we were in the centre of the typhoon – as the Captain afterwards told us. I was about at that time and shall never forget the din and row made by the wind. It really was awful. We got out of the typhoon at 10 a.m. having been in it for 13 hours.[1]

'That Mrs Rumbold behaved like a brick', wrote the Ambassador to Rumbold on September 26, '. . . goes without saying. . . . A mercy you had not the bairns with you.' The two children had been left in London with their grandmother.

On November 1 Sir Claude MacDonald left Tokyo. It was the end of his diplomatic career and he retired formally a month later. Rumbold was once more in charge of the Embassy, while waiting for the arrival of the new Ambassador, Sir William Conynghame Greene.[2] He had known Greene when they were serving together at Teheran over fifteen years before. Throughout November and most of December Rumbold worked at the Annual Report on Japan. Having been away for most of the year, he

[1] The typhoon was the worst in Japan for fifteen years. More than 500 Japanese were killed and many thousands made homeless.

[2] William Conynghame Greene, 1854–1934. Entered Foreign Office, 1877. Secretary of Legation, Teheran, 1893–96. HM Agent at Pretoria, 1896–99. Knighted, 1900. Minister to Switzerland, 1901–5; to Rumania, 1905–11; to Copenhagen, 1911–12. Ambassador to Japan, 1912–19.

had a great deal of work to do, and had to write more than half of the
sixty-page report himself.

Rumbold had only returned to Japan reluctantly. 'We hope to get away
at the beginning of April', he wrote to his father on December 8; '3 weeks
ought to be sufficient to show Greene the ropes. When I first got out here
I only had a week between my arrival & my chief's departure on leave in
which to get the hang of things.' Sir Horace sent his son regular news of
Europe. 'I gather', he wrote on 24 January 1913, 'that the feeling at
Vienna against the Servians remains very hostile; that Francis Ferdinand[1]
is extremely bellicose, but that the old Emperor continues to hold his own
for peace.'

On February 11 the Katsura Cabinet resigned. Rumbold recorded its
final day of office in his diary of February 10: 'While I was playing tennis
in the afternoon I could hear the shouts of the mob coming from the
direction of Hibiya Park and imagined that some sort of a demonstration
was going on. Towards evening the crowd got ugly and attacked the
offices of the newspapers friendly to Katsura. The staff of the "Kokumin"
defended themselves and a boy was killed by a revolver shot. Troops were
sent for and restored order, but in the course of the night many police
boxes were burnt or otherwise destroyed. About 20 people were injured.
The excitement was largely worked up by the press.' For over a week no
Government could be formed, and Katsura was said to be trying to win
the new Emperor's[2] support in an attempt to return to power. 'There have
been disturbances at Osaka, Kobe, Kyoto and Hiroshima,' Rumbold wrote
in his diary on February 14, 'these taking the form of demonstrations
against and attacks on the houses and newspaper offices of Katsura partisans and newspapers. The prestige of the Emperor is certainly no longer
what it was and people wonder whether all this would have happened
had the old Emperor been alive.' Every day Rumbold sent Sir Edward Grey
a full telegraphic account of the political developments.

The new Government was formed on February 20. Makino, the new
Foreign Minister, was a friend of Rumbold's, and was, he believed, well
disposed towards Britain. The new Cabinet, he wrote in his diary that
day, 'has a clan and bureaucratic flavour about it. . . . There is no doubt

[1] Franz Ferdinand, 1863–1914. A nephew of the Emperor Franz-Josef, and since 1889
heir to the throne of Austria-Hungary. He was assassinated at Sarajevo on June 28, 1914.

[2] Yoshihito, 1879–1926. Son of Mitsuhito. Succeeded his father as Emperor, July 30,
1912. Created a Knight of the Garter, 1912, and a British Field-Marshal, 1918. In his *Japan:
Annual Report, 1912* Rumbold wrote (p. 16): 'It is said that the Emperor is of a very kindly
disposition. He is well-disposed towards foreigners. His intellectual development is reported
to be moderate. On the other hand, the German physician, who for many years was
attached to the Court . . . states that his muscular development is somewhat extraordinary.'

that Japan is not yet ripe for party Government as *we* understand it.' On February 24 Rumbold had his first meeting with Makino since his appointment, recording in his diary Makino's comment that 'party government had not been an unmitigated success in the west'. There was no doubt, Makino told Rumbold, 'a genuine desire on the part of some politicians for real party government in Japan'; but, he added, 'these men forgot that party government, as understood and in force in Western Europe, was the result of very many years of parliamentary evolution, and did not come about in a day'. Makino asked Rumbold about female suffrage. 'Like every Japanese,' Rumbold noted in his diary, 'he is hostile to the movement and cannot understand how we can tolerate it. . . . He said he could not understand a man like Grey being in its favour.' Rumbold told Makino that he himself was 'a strong anti-suffragist' and a member of the anti-suffrage league.[1] On February 20 Rumbold sent Sir Edward Grey a detailed account of the political crisis. The new Prime Minister, Count Yamamoto[2] was, he wrote, 'especially identified with the developments of the Japanese Navy' – a 'strong man' who was believed to be well disposed to Britain.

'I am kept pretty busy here', Rumbold wrote to his father on February 18, 'with one political crisis after another'; and on March 2 he described to his father 'an absolutely necessary' telegram costing £60, which he had sent to London about the political crisis. He had drafted it, he explained, 'as if the recipient was an ass of limited intelligence, i.e. expressed so as to leave no room for misunderstanding. This is the principle on which Lord Cromer went. He said "if it is necessary to send a telegram, make the telegram full and intelligible, it is more economical in the long run".'

Rumbold was looking forward to the arrival of the new Ambassador early in March. 'Once my chargéship is over', he added, 'I shall find it difficult to get up any further interest in this place. . . . During my 4 months chargéship I have done business with 4 Foreign Ministers i.e. one a month.'[3]

---

[1] The Women's National Anti-Suffrage League was founded in 1908. Its aims were to resist the proposal to give women the vote and to prevent women from becoming Members of Parliament. Lord Cromer was a staunch supporter of the League, as well as being President of the Men's League for Opposing Women's Suffrage, which was founded in 1911. Both Leagues were wound up in 1918, when women received the vote, and were allowed to become Members of Parliament.

[2] Gombie Yamamoto, 1852–1933. Entered the Japanese Navy, 1872; Vice-Admiral, 1898. Minister of the Navy, 1898–1904. Created Count, and full Admiral, 1904. Visited England in 1907, when Edward VII decorated him with the GCMG. Prime Minister, 1913; he resigned eleven months later because of popular indignation following a scandal over naval contracts. Prime Minister for the second time, August–December 1923.

[3] The four Foreign Ministers were Uchida (who had succeeded Komura in 1911), Katsura (the Prime Minister, who had been acting Foreign Minister), Kato (who became Foreign Minister on his return from London). and Makino.

On March 5 Conynghame Greene arrived in Japan. 'He doesn't think much of Tokyo', Rumbold wrote to his father on March 14; 'He consults me about everything and implicitly follows my advice.'

Rumbold's chargéship was at an end, and he was again impatient to exchange Tokyo for a new capital. 'I should like to go to Paris', he wrote to his father on March 25. Failing Paris, he hoped for Budapest. 'But', he added, 'I have not intrigued or asked for anything.' There was still no news of his posting by April 6. 'I have completely lost all interest in this place', he wrote to his father that day; 'I have now been a month with Greene and have gone into every question with him. He is quite capable of standing on his own feet now. Nothing therefore detains us except "Tyrrell's pleasure". It is a bore to be so much at the mercy of one individual and, I admit, it does not suit my somewhat independent character.' That week, to his horror, the Japanese newspapers announced that he was going to be transferred to Chile; but the rumour was false. There was still no news by the end of April. 'I think the FO are treating you too shamefully for words!' Sir Horace wrote to his son on April 24. Rumbold decided that his wife should return to England without him, by the Trans-Siberian railway. 'We have given up speculating in despair', he wrote in his diary on April 24; 'Meanwhile I have been appointed here longer than any Counsellor or Secretary of Legation before me and am rather tired of the place – its politics and its people.' On April 26, after dining with Rear-Admiral Jerram,[1] he wrote despondently: 'He is the third Admiral I have known on this station,[2] in fact I am beginning to feel archaic or prehistoric.'

Ethel Rumbold left Tokyo on May 3. Her husband accompanied her as far as Mukden, after which he himself went south to Peking, visited the Great Wall, and then returned to Mukden. There he received, from his wife's mother, Lady Fane, a letter which she had been sent by Grey's Assistant Private Secretary, Walford Selby[3] – 'a youth called Selby', as Rumbold noted contemptuously, ignoring the fact that Selby was over thirty years old. Selby had written to Lady Fane: 'I fear I am unable to

---

[1] Thomas Henry Martyn Jerram, 1858–1933. Entered Navy, 1871; Rear-Admiral, 1908. Vice-Admiral and Commander-in-Chief of the China Station, 1913–15. Knighted, 1914. Led the Second Battle Squadron at the battle of Jutland, 1916. Admiral, 1917.

[2] While Rumbold was in Japan, the China Station was commanded by Vice-Admiral Sir Hedworth Meux (1908–10), Vice-Admiral Sir Alfred Winsloe (January 1910–January 1913) and Vice-Admiral Jerram (1913–15).

[3] Walford Harmood Montague Selby, 1881–1965. Entered the Diplomatic Service, 1904. Assistant Private Secretary to Sir Edward Grey, 1911–15. 1st Secretary, Cairo, 1919–22. Principal Private Secretary to the Secretary of State for Foreign Affairs, 1924–32. Knighted, 1931. Minister in Vienna, 1933–37. Ambassador in Lisbon, 1937–40. He published *Diplomatic Twilight 1930–1940* in 1953.

send you any definite answer about Rumbold. I think, however, that he
is certain to remain here to the end of the summer, at least that is my
impression.' Rumbold was outraged at which he considered a 'rotten
communication'. He therefore asked his father, in a letter of May 22, if he
would mind 'conniving at an innocent form of deception', whereby
Rumbold would plead by telegram his urgent personal need to return to
London in order to see his father. 'I would then, of course, sit in England
until I was appointed elsewhere. . . . I hope you will back me up.' Sir
Horace agreed to do so; he had in fact been seriously ill with appendicitis
earlier in the year. He would celebrate his eighty-fourth birthday on
July 2, and was glad enough to 'connive' at his son's return. Rumbold
remained in a pessimistic mood, writing to his father about Tyrrell: 'As
regards myself, he seems to be showing deliberate "mauvaise volonté" but
I do not know why, as I have never done him any harm. For what I am
told, nothing is of any use nowadays; it is useless to do one's best – work
hard and get on well with people – nothing of this counts. All influence is
concentrated in Tyrrell's hands and one is powerless.'

On June 1 the Foreign Office informed Rumbold that he could go on
leave whenever he wished. But no mention was made of his next posting.
Despondent about his work, puzzled about his future, he left Japan on
June 12. 'I was not prepared to spend the summer and early autumn in
Japan doing nothing', he had written to his father on June 1; 'when I get
home I daresay I shall be able to find out more authentic news in a day
than what one hears in a year at this distance. It is a great thing to be on the
spot when moves are in progress. One is apt to be forgotten when one is so
far from home.'

Rumbold reached London early in July, having crossed Russia by train,
and visited St Petersburg, his birthplace, which he had never seen before.
On reaching London he found there was no immediate news of a posting
for him. On July 6 he wrote to his father, expressing his ever-present fears
of being 'exiled to S America'; but three days later he reported with
greater optimism: 'I heard this morning from a trusty friend at the FO . . .
that we need have no fear of being sent to Monte Video or anywhere else
in South America.' He now had hopes of 'a small mission in Europe', but,
he added, 'I keep my hopes to myself'. These hopes were nearly dashed a
month later, on August 13, when Tyrrell wrote to Rumbold asking if he
would be willing to go as Minister to Guatemala. On the following day
Rumbold reported to his father that he had written to Tyrrell 'to say that
I should prefer that my name was *not* submitted for the post'. He added:
'If the FO consider that I have done well in Japan and are pleased with me,
they can show their appreciation in other ways than by offering me

Guatemala.' On the following day he wrote to his father again, to say that he had definitely turned Guatemala down. 'So somebody else can take on the job of screwing money out of shady Dagoes.'

In mid-August Rumbold set down in his diary his reflections of Japan:

I am often asked whether I like the Japanese and I answer unhesitatingly 'yes'. I saw their best side and dealt with their best officials. They treated me well and I could rely on what they told and promised me. I always treated them as if they were fellow Englishmen and they thoroughly appreciated this. When talking to or dealing with foreigners – other than Englishmen – the Japanese, I am sure, feels that the foreigner has, at the back of his mind, the persistent idea that he, the Japanese, is only a yellow man and, therefore, on a lower level. The Japanese is very sensitive. He has, so to speak, 'got into society' and is often not quite certain of himself – with foreigners. This partly explains his reserve and silence in European society.

The vulgar idea in England and elsewhere is that the Japanese are very 'deep'. It is an illusion. Often, the said Japanese has nothing to say to a foreigner. He may not even be talkative with his own compatriots except under the influence of saké and then his tongue is unloosened. A further explanation is that he is slow-thinking and, in a rapid exchange of ideas, often cannot keep pace with the faster-thinking European. Perhaps the climate has to do with this – affecting the phosphates of the brain. Foreigners come under the influence of the climate after a time. When I first arrived in Japan my French colleague[1] said to me, 'you will soon find that you will suffer from anaemia of the brain'. I eventually certainly found that when I had anything at all complicated to read I had to read it 3 times to twice anywhere else. This slow-thinking might be disastrous to the Japanese in certain contingencies. Supposing they were at war and that their enemy hustled them on the sea and did things for which they were unprepared. They would be slow to accommodate themselves to unexpected and sudden situations and might incur disaster. But where they have time to think out a plan they will think it out to the last detail. . . .

The smaller officials i.e. the provincial officials are as often as not 'Jacks in office' and very irritating. They are hidebound by regulations. Nothing is more annoying than to have to deal with such people. The Japanese at the ports are the least reputable commercially. The Japanese – to our view – have lax ideas about the sanctity of trade marks (which they imitate continually) and their constant failures to send goods 'up to sample' are responsible for their bad name commercially. But they are beginning to see that it pays to be straight. The Chinese found this out some time ago – but then they are, au fond, a peace-loving and commercial people and have been so for centuries – whilst the Japanese feudal system created the class of 'samurai' whose occupation is now

[1] Fernand Couget, 1866–1950. Entered the French Diplomatic Service, 1893. Secretary at the Teheran Embassy, 1899–1901; at Vienna, 1901–4. Counsellor, Tokyo, 1906–10. Consul-General, Beirut, 1910–16. Minister to Mexico City, 1916–20; to Prague, 1920–24. In 1928 he was appointed Minister in Rome of the Principality of Monaco.

gone and who has – in many instances – taken to trade. 60 years ago the commercial man was despised in Japan. An increasing standard of comfort amongst the official class, combined with a great increase in the cost of living without a corresponding increase in salaries has been responsible for much corruption and for many company scandals. The bulk of the nation i.e. the peasantry etc is as sound as ever. I do not believe that socialists are numerous.

By mid-September Rumbold, still in England, had been without any employment for three months. 'Nothing has been settled about the pending moves', he wrote to his father on September 15; 'I hear our fate is not yet decided. . . .' Above all, he wanted to be sent to a post where he would be the senior British representative: 'a "living" of our own', as he wrote to his father, 'and not have to serve another term as "curate" '. Early in October he was offered the British Legation in Peru. He would be the Minister, all-powerful, but Lima, his father wrote on October 11, 'seems to be an undesirable post, not only distant and politically uninteresting, but with a damp, depressing climate. If it *must* be promotion through exile to South America', his father added, Chile would be 'a far more desirable place: better paid, much more accessible through Buenos Aires & the Transandine railway, and with an excellent climate for Ethel and the children.' Rumbold rejected Peru; Chile was not offered to him. A week later the dilemma was resolved, though not as he had wished. He was instructed to go to Berlin, as Counsellor of Embassy. All hopes of being found a Legation of his own had evaporated; he was to be second in seniority to the Ambassador, Sir Edward Goschen.[1] It seemed to him that his career had not advanced at all since he had first gone to Japan as Counsellor in 1909.

On November 3, Rumbold's father died, at the age of eighty-four. Father and son had shared each others hopes and disappointments for over twenty years, had confided in each other, enjoyed their correspondence, and thrived on each others successes and enthusiasms. Father and son had shared a deep interest in their family and its history; 'We Rumbolds' had been a frequent phrase in his father's letters, and was often to reoccur in Rumbold's own letters to his son and daughter. On his father's death he succeeded to the Baronetcy, and was now the head of the Rumbold family. He watched carefully over the interests of his stepmother, and over his children. In 1913 his daughter Constantia was seven, his son two and a half. 'As regards Tony', he wrote to his brother William on

[1] William Edward Goschen, 1847–1924. Entered the Diplomatic Service, 1869. Minister at Belgrade, 1898–1900; at Copenhagen, 1900–5. Knighted, 1901. Ambassador at Vienna, 1905–8; at Berlin, 1908–14. Created Baronet, 1916.

December 5, the eve of his departure for Berlin, '. . . he is not to be a loafer on any account. He is down for Eton and I want him to go there. I am not particularly keen for him to go into the service or the FO, but I have an open mind on the subject.' As for his daughter, he wrote: 'Don't let the "trout" (should you have to deal with the matter) marry either a foreigner or a rotter. Marriages with first cousins should be strictly avoided.'

9

Berlin

1913–1914

Rumbold reached Berlin on December 6. He did not think the Foreign Office had been very tactful in sending him there, in view of his father's life-long outspoken criticisms of Prussia, which had reached a climax in his pamphlet, *Prussian Aggrandisement and English Policy*, published in 1870. His father had declared that 'the German after centuries of dreaming, has become a model man of war' and that Germany was 'a very nursery of warlike men'. Rumbold shared these sentiments, though in a less extreme form. He had liked the Bavarians, but never the Prussians, and his views of Prussian arrogance had been strengthened during his brief spell at Munich in 1909. In January 1914 Rumbold was presented to the Kaiser at the first Court Ball of the season. 'I think I know somebody of your name,' the Kaiser said. 'Probably my father, Sir,' Rumbold replied. The Kaiser stared at Rumbold for a moment and then turned away abruptly.

At dinner on March 17 Lady Rumbold sat next to Bethmann-Hollweg,[1] the Chancellor. He talked mostly about British politics, criticizing both Lloyd George's radicalism and Asquith's failure to suppress the suffragettes. 'He said that Lloyd George was not only a danger to his own country, but to others', Lady Rumbold wrote to her mother on the following day, 'as his ways of thinking were very catching. Also the Suffrage question interests him very much, & he cannot understand our methods of dealing with these criminal women. I could see that he thought our government very weak. He suggested that the ring-leaders should be deported to S Africa. . . .'

In April 1914 Karl Helfferich,[2] the director of the Deutsche Bank, published a revised edition of his detailed work on German industrial progress since 1888. The first edition, which had been published six months previ-

---

[1] Theobald von Bethmann-Hollweg, 1856–1921. Prussian Minister of the Interior, 1905–7. Chancellor of the Reich, 1909–17. His memoirs, *Reflections on the World War*, were published in English in two volumes, 1920–21.

[2] Karl Theodor Helfferich, 1872–1924. Director of the Deutsche Bank, 1908–15. State Secretary for Finance, 1915–16; for the Interior, 1916–17. An enthusiastic advocate of unrestricted U-boat warfare, 1917. Ambassador in Moscow for two weeks, August 1918. A Reichstag Deputy, and leader of the Conservative opposition, 1920–24. Killed in a railway accident in Switzerland.

ously, had been an enormous success. Rumbold asked Sir Edward Goschen if he could prepare a précis of the book for the Foreign Office. 'The summarising of this important work', Goschen wrote to Sir Edward Grey on May 16, 'has involved a great deal of hard work, and I have much pleasure in calling your special attention to the exceedingly able and careful manner in which Sir Horace Rumbold has carried out his self-imposed task.' Rumbold's précis filled seventeen printed foolscap pages, and was printed at the Foreign Office on May 18. 'Dr Helfferich considers', Rumbold noted, 'that it is not enough to have safeguarded German trade and shipping by means of treaties. An additional aim must be to secure a field of activity beyond the frontiers of the country in order to make certain of a market for German produce and to command the sources of supply of raw material.'

On June 3, at an official luncheon at Potsdam, the subject of the suffragettes was again uppermost in the minds of the Germans present. When Rumbold asked the German Foreign Minister, von Jagow,[1] how he would deal with the suffragettes, should there ever be any in Germany, Jagow replied: 'I would beat them and I would kill them'. Later Rumbold noted: 'I have little doubt from his tone and expression that he would have been as good as his word.'

On June 23 Rumbold joined Goschen at Kiel, where a British naval squadron, commanded by Sir George Warrender,[2] was being fêted by the German High Sea Fleet. It was an occasion of amity and optimism, of races, aerial displays, garden parties, balls and dances. In an account which he wrote six weeks later, and which he kept among his private papers, Rumbold recalled 'the good terms on which the officers and crews of the 2 fleets were'. On the morning of June 26 he saw the German Ambassador to Britain, Prince Lichnowsky,[3] breakfasting alone on his hotel terrace. They talked for a while. Lichnowsky asked Rumbold why *The Times* had been so unfriendly towards Germany of late. Rumbold remarked that

[1] Gottlieb von Jagow, 1863–1935. Entered the Prussian Diplomatic Service, 1895. Served as Prussian Minister in Munich; then as German Ambassador in Rome, and Minister at The Hague. Foreign Secretary, 1913–17. He published a defence of his policies, *Ursachen und Ausbruch des Weltkrieges* in 1919.

[2] George John Scott Warrender, 1860–1917. Entered Navy, 1873. 7th Baronet, 1901. Vice-Admiral Commanding the 2nd Battle Squadron, 1913–15. Removed from his command in December 1915 on account of his increasing deafness and absentmindedness.

[3] Prince Karl Max Lichnowsky, 1860–1928. Entered the German Foreign Office, 1884. German Ambassador, London, 1912–14. A member of the Prussian Upper House, he was excluded after the unauthorized publication, in 1918, of his pamphlet, *Meine Londoner Mission*, in which he declared that the German Government had failed to appreciate Britain's pacific attitude in 1914. It became impossible for him to live in Germany once the pamphlet was published, and he emigrated to Switzerland.

there were several articles in the *Kreuzzeitung*, one by a distinguished Professor, hostile to Britain. 'Nobody cares what the Professors write,' was Lichnowsky's riposte. That afternoon Rumbold was introduced to the Kaiser on board the flagship of the British squadron, the *King George V*. The meeting led to a brief incident. Rumbold had put on a top-hat in order to be presented to the Kaiser. 'Pointing to my top-hat,' Rumbold recalled, 'he said: "If I see that again I will smash it in. One doesn't wear tall hats on board ship".' The Kaiser's unexpected outburst was not mere discourtesy; being an Admiral of the Fleet in the Royal Navy, the Kaiser was in fact the senior 'British' officer present, and as such nominally in command of the squadron.

That night Rumbold attended a ball at the Kiel Naval Academy. 'I went to bed very tired', he recalled, 'and about midnight heard the well known sound of a Zeppelin. I got up and at first could not see it, but eventually I saw the Zeppelin high up in the sky, making its way over the fleet out to sea. It was very uncanny.' On June 27 he watched the naval races until noon, after which he went to a garden party given by the Admiral commanding at Kiel.[1] That night he dined on board the *King George V*. 'During the whole of my stay at Kiel', he recalled, 'I could not fail to be impressed by the great cordiality which existed between the German and our sailors.' He left for Berlin on the morning of June 28. As Goschen was returning direct from Kiel to London, Rumbold was, from that evening, in charge of the Berlin Embassy.

Rumbold's train reached Berlin just before seven in the evening. A railway porter, hurrying into his carriage, thrust into his hand an extra edition of the morning newspaper, containing the news that the Austrian Archduke Franz Ferdinand and his wife had been assassinated at Sarajevo. 'As I drove through the streets home,' he recalled, 'crowds of people were collected reading the extra. They realized how serious the news was.' Later that evening Rumbold telephoned to the Austrian Embassy for further details, but all they could tell him was that the news was true.

On the morning of June 29 Rumbold called on the Austro-Hungarian Ambassador at Berlin, Count Szögyény,[2] whom he found 'very depressed'. 'He admitted', Rumbold recalled, 'that there was no affection between the Emperor and the Archduke, his nephew', but added that 'the crime could

---

[1] Gustav Bachmann, 1860–1943. Entered the Germany Navy, 1877. Chief of Staff, German Far Eastern Squadron, 1901–3. Served under Tirpitz in the Ministry of Marine, 1907–12. Vice-Admiral Commanding at Kiel, 1913–15. Chief of the Naval Staff, February–September 1915. In March 1915, while so much of Britain's naval strength was at the Dardanelles, he wanted to force a battle in the North Sea; but he was overruled.

[2] Ladislaus Szögyény-Marich von Magyar-Szögyén und Szolgaegyhaza, 1841–1916. Austro-Hungarian Ambassador in Berlin from 1892 until his death.

not fail to affect the Emperor deeply'. On the following day Rumbold discussed the assassination with the German Under-Secretary of State for Foreign Affairs, Alfred Zimmerman,[1] 'He had little doubt', Rumbold reported at once to Sir Edward Grey, 'that this crime was the outcome of a plot hatched by the partisans of a greater Servia.' Feeling in Austria-Hungary, Zimmerman added, was very bitter against Serbia, 'and he could make allowances for this in the circumstances'. In the three weeks following the assassination, the German Press, Rumbold recalled, were urging Austria 'to take some resolute action against Servia'. It was the Press, he believed, which had 'goaded Austria into action. . . . Some German papers even did not hesitate to sneer at Austria and say that she had failed in the past to take up a strong line. Was she never going to do so?' On July 3 Rumbold sent Grey a full account of the German reaction towards the murder of Franz Ferdinand, which had, he wrote, 'produced an impression amounting almost to consternation'. That same day he attended a memorial service to Franz Ferdinand at St Hedwig's Church, at which the entire diplomatic corps were present.

During the first three weeks of July the Austrians made no official move, nor did they seem to contemplate any military action. On July 6 Grey sent Rumbold an account of a conversation which he had held with Lichnowsky on his return from Kiel to London. Lichnowsky had told Grey that 'he knew for a fact . . . that the Austrians intended to do something and it was not impossible they would take military action against Servia'. The Austrian aim, Lichnowsky believed, would not be territory, but 'some compensation in the sense of humiliation for Servia'. If Germany told the Austrians to do nothing, the Ambassador added, 'she would be accused of always holding them back and not supporting them'.

On July 9 Grey received a letter from Sir Maurice de Bunsen, who had left Spain to become Ambassador to Austria-Hungary in November 1913, stressing that there was 'a very angry sentiment against Servia' in Austria, and that many previously moderate-minded men were insisting on the need to reduce Serbia to 'impotence'. Austria's intentions were unclear. 'I have no doubts', Sir Arthur Nicolson noted on de Bunsen's letter, 'as to whether Austria will take any action of a serious character and I expect the storm will blow over.' This was also Sir Edward Goschen's view. On

---

[1] Alfred Zimmerman, 1864–1940. Entered the German Foreign Office, 1887. Served in China, 1895–1902. Director of the Eastern Division of the German Foreign Office, 1904–10. Under-Secretary of State for Foreign Affairs, 1910–16. At the end of June 1914 he was acting Secretary of State, as the Secretary of State, von Jagow, was on honeymoon. Succeeded von Jagow in November 1916. His secret telegram to Mexico proposing an alliance against the United States was made public by President Wilson in March 1917; two months later Zimmerman was removed from his post. He never held office again.

July 11 he wrote to Rumbold from London: 'I saw Grey the other day, and he seemed rather nervous as regards Austria & Servia. But I don't think he need be, do you?' Rumbold took the crisis more seriously than his absent Ambassador. Often, in the first three weeks of July, he had discussed events in detail with the Austrian Naval Attaché,[1] with whom he was on friendly terms. Rumbold recalled how:

He said that two mobilizations of recent years had cost the Austrians so much money as to practically put a stop to all trade and building operations. The Austrians felt that Russia was behind Servia and that the Russian game was to see Austria slowly ruined. If they were to be ruined they thought they had better have a run for their money. 'For after all', as the Naval Attaché said 'we shall lose some men, and perhaps some money, but anyhow we shall be done with it'. I said they stood to lose far more than that.

Throughout July the German papers urged Austria to take action against Serbia. On July 11 Rumbold wrote to Grey that 'the general upshot of their remarks is that Austria-Hungary cannot indefinitely tolerate the state of things prevailing on her Serbian frontier. Hard things are said about Servia and the Servians, and it is freely assumed by some papers that the latter will shelter themselves behind the big Slav brother [Russia]. There is a consensus of opinion that Germany will and must stand by her ally in this matter.'

Speculation in Berlin was turning from the narrow problem of Austro–Serbian relations to the wider dangers which a European diplomatic crisis might entail. On July 17 Rumbold discussed the worsening situation with the French Ambassador in Berlin, Jules Cambon.[2] Rumbold reported the conversation to Grey on the following day. 'Matters between France and Germany were by no means what they should be', Cambon had told him; 'The Germans were not behaving in a friendly way towards his country. The air would have to be cleared one way or another.' In his letter of July 18, Rumbold also sent Grey his own feelings about German relations with Russia:

As regards the general question of the relations between Germany and her eastern neighbour, I venture to think that the supposed hostile intentions of Russia have been largely conjured up by the German press itself. That press has

[1] Hieronymus, Count Colloredo-Mannsfeld, 1870–1942. Entered the Austro-Hungarian Navy, 1889. An expert in torpedo boat navigation. Naval Attaché, Tokyo, 1904–7; Berlin, 1911–18.

[2] Jules Martin Cambon, 1845–1935. Served in the Franco-Prussian War, 1870. Entered the Civil Service, 1871. Prefect of the Department of Nord, 1882; of the Rhône, 1887–81. Governor-General of Algeria, 1891–97. French Ambassador, Washington, 1897–1902; Madrid, 1902–7; Berlin, 1907–14. Secretary-General, Foreign Ministry, Paris, 1915. A signatory to the Versailles Treaty, 1919.

no doubt given expression to the feeling of irritation and anxiety caused by the determined efforts of France and Russia to develop their armaments to the utmost possible extent. Whatever confidence the Germans may have in the efficiency and quality of their army, the enormous masses of men at the command of Russia are a constant source of preoccupation to them. Speculation as to the events which might set those masses in motion against Germany seems to follow almost as a matter of course.

On July 20 Grey spoke at length about the crisis to Lichnowsky. Later that day he sent Rumbold an account of the conversation. Grey believed, as he had told the German Ambassador, that 'the more Austria could keep her demand within reasonable limits, the stronger the justification she could produce for making any demand, the more chance there would be of smoothing things over'. Lichnowsky told Grey that Austria 'was certainly going to take some step', but he did not know what. 'I hated the idea of a war between any of the Great Powers', Grey told Lichnowsky, 'and that any of them should be dragged into a war by Servia would be detestable'. On the following evening Rumbold spoke to the German Foreign Minister, von Jagow, and asked him if he knew what demands Austria-Hungary was going to make on Serbia. Von Jagow expressed his surprise that the demands had not yet been made, but he went on, as Rumbold telegraphed to Grey on July 22, to insist 'that question at issue between Austria and Servia was one for discussion and settlement by those two countries alone without interference from outside'. When this telegram reached the Foreign Office, Sir Eyre Crowe minuted:

It is difficult to understand the attitude of the German Government. On the face of it, it does not bear the stamp of straightforwardness. If they really are anxious to see Austria kept reasonably in check, they are in the best position to speak at Vienna. All they are doing is to inflame the passions at Belgrade and it looks very much like egging on the Austrians when they openly and persistently threaten the Servian Government through their official newspapers.

It may be presumed that the German Government do not believe that there is any real danger of war. They appear to rely on the British Government to reinforce the German and Austrian threats at Belgrade; it is clear that if the British Government did intervene in this sense, or by addressing admonitions to St Petersburg, the much desired breach between England and Russia would be brought one step nearer realisation. . . .

On leaving von Jagow, Rumbold felt, as he recalled in the account which he wrote after his return to London, that the Germans 'knew what were going to be the contents of the forthcoming Austrian Note to Servia'. Crowe felt likewise. 'I think we may say with some assurance', he had written in his minute, 'that they have expressed approval of those

demands and promised support, should dangerous complications ensue.'
The much-awaited Austrian Note to Serbia was delivered at Belgrade on
the evening of July 23, and published in the German papers on the following morning. It accused Serbian officials of planning the Archduke's
murder, and made a series of specific, wide-ranging demands. All anti-
Austrian propaganda in Serbia must end; all Serbian officials allegedly
guilty of inciting opinion against Austria must be arrested; Austrian
officials must be allowed to participate in all legal processes against the
conspirators, and in the suppression of all anti-Austrian activity. 'I realized
at once', Rumbold recalled, 'that we should now, only by a miracle,
escape the General European War, for it was quite obvious that the
Ultimatum was drawn up in order to force a quarrel on Servia, and it
seemed equally evident that if Austria took military action against Servia
the Russians would intervene.'

Shaken by the severity of the Austrian demands, Rumbold went early
to the Embassy on the morning of July 24. He had only just arrived at the
Embassy when Jules Cambon telephoned, asking Rumbold to come at
once to the French Embassy. Rumbold recalled how, on going into the
Ambassador's room, Cambon said to him: 'Eh bien, qu'en dites vous?
C'est la guerre.' Cambon then showed Rumbold a telegram from the
French Ambassador at Vienna, Alfred Dumaine,[1] according to which
the Austrians were prepared to attack Servia with eight Army Corps. The
telegram further stated that it was the German Ambassador at Vienna,
von Tschirsky,[2] who, as Rumbold recalled, 'was largely responsible for the
present situation as he had egged on the Austrian Government to take
forcible action'.

At five that afternoon, the Russian Chargé d'Affaires, Arkadi Bronevski,[3] called on Rumbold at the British Embassy. 'He was very pessimistic',
Rumbold noted, 'and it was quite clear that he thought that his Government could not keep out of the business. I said to him that I hoped that the
Russian Government would not be too much influenced by the pan-
Slavists.' At 7.45 Grey telegraphed to Rumbold that Lichnowsky had told
him that 'if Serbia could not accept the whole of the Austrian demands

[1] Alfred Chilhaud Dumaine, 1852–1930. Entered the French Diplomatic Service, 1877.
French Minister to Bavaria, 1904–7; to Mexico, 1907–12. French Ambassador to Vienna,
May 1912–August 1914. In 1921 he published *La Dernière Ambassade de France en Autriche*
and in 1925 *Choses d'Allemagne*.

[2] Heinrich Leonhard von Tschirsky und Bögendorff, 1858–1916. Entered the German
Diplomatic Service, 1883. Ambassador in Vienna from 1907 until his death.

[3] Arkadi Nikolaievich Bronevski, born 1867. Entered the Ministry of Foreign Affairs,
1888. First Secretary, Russian Consulate General, Cairo, 1898–1904. Counsellor, Tokyo,
1909–12; Berlin, 1913–14. Russian Chargé d'Affaires, Berlin, July 1914. Russian Consular
representative at the Vatican, 1916–17.

unconditionally Austria might be expected to move at the expiration of the time limit'. Grey had declared 'that if the Austrian ultimatum to Serbia did not lead to trouble between Austria and Russia I had no concern with it . . . but I was very apprehensive of the view Russia would take of the situation'. At 8.40 Rumbold telegraphed to Grey that he had again spoken to Jules Cambon, who believed that Austro-Hungarian and German Governments were playing 'a dangerous game of bluff, and that they think they can carry matters through with a high hand'.

Rumbold was exhilarated by the challenge of the crisis, and by his part in it. To his wife, who was in England expecting their third child, he wrote that night: 'I have come to the conclusion that, thanks to the part our country at present plays in foreign affairs, the British "chargé" here is almost as big a bug as he was in Japan.'

On reaching the Embassy on the morning of Saturday, July 25, Rumbold found a telegram from Grey urging him to go at once to von Jagow, and to press upon him the need to persuade Austria to give the Serbs more time to answer the Austrian Note. 'After working as hard as I could split for the bag', Rumbold recalled, 'I saw Jagow at twelve o'clock and read to him a memorandum which I had prepared on my instructions. Following his usual custom he drew heads on a bit of blotting paper while he was listening to what I was saying. He then looked up – he looked me straight in the face and said:—"I know many people think that I was aware of the terms of the Ultimatum, but I assure you that I did not know the contents of the Note, because had I done so I should have assumed a certain responsibility for the Note". I then said to him that it seemed to me that he had given the Austrians a blank cheque. He demurred to this description and I could not shift him from the position that the question at issue between Austria and Servia was a purely local one.' During their conversation von Jagow admitted 'quite freely', as Rumbold telegraphed to Grey during the afternoon, that the Austro-Hungarian Government 'wished to give the Servians a lesson, and that they meant to take military action'. Von Jagow also agreed with Rumbold 'that Servian Government could not swallow certain of the Austro-Hungarian demands'.

Throughout July 25 the diplomatic exchanges between the European capitals had intensified. In the succeeding week they became exceedingly confused and complex. Germany would not agree to restrain Austria. Russia felt obliged to contemplate going to Serbia's aid. If Russia went to war with Austria, Germany would have to help Austria by an attack on Russia. If Russia and Germany went to war, France could not avoid helping Russia. A war between France and Germany must almost inevitably involve Britain, particularly if German troops, in attacking France, crossed through Belgium, whose neutrality Britain was pledged by treaty to uphold. At the time of the Archduke's assassination on June 28 these possibilities were remote. But by July 25 no one could say that each of them might not come to pass. 'My darling,' Rumbold wrote to his wife at four o'clock that afternoon:

here am I having *the* time of my life in the sense that I am doing the most exciting and responsible of work. Since yesterday morning Europe is in the midst of the most dangerous crisis of modern times. As soon as I had read the terms of the Austrian ultimatum to Servia I felt that the fat was in the fire. Since then there have been nothing but telegrams of the deepest interest from the FO etc – interviews with Ambans and correspondents etc. Yesterday the whole staff & I were working at the Embassy until 8 p.m. I hoped to have got off a letter to you by the bag this morning but although I was working from an early hour I couldn't manage it. At 12.30 to-day I had a most important inter-view with Jagow and while I was with him the Crown Prince[1] rang him up from Zoppot and the Austrian Ambassador was announced. In 2 hours from now the time limit expires and the Austrians will probably be in Belgrade by Monday. The Lord only knows what will happen then and I tell you – between ourselves – that we shall be lucky if we get out of this without the long-dreaded European war – a general bust up in fact. But don't quote me. I tell you it is really *thrilling* and you know that that sort of thing isn't wasted on me.

However 'thrilling' the crisis, Rumbold still looked forward to Sir Edward Goschen's return in two days time as an opportunity for him to go back to London on leave, and asked his wife to make the necessary Bank Holiday arrangements. 'But who knows what may happen between this and Thursday?' he added; 'I see nothing but trouble ahead both at home and abroad.' Early on the evening of July 25 Rumbold learned, as he telegraphed to Grey at 8.15 p.m., 'that Austro-Hungarian Embassy here consider localisation of crisis between Austria-Hungary and Servia will depend on whether, and, if so, to what extent, Russia and France think that they can reckon on active support of His Majesty's Government in the event of a general complication'.

On his way home late that evening Rumbold passed the statue of Bismarck in front of the Reichstag. A large crowd was laying a wreath in front of it, and singing patriotic songs. 'I thought to myself', Rumbold recalled, 'what Bismarck's feelings would have been had he seen the danger being brought on his country by its want of a strong man and

[1] Frederick William Victor Ernest August von Hohenzollern, 1882–1951. Eldest son of William II. Known as 'little Willy'. Regimental Commander, Death's Head Hussars, stationed at Zoppot, near Danzig, 1911–14. Commanded the 5th Army, 1914–16; the Southern Army (Western Front), 1916–18. In exile in Holland, 1918–23. Returned to Germany, 1923, as a private citizen. In 1933 he paraded in Nazi uniform, but played no further part in politics. His eldest son, Prince William, was killed in action in May 1940.

sound diplomacy. The whole of Bismarck's endeavours had been directed to prevent Germany from being caught in a vice between Russia and France.'

On Sunday, July 26, Rumbold sent Grey an account of the demonstration which he had seen the night before. 'Up to the present,' he added, 'public were so satisfied of the strength of the Austrian case that they were convinced that conflict with Servia would remain localised. There are now indications that German public and press are beginning to appreciate the gravity of position. While not wanting war, they are nevertheless determined to see Austria-Hungary through.' That evening the correspondent of *The Times*, John Mackenzie,[1] who had only just returned to Berlin from leave, telephoned Rumbold to ask for information on the crisis. 'I asked him to come and see me at once', Rumbold recalled, 'and explained the position to him.'

On the morning of July 27 Goschen returned from leave. Rumbold's direct contact with von Jagow, and his telegrams to Grey, were at an end. But there was still an enormous amount of work to be done. 'Telegrams now began pouring in', he recalled, 'and our Staff was literally worked off its head. Three of our Secretaries and the Archivist were away, and the whole of the burden of ciphering and deciphering telegrams fell on the four of us who remained.'[2] On July 28 the Military Attaché, Lieutenant-Colonel Russell,[3] returned from leave; he and the Naval Attaché, Captain Henderson,[4] were at once, Rumbold recalled, 'impounded . . . to help us'.

On Grey's instructions, which had reached Berlin on Monday, July 27, Goschen urged upon von Jagow the idea of a Conference 'in order', as Grey had telegraphed on the previous afternoon, 'to endeavour to find an issue to prevent complications'. But von Jagow insisted that any such conference would look as if the Great Powers were sitting in judgement

[1] John Edward Nutt Mackenzie, 1877–1919. Lost the sight of one eye while a student at Oxford, 1895. Berlin correspondent of *The Times*, 1908–14. Edited *The Times History of the War* (in twenty-one volumes) from 1914 until his death.

[2] By nightfall on July 27 the following members of Goschen's staff were present in the Berlin Embassy: Sir Horace Rumbold (Counsellor), Captain Wilfred Henderson (Naval Attaché), Hugh Gurney (2nd Secretary), Godfrey Thomas (Attaché) and Richard Astell (Attaché). The three absent Secretaries were W. F. A. Rattigan (2nd Secretary), Hope-Vere (3rd Secretary) and J. Monck (Attaché). The absent Archivist was G. F. Sampson.

[3] Alexander Victor Frederick Villiers Russell, 1874–1965. 4th son of the 1st Baron Ampthill. A godson both of Queen Victoria and the Emperor Frederick of Germany. 2nd Lieutenant, Grenadier Guards, 1894; Major, 1910. Military Attaché, Berlin and Stockholm, 1910–14. Lieutenant-Colonel, 1914. Served on the Western Front, 1915–18, and mentioned in despatches six times. Special Military Mission to Chile, 1921. British Commissioner, Hungarian–Rumanian Boundary Commission, 1922–24. Brigadier-General, 1926.

[4] Wilfred Henderson, 1873–1930. Entered Navy, 1888. Commander, Admiralty, under Sir John Fisher, 1905–9. Commanded Destroyer Flotillas, 1909–13. Naval Attaché, Berlin, 1913–14. Commodore, commanding the 1st Naval Brigade, 1914. Interned in Holland after the siege of Antwerp. Rear-Admiral, 1920. Vice-Admiral, 1925.

on Austria. During the afternoon of July 27 Rumbold went to see Zimmerman, who repeated this argument. 'But I pointed out to him', Rumbold recalled, 'that in her capacity as an Ally Germany was in a peculiarly favourable position for straight speaking to Austria.' Zimmerman did not respond. 'It was evident', Rumbold recalled, 'that every hour that passed increased the danger of the situation', and by Tuesday, July 28, 'the war fever in Berlin was already high'. The Austrians rejected the idea of direct talks with Russia, nor was there any evidence that Germany was willing to exercise a moderating influence on Austria.

Rumbold still cherished hopes of going back to London on July 29. 'I am now taking it easy', he had written to his wife on July 27, 'as the responsibility is off my shoulders.' But on the following day he realized that leave would be impossible. 'I hesitate to leave this place now', he wrote to her; 'Matters are really most serious, in fact so serious that the acute stage can't last long, and we ought to know, in a week from now, what we are in for. . . . There is an *off-chance* (anything is possible in this world) of a general bust-up in which we may be involved. In this case we should all have to leave Berlin. . . . We don't *think* there will be a general bust-up, but things will be very difficult the next few days.'

During the morning of Wednesday, July 29, Rumbold asked Goschen if he could go to London for the August Bank Holiday. Goschen telegraphed his request to Tyrrell at the Foreign Office, who replied to say that the Foreign Office had no objection, provided the Embassy were not left short staffed. Goschen again consulted Rumbold, and then telegraphed the Foreign Office a second time to say that Rumbold 'had no wish to go away at the present time'. At the same time, Rumbold wrote privately to Tyrrell to say that, much as he had wanted to take his Bank Holiday leave, he was prepared to see the crisis through. 'Of course it is all very upsetting in every way', Rumbold wrote to his wife on July 28, 'but if people *will* murder Archdukes and behave in every way like the scum of the earth, what can you expect.' His antipathies were not confined to the Serbs. 'Frankly', he continued, 'I have also little patience with the Austrians & Russians. The former were always d-d fools, the latter untrustworthy barbarians. A general war will hit us hard . . . the insurance rates on tea will be so high as to swallow up all profits.' On the afternoon of July 29 Rumbold went for a walk through the city with Colonel Russell. They found themselves outside the Crown Prince's Palace at the very moment that he got out of his motor car. 'The crowd cheered wildly', he recalled; 'There was an indescribable feeling of excitement in the air. It was evident that some great event was about to happen. The olive grey motor cars of the Great General Staff were dashing about in all directions. The papers were issuing "Extras" at all hours of the day, and it was pretty evident that the situation was getting out of hand.' That evening Rumbold dined with Colonel Russell and Captain Henderson at the Hotel Bristol. 'It was like a scene in a play', he wrote to his wife on the following day, July 30:

On one side of us were sitting Moltke,[1] Gevers[2] and Beyens[3] – the 3 small Powers who are trembling. They were joined by Polo[4] – who is likewise in a blue funk. On the other side of us all the Austrians were sitting together. They didn't look very happy. There were several Germans one knew. It would be safe to say that *all*, without an exception, were wondering what we are going to do. I don't suppose we know ourselves. When I think of Kiel and now! It seems almost incredible.

One of the Germans, Baron von Stumm,[5] was, Rumbold believed, convinced that Britain would be drawn into the war. 'I had known him well at Vienna from 1897 onwards', Rumbold later wrote. 'He had then gone on to London. We were on good terms, but I always felt that his friendliness hardly concealed a substratum of Prussian arrogance. His manner was somewhat gruff, and he was a typical Prussian in appearance. He was a realist in politics, and, unlike his superiors, was convinced early in the crisis that Britain would come into the war'.

Throughout July 30 the crisis worsened. 'The work at the Embassy was so great', Rumbold recalled, 'that one or two of the Staff showed signs of collapsing and one of the two Attachés did collapse for a while.' During the afternoon Rumbold took a short walk with Colonel Russell, hoping to escape the tension building up in the Embassy. In the account which he wrote after his return to London he recalled:

. . . as we came back through the Brandenburg Gate the Danish Minister hailed us from a taxi-cab and showed us an 'Extra' which had just been issued. This

[1] Carl Moltke, 1869–1935. Lieutenant, Danish Navy, 1889–95. Entered Diplomatic Service, 1903. Minister to Washington, 1908–12. Minister to Berlin, 1912–14. Minister of Foreign Affairs, 1924–26. Danish Delegate to the League of Nations Assembly, 1926, 29, 30.

[2] Baron Gevers, 1856–1927. Joined the Dutch Diplomatic Service, 1881. Served at St Petersburg, 1884–87 and London, 1887–94. Dutch Minister, Berne, 1894–96; Bucharest, 1896–1900; Washington, 1900–4; Rome, 1904–5 and Berlin, 1905–27.

[3] Napoléon Eugène Louis Joseph Marie Auguste Beyens, 1855–1934. Principal Private Secretary to King Albert of the Belgians, 1910–12. Minister in Berlin, 1912–14. Foreign Minister of the Belgian Government in exile (at Le Havre), 1915–17. Ambassador to the Vatican, 1921–25. After the war he published *Deux Années à Berlin, 1912–14.*

[4] Luis Polo de Bernabé, 1854–1929. Entered the Spanish Diplomatic Service, 1873. Ambassador to Rome, 1904–5; to London, 1905–6. On leaving London he was awarded the Grand Cross of the Royal Victorian Order. Ambassador to Berlin, 1906–18. Senator for Life, 1919. He died after being run over by a motor-car in Madrid.

[5] Baron Wilhelm August von Stumm, 1869–1935. Served in the Army, 1894–95. Entered the Diplomatic Service, 1895; served in Vienna 1897–99. 1st Secretary, London, 1908–9. Political Director German Foreign Ministry, 1911–15; Under-Secretary of State, 1916–18.

'Extra' referred to a forged 'Extra Edition' which had come out an hour before and which had been scattered broadcast through Berlin. In this forged 'Extra' it was stated that Germany had decreed the mobilization of her land and sea forces. The German Foreign Office at once telephoned to the Russian, French and our Embassies to say there was not a word of truth in this report. Meanwhile the Russian Ambassador[1] had telegraphed the news in the forged 'Extra' to his Government, and, on receiving the telephone message from the Foreign Office, had sent a further telegram 'en clair' referring to his cipher telegram sent an hour previously contradicting the information contained therein. Whether this 'en clair' telegram ever got through to the Russian Government we do not know, and it may be that the Russian Government acted on the forged 'Extra', although there are people who think that the whole thing may have been a pre-arranged plot on the part of the German Government to induce the Russians to reveal their intentions, and so to get an excuse for ordering the general mobilization in Germany itself.

Writing to his wife that evening, Rumbold declared: 'Sometimes the whole thing seems a dream, or rather a nightmare.' Goschen, he wrote, 'has risen to the occasion – as I knew he would – but, although he has only been back 4 days, the strain is beginning to tell on him. I was with him until past midnight last night. ... Yesterday we played 2 rubbers of bridge whilst awaiting telegrams in and out.'

Each day produced new uncertainties. On Wednesday, July 29, both Russia and Austria-Hungary had begun to mobilize on the Austro-Russian frontier and these mobilizations had continued throughout Thursday, July 30. 'War is undoubtedly very popular', Sir Maurice de Bunsen telegraphed to Grey from Vienna on the evening of July 30. In his recollections, Rumbold recalled the next day's developments:

On Friday, the 31st, the correspondent of the 'Westminster Gazette'[2] came to me and said that Stumm had distinctly given him to understand that he and other correspondents would soon have to leave the country. Reuter's Agent[3] came immediately afterwards and told me the same thing, and it was therefore quite clear that Stumm foresaw that we should go to war with Germany. In his

[1] Sergei Nikolaevich Sverbeev, born 1857. Entered the Russian Diplomatic Service, 1883. 1st Secretary, Russian Embassy, Vienna, 1898–1910. Minister in Athens, 1911–13. Ambassador in Berlin, 1913–14. Worked in the Foreign Ministry, Petrograd, 1914–17. Retired to his estates, July 21, 1917.

[2] Robert Edward Crozier Long, 1872–1938. Entered journalism, 1894. Russian correspondent of the *Review of Reviews*, 1898; of the *Daily Chronicle*, 1899; of the *New York American*, 1904–5. Berlin correspondent of the *Westminster Gazette*, 1913–14. Returned to Berlin as financial correspondent of the *Economist* and the *New York Times*, from 1919 until his death. Author of several books on German, Russian and Scandinavian politics.

[3] Lester James Harvey Lawrence. Joined Reuters, 1900. Reuters' Correspondent, Berlin, 1910–14. Special Reuters' Correspondent at Gallipoli, 1915; in Egypt 1916; with the French forces in France, 1917–18 and in Italy, 1918; at the Paris Peace Conference, 1919.

position as Third in the Hierarchy of the German Foreign Office his language was as extraordinary as it was improper, and I told the correspondents that we were in close touch with the German Government throughout the day, and that we could not assume, as a fact, a war between the two countries.

That morning the German Government said that they heard that the whole Russian Army and Fleet were being mobilized. In consequence they intended to proclaim at once the 'Kriegsgefahr' and that mobilization would follow almost immediately. Meanwhile we had heard from Buchanan[1] at St Petersburg that the German Ambassador[2] had had an interview at two in the morning with the Russian Foreign Minister[3] in the course of which he broke down completely, having realized that war was inevitable.

A telegram came in from the Foreign Office during the morning instructing the Ambassador to ask the German Government whether they were prepared to respect the neutrality of Belgium so long as no other power violated it. Jagow's answer, which was really not an answer, indicated plainly enough that the German Government would not tie themselves, and of course we could only draw the conclusion that the German Army would attack France through Belgium in the event of war breaking out. Meanwhile telegrams poured into the Embassy from all over Germany containing appeals for advice from British subjects who did not know what to do. We were in great difficulty, not being able to advise them, as we could not assume that we were going to war with Germany.

From the moment that the Kriegsgefahr had been proclaimed the Military Authorities practically took charge of the situation. This meant great inconvenience, as we were only allowed to telephone in German and to send 'En clair' telegrams in German. We could only advise our subjects to leave Germany if nothing kept them there, but we did not like to go further than that.

On Friday, July 31, the Germans asked the Russians to halt their mobilization, and to demobilize at once. On August 1 Sir Francis Bertie telegraphed to Grey from Paris the information that 'the Emperor of Russia did not order a general mobilisation until after a decree of general mobilisation had been issued in Austria'. Amid these charges and counter-charges the British Foreign Office, Rumbold recalled, 'were still making desperate efforts to keep the peace ... but we felt the whole time that the

---

[1] George William Buchanan, 1854–1924. Entered the Diplomatic Service, 1876. Minister at Sofia, 1903–8; at The Hague, 1908–10. Knighted, 1905. Ambassador to St Petersburg (later Petrograd), 1910–18; to Rome, 1919–21. He published *My Mission to Russia and Other Diplomatic Memories* in 1923.

[2] Count Friedrich von Pourtalès, 1853–1928. A Lieutenant of Hussars in the German Army, 1873. Transferred to the Foreign Office, 1880. Ambassador at The Hague, 1899–1902; at St Petersburg, 1907–14. In 1919 he published *Am Scheideweg zwischen Krieg und Frieden*; in 1927 *Meine letzten Verhandlungen in Petersburg Ende Juli 1914*.

[3] Sergei Dmitrievich Sazonov, 1866–1927. Russian Minister of Foreign Affairs, 1910–15. Dismissed by the Tsar in November 1915 following his advocacy of Home Rule for Poland. Chief Representative Abroad of Admiral Kolchak, 1919–20. Died in exile in France.

situation was completely out of hand, and that in the race against time the Diplomats were always one lap behind'. During the afternoon of August 1 Grey telegraphed to Goschen that 'if only a little respite in time can be gained before any Great Power begins war it might be possible to secure peace'. On the evening of August 1 Rumbold wrote to his wife:

My darling, an English officer is going to England to-night so we are sending a bag by him to the FO – our regular messenger service being temporarily dislocated. No mail has come from England to-day and since yesterday the train service has been curtailed and a censorship established over all private and press telegrams. I got a letter from you yesterday evening, written on the 29th. I am delighted to hear that the little pair are so well. What a contrast between the peace of Boyton and Berlin on the brink of war.

The position now is that we are expecting every minute to hear whether the Russians are, in any way, going to accept or reject the German ultimatum which must have been handed in early this morning. On that depends peace or war. Meanwhile I am writing private letters as there is a temporary calm before the storm. This afternoon I packed most of the plate-chest and propose to finish all that, first thing to-morrow morning. Packing won't take me long – if it comes to that.

Last night Gurney,[1] Russell & I were cyphering until 1.30 a.m. having sent the 2 Attachés[2] to bed. The latter were dead beat. Then Gurney and I took the telegrams to the telegraph office ourselves, in order to make sure of their going through and I saw the Director at 2 a.m. I was back at work early this morning. The Amban thanked me this morning for the way I was helping him and, in doing so, showed some emotion. This crisis is telling on our nerves. Mine are good and I am fit, but I feel rather short of sleep besides being very depressed by the criminal folly of it all.

This morning Faramond[3] came round here and I took the opportunity to tell him what I thought of his Russian pals. He got very excited and I thought he was going to assault me. What an ape he is. Henderson is thoroughly fed up with him. If the French have got many officers like that, God help their navy. Sverbéeff is in a state of nerves bordering on collapse. He looks ghastly and would produce a slump on any stock exchange.

---

[1] Hugh Gurney, 1878–1968. Entered Diplomatic Service, 1901. 2nd Secretary, Berlin, 1911–14; promoted 1st Secretary, Berlin, May 31, 1914. Transferred to Copenhagen, August 1914. Served in Brussels, Tokyo and Madrid. Consul-General in Tangier, 1926–33. Minister to Copenhagen, 1933–35. Knighted, 1935. Ambassador at Rio de Janeiro, 1935–40.

[2] Godfrey John Vignoles Thomas, 1889–1968. Entered Diplomatic Service, 1912. Attaché, Berlin, 1913–14. Succeeded his father as 10th Baronet, 1919. Private Secretary to the Prince of Wales, 1919–36. Private Secretary to the Duke of Gloucester, 1937–57.

Richard John Vereker Astell, 1890–1969. Attaché, Berlin, 1913–14; served Diplomatic Service, 1915–19, when he resigned. 2nd Lieutenant, Royal Artillery, 1939; Captain, 1940.

[3] Goutram Marie Auguste de Faramond de Lafajole, 1864–1951. French Naval Attaché in Vienna, 1910–12; in Berlin, 1912–14. Vice-Admiral, 1919. After the war he wrote Souvenirs d'un attaché naval en Allemagne et en Autriche, 1910–14.

Our Amban stands out from the rest of his colleagues. As a matter of fact he is in one of the most responsible positions in Europe. Rattigan[1] has proved a 'rotter'. He is not yet back. He, Hope-Vere,[2] Monck[3] & Sampson[4] are away, but Rattigan and Monck are now starting back. Perhaps they will be too late for the fun. Your maid hasn't turned up yet. I suppose she can't get through from Vienna. You will have realized by now that there can be no question of your coming back here. What an upset it all is. Prices have gone up a lot as everybody is laying in provisions. Eggs are 1 mark a dozen dearer to-day.[5]

Sunday, August 2, opened up no new hope. 'We were practically living on our nerves', Rumbold recalled, 'and we were so hard pressed that we had to have night shifts. We could not have gone on very much longer.' That morning he wrote to his wife:

My darling, I am risking a letter to you as some Americans are going to try and get through to England to-night though we are told that the Hook of Holland and Flushing boats are not running. I can't say how thankful I am you aren't here. We are all worn out and that is the truth. I don't think we could stick it for another 48 hours – the Amban and Gurney would certainly break down. Sverbéeff received his passports at about 10 a.m. this morning and leaves with the whole Embassy and Consulate General to-morrow morning. Meanwhile the Russians have raided the German frontier at various points and are trying to blow up trains and bridges. It is only a question of a few hours when the French come in. As for ourselves, we know nothing and the government haven't given us a line. For some hours we have had no telegrams from home and, of course, no mails have come for two days. We are prepared for the worst. Everybody here assumes as a matter of course that we are going to join in and we are besieged all day long by British subjects asking for advice. The whole thing is, to me, a gigantic nightmare and I keep on wondering whether I am in a sane world. It is impossible to write about things in a letter but every hour brings some new developments. I shall be so very thankful when I see you and the children again for we all feel very cut off from home now. I would like to go to bed in some quiet place and sleep for 24 hours on end. In after years I shall

1 William Frank Arthur Rattigan, 1879–1952. Entered Diplomatic Service, 1903. 2nd Secretary, Berlin, 1913–14. Fought at the battle of Mons, 1914. Chargé d'Affaires, Bucharest. 1919–20. Acting High Commissioner, Constantinople, May–July 1921. He published *Diversions of a Diplomat* in 1924.

2 Edward James Hope-Vere, 1885–1924. Entered Diplomatic Service, 1905. Served in Madrid as an Attaché, 1906–7. 2nd Secretary, Berlin, April–August 1914. Employed in the Foreign Office, 1914–15. 2nd Secretary, Madrid, 1915–19. 1st Secretary, Belgrade, 1919–21; Buenos Aires, 1921–23. Chargé d'Affaires, Christiania (Oslo), 1923–24, when he retired.

3 John Berkeley Monck, 1883–1964. Educated at Eton; Honorary Attaché at Berlin, 1908–14. 2nd Secretary, Paris, 1917–19. Assistant Marshal of the Diplomatic Corps, 1920–36; Vice-Marshal, 1936–45. Knighted, 1938. Extra Gentleman Usher to King George VI, 1950–52 and to Queen Elizabeth II from 1952 until his death.

4 George Frederick Sampson, 1883–1948. Archivist, Berlin Embassy, 1908–14. Employed in the Stockholm Legation, 1914–19 (Acting Vice-Consul, 1918–19). Resigned, 1919.

5 In 1914 the Mark was worth one English shilling.

look back upon this with a good deal of aversion. It has been, and still is exciting to the uttermost degree but it is too awful to think what the next few months have in store. No more now. Goodness only knows when I shall hear from you again or when I shall get a letter through to you. Love to the precious pair. Goodbye for to-day, my darling.

At midday on August 2 Russia and Germany were at war. 'It was only a question of hours', Rumbold recalled, 'as to when the French came in.' The British position was still unclear, for it depended upon what the German armies would do in the west. August 2 was the first official day of the full German mobilization. 'Half the taxi cabs seemed to have disappeared', Rumbold recalled, 'and those that one saw dashing about were filled with officers and luggage, so that it was really difficult to know how to get about. Late in the afternoon Henderson and I went out into the Unter den Linden and walked up it through enormous crowds. The police were keeping the roads clear and at about half past six the Emperor dashed through the Brandenburger Tor on his way from the Offices of the Great General Staff. He got a tremendous ovation from the crowd. That was the last time I saw him.'

Rumbold could get no further letters to his wife. But from the morning of August 3 his recollections, written four weeks later, give an hour by hour account of the crisis as he saw it:

That morning the German Chancellor sent us a statement to be telegraphed to London, explaining that the French had violated the frontier at several points; he said that airmen had dropped bombs on the railway near Carlsruhe and Nuremberg, and that French aviators had flown over Belgian territory. We sent the telegram off after translating it into English, and we heard about three hours later that the telegraph office had refused to transmit the telegram until it obtained the seal of the German Foreign Office. I therefore went to the Foreign Office and saw one of the Heads of Departments and pointed out to him that if the German authorities chose to block one of their own messages, it was their fault and not ours. He was very crestfallen and gave immediate orders that our telegrams were to be allowed through. The Foreign Office said that all this was the fault of the military.

The Russian Ambassador left at about noon that day, and an enormous crowd which had gathered in front of the Embassy assaulted the motor cars in which he and his staff were, and tried to hit them with sticks. In so doing they injured one of the staff seriously.

During the day my chief made two or three attempts to see the French Ambassador, but without avail, and we had the impression that the French thought we were not going to back them up and that therefore they did not wish to meet us. It was a very unpleasant thought to us.

We did not know what to do about our private affairs, whether to pack up or to make preparations for departure. The excitement in Berlin was indescribable and it was really impossible to sleep. The Austrian Consulate happened to be in the street in which our house was, and all day there was a crowd of reservists waiting for passes and blocking up the road. The crisis was so getting on our nerves that by common consent at lunch and dinner we talked of other subjects; the Ambassador was really splendid, with a fund of anecdotes, and we all tried to help him. Two members of our staff had got through from England with great difficulty on Sunday morning, and that relieved the pressure to a certain extent.

That Monday afternoon some correspondents took refuge in the Embassy and we formed a sort of concentration camp for them, as they did not dare to show their faces outside. We had been able to send a bag home on August 2nd by an American who said he would try to get through to England, and that was our last opportunity of sending any letters.

Germany had practically declared war on France on August 3rd, and the French Ambassador received his passports that evening. We did not know this, though, until the following day. Meanwhile I had packed the silver in my house and put my papers into a case so as to be ready in case we should be withdrawn. Otherwise I had to leave the flat exactly as it stood at the tender mercies of any servant I might leave behind.

On Tuesday, August 4th, the German papers contained a mutilated fragment of Grey's speech in Parliament the night before; from that fragment it looked as if we might be coming in and when the Military Attaché showed us his map and pointed out how impossible it would be for the Germans to move their enormous army into France through the gap of twenty miles between the northernmost French fort and the Belgian frontier, we realised that they must go through Belgium.

We were still without any indication as to what our Government was going to do, and we felt in an agony of suspense. After lunch I determined to see the French Ambassador and find out whether he knew anything, so I went round and was lucky enough to see him at once. They were sealing their archives before handing them over to the Spanish Ambassador. He said to me: 'I am glad to see you, as I want to tell you what has been happening to me, but before I begin, I must tell you that I do not think you are behaving like gentlemen. Our fleet is concentrated in the Mediterranean and our northern coasts are quite unprotected.' I said to him that as we were not bound to France by the terms of an alliance, it was necessary for our Government to have a clear *casus belli*. This had not struck him before. . . .

On getting back to the Embassy at 3.15, a telegram came in from the Foreign Office saying that the King of the Belgians[1] had appealed to our King to uphold the neutrality of Belgium, which was being violated by the Germans. The

[1] Albert, 1875–1934. King of the Belgians from 1909 until his death. He married, in 1900, a daughter of Charles, Duke of Bavaria. After the outbreak of war he took command of the Belgian Army, and fought in the siege of Antwerp, where he was said to have fired the last shot before the city surrendered. In December 1914 he was given the Order of the Garter.

Ambassador was instructed to ask the German Government to immediately cancel any steps they had taken to infringe Belgian neutrality. At that moment the Chancellor was making his great speech in the Reichstag, where all the Ministers were, so my chief went to the Reichstag to carry out his instructions. The Foreign Secretary said that he regretted they could not go back, the German troops had actually entered Belgium that morning and it was a matter of life and death to the Germans to advance on France through Belgium. The Ambassador came back and we sent a telegram off to the Foreign Office in that sense. . . .

At 6 o'clock a second telegram came from the Foreign Office, saying that since the despatch of their first telegram our Foreign Office had heard that the Germans had violated the Belgian frontier at Gemmenich. In these circumstances, and in view of the fact that Germany declined to give the same assurance respecting Belgium as France gave last week, our Government must repeat the request to the German Government to respect Belgian neutrality and ask for a satisfactory reply to that request and to the previous telegram to be received in London by midnight that night; if not, the Ambassador was instructed to ask for his passports. This was the ultimatum to Germany.[1]

The Ambassador went off to see the Foreign Secretary, who said that he was not surprised, but that he could give no other answer than that which he had given a couple of hours previously. The Ambassador then went on to say good-bye to the Chancellor; he found the latter in a fury of rage and under the influence of the speech he had delivered in the Reichstag. He made a set speech in English to the Ambassador and said that he considered that England was responsible for the war; for the sake of 'a piece of paper' she had gone in against Germany. Our chief in vain tried to point out to him that we were bound in honour to observe the guarantee which we had given in common with Germany, but it was no good. He came back to the Embassy and sent his final telegram at about half past seven. This telegram was not allowed to go through, as we subsequently found out.

We then knew that we should have to leave within 24 hours. We had gradually made preparations as regards handing over the archives, etc., and we telegraphed to the Consuls to say there was war between England and Germany and that they were to ask for their passports.

That night we were all dining with the Ambassador as usual, pretty well tired out after this most exciting and critical day, when at 9 o'clock the butler brought an Extra just issued by one of the papers, containing in enormous letters the news that England had declared war on Germany and that the Ambassador had asked for his passports. No reasons were given. We heard afterwards that this Extra had been struck off in thousands of copies, packed into motor cars and sent all over Berlin, the sheets being thrown out on to the pavement wherever there were many people about. Simultaneously with the appearance of this

[1] Rumbold himself deciphered the British ultimatum with one of the Attachés at the Embassy, Godfrey Thomas. 'You and I', he wrote to Thomas twelve years later, on December 17, 1926, 'will, I am sure, never forget decyphering the Ultimatum to Germany.'

Extra, a large crowd formed up opposite the Embassy and we could hear their yells from where we were dining. At about half past nine we went into one of the front drawingrooms to smoke, when suddenly we heard the smash of glass and realised that we were being attacked. I went to the telephone and telephoned to the Foreign Office to send mounted and foot police at once, as the three men on duty in front of the Embassy were quite unable to cope with the crowd. Meanwhile, stones the size of one's fist came through all the double windows of the front rooms and people climbed up on to the window sills and smashed the windows in with sticks. One umbrella fell inside and we eventually handed it over to the 'Times' correspondent as a trophy for the 'Times' Office in London.

The attack lasted fully half an hour,[1] until strong bodies of police came along and put a stop to it. Meanwhile the yells from the crowd were not isolated, it was one continuous roar and howl of rage and had we gone out at that moment we might have been killed. At about half past eleven the police had dispersed most of the crowd so we sallied out in two bodies; three of us jumped into a motor car and went to our houses as fast as we could. We were recognised and insulted, but no violence was attempted. The others, who were more numerous, were escorted by police to another motor car, a policeman with drawn revolver got on the box seat and accompanied them. The crowd tried to get at the occupants of the car, but luckily did them no injury.

I spent most of the rest of that night putting my important valuables and papers together and winding up my affairs as best I could. Next morning I found that my wife's maid had returned from Austria, having been five days on the journey. I gave her a few final instructions and then left our apartment for good, hoping that I should see my things again but not at all certain that they would not all be smashed and looted. I then went to the Embassy for the night, picking up our Naval Attaché and one of the Secretaries.

At about 10 that morning the Emperor sent an A.D.C. to my chief to express his regret for what had occurred at the Embassy the night before. This man delivered his message in the stiffest manner possible and, after conveying the expression of regret, he added, on instructions from the Emperor, that the incident would show the Ambassador how deeply the people felt the action of England in ranging herself against Germany and forgetting how we had fought shoulder to shoulder at Waterloo. The A.D.C. also added that the Emperor had been proud of being a British Field-Marshal and an Admiral of the Fleet, but that now he would divest himself of these honours. This strange message only served to show what we had long thought, namely, that the Emperor was not a gentleman.

Meanwhile several correspondents had been locked up and some fifty or sixty British subjects were collected at the Police Station as a preliminary to being sent, as they thought, to the fortress of Spandau. We had no longer official dealings with the German Government and had handed over the protection of

---

[1] It was under cover of this attack that the French Ambassador, Jules Cambon, managed to leave Berlin without attracting any attention.

British subjects and interests to the American Embassy. I went round to that Embassy in the course of the morning to interview the Counsellor.[1] I never saw such a sight; the passages and staircases were blocked by hundreds of Americans, wanting passports, money and advice, and the Embassy had a staff of twenty secretaries working for all they were worth. The American Ambassador[2] acted with the greatest energy; he went to the Foreign Office as soon as he heard of the wholesale arrests being made and said to the Germans that they must give up their fourteenth century methods. . . .

That Wednesday afternoon the American Counsellor with one Secretary came over to our Embassy and we formally handed over our archives to him. This meant sealing some 40 cupboards, each with a label, which he and I signed, and the seals of the respective Embassies were affixed to this label. It was a lengthy proceeding, at the end of which we drew up a protocol stating that by the instructions of our respective Ambassadors we had transferred the archives to the American Embassy. He and I then signed this protocol in duplicate. While this was going on, other members of the staff burned the cyphers and other confidential documents and by dinner time we were all clear.

The 'Daily Mail' Correspondent, a man called Wile,[3] who was an American subject, had been to the Embassy earlier in the day and begged that we would take him in the Embassy train. The Germans had got their knife into him and had already arrested him, but his Embassy got him out. After a bit we considered that we must take him along with us and with the other correspondents. Meanwhile he was hidden at the American Embassy and was taken down to the station next day by the American Counsellor.

All was quiet that night, though the American Military Attaché[4] came in after dinner and said that he had heard the crowd saying that they would try to burn down the Embassy that evening. The Police had given us a Lieutenant to concert measures with us as to our departure, etc. This Lieutenant was a very nice man and came to me two or three times in the course of the day to ask what

---

[1] Joseph Clark Grew, 1880–1965. United States Deputy Consul-General, Cairo, 1904–6. Counsellor of Embassy, Berlin, 1912–16. Secretary-General to the American Peace Conference Delegation, Paris, 1919. Minister, Copenhagen, 1920; Berne, 1921. Negotiated the United States–Turkish Treaty, Lausanne, 1923. Under-Secretary of State, Washington 1924–27. Ambassador to Turkey, 1927–32; to Japan, 1932–41. He published a two-volume memoir, *Turbulent Era*, in 1953.

[2] James Watson Gerard, 1867–1951. Lawyer. Supreme Court Judge, State of New York, 1907. Ambassador to Berlin, 1913–17. Honorary Grand Cross of the order of the Bath, 1917. Returned to his Law practice, 1917. He published *My Four Years in Germany* (1917), *Face to Face with Kaiserism* (1918) and *My First Eighty-three Years in America* (1951).

[3] Frederic William Wile, 1873–1941. Journalist, Chicago, 1898–1900. Correspondent of the *Chicago Daily News* in London, 1900–1; Berlin, 1902–6. Chief Berlin Correspondent of the London *Daily Mail*, the *New York Times* and the New York *Herald Tribune*, 1906–14. In London, 1914–18, editing a column in the *Daily Mail* called 'Germany Day By Day'. Radio correspondent for various American broadcasting companies, 1923–38.

[4] George Taylor Langhorne, 1867–1962. Graduated from the US Military Academy, 1885. Served as a Major in the Spanish–American War of 1895. Stationed in the Philippines, 1899–1908. Military Attaché, Berlin, 1913–15. Colonel, 1917.

we wished. I arranged with him that we would leave the Embassy the following morning at 7 o'clock, and instead of going the usual way to the station, which would be down the Unter den Linden and through the Brandenburg Gate, that we would cut across the Unter den Linden and go by back ways. He said that the police would hold Unter den Linden in force so as to allow people to suppose that we were going that way, but as a matter of fact there were very few people about at that early hour.

I got up early on Thursday morning, and got a glimpse of the toilette of the correspondents which was really a most comic sight. We got them away at about six o'clock and we ourselves left at about seven or a little after. We left our Chancery servant in charge of the Embassy; he was a man who had been in our service for 25 years and we felt certain we could rely on him. Most of the Ambassador's servants had been mobilised, but besides the butler he had three left, who behaved in a very disgraceful way at the end. These men had been well paid; they had received a whole month's wages in advance, but directly they received the money they took off their liveries, spat and trampled on them and refused to help to carry the trunks down to the taxi cabs. It may be said that in these ways the Germans showed an entire absence of decent feeling.

The Ambassador and I left the Embassy together and we agreed that it was a rotten way of leaving one's post. On arriving at the station there did not seem to be any arrangements made for sending the Ambassador off with all proper respect. We stood about amongst the correspondents and other members of the staff until the special train was ready to leave. . . . Colonel Wedel[1] came to say goodbye on behalf of the Foreign Minister. The Belgian Minister and his staff travelled in the same train.

We left Berlin at 8.16 that morning. . . . At all the big stations we passed there were crowds on the platform, very often a band, and when they realised who we were they sang 'Deutschland, Deutschland über Alles' at us and shook their fists.

The Ambassadorial train travelled through Germany throughout Thursday, August 6, only reaching the Dutch frontier on the following morning. At noon Goschen and his staff set off by ship from the Hook to Harwich. 'At about five in the afternoon', Rumbold recalled, 'we realised that we were being chased by one of our flotillas, consisting of the parent cruiser and twenty destroyers. Our Naval Attaché at once took command, turned the ship round, and went towards them, so as to save them from using too much oil. He got on to the top of the deck cabin and semaphored to the cruiser who we were.' Reaching Harwich early that evening, the diplomats went by train to London. 'We dined in the train', Rumbold

---

[1] Botho Friedrich, Count von Wedel, 1862–1943. Lieutenant of Dragoons, 1886. Entered the German Diplomatic Service, 1888. 1st Secretary, Tokyo, 1899; Vienna, 1901. Consul-General in Budapest, 1904–7. Minister to Weimar, 1907–10. Employed in the Foreign Ministry, Berlin, 1910–16. Ambassador to Vienna, 1916–17.

recalled, 'and this was the last occasion when our whole Embassy was collected together. The Ambassador drank the health of the best staff he had ever had and we replied by drinking the health of the best chief we had ever had. We got to Liverpool Street at about eleven o'clock and the small crowd there cheered the Ambassador heartily.'

10

London

1914–1916

As soon as he reached London on 7 August 1914, Rumbold found that his interpretation of the crisis was much sought after. When he went to the Foreign Office on August 8 he was closely questioned by Tyrrell as to whether the war had been planned deliberately by Germany. 'I said no,' he recalled, 'and he said that that was also his impression.' In the account which he wrote at the end of August he set down his view of the responsibilities involved:

It will probably never be known who besides the German war party were really responsible for the war, there being various villains of the piece, two of whom are at Vienna; the one the German Ambassador at Vienna, who by his language egged on the Austrian Government, and the other one of the Austrian Under Secretaries of State, Forgach,[1] a man who was at Belgrade at the time of the Agram trial[2] and who was suspected of having forged documents for use at that trial. He had had to be withdrawn from Belgrade and it was commonly believed that he had taken his revenge by drafting the Austrian Ultimatum to Servia in such terms as to make war inevitable. This man, who was half a Jew, was all the more dangerous by reason of his ability. It will never be known really whether the Germans or the Russians mobilized first.

There was a great deal of hard swearing on both sides, but our impression was that neither the Chancellor nor the Heads of the Foreign Office really wished for war and that the same might be said of the Emperor. But whereas most people in England imagine that the Emperor dominated the situation, such was far from the case. He is not the strong man he is supposed to be and there are many who say that he has lost his nerve. In a crisis of such magnitude and where events moved so rapidly, the difficulty was to recognise the moment at which the civil

[1] Johann, Graf Forgach von Ghymes und Gacs, 1870–1935. Joined the Austro-Hungarian Diplomatic Service, 1892. Minister at Belgrade, 1907–10; Dresden, 1910–13. Head of Division at the Foreign Ministry, Vienna, 1913–17. He pressed for war with Serbia from the moment of the Archduke Franz Ferdinand's assassination. Lived in Hungary from 1918 until his death.

[2] In January 1909 the Austro-Hungarian authorities had charged 53 Serbs resident in Croatia (including 3 priests, 2 doctors and 7 schoolteachers) with conspiracy against the State. The trial was held in the Croatian capital, Agram (later called Zagreb) in March. None of the 300 witnesses proposed by the defence was allowed to appear. In *The Southern Slav Question* (1911), the historian R. W. Seton-Watson described the trial as 'one of the grossest travesties of justice in modern times'. The accused were sentenced to imprisonment with hard labour, but later released on appeal.

authorities were to hand over to the military authorities. We knew that the military authorities had been urging the German Government to issue a decree of mobilisation at least five days before it actually appeared.

And so one is forced to the conclusion that the German Government, helped on by the military, drifted into the situation in which it found itself. There was no strong man to say to Europe in the early stages of the crisis that Germany would not allow herself to be dragged into a European war by Austria. The war fever was so high from the first in Berlin that it seemed to sweep everything away with it.

Two or three factors stand out; one is, that Austria was determined to fight Servia and that she was foolish enough to believe that she could do so without interference from outside. Another fact is that the Germans never thought that we would really come in against them. When we did so, it was an absolute facer to them and explained the fury of the mob. A man who went about in Berlin the night of the declaration of war told me that he had seen groups of Germans standing about absolutely dumbfounded by the news; they realised that, now that we had come in, it was a life and death struggle for them and probably a good few appreciated the fact that they would eventually be ruined.

During his first two months in London, Rumbold was often asked about the part played by the Kaiser in the crisis. 'Whilst the Emperor has been a driving force in building up the German Navy and in other directions,' he recalled, 'it would be a great mistake to suppose that he is also the controlling force in Germany. He is surrounded by a crowd of very mediocre men, so that his superiority is all the more apparent. It was freely said that he had lost his nerve and that he in reality shrank from war.' When Rumbold put this view to Leo Maxse, the editor of the *National Review*, he received a curt rebuttal of his arguments. 'What you say about the activity of the War party in Germany is most interesting,' Maxse wrote on September 19, 'but the world will and must hold the German Emperor primarily responsible for the war because at any moment he could have stopped the crisis. . . . Of course we know that the German Emperor is a great actor and not a great man, also that he is a coward, but he has posed as the Mailed Fist, and the War Lord and he won't be able to pass himself off on the public as an injured innocent. I hear that Cassel and the Jews have already begun to intrigue to try and save Germany from the consequences of her venture should it fail, reserving to themselves of course the right to uphold her should she ultimately win, which our Potsdam Party now deems improbable. These gentry will require very careful watching because they are hand in glove with prominent Ministers with whom they have probably had financial relations.' Rumbold appears to have expressed some sympathy with Maxse's eccentric ideas. 'I am glad to find', Maxse wrote again on September 30, 'that we are in hearty agreement on the subject of German Jews, by whom our Privy Council is infested.[1] I suspect some of them to be little better than spies.'

Anti-German feeling was strong among diplomats. From the British Legation in Berne, Evelyn Grant-Duff[2] wrote to Rumbold on October 20: 'The northern Swiss are pro-pigdog but the French & Italian Swiss are behaving well. I am fighting the German Press campaign tooth & nail.' Grant-Duff's brother[3] had already been killed in action. 'The Regiment simply loved him', Grant-Duff wrote, ' & I think that if they ever get to work with their bayonets among the Pig-dogs the swines' blood will simply run.' 'If I can,' he declared, 'I will get his blood back drop by drop. Meanwhile in my little sphere I am hunting with the quiet persistence of a stoat.'

At the end of September Rumbold's third child, a daughter, was born. She was christened Bridget Margherita. Rumbold's former colleague, Captain Henderson, who had been interned in Holland,[4] wrote to congratulate him: 'I recognise the importance of a second son to you, but for my own part I prefer daughters. – I've no use for sons, the're a d-d nuisance & cost a lot for very little return.'

Rumbold's work in Berlin during July had marked him out as someone capable of working calmly and thoroughly during a period of crisis. He expected his next posting to be at Ministerial level, and to a capital of importance. But by the end of 1914 such diplomatic posts were few, for the Ambassadors and their staffs had returned from three capitals, Berlin, Vienna and Constantinople, to be joined, at the end of 1915, by those from Sofia. At the beginning of 1915 Grey asked Rumbold to take charge of the diplomatic exchanges concerning all British civilians and prisoners of war interned in Germany. For seventeen months he worked at the Foreign Office as head of the Prisoners' Department. His first political chief was

---

[1] There were only two German-born Jews in the Privy Council in 1914, Sir Ernest Cassel and Sir Edgar Speyer, both bankers. The other three Jewish Privy Councillors were all British born, Sir Rufus Isaacs, Sir Alfred Mond and Sir Herbert Samuel.

[2] Evelyn Mountstuart Grant-Duff, 1863–1926. Entered Diplomatic Service, 1888. Consul-General, Budapest, 1911–13. Minister to the Swiss Confederation, 1913–16. Knighted, 1916.

[3] Adrian Grant-Duff, 1869–1914. 2nd Lieutenant, Black Watch, 1889. Major, 1907. Assistant Secretary (Military), to the Committee of Imperial Defence, 1910–13, when he helped to prepare the War Book, which co-ordinated the action to be taken by the various Government Departments on the outbreak of war. Lieutenant-Colonel, 1914. Killed in action on the Western Front, September 14, 1914, while commanding a Battalion.

[4] Henderson had been interned in Holland on October 10, 1914, while in command of the 1st Naval Brigade (Royal Naval Division) at the defence of Antwerp. He and his men had retreated across the Dutch border in the face of overwhelming German forces.

Lord Robert Cecil,[1] who was succeeded early in 1916 by Lord Newton.[2] Rumbold's link with the prisoners of war was a member of the United States Embassy in Berlin, John B. Jackson.[3] Rumbold had to act on behalf of men he had never met, through an intermediary whom he could not confront, for the British public demanded to know that every conceivable exertion was being made on behalf of those who had been captured by the enemy.

The position of British prisoners of war in Germany was a cause for serious concern. On 4 February 1915, Captain Henderson wrote to Rumbold from his internment camp, enclosing an extract from a letter written by a Dutch friend of his. The Dutchman had described his visits to three prisoner of war camps in Germany, at Ruhleben, Doberitz and Burg. 'Burg', he wrote '(where I saw poor Colonel Gordon[4]) was simply awful – the hatred towards England in Germany is simply incredible and I am afraid the poor prisoners have to suffer for it.' Rumbold made what enquiries he could about each complaint which he received. These he passed on to Jackson in Berlin. Jackson did not always accept Rumbold's protests. On March 23, after speaking to Colonel Gordon at Burg, he wrote to Rumbold insisting that Gordon himself 'seemed to think that the letters containing reports of the bad treatment of prisoners should not be taken too seriously, as in his opinion many of them are written by men who are suffering from the nervous strain to which they had been subjected, and who exaggerate unintentionally'. But Rumbold continued, in his letters to Jackson, to give the details of alleged ill-treatment against specific individuals. 'If you will read the Debates in both Houses of Parliament on the

[1] Lord Edgar Algernon Robert Cecil, 1864–1958. Third son of the 3rd Marquess of Salisbury. Independent Conservative MP, 1911–23. Under-Secretary of State for Foreign Affairs, 1915–16. Minister of Blockade, 1916–18. Created Viscount Cecil of Chelwood, 1923. Lord Privy Seal, 1923–24. President of the League of Nations Union, 1923–45. Chancellor of the Duchy of Lancaster, 1924–27. Nobel Peace Prize, 1937.

[2] Thomas Wodehouse Legh, 1857–1942. Elder son of 1st Baron Newton. Conservative MP, 1886–99. Succeeded his father as 2nd Baron, 1899. Paymaster-General, 1915–16. Controller of the Prisoners of War Department, Foreign Office, 1916–19. He published Lord Lansdowne: A Biography in 1929 and his own memoirs, Retrospection in 1941.

[3] John Brinckerhoff Jackson, 1862–1920. Entered the US Navy, 1885. Admitted to the New York Bar, 1889. Entered the US Foreign Office, 1890. Minister at Athens, Belgrade and Bucharest, 1902–7; to Teheran, 1907–9; to Havana, 1909–11; to Athens, Belgrade and Bucharest, 1911–13. Resigned from the Foreign Service, 1913. Served as a voluntary assistant at the US Embassy, Berlin, 1914–1917, in charge of the British section.

[4] William Eagleson Gordon, 1866–1941. 2nd Lieutenant, Gordon Highlanders, 1888. Served in the Chitral Campaign, 1895, when he was wounded, and in the South African War, 1899–1902, when he was dangerously wounded and awarded the Victoria Cross. In August 1914 he went to France, as the senior Major, 1st Battalion, Gordon Highlanders. Taken prisoner, August 26, 1914. The Germans forged a letter, purporting to be signed by him on September 19, 1914, alleging that the Gordons had been issued with flat-nosed ammunition before crossing to France. In 1916 he was exchanged for Prince Salm Salm, and returned to England. He commanded No. 1 District Scottish Command, 1917–20.

treatment of prisoners of war in Germany,' he wrote on April 29, 'you will see what feeling there is in the country on the subject.' But Jackson, having visited each of the camps, was unimpressed by the mounting British complaints. 'An angel from heaven', he wrote from Berlin on April 30, 'could not satisfy all the prisoners at Ruhleben, unless he opened the gate and told them all to leave – and even then a goodly number might wish to remain. . . . *All* the prisoners would like more and different food, but none of them look as if they actually need it, and I have found very few men who claim that they have been actually badly treated themselves, although many begin by saying that others have been.'

Rumbold continued to protest. On May 31 he wrote to Jackson, enclosing copies of letters received in England from relatives interned in Ruhleben. 'They all contain the same complaint,' Rumbold pointed out, 'viz. that they are short of food.' In the same letter he protested that an officer at Gutersloh camp had complained 'that now they are only allowed to write one letter a month and three postcards'. Jackson replied on May 11:

In regard to the treatment of prisoners of war I can only say that we investigate all complaints as soon as possible and that the German military authorities, with whom we confer with absolute frankness, seem ready to do all in their power to improve conditions. . . .

In so far as dates are given in the extracts from letters which you enclosed in yours of May 3rd, I note that they are all prior to my visit to England when the Germans believed that their interned fellow-countrymen were being badly treated. Conditions generally have improved since that time, but Englishmen will obviously never be satisfied with the food which is furnished to them in the camps, as there is little on which they can *chew* and as soup digests so quickly that they never feel satiated. The soup is nourishing, however, and almost without exception the men whom I have seen look in good physical condition.

As far as correspondence is concerned, the rule is one letter and four post cards a month, and it takes an army of censors to pass them as it is. Exceptions are frequently made when there is a special reason for extra letters.

As to complaints of bad treatment, we hear of none *in the camps* at present, although there have been complaints regarding treatment of men when en route from the front, and to these we always call attention. For the first time, at Gottingen on Saturday, I heard of a man having been 'tied to a stake' – but not from any one who had been punished in that way, and the man who spoke to me of the matter said that there was no question of torture.

This defence of conditions in the camps crossed with a letter which Rumbold sent to Berlin on May 13:

Of course I need hardly say that there is no reflection on your partiality, but it appears to me that the treatment of prisoners of war falls into two divisions, i.e., their treatment after capture and until they reach the detention camps, and their treatment in detention camps. You can more or less supervise the latter but you cannot control the former.

Unfortunately we have ample evidence, based upon sworn statements, to show that great brutalities have been practised on British prisoners of war after capture, amounting in many cases to murder. The public will naturally fasten on to these stories, and the question of prisoners in detention camps will recede into the background. Moreover since the sinking of the 'Falaba' and the 'Lusitania', and the use of poisonous gases, etc.,[1] feeling in this country is so high that people will be reluctant to believe any good of a German. One cannot wonder at it. If in private life some member of one's family are in the hands of an outlaw of the worst class one would feel apprehension on their behalf. This I think sums up the situation here, though no doubt you will have gathered this for yourself.

Recent events in this country have shown the desirability of interning all male Germans, but I do not know whether this will be done.

The British decision to intern German citizens made Jackson's work in Berlin more difficult. But he made continuous efforts on the prisoners' behalf, and followed up each of Rumbold's specific complaints. During several tours of the camps in May and June, he sent Rumbold a series of reports in which he insisted that conditions had improved. On July 14 Rumbold wrote to Jackson to say that 'a considerable change has taken place in the feeling over here as regards the treatment of our Prisoners of War. . . . I think most people are quite satisfied that there has been a great improvement in the German detention camps . . . you can rest assured that all the work you are doing is fully appreciated.' The Foreign Office issued copies of Jackson's reports on conditions in the camps to the Press; this did much to allay anxiety.

Jackson's reports to Rumbold stressed the more comforting aspects of imprisonment. On May 23 he had sent a report of a visit which he had made to Ruhleben on the previous day. He had had tea 'with English white bread', and attended a Musical Review: 'There were at least four hundred people in the "theatre", but not a single German officer, soldier or official.' Once a week, he reported, 'the "theatre" (under the grand stand of the race course) is used for a prayer meeting, but almost every other evening (from 6 to 8) the stage is used for a lecture or a dramatic or musical performance of some kind. Outside the theatre last night some negroes were entertaining several hundred more men with songs and banjo music.' For the previous ten days many of the prisoners of war and

---

[1] The unarmed British steamship *Falaba* had been torpedoed on March 28, 1915; the *Lusitania* on May 7, 1915, both with heavy loss of civilian life. Poison gas had first been used, by the Germans, in the Ypres salient on April 22, 1915.

certain internees had been busy with field sports. 'There were over eleven hundred entries for these sports,' Jackson wrote, 'which would appear to contradict the stories that men are starving. That there should be such a number of entries from about four thousand men of from seventeen to fifty-five years of age, would seem to indicate a good average state of health.'

In July Jackson went to the theatrical entertainment at Doberitz camp. 'The men at Doberitz', he wrote to Rumbold on July 6, 'are apparently in good health and spirits, although more or less all of them would like new uniforms, particularly boots. I went out about seven, and found several cricket games going on, and when I left the camp, about ten, groups of men were sitting around candles playing "Crown and Anchor pitch" for pennies. . . . The present "theatre" at Doberitz has been in use for about two months, and something is "put on" about once a fortnight. Last night's show has run five nights already. Before the theatre was arranged, performances had taken place in the men's quarters.' As part of the printed programme there were several 'advertisements'. One of them contained the sentence: 'Nobody allowed to receive more than 10 parcels per day, except the C.I.V.'s, who may receive unlimited numbers.' Jackson explained to Rumbold that the abbreviation 'C.I.V.' 'means "Churchill's Innocent Victims", – the name by which the men of the Royal Naval Division (Antwerp) are known'.

Throughout 1915 and 1916 Rumbold corresponded with Jackson on the question of the return of various types of prisoner of war: severely wounded men, ship's boys, army doctors and civilians under seventeen or over fifty-five. Rumbold also initiated discussions between Jackson and the Germans for the mutual release of unfit civilians; the reduction of overcrowding in the camps; and the provision of proper clothing for prisoners during the winter months. Above all, Rumbold kept a close watch on all complaints of ill-treatment, co-ordinating all military questions with Sir Herbert Belfield[1] at the War Office. Belfield was much concerned by the constant German reluctance to answer some of Jackson's more severe complaints. 'Had the Germans nothing to be ashamed of', he wrote to Rumbold on August 22, 'they would not be so touchy. We here should feel more confidence as to the state of affairs if we heard of what is wrong as well as what is right.' Rumbold passed on Belfield's specific complaints to Jackson, commenting in his letter of August 24 that nothing

---

[1] Herbert Eversley Belfield, 1857–1934. Entered Army, 1876. Chief Staff Officer, Ashanti War, 1895–96. Lieutenant-Colonel, South Africa, 1899–1902. Major-General, 1906; Retired from the Army, May 1914, with the rank of Lieutenant-General. Knighted, 1914. Director of Prisoners of War, War Office, 1914–20.

which the Germans did, however horrible, could cause much excitement in Britain. 'Nothing surprises us', he wrote; 'We look upon them here from the highest to the lowest as "beneath the salt". Such instances as the sinking of the *Arabic*[1] and firing on the crew of the E.13 while they were in the water only provoke nausea and increasing contempt.'[2]

On September 14, after the Germans had returned only twelve of the twenty-two invalided soldiers they had agreed to repatriate, Rumbold wrote bitterly to Jackson: 'The result is very unfortunate for it seems useless for the Germans to promise to send back a certain number when they fail to do so. The consequence is we cannot attach any faith to German promises.' Rumbold was also angered because Jackson often seemed, to him, to take the German view. Yet he was the only official link the British had with the prisoners. 'Of course I know that he is a pro-German,' Rumbold wrote to Sir Louis Mallet[3] on September 5, 'but I am not certain as such he is not more useful to us than if he were anti-German. He gets off his pro-German proclivities on to me in his weekly letters but I don't mind and I give it him back.' On November 20 Jackson urged Rumbold to recognize 'that there is an earnest desire almost everywhere to improve matters and to make things as tolerable as circumstances admit. When you criticize the food, you should remember that even *we* are obliged to go without meat on two days of the week (although we have oysters and lobsters in its place) and that my own ration of bread is only 250 grammes – plenty to live on but not enough to waste.' On 7 January 1916, he wrote of a visit to Gutersloh camp, that during four hours 'I did not hear a single complaint' and that the officers there 'do not wish to go to any other camp'. When Rumbold pointed out that the number of complaints reaching him in London showed no sign of falling, Jackson replied, on January 31, that he expected the number of complaints actually to increase 'owing merely to the effect which prolonged imprisonment has on nerves and brain'.

[1] The passenger liner *Arabic* was torpedoed by a German submarine on August 19, 1915, while sailing from Liverpool to New York. Thirty-three of the 424 passengers and crew were drowned, including two United States citizens.

[2] On August 19 the British submarine E 13 had been grounded on its way to the Baltic. While the submarine was aground a German destroyer fired on her with all guns and the captain, Lieutenant-Commander Layton, gave orders to abandon ship. While the crew were in the water they were again fired upon by machine-guns and mortars. A Danish torpedo boat managed to place itself between the submarine and the destroyer, which thereupon ceased fire. The Danish ship then rescued the British crew, who were interned in Denmark for the rest of the war.

[3] Louis du Pan Mallet, 1864–1936. Entered Foreign Office, 1888. Private Secretary to Sir Edward Grey, 1905–7. An Assistant Under-Secretary of State for Foreign Affairs, 1907–13. Knighted, 1912. Ambassador in Constantinople, 1913–14. Employed in the Foreign Office, 1914–20.

On January 18 Rumbold wrote sternly to Jackson, for communication to the German authorities:

. . . we are disgusted to realise that the Germans actually did try to make some of our prisoners of war work in munition factories. This is an outrage and one of the worst things the Germans have done. The matter is now being considered by our authorities here and I should not be surprised if we adopted retaliatory measures should the Germans dare to do such a thing again. It is just as well that the Germans should realise that there is a limit to what we will stand and that they have fully if not quite reached that limit.

Another thing which the Germans would do well to realise is that in this country alone we hold many thousands more Germans both military and civil (the latter including thousands of reservists) than the Germans hold British. If we take the whole British Empire into account the disparity increases still more. German property held in the British Empire far exceeds the value of British property held by the Germans so if the authorities decide going for retaliatory measures we could hit the Germans harder than they could hit us. They had better ponder over this before committing any follies.

Six days later Rumbold wrote to Jackson again:

. . . I am afraid that any satisfaction felt by our authorities here at knowing that British prisoners of war were specially pleased with a particular Commandant would be completely discounted by the indignation aroused at hearing that British prisoners of war in Germany had been imprisoned for refusing to work in munition factories. The above is all the more true of the British public. If a man behaves decently on one day, but does something particularly villainous on the next, the world at large will judge him by his bad actions.

It is useless to shut one's eyes to the fact that there is an increasing anxiety in this country with reference to the future in store for British prisoners of war in Germany. It is not so much the fear that the Germans will starve our prisoners of war, because, after all, we cannot expect them to feed their prisoners better than their own soldiers, beside which, such an enormous quantity of parcels of food are sent to Germany every day, that we feel that the prisoners are getting enough to eat. But the feeling is really one of acute concern for what might happen to the prisoners of war in the future. The train of reasoning is that the Germans have given so many illustrations of 'frightfulness' both on land and sea, that they may possibly indulge in 'frightfulness' at the expense of the British prisoners of war. I do not wish to shock you as a neutral, by telling you all these forebodings, but it may be useful to you to know what is the feeling over here from top to bottom.

Rumbold continued to write to Jackson about the many individual cases, whether of ill-treatment or of repatriation, that were brought to the Government's attention. In many cases, Jackson was able to arrange for improved conditions, and for prisoners to return. The British Government reciprocated; but mutual suspicions and recriminations were commonplace. Each of Rumbold's weekly letters contained some accusation of German bad faith in individual cases; Jackson's letters almost equally often gave examples of alleged British duplicity in refusing specific exchanges. Rumbold was fully conscious of the special difficulties of prisoners of war. 'When a man knows that he is in for a definite term, he can chalk off the days as they go by', he wrote to Jackson on April 17, 'and knows he has an exact number of days or weeks still remaining before he completes his sentence. But with prisoners of war the case is different. They are detained for an indefinite period and in the nature of things they cannot possibly know how long that period is to last. Moreover they cannot receive papers from their own country.' Rumbold remained pessimistic as to the future of the prisoners. 'At one time many of us thought that when the Germans realised, or began to realise, that they were going to be beaten, they would mend their ways as far as possible in regard to their treatment of our prisoners', he wrote to Jackson on August 28; 'I have now come to the conclusion, and so have many others, that as the game goes more and more against the Germans they will become desperate and not hesitate to commit further atrocities.'

Sir Edward Grey had decided that the time had come to give Rumbold a Ministerial posting. In April he offered to send him to Copenhagen, but Lord Newton intervened. 'Have managed to get Rumbold kept back here for a month', he wrote in his diary on May 5 'in view of uncertainty about prisoners.' In July Grey asked Rumbold to go as Minister to Berne. Newton tried once more to keep him in England, but was unsuccessful. 'Rumbold after all is to go to Berne', he wrote in his diary on August 10, 'none of the others being considered sufficiently efficient.' It was, he added, a 'hideous nuisance'. Rumbold learned of his promotion after a visit to the Western Front, where he had watched the Germans shelling British positions on the Somme. His appointment to Switzerland, he wrote to Sir Edward Goschen on August 26, 'was rather a bomb shell which burst on me on my return from France. . . . I look forward with some apprehension to my new work. As far as I can make out Berne is an uncommonly difficult post just now and if I can stick out the War there without breaking my neck I shall consider myself lucky.'

A spate of congratulatory letters reached Rumbold after his appointment was announced. 'I expect it is pretty difficult & not very pleasant dealing with those d-d Swiss', Lord Granville[1] wrote from Paris on September 5;

---

[1] Granville George Leveson Gower, 1872–1939. Succeeded his father as 3rd Earl Granville, 1891. Entered Diplomatic Service, 1893. Counsellor of Embassy in Berlin, 1911–13; in Paris, 1913–17. British Diplomatic Agent, Salonica, 1917. Minister in Athens, 1917–21; in Copenhagen, 1921–26 and at The Hague, 1926–28. Ambassador in Brussels, 1928–33.

'At least you will be able to have the pleasure of cutting Bosches in the street ! !' The Chief Naval Censor, Sir Douglas Brownrigg,[1] wrote from the Admiralty on August 8, congratulating 'all Britishers' on the appointment, 'as I am very confident that our interests will be "well & truly" upheld by you – I have always felt that about you.' Conyngham Greene, who had been Minister in Berne from 1901 to 1905, wrote from Tokyo on September 7: 'It is a great thing to get your first post as Minister in Europe, as it will save you from exile. . . . In any case they owed you something nice after your misfortune at Berlin.'

[1] Douglas Egremont Robert Brownrigg, 1867–1939. Entered the Navy as a cadet, 1881. Succeeded his father as Baronet, 1900. Naval Attaché, Peking and Tokyo, 1910–12. Chief Censor at the Admiralty, 1914–18. Rear-Admiral, 1919. He published his wartime memoirs, *Indiscretions of the Naval Censor*, in 1920.

Berne

1916–1919

In asking Rumbold to go as British Minister to Switzerland, Sir Edward Grey had written, on 15 August 1916, of the post's 'extreme importance' since the outbreak of war. After six months in Berne, Rumbold explained what this 'importance' was in a letter to his mother-in-law, Lady Fane. 'Switzerland', he wrote to her on 12 February 1917, was a 'clearing house for intelligence' and from Berne he was 'able to keep the FO well supplied with news about all our enemies'. With no British Embassies in Vienna, Berlin or Sofia, it was his responsibility, he explained, 'to supply, as best I can, the news which would otherwise be sent from them.' But, he continued, 'that is not all. We are well situated here to report on Poland, Turkey etc. In fact my parish embraces the larger part of Europe. I sit in my room like a spider and attract every day news and information which would keep a diplomatist in pre-war days going for a month.' 'It is all-absorbing', he wrote, 'and you can imagine how I revel in it'.

In daily letters, in frequent telegrams, sometimes in five or six despatches in a single day, he kept the Foreign Office informed on a vast range of topics, and many of his reports were circulated to the War Cabinet. A month after he reached Berne the French Ambassador, Jean-Baptiste Beau,[1] told him, as he reported to Eric Drummond[2] on October 3, 'that when my appointment was first announced here, the Swiss Government was frightened to death, for they thought that our Government were sending them an official of the Prussian type, who would hector and bully them. In his opinion, the fright which the Swiss Government had had would be salutary for them. When I first arrived, I noticed myself that the Swiss were rather nervous. . . .' Rumbold found that he was soon on good

---

[1] Jean-Baptiste Paul Beau, 1857–1927. Governor-General of Indo-China, 1902–7. Minister to Brussels, 1908–11. Ambassador to Berne, 1911–19. On June 29, 1917, Rumbold wrote to Sir James Drummond that Beau 'always takes the line of least resistance and he has the misfortune of being worse served than any Ambassador I have ever met. His staff are a bye-word for inefficiency.'

[2] James Eric Drummond, 1876–1951. Entered the Foreign Office, 1900; Private Secretary to Sir Edward Grey, 1915–16, and to A. J. Balfour, 1916–18. Knighted, 1916. Attached to the British Delegation at the Paris Peace Conference, 1919. Secretary-General of the League of Nations, 1919–33. British Ambassador in Rome, 1933–39. Succeeded his half-brother as 16th Earl of Perth, 1937. Deputy Leader of the Liberal Party in the House of Lords, 1947.

terms with the Swiss Foreign Minister, Hermann-Arthur Hoffman,[1] and was able to impress upon him how important it was for Britain to maintain the blockade of Germany, even where this involved hardship for neutrals. Rumbold noted one reason why Hoffman was prepared to listen patiently, and even sympathetically, to the British view. 'I understand', he wrote to Drummond, 'that the Swiss Government are rather bored with the German Minister[2] who constantly goes and bullies them about all sorts of things.'

Throughout his time at Berne Rumbold reported any rumour which he could glean which might have the slightest possibility of truth in it. On October 6, to Lord Newton, he sent news of a particular 'Austrian Jew and possibly an enemy spy, but a man who is well thought of in radical circles', who had told the British Consul in Basle, George Beak,[3] 'that he overheard two Germans on a Bâle train the other day anticipating that an attempt would shortly be made on the life of Mr Lloyd George'. Newton replied four days later: 'I sent the warning about Ll. George to Scotland Yard. I almost wish that there was something in it!'[4]

'Continue as much as possible with political scraps', Theo Russell wrote to Rumbold on November 7, 'as they are sent to all the Big Guns from the King downwards. Anything to do with the internal conditions of Germany and Austria-Hungary is read with avidity.' On December 6 Rumbold informed Grey that a German socialist who had just reached Switzerland had said that the Germans were 'sick of war' and that a German victory was 'out of the question'. Coming so soon after the German

[1] Hermann-Arthur Hoffman, 1857–1927. Lawyer and parliamentarian. Head of the Swiss Radical Party. Member of the Council of States, 1896–1911; and of the Federal Council, 1911–17. Minister for Foreign Affairs, 1914–17. President of the Swiss Federation, 1914.

[2] Gisbert Freiherr von Romberg, 1866–1939. Entered the Foreign Service, 1889. Served in Vienna, 1897–1901. Consul-General, Sofia, 1905; Minister in Sofia, 1909. Minister in Berne, 1912–18. Head of the Eastern Department of the German Foreign Ministry, April–June 1919. On November 14, 1916, Rumbold wrote to Lord Newton: 'Romberg . . . said that I was an old friend of his. I said . . . I could no longer consider Romberg, or any other German I had known, as a friend.'

[3] George Bailey Beak, 1872–1934. Schoolmaster; Assistant Master, Lancing College, 1895. Served in the South African War, 1899–1902. Vice-Consul, Katanga, 1911. Consul, Genoa, 1911–13; Zanzibar, 1913–14; Venice, 1915; Basle, 1916. Acting Consul-General, Zurich, 1917–19. Consul-General, Frankfurt-on-Main, 1919–20; Prague, 1920; Lisbon, 1921; Seville, 1923–27; Leipzig, 1928–31; the Eastern Seaboard States of the United States (based on Boston), 1931–33.

[4] A plot to poison Lloyd George was actually discovered at the beginning of 1917. All the conspirators were English pacifists; their aim in trying to kill Lloyd George was to force his successor to abandon Conscription. The conspirators had received neither encouragement nor assistance from the Germans and were caught before they could attempt the assassination. Their leader, Mrs Weeldon, was sentenced to ten years' penal servitude.

victories over Rumania, and the heavy British losses on the Somme, such information was cheering to the Government, and Grey caused it to be circulated to all senior Cabinet Ministers.

On December 7 Lloyd George replaced Asquith as Prime Minister. Grey was succeeded as Foreign Secretary by A. J. Balfour. 'I give this Govt a short lease of life', Lord Newton wrote to Rumbold on December 9, 'and then an election which will bring about an inconclusive peace.' People at the Foreign Office, he added, were relieved that Lord Curzon had not been appointed Foreign Secretary. 'All the same,' he commented, 'I don't think the choice of AJB a happy one.' Three days later Newton wrote again: 'No one quite knows what is going to happen here. Balfour is going apparently to begin by 3 weeks rest! and I feel some doubt as to whether he will ever get there....In a few months time, the new Govt will be as unpopular as the old, and my belief is that we and every other country will fall into the hands of the socialists before we are very much older. Asquith & his crowd will join with the Irish and the Labour people and constitute a solid opposition which will gradually become a stop the war opposition.'

At the end of 1916 the Germans offered to open peace negotiations. A mood of depression in England made many people receptive to talk of peace. Rumbold did not approve; despite the often adverse military situation, he was convinced that Britain would win in the end, and deprecated a negotiated settlement. 'If ever I feel depressed', he wrote to Newton on December 4, 'I think of the last sentence of a letter from somebody in Germany to a German outside which recently came before our notice. It said "who would have thought that England could have brought us to such a pass".' 'I hope we shall turn down this latest peace offer', he wrote to Newton nine days later: 'Bethmann Hollweg is a knave and an imposter of the first order.' Rumbold was convinced that 'the serious economic conditions of the Central Empires is at the bottom of this peace offer'. He was also convinced, he added, 'that although we shall have to make great sacrifices, we must kill and maim two million Germans at least before we have done with them'.

In almost daily telegrams to Balfour and Hardinge[1] at the Foreign Office, Rumbold reported on the reiterated desire of all the Germans then in Switzerland for a negotiated peace. 'The Rhine-whine is very audible now,' he wrote to Newton on December 19, 'but I hope that nobody in any of the countries of the Entente will listen to it.' 'To my mind', he wrote to Lord Hardinge on the same day, 'the position of Germany is in

[1] Hardinge, who had been Viceroy of India from 1910 to 1916, returned to the Foreign Office in May 1916 as Permanent Under-Secretary of State.

some respects precisely similar to that of Japan at the time of the conclusion of the Treaty of Portsmouth. At that moment, Japan was in reality fought to a standstill. The rice crop which is of such importance to the Japanese had been a failure. The effectives of the Russian army in Manchuria were considerably larger than those of the Japanese army. This is what the late Count Komura told me himself. In these circumstances the intervention of the American President[1] was a perfect god-send to the Japanese. It is true that the Germans are still prosecuting their adventures in Rumania but in other respects their position to my mind is the same as that of the Japanese, as described above. You have to substitute the failure of the potato crop for that of the rice crop. In the present case I hope there will be no question of American intervention and we are all anxiously waiting to hear what answer will be returned to the peace proposals of the Central Empires.' Lloyd George rejected the German peace proposals. In Berne, Rumbold took the initiative in impressing upon the Swiss Government, as he wrote to Newton on December 21, that the British 'were bound to win, owing to our superiority in reserves and munitionment'. Newton was due to visit Switzerland shortly. 'It is absolutely essential', Rumbold wrote, 'that you should speak in the same sense here when you come out.'

Businessmen and diplomats coming from Germany provided Rumbold with an encouraging stream of news, which he invariably passed on to London. 'Morale of people is low . . . ,' he informed Balfour on 1 February 1917, 'nobody thinks or talks of anything but peace.' Two days later he wrote of how an outbreak of scurvy was 'said to be causing great and increasing havoc on large towns and industrial areas of Northern and North Western Germany'; that stocks of cereals had risen, but that meat and potatoes were in diminishing supply. On February 6 he telegraphed again, reporting the opinion of two German bankers then in Switzerland 'that hopes of German victory are discounted in intelligent circles'. On February 10 the Danish Minister in London,[2] who had just come from Berlin, told Rumbold – with whom he had long been on friendly terms – 'that he could never forget the wistful and hungry look in the eyes of the population', but that the patriotism of the German people 'would induce them to hold out for some time longer'. Rumbold telegraphed this information to London that same day.

Rumbold's confidence in an eventual British victory pervaded all his

[1] Theodore Roosevelt, 1858–1919. Twenty-sixth President of the United States, 1901–10. As a result of his efforts to bring peace between Japan and Russia in 1905 he was awarded the Nobel Prize for peace. He was the first head of state to send an international dispute for settlement at the International Court of Arbitration at The Hague.

[2] Henrik de Grevenkop Castenskjold, 1862–1921. Entered the Danish Diplomatic Service, 1888. Minister in both Vienna and Rome, 1910–12; Minister in London, 1912–21.

correspondence. On 6 January 1917, Sir Edward Goschen replied to one of Rumbold's letters that 'it was a most cheering and encouraging letter in these rather depressing times'. On February 6, following repeated German submarine attacks on American ships, President Wilson[1] broke off diplomatic relations with Germany. Three days later Hardinge wrote to Rumbold of how disappointed the British were that the neutral powers contiguous to Germany – Denmark, Sweden, Holland and Switzerland – had 'not felt justified in following President Wilson's lead'. But, as he wrote, 'one cannot blame them. They are too uncomfortably close to the mad dog which Germany has now become.'

As soon as German–American relations were broken off, the American Ambassador in Berlin, James W. Gerard, and his staff – 120 people in all – passed through Switzerland on their way back to the United States. 'They looked like boys just escaped from an unpleasant school', Rumbold wrote to Lady Fane on February 12. Gerard had spent an hour and a half with Rumbold at the British Legation, and had 'poured a stream of the most absorbing information into my willing ears'. Rumbold's optimism was enhanced by his conversation with Gerard, and he at once sent the Foreign Office details of the increasing food shortages in Germany, and the widespread demoralization there. Gerard had told Rumbold of 'great distresses and suffering' among working people in the towns, as a result of the allied blockade, and of the virtual disappearance of coffee, sugar and fats from the shops. Infant mortality, he said, was 'very high' and 'privations were telling on the health of the people'. Rumbold telegraphed this information to the Foreign Office on February 13. But Gerard had also confirmed, as the Danish diplomat had reported, that the call for patriotism overrode the demoralization of hunger, and that the 'Military Party and Nation are still full of confidence'. Ten days later the United States Consul-General in Hamburg, Harry Morgan,[a] who had only just been allowed to leave Germany, went to see Rumbold with more encouraging news. The morale of German troops in the Hamburg region, he said, 'had deteriorated by 75%; soldiers would subscribe to any peace conditions if only they could get peace'. The Consul-General had even heard German officers criticize the Kaiser 'unsparingly'. Rumbold telegraphed this report to the Foreign Office as soon as the American had left him. The blockade of Germany

[1] Thomas Woodrow Wilson, 1856–1924. Twenty-eighth President of the United States, 1912–21. In 1919 he sought to devise a just and lasting peace treaty. Awarded the Nobel Peace Prize, 1920.

[a] Harry Hays Morgan, 1860–1933. Entered the United States Consular Service, 1882, as Secretary to the Legation in Mexico City. Consul-General, Barcelona, 1910–13; Hamburg, 1913–17. United States Representative in Cuba for war trade and shipping, 1917–19. Consul-General, Antwerp, 1918–19; Brussels, 1919–23; Buenos Aires, 1923–25.

was undoubtedly effective; 'Misery in Germany is intense', Rumbold
telegraphed to London on March 14, after receiving a secret coded
message from Germany, 'and mortality from underfeeding is high. Want
of food is also producing cases of consumption.'

Rumbold's news was correct. The blockade, which had led to some
120,000 German deaths in 1916, led to over 250,000 in 1917, and nearly
300,000 in 1918, sapping civilian morale and encouraging republican,
revolutionary and defeatist tendencies throughout Germany, above all in
the great industrial cities, and the northern ports. 'I have a firm conviction', Rumbold wrote to Lady Fane, 'that we shall "down" the un-
speakable Bosche this year and that there will not be a fourth winter
campaign. I am glad to say that conditions in Prussia are terrible and made
all the worse by this severe winter. But the Bosche must be licked in the field.'

During his wartime years at Berne Rumbold served as the link between
the British Foreign Office and the Polish National Committee, whose
centre was at Lucerne and whose objective was an independent Polish
State. Polish politicians frequently confided in him their national aspirations and their desire to be totally independent both of Russia and
Germany. He did not totally relish his work. The émigré Poles, he wrote
to George Clerk[1] on 9 September 1918, 'are more often than not unreliable
and are simply playing for their own hand. They seem to think that the
Polish question is the only question that counts, quite forgetting the
innumerable other questions which will have to be settled and about which
we are fighting.' Rumbold's letter continued:

We here see a good deal of their jealousies. On the one hand we have the
national committee which arrogates to itself the whole right of representing
Polish opinion abroad and is more and more intolerant of any views differing
from those they hold. On the other hand, we have a certain number of Poles of
various shades of opinion, each of whom maligns the other and states that the
other does not represent any opinion worth considering, but all combining in
hostility to or criticism of the national committee. Whether all these Poles will
pull together, once a Polish kingdom comes into being, remains to be seen, but
my own impression is that Poland will be an hot-bed of intrigue after the war
and that the Germans and Russians will take advantage of this fact. But perhaps
I am rather pessimistic.

While he was in Switzerland Rumbold was helped in his dealings with
the Poles by a member of the Legation who spoke fluent Polish, Frank

---

[1] George Russell Clerk, 1874–1951. Entered Foreign Office, 1899. Senior Clerk, 1913–17.
Knighted, 1917. First British Minister to the Czecho-Slovak Republic, 1919–26; Ambassador
to Turkey, 1926–33; to Belgium, 1933–34; to France, 1934–37.

Savery,[1] who interviewed many of the émigré Poles on Rumbold's behalf, and scrutinized the Polish Press. From these sources, and from his own interviews and enquiries, Rumbold sent regular despatches to London about Polish opinion, and conditions inside Poland. To all the Poles with whom he was in contact, he insisted that the British intended, as Lloyd George had publicly declared, to support a fully independent Poland as soon as Germany was defeated. To Balfour he telegraphed repeatedly with information of German activities inside Poland, pointing out that these activities could only strengthen Polish support for the allied cause. Panic had been created in the Cracow region, he reported on 24 May, 1918, by the German seizure of 20 per cent of the cattle. He also reported on the 'deliberate anti-Jewish policy on the part of Germany' in Russian Poland. Two months later, on July 29, Prince Lubomirski,[2] a member of one of Poland's aristocratic families, came to see him. Rumbold recorded their conversation in a letter to Balfour on the following day:

He said that he was returning to Warsaw in about 10 days time via Vienna and wished to take back with him some message of encouragement to the Polish regents and the Polish Government. The war had gone on for a very long time and the Poles were beginning to be discouraged. They knew that economic conditions in Germany and Austria were very bad and they felt that if matters came to the worst the Poles would be made to die of starvation before the Germans allowed themselves to be famished.

. . . Prince Lubomirski said that the Poles had been greatly heartened by the announcement regarding the re-establishment of Poland made as the outcome of the recent meeting of the Supreme War Council at Versailles. . . . Prince Lubomirski also said that the present successes of the Allied armies on the western front had caused him great gratification.

I told Prince Lubomirski that he should make the utmost of those successes and publish them widely; that he should dwell on the extent of the American effort and of the determination of the Allies not to rest until they had beaten Germany. He should not allow the Poles for one instant to doubt the determination of the Allies to go through with their programme. . . .

Prince Lubomirski hoped that the Allied Governments would not misunderstand the action of the present Polish Government in working with the occupying Powers. The Polish Government thought solely of the interests of Poland and felt that they ought to do what they could for their country.

Prince Lubomirski admitted that he himself had at one time worked for the

[1] Frank Savery, 1883–1965. Employed at the British Legation in Munich, 1911–14; Berne, 1915–19. Consul at Warsaw, 1919–39; Consul General, 1939. Counsellor, HM Embassy to Poland (in London), 1939–45.

[2] Prince Ladislas Lubomirski, 1866–1934. A first cousin of one of the three Regents of German-occupied Poland, Zdzislaw Lubomirski. Owner of estates in White Russia and Galicia. A patron of art and music, Artur Rubinstein was among his protégés.

Austro-Polish solution of the Polish question as a means of escape from German domination, but he had speedily come to the conclusion that Austria was so rotten that such a solution was not desirable. It was no good tying Poland to a corpse. . . .

I asked Prince Lubomirski whether he had been in Poland at the time of the Austrian defeat on the Piave, and what impression it had produced on the Poles. He replied that the latter were so accustomed to hearing that the Austrians had been beaten that they took the last Austrian defeat as a matter of course. He said that although the Germans did their utmost to prevent news of military operations etc. from getting known in Poland there was no doubt that the Poles would learn of the Allied successes on the western front from Austrians who were constantly going from Vienna to Poland. They were smarting under the jeers and sarcasm of the Germans with regard to their defeat on the Piave. Now that the Germans had likewise suffered a serious reverse on the western front the Austrians, from a spirit of 'Schadenfreude' would be certain to rub it in.

I told Prince Lubomirski that he would do well to point out to the regents that the Allies were cooperating in a spirit of the greatest harmony whereas, as the war proceeded, the differences amongst their enemies became more and more acute.

In every meeting with the Poles passing through Switzerland, Rumbold reiterated that neither Austria nor Germany could be trusted, and that if Poland wanted a future as an independent state, it must look to the Allies, whose victory was certain. For Rumbold this insistence upon the inevitability of an allied victory was neither propaganda nor bravado; he believed in it absolutely.

From his vantage-point at Berne, Rumbold was an important source of information about conditions inside Germany and Austria-Hungary. As Hardinge wrote to him on 26 April 1917, Switzerland appeared 'to enjoy the distinction of being a sort of happy hunting ground for all the political malcontents and intriguers of Europe'. A stream of visitors provided Rumbold with his information. Although he refused to speak to Germans face to face, their stories and opinions were quickly reported to him. Not all of it could be reliable. On March 1 he wrote to Newton of contradictory reports from Germany. According to one, 'the hatred of England is dying out, largely owing to our good treatment of German prisoners of war, those who have been repatriated having reported enthusiastically on the subject'. But another report that same week suggested that feeling against England 'is stronger than ever, for all the misfortunes which have overtaken Germany are laid to our door'.

Rumbold himself was convinced that German morale was weakening, and that by maintaining the blockade, and attacking whenever possible, Britain and France must eventually win the war, and might possibly win it soon. 'There have been persistent reports in the last few days', he wrote to the Controller of Commercial and Consular Affairs at the Foreign Office, Victor Wellesley,[1] on March 28, 'of serious riots at Berlin and Hamburg. I was even told that the German Legation had been without news from Berlin for 3 days. There is no smoke without fire and I have little doubt that there have been disturbances. . . . I am convinced that the Germans will only last till the next harvest by putting up with the very greatest sacrifices.' It was difficult to make out, Rumbold continued, 'whether or not the Germans can hold out until the next harvest. I think it is a toss up myself so that if we can hammer them effectively in the course of the summer we may produce a collapse.' From the information reaching him in Berne, Rumbold believed 'that of the four members of the Alliance against us, Austria and Turkey are by far the most exhausted. Bulgaria is "standing by" very uneasy as to the outcome of the war. The Germans are stretched to the absolute limit and cannot make any further efforts as regards men or money.' Rumbold had confidence in his opinions. 'I sit here,' he told Wellesley, 'and day after day all sorts of fat spies walk into my parlour with really good information.' He knew the tendency of informants to tell their listeners what they wanted to hear, but despite this, his belief in Germany's weakness was strong, and made its impact in London. To an American friend, Irwin Laughlin,[2] he wrote on April 4:

I think that we shall break the back of Germany this summer and it will be interesting to see whether they collapse at once or drag on hostilities until the end of the year or even over the winter. Their internal condition is now deplorable and it is even said that the army will go short of food. You know Germany better than I do but do you think that Fritz is the sort of person to have his heart in the fight if he is being underfed? I don't. Good judges prophesy that there will be a revolution in Germany of the very worst kind, one accompanied by massacres of people in high places and which will reproduce in an aggravated form the worst features of the French revolution. I hope this may be so but in any event I feel that we are now assisting at a new 'Götterdämmerung' but that instead of it being a twilight of the gods it is the twilight or eclipse of 'war lords' who are an anachronism. Since I last saw you the Germans

[1] Victor Alexander Augustus Henry Wellesley, 1876–1954. A godson of Queen Victoria; Page of Honour to the Queen, 1887–92. Educated in Germany. Entered Foreign Office, 1899; Superintendent, Treaty Department, 1913–16; Controller of Commercial and Consular Affairs, 1916–19; Counsellor in charge of the Far Eastern Department, 1920–24; Deputy Under-Secretary of State, 1925–36. Knighted, 1926. A painter of landscapes and portraits, his pictures were frequently exhibited at the Royal Academy. He published his memoirs and reflections, *Diplomacy in Fetters*, in 1944

[2] Irwin Boyle Laughlin, 1871–1941. On the staff of the Jones & Laughlin Steel Corporation, 1894–1903. US Consul-General in Bangkok, 1906–7. First Secretary in Berlin, 1909–12; in London, 1912–17. Counsellor of Embassy, London, 1917–19. Minister to Greece, 1924–26. Ambassador to Spain, 1929–33.

have managed to perpetrate even greater bestialities and crimes than before, in fact there seems no limit to their power for evil.

As the Germans intensified the war at sea, sinking not only unarmed merchant ships, and neutral shipping, but also allied hospital ships, Rumbold's hatred of the Germans intensified. In February 1917 the Germans torpedoed the hospital ship *Asturias*, and in March the *Gloucester Castle*. There were no deaths, although the *Gloucester Castle* was carrying 450 wounded soldiers. When the Franco-Russian hospital ship *Portugal* was torpedoed in the Black Sea, 100 non-combatants were killed. 'I think you must make up your mind', Rumbold wrote to Newton on April 2, 'to go to all lengths with the Germans now and not to shrink from shooting some of the most prominent of them.' He noted angrily that 'with the exception of ourselves, all the nations at war are shrinking from the tremendous blood letting which is bound to take place this summer'. Rumbold believed that the next allied offensive on the Western Front would break the German line. Newton was less certain, either of German weakness or of British preparedness, replying on April 7: 'I don't think that our military pundits know in the least what the Hun is going to do. Anyhow he has a big lot of men in reserve, although they may not be of a high class. I should think myself that he would make a desperate effort to smash us, before American intervention has really made itself felt.' Rumbold wanted British ferocity to match that of the Germans. 'I am glad that we at last raided an open town', he wrote to Newton on April 23, 'and wish we had killed a lot more people.'[1]

The allied offensive on the Western Front, which Rumbold believed might be decisive, opened with a British attack east of Arras on April 9, and continued, almost without interruption, and at enormous loss of life on both sides, until the end of the battle of Passchendaele seven months later, on November 10. 'The military news is first rate', Rumbold wrote to his stepmother on April 17, 'and the horrible Boche is at last getting the hammering which is long overdue.' Of thirty German prisoners interviewed after the first phase of the battle, he reported, 'only one expressed belief in a German victory, the rest holding that Germany is done for'. On the following day he wrote to his brother William: 'I am firmly convinced that the Boche will be back to the line of the Meuse – if not beyond it – by June 30 and then you will have 4 months good campaigning weather in which to throw him out of Belgium and finally break his spirit.' For as

---

[1] As a reprisal for the repeated German sinking of unarmed allied ships, on April 14, 1917, thirty-five British and French aeroplanes bombed Freiburg-im-Breisgau. Seven women, three men and one soldier were killed in the raid (and twenty-seven people injured). The university buildings, the new municipal theatre, and several business streets were severely damaged.

long as an allied victory seemed possible in 1917, Rumbold was treated with great respect in Berne. 'The battle of Arras', he informed his brother, 'has produced a considerable impression on the Schweitzers who are feeding out of my hand at the present moment... they consider that the Boche's goose is cooked.'

Rumbold felt that allied propaganda did not sufficiently exploit military successes. Press comments, he wrote critically to Charles Montgomery[1] at the Foreign Office, on April 23, did not seem 'to bring out facts which would impress the Swiss', or other neutrals. The Germans always made journalistic capital out of their successes: 'Why cannot we do the same?' There was one particular story to which he felt special publicity could be given with good advantage to the allied cause. 'I hope that the utmost use will be made', he wrote, 'of that gruesome description of the use to which the Germans put the corpses of their dead. I reported officially some time ago that I had heard that the Germans were turning the bodies of those who had died in hospital at Dresden into soap. I found it difficult to believe this at the time but it appears to be quite true. The point to bring out seems to me to be this, that a nation which will submit to see its dead soldiers turned into soap or fodder for pigs must be on an absolutely lower plain and lost to every vestige of decency. Or it proves that the Germans are even more a race of serfs than we thought they were. But in any event the psychology of the German mind in connection with their disposal of their dead ought to be brought out.'

In March 1917 all allied calculations had been cast into chaos by the revolution in Russia. Following the abdication of the Tsar, a Provisional Government had come to power, of whose intentions little was known, and whose ability to keep Russia in the war was, from the outset, uncertain. 'The Russian Revolution was a regular bombshell', Newton wrote to Rumbold on March 17; 'The great danger is, of course, that if the extreme people get their way, they will stop the war.' Newton was bitter against the Tsar. 'I suppose that, when it is all over, he will come here and live like a retired MP. That seems to be about all he is fit for. It is lamentable when people in high places are deficient in brains: and war finds them out.' By the end of March it was becoming clearer that the influence of the anti-war factions inside Russia was not strong enough to force the new Government to pull Russia out of the war. But on March 24 Newton warned Rumbold that 'we are by no means out of the wood. The

---

[1] Charles Hubert Montgomery, 1876–1942. Entered the Foreign Office, 1900. Précis-writer to Sir Edward Grey, 1905–7 and 1908–10; Marshal of the Ceremonies, 1913–20; Chief Clerk, 1919; Assistant Under-Secretary of State, 1922–30; Deputy Under-Secretary, 1930–33. Knighted, 1927. Minister at The Hague, 1933–38.

revolutionary people are very strong, and the Petrograd regiments seem to have sacked their officers right & left & announce that they will only work 4 hours a day'.

If Germany and Austria could encourage Russia to leave the war, all Germany's military forces could be thrown into the Western Front, and the advantage gained by the Allies at Arras would be put in jeopardy. The Germans and Austrians, Rumbold wrote to his stepmother on April 17, 'are banking on coming to an arrangement with Russia and are moving heaven & earth to bring this about. Amongst other things they have collected a good number of Russian extremists, nihilists etc who were living in exile in this country and have shipped these gentry off to Stockholm via Germany in order to work on the Russian socialists in favour of peace.' Among these 'gentry' was the Bolshevik leader, Lenin,[1] who had been in exile in Switzerland since the early months of the war, and for whom the German Government had on April 9 provided a special train to take him and forty-two fellow Marxists across Germany to Sweden, from where, on April 16, he reached Petrograd. There, he at once demanded an end to the war with Germany. Rumbold had informed the Foreign Office in some detail of these plans. The 'Russian Socialists and anarchists resident in Switzerland', he had telegraphed on April 3, favoured an 'immediate peace with Germany', and would therefore be asked 'to make violent propaganda in this sense amongst working classes in Russia and amongst the troops at the front'. On April 13, he had telegraphed again, to say that Lenin, together with the Swiss socialist, Fritz Platten,[2] and forty-two other Russians, had left Zurich on April 9 for Germany. 'There was a small demonstration at the railway station', he added, 'in favour of departing Russians, and counter-demonstration against them as traitors and German agents.' 'All this sort of thing', Rumbold wrote in his letter of April 17 to his stepmother, 'tends to paralyse the Russian Govern-

---

[1] Vladimir Ilich Ulyanov, 1870–1924. Known as 'Lenin'. Son of an inspector of schools. In 1887 his elder brother was executed for the attempted assassination of Alexander III. Joined a Marxist circle in Kazan, 1887; banished to Siberia, 1897–1900; an émigré in Europe, 1900–5 and 1906–17. Founded the 'Bolshevik' faction of the Russian Social Democratic Labour Party, 1905. Chairman of the Council of People's Commissars (Prime Minister) from the revolution of October 1917 until his death.

[2] Fritz Platten, 1883–1942. The son of a Prussian, he became a Swiss citizen in 1890. Secretary of the Swiss Socialist Party, 1915–19. A close collaborator of Lenin while the latter was in Switzerland, 1915–17, and a leading figure in the Third International. Imprisoned for six months for his part in the Swiss General Strike of 1918. A Deputy in the Swiss National Council, 1918–19 and 1921–22. Secretary of the Swiss Communist Party, 1920–23. Emigrated to the Soviet Union, October 1923, where, with fifty other Swiss Communists, he established a Collective Farm near Lenin's birthplace, Simbirsk. Sentenced by Stalin to four years in a Labour Camp, October 1939, he died in Siberia. He was rehabilitated posthumously by Marshal Bulganin in 1956.

ment for effective purposes. The Russian extremists & pacifists don't or won't realise that the German Govt are using their own Socialists as will-ing tools in order to ensnare their opponents.'

It was several months before Lenin's anti-war agitation gained strength. Rumbold still had faith in a swift allied victory. 'I expect to see the Boches thrown out of France by June 30 at latest', he wrote con-fidently in his letter to his stepmother on April 17. He was even optimistic about Russia, believing that it might still be possible 'to detach Turkey from the alliance against us', as he wrote to Newton on April 23, by persuading Russia to agree to let Turkey keep Constantinople in return for peace. Were Russia to give up the city which Britain and France had promised her in March 1915, Rumbold felt that Turkey would agree that henceforth 'none but Russian warships should pass in and out of the Black Sea'. But the new Russian Government, while willing to continue fighting Germany, did not intend to relinquish the possibility of Russian rule in Constantinople.

In Berne, Rumbold continued to be troubled by emissaries of varying degrees of credibility. An Englishman named Pilling[1] asked Rumbold to send his letters back to England in the security of the diplomatic bag. Rumbold declined to do so. Pilling informed him that these letters went, through two intermediaries, to Lloyd George, and that his 'mission' was an official one. Rumbold was sceptical. 'Whilst there is no harm in Mr Pilling as far as I can see', he wrote to Ronald Campbell[2] on February 27, 'he seems rather a muddle headed person and I do not think he should be playing about in Switzerland interviewing Turks. Amongst others, he has seen the ex-Khedive. These free lances are rather a nuisance.' Campbell replied on March 3 that when Lloyd George had, while Secretary of State for War in 1916, seen Pilling at the War Office, he had 'formed a rather low opinion of him'; that he had passed Pilling on to the General Staff, 'who also gave him no encouragement'; and that neither Lloyd George nor the General Staff had given him 'any sort of mission'. Nevertheless, Pilling had apparently 'persuaded Mr Lloyd George to give instructions for

[1] John Robert Pilling, born 1849. A Manchester solicitor, banker and undischarged bank-rupt. In the 1890s he formed the Syria-Ottoman Railway Company. Only seven miles of line were built; in 1906 Sir Edward Grey refused to allow Pilling to assume the Presidency of the Company. The Germans submitted a counter-claim for the same railway on behalf of Fraülein Therese de Kroelle, with whom, it transpired, Pilling was living at the Pera Palace Hotel in Constantinople. The Foreign Office believed her to be a German agent. In 1915 Pilling had made an unsuccessful claim for £5,000,000 for the loss of his railway interests.
[2] Ronald Hugh Campbell, 1883–1953. Entered Foreign Office, 1907. Private Secretary to the Permanent Under-Secretary of State for Foreign Affairs, 1913–19. Private Secretary to the Foreign Secretary, 1919–20. Minister at Paris, 1929–35; at Belgrade, 1935–39. Knighted, 1936. Ambassador to Paris, 1939–40; to Lisbon, 1940–45.

him to be allowed to proceed to Switzerland. . . . Probably what happened was that he unfolded his plans to the Prime Minister who thought it rubbish, but, not realising the harm that these people can do, saw no reason to prevent him going off and nosing around as a free-lance, if he wanted to.'

Campbell approved Rumbold's decision not to let Pilling use the security of the diplomatic bag. But Pilling persevered in his efforts. In the middle of March he asked the assistant Military Attaché in Berne, Captain Harran,[1] to telegraph direct to the War Office 'that his business was getting on well but that the work involved was too much for him' and that he wanted a lady friend to be sent out 'at once' to assist him. This request was shown to Lloyd George, who gave instructions that 'Pilling should be brought back from Berne – as he is likely to do more harm than good. The Lady . . . will *not* be allowed to join him.'[2] Campbell sent a copy of Lloyd George's wishes to Rumbold. 'It remains to deal with Mr Pilling in the Prime Minister's dictum', he wrote on March 22; 'Lord Hardinge thinks the best plan would be to warn him that, after careful reflexion, the authorities at home (quoting if necessary the Prime Minister) consider it undesirable that he should remain any longer in Switzerland. If that does not have the desired effect the only course would be to impound his passport which would presumably be followed by his expulsion from Switzerland'. Pilling returned to England early in April. But Rumbold's relief at his departure was short-lived. On May 5 Campbell informed him that Pilling had been interviewed on his return to London by the Director of Military Intelligence, Major-General Macdonogh,[3] who had thought him 'fairly reasonable', and was not sure that 'there was not something in what he said'. Pilling persuaded Military Intelligence to let him go back to Switzerland, and to attempt to enter into negotiations with the Turks. 'He has been allowed to go', Campbell explained, 'on the understanding that he had no official mission, and that he makes this clear to any Turks he may meet.' What had impressed the War Office about Pilling was his belief that Djemal Pasha,[4] who commanded the Turkish

---

[1] Edward Bela Harran, born 1878. Lieutenant, British Expeditionary Force, March 1915; Captain, 1917. Assistant Military Attaché, Berne, September 1917–July 1918. Military Control Officer, New York, 1918–21.

[2] Lloyd George's instructions were sent by his Private Secretary David Davies on March 21 to Brigadier-General Cockerill, Director of Special Intelligence at the War Office.

[3] George Mark Watson Macdonogh, 1865–1942. Entered Army, 1884; Major-General, 1916. Director of Military Intelligence, 1916–18. Knighted, 1917. Lieutenant-General, 1919. President of the China Association, 1930–35. President of the Federation of British Industries, 1933–34. Member of the Central Committee for the Regulation of Prices, 1939–41.

[4] Ahmed Djemal, 1872–1922. Member of the Young Turk triumvirate, 1908. Military Governor of Constantinople, 1913. Minister of Marine, 1914. Commanded the 4th Army in Syria, November 1914. Fled Turkey, 1918. Assassinated by Armenians in Georgia.

army in Syria, might be induced to hand over Jerusalem to the British without a fight. He believed that another leading Turkish politician, Talaat Pasha,[1] could also be persuaded, particularly if bribed, to make peace. Pilling also told Macdonogh that Bulgaria would join the Turks in any anti-German revolt. These possibilities were enticing to the War Office, for the war against Turkey was not going well. In Mesopotamia a vast allied army was making only slow advances; in Palestine the capture of Jerusalem seemed a long way off. They therefore instructed Pilling to return to Switzerland and enter into negotiations with the Turks.

Rumbold tried to prevent Pilling's return to Switzerland. 'The Germans will shadow him very closely', he warned Campbell on May 14, for Pilling on his earlier visit had been far from discreet in his contacts. But unknown to Rumbold, Pilling had already returned to Switzerland, and had given a letter for Talaat to the Turkish Legation there. On June 7 Rumbold wrote to Campbell with some annoyance that Pilling 'has now been in this country about a month waiting a reply from Talaat'. Rumbold believed that there was no chance of a reply: 'I think that after Talaat's recent visit to Berlin he is not at all likely to fall in with any suggestions Pilling may have made for getting rid of the German alliance.' Rumbold proposed 'that Pilling should now return to England'. Ten days later he saw Pilling, and with the Foreign Office's approval, told him that he must leave within twenty-four hours. 'He is very crest-fallen,' Rumbold wrote to Campbell on June 18, 'but I do not think he is doing any good here and the gossip about him complicates my work.'

Rumbold's work was repeatedly complicated by intermediaries for whose actions he was ultimately responsible. Of one such he wrote to Newton on May 26: 'I always suspected him of being a bit of an imposter but he seems to be almost worse than that'; and of another that 'he is embarrassingly patriotic and scents the enemy everywhere. . . . we have recently employed him as a colporteur to distribute propagandist litera-ture. But we have now dispensed with his services.' A major difficulty arose in May when a War Office agent in Switzerland, Mr Lang,[2] of whose presence Rumbold had been ignorant, sent a letter back to the War Office in London giving details of Swiss troop movements and military stores. By accident, this letter had been returned unopened to Switzerland by the War Office Censor in London. On its return it was opened by the Swiss authorities. Lang was promptly arrested by the Swiss, who informed

---

[1] Mehmed Talaat, 1874–1921. Member of the Young Turk Triumvirate, 1908. Minister of the Interior, 1913–17. Grand Vizier, 1917–18. Left Turkey, 1918. Assassinated in Berlin.

[2] Alfred Lang, born 1876. An English businessman, resident in Lausanne. In 1916 he sent the Board of Trade economic and sometimes military information from Switzerland. Employed as a War Office agent, 1916–17. Expelled from Switzerland in November 1917.

Rumbold that they had a British captive. The whole affair, Rumbold wrote to Campbell on May 21, was 'an incredible performance', and he hoped that somebody would be severely dealt with for the blunder. 'I am sure you will appreciate better than most', he told Campbell, 'that if our agents are going to be the victims of gross carelessness or imbecility on the part of the censor or some other person at home, there will be difficulty in getting agents at all . . . my feelings about this business are very sulphurous.' Fortunately for Rumbold, the Swiss Government recognized that the British Legation had not been involved in any way in Lang's activities. But it was with some difficulty that he persuaded them at the end of June, to release Lang on bail, after he had been sentenced to ten months' imprisonment.

On April 26 another visitor arrived in Berne, this time with Foreign Office approval. That day Ronald Campbell wrote to Rumbold in a letter headed *'Private and Secret'* that a British subject of Armenian origin, born in Bulgaria, was coming to Switzerland in the guise of a businessman to make contact with any Bulgarians in Switzerland. The man, Manouk Kouyoumdjian,[1] was, Campbell wrote, 'to obtain for us any information he can about what is going on in Bulgaria, and is also in talking to any Bulgarians he comes across to instil the idea (without of course mentioning that he has been told to do so) that this country entertains no animosity towards the Bulgarians and would welcome any arrangement acceptable to both parties etc., etc.' 'Kouyoumdjian', Campbell continued, 'is a dreadful little object to look at, but we believe him to be entirely loyal and trustworthy. . . . He will send his reports to you. Will you send them on to me by bag, telegraphing anything that you consider sufficiently important, if ever there is anything. Judging by his efforts from Bucharest we are not expecting very much, but our news from Bulgaria being almost non-existent we snatch at any straw.'

On May 25 Ronald Campbell wrote to Rumbold that in order to carry out his instructions successfully Kouyoumdjian 'has to spend money from time to time in entertaining and generally propitiating his friends'. Rumbold had to supply this money, which Campbell then reimbursed. On June 4 Rumbold warned Campbell that 'some of K's Turkish information'

[1] Manouk Kouyoumdjian, 1870–1921. Born in Rustchuk, Bulgaria. Worked in Manchester, as a cotton shipping agent. Naturalized as a British citizen, 1897. Returned to Bulgaria, 1914, as British Consular Agent, Philippopolis, June 1914. Expelled from Bulgaria, October 1915. Sent by the Foreign Office to Rumania in 1916, but recalled after he had failed to obtain any information of value about conditions inside Bulgaria. Sent by the Foreign Office to Switzerland, 1917. Awarded the OBE for having 'rendered gratuitously valuable service through his knowledge of Bulgarian personalities', 1918. He lived in Southport from 1918 to his death, working for his family cotton shipping firm.

– for he had branched out from his Bulgarian brief – 'appears to me somewhat fantastic', such as his report that a million Turkish soldiers were being
sent to reinforce the Syrian front. Rumbold pointed out, 'I do not believe
that there are a million Turks all told fighting at the present moment'.
When reporting on Bulgaria, Kouyoumdjian seemed more reliable. But
on June 11 he amazed Rumbold by asking for £80,000, with which he
believed he could stimulate a pro-allied movement in Bulgaria, and
possibly pull Bulgaria out of the war. The Foreign Office could not afford
to neglect such an opportunity. 'Your telegram did rather startle us,'
Campbell wrote to Rumbold on June 19, 'but on thinking it carefully over
I came to the conclusion that it was worth trying and succeeded in so
persuading the authorities. . . . if successful the results might be so far-
reaching and the object ultimately aimed at is a thing about which the
War Cabinet are very keen.' Rumbold believed that 'the present discontent in Bulgaria' – as he wrote to Campbell on July 7 – would make
the money worth spending. He had told Kouyoumdjian to impress upon
the Bulgarians to whom he gave the money the importance to the allied
cause of both 'the Russian offensive and . . . the arrival of the American
troops'. The Bulgarians ought to ask themselves, Rumbold added, 'what
possible future lay before them if they remained in the war'. The successful
Russian advance, which looked as if it might drive the Austrian troops
back to the Austro-Hungarian border, might make the Bulgarians realize,
Rumbold wrote to Campbell on July 16, 'that the game is up, apart from
any question of having to grease the palms of some of them'. Kouyoumdjian asked for another £25,000 before he could guarantee any
progress. 'Surely £80,000 are ample', Rumbold asked Campbell in his
letter of July 16, 'with which to buy a few Bulgarian generals and
politicians?'

On July 21 Rumbold summoned Kouyoumdjian to the British Legation, and informed him that £80,000 was the maximum the British
Government were willing to pay out. As soon as the money was paid over,
Rumbold wrote to Campbell on July 23, it would be wise for Kouyoumdjian to return to England, 'because he tells me that he is looked
upon as a spy and we do not want to have any trouble in this matter. In
any event it is pretty certain that he is being watched.' 'Mr K' had reported
to Rumbold, and Rumbold passed on the report to Campbell, 'that our
friends in Bulgaria would like to know what Bulgaria would probably get
out of this war'. The Bulgarians, Rumbold commented, 'open their
mouths rather wide. I told K that I had no idea what were the views of
our Government with regard to a settlement in the Balkans'. It was
unlikely, Rumbold told Kouyoumdjian, that Bulgaria would be offered

any territory on the Aegean belonging to Greece, as Greece had recently adopted a pro-allied policy itself. The money would have to be sufficient incentive, together with the inevitability of an allied victory.

In the last week of July Kouyoumdjian pressed again for more money as a matter of urgency. Despite Rumbold's initial hostility to the idea of giving more, the Foreign Office agreed to a further £20,000, making a total of £100,000. Not long afterwards he was given a further £20,000. Rumbold encouraged Kouyoumdjian to use this British money as speedily and effectively as possible. But he was beginning to doubt whether it could be decisive in persuading the Bulgarian leaders to abandon Germany. On July 25 the War Cabinet was circulated with a telegram in which Rumbold reported the opinion of Alexander Naoum,[1] until three weeks before Greek Minister to Bulgaria, that 'it was hopeless to detach Bulgaria from her Allies. The Bulgarians were entirely in the grip of Germany.' Only an allied victory on the Salonika front would influence the Bulgarians, the diplomat stressed, and Rumbold agreed with him. The military situation, not British gold, would determine the attitude of Germany's allies.

By the end of July Kouyoumdjian had handed over the £120,000 to his Bulgarian contacts. Rumbold was keen to see him return to England. 'It is obvious', he wrote to Campbell on July 30, 'that his continued presence in Switzerland and especially at Geneva which is teeming with spies would excite suspicions.' Kouyoumdjian left Switzerland on August 14, his expensive mission a failure, for Bulgaria remained at war with the Allies until October 1918.

In recognition of his services in Berne Rumbold was given the KCMG in June 1917. 'You have had a great chance at Berne in these times', Ronald Graham wrote from the Foreign Office on June 8, '& are certainly making the most of it. Personally I feel especially grateful to you for the touch of optimism which characterises your interesting reports & which is very welcome in these days of depression & pacifism.' Replying to Graham on June 23, Rumbold described his work as 'harassing and strenuous . . . it never lets down for one moment'. 'This country', he added, 'is crammed full of spies and rascals of every description, and it is incredible that such a small country should be able to hold so many of these gentry. We have everything here of every nationality. . . .'

Rumbold was critical of his Entente colleagues, particularly the French

---

[1] Alexander Naoum, 1857–1936. Entered the Greek Diplomatic Service as an Interpreter at the Greek Embassy in Constantinople, 1884. Minister at Sofia, July 1914–July 1917; at Bucharest, 1920–23.

and American[1] Ambassadors. They were constantly promising to back
him up, he wrote to Eric Drummond on June 29, 'but they did not do so'.
In fact, he added, 'not one of these Representatives appears to have any
fight in him and the strength of the coalition against the Central Empires
is not reflected by their representatives at Berne'. But it was the spies
rather than the Ambassadors who gave Rumbold the greatest anguish. On
July 30 he wrote to Campbell outlining his complaint:

> The free-lances who are sent out here from time to time by the Intelligence
> Division or by others or who come of their own accord, cause me a certain
> amount of anxiety. It is almost certain that they have not been here for two or
> three days without the enemy getting wind of their presence. I am told that,
> during the recent trial of a German spy, the proceedings at which were not
> made public, some remarkable revelations were made about the German
> espionage system in Switzerland. It seems that the Germans have 1100 spies in
> this country. . . .
> I am the only person here who has the threads of our Turkish policy in his
> hands and who knows what the free-lances are after.

The difficulties created by so many agents and organizations did not
diminish. As more of them agreed to work through the Legation, Rumbold's own work increased. 'I know what hard work is', he wrote to Theo
Russell on August 22, 'and I have no hesitation in saying that Berne is
a hard worked post.' On October 22 Rumbold explained, in a letter to
George Clerk at the Foreign Office, the system which he had evolved:
'Under an arrangement I made some little time ago the Military Control
Office here send us all the political information which is furnished to them
by their agents in Switzerland. We sift and carefully analyse this information and pass as much of it as seems to us really good stuff, based on
reliable authority, on to you in the form of short memoranda. I know that
you at the office must have a great deal to read and so we endeavour to
let you have the information in tabloid form. . . . I try to satisfy myself
that the agents who are responsible for the reports we send on to you are
reliable. Would you let me have a line sometime as to whether you
approve of our method of passing on these intelligence reports to you. If
any criticism occurs to you please let me know and I will attend to it. Of
course I have several other sources of information besides the agents employed by the Military Control Office and I generally report by despatch
or by telegram reliable items of information from these other sources.'

---

[1] Pleasant Alexander Stovall, 1857–1935. Newspaper editor. Founder, 1891, and owner of
the *Savannah Press*. Represented Georgia in the House of Representatives for five years.
US Minister to Switzerland, 1913–20. Chairman of the Georgia Delegation to the Democratic National Convention, 1920.

Rumbold's anti-German feelings intensified during 1917. At the beginning of May he had read an Admiralty communiqué, published in *The Times*, which stated that 'we were fortunate in having been able to save a certain number of Germans' at sea. This, Rumbold wrote to Newton on May 3, 'is the absolute limit. If I saw a German drowning I should try to save him, but I should consider myself unfortunate in having to try to save him'. He believed that Germany's allies were likewise worthy only of contempt. 'I hope we shall manage to give the Bulgarians a sound thrashing first', he wrote to Campbell on May 10, 'before we come to any arrangement with them. Otherwise they will suffer from swelled heads.' When Newton wrote of how the Germans were putting up with increased food shortages and privations, as a result of the allied blockade, he replied, on May 26, that 'it would not be accurate, I think, to ascribe the apparent willingness of the Germans to undergo these privations entirely to an highly developed sense of patriotism. The fact is that, being a servile race, the Germans will put up with a condition of things which an independent race like ours would not be disposed to tolerate. I am sure that our women and older men are absolutely sound, however, and will work themselves to the bone.' The younger British trade-unionists, Rumbold added, 'would, it seems to me, be all the better for a spell in the front trenches'.

The initial hopes raised by the battle of Arras dwindled as 1917 progressed. 'The French are very depressed', Newton had written to Rumbold on May 12, '& the Italians are doing next to nothing.' The main fear was still a possible peace treaty between Russia and Germany. 'The Russian situation', Newton wrote, 'looks as bad as it can be. It makes me gasp to think what the effect will be if they drop out. We hear that the Huns are counting confidently upon a separate peace in a week or two, & that the Kaiser, Hindenburg[1] & Ludendorff[2] are in tearing spirits.' But the Russian

---

[1] Paul von Hindenburg, 1847–1934. Entered the Prussian Army, 1866; wounded in the Austro-Prussian War. Won the Iron Cross in the Franco-Prussian War, 1870–71. General, 1903. Retired at his own request, 1911, because 'there was no prospect of war'. Appointed to command the 8th Army in East Prussia, August 1914; defeated the Russians at Tannenberg. Field-Marshal, November 1914. Commander of all German Forces in the East, 1915. Chief of the German General Staff, 1916–18. Lived in retirement, 1919–25, when he wrote his memoirs, in which he declared that Germany had not been defeated by force of arms, but by treachery and revolution inside Germany. Chancellor of the Reich, 1925–34.

[2] Erich Ludendorff, 1865–1937. Entered the Prussian Army, 1883. Served on the General Staff, 1894–1913. Quartermaster-General of the 2nd Army, August 1914, when he took over command of the 14th brigade of infantry, whose General had been killed, and captured Liège. Chief of Staff to Hindenburg in East Prussia, 1914–15; First Quartermaster-General of the German armies, 1916–18; with Hindenburg, he controlled entirely German war policy. Fled to Sweden, November 1918. Returned to Germany, April 1919. Joined Hitler's unsuccessful attempt to seize power in Munich, November 1923. Entered the Reichstag as a National Socialist, 1924. He published *My War Memories* in 1919.

Government remained in the war, despite the growing demand for peace inside Russia, and the grave shortages of ammunition and military supplies at the front. 'The news from Russia seems a bit better today', Rumbold replied on May 19, 'but what it amounts to is this that the western Allies are bleeding and paying through the nose in order that the Russians should gas and issue daily manifestoes which do not advance matters one bit. I fancy that our General Staffs have entirely left the Russians out of their calculations and that if the latter make any sort of push in the course of the summer it will be so much to the good. Of course, if they could really make a sustained push or even one like Brusilov's[1] push of last year they would end the war this summer or by the autumn. But they are a rotten lot and, I am afraid, will be helpless for many years to come.'

During June the Russian Provisional Government, pressed by Britain, agreed to a further military offensive on the Eastern Front, with the aim of driving the Germans out of Russia, and taking the war westwards into Germany itself. Rumbold was optimistic about the outcome. 'The last news', he wrote to Ronald Campbell on June 22, 'certainly looks as if the Russian army were slowly getting under weigh. They still have more than three months of campaigning weather and even if they only begin operations on August 1, they can do an enormous amount of harm to the Austrians and Germans and appreciably hasten the end.' Rumbold realized that the war might last until 1918, but he believed, as he wrote on June 23 to his American friend Irwin Laughlin, that 'a campaign of 1918, if there is one, must settle the Boche for good and all'. At worst, he told Laughlin, the American army then on its way to Europe would 'take the place of the Russian army'. As for the Germans, 'I know for a fact', he wrote, 'that they are most anxious for the termination of the war this autumn at latest because, amongst other things, they dread having to face your perfectly fresh army next spring.'

By the end of July, Rumbold's hope of a Russian military success began to evaporate. 'News from Russia still very bad', Newton wrote on July 27, seeing little chance of a successful offensive. The Russian army, having advanced briefly into Austria, began falling back to the Russian frontier at the end of July. Whole units mutinied, and the gains of Brusilov's 1916 offensive were lost. Rumbold wrote to Newton on July 30:

---

[1] Alexei Alexeievich Brusilov, 1853–1926. Commanded the Russian Armies south of the Pripet Marshes, 1916–17. His successful offensive, launched on June 4, 1916, was halted in September through lack of artillery munitions, having at one point advanced seventy miles. Supreme Commander of the Russian Armies, May–July 1917. Put his services at the disposal of the Red Army during the Russo-Polish War, 1920; Inspector of Cavalry, 1923–24; Head of the State Horse-breeding Establishment, Moscow, 1924–26.

I hope the Russians will fetch up somewhere to the west of the Urals and not become absolutely an Asiatic Power. The Austro-boches seem to be having a bit of a walk over in Galicia but, as an intelligent friend of mine who spent several years at Petrograd wrote to me to-day, Russia is a 'boîte à surprises' and it would be just as great a mistake to be enthusiastic about Russian successes as to be downcast about their reverses. . . . All the same, I shall be glad when they turn on the enemy and cease running away.

'I feel in my bones that the news is bad', Lady Rumbold wrote to her mother that same day, 'the Bosch element is looking disgustingly elated.' The Germans had every reason for elation. The mutinies on the Russian front made it certain that there could be no further Russian offensive; yet the British desperately wanted a diversion on the Eastern Front to give their own attack at Passchendaele a greater chance of success.

As the American troops would not be ready to go into action on the Western Front until the spring of 1918, Russia's military effort was all-important. The mutinies were a setback to the allied cause, but did not seem decisive. 'News from Russia looks a bit better now', Rumbold wrote to Newton on August 3, having learned that the Germans had failed to break through the gaps in the Russian line where the mutinies had been, and that these gaps had quickly been filled. But no further advances could be made, and in Petrograd the anti-war propaganda gained ground week by week. 'The Russians have let us down badly again', Rumbold wrote to his stepmother on August 7; 'They are dreadful allies in a way because one never can tell what to expect from them. We have poured out money and munitions for them and are now bleeding freely. It is very disgusting, and if only they had played up properly the war would have been over this autumn'.

Rumbold was becoming depressed at the slow progress of the war. His hopes for a decisive breakthrough on the Western Front by the autumn of 1917 had been clearly falsified by the beginning of August. 'Even after 3 years' war', he wrote to his stepmother, 'things don't go as well for us as we have a right to expect. What a slow business it all is and how one longs sometimes for some explosive which would blow the German army to the hell from which they originally came.' When the Germans drove the Russians from Riga at the beginning of September, Rumbold wrote despondently to Hardinge, on September 10, that the Swiss General Staff, who a month earlier had 'whined in the true Teutonic fashion' were again exhilarated, and 'as pro-German as ever'. Writing to Sir Maurice de Bunsen on September 14, Rumbold was in a pessimistic mood. 'I wish we could detach one of our enemies from the Alliance against us', he wrote; 'The three subordinate members of the Alliance are all in their several ways sick of the war but do not know how to get out of it. I am convinced that there is nothing to be done with Austria just yet for she cannot get rid of the German yoke.' At Constantinople, a group of leading Turkish politicians seemed to be active 'working hard to get Turkey out of the war'; in Bulgaria there was 'much discontent' with the war. But the failure throughout of the Russians to take the offensive 'will throw everything back and of course the Germans will make the utmost use of the débâcle in Russia'.

Throughout 1917 Rumbold sent the Foreign Office detailed information about conditions inside Germany and Austria-Hungary. Many of his telegrams were circulated to the War Cabinet. On April 5 he reported on a meeting between the former Austrian Ambassador in London, Count Mensdorff,[1] and Mrs Barton,[2] the widow of a former British Consul at Geneva. Mensdorff told Mrs Barton that Germany and Austria both wanted peace, and that as 'military operations had reached a deadlock' on the Western Front, 'there did not seem much point in continuing the war'. Mrs Barton was not impressed, telling Mensdorff that the British people 'were determined to pursue the war to its proper conclusion'.[3] Mensdorff hinted at the desirability of a talk with Rumbold himself; but neither Mrs Barton nor Rumbold were willing to see him again, and he returned to Vienna.

All the information arriving from inside Austria-Hungary during the summer and autumn confirmed the peace-seeking mood. On October 3 Rumbold telegraphed information which had come from 'a leading merchant arrived from Budapest'. These were the details:

Austria-Hungary is totally exhausted and cannot last over the winter. Her supply of corn will run out in February.

Feeling in Austria is bitter against Hungary and Bavaria, owing to refusal of latter to allow export of their foodstuffs.

Very little oil reaches Austria from Roumania. Of the 27 'Gisements' (of 50 wells each) very few are working. Owing to thorough nature of destructive measures taken it will take 5 years to arrive at pre-war production.

This telegram was circulated to all Cabinet Ministers concerned with war policy. But Rumbold was sceptical of drawing too much hope from such

[1] Albert, Count von Mensdorff-Pouilly-Dietrichstein, 1861–1945. Attached to the Austro-Hungarian Embassy in Paris, 1886; transferred to London, 1889. Ambassador in London, 1904–14. An advocate of a negotiated peace from the outbreak of war in 1914.

[2] Victoria Alexandrina Julia Peel, 1870–1935. A granddaughter of Sir Robert Peel, and a goddaughter of Queen Victoria. In 1887 she married Daniel Fitzgerald Pakenham Barton (Consul, Geneva, 1886–97); he died in 1907. She lived at the Villa Lammermoor, Geneva.

[3] Rumbold's report of Mrs Barton's meeting with Mensdorff was circulated to the King and War Cabinet.

information. 'Austria', he wrote to Mrs Barton on October 9, 'either will not or cannot break away from Germany, which means of course that there can be no question at present of a separate peace with Austria. . . . Germany is behind Austria in everything she does.'

Conditions inside Germany were worsening throughout 1917, largely as a result of the allied blockade. Rumbold made strenuous efforts to obtain detailed information from anyone who reached Berne from Germany, and to send it back to London. At the end of November he spoke at length with Bishop Bury,[1] who had been allowed by the Germans to visit the British prisoners of war at Ruhleben, and who had also stayed for a while in Berlin. 'He was most interesting', Lady Rumbold wrote to her mother on December 1. 'The description of his only meal in Berlin was cheering. He breakfasted at a 1st class hotel, and it consisted of *acorn* coffee which nearly "turned him up", *no* milk *no* sugar (saccharine instead) *no* butter, kriegs-brot, and a horrible jam of rhubarb with *no* sugar in it! He lived a week in Ruhleben, and was allowed complete freedom. The poor men are in a very highly nervous state, constantly on the verge of tears, or laughter and in many cases their minds have given way. They all said that their treatment was better now, but if it was not for their parcels they would be dead in 3 weeks. I wish I had time to tell you all he told us. Of course he was escorted from here and back by a German officer. He said the people in Berlin look very sad, but the officers very hilarious, while again the soldiers look apathetic and unhappy.'

On Russian affairs also, Rumbold's information was detailed, and ominous. On October 29 he sent Balfour an account of an imminent agreement between the Russian Bolshevists – or Maximalists as they were also known – and the Germans. It was accurate in each particular. 'As a result of their negotiations with the Germans', Rumbold reported, 'the Maximalists in the Soviet have agreed to work for the fall of Kerensky[2] and the establishment of a purely Nationalist Government, which is to issue to the Allies an ultimatum laying down conditions of peace on the basis of no annexations and no indemnities. Should the Nationalists still refuse to make a joint peace with Germany, the Maximalist Government would

[1] Herbert Bury, 1853–1933. Cattle-farmer in the Argentine, 1875–77. Ordained, 1878. Bishop of British Honduras and Central America, 1908–11. Bishop of Northern and Central Europe, 1911–26. Among his publications were *A Bishop Among Bananas* (1911), *Here and There in the War Area* (1916), *My Visit to Ruhleben* (1917), *Russia from Within* (1927) and *Experiences of a Travelling Bishop* (1930).

[2] Alexander Feodorovich Kerensky, 1881–1970. A Labour member of the Duma, 1912. Minister of Justice, February 1917. Minister of War, May 1917, when he successfully raised army morale. Prime Minister, July–October 1917. Fled from Petrograd, October 1917, and failed to recapture the city by force. In exile, first in France, then in the United States.

make a separate peace with the Powers.' Rumbold then pointed out the consequences of such a Russo-German peace. 'Thus relieved from the necessity of keeping troops on the eastern front', he wrote, 'the Central Empires would attack on each of the western powers in turn and force the Allies to make peace as a result of total defeat in the field. It is thanks to this same agreement with the Maximalists that the Russian fleet has been allowed to escape from the Gulf of Riga and will be further allowed to take refuge in Swedish ports where it will be disarmed. The Germans have no intention of carrying out any further military operations in the Baltic or against Petrograd, and more confidence than ever is felt in Austro-German circles that peace will soon be concluded with Russia.'

During 1917, in over a thousand telegrams, Rumbold sent the Foreign Office details of conditions inside Turkey, and of the Turkish desire to make peace. He was helped in collecting his information by a former employee of the Egyptian Government, Humbert Parodi,[1] who was in direct contact with the various Turks who visited Switzerland, and who passed on all that he heard direct to Rumbold. The Turks, Rumbold reported to the Foreign Office on May 12, 1917, were said by one informant to be unable to last 'another winter'; the Bulgarians 'were sick of war, and would be only too glad to make peace'. On June 7, in a letter to Lord Robert Cecil, Rumbold speculated on the possible assassination of Enver Pasha,[2] but pointed out that, according to another informant, 'the impression produced on malcontents by the extermination of hundreds of thousands of Armenians has been such as to deter everybody from attempts on the lives' of the Turkish leaders. Several non-Turks who had been in Constantinople, brought news of conditions inside Turkey direct to Rumbold.[3]

From mid-June, Rumbold reported on the increasing number of Turks

[1] Humbert Denis Parodi, 1878–   . Son of an Italian father and a French mother. A Swiss citizen, he worked for the Egyptian Government as Inspector-General of Public Instruction, Cairo, 1910–14. During the war he worked in Switzerland, as a representative of Egyptian interests. Head of the Interpreters' and Translators Bureau, League of Nations, Geneva, 1919–21; employed by the League as a translator and interpreter, 1922–38. 'Even when matters were looking their worst for us', Rumbold wrote to him on November 21, 1918, 'you saw a fly in the ointment of our adversaries.'

[2] Enver Pasha, 1881–1922. Member of the Young Turk triumvirate, 1908. Military Attaché, Berlin, 1909. Commanded Turkish units in the Libyan and Balkan Wars, 1911–13. Minister of War, 1914. Commanded the Turkish forces against the Russians in eastern Turkey, 1915. Fled to Russia, 1918. Killed leading an anti-Bolshevik movement in Turkestan.

[3] Among Rumbold's informants during 1917 were the former Greek Minister in Constantinople, Monsieur Kalergi, and three members of the United States Embassy at Constantinople, Mr Elkus (the Ambassador), Mr Ravndal (Consul-General) and Mr Tarler (Counsellor of Embassy).

who appeared to want a negotiated peace with the Allies.[1] One Turkish condition, however, could not be granted. 'It is indispensable', Rumbold telegraphed on June 15, 'that Constantinople should remain Capital of Ottoman Empire.' But, since March 1915, Constantinople had been promised to Russia. The anti-war Turks, unaware of this, persevered in their efforts to enlist allied support. On June 27 several prominent Turks then in Switzerland formed an Ottoman League of Peace and Liberation; their aim, Rumbold telegraphed to Balfour on June 30, was 'to shake off military and financial yoke of Germany', and to seek allied support for this task.[2] Lord Robert Cecil wrote to Balfour on July 8: 'I suggest that Sir H. Rumbold should be instructed that if the Turks make any advances to him he should give them a sympathetic reception.' Lord Milner,[3] he added, was 'keen in this direction'. As a result of the information which Rumbold had sent them, the War Cabinet decided to send an emissary to talk to the Turks; and on July 20 a Conservative MP, Aubrey Herbert,[4] arrived in Berne.

Discussions between the two emissaries soon began. Rumbold arranged for Herbert to meet several of the Turks 'accidentally' at Interlaken. They all declared, Rumbold telegraphed to Balfour on July 24, 'that Enver's present policy is disastrous, and that immediate steps should be taken to defeat it and to bring about an Anglo-Turkish understanding'. 'The Anglophile Turks', Rumbold added, 'want moral and financial support from England and guarantees that there will be no complete partition of Turkey'. This Britain could not promise; under the Treaty of London of 26 April 1915, and the Sykes–Picot secret agreement of 16 May 1916, Britain, France, Russia, Italy and Greece had allocated each other major territorial prizes on Ottoman soil. These agreements could not be abandoned. When the Turks asked Herbert about possible peace terms he

---

[1] Among the Turks in Switzerland during the summer of 1917 were Rifaat Bey (President of the Senate), Mutak Effendi (Secretary to the Senate), Fethy Bey (Minister at Sofia), Hadji Adil Bey (President of the Chamber of Deputies), Hakki Halid Bey (former Director of the Mint at Constantinople), Noureddin Bey (an influential member of the Committee of Union and Progress) and Kamil Bey (a member of the Turkish Council of State).

[2] Rumbold's telegrams of June 15 and June 30 were both circulated to the War Cabinet.

[3] Alfred Milner, 1854–1925. Under-Secretary for Finance, Egypt, 1889–92. Chairman of the Board of Inland Revenue, 1892–97. Knighted, 1895. High Commissioner for South Africa, 1897–1905. Created Baron, 1901. Created Viscount, 1902. Member of the War Cabinet, 1916–18. Secretary of State for War, 1918–19; for the Colonies, 1919–21.

[4] Aubrey Nigel Henry Molyneux Herbert, 1880–1923. 2nd son of the 4th Earl of Carnarvon. Hon Attaché, Constantinople, 1900. Conservative MP, 1911–18 and 1918–23. Lieutenant, Irish Guards, August 1914. Captain, General Staff, Mediterranean Forces, January 1915. Present at the Gallipoli landings of April and August 1915. Lieutenant-Colonel, Adriatic Mission, December 1915. Served in Mesopotamia, 1916 and Italy 1917–18.

replied 'that he was not authorised to discuss the question'. But the Turks insisted that direct Anglo-Turkish talks were what they wished; they did not want Italy, Russia or France to be brought in. The Turks returned to Constantinople; Herbert to London. The negotiations were not taken up again for nearly six months; in Palestine and Mesopotamia Turkish weakness encouraged the British to seek a military solution. Rumbold's telegrams gave support to this attitude.

On October 4 he reported that a recent visit to Germany by Enver Pasha was 'intended to impress on the German military authorities the urgent need of further German troops in Turkey'. On October 25 he told of Turkish discontent because the Central Powers 'were not giving her adequate help in return for Turkey agreeing to sacrifice territorial ambitions in Europe'. On November 17 he telegraphed, in his 1103rd telegram that year, that the Turkish economic situation was growing steadily worse, that there were daily 'deaths from starvation' in the Turkish provinces and that 'for the purpose of keeping up the spirits of the people', the Turks were letting it be 'known' that peace would be signed in January 1918. Pillaging was rife near Constantinople. These reports were studied by the War Office, and their contents passed on to the military staffs on the Palestinian and Mesopotamian fronts. Rumbold's telegram of November 17 was sent to the King and to the War Cabinet.

Towards the end of October an Irish Nationalist MP, Arthur Lynch,[1] wrote to Balfour to protest that British propaganda in Switzerland was weak, and that the work of innumerable German agents was not counteracted at all by any British propaganda. Lynch argued in favour of a special agency in Switzerland, 'presided over', he wrote to Balfour on October 22, 'by a man . . . of great activity, intelligence, savoir-faire etc. knowing well three languages, well supplied with money, and entrusted with considerable freedom of action'. Rumbold did not see the value of setting up a propaganda agency in Switzerland. 'My belief is', he wrote to Ronald Campbell on October 29, 'that the Germans have overdone their propaganda here and even some of the German Swiss are bored with it. There is only one really effective form of propaganda and that is victories in the field. There is no doubt that the Germans are doing their utmost to absorb Switzerland economically and financially and we have warned the Swiss against this. They are waking up to the fact. . . .'

Swiss sympathies for Germany often affected Rumbold's work. 'The

---

[1] Arthur Lynch, 1861–1934. Born in Australia, of Irish parents. Served in the South African War, on the Boer side, as Colonel Commanding the Irish Brigade, 1900. Imprisoned in Brixton Gaol, 1901. Nationalist MP, 1901–18. Appointed Colonel in the British Army, 1918. The author of twenty-six books, including several works on philosophy and ethics, and My Life Story, published in 1924.

Swiss', he wrote to his stepmother at this time, 'are influenced by the military events round them. They think that the Entente are very much en baisse and that the Germans are going to win, if anybody is going to win. This belief makes them very stiff and difficult to deal with. . . . The fact is that this small nation takes small views. . . . On the whole I heartily dislike neutrals and am quite pleased that they are suffering.'

German pressure on the Allies increased during October 1917. The Italian defeat at Caporetto had, as Campbell wrote to Rumbold on November 1, 'rather depressed' the Foreign Office although, in one respect, 'it has not been a bad thing as it seems really to have pulled the Italian nation together'. Nevertheless, the Italian front was broken, and the Italian army fell back almost to Venice. Learning of further German air raids on London, Rumbold wrote to his stepmother on November 4: 'I hope no bombs fell anywhere near you and that the servants behaved well. We shall never stop these air-raids until we begin liberally strewing the Rhine towns with bombs.'

In Russia, on November 7, the Provisional Government was overthrown and Lenin came to power. On the following evening to an excited meeting of the Soviet Congress, he read his 'Proclamation to the Peoples of All the Belligerent Countries', proposing an immediate armistice on all fronts, and a peace with neither annexations or indemnities. The delegates approved his proposal by their applause. This Decree of Peace was the first official act of the Bolshevik Government; the Russo-German armistice was signed at Brest-Litovsk on December 15. Rumbold had feared this outcome since the fall of the monarchy seven months before. 'I am afraid the Russian débâcle,' he told his stepmother, 'followed by the Italian defeats will prolong the war.' November was a month of gloom. 'It was not so much a military defeat in the first place', Hardinge wrote to Rumbold on November 9 to explain the Italian collapse at Caporetto, 'as a kind of strike on the part of the Italian 2nd Army. They simply laid down their arms and walked away crying "viva la pace" – the result chiefly of clerical and socialist propaganda assisted and played upon by German agents.' Hardinge expressed the fears of the Foreign Office 'that when her last reserves of wheat are exhausted Switzerland will throw in her lot with the Central Empires in exchange for some of the wheat which Germany is supposed now to possess enough and to spare, thanks to the excellent harvest in Roumania and the large stocks they seized at Riga'. If Switzerland joined Germany, it would involve, Hardinge wrote, 'a considerable diversion of French troops and be a very serious matter'.

'What dreadful Allies we have!' Rumbold wrote to Campbell on November 10; 'First of all we are let down by the Russians and now by the Italians. . . . We must be under no illusions. The French, the Americans and ourselves will have to win this war, and we are capable of doing it, but it is very disagreeable to think that so many lives should have been lost for the sake of people like the Russians and the Italians.' On the same day he wrote to Newton: 'I always had my doubts about the Russians from the very first, even during the crisis preceding the war. As for the Italians, what can you expect from a nation the majority of which would be better employed selling ice-cream.' Bitterness against the Italians was widespread. 'I hope we shall not allow our men to be sacrificed', Newton wrote to Rumbold on November 16, 'because the Italians won't fight for their own country.' It was Russia's withdrawal from the war that seemed more serious. British and French troops could easily be hurried to the Italian front, but in the east the situation could not be retrieved once the Bolsheviks decided to abandon the war. 'I long ago imagined', Rumbold wrote to Hardinge on November 19, 'that we must write off Russia as a bad debt and consider that the Americans had taken the place of the Russians.' Rumbold was sure that the Allies would gain by the exchange 'as half a million well organised Americans with powerful artillery are worth more than twice that number of Russians'. On December 1 Rumbold learned that Lenin had definitely taken Russia out of the war. 'The Maximalists are the absolute limit', he wrote to Campbell that day; 'It seems to me there is nothing they have left undone to dishonour Russia. Incidentally of course they have presumably given away all the Russian cyphers by publishing the secret documents. I hope it is not true that Buchanan has been arrested by the Jew Trotzky alias Bronstein.[1] It is an awful situation for Buchanan and his Embassy. I wish we could get hold of Lenin and his gang and string them up. I would willingly assist at the operation.'

Despite the Russian blow to the allied cause, winter brought other successes, and cause for hope of victory in 1918. On the Palestine front, the Turks had been driven northwards by the British forces, who entered Jerusalem on December 9. The Turkish commander, Djemal Pasha, was

[1] Lev Davidovich Bronstein, 1879–1940. Son of a Jewish farmer. Studied mathematics at Odessa University, 1896. Gave up his studies to devote himself to revolutionary activity. Exiled to Siberia, 1898; escaped to England, 1902, with a forged passport in the name of 'Trotsky'. Joined the Mensheviks against Lenin, 1903. Returned to Russia, 1905. Again deported to Siberia, he again escaped, to London, in 1907. In exile in Vienna and Paris. Expelled from Paris, 1916, he went to New York. Returned to Russia, 1917, where he was reconciled to Lenin and became head of the Petrograd Soviet. Directed the armed uprising of November 7, 1917. Commissar for Foreign Affairs, 1917–18; for Military Affairs, 1918–25. Expelled from the Communist Party by Stalin, 1927. In exile in Turkey (1929), Norway (1936), and Mexico. where he was assassinated, probably on Stalin's orders.

replaced by the German General von Falkenhayn,[1] the 'conqueror' of Rumania; but even under German command the Turks could not recapture Jerusalem. The Italian army, reinforced by British and French troops, remained at war. At Passchendaele the British attack, while failing to break across German-occupied Belgium to the borders of Germany, took a heavy toll of German lives, and, though at great cost, pushed the trenches of the Ypres salient further east than they had been at any time since the line was established three years before.

These allied successes made a strong impression in Austria-Hungary. In November Count Karolyi[2] reached Berne, and, as Rumbold telegraphed to the Foreign Office on November 27, 'wished to get into touch with the Entente with a view to seeing whether in spite of the continuation of hostilities, it might be possible to bring about, in conjunction with the Western Powers, action against Germany'. Karolyi envisaged a Hungarian–Slav block in Austria-Hungary which would 'swamp' the German element of the dual monarchy, and pursue democratic policies acceptable to the Allies. Karolyi also reported that in Germany 'the stories or privation and suffering . . . were by no means exaggerated' and that the allied blockade 'was hitting the class which might have engineered troubles or a revolution'.

On November 21 Rumbold learned, from one of his most trusted informants, Dr Parodi, that the Austrian Foreign Minister, Count Czernin,[3] was willing to send to Switzerland, for discussions with a senior British official, an equally senior Austrian. Czernin suggested Count

[1] Erich von Falkenhayn, 1861–1922. Prussian Minister for War, 1912–15. Chief of the German General Staff, 1914–16. Dismissed by the Kaiser in August 1916. Commanded the German forces in Rumania, 1916–17. Commanded the Turkish forces in Palestine and Syria, 1917–18. In defence of his strategy he published, in 1919, *General Headquarters 1914–1916 and Its Critical Decisions*.

[2] Count Mihaly Karolyi, 1875–1955. Member of an aristocratic Hungarian family. Elected to the Hungarian Parliament as a Liberal, 1905. Became the leader of the radical wing of the Independent Party. He wanted to break the union between Austria and Hungary, and to create a Russo-Hungarian *rapprochement*; he also wished to destroy the capitalist system. Interned in France, August 1914, but soon released. Advocated a complete break with Germany, 1914–18. Prime Minister of Hungary, November 1918; President, January–March 1919. In exile in Czechoslovakia, Italy and France, 1919–40. Leader of the Free Hungarian Movement in London, 1941–45. Hungarian Minister in Paris, 1946–49. In exile for the second time, in France and England, from 1950 until his death. His son Adam, a Royal Air Force pilot, was killed in 1939.

[3] Count Ottokar Czernin, 1872–1932. Member of the Austrian Upper House, 1912; advocated a vigorous external policy for Austria–Hungary. Minister to Bucharest, 1912–16; he played a large part in keeping Rumania neutral for two years. Austro-Hungarian Foreign Minister, December 1916–April 1918. He tried in vain to persuade the German Emperor to accept a negotiated peace. Member of the Bürglichen Arbeitspartei, Vienna, 1920–23. He published *Im Weltkriege* in 1919.

Mensdorff, the former Austro-Hungarian Ambassador in London, as a possible emissary. Rumbold at once telegraphed this news to London, and on November 30 informed Parodi that the British Government would welcome the visit of an Austrian intermediary to Berne, and that Rumbold himself would 'listen to what he has to say', and forward his proposals to London. On December 1 Rumbold learned that Lloyd George had authorized a special British delegate to go out to Switzerland, and passed this news on to Parodi that same day. Lloyd George's choice was General Smuts,[1] who, to avoid arousing undue curiosity, was to be called 'Mr Smith'. He was to stay at the Hotel de Russie, whose proprietor was known for his pro-English sentiments, and whose hotel tended to be avoided by visitors from Germany and Austria-Hungary. On December 13 Parodi informed Rumbold that the Austrian Government accepted Smuts as the British delegate, and that Mensdorff would arrive at Geneva on the evening of December 17.

Mensdorff and Smuts held three meetings at Geneva on the morning, afternoon and evening of December 18. Smuts pointed out, as he recorded in a memorandum of the conversations on December 19, that 'the friendly feelings towards Austria which had existed among the British people before the War had by no means disappeared', and that since the revolution in Russia 'it was feared in many influential quarters that unless some counterweight was established on the Continent to Germany in place of Russia, the future peace of Europe might continue to be precarious'. If Austria could be 'emancipated from German domination', Britain would help her to 'make a fresh start of complete independence vis-à-vis the German Empire'. In such circumstances, Britain would give Austria the necessary support 'to uphold and strengthen her and to assist her economic reconstruction'. But Mensdorff replied firmly that Austria could not possibly break away from Germany 'while the war lasted', and asked whether Britain was prepared to discuss possible peace terms with Germany. Smuts said bluntly that 'neither the British public nor the British Government were in a temper to discuss peace with the German Government'. Mensdorff then declared that if Britain was not willing to contemplate peace negotiations with Germany 'this horrible War must go on'. 'Europe', he said, 'was dying at the centre, America was becoming the

[1] Jan Christian Smuts, 1870–1950. Born in Cape Colony. General, commanding Boer Commando Forces, Cape Colony, 1901. Colonial Secretary, Transvaal, 1907. Minister of Defence, Union of South Africa, 1910–20. Second-in-Command of the South African forces that defeated the Germans in South-West Africa, July 1915. Honorary Lieutenant-General commanding the imperial forces in East Africa, 1916–17. South African Representative at the Imperial War Cabinet, 1917 and 1918. Prime Minister of South Africa, 1919–24. Minister of Justice, 1933–39. Prime Minister 1939–48.

financial and economic centre of the world, while Japan at the other end was gathering to herself immense power and resources and the whole trade of Asia. Why were we going on fighting? The British Prime Minister had said that we must have victory; Asquith had said that Prussian militarism must be crushed. If another year of this destruction had to pass, the position of Europe and civilisation, already so pitiable, would be beyond repair.' Mensdorff pleaded for the opening of Anglo-German negotiations. Smuts insisted that Britain would accept only a separate peace between Austria-Hungary and Britain. The two men held a fourth meeting on December 19, but made no progress.

Rumbold took the opportunity of Smuts's visit to raise the question of possible negotiations between Turkey and Britain, which, like the discussions about Austria-Hungary, had been authorized by the War Cabinet. Lloyd George's Private Secretary, Philip Kerr,[1] who had accompanied Smuts to Geneva, travelled to Berne for talks with Dr Parodi about possible Turkish negotiations. Kerr told Parodi that – as he recorded in a memorandum after his conversations – Britain was 'quite prepared that Turkey should occupy an adequate place among the people of the world, provided she was willing to break with Germany and make an immediate peace with the Allies'. In return for an immediate peace, Britain would allow Turkey to keep Constantinople; but the Turks must agree to withdraw from Armenia, Syria, Mesopotamia, Arabia and Palestine, 'so that the inhabitants of these territories might conduct autonomous Governments of their own, or be governed by a mixed system of local and European officials under the protection of one or more of the Allied Powers'. Were Turkey to make peace at once, Britain would be willing to consider in Mesopotamia, Syria and Palestine, 'the retention of the Turkish flag as a symbol of Turkish suzerainty, provided it carried with it no executive authority'. Just as Smuts had told Mensdorff, so Kerr told Parodi that Britain would provide 'liberal financial and other economic assistance'. Parodi believed that Britain's terms would appeal to the anti-German forces in Turkey, who might be stimulated to take swift action, possibly, first, by murdering Enver Pasha, and then by opening the Dardanelles to British warships. But within a few days of Kerr's discussions, Turkish war-making zeal returned, for at the end of December the Bolsheviks declared an end to all hostilities, including those against Turkey, and began peace negotiations at Brest-Litovsk. The Turkish

[1] Philip Henry Kerr, 1882–1940. Worked as a Civil Servant in South Africa, 1905–8. Editor, *The Round Table*, 1910–16. Secretary to Lloyd George, 1916–21. Secretary of the Rhodes Trust, 1925–39. Succeeded his cousin as 11th Marquess of Lothian, 1930. Chancellor of the Duchy of Lancaster, 1931. Chairman of the Indian Franchise Committee, 1932. Ambassador in Washington from 1939 until his death.

armies on the Black Sea, around Lake Van, and in Persia, were released from the pressures which had tied them there since October 1914. 'The Russians have promised', Parodi wrote to Rumbold on 2 January 1918, 'to evacuate their troops from the occupied regions of Armenia, Trebizond, Erzerum etc, and Persia. Georgia will become an independent state, friendly to Turkey.' As a result of Russia's defection from the Entente, 'the moral of the Turks had risen, and they feel they can wait upon events, without trying to force them'. So ended the chance of a negotiated peace, either with Austria or with Turkey. Slim though the chances had been, Britain had taken them seriously. Rumbold drew the same lesson he had drawn during the Bulgarian discussions five months earlier, that none of Germany's allies was willing to take the risk of seeking a separate peace, and that only by a military victory could peace be secured.

Rumbold continued to obtain information from the Turkish officials in Switzerland.[1] But there seemed little chance of any agreement. In a letter to Balfour on January 7 he described the adverse effect which the Brest-Litovsk discussions was having on them:

Our conversations with the Turks have, of course, been prejudiced by the conference at Brest-Litovsk. In the last week we have ascertained from a number of Government Turks at Geneva that the conference in question has filled the Turks with extravagant hopes for the future of their empire. Not only do they hope to recover Mesopotamia, Palestine, etc., with the help of the Germans, but they also expect to get portions of the Caucasus and to enter into an alliance with such a state as Georgia. In fact they seem really to believe in the possibilities of the Turanian movement. We feel, therefore, that we should not at this moment shew undue eagerness to come to an arrangement with the Turks as we may appear to be competing with the negotiations at Brest-Litovsk.

The Turk to whom Parodi had given Philip Kerr's 'peace terms', Mouktar Pasha,[2] was reluctant to abandon negotiations. He was in Switzerland for several months in order to discuss a possible exchange of British and Turkish prisoners of war, and wanted to use his visit to strengthen his political position at Constantinople, and also, so Rumbold believed, to enrich himself. 'This man is well known to be dissolute',

[1] The three principal Turks with whom Rumbold had dealings were Chevky Bey (a Secretary at the Turkish Legation in Berne who had formerly been at the Embassy in London); Begjet Wahby (a former employee of the Egyptian Government whose Egyptian pension was paid through the British officials in Berne, and whose brother was an Ottoman official previously attached to the Grand Vizier's office in Constantinople); and Mouktar Pasha (former Turkish Ambassador in Berlin).

[2] Mahmud Mouktar Pasha, 1867–1935. Commanded the Turkish 1st Army, 1908–9. Minister of Marine, 1912. Ambassador to Berlin, 1913–15. Lived in retirement in Switzerland from 1915. The son of a Grand Vizier, he nevertheless had tried to work in co-operation with the Young Turks of the Committee of Union and Progress.

Rumbold wrote in his letter to Balfour, 'and to be constantly in want of money.' As soon as he arrived in Switzerland 'a German and a Turkish spy were detailed to watch him. The German spy . . . was occupying the next room to him at the hotel.' Rumbold did not regard Mouktar as a satisfactory intermediary. He was 'evidently a first class liar', Rumbold wrote to Newton on January 9; and on the same day he wrote to Parodi that 'it would be undesirable to make any further attempt to approach Mouktar and also that it would probably be injudicious to make him any payment at present. So please do not promise him any money.' It was useless negotiating further with the Turks, Rumbold wrote to Newton five days later, as 'they have got their tails up now and expect a good deal from the negotiations with Russia'.

Rumbold saw clearly that Germany would not allow its allies to make a separate peace. 'There is nothing to be done with the Austrians,' he wrote to Newton on January 28, 'ie in the direction of detaching them from Germany. But the Austrians are simply howling for peace. . . .' On February 2 he wrote again to Newton of his belief that, inside Germany, 'the military, of course, are top dogs now and their arrogance is as great as ever'. He disapproved strongly of direct peace negotiations with Germany:

I cannot understand how anybody who is not an absolute lunatic can talk of a peace of conciliation with the Germans for how can you ever admit such a race into the Society of Nations? I am all for the Society of Nations if it means a league of the whole world against Germany, but it is clap-trap if the league is to include Germany. I do not suppose you or I will ever ask a German to our house or shake hands with one if we can possibly help it in the future. Why, therefore, should we admit to the Society of Nations a people which is composed of individuals who are beneath the salt?

Throughout February Rumbold sent the Foreign Office all the information he could glean about conditions inside Germany, Austria and Turkey. His Turkish contacts in particular gave accounts of much anti-war feeling inside Turkey. 'Continue to pump as much optimism as you can into us,' Ronald Graham wrote from the Foreign Office on February 18, 'for we want it and your interesting notes & telegrams carry considerable weight.' Of greatest concern to the Foreign Office was the much talked of German offensive, for it was widely believed that the Germans would launch an attack on the Western Front during the spring, in an attempt to break the allied line. Since November 1914 only the British and French had launched attacks in France and Flanders; the Germans had remained on the defensive. By February 1918 the success of the allied blockade, the cease-fire on the Eastern Front, and the growing anti-war feeling shared by all her allies, made it certain that Germany would seek a dramatic military victory. 'The Generals have got Germany into an impasse', Rumbold wrote to his stepmother on February 18, 'and know that only a successful offensive can get her out of it.' His own optimism was undiminished. 'I do not for a moment believe the offensive *will* be successful', he added, 'and then, given the situation at home, the game is up.' He had no doubt that the results of the offensive would be decisive, not only on the Western Front. 'My belief is', he wrote to Newton on February 25, 'that Germany's satellites will watch and see what is the issue of the much proclaimed offensive on the western front before they commit themselves definitely to anything pointing to a breaking away from Germany. If, as I hope and trust, the offensive fails, there will then be an undignified scramble on the part of Austria and Turkey to cut their losses.' But he was convinced that 'until something is decided one way or the other on the western front', any peace overtures from Austria or Turkey 'only mean a desire to play for time'. To Ronald Campbell, Rumbold wrote pugnaciously on March 4:

The Germans are very much on top now, at least outwardly, and they have impressed the Swiss by the manner in which they suppressed the recent strikes in Germany and forced the Maximalists to make peace. As matters stand now I see no chance of securing a decent ending to the war unless and until we kill and put out of action another million or so Germans. I do not believe their country would stand a bigger drain than that. Of course it is not a pleasant prospect but it is the only way.

No German offensive had been launched by the end of the first week in March. But Rumbold received continual messages from Parodi that the Austrians wanted to reopen talks with General Smuts. Once more Smuts went to Switzerland, reaching Berne on March 9. Philip Kerr again went with him. Discussions began at once between Smuts and an Austrian emissary, Skrzynski[1], who had been in Switzerland for some months, and had been in continual touch with Parodi. But the talks were indecisive. Smuts insisted that in any peace settlement 'justice must be done to all peoples'; this pressure for some form of Home Rule, or even autonomy, for the Poles, Czechs, Croats and other minorities of the Habsburg Empire was a condition which the Austrians could not accept. On March 14 they

[1] Count Alexander Skrzynski, 1882–1931. Born in Galicia. Educated at Cracow and Munich. Entered the Austro-Hungarian Diplomatic Service, 1906; Secretary, Paris, 1914. Polish Minister, Bucharest, 1919–22. Minister for Foreign Affairs, December 1922–May 1923. Polish Delegate, League of Nations, 1923–24. Foreign Minister (for the second time), August 1924–November 1925. Prime Minister and Foreign Minister, November 1925–March 1926.

broke off the negotiations. Six days later Kerr wrote to Rumbold from 10 Downing Street that the War Cabinet believed that Austrian 'expectations about the possibilities of a Western offensive' had caused the abrupt change in the Austrian attitude. 'They think', Kerr explained, that Czernin, the Austrian Foreign Minister, 'had decided against negotiation either because he had decided to wait on military events, thinking that we shall ere long go to him for terms, or because he had realised that in existing circumstances it is impossible for him to "carry" a peace on Allied terms in Austria-Hungary itself. . . . Or having come to the edge of the precipice he may have realized that once he had started negotiations public opinion would never allow him to draw back if the Entente terms were reasonable & that once he had started negotiations it was rather a case of a separate peace or a break up of Austria-Hungary. . . . Anyhow there is nothing to do now but to await events.' In his letter of March 20 Kerr told Rumbold that he looked forward to further reports from Parodi about his talks with Skrzynski; but events moved more quickly than he anticipated.

The German offensive was launched on 21 March 1918. All along the Western Front the allied armies were thrown back. 'We are passing through a very anxious moment', Rumbold wrote to Hardinge on March 25, 'but I have every confidence in our ability to hold the Germans. It is Waterloo over again on a gigantic scale.' If the German offensive were to fail, he added, 'then I think there will be no difficulty in detaching Austria and Turkey'. 'We have been very anxious these last few days', he wrote to Newton on March 30, 'and this week has seemed interminable to me. But I have a feeling that if we can safely stick it for another two or three days, the tide will turn and the Boche will be chased back again.' That same day he wrote to Philip Kerr that although 'these are anxious days for all of us' he was firm in his belief the Germans were 'even more anxious than we are. It is neck or nothing with them.'

For a further month the battle on the Western Front continued. All potential negotiators, all regular intermediaries, waited to see what the result of the fighting would be. Bombing raids on Germany were one retaliation which Rumbold believed could hasten the moment when German morale would crack. To Philip Kerr he sent details, in his letter of March 30, of a successful British air raid on Mannheim in which an important factory was destroyed. 'The workmen who escaped', he reported, 'said that nothing would induce them to work there again.' Rumbold was angered by rumours that the bombing policy was not being pursued as rigorously as it might be, informing Kerr:

There is a story current here that we refrain from bombarding Frankfort because of the interests which certain of our Jews in England have in that city.

I do not suppose that that is true. It would be deplorable if it were. I suppose that we would say that we only bombard places of military utility such as factories, railway stations, etc. But if I know anything about Germany, the bombardment of Frankfort would cause a tremendous impression in that country. After all, rich Jews are objects of military utility, as they provide the sinews of war.

On April 15 Rumbold set out his views on both Germany and Austria-Hungary in a letter to Sir Maurice de Bunsen. 'If there is to be any justice in this world', he wrote, 'the Central Empires ought to be completely smashed. . . . I find it difficult to decide which is the stronger feeling in my mind, i.e. hatred of Germany or contempt for Austria. They are a pretty pair and I still hope and believe that they will receive proper chastisement. But it is a long time coming and it is causing a frightful lot of carnage.' That same day he wrote to Newton: 'Though our losses must be heavy in men and material, I feel that we are inflicting losses on the Germans such as they never dreamt of.' On April 21 he wrote to Newton again that the French Ambassador had told him 'that the French had certain information that the German General Staff were greatly disappointed with the results achieved'. But Rumbold realized that 'we must look forward to a period of anxiety lasting certainly for the next two months'.

Throughout April the German advance continued. 'The military situation remains fearfully anxious', Newton wrote on April 27. But he also sent the 'cheering news' that 120,000 American troops would have arrived by the end of April, and a further 150,000 during May. On May 4 Rumbold was able to report to Campbell at the Foreign Office that the German losses 'are really beginning to tell on them and there is considerable depression in the Fatherland'. But, as he warned Newton that same day, there would be another two or three months of equally fierce fighting; then, he believed, 'the Boche will have shot his bolt for good and all'.

By the first week in June the momentum of the German advance was much weakened. Ypres remained in British hands, Paris was not seriously threatened, and the Channel Ports were secure. 'The Germans', Rumbold wrote to Newton on June 7, 'will go on hammering at us until August when they and we will be pretty exhausted. Then I suppose the Yankees will come in and knock out the exhausted Boche.' On June 14 Hardinge sent Rumbold confirmation of his view. 'The next two to three months will inevitably be very critical for us', he wrote, 'as we are really at the bed-rock of our man power and the French are very much in the same position.' There was consolation, and hope, Rumbold believed, in the internal problems of Germany and Austria; grave shortages of food and raw materials, social unrest, and the determination of national minorities to secure autonomy or independence. 'Only a race of waiters and hair-dressers', Rumbold wrote to his stepmother on June 18, 'would put up with what the Boches stand. And yet it must be confessed that the said waiters etc are brave enough.'

The final German offensive on the Western Front was launched on July 15. Within two days it had been halted, and on July 18 the first allied advances were begun. Nearly four months of German victories were at an end. Rumbold was convinced that it could only be a few months before the Germans, exhausted by the efforts they had made, and despondent at their failure to break the allied resolve, were driven back to Germany. The morale of the Central Powers was clearly broken. On July 15 Rumbold informed Hardinge 'that the confusion and troubles in Austria are such that for all practical purposes the Austrian half of the monarchy is in process of dissolution'. Germany, he added, was 'practically staking her fortunes on the coming offensive'. On July 22 Rumbold wrote to his brother that 'it looks to me like the turn of the tide at last. Matters may go quickly now.'

The purpose of Rumbold's letter was a sad one. It was to inform his brother that his youngest child, Bridget, had died three days earlier:

She put up a gallant fight for her life but practically a month's fever was too much for her and she could not grapple with meningitis which declared itself last Thursday. I don't think we have anything to reproach ourselves with for we procured the best medical and surgical assistance in Berne – it is certain that, although she was in a children's hospital – she got the influenza bacillus, which has been one of the most virulent kind at Berne. This is responsible for her meningitis. Her operation was successful and she was recovering from it in a normal way when she went down with fever and from that moment I had a foreboding that she wouldn't live. Her death is an absolute knock-out blow to Ethel and myself and you – who are so keen about your own children, will understand this better than most. Bridget had managed to acquire any good looks there are in the Fane and Rumbold families and she was well-known in Berne as a beautiful child. She was just as jolly as she could be – in fact she was just about too good for this world. Well, this war has broken up hundreds of thousands – even millions of homes – and there was no particular reason why we should not have trouble also. And now we have got it in the neck.

'If Bridget had grown up', Rumbold wrote to his stepmother on July 22, 'she would have been unique.' Six days later he wrote that his wife 'is behaving with the greatest fortitude. . . . We find that this enormous Legation – as also many foreigners, look to us for support. Therefore it is up to us, in these times, to give an example of fortitude.' But, he added, 'nothing will ever replace our little Bridget'. On August 3 he wrote to

Newton: 'The house seems empty without her. . . . I have a great deal of absorbing work to do, but I have found it difficult lately to concentrate on it as I should.'

During August the allied advances continued slowly, but without set-back. 'There is great depression in Germany', Rumbold wrote to his stepmother on August 10. 'The new British attack should increase that depression.' 'The Kaiser', he added, 'is completely neurasthenic. I don't believe that any neutrals any longer believe in the possibility of a German victory; certainly the Swiss don't'. On August 14 Rumbold telegraphed to Balfour with news of 'complete disorder' inside Austria-Hungary. Bolshevism, he reported, was spreading in the eastern provinces. The minority races – in particular the Poles and Czechs – were working 'in close collaboration' against the Austrians. There was no one at Vienna 'strong enough to carry on the public business of the State'. In Germany, however, his informants had told him that 'complete order prevails', despite the gloom which followed the failure of the March offensive. Balfour circulated Rumbold's telegram to the War Cabinet. On August 24 Rumbold wrote to Newton: 'The Germans would give a great deal to be able to make peace but they are not yet in a frame of mind to accept our conditions.'

Bulgaria was the first of the Central Powers to sue for peace, and an armistice was signed on October 3. 'What extraordinary times we are living in', Rumbold wrote to Campbell four days later; 'History was never made at such a rapid rate as it is at present. I really think that our £120,000 did after all help to bring about the Bulgarian débâcle. Anyhow it probably sowed some of the seeds thereof and I do not think we need for a moment regret the expenditure. . . .' The main causes of the Bul-garian collapse, he believed, were 'the drought which made their harvest a failure, combined with intense war weariness. It is very satisfactory and I hope that Turkey will soon follow suit. You will notice that the Turks are round us like flies round honey and I am sure by the end of the year we shall have got rid of all our enemies except Germany.'

Throughout October Rumbold telegraphed to the Foreign Office, often several times each day and at great length, about the negotiators and inter-mediaries of the three remaining Central Powers. These telegrams were carefully studied at the Foreign Office, and frequently circulated by Balfour to the War Cabinet. Their tone was optimistic. 'A man who came from Cologne recently', he wrote to his stepmother on October 10, 'said that the feeling in the Rhine cities was that *we* had got Germany by the throat. The British bull-dog won't let go in a hurry – in fact he will never let go until his object is accomplished.' His own work, he added, 'has been

most strenuous lately and I can only compare it with the work I put in
during the 12 days of the crisis at Berlin.' Rumbold's fear was that the
Germans would ask for an armistice too soon. 'It will be a thousand pities',
he wrote to Ronald Campbell on October 14, 'if we are called off before
we hammer him completely on the Western Front. We ought to get into
his beastly country, for that is the only way of really bringing home to
him or to his population what war means. . . .'

On October 17, exhausted by his incessant work, Rumbold returned to
London for three weeks' leave. Two days later he met the Secretary of
State for War, Lord Derby,[1] who recorded in his diary: 'I have read with
intense amusement for the last 2 years the telegrams he has sent from Berne.
The most extravagant rumours have been detailed in length in his various
communications and if they were put together now they would show even
greater flights of imagination than H. G. Wells' book. All interest in
the telegrams has gone since I have seen him as I recognize now that it was
not a spirit of imagination that prompted him to send them. It was sheer
stupidity. I never came across a more stupid man in my life, both in
appearance and in conversation.'

On October 30, while Rumbold was still on leave in London, Turkey
signed an armistice with Britain. On November 3 Austria-Hungary
signed an armistice, and the ceasefire came into effect on the following
day. By November 5 only Germany remained at war with the Allies.
On reaching Berne in the first week of November Rumbold was confronted, to his surprise, by Mensdorff, whom he had not seen since the
outbreak of war. Mensdorff appealed to Rumbold for British food to be
sent to the starving population of Vienna. Because Mensdorff was a distant
relative of the King, Rumbold sent the King's Private Secretary, Lord
Stamfordham,[2] an account of the meeting on November 11:

He is rather bald and has grown much grayer. He was very quiet and depressed. The situation of his country would be sufficient to account for that but
I think he also felt that all hope of returning to England as Ambassador had gone
for ever. He asked after various people in England. He told me he had come
out of Austria by what he thought would be the last passenger train and he
travelled with various prominent Austrians. I do not know how long he intends
to remain here but he has got a secretary with him and told me somewhat sadly

---

[1] Edward George Villiers Stanley, 1865–1946. Conservative MP, 1892–1906. Postmaster-General, 1903–5. 17th Earl of Derby, 1908. Director-General of Recruiting, October
1915. Secretary of State for War, December 1916–18. Ambassador to France, 1918–20.
Secretary of State for War, 1922–24. He held no further political office after 1924.

[2] Arthur John Bigge, 1849–1931. Entered the Royal Household, 1880. Private Secretary
to Queen Victoria, 1895–1901; to King George V, 1910–31. Created Baron Stamfordham,
1910. His only son was killed in action on the Western Front in May 1915.

that he had not been able to get into the best hotel in Berne. If someone had said to me five years ago or less that Count Mensdorff would one day come to my room and implore me to get food sent to Vienna, I should have said that that person was a proper inmate for a lunatic asylum.

On November 11 the Germans signed their armistice with the allied powers. The Kaiser abdicated and sought refuge in Holland. A month later, in a letter to Hardinge on December 9, Rumbold recalled how armistice day had been received by the Swiss:

The news of the armistice fell absolutely flat at Berne and, in fact, was received, outwardly at least, with glacial indifference. It is true that there was a general strike on at the time but this is hardly sufficient to account for the indifference of the Bernese. I am myself inclined to think that the said Bernese used their anxiety about the strike as an excuse for hiding their feelings which were those of dismay. Neither the French Ambassador nor I received any card or letter of congratulation, and not a single Swiss here at Berne made a sign to either of us. I had often wondered what the day would be like when we heard that hostilities had ceased. The reality was utterly different to anything I had anticipated and I could not have imagined anything more depressing than Berne that day. The Bernese are singularly unattractive. In French-Switzerland of course the flags were flown everywhere and there was general rejoicing.

The war was over, but in Switzerland the first days of peace were troubled ones. 'Just at the present moment', Rumbold wrote to his step-mother on November 13, 'the Bolshevik and advanced elements in this country have engineered a general strike. No trains or trams are running and no papers appear so that, except for a few Reuter telegrams we do not know what is going on in the outside world.' The social unrest which Switzerland had avoided for four years had suddenly arrived. 'The Government', Rumbold added, 'have called out large number of troops and most of the Legations are protected.' For a few days there were fears of a Bolshevik uprising in Berne. Rumbold telegraphed to the Foreign Office details of Swiss Bolshevik activities. But the danger passed. Switzerland filled again with intermediaries, this time anxious to put forward national claims. 'The representatives of all the different nationalities which are now emerging as separate States', Rumbold wrote to Theo Russell on November 30, 'besiege this Legation with Memoranda etc.' 'The work here', he wrote to Campbell on December 2, 'is still very heavy though of a different order to what it was before the armistice with Germany. We are flooded with memoranda from Georgians, Ukrainians and others advocating the claims of their respective countries as also claims to territories belonging to their neighbours. I have collected quite a lot of maps put in by various nationalities; each representative is busy insinuating that the other man is a liar.' 'I still have plenty to do', he wrote to Newton on December 16; but, he added, 'of course most of the kick has gone out of it. My colleagues are suffering badly from reaction after the excitement of the last two years or more. I am also feeling the reaction. The work was so absorbing and delicate before the various armistices were signed that it is impossible not to feel the reaction. I had to take great risks from time to time and had to trust to luck not to make a mistake for a mistake might have led the Government into serious difficulties with our Allies. This made the work very exciting; all that is now over and I can only hope that I will be given a big and important post in Europe – with any luck an Embassy – after peace has been signed.' Rumbold told Newton that he was 'rather anxious to go to Warsaw', particularly as 'all the Polish business not transacted in London has passed through my hands during the war and I have got to know something about Poland and the Poles'. But the Foreign Office decided that he should remain in Berne.

On 30 November 1918, James Joyce,[1] who was then resident in Zurich, wrote to Rumbold to complain that a theatrical troupe which he had founded in Zurich, the English Players, had been boycotted by the British Consul-General, Andrew Bennett.[2] Joyce also accused Bennett of trying to conscript him into the British Army, and of not supporting him in a legal action connected with his theatrical work. In his letter of November 30 Joyce demanded 'that protection and redress from the insult of violence which are the right and privilege of the least of His Majesty's subjects'. Joyce was supported in his complaints by Ezra Pound,[3] who wrote to Rumbold on April 11, 1919:

If it be not already too late, I should like to caution you that you can find no surer means of making a few converts to Bolshevism or to the more violent revolutionary factions than by continuing or permitting to continue the persecution of James Joyce by the Zurich officials within the sphere of your influence.

I don't want to write 'scare heads' to you, and I don't imagine converts would be numerous, but they would probably be extremely vocal and active, a number

---

[1] James Augustine Joyce, 1882–1941. Irish novelist. He lived in Zurich from 1915 to 1919; in April 1918 he founded the English Players Company, for the production of plays in English. His novel *Ulysses* was published in Paris in 1922.

[2] Andrew Percy Bennett, 1866–1943. Entered the Consular Service, 1893. Consul-General, Zurich, 1899–1918. Minister to Panama, 1919–23; to Costa Rica, 1920–23; to Venezuela, 1924–27.

[3] Ezra Pound, 1885–1972. American poet; his first volume of poetry was published in 1908. London editor of *The Little Review*, 1917–19. Broadcast on Rome Radio after the Japanese attack on Pearl Harbor, 1941. Tried for treason, but found unfit to plead, 1945. Confined in a mental home, 1945–57. Resident in Italy from 1957 until his death.

of young men are not far from the borderline of these opinions; and a case like Joyce's would considerably enflame their imaginations. I would therefore request that some ambassadorial courtesy might be extended to this without exception, the most distinguished of the younger English prose authors. After all, literature was once considered an honourable calling. . . . I should very much regret having to undertake a publicity campaign on his behalf.

Rumbold did not reply, either to Joyce or Pound. Joyce was so angry that he changed the name of the English barber in *Ulysses* (which he was then writing) from Billington to Rumbold. On his way back from an Irish holiday, the barber offered the Sheriff of Dublin his services as a hangman, and after describing his skill in fastening and pulling nooses, was accepted. Joyce's story continued:

Quietly, unassumingly, Rumbold stepped on to the scaffold in faultless morning dress and wearing his favourite flower the *Gladiolus Cruentus*. He announced his presence by that gentle Rumboldian cough which so many have tried (unsuccessfully) to imitate – short, painstaking yet withal so characteristic of the man. The arrival of the world renowned headsman was greeted by a roar of acclamation from the huge concourse, the viceregal ladies waving their handkerchiefs in their excitement while the even more excitable foreign delegates cheered vociferously in a medley of cries, *hoch, banzai, eljen, zivio, chinchin, polla kromia, hiphip, vive, Allah.* . . .

In a private letter in July 1919 Joyce referred to Rumbold as 'Sir Whorearse Rumhole'.

At the end of November Rumbold and his wife went for two days to Strasbourg, reaching it less than forty-eight hours after the Germans had left. 'There are some eighty thousand Germans left in Strasbourg', Rumbold wrote to Newton on November 28, 'but the majority of those persons had, apparently, rushed out and bought rosettes with the French colours.' Shortly after reaching the city, Rumbold set off in search of a meal:

The French had not had time to pour provisions into the town, nevertheless, we got a wonderful lunch consisting of a very good soup, chicken and goose a la milanaise, a saddle of roe-deer and a sweet. The only evidence of the blockade was a paper table-cloth and some substitute coffee. Otherwise, we had as much sugar and butter as we wanted and they gave us small white rolls. . . . I was told that certain German officers had stayed behind at the Casino on the previous Friday and had photographed the French troops as they entered the town. The Boche is a surprising animal and seems to have no sense of dignity.

During December the influenza epidemic, which in a few months was to kill several million civilians throughout Europe, reached Switzerland. 'It is a beastly disease', Rumbold wrote to his stepmother on December 16. 'If only it would carry off the Bolsheviks and similar ruffians I wouldn't mind.' On New Year's Day, 1919, in a speech before the President of the Swiss Confederation, Gustav Ador,[1] Rumbold declared that 'the political horizon is far from free of clouds. The scourge of Bolshevism threatens the very foundations of civilisation.' Whether the new states being set up in Europe could act as a barrier to Bolshevism, no one could say. 'I have no great belief in the stability of these new states we are setting up,' Sir Maurice de Bunsen wrote to Rumbold on January 17, 'but it had to be done, as a means of breaking Germany, a job now so thoroughly accomplished.' Rumbold followed the peace negotiations in Paris closely, but was not concerned in them directly. 'I hope the new armistice terms will be really stiff', he wrote to Ronald Graham, who was at the Peace Conference, on February 17.

Rumbold looked forward to at least two months' leave, which he hoped to take at the end of April. 'I have had enough of work', he wrote to Newton on February 10, 'and need a rest.' To Theo Russell at the Foreign Office he wrote on March 7: 'The fact is that I am thoroughly tired and in need of a rest. I cannot sleep properly and I shall not recover my sleep until I have a complete change. One cannot go on indefinitely and I have had no leave since the autumn of 1913.'

Early in April Rumbold's leave began. He went first to Italy, then to England. The death of his daughter had much saddened him; it was a loss which he could not forget. While in London he received a letter from Lord Hardinge, sent from the Paris Peace Conference on June 4, formally offering him the post he had wanted, that of Minister to Poland. He returned to Berne in September to wind up the affairs of the Legation there, and to hand them over to Theo Russell, who had been appointed his successor. On October 27, when Rumbold had reached Warsaw, Russell wrote to him: 'You are both enormously regretted on all sides and I hope and feel sure you will establish an equally good position in Warsaw. When I was in London last, those in authority were seriously discussing you as a candidate for Berlin.' This rumour of a Berlin posting had been a persistent one. At the end of August the French newspaper *Le Temps* had announced 'as a fact' that Rumbold was to go as Ambassador to

---

[1] Gustave Ador, 1845–1928. Entered the Swiss Parliament, 1879. National Councillor (deputy for Geneva), 1891–1917. President of the Swiss Federation, 1919. President of the International Committee of the Red Cross. The only person mentioned by name in the Versailles Treaty. Honorary President of the League of Nations Assembly, 1921.

Germany and, this had been 'confirmed' by the *Daily Mail*, and applauded by the *Evening Standard*. 'The result', Lady Rumbold had written to her mother on August 28, 'is that H is bombarded with questions and telephones, as well as letters from *German* papers, if you please, asking for his photo.' But it was to Warsaw that Rumbold wanted to go, and to which he went.

James Joyce, who was still in Zurich, parodied Rumbold's appointment in a poem entitled 'The Right Man in the Wrong Place':

> The pig's in the barley,
> The fat's in the fire:
> Old Europe can hardly
> Find twopence to buy her.
> Jack Spratt's in his office,
> Puffed, powdered and curled:
> Rumbold's in Warsaw –
> All's right with the world.

12

Warsaw

1919–1920

At the beginning of October 1919 Poland had been independent for only a year, after more than a century under the triple rule of Germany, Austria and Russia. Its reconstituted territory came from the German, Russian and Habsburg Empires, each of which the war had destroyed. The frontier with the new German and Austrian states had been laid down at the Paris Peace Conference in the early months of 1919, with the exception of the areas of Teschen, Upper Silesia, Allenstein and Marienwerder, in each of which plebiscites were to be held under allied auspices. The frontier with Russia, which the Allies wanted settled on ethnic lines, did not yet exist; the Polish Army was moving steadily eastwards, and the Red Army was unable to halt their slow but persistent advance. The British Government wanted to limit Polish expansion eastwards to the eastern limit of 'ethnographic' Poland; but this line did not satisfy the Poles, who wished to include within their eastern boundary areas with a predominantly Lithuanian, White Russian and Ukrainian population.

Rumbold's initial impressions when he arrived in Warsaw in October 1919 did little to dispel the pessimism which had beset him while he had been in Switzerland. The Poles seemed to him to be as prone to intrigue in Warsaw as they had been in Berne. 'Poland', he wrote to his stepmother on October 18, 'is rather "oriental" in many ways.' Warsaw itself reminded him of Budapest and Petrograd: 'There are fine broad streets and good houses and any amount of Jews and poverty.' Lady Rumbold described Warsaw to her mother on 3 October 1919, as 'a large, extremely dirty, shoddy looking town, with everything looking as though it were tied up with string'. The aristocracy, however, impressed her. 'Without doubt the Poles have more than their fair share of charm', she wrote a week later. 'No other nationality possesses so much. The women are *very* pretty. . . .' But the populace were less attractive. 'I never saw such crowds, like Oxford Street in London. The Jews are too repugnant, in long dirty kaftans with *red*, or black beards and ringlets.'

Polish officialdom, Rumbold found, was hard to stir into action. But, he explained in his letter to his stepmother of October 18, 'I have hustled the Poles in a way to which they are not accustomed.' On October 27 he

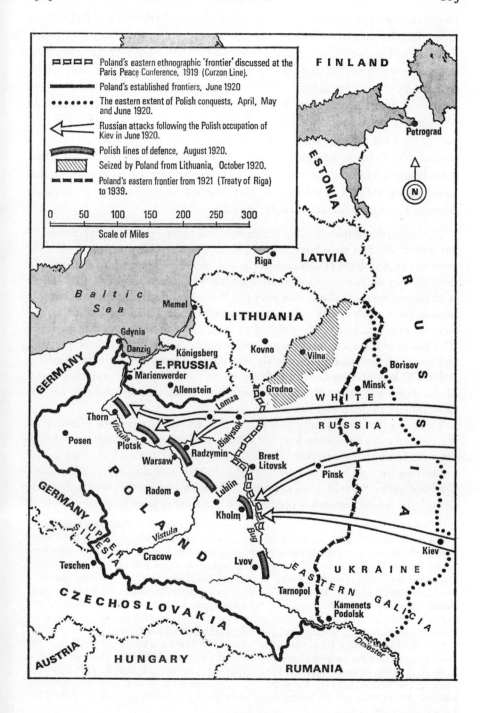

wrote to Lord Hardinge: 'I realised before I came here that the Poles were rather unreliable and excitable, but this has come home to me with much force since I arrived here.' Even Paderewski,[1] the Polish Prime Minister, 'let me down the other day', he added; 'but once bit twice shy, and we all have to buy our experience'. These sceptical sentiments did not prevent Rumbold from seeing the Polish point of view. 'I feel considerable sympathy', he wrote to Charles Wingfield[2] on October 23, 'for this country which is in the most unenviable geographical position. The business of the Poles is to get as strong as possible before their two great neighbours recover their strength.' On November 16 he set down his thoughts on Poland in a letter to Hardinge, which Hardinge showed to the new Foreign Secretary, Lord Curzon:

The original enthusiasm of the Poles over the recovery of their independence has passed off, and they have now realised that they have got to turn their attention to problems of reconstruction and to the building up of the state. In this task they are handicapped by an utter lack of efficient administrators. There is, of course, no particular reason why the Poles should have a supply of capable officials since such officials were not encouraged under either the Russian or the German regimes. The result is that they have had to scrape together anybody who has ever filled any post before under either of the former three empires, and many of the prominent officials are recruited from amongst the Austrian Poles. The lack of capable officials added to the natural slackness and insouciance of the Poles and especially the Russian Poles makes it very difficult for the Government to get things done.

There is a further difficulty and that is the attitude of the Jews. I have it on the authority of a prominent Jew, not a Pole, who is in the best position to know what the feelings of the Jews are in this country, that a large section of the Jewish population have no belief in Poland continuing to exist as an independent state. I did not gather that this is an instance of the wish being father to the thought, though the above mentioned opinion of a great many Jews may coincide with

[1] Ignacy Jan Paderewski, 1860–1941. Pianist and Composer. A leading propagandist for Polish independence, 1914–17, based at Vevey in Switzerland. Organized, in the United States, a Polish army to fight in France, 1917. Representative of the Polish National Committee in the United States, 1917–18. Disembarked at Danzig from a British cruiser, December 24, 1918. Prime Minister of Poland, and also Foreign Minister, January–November 1919. One of the two Polish signatories of the Versailles Treaty, June 1919. Polish Representative at the League of Nations, Geneva, 1920–21. An opponent of Pilsudski's regime, he lived in Switzerland, and on his estate in California, 1921–39. Chairman, Polish National Council (in exile), 1939–41. He died in New York.

[2] Charles John FitzRoy Rhys Wingfield, 1877–1960. Served in the Royal Fusiliers, 1896–1901, retiring with the rank of Captain. Entered the Diplomatic Service, 1901. Counsellor, Madrid, 1919–22; Brussels, 1922–26; Rome, 1926–28. Minister at Bangkok, 1928–29; Oslo, 1929–34; the Vatican, 1934–35. Knighted, 1933. Ambassador in Lisbon, 1935–37. Adviser on Foreign Affairs, Ministry of Information, 1939–41. He married Lady Rumbold's sister, Lucy Evelyn Fane, in 1905.

their wishes. But it is obvious that such an attitude on the part of a considerable section of the community must tend to weaken the state as a whole. I fear that the Jews are amongst the most shameless of the profiteers, and profiteering in this country has reached considerable dimensions.

Paderewski is to me a very sympathetic personality, but he has the defects of his qualities. His artistic temperament betrays itself in a disregard for the necessary economy, and I am told that the Foreign Office here is an example of scandalous waste. You have only to look at the diplomatic establishments maintained by Poland in London and Paris for instance for an illustration of what I mean. We are content here with one first secretary and perhaps two other secretaries, but the Poles have two Counsellors in London and the same in Paris, while they maintain a most expensive messenger service between Paris and Warsaw.

The Poles are also very difficult people to deal with. They are very sensitive and while they know quite well that they need foreign help and advice to enable them to put their administration on a sound footing, it is difficult to talk very straight to them, although I have done so once or twice to men I have known properly. I do not consider that it is the act of a friend to go on flattering these people and telling them what fine people they are. They want some wholesome advice, and they know it, but the difficulty is how to impart such advice.

During the winter months of 1919 the Poles were eager to push their frontier as far eastwards as possible. The Bolsheviks were little able to resist Polish military pressure, but Rumbold was sceptical that it could be prolonged. 'According to a secret report which I have just read', he reported to Hardinge on October 27, 'and which is confirmed by something Paderewski said to me the other day, the morale of the army on the eastern front is beginning to go.' As winter approached, lack of adequate supplies of greatcoats and boots added to the problem.

Rumbold was confronted by a variety of facts and rumours. 'The intrigues are even worse than in Switzerland', he wrote on November 22 to Lord St Cyres,[1] who had been on his staff at Berne, 'and the people of the place more difficult to deal with, being extraordinarily touchy, prone to exaggeration and generally unreliable'. The social inequalities of Warsaw also made a strong impression on him. 'Polish society', he told St Cyres, 'reminds me a good deal of Austrian society in the old days. They love amusing themselves and seem to do so regardless of the poverty and misery. . . . It was pathetic to see the long lines of people outside the bread shops, who on one or two days could not get anything to eat.

---

[1] Stafford Harry Northcote, Viscount St Cyres, 1869–1926. Only son of the 2nd Earl o ddesleigh. Clerical Assistant, Queen Alexandra Military Hospital, Milbank, London, 1915–17. Honorary Secretary, British Legation, Berne, April 1917; Honorary Counsellor, April 1918. Resigned through ill-health, December 1918. He died a year before his father.

Meanwhile there was everything in the restaurants.' To his stepmother he wrote on December 8: 'It cannot be said that *the* society – however pleasant they are – contribute much if anything to set Poland on her legs. They just amuse themselves as if there were no crisis at all. But the situation is far from healthy. . . .'

Rumbold soon won the confidence of the Poles, even if he could not easily influence their policies. A junior member of his staff, Victor Cavendish-Bentinck,[1] later wrote:

Whilst HR had to give much unpalatable advice to the Poles and represented a Government hostile to their ambitions, he was greatly respected and well liked. . . . He had the most important attributes for a Chef de Mission, viz: calmness – he was never flustered – shrewdness in observation, clarity in reporting and a capacity for inspiring trust and confidence; all who dealt with him knew that he was imbued with deep moral honesty. His appearance tended to disguise his ability. I have often seen someone, who was under the illusion that HR was not very intelligent, try to put something across him. HR would listen, then drop his eyeglass into his hand, shoot out his cuffs and make a couple of comments that swiftly dispelled any doubts about his mental capacity.

The Polish attitude towards Britain was at times hostile, despite British support for the new Polish state. The British Government, while encouraging Poland as a buffer between the defeated Germany and Bolshevik Russia had refused, categorically, to support Polish territorial claims over Eastern Galicia, which until 1918 had been part of Austria-Hungary. Britain's refusal led to an incident at the British Legation early in December. Rumbold gave a dinner for various leading Poles, to be followed by a dance. One of the Poles who had been invited, Prince Lubomirski,[2] was responsible for sending an anonymous note to all the guests to say that, on account of Britain's rejection of Polish claims to Eastern Galicia, they could go to the dinner, but were not to dance. 'The music tuned up', Rumbold wrote to Hardinge on December 13, 'and we thought we had primed our guests well with a good dinner. But they would not dance and sat about looking very sheepish and uncomfortable.'

[1] Victor Frederick William Cavendish-Bentinck, 1897–   . Entered the Diplomatic Service, 1915. Served under Rumbold in Warsaw, as 3rd Secretary, and was present at the Lausanne Conference, 1922–23. Assistant Under-Secretary of State at the Foreign Office, 1944. Ambassador to Warsaw, 1945–47. Since 1947 active in the Chemical industry, and a Director of several companies, including Baywood Chemicals Ltd., Bayer Dye-stuffs Ltd, Philip Hill Investment Trust and Metrogate Property Holdings Limited.

[2] Zdzislaw Lubomirski, 1865–1941. A member of one of Poland's aristocratic families. President of the City Council of Warsaw, 1915–17. After Poland was given semi-autonomous status by the Germans in 1916, he was appointed one of the three members of the Regency Council, a position which he held from 1917–18. In 1917, in a letter to Balfour, Rumbold described Lubomirski's language in Berlin and Vienna as 'so obsequious as almost to be grovelling'.

The head of the British Military Mission, Carton de Wiart,[1] who was present, thereupon told the Poles 'what he thought of them in no measured language'. 'General Carton de Wiart was white with fury', Lady Rumbold wrote to her mother on December 11, 'and said in a loud voice "*I should turn the whole lot out of the house if I were you*". He is very popular (a VC with 10 wound stripes) and knows these Poles well, so he gave them a bit of his mind all round.'

De Wiart's outburst roused the pro-British sentiments of another of the guests, Adam Zamoyski,[2] who at once challenged Prince Lubomirski to a duel for insulting the British. Fortunately de Wiart, whom Zamoyski chose as one of his seconds, was able to mediate, and the duel was called off. 'I have told you the above', Rumbold explained to Hardinge, 'in order to show you the sort of people one deals with here. Many of them have an exaggerated idea of their own importance, and the feelings, certainly of people in society are, I am sure, only skin deep. There are precious few of the latter category who have done anything for Poland. They all crab each other to me, and not only crab each other, but they crab my colleagues and their own Ministers to me. They are a curious race, and I sometimes wonder if they will ever make anything of their country.' Rumbold did not allow the incident to depress him unduly. 'I still hope for the best', he wrote to Hardinge, 'and I do not despair of their pulling themselves together. They have been heavily handicapped at the start and need and deserve encouragement.' Hardinge was also dubious about the Poles' ability to 'make anything of their country. They never have so far', he replied on January 6, 'and as they always seem to be quarrelling among themselves, I don't see why they ever should pull themselves together in the future.' Lady Rumbold shared these pessimistic beliefs. 'These people are charming to meet', she had written to her mother on November 10, 'but one can't believe a thing they say, and they are thoroughly corrupt. One wonders whether they will be able to get along as a nation.'

In an attempt to improve Anglo-Polish relations, Rumbold wrote to Philip Kerr, hoping to enlist Lloyd George's sympathy. He explained to

[1] Adrian Carton de Wiart, 1880–1963. Born in Brussels; educated at Oxford. Served in the South African War, 1901 (twice wounded) in Somaliland, 1914–15 (severely wounded) and on the Western Front, 1915–18 (eight times wounded, and awarded the Victoria Cross). Commanded the British Military Mission to Poland, 1918–24. Retired, 1924. Recalled, 1939. Commanded the Central Norwegian Expeditionary Force, 1940. Taken prisoner of war in the Middle East, 1941; freed, 1943. British Military Representative with Chiang Kai-shek, 1943–46. Knighted, 1945. He published his memoirs, *Happy Odyssey*, in 1950.

[2] Count Adam Zamoyski, 1873–1940. Member of a leading Polish aristocratic family. Aide-de-Camp to Tsar Nicholas II, 1914–17. Returned to Poland after the assassination of the Tsar, 1917. President of the Polish Gymnastic Society between the wars.

Kerr, in a letter on December 6, that the Poles regarded Britain's setting up of Danzig as a Free City outside Polish jurisdiction, and her refusal to support Polish claims to Eastern Galicia, as 'proof of our unfriendly feelings'. They ask, he went on, 'what is the good of having brought a child into the world if you do not endow it with the gifts usually presented by godfathers'. Rumbold told Kerr that to this he always replied 'that if it had not been for us there would not have been a child at all', but he felt that the time had come for a more positive British act of friendship. As he wrote in his letter to Kerr, the Polish Army, alone of the many anti-Bolshevik armies which had been in existence at the beginning of 1919, still had sufficient strength to keep the Bolsheviks at bay, and even, if encouraged, to advance against them. He asked Kerr if Lloyd George might not see his way 'to give the Poles a pat on the back'.

Kerr replied from 10 Downing Street on December 15. 'Lloyd George had always believed', he wrote, 'that the best friend of Poland was the man who set his face against the inclusion in Poland of non-Polish minorities.' There was little comfort for the Poles in such advice, nor in the rest of Lloyd George's opinions, as set out bluntly in Kerr's letter:

If the Poles, and their short-sighted friends, had had their way Poland would have had as its bitterest enemies all her neighbours, each one of whom would be spending its time in trying to get back what it regarded its own, by fomenting discord within Poland through the members of its own race.

Mr Lloyd George has always said that the real thing for Poland was a settlement which both the German people and the Russian people would recognise to be just. That is why he has always insisted that German majorities, except where they are scattered, should not be under Polish rule, and that Danzig should be a Free City. He takes exactly the same view about Eastern Galicia. There is a two thirds majority of Ruthenians in that country. Sooner or later Russia and the Ukraine will regenerate. Is it going to be for the strength of Poland or the stability of Europe that Poland should be permitted to create permanently a glorified Alsace Lorraine in Eastern Galicia?

Everybody agrees that there is a wonderful spirit in Poland today, and that to enter Poland from Russia is to pass into light from darkness, but there is a section of Polish opinion which undoubtedly has lost its perspective. Some of the French militarists who encouraged Poland to annex because they think it means a larger anti-German army are just as bad. They forget that Poland as yet has done little or nothing to establish the fact of its ability to maintain a modern progressive state, except that it has clung to its nationality and endured terrible hardships for that cause.

Kerr went on to ask Rumbold to tell the Poles that 'there is no hostility to Poland at all in the Prime Minister's mind', but that he was looking at the Polish problem 'not merely in terms of 1919–1920, but in the light of a thousand years of European history, and of the inevitable fact that Poland's neighbours, which today are prostrate, will ere long become strong, vigorous and patriotic nations'.

Before learning of Lloyd George's opinions, Rumbold had written to the Foreign Office to ask if it were possible to obtain Treasury sanction for a three million pound loan to Poland. Such a loan, he believed, would do much to offset Polish bitterness towards Britain over its territorial frustrations. But when Ronald Campbell wrote to him from the Foreign Office on December 18, it was to state emphatically that no such loan was possible. 'We have poured enormous sums into every corner of Europe', Campbell wrote, 'none of which there seems any immediate prospect of getting back.' The Treasury, he added, 'are determined to call a halt'. There was no consolation for Rumbold, or the Poles, in Campbell's own belief that Britain had 'already spent so much that it would be well to spend just a little more if it were going to make all the difference, as I think it would, towards getting a return for our money'. No loan was forthcoming; nor were Rumbold's efforts or Campbell's sympathy enough to counteract the growing Polish belief that, if a crisis came in their relations with Bolshevik Russia, Britain might withhold its support.

During December, Rumbold was busy trying to ascertain Poland's military intentions towards Russia. It was not easy to do so; Pilsudski,[1] who was both Chief of the Polish State and Commander-in-Chief of the Polish Armed Forces, had, as Rumbold wrote to Hardinge on December 19, 'been a conspirator nearly all his life, through force of circumstances. . . . He has interviews etc. all through the night, sometimes not going to bed until six or seven in the morning. He is one of those persons who thinks he must do everything himself, and the result is that he is working himself to death. He is very much like Kitchener in many ways.' With Kitchener, he shared also a heightened sense of secrecy, which was intensified by the atmosphere of suspicion and intrigue with which he and his policies were surrounded. Rumbold persevered in trying to reach a clear picture of Pilsudki's intentions. On December 29 he wrote to Lord

[1] Joseph Clemens Pilsudski, 1867–1935. Born in the Vilna Province of Russian Poland. Involved in an anti-Tsarist plot and deported to Siberia, 1887–92. Edited, printed and distributed a secret Radical paper, *Robotnik*, 1894–1900, when he was arrested in Lodz and imprisoned for a year. Escaped from prison in St Petersburg, 1901. In exile in London, 1901–2. Established a Polish army in Austrian Poland, 1908–14; in 1914 his 10,000 men fought in the Austro-Hungarian Army. Minister of War in the Council of State, Warsaw (under Central Power auspices), 1916–17. His army refused to support the Germans in July 1917; he was imprisoned by the Germans, July 1917–November 1918. Chief of the Polish State, November 1918–December 1922. Chief of the General Staff, 1923. Retired from public life, July 1923. Occupied Warsaw, May 1926. Minister of War from 1926 until his death. Prime Minister, 1927–28 and 1930.

Acton, who had served under him in Switzerland, that the weakness of Poland's military situation would prevent an anti-Bolshevik offensive that winter. There was a serious lack of winter clothing, and also, as Rumbold explained, the front line was 'a good deal in advance of any railway running parallel to the front and has to be revictualled by carts'. It seemed to him that Pilsudski 'always preferred to nibble away at the Bolshevist front rather than go in for any big operations'. It was by such a method, Rumbold believed, 'that he has pushed the Bolshevists back a very considerable distance and they have never been able to make much impression on the Polish army'.

In the middle of December General Denikin,[1] the Russian anti-Bolshevik leader who had hitherto refused to co-operate with the Poles, expressed his willingness to contemplate some joint action with Pilsudski. With the approval of the Cabinet, the British representative with Denikin's Army, Sir Halford Mackinder,[2] visited Warsaw, and on December 16 he and Rumbold called on Pilsudski to urge a joint effort. 'Sir H Mackinder and I', Rumbold wrote to Lord Cromer's son Rowland[3] on February 1, 'proposed a combination of Poland and General Denikin against the Bolshevists. Roumania might also have joined this combination.' But Pilsudski did not intend to follow up this proposal, fearing that if, with Polish help, Denikin were to reach Moscow and overthrow the Bolsheviks, he might then turn against the Poles, and try to put eastern Poland and Warsaw once more under Russian rule. At their meeting, Pilsudski reassured Rumbold that Poland had no 'imperialist desires' over western Russia, and would accept plebiscites in the disputed border areas. Both Rumbold and Mackinder believed that Pilsudski and Denikin would work together. But Denikin sabotaged the plan by insisting that Pilsudski

---

[1] Anton Ivanovich Denikin, 1872–1947. Entered the Tsarist Army in 1887; served in the Russo-Japanese War, 1904–5. Commanded, first a Division, then a Corps, in the First World War. Deputy Chief of Staff, February 1917. Commander of the Western Front, March 1917; of the South Western Front, May 1917. Commander-in-Chief of the Armed Forces of the South (anti-Bolshevist), 1918–19. Escaped first to Constantinople, then to France, 1920. Emigrated to the United States, 1945.

[2] Halford John Mackinder, 1861–1947. Reader in Geography, Oxford University, 1887–1905. Professor of Geography, University of London, 1905–25. Made the first ascent of Mount Kenya, 1909. Conservative MP, 1910–22. Head of British Mission to Denikin, 1919. British High Commissioner for South Russia, 1919–20. Knighted, 1920. Chairman of the Imperial Shipping Committee, 1920–45.

[3] Rowland Thomas Baring, 1877–1953. Served in the Diplomatic Service, 1900–7 and the Foreign Office, 1907–11. Managing Director, Baring Brothers, merchant bankers, 1912–13. Aide-de-Camp to the Viceroy of India, 1915–16. Assistant Private Secretary to George V, 1916–20. Succeeded his father as 2nd Earl, 1917. Lord Chamberlain of His Majesty's Household, 1922–38. British Government Director of the Suez Canal Company, 1926–50. Lord-in-Waiting to George VI, 1938–52 and to Elizabeth II, 1952–53.

attack the Bolsheviks first, and by refusing to offer Poland anything approaching the eastern frontier which she demanded. By the end of December Denikin's army was being seriously mauled by the Bolsheviks and by mid-January it was clear to all observers that if Pilsudski were to launch an offensive against the Bolsheviks he would have to do so alone.
Rumbold did not believe that the Poles could fight the Bolsheviks without assistance. If such assistance were not forthcoming, Poland ought to make peace. But Britain must not abandon Poland to destruction. On January 19 Rumbold sent Curzon a long telegram, explaining his advice. 'The situation here is undoubtedly serious', he reported, 'from every point of view. Prices are rising daily; meat is no longer within reach of the poor and economic conditions generally are favourable for the spread of Bolshevism. Typhus is spreading throughout the country. The value of the mark is steadily depreciating, nothing is being exported and the Poles are now in a vicious circle from which there are only two avenues of escape i.e. a settlement of one sort or another with the Bolshevists and, eventually, the resumption of exports.' By itself, he believed, the Polish Army could not 'finally dispose of the Bolshevists', even though the Polish troops, man for man, were 'infinitely superior' to the Russian. Yet Poland could not, in Rumbold's opinion, be allowed to succumb to Russian attack. 'If the Polish barrier against Bolshevism goes', he added, 'the barrier will be shifted much further west and an opportunity will be given to latent Bolshevism in Czecho-Slovakia to join hands with Russian Bolshevism, thereby creating a very serious state of things for Central Europe and the Western Powers. . . . To sum up, whilst I would strongly deprecate a Polish offensive against the Bolshevists if the Poles are to stand alone, I am of the opinion that everything should be done to assist them to withstand a Bolshevist offensive.' British aid, he believed, given even for a purely defensive policy, would give Britain a hold over the Poles 'to check any imperialistic tendencies'.

Since November 1919 Lloyd George had been urging his Cabinet to agree to the restoration of trade and amicable relations with the Bolsheviks. On November 8, speaking at the Guildhall, he had stated that 'the world cannot afford a continuance of the struggle in Russia, which is devastating a country essential to the world's prosperity'. In January 1920 he announced publicly that Britain would soon begin trade negotiations with Russia. The Poles received this news with 'consternation', Rumbold reported to Curzon on January 19. Ten days later the new Polish Foreign Minister, Stanislas Patek,[1] saw Lloyd George at 10 Downing Street. The

---

[1] Stanislas Patek, 1866–1945. Barrister; in 1905 he defended several Poles accused by the Russians of subversive activity. A member of the Polish National Committee in Paris, 1919,

Prime Minister told Patek that if Poland invaded Russia in the spring, Britain would refuse to help. Lloyd George added that he 'wished to make it perfectly clear to the Polish Government that the British Government did not wish to give Poland the slightest encouragement to pursue a policy of war, because if it were to give that advice it would incur responsibilities which it could not discharge.' He went on to criticize the fact that the Polish Army had advanced 'far beyond the racial boundary into territories which contained large Russian majorities'. If Poland insisted on retaining these boundaries, and if the Soviet Government then attacked Poland 'in order to recover Russian districts for Russia', then the British Government would, Lloyd George insisted, be unable to persuade public opinion 'to support any military or financial outlay'. Above all, 'His Majesty's Government did not want Poland, which was itself short of food and raw materials, to maintain an economic barrier owing to her warlike operations against Russia, whilst the Allies were themselves trading to the best of their ability with the Russian people'. On the following day the Cabinet endorsed Lloyd George's remarks. Curzon was instructed to inform Rumbold that owing to British economic weakness, and in view of the growing concern of British public opinion, there was no question of Britain again making war against the Bolsheviks. It is fairly clear', Rumbold minuted on Curzon's telegram, 'that the Poles will now have to come to terms with the Bolsheviks.'

At the end of January the Bolsheviks offered to make peace with Poland. This offer, Rumbold wrote to Hardinge on February 1, 'coming on the top of the Prime Minister's conversation with Patek is pretty sure to result in Poland coming to terms with the Bolshevists'. Then, he believed, the real danger to Poland would come from Germany, not Russia. There were nearly three million German-born subjects in Poland, mostly in the Posen Province. 'The Germans', Rumbold wrote to Lord Cromer on February 1, 'are going in for propaganda in Posen against Poland. . . . Thinking Poles openly admit that the Germans will never forgive them for the loss of Posen and other districts. I do not envy the position of this country and am sorry for it.' The Poles, he wrote on the following day to Francis Lindley[1] in Vienna, 'want peace and quiet in

---

and of the Polish Delegation to the Paris Peace Conference. Minister of Foreign Affairs, 1919–20. Minister to Tokyo, 1921–26; to Moscow, 1926–32. Ambassador to Washington, 1933–35. Senator, 1936–39. In a letter to Lord Hardinge on July 10, 1920, Rumbold described Patek as 'a chattering lawyer'.

[1] Francis Oswald Lindley, 1872–1950. 4th son of Baron Lindley. Entered Diplomatic Service, 1897. 3rd Secretary at Vienna, 1899. 2nd Secretary, Cairo, 1904–6. Counsellor of Embassy, Petrograd, 1915–17. Commissioner in Russia, 1918; Consul-General, Russia, 1919; High Commissioner Vienna, 1919–20. Minister to Athens, 1922–23; to Oslo, 1923–29.

order to get on with the task of building up their country'. Although the idea of Poland or of Britain recognizing the Bolshevik regime was, he told Lindley, 'repugnant to me', he did not see how recognition could be avoided. 'This would be welcomed by our dear friends in the Labour Party at home', he wrote, 'not to speak of others not belonging to the Labour Party. It will be another case of evil triumphing.' In Poland itself, he warned Curzon on February 2, 'a very large section of public opinion will be most reluctant to come to terms with the Bolshevists. Those in favour of doing so principally include the Socialists and the Jews.'

On February 9 Pilsudski saw General de Wiart, and declared – as Rumbold telegraphed to Curzon on the following day – that he wished to avoid 'all appearance of capitulating to Bolsheviks'. He felt confident that if necessary Poland could carry on the war with Russia 'for several months' and added 'that his latest information from Russia indicated that the Soviet Government were badly in need of peace'. During the conversation Pilsudski remarked that one positive effect of Britain's refusal to support a forward military policy was 'that Poland which had hitherto been accustomed to lean on Western Powers should realise that she must stand alone'.

Largely as a result of Britain's insistence Pilsudski was preparing a set of peace terms to present to the Russians. But he did not really want to make peace. On February 17 he told Rumbold – who sent a report of the conversation to Curzon – 'that the Western Powers could afford to await developments in Russia. Poland, being a limitrophe State, could not afford to do so.' Rumbold pointed out that the anti-Bolshevik armies of Denikin, Kolchak[1] and Yudenitch[2] had each failed, and that it was 'not surprising that the British nation was tired of helping people who could not help themselves'. Britain, Rumbold emphasized, 'did not wish to be involved in further adventures, as might be the case supposing it

---

Knighted, 1926. He published his memoirs, *A Diplomat off Duty*, in 1928. Ambassador to Portugal, 1929–31; to Japan 1931–34. Member of the Home Office Advisory Committee on Interned Aliens, 1939–45.

[1] Alexander Vasilievich Kolchak, 1870–1920. A Crimean Tartar by birth. Entered the Tsarist Navy, 1888. Admiral and Arctic Explorer. Commanded the Black Sea Fleet, 1916–17. Leader of the anti-Bolshevik forces in Siberia, 1918–19; proclaimed himself Supreme Ruler of Russia, November 18, 1918. Taken prisoner by the Bolsheviks at Irkutsk, and shot, February 7, 1920.

[2] Nikolai Nikolaievich Yudenitch, 1862–1933. Entered the Tsarist Army, 1879. General, 1905. Chief of Staff of the Russian Army, 1913–14. Commander-in-Chief of the Caucasus Front, October 1914–October 1915, and March–October 1917. Commander-in-Chief of the North-Western Army (anti-Bolshevist), June 1919. Arrested by another General after the failure of his attack on Petrograd, he was released as a result of allied intervention, and emigrated to Britain.

encouraged the Poles to undertake offensive operations against the Bolshevists'. When the acting British High Commissioner to South Russia, Brigadier-General Keyes,[1] suggested a meeting between Denikin and Pilsudski to co-ordinate anti-Bolshevik activities, Rumbold on his own initiative, refused to broach the suggestion to Pilsudski. 'I concur in your views', Curzon telegraphed on February 26. 'We cannot any longer act as intermediaries between General Denikin and the neighbouring Governments in negotiations which might involve the latter in aggressive action against the Bolsheviks.'

On March 8 the Polish peace terms were presented to the Polish Cabinet. Five days later Patek handed them to Rumbold, for transmission to London. As soon as he saw them, Rumbold realized that they would be unacceptable to Russia, and told Patek so in blunt terms. He expressed amazement at Poland's demand for the frontiers of 1772, pointing out, as he telegraphed to Curzon on March 14, that these frontiers 'included a large part of historical Lithuania as well as a large portion of the Ukraine'. Rumbold told Patek that, in his opinion, 'if Bolsheviks made peace with Poles on basis of present peace conditions, and then violated their agreement and attacked Poles, latter could count on no help whatever from Great Britain'. Curzon approved this severe warning. In April Curzon's Assistant Secretary, John Gregory,[2] wrote to Rumbold to say that the Foreign Secretary had 'expressed the utmost confidence in your judgement and told me that he looked on you as one of our ablest representatives abroad etc. This was à propos of your long telegram on the Polish peace terms. . . . He said, if I remember right, that we could safely leave it to you to direct us in the way we should go. It is unusual for him to be so enthusiastic!' In his telegram to Curzon, Rumbold expressed his belief that the Poles were 'quite prepared for a rejection of their proposed basis of discussion', and that they believed they would gain either by such a peace, or by war. What Pilsudski really intended, Rumbold did not guess at. 'He keeps his own counsel', Rumbold wrote to Curzon on March 21. 'He will only reveal his policy at the moment it suits him, and, in the meantime, he is very skilful in the art of suggestion.'

On March 27 Patek informed the Russians that Poland was willing to

[1] Terence Humphrey Keyes, 1877–1939. Entered Army, 1897. Wounded in the Tirah Campaign, 1898. On Famine Duty, Central Provinces, India, 1900. Political Agent, Bahrein, 1914. Served in Mesopotamia, 1915–16. Attached to the Russian Army in Eastern Rumania, 1917–18. Brigadier-General, General Staff, Army of the Black Sea, 1919. Acting High Commissioner, South Russia, 1919–20. British Envoy, Nepal. Resident, Gwalior, 1928–29. Resident, Hyderabad, 1930–33. Knighted, 1933.

[2] John Duncan Gregory, 1878–1951. Entered Foreign Office, 1902; Assistant Secretary, 1920–25; Assistant Under-Secretary of State, 1925–28. He published his memoirs, *On the Edge of Diplomacy*, in 1929.

open peace negotiations on April 10. But Rumbold believed, as he wrote to Curzon two days later, that while Patek would do 'his utmost to conclude a speedy peace', Pilsudski would 'continue to hit the Bolsheviks as hard as possible'.

While waiting for peace negotiations to begin between Russia and Poland, Rumbold made two suggestions which he hoped would ameliorate Anglo-Polish relations, and help to undermine the growing belief in Europe that Poland was essentially a French, rather than a British area of concern and influence. On March 29 he sent Curzon a long letter arguing in favour of concessions to Poland over the Free City of Danzig. The Poles, he wrote, saw in the German citizen of Danzig 'a representative of militant Germany, the old enemy, seeking to throttle his free access to the sea and to the markets of the world'. One argument against giving the Poles administrative powers in Danzig had been that for over a hundred years they had been allowed little experience in administration. If this were a valid objection, Rumbold wrote, 'then it would seem illogical to have handed over a well-administered country like Prussian Poland to the new Polish State. Unless the Poles begin to administer, how can they learn, and who is to be the judge of the moment at which they may be supposed to have attained sufficient training and sagacity?' Rumbold's arguments were of no avail. Danzig remained a Free City outside Polish jurisdiction, and the Poles had to build up a new exit to the sea, at Gdynia.

Rumbold's second effort to improve Anglo-Polish relations took the form of a request to Curzon, on March 30, not to recall the British Naval Mission from Poland.[1] The Treasury were insisting on recalling the Mission unless the Poles would pay for its cost. To withdraw the Mission, Rumbold insisted, 'would be politically a grave mistake, and would be considered as another proof that Great Britain was disinteresting herself in Poland'. There was another reason which Rumbold urged; if the British Mission had to go, the French would probably set up a Naval Mission of their own, and gradually come to superintend the Polish merchant navy. This would deprive Britain of a valuable economic advantage, because, Rumbold wrote, in a few years time, as British trading increased, and if good relations had been preserved with the Poles and naval links maintained, there would open up 'a lucrative field for British commercial

---

[1] The British Naval Mission, consisting of five officers under Commander F. Wharton, RN, had, throughout 1920, advised the Polish Naval Department on (i) organizing a merchant marine training college, (ii) drafting a Marine Shipping Act for Poland, (iii) setting up a Polish Hydrographical Department, (iv) establishing naval wireless stations, and (v) maintaining and supervising work on the six torpedo-boats handed over to Poland by Germany. The mission was withdrawn on January 15, 1921.

enterprise'. None of these arguments were effective; ten months later the Naval Mission was withdrawn.

The Polish–Russian peace negotiations foundered at the outset, ostensibly on the question of where they were to take place. The Poles suggested the town of Borisov, in the zone of the two armies. The Bolsheviks wanted another site, and appealed to Britain and France to put pressure on the Poles to secure it. 'If the Allies are wise', Rumbold wrote on April 12 to Lord Kilmarnock,[1] the British Chargé d'Affaires in Berlin, 'they will not pay any attention. . . . I have advised our Government to let the Poles come to the best agreement they can with the Bolsheviks without any interference.' Curzon accepted Rumbold's advice. Behind it lay Rumbold's belief, which he explained in a letter to Lord St Cyres on April 21, that Bolshevism might collapse entirely in Russia 'within a month or two', and that the Poles had 'only to sit tight' to reap the benefit.

Throughout April Rumbold was at work drafting the first 'Annual Report' on Poland. Its forty-seven pages dealt with political, diplomatic and economic events throughout the previous year. 'The Poles', Rumbold stated 'with General Pilsudski at their head, have a profound mistrust of the Bolshevik Government.' Rumbold's diagnosis was correct; on April 24 Pilsudski launched his military offensive against Russia. The Bolsheviks fell back, surprised by the severity of the Polish attack. Within ten days the Poles had captured 25,000 prisoners. On May 3 the Bolshevik forces evacuated Kiev, the capital of the Ukraine, which was entered by Pilsudski four days later. 'There was much loose talk in Warsaw', Rumbold telegraphed to Curzon on May 12, 'about an advance on Moscow'; talk which, Rumbold warned the Director of the Political Department, Zdzislaw Okencki,[2] could do them 'much harm' among those who sympathized with their aspirations. As a result of their successes, Rumbold advised, the Poles 'had an unique opportunity of showing modification and commonsense in their future dealings with Soviet Russia'.

The success of the Polish attack rallied many anti-Bolshevik Russians to the defence of their native land. General Brusilov offered his services to the Soviet Government, and over 12,000 anti-Bolshevik prisoners of war, from the defeated armies of Denikin, Kolchak and Yudenitch, volunteered to fight against the Poles. In Britain too there was an outburst of anti-Polish feeling, particularly throughout the Labour movement. On May 19

[1] Victor Alexander Sereld Hay, Baron Kilmarnock, 1876–1928. Elder son of the 20th Earl of Erroll. Entered the Diplomatic Service, 1900; Chargé d'Affaires, Berlin, 1920; Counsellor of Embassy, 1921. British High Commissioner, Inter-Allied Rhineland High Commission, 1921–28. Succeeded his father as 21st Earl of Erroll, 1927.

[2] Zdzislaw Okencki, 1874–1940. Director of the Political and Diplomatic Department of the Polish Foreign Office, 1919–20. Subsequently Polish Minister in Belgrade.

London dockers refused to load a consignment of munitions due to go to Poland on board the *Jolly George*. That same day the *Daily Herald* reported Ernest Bevin,[1] a leading trade-unionist, as saying: 'I do not believe that the present Government have the authority of the democracy of this country to lend a single penny or supply a single gun to carry on further war against Russia.' On May 22 the National Union of Railwaymen instructed its members to refuse to handle any material intended for Poland that might be used against Russia.

The Poles were outraged by this outburst of British hostility in their hour of triumph. 'It is only right to report to your Lordship', Rumbold wrote to Curzon on May 22, 'that there is considerable bitterness against England at the present moment.' When Rumbold called on Patek on May 19 he had told the Polish Foreign Minister – as he reported to Curzon in his letter on May 22 – 'that we felt that as long as the war continued in this or any other part of Europe it was impossible for Europe as a whole to return to normal conditions, and yet a return to approximately normal conditions was more than ever essential'. The Poles continued to hope for a decisive victory, and to deride Britain's cautious, pacific attitude. On May 29 the *Kurier Poranny*, the newspaper controlled by Pilsudski's supporters, declared that the three principal enemies of an independent Poland were the British Labour Party, under Bolshevik influence; certain leading British politicians, anxious to restore the Russian Tsar; and International Jewry, making full use of its influence over Lloyd George.

Lloyd George had lost patience with Pilsudski and the Poles, and was much angered by the Polish attack on Russia. On June 10 Philip Kerr sent Rumbold an account of Lloyd George's attitude:

As you remember, the PM has throughout warned the Poles against inflated aspirations. He has always said the same thing to them: that while they have suffered badly in the war, they had really done nothing to gain their own freedom. They were very dangerously situated with the Slavs on one side and the Germans on the other. This difficulty was accentuated by the fact that they had large minorities of both Russians and Jews as well inside their own frontier. He, therefore, has always counselled them to put sternly away from them ambitious projects or quarrels with their neighbours and to concentrate upon laying real foundations of national life on the basis of ethnographic Poland. Otherwise in his opinion Poland will come to disaster.

For that reason and also because he felt that peace was essential to Europe, he sent for Patek last January and made the declaration to him of which you know.

---

[1] Ernest Bevin, 1881–1951. National Organizer of the Dockers' Union, 1910–21. General Secretary, Transport and General Workers' Union, 1921–40. Labour MP, 1940–51. Minister of Labour and National Service in Churchill's wartime Coalition, 1940–45. Secretary of State for Foreign Affairs in the third Labour Government, 1945–51. Lord Privy Seal, 1951.

His present view is that whatever may be the merits or demerits of the recent negotiations between Soviet Russia and Poland, the Poles have put themselves in the wrong from the start, first, by occupying, contrary to the views of the Supreme Council, great areas of Russian territory and then making a further advance into the Ukraine and seizing Kieff. To do this they not only endangered their own future but precipitated a quarrel in Eastern Europe which it would be very difficult to heal. He is perfectly aware of the difficulties and dangers of Bolshevism, but the Poles have put themselves in the wrong by plunging madly into conquest and adventure, the fundamental purpose of which is the occupation of vast areas in which the overwhelming majority of the population is not Polish. He is, therefore, much afraid of Poland going to disaster because she is attempting a policy which is wrong in itself and for which she has no adequate resources, and for which the Allies can give her no support. If she pursued the other policy, the policy he really recommended, of doing her level best to make a fair peace with Soviet Russia, making it clear to the Allies that she was ready to make that peace because she wanted to do what all the other sensible nations in Europe were doing – concentrating on internal reform – she would now be in a strong position. She would either have got peace or she would have got the sympathy and support of the Great Powers, as it is she has got neither, and the future, therefore, in his opinion, is not very bright.

Before Kerr's letter reached Warsaw, the Polish Army met its first setback. On June 11 the Bolsheviks regained Kiev, and threatened the Polish forces in Eastern Galicia. At that moment Poland was without a government, that of Leopold Skulski[1] having resigned a few days earlier. For nearly three weeks, during which time the Bolsheviks advanced rapidly in the south, no administration could be formed. 'It is almost incredible', Rumbold wrote to Hardinge on June 21, 'and would not have happened in any other country but this. It is very difficult to help people who do not help themselves.' On June 23 the political crisis was resolved and Wladislaw Grabski[2] became Prime Minister.

The new Polish Government could not influence the deteriorating military situation. Rumbold was convinced that Pilsudski's offensive had been a mistake. 'I regret his adventure', he wrote to Philip Kerr on June 18, 'because I think that Poland has now got herself into a very serious position. She has weakened herself from a military point of view. Her easy successes against the Bolsheviks throughout last year have tempted her to

[1] Leopold Skulski, 1878–1942. Member of the Polish Parliament, 1919–22. Prime Minister, December 1919–July 1920. Minister of Internal Affairs, 1920–21.

[2] Wladislaw Grabski, 1874–1938. Born in Russian Poland. A member of the Russian Duma, 1905–17, for the Warsaw district. Interned by the Germans in Warsaw, October–November 1918. Minister of Agriculture in the first Polish Government, 1919. Third Polish delegate to the Paris Peace Conference, 1919. Minister of Finance, 1919–20. Prime Minister, June–July 1920 and December 1923–November 1925.

undertake a task beyond her strength.' Rumbold believed that he had acted throughout in harmony with Lloyd George's policies. 'I have impressed on the Poles time and time again', he told Kerr, 'the necessity for coming to terms with the Bolsheviks as soon as possible and above all of putting forward the most moderate conditions of peace.'

Rumbold was depressed by the refusal of the Poles to accept his advice. To Hardinge, in his letter of June 21, he described the difficulties he had faced in dealing with 'these extremely sensitive and shortsighted people. . . . I do all I can to instill sense into these people. . . . If one were to wait until all the crises were over one might wait until one died.' He was, he added, 'very tired indeed – a sort of brain fag which is not pleasant and I cannot undertake to carry on much longer without a change'. He was most anxious to go on leave; but the uncertainty of the military situation made it essential that he remain in Poland. On July 27 he wrote despondently to his stepmother that were Providence to solve all Poland's difficulties 'at a stroke, and start her with a clean sheet the Poles – or many Poles – would be so bored that they would get up a crisis in a few months'. The Poles, he added, were much in need of peace, 'and if they don't get it soon they will go to disaster'.

The storm provoked by Pilsudski's attack on Russia showed no sign of subsiding. On June 28 Rumbold sent his wife and children back to London. That afternoon he went to see Stanislas Patek, and 'finding him unduly optimistic' as he wrote to his wife two weeks later, 'succeeded in impressing him with the gravity of the situation'. That evening, at 8.30, Rumbold telegraphed to Curzon that 'a renewed Bolshevik attack in northern sector is impending'. Pilsudski, he reported, believed that the Bolshevik regime 'was nearing its end' and that if the Polish Army could check the offensive it would lead to the exhaustion of the Soviet troops, and could bring about 'a collapse of Bolshevik regime . . . thus avoiding necessity of making peace with a treacherous neighbour'. Rumbold added his personal opinion that he doubted whether Polish morale could withstand 'the strain of another three months hard struggle'. An hour later Rumbold telegraphed to Curzon again. The Bolshevik cavalry had broken through the Polish defences: 'British Military Mission considers military situation very grave.' Ten minutes later, at 9.40 p.m., Rumbold sent Curzon a third telegram, urging immediate British intervention 'to tell Poland categorically that she must try to come to terms with Bolsheviks at once'. His telegram continued:

There is a real and general desire for peace on the part of the Poles, but as Your Lordship will have seen from my recent telegrams those at the head of affairs here seem reluctant to propose resumption of peace negotiations whilst

military situation is unfavourable to Poland. There is, however, no reason to
think that military situation will get more favourable. It may even get much
worse and end in invasion of ethnographical Poland by Bolsheviks. It would
therefore seem advisable in true interests of Poles themselves that they should
propose renewal of peace negotiations whilst their army is still more or less
intact rather than wait until that army has been weakened or even utterly
demoralised by impending Bolshevik offensive in North or by attacks on
Southern sector. . . .

I feel prolongation of this war may lead not only to disaster to Poland herself
but to serious complications for Allies, inasmuch as an invasion of ethnographical Poland would presumably raise in an acute form question of authorised strength of German army. . . .

I feel that it is a matter which ought to be taken up without delay, for whilst
Bolsheviks may very likely refuse to listen to peace overtures now, Poles at all
events should do all in their power to terminate war rapidly even at cost of great
sacrifices. I consider that men at head of affairs here are practically gambling
with existence of this nation at present moment and are showing an absence of
foresight and judgment. The sacrifices which the Allies have made in the war,
one of the results of which has been revival of Poland, certainly entitle them to
bring pressure to bear on this country at this critical moment.

Curzon acted on Rumbold's advice, speaking to Prince Sapieha,[1] who
was leaving London on June 30 to return to Warsaw as Minister of
Foreign Affairs. 'I spoke to him very strongly', Curzon telegraphed to
Rumbold that day, 'about . . . desirability of making an early peace with
Russia. . . . I told him that Poland by her foolish conduct was alienating
sympathy of Allies. . . . She must abate her pretensions, or worse would
ensue'. Curzon took the opportunity of warning the Poles against several
of their 'pretensions', their desire to keep the city of Vilna and not allow it
to go to the new Lithuanian State, their dislike of holding plebiscites in the
disputed territories in East Prussia and Teschen, and their hopes of in-
corporating Danzig inside Poland. Sapieha refused to contemplate allowing the Lithuanians to have Vilna. 'Conversation did not leave very
favourable impression upon me', Curzon reported to Rumbold.

On June 30 Rumbold went to the Polish Foreign Ministry, where he
was told – as he telegraphed to Curzon on the following day – that in the
opinion of the Polish military authorities 'Poland was engaged in a task
beyond her strength'. Rumbold reiterated his view that 'it was indispensable' for the Poles to make an immediate offer of peace. On July 2 Prince
Sapieha, who had just reached Warsaw, called on Rumbold at the British

[1] Eustace Sapieha, 1881–1963. Educated in Britain before 1900, he returned to Russian
Poland and became a Russian subject. Polish Minister to London, 1919–20. Foreign Minister,
1920–21. Member of the Polish Parliament, 1928–30. Left Poland during the German
occupation, 1944, and settled in Kenya, where he died.

Legation, and told him that although Pilsudski and the military authorities were likely to obstruct any internal peace moves, some international pressure might be more effective. But Sapieha added that he agreed with the Polish military authorities that if Poland could fight on for another six to eight weeks, 'transport system in Russia would collapse and Bolsheviks would be unable to continue war'. With such hopes did the Poles justify remaining at war. On July 4 Philip Kerr sent Rumbold a terse account of Lloyd George's attitude:

He says that not only have the Poles been extremely short-sighted, but they have deliberately disregarded the advice given to them by the Allies. Therefore he will not agree to intervention on behalf of the Poles except on four conditions. First, that they take the initiative in asking the Allies to intervene. Otherwise, they would always say that but for the Allied intervention they would have been all right. Secondly, they must take the initiative on their own account in asking the Bolsheviks to make peace. Three, they must come to fair terms with Lithuania. Fourthly they must make peace with Czecho-Slovakia and be reasonable both in regard to Eastern Galicia, and Danzig.

Finally as to peace terms themselves, I am quite certain he would not look at the sort of peace terms which the Poles themselves contemplate. He will go for an ethnographic Poland as the only kind of Poland which can possibly survive in the future.

The Bolshevik advance continued. On July 7 Rumbold telegraphed to Curzon, who was at an inter-allied meeting being held at Spa in Belgium, that Sapieha feared that the Red Army might reach Warsaw within three weeks, and that the Polish troops in the southern sector 'were completely demoralised'. The Poles appealed to Britain and France for military support. But Lloyd George, who was also at Spa, proposed instead an immediate armistice between the two armies, and the withdrawal of the Poles further westward, to the 'ethnographic' boundary laid down by the Paris Peace Conference, and which the Poles had long before rejected out of hand.

Although Rumbold had taken several initiatives in trying to persuade the Poles to make peace with Russia, the possibility of the Red Army crossing the Peace Conference 'frontier' and driving across ethnographic Poland to Warsaw, caused him some alarm. It was essential, he wrote on July 9 to Rex Leeper[1] at the Foreign Office, to give the Poles 'moral and

---

[1] Reginald Wilding Allen Leeper, 1888–1968. Intelligence Bureau, Department of Information, 1917. Entered Foreign Office, 1918; 2nd Secretary, 1920. 1st Secretary, Warsaw, 1923–24; Riga, 1924; Constantinople, 1925; Warsaw, 1927–29. Counsellor, Foreign Office, 1933–40; Under-Secretary, 1940–43. Ambassador to the King of the Hellenes, 1943–46. Knighted, 1945. Ambassador, Buenos Aires, 1946–48. Vice-President of the British Council, 1949–68. Director, De Beers Consolidated Mines Ltd., 1950–65.

some slight material assistance . . . we should now do our utmost to hearten them in their struggle', at least until the Bolsheviks agreed to peace negotiations. 'It seems all important', Rumbold reiterated on the following day in a letter to Hardinge, 'to back these people up . . . and not let them feel that they are abandoned.' If the Allies decided to help Poland, Rumbold hoped they would say 'once and for all' exactly what Poland 'may or may not do'. The Poles, he explained, 'are like children; they need guidance and advice given in no uncertain manner'.

On July 11 Rumbold wrote to his wife of 'a great wave of patriotism throughout the country', which, he added, 'needs stiffening by us'. If the Russians reached Warsaw, he told her, it might spark off a revolution in Germany.[1] 'I feel like a rat in a trap', he commented. On July 13 Hardinge wrote to Rumbold from the Foreign Office to say that he expected the Bolsheviks would make peace with Poland. 'The Poles', Hardinge added, 'made great fools of themselves and have only themselves to thank for their troubles.'

By July 16 it looked as if the Soviet Government would accept the British request for an armistice, to be followed by a peace conference to be held, as Lloyd George had proposed, in London. 'If it is accepted', Rumbold wrote to his stepmother on the following day, 'there will be an immediate detente in the situation and the contemplated conference in London to follow it will or should clear up all pending and dangerous questions in this part of Europe.' He felt convinced that the Bolsheviks would agree to negotiate; 'Russia is in a very bad way', he explained. 'Our latest information', Rumbold wrote to his wife on July 18, 'is that Lenin and Tchitcherin[2] are for the acceptance of the whole proposal whilst Trotsky wants to go on with the war and make peace at Warsaw.' If Trotsky had his way, and the Red Army approached Warsaw, Britain and France, Rumbold wrote, 'will have to go to war with the Bolsheviks in defence of ethnographic Poland'. He did not believe that such a war need necessarily go badly. The 'best thing' Britain could do, he wrote, 'would be to send masses of aeroplanes over here. These would speedily utterly demoralise the Bolsheviks. We ought also – in that contingency – fit out a

[1] Lenin and Trotsky also believed that, once Poland was overrun, contact between the Red Army and the German revolutionaries would spark off a revolution in Germany. Lenin later declared: 'all Germany boiled up when our troops approached Warsaw'. (Lenin, *Collected Works*, Vol. XVII, p. 308.)

[2] Georghy Valentinovich Tchicherin, 1872–1936. A Russian diplomat and landowner, he resigned from the Imperial Diplomatic Service in 1905, renounced his estates and joined the Social Democratic Movement. Arrested near Berlin, 1908, and expelled from Germany. Lived in Paris and London, 1908–17. Imprisoned in Brixton Gaol, November 1917; expelled from England, January 1918, in exchange for the British Ambassador in Petrograd, Sir George Buchanan. People's Commissar for Foreign Affairs, 1918–30.

powerful bombing squadron, provided with the biggest bombs and go and blot out Moscow – a perfectly feasible operation I imagine.'

By Monday, July 19, the Poles – as Rumbold reported to his wife in a long letter five days later – 'were becoming dreadfully depressed . . . no reply having come from the Bolos'. During the day he learned that 'there was nothing between the Bolos and Warsaw except a disorganised rabble. . . . Most of the Polish officers had hooked it or were not to be found.' That day the Soviet Government informed Curzon that they were willing to enter into negotiations with the Poles. Curzon telegraphed the news to Rumbold. At 7.30 p.m. Rumbold explained to his wife 'the long expected telegram came from London and after hastily decyphering it etc. I rushed off . . . sent for Sapieha out of the Council and read the contents to him. I never saw a man so relieved.'

Rumbold told Sapieha that the Polish Government 'must at once send a radio to Moscow to propose peace and asked for an armistice'. But on the following morning, when Rumbold went to see Sapieha again, he found that no message had yet been sent to Moscow. 'I protested and expostulated', he told his wife. The reason for the delay 'was the obstruction of Pilsudski and the Guards who hoped even at the eleventh hour to bring off some coup in the north'. He therefore told Sapieha 'that the military party were rotten and had let the nation down time after time'. Sapieha agreed to take up the Soviet offer. But on the morning of July 21 when Rumbold went to the Foreign Ministry, he found that still no message had been sent. 'I threatened unless the messages were sent immediately to see Pilsudski myself that afternoon', Rumbold wrote to his wife, 'and to protest formally at the attitude of the Polish Government and throw all the responsibility for the consequences on him. This did the trick and the messages went out.'

Lloyd George decided to send a special mission to Warsaw to advise the Poles during the negotiations. It was headed by Lord D'Abernon,[1] and had two other members.[2] On July 24 Rumbold telegraphed to Curzon that the announcement of the impending arrival of the Mission 'has greatly encouraged Poles', particularly as the French Government was at the same

---

[1] Edgar Vincent, 1857–1941. Served in the Coldstream Guards, 1877–82. Financial Adviser to the Egyptian Government, 1883–89. Knighted, 1887 (at the age of thirty). Governor of the Imperial Ottoman Bank, 1889–97. Conservative MP, 1899–1906. Created Baron D'Abernon, 1914. Chairman, Central Control Board (Liquor Traffic), 1915–20. Mission to Poland, 1920. Ambassador to Berlin, 1920–26. Created Viscount, 1926. Chairman, Medical Research Council, 1929–33. In 1931 he published an account of the battle of Warsaw, *The Eighteenth Decisive Battle of the World*.

[2] Major-General Sir Percy Radcliffe (Director of Military Operations at the War Office) and Sir Maurice Hankey (Secretary to the Cabinet).

time sending General Weygand[1] to Warsaw. 'I hope the armistice negotiations will be put quickly through', Rumbold wrote to Hardinge that day.

Rumbold was weary both of the crisis and of the Poles; even of diplomacy. 'I think I shall be quite ready to go altogether', he wrote to Hardinge, 'when I have completed my time here.' He explained the reason for his disillusionment in his letter to Hardinge:

The Poles are entirely to blame for the mess in which they find themselves, and I have come to the conclusion that the chief offender is Pilsudski. You are right when you say that I do not have an easy time of it with these people. They are exasperating to deal with, and their dilatory conduct in sending out the armistice and peace proposals to the Bolsheviks is a case in point. It is obvious that they will require some form of tutelage for several years to come. I am certain of one thing, and that is that our Government ought to send here a constant succession of British Ministers at comparatively short intervals, because the Poles are calculated to wear out the patience and spoil the temper of the calmest person. To run this country with full power to do so would not be nearly such a wearing task as constantly to advise the Poles against committing follies and trying to save them from the consequences of these follies.

Despite their agreement to begin armistice negotiations, the Bolsheviks continued to advance towards Warsaw, crossing the 'ethnographic' line on July 24. On the following day the British and French Missions reached the city. 'As soon as they arrived', Rumbold wrote to his wife later that day, 'both missions . . . came to this Legation where we held a Council of War in the drawing room.' The Poles, under pressure from the two Missions, agreed to open negotiations with the Russians on July 30. Meanwhile the Russians continued to advance, and by July 30 were within seventy miles of Warsaw. 'The Polish troops defending the capital', Rumbold wrote to Curzon on July 31, 'are disorganised because there is no leadership and they are worn out as a result of a retreat of 200 kilometres in great heat.' 'The population of Warsaw', Rumbold added, 'remains calm, but it is a calm born of apathy.' In his report written later in the year, General Radcliffe[2] described his own alarm when confronted by 'an army that did not fight, a staff which did not function, a Govern-

[1] Maxime Weygand, 1867–1965. Sub-lieutenant, 1888; Colonel, 1914; General of Brigade, 1916. Chief of the General Staff of the Army, 1914–16 and 1918. French Military Expert at the Lausanne Conference, 1922. High Commissioner in Syria, 1923–24. General Inspector of the Army, 1931–35. Minister of National Defence, 1940. Governor-General of Algeria, 1941. Imprisoned by the Nazis, 1942–45.

[2] Percy Pollexfen de Blaquiere Radcliffe, 1874–1934. 2nd Lieutenant, Royal Artillery, 1893; Major, 1910; Major-General, 1918. Director of Military Operations, War Office, 1918–22. Knighted, 1919. While in Poland he assisted Weygand in the reorganization of the Polish Army. Commanded Scottish Command, 1930–33; Southern Command, 1933–34.

ment of all the vices that were making no serious attempt to rally the people for the defence of the country. . . .'

On August 1 the Red Army was only fifty miles from Warsaw. 'In view of the feeble resistance offered by the Polish troops', Rumbold had written to Dr Parodi on July 31, 'it looks as if the Bolsheviks finding nothing in front of them are pushing on. The situation is very disquieting because the question of Poland *v*. Soviet Russia must necessarily become merged in the larger question of Soviet Russia *v*. the civilised world.' Rumbold's bitterness against the Poles was undiminished. To Parodi he continued:

The Poles are themselves to blame for the mess into which they have got. As far as I can make out the Government of the country has been run by a kind of camarilla or militarist clique at the head of which is Pilsudski, the Chief of the State. This man is a somewhat sinister figure and has been a conspirator all his life. He is profoundly interested in military questions and has an inordinate ambition for military renown. He has been attempting what even a Napoleon might attempt in vain, i.e., he has combined in his person the active command of the army, the direction of military operations, and the conduct of foreign policy. He is anything but a Napoleon, however, and his military strategy has shocked all good soldiers. There is no doubt that he is largely responsible for the present disaster to the nation.

During the advance of the Red Army on Warsaw, Rumbold asked General Carton de Wiart to take him to the front. In his memoirs, *Happy Odyssey*, the General recorded:

I agreed, and drove him myself in my car, followed by another car belonging to the Naval Mission armed with a machine-gun. . . . On getting near the front, we met a very scared-looking Polish soldier who told us he had just escaped from the Bolsheviks, and he pointed to a village that we could see about a mile away. I turned to the Naval Mission and said that we would go on but that they must follow close behind, and be ready to shoot when I gave them the signal. We arrived at the village and found the population looking terrified and it was clear that the Bolsheviks could not be far away. We went through, and on the other side of the village I saw a Cossack right on top of a telegraph pole busy cutting the wires. At the foot of the pole he had an admiring audience of half a dozen mounted Cossacks busy holding his horse. They were a lovely target, and I signalled the Naval car to come up and shoot. Either the Naval Mission were too slow or the Cossacks too fast, but all the Cossacks galloped away unhurt, and getting cover behind a ridge about six hundred yards off, turned their fire on us. Sir Horace was enjoying every moment of his outing, it being the first time he had been under fire, and I believe he even enjoyed the last few minutes when I had to turn my large car round in a very narrow road. Personally I was relieved to return him intact.

There seemed no reason why the Bolsheviks should not enter Warsaw by the second week in August. Pilsudski was refusing to co-operate with Weygand, and Rumbold began to make arrangements to move the Legation westwards to Posen. 'I have packed up all the plates, pictures, prints, lacquer objects, china, photographs, best books, papers, best china and glass, carpets etc', he wrote to his wife on August 1, 'probably about 16 cases.' All British subjects were being evacuated. Rumbold considered the Bolshevik decision to continue the advance less serious than the earlier Polish decision to invade Russia. 'The villain of the piece is Pilsudski', he wrote to his wife, 'and he is backed by a military clique, but even the restless Poles are sick of war and want peace, so that I hope they will keep quiet for a bit now.'

For four days the Red Army continued to advance. 'We may all be in flight in 2 or 3 days from now', Rumbold wrote to his wife on August 5. 'I wonder what will happen to all the nice furniture and good beds etc. which I could not pack up. The Bolos, if and when they get here, will make hay of these. It is very depressing but there it is. Some fate pursues me. Just 6 years ago I was burning archives at Berlin before our departure and we are doing the same thing now.' He could not understand why Warsaw had not already been evacuated. 'We have warned the Poles that the Bolshevik cavalry will work round their left flank and try to cut the lines to Posen and Danzig. . . . I have very little patience left. The Polish Government ought to have moved 10 days ago but they show no intention of doing so just yet. They just slap their chests and declare that they mean to stay until the last minute – even until Warsaw is under fire. There will be a pretty debandade when they *do* go.' Rumbold could not understand why the British Government allowed the Bolsheviks to continue to advance, despite their agreement to enter into negotiations. 'There has been no telegram of importance from the FO for 3 days', he wrote to his wife in his letter of August 5. 'It is a repetition of the Berlin days over again.' His own view was that the British Government 'have been flouted by the Bolsheviks and have eaten more dirt than is good for anybody. They ought to declare war on Russia. But will they?'

In the early hours of August 6 the Red Army reached a point only twenty-five miles from Warsaw. Twelve hours later Lord D'Abernon telegraphed to Curzon suggesting the despatch of a Franco-British Expeditionary Force of at least 20,000 men. 'The force', he added, 'should rigorously exclude any elements liable to be affected by Bolshevik or Sinn Fein propaganda'. But Lloyd George believed he could convince the Soviet Government to halt the advance without actually sending troops. Instead, he threatened to restore the blockade of Russia which had been in

3 Tony Rumbold in Berne during the First World War: the uniform was made for
him by British soldiers interned in Switzerland. They made him a private soldier's uniform
from an officer's cloth.

14   The British Legation in Berne, 1917.

15   Rumbold in his study, Warsaw, 1920.

16 The dining-room in the British Embassy,
Constantinople, 1922.

17 Allied warships at anchor in the Bosphorus; a photograph taken from the European shore, looking towards Asia. This photograph was taken on 22 February 1920. Six British battleships are shown: *Ajax, Revenge, Resolution, Royal Sovereign, Royal Oak* and *Ramillies*. In the foreground are three French destroyers.

18　The Allied High Commissioners in Constantinople, 1922: Marquis Garroni, Rumbold, and General Pellé.

19　Mehmed V; the last of the Turkish Sultans.

20   Rumbold in Constantinople, 1922.

21   Constantia, Horace, Ethel and Tony Rumbold at Yenikeui, on the Bosphorus, 1922. Their house had formerly been the Austro-Hungarian summer Embassy. The Asian shore is in the background.

force during the anti-Bolshevik Intervention of 1918. 'Britain plunging into war with Soviet Russia' was the *Daily Herald*'s main headline on August 6, and in a leading article *The Times* demanded of the nation 'the same unanimity and the same courage with which we faced the crisis of 1914'.

On August 8 Rumbold informed Curzon that the Bolsheviks had set up 'Soviets' in three eastern Polish towns, Bialystok, Lomza and Tarnopol, 'thereby furnishing an indication of the procedure they would follow if they succeeded in capturing Warsaw'. The Polish Army was preparing for a 'pitched battle' outside Warsaw. The diplomatic Missions were leaving that night for Posen, although, Rumbold wrote, the Ministers themselves would stay in Warsaw and 'in case of necessity, leave by motor or in a special train which it is hoped the Polish Government will provide at the last minute'. Rumbold was confident, as was General Radcliffe, that the Poles still had the strength to repulse the Bolshevik attack. 'The Russian troops', he wrote to Curzon in his letter of August 8, 'are much exhausted and there is a consensus of opinion that it would take a comparatively small effort on the part of the Poles to inflict a defeat on their enemies.'

On August 9 Lloyd George met the French Prime Minister, Alexandre Millerand,[1] at Lympne, on the channel coast. The Russians still professed their desire to negotiate peace with Poland. The two Prime Ministers gave Poland a pledge that if these negotiations failed, Britain and France would intervene and preserve Polish independence, but that if they were to do so, the Poles must accept whatever military advice, and advisers, that Britain and France felt were needed. That night Curzon telegraphed these decisions to Rumbold, who was still in Warsaw. 'The real meaning of the Allied declaration', he explained, 'is that the Allies are not prepared to undertake the responsibility involved in assisting Poland unless the Poles are really prepared to fight as vigorously and tenaciously for their independence as the Allies were for their own freedom in the late war.' The Poles, Curzon insisted, would have to 'accept and act upon the advice of Allies'. The British Government had given a bold pledge. But, Curzon explained in his telegram, 'the present plight of Poland is mainly due not only to her grave mistakes of policy in the past, but to her military and administrative incompetence in the present. French Government . . . tell us that Poles even scout advice of General Weygand, the ablest and most

[1] Alexandre Millerand, 1859–1943. Elected to the French Chamber of Deputies as a Radical Socialist, 1885. Minister of War, January 1912–January 1913; and again from January 1914–October 1915. He resigned following accusations that he had failed to find sufficient heavy artillery. Prime Minister, 1920. President of the Republic, 1920–24.

experienced Chief of Staff in the world.' Curzon also passed on to
Rumbold the fears of the French Government 'that Pilsudski means to
compromise with the Bolsheviks and Sovietize Poland provided his own
power is safeguarded'.

On the morning of August 10 the Poles agreed that Pilsudski would not
issue any orders without Weygand's approval. That evening the Russians
produced a set of terms which they said they were prepared to offer to the
Poles. At ten that night Curzon telegraphed the terms to Rumbold,
commenting that the British Government 'could not assume responsibility
of taking hostile action against Russia' if the Poles refused these terms.
Under them, the Polish Army was to be reduced to a maximum of
60,000 men; all arms not needed for these men were to be handed over to
the Russians; the Polish Army, and all Polish war industries, were to be
demobilized; and no troops or war materials were to be allowed to come
to Poland from abroad. In return, the Russians agreed to withdraw to the
'ethnographic' line which had been laid down at the Paris Peace Conference, and modified slightly by Curzon himself in a Note of July 20.
'The Russian terms', Curzon told Rumbold, 'would appear to leave the
independence of Poland within her ethnographic frontiers unimpaired.'

On August 11, as soon as it reached him, Rumbold took Curzon's
telegram to the Polish Foreign Ministry. Prince Sapieha was aghast, as
Rumbold telegraphed to Curzon that evening:

Minister for Foreign Affairs stated even if Poland were to be deprived of all
Allied support she would fight to the end rather than accept terms indicated. He
said that in putting themselves in hands of Allied Powers Poles would never
have believed they would be advised to accept terms which amounted to
a shameful capitulation. Minister for Foreign Affairs added that if it were known
to public that British Government had declared that they would not assume
responsibility of taking hostile action against Russia if Soviet Armistice conditions in their general substance were refused this knowledge would create
utmost bitterness in Poland against England.

'My interview', Rumbold added, 'was of a very painful character.' On
the following day he telegraphed to Curzon to say that the French
Minister in Warsaw, de Panafieu,[1] 'is informing Polish Government today
that French Government consider armistice proposals of Soviet Government as totally inacceptable'. Curzon was angered, both by the Polish
refusal to accept the Soviet terms, and by the French decision not to
support Britain. On August 13 he telegraphed to Rumbold:

---

[1] Hector André de Panafieu, born 1865. Entered the French Diplomatic Service, 1883.
Minister to Sofia, 1912–15. High Commissioner, Sofia, 1920. Minister in Warsaw, 1920–23.

I greatly regret that advice which we gave to Polish Government was not well received by them. It was dictated solely by desire to acquaint them with point of view, strongly and indeed unanimously held by public opinion of every shade in England, which will not tolerate renewal of war with Russia save on grounds of incontestable justification, and in order to prevent Polish Government, in entering negotiations, from making the mistake of relying too confidently upon Allied military support. Fullest opportunity was conceded to Polish Government of disputing individual terms, and there was little doubt that they would do so. But it was our duty to acquaint them with our general impression, for their warning and guidance.

Situation has, I fear, been gravely complicated by information contained in your telegram No. 684,[1] which is in absolute contradiction of assurance given to me by French Minister[2] here this morning. I must trust you in these difficult circumstances to keep the head of the Polish Government straight, and not to encourage them in an attitude which may result in their finding themselves alone with only the French behind them.

The Poles were determined to decide their own future despite British pressure. 'Poland will not agree to any humiliating terms', Prince Sapieha telegraphed direct to Curzon on August 13, 'there can be no question of demobilisation and disarmament'. That night Russian troops were reported just to the east of Warsaw. Lord D'Abernon's Mission decided to leave the capital for Posen, and asked Rumbold to accompany them. 'I was reluctant to go', he wrote to Hardinge four days later, 'because I wanted to remain in touch with the Polish Government and had made the necessary arrangements for leaving in a motor car in case the Bolsheviks were on the point of entering the town.' The only foreign diplomat who refused to leave the capital was the Papal Nuncio, Achille Ratti.[3]

Rumbold reached Posen at midday on August 14. For three days Polish and Soviet troops were locked in battle outside Warsaw, and along the Vistula. 'Now that they have got their backs to the wall', Rumbold wrote to Hardinge in his letter of August 17, 'and perhaps stimulated by the proximity of the capital, the Poles seem to be fighting well.' Even on his last day in Warsaw he had sensed a new attitude, telling Hardinge that 'several Poles who showed cowardice on previous occasions have been shot at Warsaw. The officers are principally to blame for the recent demoralisation of the Polish army. They are very much in evidence at Warsaw and

---

[1] Rumbold's telegram to Curzon of August 12, 1920, cited above.

[2] Aimé Joseph de Fleuriau, 1870–1938. Entered the French Diplomatic Service, 1895. Counsellor of Embassy, London, 1913–20, and close friend of Paul Cambon, the Ambassador. Minister to Peking, 1921–24. Ambassador to London, 1924–33.

[3] Achille Ratti, 1857–1939. Ordained priest, 1879. Professor of Theology, College of San Carlo, Milan, 1882. Apostolic Visitor to Poland, 1918. Papal Nuncio to Poland, 1919–21. Archbishop of Milan, 1921. Cardinal, 1921. Pope, as Pius XI, from 1922 until his death.

swagger about the streets, but they are not so much in evidence when it is a case of facing the enemy. They appear, however, to be doing better now.' Rumbold felt convinced that the Bolsheviks were about to suffer 'a real defeat', writing to Hardinge:

I think it is now certain that they will not get Warsaw. A defeat so far from their base may turn into a disaster and destroy their military prestige. I hope that this may come about because we here are all convinced that it is useless to negotiate with such treacherous people as the Bolsheviks and that the only thing they understand is force. . . .

A real success in front of Warsaw may enable the Poles to get better armistice terms than those presented through our Government. . . . The Poles would certainly not look at those terms unless they were completely crushed, which is far from being the case. . . .

Should the Poles succeed in beating the Bolsheviks decisively in front of Warsaw they would probably want to chase them out of ethnographic Poland or at least across the Bug before seriously discussing armistice and peace preliminaries and nobody could blame the Poles for following this course. On the other hand there is a real and genuine desire for peace in this country. The bulk of the nation is as sick of war as we are in England. . . .

Rumbold was critical of the British policy of the previous week. 'I can understand our Government taking up the perfectly sound line that we are sick of war', he wrote to Hardinge, 'and will not be dragged into another war except in the last extremity. That is sound ground, but there seems to me to be a great difference between that position and what the Government have actually done, which is to send minatory notes at intervals to Moscow whilst allowing the Bolsheviks to advance within sight of Warsaw.' In a telegram to Curzon on August 15, Rumbold pointed out that the Polish Peace Delegation chosen by the Poles to negotiate with the Russians 'may be regarded as the most conciliatory delegation which could have been sent'.

By August 16 the impetus of the Russian advance had been checked at all points, and the Poles were ready to launch a counter offensive. On August 17, Lenin telegraphed to Trotsky: 'We must get a move on. At whatever cost Warsaw must be taken in three to five days.' But Lenin's exhortation came too late. The Russian troops had reached the limit of their military energies, and had gone too far ahead of their supplies. All indications pointed to an imminent Polish advance. 'If the Poles win the battle of Warsaw', Rumbold wrote to his wife from Posen at noon that day, 'they will have reason to be proud.' The Poles, he wrote, would be able to reject the Bolshevik armistice terms, which were, in his view, 'entirely unacceptable'. He was not at all impressed by British policy, writing to his wife:

The Poles will refuse any proposal for disarmament. If this were forced on them they would be entirely at the mercy of the Bolsheviks. What our luminaries in London cannot grasp is that the Bolsheviks are essentially treacherous. You cannot negotiate with them. They will violate their engagements at the first opportunity. But Lloyd George, Philip Kerr and others are so anxious to enter into relations with the Bolsheviks that they accept any flapdoodle from the latter. Our Government have correctly interpreted public opinion in one matter, i.e. that we are sick of war and don't want to be dragged into another war at any price. But between that and the policy they have pursued in the Russo-Polish conflict there is a wide gulf. We have cut a sorry figure in this business and have eaten more dirt than any powerful Government of recent years. The Bolsheviks must be laughing in their sleeves in London and Moscow.

Rumbold was physically exhausted; but, he wrote in his letter of August 17, 'I see no prospect of getting away at all for some time to come, i.e. until these people settle their wretched affairs with the Bolsheviks and heaven knows when that will be.' His patience was exhausted with all parties. 'I don't know whom I dislike worse', he added, 'Poles, Bolsheviks or Lloyd George. They are all very trying and I have little use for Curzon in spite of the almost oily expressions of approval I receive from him.' He was, he wrote, 'entirely tired' of the Diplomatic Service, and wanted 'to be my own master, accountable to nobody'. If only, he ended, he could 'escape to some Swiss valley. . . .' On August 18, while still in Posen, he wrote to his stepmother: '. . . heaven knows when I shall be able to get away from this God-forsaken country of which I have had more than enough. . . . I regret ever having suggested Warsaw as a post.' The war, he believed, would go on for some time, with the Poles gaining the ascendant. 'Both armies are rotten', he declared.

On August 18 the Russians began to retreat. Rumbold returned to Warsaw on the following day. On August 20 Sir Maurice Hankey[1] wrote to him from Switzerland: 'I am glad that your own hopes that the Poles would pull themselves together when the Russians got to the gates of

---

[1] Maurice Pascal Alers Hankey, 1877–1963. Entered Royal Marine Artillery, 1895; retired, 1912. Secretary to the Committee of Imperial Defence, 1912–38. Lieutenant-Colonel, Royal Marines, October 1914. Secretary to the War Council, November 1914–May 1915; to the Dardanelles Committee, May–November 1915; to the Cabinet War Committee, December 1915–December 1916. Knighted, February 1916. Secretary to the War Cabinet, 1916–18; to the Cabinet, 1919–38. Created Baron, 1939. Minister without Portfolio, September 1939–May 1940. Chancellor of the Duchy of Lancaster, 1940–41. Paymaster-General, 1941–42.

Warsaw have come true. I hardly hoped for it myself, but with emotional people like the Poles all things are possible.' Writing in his diary on September 18, Hankey described Rumbold as 'a tower of strength' during the August crisis.

The causes of the Bolshevik defeat were henceforth to be much discussed. In his book *The Eighteenth Decisive Battle of the World*, Lord D'Abernon ascribed the change in Polish morale to the presence of General Weygand. In his secret 'Report on the Franco-British Mission to Poland', printed for the War Office in September 1920, Sir Percy Radcliffe stressed what he believed had been the underlying weakness of the Bolshevik troops. 'The Russian "armies" ', he wrote, 'were nothing but untrained levies herded by Jewish Commissars and only kept going by fear of being shot from behind. Their forces also spread out on an inordinately wide front, with no depth of reserves, and although discipline was said to be good in the interior, at the front it was conspicuously bad.' After the battle, on September 10, in a letter to Lord Newton, Rumbold reported on several other opinions, and gave his own:

The Bolsheviks nearly did the trick but not quite. They actually came within sight of Warsaw and one of their patrols was caught in the yard of a spinning factory some 7 miles from Warsaw.

According to a French officer, the situation was saved by the Poles being able to bring up two or three batteries with which they opened fire on the Bolsheviks who had taken a small town called Radzymin which is only 12½ miles from Warsaw. The Bolos were so unaccustomed to being shelled that they fled.

The Naval Mission, however, claim that they saved the situation by appearing on the scene at a critical moment and giving the Polish General[1] a stiff tot of whiskey. He then personally rallied his troops who were retiring in disorder. However this may be it was touch and go on the day and night of August 13....

The change in the military situation here certainly was nothing short of a miracle. I put it down largely to the fact that the Bolsheviks had shot their bolt and were literally at the end of their tether when they arrived in front of Warsaw. It was a competition in rottenness between two armies and in the end the Bolshevik army proved the more rotten of the two. The Poles felt that they had a good man behind them in the shape of Weygand and this gave them confidence and enabled them to make the small effort needed to turn the scale.

By August 24 the Poles had driven the Russians out of 'ethnographic' Poland, capturing over 60,000 Russian troops and over a thousand

[1] Lucian Zeligowski, 1865–1947. Served in the Russian Army in the Russo-Japanese war, 1904–5. Commanded a Russian Brigade during the first world war. Commanded the Polish forces, outside Warsaw, August 1920. Led the force that seized Vilna, and established a military government there, October 1920. Inspector-General of the Polish Army, 1922–4. Minister of War, 1925–26.

machine guns. That day Rumbold sent Curzon a detailed account of the
Polish military successes. Not only had Warsaw itself been saved, but, he
declared 'the final ruin and probable disappearance of Poland' had been
avoided. 'It is certain', he added, 'that if the Soviet troops had captured
Warsaw a Soviet regime would have been set up in that town.' As a result
of the Polish victory, 'the flood of barbarism which threatened to over-
whelm Europe has been rolled back. It is a repetition of the defeat of the
Turks under the walls of Vienna in 1683.'[1] The Polish success could not
fail, in his opinion, 'to depress the extremist elements in every country in
Europe'. Yet he doubted whether the Poles could advance very far,
certainly not to Moscow as they had done at the beginning of the seven-
teenth century. Although the Russian position was 'gloomy', the Poles,
he told Curzon, 'are also exhausted. They are equally in need of peace. . . .
They have I think been cured of unreasonable and far-reaching ambitions.'

Henceforth, until he left Warsaw early in November, Rumbold continually urged the Poles to adopt a moderate policy in their negotiations
with Russia, which began at Minsk at the end of August. On August 28
he saw Prince Sapieha just before he set off to the peace talks. 'I again
urged on Minister for Foreign Affairs', Rumbold telegraphed to Curzon
that evening, 'not to take advantage of military successes of Polish army
to demand extravagant terms.' But while an increasing number of Poles
were anxious for peace, there was, Rumbold telegraphed to Curzon on
August 31, 'a strong movement in Pilsudski's immediate entourage to go
further than Polish troops are at present and indeed beyond any reason-
strategised lines'. The Poles, he warned, 'are in many ways like children
who require guidance at every turn', and he had little faith in a moderate
policy emerging by the light either of reason or experience. In a second
telegram to Curzon that same day Rumbold commented on the general
Polish apprehension about a second attack towards Kiev. 'The bulk of the
nation', he reported, 'will certainly set its face against any advance into
purely Russian territory.' The morale of the Polish soldier was such, he
added, that he would 'probably refuse to be led into further adventures'.

Rumbold was exhausted by a summer of continual crisis. For two
months he had worked without a break, from seven in the morning until
well after midnight, in a situation always of uncertainty, and for several
days of impending danger. His powers of collating and transmitting
information had been put to a severe test. The strain of events had told on
him and by the end of August he was ready to leave Warsaw for ever.

---

[1] In September 1683 Jan Sobieski, King of Poland, had commanded an army of Polish,
Austrian and German troops which defeated the Turks at the battle of Vienna, halting the
Turkish advance into central Europe.

On August 25 he wrote to Lord D'Abernon, who was returning to London:

You will have appreciated the nature of the work here. This is a most exacting post calculated to take heavy toll of the energy and good temper of the most hardworking and evenly balanced person. Owing to the utter want of resources in the place it is a post which is all work and no play. This is not good for anybody indefinitely. I have now been here eleven months, during which time the crisis has been more or less chronic. The summer has been a particularly trying one.

I think that Lord Curzon ought to realise what sort of post this is. In some ways it is perhaps the most trying post in the service. I am a willing horse but it does not do to work a willing horse too hard. It is false economy.

While D'Abernon and his Mission had been in Warsaw, Rumbold had worked well with them. But he had regarded their arrival with alarm, fearing that he was to be superseded, and on August 28, once they had gone, he wrote bitterly to Hardinge of Lloyd George's request that D'Abernon stay on in Warsaw in order to act as a check on Polish intentions. Lloyd George's request had not been decyphered in time for D'Abernon to receive it. If D'Abernon were to return, Rumbold wrote to Hardinge, 'the situation really becomes impossible'. His letter continued:

I have done hard and exacting work here for 11 months, not in anticipation of any reward or advancement – incidentally the recent appointments in our service show clearly enough that we cannot expect advancement[1] – but because I wished to do my utmost to keep the Poles straight and to contribute to bring about peace in this part of the world in the interests of my own country principally and of Poland in the second place. But if I am practically superseded the result must inevitably be to discourage me and to impair my authority with the Poles. This is no ordinary post. The man here must take considerable responsibility involving great risks. He is at full tension the whole time. But all this seems to be in vain.

To sum up, what I feel is that no matter how hard one works and how much satisfaction one may give one's own department, nothing counts. Nothing could be more discouraging than this reflection.

In his reply on September 4 Hardinge assured Rumbold that the Foreign Office had 'no intention' of sending D'Abernon back to Warsaw. 'In any case', he added, 'you need not fret about your own position. I can only tell you that Curzon has written to me that he has nothing but praise

[1] Many career diplomats were dismayed when Lloyd George appointed Lord Derby, Sir Auckland Geddes and Lord D'Abernon as Ambassadors to Paris (April 1918), Washington (March 1920) and Berlin (June 1920) respectively. Derby and Geddes were politicians, D'Abernon a banker. In December 1922 a senior Liberal politician, Lord Crewe, was sent to Paris as Ambassador by Bonar Law.

for your work and that he hopes for some opportunity of recognising it.' But Rumbold's bitterness increased when D'Abernon, who was not a career diplomat, was appointed as Ambassador to Berlin. This news was made more galling when Rumbold learned, direct from Hardinge, that the Foreign Office had wanted Rumbold himself for the Berlin Embassy. Hardinge tried to assure him that Lloyd George's patronage of D'Abernon would not threaten his own future. 'Lloyd George', Hardinge wrote in his letter of September 4, 'is not like other people, and at the present moment he is going through a phase of a sort of blind admiration and hero worship of D'Abernon and thinks that nobody can do anything except D'Abernon: all that will pass, as has already passed with so many others, and you needn't be a bit afraid as to your future prospects.'

Rumbold wanted a new posting. 'I am pretty tired', he wrote to Sir George Clerk on September 2, 'and longing to get away for a change of air and scene. This post is all work and no play. It is as if one were in the front trenches the whole time and never got pulled out for a rest.' To his stepmother three days later he wrote scathingly of Curzon: 'the belted Earl at the head of the FO snaps his fingers at us and doesn't care a brass farthing for what we think'.

The Russo-Polish negotiations continued throughout September, first at Minsk, then at Riga. 'At the present moment both sides are most anxious for peace', Rumbold wrote to Clerk in his letter of September 2. 'Whilst I do not share the view of the Anglo-French Mission that the Bolshevik army is broken for good, I do not think they will be able to organise a fresh attack on Poland before next Spring, supposing the war goes on.'

On August 26 the French newspaper *Le Temps* reported that the Bolsheviks deeply resented Rumbold's refusal to be flustered when the battle of Warsaw was at its height, believing that by his calmness he had contributed to a stiffening of Polish morale. 'I am more pleased at having enraged the Bolos', Rumbold wrote to his stepmother on September 5, 'than about anything that has happened recently. I did my utmost to harm the Germans during the war and I have equally little compunction for the Bolsheviks.' He was angered by news of an impending miners' strike in England. 'The whole world is watching England', he wrote to Newton on September 10. 'The Bolsheviks above all are ready to profit by our troubles at home and I am afraid that they will procrastinate in the matter of the peace negotiations with Poland until they see which way the cat is going to jump . . . if there is a strike I hope we shall fight it and down the miners for good and all. This perpetual labour unrest is intolerable and the men want a good lesson.'

Throughout September and early November a series of Polish military advances repeatedly jeopardized the peace talks being held at Riga. On several occasions Rumbold was instructed by Curzon to protest strongly to the Polish Government. This he did, but, as he telegraphed to Curzon on October 3:

My own impression is that Government are sincere but that they are not kept fully acquainted with military plans and may at any moment find themselves confronted by a *fait accompli*. General Pilsudski, whose double rôle of Chief of State and active Commander-in-Chief of the Army is prejudicial to the interests of the State, keeps his own counsel. He is constantly away at the front and therefore not in continuous contact with his Ministers. His rôle is somewhat like that played by Ludendorff. At the present moment he appears to be engaged in trying to retrieve his military reputation regardless of other considerations and I am sceptical of statement twice made to me by Minister for Foreign Affairs that he (General Pilsudski) is now a convinced believer in necessity for peace. He does not seem to have learnt anything from the events of last August and I feel sure that we are constantly up against him when we advise moderation both as regards Lithuania and as regards Polish Russian frontier.

The British appeals for moderation had some effect. On October 5 the Russian and Polish delegates at Riga reached a provisional agreement, and the long-awaited armistice was signed three days later. When peace was finally signed at Riga between Russia and Poland in March 1921, the Polish frontier ran much further to the east than the British Government regarded as wise, for the lands conquered since August contained an overwhelming majority of Ukrainians, White Russians, Jews and Lithuanians, for most of whom Polish rule was irksome and unjust.[1]

Four months before the final peace was signed at Riga, Rumbold left Poland, for on September 29 Curzon telegraphed to ask if he would be willing to go to Constantinople as Ambassador and High Commissioner. 'The ability and sound judgment with which you have represented His Majesty's Government at Berne and Warsaw', Curzon declared, 'give me every confidence in your power to attain a similar success in the no less difficult sphere of eastern politics'. Rumbold telegraphed that same day, accepting both the post and the promotion. On October 4 he went back to London on leave.

While he was in London, Rumbold discussed the problems which would confront him in Constantinople with the Chief of the Imperial General

---

[1] The territory east of the Curzon line over which Poland established sovereignty in 1921 included nearly four million Ukrainians, two million Jews (there were a further million in the rest of Poland), a million White Russians and 700,000 Lithuanians. There were also a million Germans in western Poland. The number of Poles throughout Poland was just over eighteen million.

Staff, Sir Henry Wilson.[1] In his diary for October 27 Wilson recorded that Rumbold was 'lamentably ignorant of the Turkish & Greek situation & said he had learnt more in our $\frac{1}{2}$ hour talk than in all the FO palavers and papers, that FO & Curzon are hopeless. They haven't even got maps!'

Rumbold returned to Warsaw on November 1, to wind up his affairs. On November 5 he presented his letters of recall to Pilsudski, and two days later sent Curzon his final despatch from Poland. In it he gave a character sketch of Pilsudski:

His whole record as a conspirator and his life of adventure have predisposed him to work by subterranean methods if he cannot obtain his object in an open and direct manner. He is a man who knows what he wants but who takes nobody into his counsel. He maintains his own espionage and secret intelligence system. His ambition may prove dangerous and, in my view, he is a restless element in this part of Europe. He is ignorant of Western mentality and, I suspect, has little belief in organisations such as the League of Nations. . . . His Ukrainian adventure proved that he is also a gambler and his initial success threw him off his balance. He reasons well and logically up to a certain point after which his judgment seems to fail him. The disaster brought on by his expedition to Kieff naturally reacted on his position in Poland. When matters were at their worst during the summer and the Soviet troops were threatening Warsaw he was sunk in apathy for several days. But he pulled himself together and personally took command of the counter-offensive from the south-west which forced the Bolsheviks to beat a hurried retreat. He succeeded in regaining his military prestige and in rehabilitating himself in the eyes of his countrymen.

His influence is probably as great as ever and he makes it felt in the Diet. He considers that he is identified with the fortunes of his country. He has hitherto relied mainly on the Socialist Party, but it does not follow that he is a Socialist at heart or by inclination. He has suffered much in the past owing to his devotion to the cause of liberty and his years of exile in Siberia and his imprisonment under rigorous conditions at Magdeburg have inevitably left their mark on him. Such is the man who, as far as can be seen, largely controls, and will for some time to come control, the destinies of this nation. He is an interesting study – and almost an anachronism in the twentieth century.

Rumbold was pessimistic about Poland's future. 'Both Germany and Russia will count again some day', he wrote in his final despatch from Warsaw, 'and possibly become a serious menace to Poland.' He was certain that the Polish corridor 'must and will be a perpetual irritant to Germany', and he wrote with foreboding of 'the hatred and distrust which

[1] Henry Hughes Wilson, 1864–1922. Entered Army, 1884. Director of Military Operations, War Office, 1910–14. Lieutenant-General, 1914. Chief Liaison Officer with the French Army, 1915. Knighted, 1915. Commanded the 4th Corps, 1916. Chief of the Imperial General Staff, 1918–22. Shot dead by Sinn Feiners on the steps of his London house.

Germans and Poles feel for one another'. What Poland's future would be, he could not say. 'The Poles', he wrote, 'are much to be pitied for the great handicaps under which they have restarted their existence. . . . A considerable number of years must necessarily elapse before the Poles possess an adequate supply of trained statesmen and administrators.' As for the Polish Press, it was, he declared, 'a thoroughly irresponsible press unworthy of a considerable nation'. His report ended:

The difficulties of the agent of one of the Allied Great Powers in this country are manifold. He is dealing with an inexperienced, wayward and impulsive people. He realises that he is rarely able to arrive at the real truth of what is going on. There is something which eludes his grasp. He often sees quite clearly the imprudence of the course of action decided on by the Polish Government. He offers advice and is listened to with attention. His advice even carries some weight. Other influences, however, which he can only suspect, tend as often as not to prevent his advice from being followed. He has to be on the alert the whole time for, given the number and complexity of the questions which this country has had to solve and which remain to be solved, he passes literally from one crisis to another.

The Rumbolds went direct from Warsaw to Constantinople. At Vienna the wagon carrying their luggage was detached from the train while it was in a siding, and thieves took all their personal linen and cutlery, most of their clothes, books, china and pictures. The stolen goods were never recovered. On November 11 they reached Trieste. The trials of the journey were not over; when they left the train at Trieste station, Rumbold's cases of claret, which were stacked up on the platform, were caught by the fender of an engine, and smashed. Rumbold's son later recalled: 'The porters got down on their hands and knees and lapped it up.' That night the family embarked on HMS *Surprise*, reaching Constantinople six days later.

13

Constantinople

1920–1922

Rumbold's appointment as High Commissioner to Constantinople delighted his friends and colleagues. He was fifty-one; his father had not been appointed Ambassador until the age of sixty-seven. 'What a combination of Merit and Magnificence!' his friend Irwin Laughlin wrote from Washington. Rumbold went to Turkey as the representative of a victorious and occupying power, for Turkey had surrendered to the Allies on 30 October 1918, signing, at Mudros, an armistice which was still in force two years later. The Ottoman Empire of 1914 had disappeared. Its southern provinces – Syria, Mesopotamia, Palestine and Arabia – had been detached in October 1918, and had come under British, French or Arab control. With British encouragement, Smyrna, and much of western Anatolia had been occupied by Greece. In eastern Anatolia, Armenians and Kurds strove to establish independent regimes. Constantinople itself, the Bosphorus and the Dardanelles were under British, French and Italian military occupation, ruled nominally by the Sultan, Mehmed VI,[1] and his cabinet.

In May 1919, Mustafa Kemal,[2] the hero of the Gallipoli campaign of 1915, had left Constantinople for eastern Anatolia, where he became the leader of a national movement which extended its authority throughout eastern and central Anatolia. In September 1919, at a congress at Sivas, the Nationalists issued a manifesto declaring all Anatolia, and all European Turkey, to be an indivisible whole. No independent Greek or Armenian state would be tolerated within this area; the Allies must halt their plans for partition or spheres of influence; the occupation of Constantinople must cease; the existing Government at Constantinople, surviving only because of allied protection, must go. Such were the principal claims of the Nationalists, who, in 1920, established their centre at Angora, convened a Grand National Assembly, and declared themselves a separate,

---

[1] Mehmed Vahid-ed-Din Efendi. Became Sultan, as Mehmed VI, in July 1918. Fled from Constantinople, November 17, 1922. Lived in exile at San Remo until his death.

[2] Mustafa Kemal, 1881–1938. Served in the Libyan and Balkan campaigns, 1911–13. Military Attaché in Sofia, 1913–14. Served at Gallipoli, 1915, in the Caucasus, 1916, and in Syria, 1917. Assumed command of the Turkish National Movement, 1919. First President of the Turkish Republic from 1922 until his death. Known as Atatürk.

ALBANIA

SERBIA

BULGARIA

B l a c

Adrianople

Constantinople
Scutari

Ineboli

G R E E C E

LEMNOS

Chanak

Bursa

Eskishehir

Sakarya

Aegean
Sea

Inönü

Angora

Kutahia

TU

Athens

Smyrna

Afion Karahissar

A N A

Aidin

BERLIN-BAGHDAD
RAILWAY(incomplete)

CILICI

Mersina

RHODES
(Italian)

CASTELLORIZO

Alex

CRETE

CYPRUS

M e d i t e r r a n e a n
S e a

Beirut

Haifa

Alexandria

Je

P A L E S T

N

Suez
Canal

Cairo

The Turkish frontier, 1914.

Territory allocated to France in 1916,
but transferred to Turkey in 1921.

E G Y P T

SINAI

Akaba

Territory transferred to Turkey by
Russia in 1921.

Nile

0   100   200   300

Scale of Miles

Red
Sea

autonomous entity. This Angora Government announced that it was the 'sole exponent of the will of the Turkish people', and took upon itself the task of driving all foreign armies from Turkish soil. It denied the right of the Constantinople Government to make any decisions or enter into any agreements on Turkey's behalf.

The Allies refused to recognize any of the claims of the Angora Government, and denounced Mustafa Kemal as a bandit and a brigand. During 1920 they strengthened their control over the Sultan, and the Constantinople administration of which he was the nominal suzerain. In March 1920 the Allied High Commissioners made themselves responsible for the Turkish War Office, which was put under the joint charge of a British, a French and an Italian officer. On 11 March 1920, they formally occupied Constantinople. Shortly before Rumbold reached Constantinople, General Sir Charles Harington,[1] took command of the 8,000 British troops in the city.

On 10 August 1920, the Allied Governments signed the Treaty of Sèvres, as part of which Greece formally annexed eastern Thrace and the Smyrna region of western Anatolia. Although the Treaty established Greek sovereignty in Asia Minor for the first time since the Middle Ages, and brought the Greeks to the shore of the Sea of Marmora and the outskirts of Constantinople, the Constantinople Government agreed to sign it on behalf of Turkey. The Angora Government at once denounced the Treaty as a betrayal of Turkey's national rights, and pledged themselves to the total restoration of Turkey in Asia Minor and eastern Thrace. Mustafa Kemal announced that the Treaty constituted a direct blow to the Turkish nation and an open act of aggression by Britain, France, Italy and Greece. Henceforth, he declared, the Angora Government was at war with the Allies, and would drive them from Constantinople, just as it would drive the Greeks from Smyrna and eastern Thrace.

In October 1920 Tewfik Pasha[2] became Grand Vizier – the head of the Turkish Government at Constantinople. With the reluctant approval

[1] Charles Harington, 1872–1940. Known as 'Tim'. Entered Army, 1892. Served in the South African and First World Wars; Major-General, 1918. Deputy Chief of the Imperial General Staff, 1918–20. Knighted, 1919. Lieutenant-General Commanding the Army of the Black Sea, 1920. General Officer Commanding the Allied Forces of Occupation in Turkey, 1920–23. General, 1927. Governor and Commander-in-Chief, Gibraltar, 1933–38. He published *Tim Harington Looks Back* in 1940. When the Turks, unsuccessfully, claimed the Vilayet of Mosul in 1925, Rumbold wrote to Sir Andrew Ryan: 'Harington, whose slogan was always "Trust the Turk", must be feeling rather foolish just now.'

[2] Ahmed Tewfik Pasha, 1845–1936. Born in Constantinople. Entered the Turkish Foreign Ministry, 1866. Minister in Athens, 1878–85. Ambassador to Berlin, 1885–95. Minister for Foreign Affairs, 1895–1909. Ambassador to London, 1909–14. Grand Vizier, 1919–22. He was a life-long advocate of conciliation with Greece and the Balkan states, and had wanted Turkey to remain neutral in 1914.

of the Allies he entered into negotiations with the Angora Government, hoping to reach some compromise with them. He chose for his emissary to Angora, Marshal Izzet Pasha,[1] the new Minister of the Interior. 'He is personally honest and straightforward', Rumbold wrote of Izzet in his Annual Report for Turkey of 1920, 'and, if not a man of commanding intelligence or really strong character, he has a good deal of common-sense and is capable, under guidance, of becoming a centre of relatively moderate nationalism. . . . The Sultan is prejudiced against him, but he stands well with the Heir Apparent.'[2] Much depended upon Izzet's mission to Angora. If the Nationalists would agree to a compromise, the Treaty of Sèvres might be allowed to stand in some modified form, and the dominant allied position in Constantinople preserved. But Izzet's mission was a failure. Mustafa Kemal had no intention of making any bargain with the Government in Constantinople.[3]

Rumbold's task as High Commissioner extended beyond relations between Constantinople and Angora. He was also responsible for the administration of Constantinople itself. This responsibility was an onerous one; the city was virtually bankrupt, its officials demoralized, and its public services in a state of near chaos. Even the policing of the city caused Rumbold anxiety; but he was prepared to act on his own initiative to avert a crisis, as he wrote to Curzon on November 26:

The apparent chronic monthly financial crisis became acute a few days ago. Colonel Ballard,[4] commanding the Inter-Allied Police, called on me on the

[1] Ahmed Izzet Pasha. Commanded the 2nd Army in Eastern Anatolia, 1916–17. Appointed Grand Vizier, October 14, 1918; he also made himself Minister of War and Chief of the General Staff (Mustafa Kemal had hoped to be made Minister of War); sixteen days later he authorized the signature of the Armistice of Mudros. Replaced by Tewfik Pasha as Grand Vizier, November 10, 1918. Minister of the Interior, 1920–21. Foreign Minister, 1921. Resigned on Mustafa Kemal's insistence, 1921; thereafter he gave Nationalists both moral support, and weapons.

[2] Abdul Mejid Efendi, 1868–1944. Second son of Abdul Azziz. The Sultanate was abolished by the Nationalists before he could succeed to the throne. In November 1922, after the flight of his cousin, Sultan Mehmed, he accepted the Caliphate, shorn of all but its spiritual functions. In March 1924 he was expelled from Turkey, and went into exile in Switzerland. He died in Paris.

[3] The Government at Constantinople was variously referred to as: the Turkish Government, the Sultan's Government, the Central Government and the Constantinople Government. The Turks at Angora under Mustafa Kemal's leadership were known as: the Kemalists, the Nationalists, the Angora authorities, and the Angora Government.

[4] Colin Robert Ballard, 1868–1941. Entered Army, 1888; Commanded the 7th and 95th Brigades, on the Western Front, 1914–16. Wounded on the Somme, 1916. Military Attaché, Rumania, 1917–18. President of the Allied Police Commission, Constantinople, 1920–23. He published Russia in Rule and Miss Rule (1920) and biographies of Napoleon (1924) and Abraham Lincoln (1926).

19th instant and stated that whilst he did not apprehend disturbances on the part of the police it was most desirable that the latter should receive their pay for October. As I understand that General Harington was also somewhat nervous on the subject, and as I did not wish that any strain should be thrown on his slender forces, I made arrangements that the receipts of the Turkish Government should be at once ear-marked for the payment of the police salaries of October. In doing this I was well aware that other categories of officials would become vociferous in their demand for payment. Reports reached me at the same time that the large numbers of Turkish officers in Constantinople – some 8,500 – who are living in very poor circumstances were showing signs of discontent, and were holding meetings as a preliminary to demonstrations. . . .

The financial weakness of the Constantinople Government remained acute throughout Rumbold's period as High Commissioner. The Provisional Financial Commission, under the control of the High Commissioners, was unable to influence the financial policy of the local Constantinople authorities. On December 18 Rumbold sent the Foreign Office a report in which he stated bluntly: 'I see no permanent solution of the exchange difficulties until there is a reconciliation between the Government and the Kemalists and Anatolia is opened up again to foreign intercourse. . . .'

On December 6 Rumbold was received by the Sultan, who, as he wrote to King George V a week later, 'was extremely nervous at the beginning of the audience . . . he remained absolutely silent for a considerable time, his mouth twitching nervously'. The Sultan, Rumbold continued, insisted 'that he had always considered that the friendship of England was necessary to Turkey'. On December 23 Lord Stamfordham replied on behalf of the King, thanking Rumbold for his letter, and asking: 'Who will eventually reign in Constantinople? Some people think it will be Kemal, others even back Constantine[1] – but one thing is evident, that until Bolshevik rule is crushed there will be no peace in Eastern Europe, and no return of anything like prosperity in the world.'

Rumbold could see no prospect of a Turkish settlement. He had some hopes that the Angora Government might quarrel with the Bolsheviks about which of them should control the Black Sea port of Batum, and that a conflict between Lenin and Mustafa Kemal might embroil the Nationalists in warfare in the Caucasus. But he knew that it was just as

[1] Constantine, 1868–1923. Became King of Greece in 1913, when he was created a Field-Marshal in the German Army. Vetoed Greek co-operation at the Dardanelles, 1915. Refused to help the Allied Army at Salonika, 1916–17. Forced to leave Greece by the Allies, 1917. In exile, 1917–20. Returned as King, 1920. Abdicated after a military revolt, 1922.

likely that Angora and Moscow would come to terms, leaving the Nationalists free to concentrate their attacks upon the Greeks and the Allies. 'The situation here is pretty black', he wrote to Eyre Crowe on New Year's Day, 1921, 'and I do not see any light.' On January 4 he wrote to Carton de Wiart, who was still head of the British Military Mission in Warsaw: 'I begin to think that I am the stormy petrel of the Diplomatic Service for there seem to be troubles wherever I go. However, difficulties are made to be overcome, and I hope we shall pull through our difficulties here. The training I got in Warsaw has been very useful to me, for I think nothing of crises now.'

In mid-December, Tewfik Pasha told Rumbold that as a result of Izzet's unsuccessful mission to Angora, ratification of the Treaty of Sèvres must be delayed. 'The Turks', Rumbold wrote on January 4 to his predecessor as High Commissioner, Vice-Admiral de Robeck,[1] 'are in a stubborn mood now, almost amounting to arrogance.' He went on: 'I have never dealt with people who have so little political sagacity as the Turks. Some time ago I told them they ought to show goodwill in the matter of ratification, and thereby acquire merit in the eyes of the Allies. . . . But they could not or would not see this.' A debate about the ratification of the Treaty of Sèvres took place within the Foreign Office. Curzon argued the need to modify the Treaty before seeking Turkish ratification, writing in a Foreign Office minute on January 7 that an alternative to the existing terms might be the admission of Turkish sovereignty over Smyrna 'in some more palpable form than a flag on a fort' retaining some form of Greek administration there, and allowing the Turks the Enos–Midia line in Europe, rather than the Chatalja line as laid down in the Treaty. If given the Enos–Midia line, the Turks would then control the Gallipoli Peninsula, which the Treaty allocated to Greece. 'I cannot but think', Sir Eyre Crowe minuted on January 8, 'that the re-establishment of the Turk on both shores of the Dardanelles would be far more dangerous to our interests than a division of the two shores between Greeks and Turks.' A member of the Central European Department of the Foreign Office, Harold Nicolson,[2] deprecated any concessions to Turkish

---

[1] John Michael de Robeck, 1862–1928. Entered Navy, 1875. Rear-Admiral, 1911. Commanded the 9th Cruiser Squadron, charged with protecting British merchant ships in the mid-Atlantic, 1914–15; commanded the Allied naval forces at the Dardanelles, March 1915–January 1916. Knighted, 1916. Commanded the 2nd Battle Squadron in the North Sea, 1916–18. Created Baronet, 1919. Admiral, 1920. High Commissioner at Constantinople, 1920. Commander-in-Chief of the Mediterranean Fleet, 1920–22. Commander-in-Chief of the Atlantic Fleet, 1922–24. Admiral of the Fleet, 1925.

[2] Harold George Nicolson, 1886–1968. Son of Sir Arthur Nicolson (1st Baron Carnock). Entered Foreign Office, 1909; Counsellor, 1925. Served at Teheran, 1925–27 and Berlin,

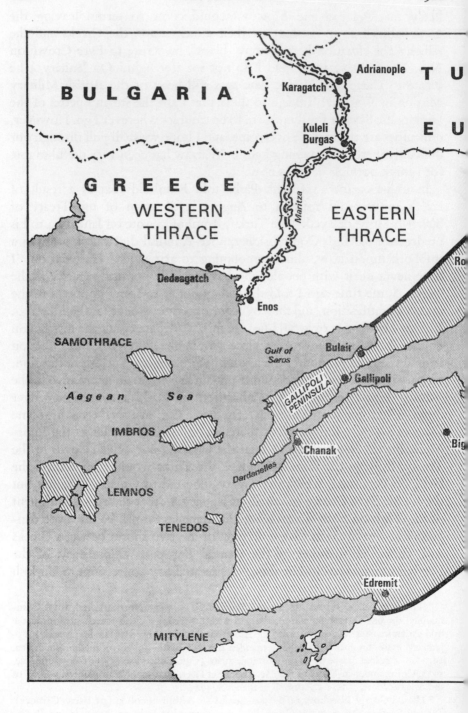

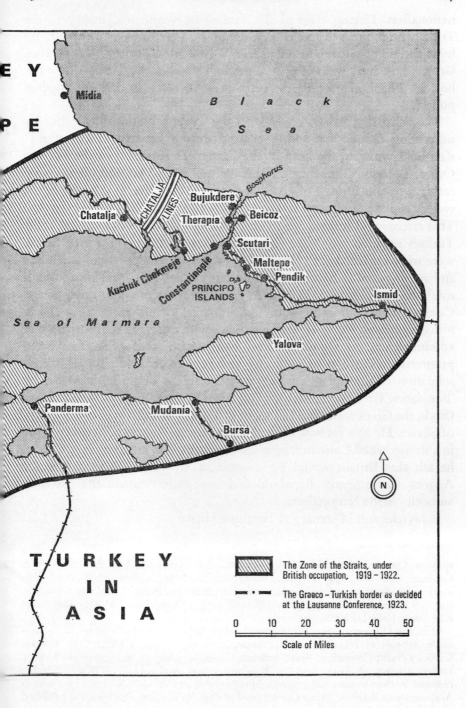

Midia

B l a c k

S e a

Bosphorus

CHATALJA LINES

Bujukdere

Chatalja

Therapia

Beicoz

Scutari

Maltepe

Kuchuk Chekmeje

Constantinople

Pendik

Ismid

PRINCIPO
ISLANDS

Sea of Marmara

Yalova

Panderma

Mudania

Bursa

N

T U R K E Y

I N

A S I A

The Zone of the Straits, under
British occupation, 1919 – 1922.

The Graeco – Turkish border as decided
at the Lausanne Conference, 1923.

| 0 | 10 | 20 | 30 | 40 | 50 |

Scale of Miles

nationalism. Having claimed the Straits, he wrote on January 8, the Turks would 'proceed to claim Adrianople'. There was, he believed, 'no logic and no conviction in the phrase "a contented Turkey" '. A satisfied Greece, however, was not only a possibility under the Treaty of Sèvres, but, in Nicolson's words, 'a very positive asset in British imperial policy'.

The belief that Britain could keep the Turkish Nationalists at bay by supporting Greece was losing ground during January. 'I am afraid', Rumbold wrote to the head of the Eastern Department of the Foreign Office, Lancelot Oliphant,[1] on January 20, 'it will be difficult to avoid eating a certain amount of dirt if we are to have place in this part of the world, and we are bound to antagonise either the Turks or the Greeks'. That afternoon Rumbold telegraphed at length to Curzon, stating that the Turkish situation would be 'quite inextricable' if the Treaty of Sèvres were to be regarded as the basis of future policy, 'unless Allies are united and are prepared to fight new war on large scale'. Rumbold hoped that it might be possible to confront the Angora Government with a strengthened Constantinople administration 'the Sultan as corner stone . . . giving him definite and whole-hearted assistance with a view to reconstruction of administration on sound financial basis, creation of gendarmerie and progressive extension of authority outward from here'. But this consolidation of the Sultan's power could only be done, he believed, by 'liquidating Greek complications imported by ourselves into Asia Minor', that is, the Greek annexation of western Turkey as laid down in the Treaty of Sèvres. He also foresaw difficulties in finding 'suitable' Turks to serve in a strengthened Constantinople Government. Yet unless this were done, he felt that Britain would be 'compelled' by events to recognize the Angora Government. Rumbold did not underestimate the growing authority of the Nationalists.

In his telegram of January 20 he stressed that:

1927–29. On editorial staff of *Evening Standard*, 1930. National Labour MP, 1935–45. A Governor of the BBC, 1941–46. Joined the Labour Party, 1947. Knighted, 1953. Among his many publications were *Some People*, a satire in which the Foreign Office was prominent (1927), a biography of his father, *Lord Carnock* (1930), *Curzon: the Last Phase* (1934) and *King George V: his Life and Reign* (1952).

[1] Lancelot Oliphant, 1881–1965. Entered Foreign Office, 1903. 3rd Secretary, Constantinople, 1905–6; at Teheran, 1909–11. Returned to the Foreign Office, 1912; Assistant Secretary, 1920; Counsellor, 1923; Assistant Under-Secretary of State, 1927–36; Deputy Under-Secretary of State, 1936–39. Knighted, 1931. Ambassador to Belgium, 1939; captured by the Germans and interned, June 1940–September 1941. Resumed his duties as Ambassador to Belgium (to the Government in Exile, in London), 1941–45. He published *An Ambassador in Berlin* (1946).

It is useless to regard Mustapha Kemal any longer as a brigand chief. Angora Government has tight grip on the whole of Asia Minor not in effective foreign occupation with probable exception of certain more or less Kurdish areas in the South East. It exercises all functions of Government with average efficiency as efficiency goes in Turkey. Bulk of population sheep-like as always, recognized its authority without demur and majority. . . . Moslem element support it strongly as standing for best interests of Turkey and individual Turks. It has been strong enough to repress quickly and thoroughly any attempts at local risings by anti-Kemalist Turks. It has strangle hold on native Christians though they do not fare badly at present except in marginal areas which are more or less the theatres of war. . . .

Foreign orientation of Angora Government still turns mainly on question of relations with Bolsheviks. These are undoubtedly subject to frequent strain owing firstly to frequent differences over Caucasus question and secondly to mistrust of Bolsheviks amongst large numbers of Turks who fear penetration of Bolshevik principles into Asia Minor or who simply see old Russian menace behind present Bolshevik friendship. Nevertheless all recent indications point to conclusion that guiding spirits on both sides attach utmost value to continued co-operation and desire to avoid anything in the nature of rupture.

I am familiar with theory that Nationalist movement contains sufficiency of moderate element to be capable of being drawn into our orbit by relatively small concessions. There was a time when, if we had been prepared to drive Turkey less hard in the matter of territorial sacrifices, we might have divided moderate Nationalists and irreconcilable Extremists. But as things have worked out movement has maintained its cohesion and extremists are entitled to claim that its present strength justifies their attitude. I do not say it would be impossible even now to make bid for cohesion of more moderate elements to allied point of view. For this, however, it would be necessary not merely to offer substantial concessions but to show that Allies both disposed of and intended to use force necessary to impose any new settlement.

Whatever their difficulties, leaders of Nationalist movement are now elated and self-confident and their acts and pronouncements show them to be intensely hostile to Allies with the exception of Italy, whose complaisance is however her only recommendation in their eyes. They are especially hostile to Great Britain. That is their chief common ground with Bolsheviks. Many of them still cherish hope of not merely saving Thrace and whole of Asia Minor but of establishing Turkish hegemony in the East at the expense of Great Britain. Others do not go so far as this and some of them would even like to revert to traditional friendship with Great Britain if only Great Britain would transfer her affections from Greece to Turkey; but even these would now regard retention of whole 'Turkey proper' with complete sovereign rights subject perhaps to mitigation by financial control as object to be attained.

Rumbold warned Curzon that it would be a mistake to regard the Constantinople Government 'as submissive to Allied point of view'. It regarded Treaty revision as a 'forgone conclusion', and was as sympathetic to the moderate Nationalists as it was afraid of the extremists. Britain's task, he believed, was to 'keep our hold here and maintain semblance of legitimate Government'; but this would not be easy, as the economic situation was precarious, and an influx of Russian refugees fleeing from the Bolsheviks added to the distress, and near starvation of the city. Vice-Admiral de Robeck doubted whether Britain could maintain its control over Constantinople. 'If it is our intention', he wrote to Rumbold from Malta on January 21, 'to retain our position in Constantinople and in the Straits the advance of the Turkish Nationalists assisted by the Bolsheviks having for its objective Constantinople and the Straits will be difficult to deal with, especially if the Greek Army proves to be untrustworthy. . . .' De Robeck had reason to be concerned; as Commander-in-Chief of all British Naval Forces in the Mediterranean, he would have to provide the ships to keep both the Bosphorus and the Dardanelles under allied control if the Nationalists attacked. The Commander of the British Military Forces at Constantinople, General Harington, shared de Robeck's scepticism about the ability to defend Constantinople against a concerted Kemalist attack.

By the beginning of 1921 the financial situation had deteriorated so far that the local banks were refusing to lend the Constantinople Government any more money. Most Government officials had only been paid three-quarters of their salaries for October 1920, and nothing at all for November and December. At the beginning of December Rumbold had informed the Minister of Finance, Rashid Bey,[1] that 252,000 Turkish gold pounds would be made available from Turkish funds held by the Allies if, in return, the Turks accepted allied control over their finances. But the Turks had refused to abandon control over their economy. 'Turkish Government', Rumbold telegraphed to Curzon on January 3, 'are stubbornly opposing form of control of their finance desired by Provisional Financial Commission.' Nine days later he telegraphed again; the Turks still refused to accept allied financial control; Rumbold therefore held back the gold. On January 19, in an attempt to put pressure on Rashid Bey, Rumbold sent a message direct to the Sultan pointing out – as he explained to Curzon six days later – 'that I was only too anxious to raise embargo on gold in order to permit a payment on account to be made to officials who were in such terrible straits. I added that the person of the Finance Minister stood in the way.' The Sultan, eager to cure the distress of the Government's

---

[1] Mustafa Rashid Bey, 1858–1921. Ottoman Minister in Bucharest, 1893; Rome, 1896; The Hague, 1897; Vienna, 1908. Minister of Commerce and Agriculture, 1912. Foreign Minister, 1918. Ambassador to London, 1920. Minister of Finance, 1920–21.

officials, acted as Rumbold hoped. On January 22, bowing to the Sultan's intervention, Rashid Bey accepted the allied terms. Henceforth the Turkish Finance Ministry would be under the same strict allied surveillance as had been imposed on the War Ministry ten months earlier. This decision, like all those concerning the administration of Constantinople, had to be approved by Albert Defrance[1] and Marquis Garroni,[2] the French and Italian High Commissioners, who, with Rumbold, formed a High Commissioners' Conference, and met regularly to co-ordinate allied policy. One of the Secretaries to the Conference, Henry Mack,[3] later recalled how Rumbold 'dominated the proceedings'. Rumbold's comments, he added, were usually 'brief and decisive; downright when the occasion demanded'.

During his first month at Constantinople, in a private letter to King George V, Rumbold had written, on December 13, of how the streets of the city were full 'of famished and utterly demoralised Russians who are a danger to the security and health of the town'. These Russians had been forced to leave Russia on the defeat of General Wrangel[4] and his anti-Bolshevik army in the Crimea. Together with the French High Commissioner, Rumbold was, he explained to the King, 'trying to have undesirable elements collected and interned on board ship, after the ships have been disinfected. . . . The conditions in which many of these unfortunate Russians travelled from the Crimea here defy description. The whole episode is most depressing. Many of the Russians seem incapable of helping themselves.'

Among the Russian refugees in Constantinople was one of the most

[1] Albert Defrance, 1860–1936. Entered the French Dipomatic Service, 1880. Minister in Bangkok, 1895–1902; Teheran, 1902–9; Stockholm, 1909–10. French Consul-General, Cairo, 1910–18. Minister in Brussels, 1918–19. High Commissioner, Constantinople, 1919–21. Ambassador in Madrid, 1921–23.

[2] Marquis Eugenio Camillo Garroni, 1852–1935. Prefect of Genoa, 1896–1912. Senator, 1905. Italian Ambassador in Constantinople, 1912–15 and 1920–22. Head of the Italian Delegation at the Lausanne Conference, 1922–23. In his report of January 4, 1921 to Curzon, Rumbold wrote of Garroni: 'His appearance is that of an easy-going elderly gentleman but he is very alert.' Known as 'the turtle'.

[3] William Henry Bradshaw Mack, 1894–   . Served on the Western Front, 1916–19. Entered the Diplomatic Service, 1921. 3rd Secretary, Constantinople, 1921–22. Head of the French Department, Foreign Office, 1940. Chief British Liaison Officer to General Eisenhower, North Africa, 1942. Deputy Civil Commissioner for Austria, 1944; Minister in Vienna, 1947–48. Ambassador. Baghdad, 1948–51; Buenos Aires, 1951–54. Knighted, 1947.

[4] Peter Nikolaevich Wrangel, 1878–1928. Served in the Russo-Japanese and First World War. Joined the anti-Bolshevik forces of General Denikin, 1918. Assumed command of the anti-Bolshevik forces in southern Russia, November 1919. Launched an offensive against the Bolsheviks, June 1920, whereupon the British at once withdrew their support for his actions. Evacuated his forces from the Crimea, November 1920. In exile in Belgium. His memoirs, Always With Honor, were published in New York in 1958.

distinguished of the Imperial Diplomats, Nicolai Tcharykoff,[1] a former Tsarist Ambassador in Constantinople. Tcharykoff often dined at the Embassy, where his plight and poverty revealed the all-consuming effects of the revolution. One of General Harington's staff, Colonel Farmar,[2] befriended Tcharykoff while he was in Constantinople. 'M. Tcharykoff told me', he recorded in his recollections, 'that Lenin and Trotsky (Bronstein) were subordinates in an organization which existed to foment world revolution. . . . No one knows the principals in name.' When Colonel Farmar asked Rumbold his opinion of the existence of such a conspiracy, Rumbold told him that 'the existence of this menace was known to every Chancery in Europe before 1914 and its headquarters were believed to be in Austria: to await an opportunity which might offer for their activities on the death of Francis Joseph. When the Germans gave the chance in Russia to upset the weak Kerensky, the HQ moved, leaving behind Bela Kun.'[3]

Lady Rumbold was particularly concerned to help the Russian refugees, whose plight was a severe one. When the Rumbolds had reached Constantinople in November 1920 there were 120,000 Russians crowded into sixty ships in the Sea of Marmora. Lady Rumbold helped to organize the British Emergency Committee, which undertook the feeding, bathing and clothing of 10,000 Russian women and children. Unknown to her husband, Lady Rumbold took pity on a young Russian officer, wounded in both legs, whom she hid in an Embassy bathroom for three weeks before a place could be found for him in hospital. From a hut in the

[1] Nicolai Valerianovitch Tcharykoff, 1855–1922. Fought against the Turks as a trooper in the Imperial Guard, 1877; wounded and decorated for valour by the Tsar. Entered the Foreign Service, 1878. Russian Minister at the Court of Bokhara, 1880–90; at Sofia, 1896–1905; at The Hague, 1905–9. Ambassador in Constantinople, 1909–12. The advocate of a Russo-Turkish *rapprochement*, he was recalled in March 1912. Senator, 1912–17. A friend of Nicholas II, he was with him at his abdication. Fled to Constantinople as a refugee, 1920.

[2] Harold Mynors Farmar, 1878–1961. 2nd Lieutenant, Lancashire Fusiliers, 1898; present at the battle of Omdurman. Captain, 1914. Assumed command of the 86th Infantry Brigade at the 'W' Beach Landing, Gallipoli, April 25, 1915, after the Brigadier had been wounded and the Brigade Major killed. Lieutenant-Colonel, 1916. Served on the Western Front, 1916–18; at Constantinople, 1920–22; in India, 1922–28. Colonel, 1924. His son, Hugh William Farmar (born 1908) married Rumbold's daughter Constantia in 1944.

[3] Bela Kun, 1886–1936. A Hungarian Jew, he worked before 1914 as a journalist on a Socialist newspaper in Budapest. Served as a Lieutenant-Commander of an ammunition supply column, 1914. Captured by the Russians on the Eastern Front and imprisoned in Russia, 1915–17. He supported the Bolsheviks in 1917; in October 1918 he returned to Hungary as leader of a revolutionary party. Prime Minister of Hungary, March–August 1919, when he instituted a communist regime. In July 1919 the Allies halted his invasion of Slovakia. He fled to Vienna in August 1919, and was interned in a lunatic asylum. Allowed by the Allies to go to Russia, 1920, he became a leading figure of the Comintern. Eventually he was imprisoned, then murdered on Stalin's orders.

Embassy garden clothes were distributed to the Russians by the English ladies of the Emergency Committee. Early in 1921 Rumbold requisitioned the Sultan's derelict stables in which 1,500 refugees were able to find room to sleep. But the majority had nowhere so palatial to go. 'The wretched Russian refugees look more miserable than ever', Lady Rumbold wrote to her mother on 8 February, 1921. 'You see cadaverous looking officers selling newspapers in the streets.'

The number of refugees and vagabonds in the city created a security problem. Forty Indian soldiers with a machine-gun mounted guard each day in the Embassy forecourt, and patrolled each night. But there was also a surfeit of labour in the city which worked to the Embassy's advantage. Ten nationalities were represented on the domestic staff, including an Armenian housemaid, a Montenegrin footman, a Hungarian and a Serb servant, a Belgian gardener, an Albanian porter and an Italian chef. The latter had done very well out of his activities, being, Lady Rumbold wrote to her mother, 'an excellent *cook*, but a villain of the deepest dye, owning a *motor*, an Hotel, and he is now buying a launch!'

In February 1921 the British Government decided to take the initiative in reducing the tensions created by the Treaty of Sèvres. Both the Constantinople and Angora Governments were invited to London to discuss with the Greeks possible modifications of the Treaty. Treaty revision was strongly advocated both by Lord Curzon, and by Winston Churchill, the Secretary of State for War,[1] who believed that a drastic revision of the Treaty was necessary in favour of the Turks if peace were to be secured in Anatolia. For several weeks it was uncertain whether Mustafa Kemal would agree to send a delegation to London. 'At the present moment we have reached a deadlock', Rumbold wrote to the American Minister in Warsaw, Hugh Gibson,[2] on February 2, 'and the issue would appear to depend on Mustafa Kemal. The latter is suffering from swelled head, and does not seem inclined to go to the Conference.' The Kemalists, Rumbold telegraphed to Curzon on February 6, were 'immovable up to date in their pretension to be regarded as sole Government of Turkey'. On February 11 Curzon replied that the 'Angora delegation' could only be received in London 'as part of the Constantinople delegation, having no independent

---

[1] Churchill had been Secretary of State for War since January 1919; on February 13, 1921, he was appointed Secretary of State for the Colonies.

[2] Hugh Gibson, 1883–1954. A United States diplomat, he was a 2nd Secretary in London, 1909–10 and 1st Secretary in London, 1916. Member of the Interallied Mission to the countries of the former Austro-Hungarian Empire, 1918–19. Minister to Warsaw, 1919–23; to Berne, 1924–27. Ambassador to Belgium, 1927–33; to Brazil, 1933–37. He was Chairman of the Three-Power Naval Conference at Geneva, 1927, and a Delegate at the Geneva Disarmament Conference, 1932.

status or title of their own'. The two delegations eventually reached London, and the conference lasted from February 21 to March 17. No settlement was reached and on March 24 the Greeks launched a military offensive eastwards towards Angora from their western Anatolian territories. During the early months of 1921, and throughout the period of the London conference, Rumbold was worried about the divergence between French and British policy at Constantinople. It was almost certain that the French would try to come to terms with Mustafa Kemal. When, at the beginning of February, the French General at Constantinople, General Charpy,[1] proposed to organize a special Battalion of Gendarmes for Scutari, a suburb of Constantinople on the Asian shore of the Bosphorus, Rumbold sensed a French attempt to take eventual control of the policing of the capital itself. Britain, he wrote to the Commander-in-Chief of the British forces, General Harington, on February 11, must 'prevent any attempt of the sort on the part of the French'. His letter continued:

It is an unfortunate fact that the French are of a jealous disposition, and they seem to me to be trying to get a grip over nearly every country in Europe. For the moment we hold most of the cards at Constantinople. You are the General in Command of this place; the Allied Police are under your orders; we have two or three battleships always in port; and, finally, Sir Adam Block[2] is by far the best known personality on the financial side, and probably the man who carries most weight with the Turks. Thus we are top dogs, and the French probably do not like it.

Writing to Curzon on the following day, Rumbold reiterated these arguments, adding that 'the fact that the Conference . . . is taking place in London must tend to show the Turks that we are the real arbiters of their destinies'.

If the Constantinople Government were to survive it was essential, Rumbold believed, to strengthen the Sultan's position, and to make him, as he telegraphed to Curzon on March 8, a 'rallying point for moderate element in Turkey'. Curzon had no desire to see Mustafa Kemal extend

[1] Charles Antoine Charpy, 1869–1941. Entered the French Army, 1888. Commanded the 84th Infantry Battalion during the battle of the Marne, 1914. Chief of Staff of the 1st Corps, 1915. Général de Brigade, 1918. Commander of the French forces in Constantinople, 1920–22. Général de Division, 1924. Chief of French Military Mission to Poland, 1926. Commanded the 3rd Corps at Rouen, 1927.

[2] Adam Samuel James Block, 1856–1941. Student Interpreter, Constantinople, 1877; Consul, 1890; Secretary of Legation, 1902. Represented the British Bondholders on the Council of Administration of the Ottoman Public Debt, 1903–29. Vice-Chairman, Constantinople Telephone Company. Knighted, 1907. Worked at the Admiralty, and at the Ministry of Blockade, during the First World War. Advised on the Blockade of the Black Sea (against the Bolsheviks), 1919–20.

his power to Constantinople, and had consistently refused to grant British recognition to the Grand National Assembly at Angora. On March 12 he replied to Rumbold's telegram by asking him to inform the Sultan that Britain wanted 'a united Turkey under his authority'.

During March, Britain's hopes of bolstering the Constantinople Government suffered a triple blow. On March 11 the French, without either consulting or informing the British, signed an agreement direct with the Angora Government to settle frontier problems between southern Anatolia and the French administration in Syria.[1] Two days later, on March 13, the Italians also made a separate agreement with Angora to settle disputes which had arisen between them in the Cilician province of southern Anatolia, where the Italians had hoped to establish a dominant influence. The Italians also agreed to support the Nationalist demands for the restitution of Smyrna.[2] On March 16, in Moscow, the Angora Government signed a Treaty with the Soviet Government of far-reaching implications. The Russians agreed to recognize no treaties relating to Turkey which had not been approved by the Grand National Assembly, and gave explicit support to Mustafa Kemal's claims that Anatolia and Turkey-in-Europe were a territorial entity that could not be partitioned or divided. For their part, the Angora Government ceded the port and province of Batum to the Georgian Republic.[3] The Russians agreed to release Turkey from all debts and obligations owed to the Tsarist regime.

At an audience on March 22 Rumbold found the Sultan very depressed, and threatening to resign unless Britain took active measures against Angora. On the following day Rumbold sent Curzon an account of their conversation. The Sultan, he wrote, had spoken 'rather contemptuously' of his own Government; as for Angora, the regime there, he had declared 'was a mad-house'. In a second letter to Curzon on March 23, Rumbold reported at greater length the Sultan's bitter comments about the Angora Government:

A handful of brigands had established complete ascendancy. They were few in number, but they had got a strangle-hold on the people as a whole, profiting

---

[1] Although the agreement between France and Angora was negotiated and signed in London, during the Allied Conference with the Turks, its text was not communicated to the British until April 2, two weeks after the Conference had ended.

[2] The British only learnt of the full agreement between Italy and Angora on April 15, when Curzon described it, in a telegram to Sir George Buchanan in Rome, as 'an indefensible breach of faith with an ally'.

[3] Although a concession to Russia, because Batum was at that time occupied by Turkish troops, the Soviet-Turkish agreement in fact benefited Turkey most, extending the Turkish frontier further eastwards than in 1914, and adding the formerly Russian towns of Artvin, Ardahan, Kars, Sarikamish and Igdir to Turkey. These had all been transferred from Turkey to Russia in 1878.

by their submissiveness, their timidity, or their penury. Their strength lay in the backing of 16,000 military officers who were concerned for their own future personal interests. . . .

The Angora leaders were men without any real stake in this country, with which they had no connection of blood or anything else. Moustafa Kemal was a Macedonian revolutionary of unknown origin. His blood might be anything, Bulgarian, Greek or Serbian, for instance. He looked rather like a Serbian! Bekir Sami[1] was a Circassian. They were all the same, Albanians, Circassians, anything but Turkish. There was not a real Turk among them. He and his Government were nevertheless powerless before them. The hold was such that there was no means of access to the real Turks, even by way of propaganda. The real Turks were loyal to the core but they were intimidated, or they were hoodwinked by fantastic misrepresentations.

The influence of Angora continued to grow. On March 24, the Smyrna Representative of the British High Commission, Sir Harry Lamb,[2] wrote to Rumbold of 'an active propaganda' being conducted among the Turks 'to prepare for the moment when the national forces could return' to Smyrna. The Greek administration in Smyrna, Lamb continued, were afraid 'that the return of the Turk, *uncontrolled*, in his present mood would be a calamity worse than any that had gone before!' That same day the Greeks in western Anatolia, confident of their ability to destroy the Angora Government, launched a further military offensive eastwards from Bursa. Rumbold did not intend to help towards a Greek victory. At a meeting on March 26, he, the new French High Commissioner, General Pellé,[3] and Marquis Garroni agreed, as Rumbold telegraphed to Curzon that evening, not to allow the Greeks to use any of the facilities of the Smyrna–Aidin railway[4] in the course of their military operations against the Nationalists. 'The Greek offensive', Rumbold wrote to Lancelot

---

[1] Bekir Sami, died 1932. A deputy in the First National Assembly, April 1920. Minister for Foreign Affairs, May 1920–March 1921. Head of the Turkish delegation to Moscow, 1920, and to London, 1921. Took the surname of Kunduk.

[2] Harry Harling Lamb, 1857–1948. Entered Consular Service, 1885. Served, 1885–1903 in Van, Mosul, Scutari, Suakin and Erzerum. Chief Dragoman, British Embassy, Constantinople, 1903–7. Consul-General, Salonica, 1907–13. Employed in the Foreign Office, London, 1914–18. Knighted, 1919. Attached to the British High Commission, Constantinople, 1920–21. High Commission Representative and Consul-General, Smyrna, 1921–3.

[3] Maurice César Joseph Pellé, 1863–1924. Served before 1914 in the French Artillery, and as Military Attaché in Berlin. On the Staff of General Joffre, 1914–16. Commanded the 15th Corps on the Western Front, 1917–18. Head of the French Military Mission to Czechoslovakia, 1919–20. High Commissioner in Constantinople, 1921–22; in Syria, 1923–24.

[4] Over five million pounds of British capital were invested in this railway, known officially as the *Ottoman Railway from Smyrna to Aidin of his Imperial Majesty the Sultan*, which had received its original concession in 1856 and was opened ten years later. It had begun to make a profit only after 1900, and was flourishing on the eve of war. Although the railway, its stock and its property, were badly damaged in the fighting of 1922, the Company survived.

Oliphant on March 30, 'has upset the apple-cart here and has deferred for some time to come all hope of peace. As the Greeks have elected to start fighting again the best thing which could happen would be for the two parties to fight to a stalemate and be thoroughly exhausted. Then there may be some chance of their proving tractable. As it is, it would never do for either the Kemalists or the Greeks to have a walkover.'

On March 30 the Greeks reached Eskishehir, an important town on the railway between Constantinople and Angora. 'My information', Rumbold wrote to Lamb on March 31, 'is that the Greeks will pause and re-organise their forces and then advance on Angora in about a fortnight's time. I suppose they will take that place but the war is not over then.' Rumbold's forecast was quickly falsified. The Nationalist forces checked the Greeks in front of Eskishehir and drove them back to their point of departure. Reinforcements were hurried from Greece, and the line held. On April 4 General Harington wrote to Rumbold that he was not altogether surprised at the Nationalist success, as he was 'convinced that the Greeks were doing everything they could to destroy their chances by putting in all these useless Commanders, and that their wave of en-thusiasm would disappear as soon as they met anything solid'. That same day Sir Harry Lamb telegraphed to Rumbold that the Greek military authorities at Smyrna, in response to the Greek appeal for reinforcements, had set up a commission to mobilize all railway employees in the province 'whether Hellenic or Ottoman subjects'. On learning this Rumbold telegraphed at once to Lamb: 'You should protest against mobilisation of Ottoman subjects which is contrary to international law.' He also pointed out that 'although Greeks may contend that Treaty of Sèvres is not yet in force, article No 74 of that Treaty deprives Greeks of right to enforce military service in Smyrna area'. Curzon approved Rumbold's initiative.

The Nationalists' successes against the Greeks were proof both of the military strength and the moral fervour of the Angora Government. 'You have not only defeated the enemy', Mustafa Kemal telegraphed to the commander of his western army, General Ismet,[1] on April 1, 'but at the same time have reversed the unhappy fate of the nation. . . . The storm-wave of the enemy's attack has been shattered against the hard rock formed

---

[1] Ismet, 1884–   . Born in Smyrna. Captain, General Staff of the 2nd Army (Edirne), 1906. Major, Army of the Yemen, 1912. Colonel, 1915. Commanded the 4th Corps, 1916; the 20th Army Corps, 1917. Under-Secretary for War, 1918. Chief of the General Staff of the Nationalist Forces, 1920. Commanded the Turkish troops in western Anatolia at the 1st and 2nd battles of Inönü, 1921. Lieutenant-General, 1922. Foreign Minister, 1922–23. Prime Minister, 1923–24 and 1925–37. Given the name of Inönü. President of Turkey, 1938–50. Leader of the Opposition in the Turkish Parliament, 1950–60. Prime Minister, 1961–65. Leader of the Opposition, 1965–72.

by your patriotism and energy . . . the high pinnacles on which you stand overlooks a glorious battlefield strewn with the bodies of thousands of the enemy, and from its summit the eye can also discern the horizon of a future for our people, and yourself that is resplendent with glory.' Flushed by their victory, the Nationalist troops were expected to continue the advance. Greek morale was deteriorating, Rumbold wrote to his stepmother on April 6, 'and we do not think that the men will be induced to advance again. . . . I am hoping that both sides will fight to a standstill in which case there is more likelihood of their listening to reason and to sound advice.' But General Harington feared a Nationalist advance as far as the zone of allied occupation, and a direct military confrontation between allied and Nationalist troops. He even foresaw the possibility of Nationalist bands reaching the Asian shore of the Bosphorus, thereby endangering the safety of the allied warships. 'I can hold position covering Scutari . . .', he telegraphed to the War Office that same day, 'with one French and one British brigade.'

On April 7 Rumbold telegraphed to Curzon that it was still hoped 'that Greeks will put up a good fight', but that there was every danger 'that they may be compelled to retreat to the coast', leaving Constantinople open to Nationalist attack. 'An awkward situation would arise here', he declared, 'if Nationalists decided to advance on Constantinople for we do not see what could stop them. . . . If Greeks were definitely beaten the Kemalists would, it was to be feared, prove intractable.' The French High Commissioner, General Pellé, asked Rumbold whether the moment for allied intervention 'had not already come'. But Rumbold believed that the Greeks must first be allowed to try to halt the Nationalist advance. This, they succeeded in doing. The front was stabilized. Bursa remained under Greek control, and no Nationalist forces threatened the allied zone of occupation.

At the end of March Izzet Pasha had returned from Angora. His four months in Angora had impressed on him the strength and potential of the Nationalist movement. On April 8 he announced his resignation from Tewfik's Cabinet. On the following day Rumbold telegraphed to Curzon that it was quite possible that Izzet would 'go over bag and baggage to the Nationalists'.

Sympathy for the Nationalist movement spread rapidly in Constantinople. On April 13 Rumbold informed Curzon 'that the majority of the principal Turkish newspapers have openly espoused the Nationalist cause'. The Greek offensive had likewise stimulated Turkish Nationalist sentiment, and the presence of large numbers of Greek officers in Constantinople had exacerbated feelings. The Constantinople Government had even organized a medical aid mission for service with the Nationalist forces. More ominously, as Rumbold wrote to Curzon, 'General Harington reports that a considerable number of arms have disappeared from the stores which are under the control of the Minister of War. Steps have been taken to make an inventory of the contents of these stores with a view to checking any further withdrawals of arms or munitions. There can be no doubt that these arms have found their way to the Nationalist forces.'

On April 20 Rumbold wrote again to Curzon about the guns which were reaching the Nationalists. It was impossible, he said, 'to disregard the numerous reports to the effect that the Italians are supplying the Nationalists with a considerable quantity of arms and munitions'. On the other hand, he pointed out, the Greeks, without allied protest, 'are freely using the Sea of Marmora for belligerent operations', and had even used Constantinople itself 'as a Naval base from which to prevent Turkish subjects returning to Turkey and three days ago a Greek destroyer took 157 Turkish subjects, who were returning to Constantinople, off a Bulgarian ship coming from Varna. The Greek destroyer subsequently returned to Constantinople.' Two days later Rumbold telegraphed to Curzon that 'Greeks are undoubtedly using Constantinople as a supply base. They have lately bought here horses, mules and military lorries and General Harington has refused a direct offer from Greek military authorities to buy at a fantastic price 4,000 sets of old equipment.' He added that Greek ships were 'daily loading large quantities of stores and material at Galata, Stamboul and in Golden Horn'. 'The use of Constantinople by the Greeks', Rumbold wrote to Sir Harry Lamb on April 19, 'was a most incorrect proceeding . . . no Greek ships ought to be allowed here'.

The behaviour of the Greeks gave Rumbold frequent cause for concern. On May 7 he telegraphed to Curzon that 'grave excesses' had been committed against the Turkish population on the southern shore of the Sea of Marmora, 'and that these outrages are the work of Greek bands'. A 'regrettable feature of these excesses', he wrote to Curzon eleven days later, 'is that in some cases Greek regular troops have been a party to them'. Nevertheless, Rumbold had written to Lancelot Oliphant on May 3, 'if one side should triumph over the other I had rather that the Greeks won. We have means of exercising pressure on the Greeks but I do not see what we could do to Mustafa Kemal if he were to triumph over the Greeks. He would be impossible unless I am very much mistaken and our job here would become very difficult for years to come.'

During April, Rumbold and his staff compiled the forty-seven page Annual Report for 1920. In one of the sections, written by Rumbold himself, was a description of Mustafa Kemal of whose 'administrative capacity, political ability and determination there could be no doubt'. His speeches, Rumbold wrote, 'if composed by himself, as seems probable, show considerable skill in handling people and situations. He is spectacular and domineering, but there is no reason to accuse him of lack of patriotism of a chauvinistic type or of personal dishonesty.' Rumbold sent the Report to Curzon on April 27. The events of the following month gave him no reason to doubt the strength of Mustafa Kemal's position. In a telegram to Curzon on May 24, reporting on Cabinet changes in the Angora Government, he added: 'Cabinet, is, probably, of minor importance as compared to the dictatorship of Mustafa Kemal and military leaders among whom there is no real sign of disintegration to date.'

Rumbold anticipated a bitter struggle between Greeks and Turks once the Greeks felt strong enough to launch another attack across the Sakaria river towards Angora. In his letter to Oliphant on May 3 he asked if he could be given two months leave as soon as possible, so as to be back at Constantinople before the next crisis. 'I am really rather tired', he wrote, 'and feel that I should work better after I have had a bit of a rest.' Rumbold's leave was granted. To Carton de Wiart, who was still in Warsaw, he wrote on May 10: 'I am having a pretty strenuous time here trying to maintain the neutrality of Constantinople, which both Greek and Turks would violate with impunity if they could. . . . Turks and Greeks hate each other about as much as Poles and Germans.' The Russian refugees also continued to be an anxiety, having, he wrote, 'further debauched this already debauched capital'.

On May 26 Rumbold left Constantinople for London. On his way back, he spent two weeks in Switzerland, explaining why in a letter to Lancelot Oliphant on June 6:

The few days I have spent in Switzerland have bucked me up a lot and I look very fit but am still thoroughly stale and tired mentally. I have suffered from sleeplessness for ages and have at various times applied to 4 different doctors including Parkinson,[1] for relief. All have told me to knock off work for a time but this is more easily said than done. I also get blood pressure. Luckily I am very strong constitutionally and lead a most temperate existence – otherwise I should have cracked up some time ago.

I apologise for writing at such length about myself but I want to forestall any criticism of having applied for and come away on leave at this juncture so please make any use you like of this letter with the S. of S. or anybody else – should this be necessary. . . .

[1] Thomas Wright Parkinson, 1863–1935. A sheep and cattle farmer in New Zealand, he went to Edinburgh to study medicine, 1886. Came to London, 1900; physician to Prince Louis of Battenberg, and to the Lady Lytton Hospital. Knighted, 1916.

Towards the end of June, while Rumbold was still on leave, Curzon went to Paris to discuss a possible Anglo-French mediation between the Greek and Angora Governments. Britain and France agreed that Smyrna must revert to Turkish sovereignty. But in a memorandum of June 23 the Greek Government not only asserted its geographical rights to the eastern shores of the Aegean, but asked to be recognized 'as a faithful and sincere guardian of the Straits'. At the beginning of July the Constantinople Government reasserted, in a secret memorandum handed to William Rattigan, the acting High Commissioner in Rumbold's absence, the need for all of Asia Minor to be under Turkish sovereignty, as well as Turkey-in-Europe, including Adrianople.

On July 8 the Greeks opened another military offensive towards Angora. Within two weeks they had driven the Nationalists from the three important towns of Afion Karahissar, Kutahia and Eskishehir. A Nationalist counter-attack on July 21 was a costly failure, and Ismet Pasha's forces fell back to the Sakaria river. Rumbold returned to Constantinople on July 31. Two days later Izzet Pasha, whom Tewfik had appointed Foreign Minister in the Constantinople Government, called to see him at the British Embassy. 'He seemed very depressed', Rumbold telegraphed to Curzon on August 2, 'and I hear on all sides that Turks are very down in the mouth.' On the following day Tewfik himself asked Rumbold if the British would be willing to mediate between the Greek and Nationalist forces. But in a telegram to Curzon on August 4, Rumbold declared that the Angora Government 'will only prove amenable when and if they sustain another defeat'. Rumbold passed on to Curzon the opinion of General Harington that the Turkish forces were 'incapable of much further resistance and of a counter-offensive, and will withdraw into the interior if seriously threatened'. This was not the view of the Constantinople Turks, however; on August 6 Rumbold wrote to Curzon that although they were still depressed, 'they are recovering confidence in the Nationalist Army and count on the exhaustion of the Greeks at no distant date'. That same day Rumbold was received by the Sultan, who asked why Britain did not intervene to end hostilities. 'I said', Rumbold wrote to Curzon on August 9, 'that I failed to perceive what practical means the Allies had of stopping the war in Asia Minor, or of coercing either the Greeks or the Nationalists.'

On August 10 Lloyd George announced, to an Allied Conference in Paris, his view of the Graeco-Turkish conflict. He declared himself opposed to the policy, for which Rumbold had pressed, of denying Greece the use of Constantinople as a naval base. 'Prime Minister pointed out', Curzon telegraphed to Rumbold on August 12, 'that to close bases would amount to taking steps against Greece since it would prevent Greece from delivering decisive blow.' Lloyd George also declared that the Bosphorus and Dardanelles 'could not be left in hands of Turks'. Rumbold did not approve of so blatant a pro-Greek policy. But the military situation pointed to an eventual Greek victory. On August 14 Greek troops began to advance towards the Sakaria river. 'This battle', Rumbold wrote to his stepmother ten days later, 'will decide the fate of the campaign and of the Nationalists.' He still saw the ideal solution, not in a Greek victory, but in 'the complete exhaustion of both sides'. Rumbold saw no superior virtue on either side. It was essential, he telegraphed to Curzon on August 31, to avoid actions which might confirm the Nationalists 'in their belief that we are favouring the Greeks at their expense'. If the Greeks were allowed to continue seizing Turkish ships in the Sea of Marmora, he warned, 'result can only be to bring trade with Constantinople to a complete standstill' and increase Nationalist feeling.

Throughout 1921 there was friction among the allied powers in Constantinople. The French and Italian High Commissioners resented both Rumbold's influence, and General Harington's control of the allied forces. Rumbold himself was angered by the American High Commissioner, Admiral Bristol,[1] who represented the interests of the United States at Constantinople, whose anti-British feelings were undisguised. 'The fact is', Rumbold wrote privately to Curzon on September 14, 'that Admiral Bristol is a man of limited intelligence and outlook. He is jealous of the three High Commissioners, partly on his own account and partly on account of his country. He is one of those Americans who believes everything written against us in the yellow press such as that we are seeking to create an oil monopoly in Mesopotamia and elsewhere.' Curzon sympathized with Rumbold's complaint. 'I have told Crowe to send you a selection of our secret sources of information', he replied on September 23, 'which more than confirm your impression of the American Admiral. We have had abundant proof for nearly 2 years that he is suspicious, anti-British, stupid, and at times malignant. You must be careful with him, for he reports everything in an unfavourable spirit.'

In June a demobilized British Army officer, Major Henry,[2] who had

[1] Mark Lambert Bristol, 1868–1939. Entered the US Navy, 1889; Captain, 1913. In charge of the aeronautical development of the Navy, 1913–16. Commanded the *North Carolina*, convoying troops to Europe, 1917. Rear-Admiral commanding the US naval base, Plymouth, 1918–19. Commanded the US naval detachment, Eastern Mediterranean, 1919 High Commissioner, Constantinople, 1919–27. Admiral commanding the US Asiatic Fleet, 1927–29.

[2] James Douglas Henry, 1881–1943. Before 1914 a mining engineer in Queensland. 2nd Lieutenant, Australian Tunnelling Company, December 1915; Major, November 1916. Commanded the 1st Australian Tunnelling Company in the Ypres Salient, 1916–17.

been in Anatolia to negotiate a private mining concession, informed General Harington that Mustafa Kemal wished to meet him at Ineboli, a Black Sea port controlled by the Nationalists. On July 5 Harington agreed to meet Kemal on board a British battleship off Ineboli. Mustafa Kemal replied that he would come to the meeting only if Harington would agree in advance to the 'complete liberation of the national territory and unqualified independence in the political, financial, economic, judicial and religious spheres'. But he rejected 'a mere exchange of views'. Rumbold noted in his Annual Report for 1921 that 'no answer was returned to this communication'. He had been angered to discover that Major Henry had told the Nationalists that it was the British who wanted to begin negotiations, while he had told the British that it was the Nationalists who wished to talk.

The French Government shared none of the British reluctance to open negotiations in Angora. On September 15 a French diplomat, Franklin-Bouillon,[1] left Constantinople in a French destroyer for Ineboli, whence he proceeded overland to Angora. It was announced that the purpose of his mission was to discuss an exchange of French and Turkish prisoners on the Syrian frontier. But on September 20 Rumbold wrote to Curzon that 'there is little doubt in my mind' that the discussions would range more widely. On September 27 he wrote again. The future 'struggle for influence' at Constantinople, he believed, would be between Britain and France. 'If this struggle comes', he added, 'it will not be so much owing to any action taken by England but rather the direct result of French jealousy. . . . There is no doubt that they have allowed the Turkish Authorities to gather that they look with sympathy on the Nationalist cause.'

As 1921 progressed Rumbold came to realize that no efforts or reforms of the Constantinople Government were likely to be effective in rallying Turkish opinion. Territorially, Angora was already in control of 90 per cent of Turkish soil. The Sultan's authority went no further than the area occupied by British, French and Italian troops. The Greek Army, although dominant in western Anatolia, was unable to reach Angora. Its summer offensive was driven back as its spring offensive had been. 'The Greeks cannot crush the Kemalist army', Rumbold wrote bluntly to Curzon on October 4. They would, he believed, attack yet again in the spring of

---

Awarded the DSO, 1918. Seconded to the 1st Camel Brigade Headquarters, Cairo, August 1918. Attached to the Royal Air Force, Middle East, October 1918. Demobilized, 1919.

[1] Henri Franklin-Bouillon, 1870–1939. Entered the Chamber of Deputies, 1910. Minister of State in Charge of Propaganda, 1917. In charge of negotiations with Mustafa Kemal, 1921–22. Known to the British in Constantinople as 'boiling Frankie'.

244   CONSTANTINOPLE   1921

1922. But, he added, 'I do not know whether the Greeks are in a position to stand an indefinite war which will cost them more than it will cost the Turks!' Rumbold's assessment of Nationalist strength was not based on speculation alone. The officer in charge of General Harington's Secret Service, Major Cornwall,[1] had gathered detailed information on Kemal's military resources from a wide spectrum of agents, not only dissident Greeks, Armenians and Levantines, but from Turks themselves, who had travelled into the interior and had seen the Nationalist forces at first hand. One of Cornwall's informants was actually an officer at Kemal's headquarters.

On October 7, in a lengthy memorandum circulated to the Cabinet, Curzon emphasized that 'the nationalist movement, with Mustafa Kemal either as dictator or figurehead, has a real hold in Asia Minor'. It would probably be impossible, Curzon stressed, for Britain alone 'to enable Greece to defeat the Kemalists and to hold Smyrna'. Yet the French Government refused to support Lloyd George's policy of encouraging Greece to maintain itself in western Anatolia, and on October 20, to the chagrin of the British Government, an agreement between France and the Nationalists was signed in Angora. Under this agreement, negotiated in Angora by Franklin-Bouillon, the French agreed to a frontier between Nationalist Turkey and Syria much further south than had been drawn in the Treaty of Sèvres, and including several hundred miles of the Bagdad railway within Turkey. The agreement gave Mustafa Kemal's regime the recognition which it had sought, and had the result, Rumbold wrote in his Annual Report for 1921, of 'surrendering to Turkey territory which it was not in the power of the French to surrender'. It was, he believed, 'a violation of the engagement that no separate agreement should be concluded with Turkey', and above all it 'compromised the whole Allied position vis-à-vis the Nationalists, who were already elated by what they chose to consider their recent victory over Greece'. The Angora Government, he concluded, 'whose fortunes had been at a low ebb in July and August, now seemed triumphant'.

In a telegram to Curzon on November 9, Rumbold reported:

---

[1] James Handyside Marshall Cornwall, 1887–   . Entered Royal Artillery, 1907. Served as an Intelligence Officer in France and Flanders, 1914–18; awarded the Military Cross and mentioned in despatches five times. Lieutenant-Colonel, 1918. Attended the Paris Peace Conference, 1919. Officer Commanding the Dardanelles Defences, 1920. Intelligence Officer, Constantinople, 1920–22. British Delegate, Thracian Boundary Commission, 1924–25. Served with the Shanghai Defence Force, 1927. Military Attaché, Berlin, April 1928–April 1932. Took the surname Marshall-Cornwall, 1929. Director-General, Air and Coast Defence, 1938–39. Knighted, 1940. General Officer Commanding the British Troops, Egypt, 1941; Western Command, 1941–42. Editor-in-Chief, Captured German Archives, 1948–51. President, Royal Geographical Society, 1954–58. Military historian.

'Nationalists are greatly elated by conclusion of this agreement.' By it, he asserted, they would be strengthened in their resolve not to enter into a compromise agreement on the territorial integrity of an independent Turkey. On the following day he telegraphed again:

I am convinced that Franco-Kemalist agreement will make it impossible for French to participate in any energetic measures against Nationalists, should such prove necessary as result of an eventual Nationalist advance on Constantinople. We must therefore expect French defection in the above contingency. The more I reflect on French agreement the more it is evident that it has undermined the whole position of the Allies *vis-à-vis* the Nationalists, and having regard to real necessity for presenting a united front towards the Nationalists if intervention is to be successful on acceptance of terms, I can only characterize French independent action in this matter as dishonourable, and as having greatly increased our difficulties.

During November the British Government began to contemplate an agreement with Mustafa Kemal. But Rumbold doubted whether such an agreement were possible. The Nationalists, he telegraphed to Curzon on November 13, were in a 'most intractable frame of mind'. To King George V he wrote two days later: 'I am pessimistic as to the chance of a settlement in this part of the world in the immediate future.' On December 1 he informed Sir Harry Lamb of the Nationalist mood. 'All our information shows', he wrote, 'that they are in an unyielding and intractable frame of mind.' This, he added, 'is of course due to the deplorable action of the French. The latter seem incapable of appreciating the harm they have done.'

During November Major Henry made a second attempt to mediate between Britain and the Nationalists. While at the Black Sea port of Samsun, nominally pursuing once more his mining activities, he had a number of interviews with the Minister of Defence of the Angora Government, Raffet Pasha.[1] Henry and his companions were received at Samsun with a guard of honour, Rumbold telegraphed to Curzon on December 10, 'because it was supposed that the party constituted a semi-official mission from His Majesty's Government to the Nationalist Government'. When, on December 11, Rumbold informed Pellé and Garroni that the Henry 'mission' was devoid of official support, his remarks, he telegraphed to Curzon that day, were 'received with ill-disguised incredulity. We are suspected of playing the same game as the

---

[1] Raffet Pasha, 1881–1963. Born in Istanbul. A graduate of the War Academy, he served in Palestine, 1915–17, rendering outstanding services on the Gaza front. Joined Mustafa Kemal, 1919. Commanded the 3rd sub-Army at Sivas, 1919–20. Member of the First National Grand Assembly, 1920. Minister of the Interior, 1920–21; of Defence, 1921–22. Member of Parliament, 1922–26 and 1939–50. He changed his name to Refet Bele.

French in the early stages of the Franklin–Bouillon negotiations.' In Constantinople itself, Rumbold wrote to Oliphant two days later, there was 'a natural impression that this individual . . . was sent on an unofficial mission to get into touch with the Nationalists and that I was a party to this move. . . . Nothing could queer my pitch more than Henry's proceedings.' Rumbold was particularly angered because Major Henry had drawn up a report of his interview with Raffet Pasha which was being taken direct to London without his being allowed to see it. His letter to Oliphant continued:

I do not know Henry and his three companions; nor do I wish to know them. This post is difficult enough without being further complicated by the escapades of amateur diplomatists. I had a considerable experience of unofficial agents during the war in Switzerland. I cannot recall a single case in which any of them did any good. On the contrary, several of them did positive harm, and I turned one man out of Switzerland twice, much to his annoyance. He was one of the PM's agents but the Foreign Office when they heard of it were equally annoyed and entirely approved of what I had done.

The Foreign Office again supported Rumbold's hostility to unofficial intermediaries. But Major Henry had the support of the War Office, and on his return to London his report was treated seriously. 'Henry had been "the very devil" ', Oliphant wrote to Rumbold on December 19; Curzon was 'extremely angry' when he called at the Foreign Office, 'and most stringent orders have now been given that he is to be seen by nobody'. Curzon informed the War Office that he could attach no credibility to Major Henry's activities, and was, Oliphant informed Rumbold, 'supporting you completely without any reservation'. Rumbold believed that Henry had been encouraged in his activities by a member of Harington's staff, Colonel Gribbon.[1] 'Harington realises that some of his officers have been indiscreet', Rumbold wrote to Oliphant on December 27, 'and tells me that he has given the strictest instructions that they are in future to confine themselves to their military duties and to abstain from political activities.'

The war between the Nationalists and the Greeks continued throughout the winter. 'The work here is awfully strenuous', Rumbold wrote to Carton de Wiart on December 20, 'and reminds me of the hectic days preceding the Bolo advance on Warsaw. . . . The Turks are a very irritating people to deal with – they have even less political instinct than

[1] Walter Harold Gribbon, 1881–1944. 2nd Lieutenant, Royal Lancashire Regiment, 1901. Staff Captain, India, 1912–13. Major, 1915. Served on the Staff in Mesopotamia, 1916–18. Chief Staff Officer, Constantinople, 1920–22. Colonel, 1921. Commanded the Suez Canal Brigade, Egypt, 1931–32. Officer-in-Charge of the Infantry Record and Pay Office, England, 1932–36. Retired, 1936. Commanded the 8th Battalion, Kent Home Guard, 1942–44.

the Poles.' He was in a reflective mood. 'I often feel', he wrote, 'that it would be pleasant to live in normal times and not to have to deal continually with hectic and exceptional situations. But then one might get slack. There is no doubt that this place applies plenty of ginger.'

Rumbold saw little chance of an agreement with the Nationalists unless, as he wrote to Oliphant on December 27, 'the Powers would agree to hand Smyrna district over, lock, stock and barrel, to the Turks'. Four days later he wrote to Sir Harry Lamb: 'The Nationalists will never accept a dictated solution of the Near Eastern question.' On 15 January, 1922, seeing no prospect of a compromise peace between Greece and Angora, even if sponsored by Britain, he telegraphed to Curzon that the Nationalists 'are out not merely for recovering Smyrna and Thrace in complete sovereignty but they are against real safeguards for minorities . . . and any form of control, financial or otherwise'. Mustafa Kemal, he added, was unswerving in his determination to uphold the 'right of Turks to manage their own affairs', and with the sole exception of the transfer of Batum to Russia in March 1921 'he has not once wavered from that programme since inception of national movement'. Only if the Allies could persuade the Greeks to evacuate both Smyrna and eastern Thrace was there any chance of persuading the Angora Government to enter into negotiations.

On January 26, Rumbold informed Curzon that even the Constantinople Turks, dependent as they were upon allied support, would refuse to contemplate any settlement which allowed the Greeks to remain on the shores of the Sea of Marmora or the Dardanelles. 'Not even the most moderate Turk would accept such a frontier', he reported. 'There is no doubt', he telegraphed again to Curzon four days later, 'that Turks attach great importance, for historical and sentimental reasons, to retention of Adrianople.'[1]

Rumbold hoped that the Allies would offer generous terms in eastern Thrace to the Constantinople Government which, by accepting them, would gain the support of many Nationalist supporters. His aim, he had written to Oliphant on January 16, was that the Sultan 'a friend of ours' would 'figuratively speaking' go to Angora, 'instead of Kemal coming here in close relation with the French'. To Francis Lindley, who had just been appointed Minister in Athens, Rumbold wrote that same day that once a Treaty were signed with the Sultan he hoped that Britain would be

---

[1] The Turks had conquered Adrianople in 1361, nearly a hundred years before the conquest of Constantinople. During that time it was the residence of the Sultans. In a heroic defence, the Turks had held off the Russians for several months in 1878. In 1914 half the population had been Turks; the other half Jews, Greeks, Bulgars and Armenians. Both the Greek and Bulgarian Governments hoped to annex the city, but it remained Turkish.

able to 'bring him into the limelight and get him to work on the population of Anatolia by pointing out that the Turks had got the substance of what they wanted and that it would be foolish to go on fighting. Such an appeal ought to fall on receptive ears.' But it was not longer possible to bolster the Sultan's power; the appeal of the Nationalists gave them the real authority in any future negotiations. Rumbold saw this; but, as he wrote to Lord Bryce[1] on January 26: 'I have no confidence whatever that the Kemalists will respect any guarantees we will be able to extract from them for the protection of minorities. They will observe any stipulations of the kind just as long as it suits them and no longer.' Two weeks later, on February 14, Rumbold wrote to Oliphant at the Foreign Office: 'The French seem to be unduly nervous about Mustafa Kemal's power and forget that he has his difficulties which are by no means small, they also forget the progressive exhaustion of Anatolia which will make it more and more difficult for the Nationalists to embark on schemes of conquest in Mesopotamia and elsewhere. I do not mind confessing privately that I should be rather glad to see the Greeks give the Nationalists one big knock before hostilities come to an end. I am neither pro-Greek nor pro-Turk. There is little to choose between them and their methods.'

Early in February the Angora Government decided to take its claims direct to Paris and London. Mustafa Kemal's Foreign Minister, Yussuf Kemal,[2] headed the mission. He reached Constantinople on February 15, and two days later called on Rumbold at the British Embassy. 'He spoke with studied moderation throughout the interview', Rumbold telegraphed to Curzon that midnight, 'and made a good impression.' During the course of a long conversation, Yussuf Kemal stressed that 'it was essential that Adrianople should be restored to Turkey and with it Eastern Thrace. . . . If Greeks were allowed to retain any portion of the shores of the Sea of Marmora they would not only be a menace to Constantinople but to the southern coast of that sea.' The Nationalists accepted, Yussuf Kemal continued, 'that old Ottoman empire composed of so many heterogeneous elements should disappear. A new Turkey had arisen which

---

[1] James Bryce, 1838–1922. Lawyer, historian and philosopher. Founder of the *English Historical Review*, 1885. Liberal MP, 1885–1907. Fellow of the Royal Society, 1893. Order of Merit, 1907. Ambassador at Washington, 1907–13. President of the British Academy, 1913–17. Created Viscount, 1914. Presided over the Committee set up to inquire into alleged German atrocities in Belgium, September 1914; his report concluded that excesses had been committed. An early, wartime, advocate of the League of Nations.

[2] Yussuf Kemal, 1878–1968. Professor of Criminal Law, Constantinople, 1906. General Inspector, Ministry of Justice, 1914–15. Minister for Economic Affairs at Angora, May 1920–May 1921. Signed the Turco-Soviet Friendship Treaty in Moscow, March 16, 1921. Minister for Foreign Affairs, May 1921–October 1922. Turkish Ambassador in London, 1923. Minister of Justice, 1930. Took the surname of Tengirşek.

repudiated bad traditions of former Ottoman Empire.' To Rumbold's suggestion that a territorial compromise might be necessary, Yussuf Kemal replied 'that compromise must not always be at the expense of Turkey'.

Rumbold was impressed by the strength of Yussuf Kemal's convictions, and by the determination of the Nationalists not to be deflected from their goal of a unified and independent Turkey. But he was angered when he learnt a few days later that General Pellé – as he telegraphed to Curzon on February 21 – had apparently told Yussuf Kemal 'that France would be the advocate of Turkey against Great Britain who is supporting Greece'. It was evident, Rumbold commented, 'that French here are entirely un-scrupulous in their attempts to curry favour with Nationalists and that their proceedings will greatly increase the difficulty of a settlement'. 'General Pellé', Rumbold wrote to Curzon on February 28, 'appears to have changed a good deal since he first came here and it is evident that the local atmosphere of intrigue has begun to affect him.' French support for the Nationalists continued to upset Rumbold. 'They are dreadful Allies', he wrote on March 6 to a member of his Embassy, Andrew Ryan,[1] who was in London at the time. 'If the Greeks crack', he added, 'we may expect to have to eat dirt to an unlimited extent and this is not a form of diet that has ever agreed with me, though Pellé and Garroni may flourish on it.'

Greek prospects in western Anatolia were beginning to wane. On March 13 Rumbold telegraphed to Curzon: 'I hear from Sir H. Lamb that news he has of morale of Greek troops is bad and they appear disheartened and he fears that if Nationalists are ever in a position to press on attack home they will crumple.' In an interview with Curzon on March 18, Yussuf Kemal insisted that 'the evacuation of Asia Minor by the Greeks' must be the first condition of any settlement.

In Paris, from March 22 to March 26, Curzon, Raymond Poincaré[2] and Carlo Schanzer[3] – the Foreign Ministers of Britain, France and Italy – examined the Turkish question in exhaustive detail. On March 26 they proposed an immediate armistice between the Greek and Turkish forces,

---

[1] Andrew Ryan, 1876–1949. Entered Levant Consular Service, 1897. 1st Dragoman, Constantinople, 1911–12 and March–October 1914. Employed in the Contraband Depart-ment, Foreign Office, 1914–18. Political Officer, British High Commission, Constantinople, 1918–21; Chief Dragoman, with the rank of Counsellor, 1921. Member of the British Delegation at Lausanne, 1922–23. Consul-General at Rabat (Morocco), 1924–30. Knighted, 1925. Minister at Jedda (Saudi Arabia), 1930–36; in Albania, 1936–39. His memoirs, *The Last of the Dragomans*, were published in 1951.

[2] Raymond Poincaré, 1860–1934. Minister of Public Instruction, 1893 and 1894. Minister of Finance, 1894 and 1906. Prime Minister, 1911–13. President of the Republic, 1913–20. Prime Minister and Minister for Foreign Affairs, 1922–24. Minister of Finance, 1926–28. Prime Minister for the third time, 1926–29.

[3] Carlo Schanzer, 1865–1953. A deputy in the Italian Parliament, 1900–13. Minister of Posts, 1906. Senator, 1919. Minister of Finance, 1919–20. Foreign Minister, 1922.

to be followed by negotiations for a new peace Treaty with Turkey. But within a month the scheme had collapsed. The Greeks insisted on remaining in occupation of western Anatolia during the Treaty negotiations; the Turks demanded a total Greek withdrawal as soon as the armistice was concluded. 'Even if the Nationalists do accept the Armistice and Conference proposals', Rumbold wrote to Curzon on April 4, 'they are sure to hedge their acceptance round with many conditions. I do not believe that any Turk is capable of giving a straight answer to a straight question.' On the following day Lindley wrote to Rumbold from Athens that the Greeks did not seem to want the proposals to go forward any more than the Turks did. 'The Greeks are certainly an odd people', Lindley wrote. 'They have been at war for ten years and it is perfectly evident to everyone that peace is the thing which the country needs most. Yet I believe I am right in thinking that there will be genuine relief here if the Turks refuse the proposals altogether and the war continues. The Greeks are confident that the Turks can not turn them out either of Smyrna or of Thrace. . . .'

On April 23 Yussuf Kemal passed on to Rumbold, Pellé and Garroni an appeal for their respective Foreign Ministers. Rumbold telegraphed its contents to Curzon that night. The Angora Government insisted upon the evacuation of all Greek forces from Anatolia and eastern Thrace 'simultaneously with armistice'. It refused to wait the results of a Peace Conference, which might take many weeks, or indeed months. Yussuf Kemal quoted Lloyd George's own words, in a wartime speech of 5 January, 1918: 'Nor are we fighting . . . to deprive Turkey of its capital, or of the rich and renowned areas of Asia Minor and Thrace, which are predominantly Turkish in race. . . .' Two days later Rumbold telegraphed to Curzon that he regarded Yussuf Kemal's appeal as nothing 'but tactical manoeuvre in attempt to drive us into a position where responsibility for breakdown of negotiations can be thrown upon the Allies'. The Angora request to hold preliminary talks at Ismid, a town under Nationalist control, would Rumbold added, give Mustafa Kemal 'opportunity for strengthening his own prestige at the expense of allied representations'. The telegraphic exchanges continued; both Turks and Greeks holding stubbornly to their positions, but insisting that they were flexible in their attitudes. 'Neither is behaving with sincerity', Curzon telegraphed to Gregory at Genoa on April 25. 'We cannot give any encouragement', he telegraphed to Rumbold four days later, 'to tactics which are obviously designed to wreck the whole scheme.'

By the beginning of May no chance remained of a negotiated settlement between Angora and Athens. The Turks accused the Greeks of brutal massacres of Turks. In areas under Greek control, conditions for the

Turkish population were worsening considerably. Sir Harry Lamb had warned Rumbold of what might happen in a letter written from Smyrna on February 27. 'The Greeks', he wrote, 'have realised that they have got to go, but they are decided to leave a desert behind them, no matter whose interests may suffer thereby. Everything which they have time and means to move will be carried off to Greece; the Turks will be plundered and burnt out of house and home. . . .' Unless, Lamb warned, the Allies were prepared to cover the Greek withdrawal from Smyrna with an adequate force, 'the fate of Anatolia will be settled by blood and fire alone. Nothing will be spared and our railways will be among the first things to go phut!'

For more than six months. Rumbold had assiduously reported details of atrocities. On 21 November 1921, he had telegraphed to Curzon with details of the massacre of over 3,000 Armenians near Erzerum in eastern Turkey, and the condition of 400 Greek women near Trebizond 'without food or warm clothing' whose sufferings were 'impossible to describe'.[1] Three days later he reported 4,000 Greek refugees, women and children, on the road from Samsun to Sivas 'in deplorable condition, some actually dying'.[2] On December 13 he sent the Foreign Office a report from Sir Harry Lamb enumerating Turkish atrocities against the Circassian minority. On 22 February 1922, he saw Mustafa Kemal's representative in Constantinople, Hamid Bey,[3] and warned him 'that British public opinion attached great importance to questions of protecting minorities'. But atrocities were being committed by the Greeks as well; on February 27 Rumbold sent the Foreign Office a long telegram in which he pointed out that 'systematic destruction carried out by Greek army in its retreat from Sakaria river produced an effect on Anatolian peasant who witnessed the destruction of villages etc. He is therefore willing to do everything possible to expel Greeks from Anatolia.'[4] Turkish atrocities against the Greeks caused the Greek communities to flee in panic; but Greek atrocities against the Turks strengthened the Nationalist will to fight.

During the first four months of 1922 Rumbold noted that the Angora Government, the 'bandits' of a year before, were being treated as if they were a sovereign body, particularly by the French. 'The Nationalists', he

---

[1] Rumbold's informant was Colonel Alfred Rawlinson, who had gone on a special mission to Erzerum in 1919 and had been held prisoner by the Turks for 18 months.

[2] Rumbold had received this information from a team of American relief workers.

[3] Hamid Hasancan Bey. Administrator of the Ottoman Bank, 1912–25. Joined the Board of Directors of the Turkish Red Crescent Society as an expert in financial matters, 1913. Constantinople representative of the International Organization for the Protection of Children, 1920. Constantinople Agent of the Angora Government, 1921–22. Rumbold described him to Lancelot Oliphant, on August 15, 1922, as: 'a particularly objectionable specimen of a Turk; I have never met such an oily individual'.

[4] Rumbold's informant was Monsieur Mery, an official of the Ottoman Public Debt.

wrote to George V on May 1, 'wilfully forget that Turkey has been beaten in the war and almost pose as victors over the Allies.' His hopes of a revived Sultanate, and of a strong Constantinople Government, had evaporated. 'The Sultan's Government is impotent', he informed the King; 'it watches Angora the whole time and tries to frame its replies to the Allied Notes in such a way as not to cause umbrage to the Nationalists. In return for this the Nationalists freely abuse the Central Government. The latter's territorial demands do not differ from those of the Nationalists; indeed the Sultan, of whom I had an audience of two and a quarter hours recently, stated frankly that, as Caliph,[1] he was bound to claim Adrianople.' During May, further news of Nationalist atrocities, authentic and incontrovertible, received wide publicity in the British Press. 'The Turks', Rumbold telegraphed to Curzon on May 10, 'appear to be working on a deliberate plan to get rid of minorities . . . whole Greek male population from the age of 15 upwards of Trebizond area and its hinterland is being deported apparently to labour battalions at Erzeroum, Kars and Sari Kamish.' In a second telegram that day he reported further news of deportations, and of the killing of women and children. Two days later Curzon replied that it was 'inconceivable that Europe should agree to hand back to Turkish rule, without the most stringent guarantees, communities who would be liable to be treated in the manner described. . . .' On May 15, in answer to Parliamentary pressure for information, Austen Chamberlain,[2] the Lord Privy Seal and a senior member of Lloyd George's Cabinet, read Rumbold's two telegrams of May 10 to the House of Commons. The outspoken British attitude towards the Turkish atrocities brought all hopes for armistice negotiations to an end, and was, Rumbold telegraphed to Curzon on May 22, 'stiffening Kemalists in their hostility to Great Britain'. The Constantinople ministers, he informed Curzon, were 'too impotent to divorce their own foreign policy from that of the Kemalists'.

The atrocities continued on both sides. On June 7 the Greeks bombarded the Black Sea port of Samsun, allegedly to destroy military stores belonging to the Nationalists. 'Just as one begins to hope that a settlement may be achieved', Rumbold wrote to Sir Maurice de Bunsen on June 12, 'something seems to spoil the chances of a settlement.' It was not only the Angora Government, or the Greeks, whom Rumbold blamed. 'The

---

[1] In addition to being Sultan (temporal ruler) of Turkey, Mehmed was also Caliph (spiritual ruler) of the Muslims of his Empire.

[2] Joseph Austen Chamberlain, 1863–1937. Conservative MP, 1892–1937. Chancellor of the Exchequer, 1903–5. Secretary of State for India, 1915–17. Minister without Portfolio, 1918–19. Chancellor of the Exchequer, 1919–21. Lord Privy Seal, 1921–22. Foreign Secretary, 1924–29. Knighted, 1925. First Lord of the Admiralty, 1931.

French are far too ready to give way to the successive demands of the Kemalists', he added. 'If they and the Italians had maintained a stout front from the first I think we should have brought Mustapha Kemal and Company to reason before now.'

Since June 9 Rumbold had been in a further dispute with the French and Italian High Commissioners. General Pellé wanted to transfer to the Angora authorities all administrative authority over those parts of Anatolia which might be evacuated by the Greeks. He was strongly supported by Garroni. But Rumbold could not agree. Both he and General Harington believed – as he wrote to A. J. Balfour[1] on June 13 –

... that if massacres or acute disorder occurred in any particular district after it had been evacuated, it might be necessary to suspend the further progress of the evacuation until order had been restored. The French and Italian High Commissioners demurred very strongly to anything of this kind, and held that nothing whatsoever should be allowed to hold up the evacuation once it began, and that, even in the event of acute disorder, it would be a matter not for the authorities in charge of the evacuation, but for whatever machinery might be created for the protection of minorities.

Rumbold appealed to Balfour 'to reach some agreement with the French and Italian Governments' on the question. But no agreement was possible. The French, Rumbold wrote to Oliphant on June 19, 'are too much committed to the Nationalists'. In Constantinople itself the full burden of defence fell upon the British forces, both military and naval.

Among the British troops recently arrived in Constantinople were the Irish Guards. Their Colonel, Alexander,[2] often lunched with the Rumbolds during the summer. The British strength was much in evidence. 'We are very grand', Lady Rumbold wrote to her mother on July 18, 'with *three* Super Dreadnoughts lying opposite. . . . Off Bujukdere there are ten destroyers, and a hospital ship.' A month later she wrote: 'We have a new ship opposite us now *King George V*, celebrated for being the ship on which the Kaiser hoisted his flag as British Admiral, the last Kiel-week 1914. Horace was on board her too then.'

After eleven months at Constantinople, Rumbold was eager for leave. But the opportunity did not arise. 'I don't see much prospect of getting away *this* summer', he had written to his stepmother on April 3. 'In fact

---

[1] Balfour was in temporary charge of the Foreign Office from May 25 to August 10, as Curzon was ill.

[2] Harold Rupert Leoffric George Alexander, 1891–1969. Son of the 4th Earl of Caledon. Served on the western front, 1914–18 (twice wounded), in Russia, 1919, and in Turkey, 1920–22. Lieutenant-General, 1940. Commanded the British forces in Burma, 1942; the Middle East, 1942–43 and Italy, 1943–44. Field-Marshal, 1944. Governor-General of Canada, 1946–52. Created Viscount, 1946; Earl, 1952. Minister of Defence, 1952–54.

once one has been pitch-forked into a place like this it is difficult to get out of it again. My colleagues are looking old and tired and are longing for an holiday.' Rumbold's hopes of going on leave revived as the chances of a Peace Conference declined. To Oliphant, on June 6, he had written: 'The Frenchman and the Italian are getting restive and are anxious to go away on leave, for they see no use in staying here if there is not going to be a conference. I agree with them, and likewise propose to take a change of air.' But by mid-June he felt that it would be unwise to leave Turkey and decided to hand over the Embassy for four weeks to his Counsellor, Nevile Henderson, and for a brief respite to go to the former Austrian Embassy at Therapia, on the Bosphorus, which the British had taken over in October 1918. Rumbold was disappointed at not being able to go back to England, 'not', he wrote to Oliphant on June 19, 'because I am hankering after the Fleshpots of London, but because I wanted to see my boy at school and bring him back here for his summer holidays'. But a week later he decided that, despite the distance, he would go to England; on July 1 he left Constantinople by train for London; four weeks later on July 30, he was back. Ten of these days had been spent in travelling.

The impending crisis which had made Rumbold hesitant to go on leave developed in his absence. At the end of June the Angora Government had protested against the use of Constantinople by the Greek Navy. The Greek ships which had bombarded Samsun had used Constantinople as their base of operations. Rumbold had warned the Greeks against abusing their right – as one of the powers associated with the Allies – to use the city's harbour for their warships; a right which Rumbold had described to Balfour on June 24 as 'illogical and vulnerable'. In mid-July the Greeks, fearing that the Allies would soon desert them in their attempt to retain at least some of the territory of the former Ottoman Empire, threatened to march on Constantinople. In Rumbold's absence, Nevile Henderson drafted a proclamation, which was issued by General Harington on June 28, announcing that any attacks, Greek or Turkish, would be met by force. 'Greece is undoubtedly determined to force a solution of the Near East impasse', Nevile Henderson telegraphed to Balfour on July 29.

Throughout July 29 Henderson and Harington pursued their resolve to confront the Greeks with the maximum of force. Henderson saw the Greek Chargé d'Affaires[1] at Constantinople and 'warned him against madness of any precipitate action which would bring Greece in conflict

---

[1] Constantine Sakellaropoulos, 1884–1971. Born in Corfu. Entered the Greek Diplomatic Corps, 1909. First Secretary, Constantinople, January–August 1921. Greek Ambassador in Ottawa, 1950. In 1954 he published *The Shadow of the West, A History of a Catastrophe*, a study of Greek political history from 1914 to 1922.

with the allied powers'. 'Britain', he asserted, 'had no intention of permitting any violation of neutral zone.' Harington toured the Thracian frontier and inspected the Chatalja Lines, which were reinforced by French and British troops commanded by General Charpy. From Malta, the 3rd Light Cruiser Squadron took on fuel and ammunition and steamed eastwards at full speed towards the Aegean. The newly appointed Commander-in-Chief of Britain's Mediterranean Fleet, Admiral Sir Osmond Brock,[1] who was then at Constantinople, consulted with Harington and, fully prepared to intercept any Greek warships that might approach the city, put out to sea in his flagship, the *Iron Duke*, taking with him into the Sea of Marmora a powerful fighting force; five heavily armed ships, *Benbow*, *King George V*, *Marlborough*, *Ajax* and *Centurion*, a seaplane carrier and nine destroyers. The Constantinople Government offered Harington 20,000 Turkish soldiers to help in the defence of the city.

By the morning of July 30 the warlike preparations were complete; only the Greek attackers were missing. That morning Rumbold returned to Constantinople. 'We have just watched our three Dreadnoughts leave Beicos', Lady Rumbold wrote to her mother, 'looking most imposing and steaming towards the town, to join the rest of the fleet and to do a bit of "impressing"! Horace *groans* and wishes he had stopped for a week in Switzerland! He remains most annoyingly calm! I believe if the last trump sounded he would gaze unperturbed through his eye glass and wish there were not so many d . . . foreigners about. The place is humming with launches and cars, and a small crowd has collected outside. H thinks it is bluff on the part of the Greeks, this threat to occupy Constantinople. The cheek of them!'

As soon as he reached the British Embassy, Rumbold called a meeting of General Pellé, Marquis Garroni and the Allied military representatives. Pellé was eager to take some dramatic initiative against the Greeks, such as suppressing the Greek naval and military missions in Constantinople, or insisting that the Greeks withdraw to eastern Thrace all the troops which they had sent to Mudania, in Asia Minor. Rumbold deprecated such a move, telling Pellé – as he telegraphed to Balfour on July 31 – that 'I was strongly opposed to any action which might force the very issue which we desired to avoid'. His own belief, he told Balfour, was that the Greek

---

[1] Osmond de Beauvoir Brock, 1869–1947. Entered the Navy, as a cadet, in 1874. Assistant Director of Naval Mobilization, 1910. Rear-Admiral, 1915. Served at the battle of Jutland, 1916. Chief of Staff to the Commander-in-Chief, Grand Fleet, 1916–18. Knighted, 1917. Deputy Chief of the Naval Staff, 1919–21. Succeeded de Robeck as Commander-in-Chief Mediterranean, May 15, 1922. Admiral, 1924. Commander-in-Chief, Portsmouth, 1926–29. Admiral of the Fleet, 1929.

menace to Constantinople 'is 50% bluff and 50% serious'. Balfour replied on August 1, approving Rumbold's caution.

In a private letter to Oliphant on August 8, Rumbold described his motives in applying so swift a brake to the men who, in his absence, had been eager to challenge the Greeks:

It was evident from the outset that the French were out to make the most of the Greek threat to Constantinople in pursuance of their policy of downing the Greeks. Harington's energetic attitude therefore delighted them and the interesting spectacle was presented of Pellé, and in a lesser degree Garroni, slobbering over Harington, telling him what a fine fellow he was and what confidence they had in him. When one remembers how they both disliked the assumption by Harington, rather more than a year ago, of the supreme command over the Allied forces, it was difficult to restrain a smile at this volte-face. My colleagues have even gone so far as to place their sections of the Inter-allied Police at Harington's disposal. As you recollect, they have always disputed Harington's claim to command the Inter-allied Police.

There is no doubt Harington has done very well indeed in this crisis and that his prompt measures did more than anything else to nip the Greek adventure in the bud. It was therefore all the more embarrassing for me to have to damp down, at the meeting, the premature proposals for action against the Greek ships. Brock and I found ourselves in opposition in this matter to Harington, egged on by the Allied High Commissioners, Generals, etc. In fact I was a wet-blanket at the meeting rather, I think, to the mortification of Pellé. Coming fresh from England it was perhaps more easy to take an objective view. I hope the crisis is now over. Anyway we have had two or three days calm.

On August 4, Lloyd George, speaking in the House of Commons, gave the impression that Britain, far from being in bellicose mood towards the Greeks, wanted to give them moral, if not material, support against the Turks. 'I do not know of any army that would have gone as far as the Greeks have gone', he said. 'It was a very daring and a very dangerous military experiment. They established a military superiority in every battle.' This speech, Lindley wrote in his Annual Report for 1922, 'raised a wave of enthusiasm in Greece, and was the occasion of an imposing demonstration before His Majesty's Legation. Parts of it were circulated to the army as an order of the day'. But as Lindley noted, Lloyd George's remarks, however flattering, 'contained no promise that Greece would be allowed to retain any of the fruits of the campaign'. But they did, in his view, produce in Turkish minds 'the feeling that, if they did not act quickly, they might find themselves faced by the British'.

Throughout August Rumbold persevered in his attitude of caution and conciliation, putting his hopes in a conference between the Turks and the Greeks. The British were prepared to hold the conference either on territory controlled by the Nationalists, or on board a British battleship. The French preferred, Balfour telegraphed to Rumbold on August 9, the Italian island of Rhodes, 'or a Swiss or North Italian town'. On August 10 Curzon, who had returned to the Foreign Office after his illness, telegraphed to Rumbold to say that the French were in favour 'of earliest possible meeting', even before a formal armistice had been signed. On August 12 Rumbold replied to Curzon suggesting Venice as the meeting-place. Were the Conference to be held at Venice, Rumbold hoped that he would be made Chairman. 'Whilst I do not wish to exalt my own name', he wrote to Oliphant on August 28, 'I do feel that an Englishman always has a better sense of fair play that a foreigner.'

Rumbold doubted whether the Angora Government had much reason to agree to meet the Greeks at all. 'Although their own position is most unsatisfactory', he telegraphed two days later, 'Nationalists may elect to delay a reply to a preliminary conference even at Venice, in knowledge that Greeks are nearing the end of their resources.'

Harry Lamb confirmed Rumbold's impression of Greek weakness. 'I think Your Excellency is right', he wrote on August 18 from Smyrna, 'in believing the Greeks to be at the end of their tether. The vision of Constantinople in the spring *might* just sustain them through another winter, but it would mean complete exhaustion and financial ruin.' Lamb also reported that an Italian steamer had reached Smyrna on the previous day, carrying a party of Italians 'on their way home from Angora, where they had been delivering aeroplanes to Kemal. They said openly that Kemal was preparing for a push somewhere on the Eskishehir front and thought it had a good chance of success.' The Italians, Lamb reported, had seen 'many French officers' serving in the Kemalist army. Rumbold telegraphed these details of Italian and French military help to the Nationalists to Curzon on August 21, and suggested a protest by Britain. But Curzon took the precaution of minuting on Rumbold's telegram: 'Are our firms supplying anything to the Greeks?' The answer was provided by a Foreign Office official, Eric Forbes Adam,[1] who wrote, in a memorandum of August 23, that the British had supplied the Greek Government, in the previous six months, with £120,000 worth of aeroplanes and parts, and twenty-four machine-guns. 'How then can we protest?' Curzon noted on August 26. The time to protest had passed. That same day the Angora Government launched a major attack on the Greek forces. Mustafa Kemal

---

[1] Eric Graham Forbes Adam, 1888–1925. Entered Foreign Office, 1913. 3rd Secretary, Diplomatic Service, at the Paris Peace Conference, 1919. 1st Secretary, Foreign Office, 1922. With Lord Curzon at the Lausanne Conference, 1922–23. Transferred to Constantinople as 1st Secretary, at his own request, 1923; he died there suddenly on July 7, 1925.

told his troops that their goal was the complete liberation of Asia Minor from Greek control. Within four days the Greek forces had been savagely mauled, and the Greek Commander-in-Chief, General Trikoupis,[1] taken prisoner. The seriousness of the Turkish attack was not immediately understood in Constantinople. 'I think everything depends on whether the Greek soldier will fight', General Harington wrote to Rumbold on August 31; 'if he doesn't, the Greek Army may fall to pieces, which will elate the Nationalists, though I doubt if they are capable of pressing their attacks really home. Charpy told me only a few days ago that he didn't think that operations on a large scale were contemplated.' Both Charpy and Harington were over-optimistic. The Kemalist forces continued to advance, defeating the Greeks in a series of ferocious battles, and driving them towards the Aegean and the Sea of Marmora.

'Whilst every Turk must naturally rejoice at the initial success of the offensive', Rumbold telegraphed to Curzon on September 2, 'the Sultan, and at all event some of his Ministers, cannot fail to realize that if the Nationalist army succeeds in inflicting a decisive defeat on the Greek army, the waning prestige of Mustapha Kemal will be completely restored and he will stand out as the saviour of his country.' Rumbold added that the Greek General Staff had been taken 'entirely unawares'.

The Nationalist advance continued during the first week of September. It was 'cruel bad luck' to have encouraged the Greeks as Britain had done, Lady Rumbold wrote to her mother on September 5, 'and they must *hate* us'. Her husband, she commented, was 'wild with LG, but of course can say and do nothing, as it is the policy of the Government'. The main Turkish army drove westwards towards Smyrna. On September 5 British Marines landed at Smyrna to supervise the evacuation of British subjects, and, at the request of the Dutch Government, to evacuate all Dutch nationals.[2] On September 8 the last of the British and Dutch refugees were embarked. Two British battleships, the *Iron Duke* and *Ajax*, lay at anchor in Smyrna Bay, commanded by Admiral Brock. During the day a Turkish aeroplane was seen circling above the town. On September 9 the first Turkish troops arrived, followed, on September 10, by Mustafa Kemal himself.

The British authorities in Smyrna maintained an uneasy truce with the Turks. When, on September 10, Harry Lamb was walking through the

[1] Nikolaos Trikoupis, 1868–1959. Major-General, commanding various Greek forces in Asia Minor, 1918–22. Appointed Commander-in-Chief of all Greek forces in Asia Minor, August 1922, but taken prisoner by the Turks before he could take up his appointment, which he only learnt of after his capture. He had been captured because, while leading a counter-attack, he had not been followed by his men.

[2] There had been a flourishing Dutch trading community in Smyrna for over 200 years.

streets of the city, he met Mustafa Kemal by chance. The Turkish leader told him bluntly that he still considered Turkey to be at war with Britain. But when Admiral Brock's Chief of Staff, Commodore Domvile,[1] called on the Turkish leader later that day, Mustafa Kemal told him that he had spoken in haste. Late that night Lamb wrote to Rumbold:

The urgent question for me now is what are to be the mutual relations of myself & the Kemalist government? Noureddin Pasha,[2] the Commander-in-Chief, when I called on him about sundry matters this morning, put it to me that a 'state of hostility' existed between us & that he could not recognize me in any official capacity.

In the afternoon I went again with the C-in-C & Admiral Tyrwhitt,[3] when the question of the attitude of each to each was threshed out. The Admiral explained that, whilst we had, together with the other allies, concluded an Armistice with Turkey in 1918, we had subsequently recognized that a state of war existed between a certain section of the Turks and the Kingdom of Greece and we have in May 1921 made a declaration of neutrality in respect of those hostilities. Our attitude towards the two belligerents had since then been one of strict neutrality. There was therefore no question of a state of war existing between us, the best proof of which was that his own presence there and the further arrival of Admiral Tyrwhitt this very day.

Noureddin Pasha said that it gave him great pleasure to hear this and he guaranteed the safety of the British community here and that they should be treated on exactly the same footing as subjects of other foreign powers.

The question now arises: to what extent and in what form are we going to recognize the Government of the Great National Assembly.

[1] Barry Edward Domvile, 1878–1971. Entered the Navy as a cadet, 1892; Lieutenant, 1895. Assistant Secretary, Committee of Imperial Defence, 1912–14. Commanded various ships, 1914–18; Captain, 1916. Director of Plans, Admiralty, 1920–22. Chief of Staff, Mediterranean, 1922–25. Director of Naval Intelligence, 1927–30. Vice-Admiral Commanding the 3rd Cruiser Squadron, 1931–32. Commanded the War College, 1932–34. Knighted, 1934. An early supporter of Nazi Germany, he published his enthusiasms in *By and Large* in 1936. Interned under Regulation 18B, in Brixton Prison, 1940. He published his memoirs, *From Admiral to Cabin Boy* in 1947.

[2] Noureddin Pasha, 1881–1937. Born in Salonika. Served at Benghazi during the Italo-Turkish war of 1912, and at the Dardanelles, 1915. Military Attaché, The Hague, 1917–18. Joined Mustafa Kemal in Anatolia, 1919. Commander-in-Chief of the Turkish forces, and Deputy Governor of Angora, 1920–21. Sent to Berlin as the representative of the First Turkish National Assembly, 1921. Member of Parliament, 1923–37. Took the surname 'Conker'.

[3] Reginald Yorke Tyrwhitt, 1870–1951. Entered Navy, 1883. Commodore, commanding the Destroyer Flotilla of the First Fleet, 1913–16. Knighted, 1917. Created Baronet, 1919. Commanded the Third Light Cruiser Squadron, Mediterranean, 1921–22. Commanding Officer, coast of Scotland, 1923–25. Commander-in-Chief, China Station, 1927–29. Admiral, 1929. Commander-in-Chief, the Nore, 1930–33. Admiral of the Fleet, 1934.

In Constantinople the Turks rejoiced at Kemal's successes. 'Anti-Greek feeling has of late years got such a hold on the whole Turkish people', Rumbold wrote to Curzon on September 12, 'that the reconquest of Smyrna really does mean something to the usually inert Constantinople Moslem. . . . The Turkish flag is being flown in all Turkish quarters.' The Sultan's Ministers realized, he wrote, that 'the new situation will make Angora more arrogant in its pretension to be the sole government of Turkey'; the Sultan himself was most likely 'nervous as to his tenure of the throne'. In a later despatch to Curzon that same day Rumbold reported that the French were 'somewhat taken aback and are slightly apprehensive at the extent of the Kemalist successes'. They were beginning to realize, he added, 'even although it may be dimly at the moment, the potential danger of a strong and chauvinistic Turkey'. As a result, he hoped that they might adopt 'a more loyal attitude in regard to the Near Eastern question'.

The crisis was acute; in a telegram to Curzon on September 19 Rumbold warned that even if Britain allowed the situation to drift, 'Kemal will not rest quiet'. He had told his army that their first objective was Smyrna and the Mediterranean. Their second objective, Rumbold believed, 'is almost certainly Thrace'. Unless negotiations could begin soon, Kemal would try to reach Thrace 'either via Constantinople or Chanak'.

Having driven the Greeks out of the Smyrna province, the Nationalist forces turned northwards, pressing the Greek troops at Bursa back towards the southern shore of the Sea of Marmora. Much of this shore formed part of the Zone of the Straits, under British, French and Italian control. The principal defensive position, at Chanak, was guarded by a single British battalion supported by a squadron of Cavalry, and a Battery of Artillery. On September 11, Colonel Shuttleworth,[1] the British officer who had been put in charge of the Ottoman War Office in Constantinople, arrived from Constantinople to take charge of this small force of only a thousand men. A day later the battleship *Ajax*, which had come north from Smyrna, anchored in the Narrows.

The British Cabinet met at 10 Downing Street on September 15 to decide what steps to take to keep Mustafa Kemal's armies out of the neutral zone. The Secretary of State for War, Sir Laming Worthington-

[1] Digby Inglis Shuttleworth, 1876–1948. Entered Army, 1896; Major, 1914. Lieutenant-Colonel, Mesopotamian Expeditionary Force, 1917–19. Commanded the 39th Infantry Brigade in the Caucasus, 1919–20. Colonel, 1920. President, Allied Commission of Control, Ottoman War Office, 1920–22. Commanded the 83rd Infantry Brigade, Chanak, 1922–23. Colonel Commandant, Jullundur Brigade, India, 1924–28. Major-General, 1929. Quarter-Master-General, Northern Command, India, 1930–32. Knighted, 1937.

Evans,[1] with the help of a map, showed that 7,600 allied troops in the neutral zone, including those at Constantinople, confronted 6,000 Turks in Thrace and 5,000 around Chanak; a further 40,000 Turks were in the Smyrna area, where the defeat of the Greeks had been completed. Curzon deprecated all thought of a military confrontation aimed at frightening the Nationalists into submission; Rumbold had warned him in a telegram on September 13 that it would not be safe to try to bluff Mustafa Kemal. Curzon proposed another conference, in Paris. Churchill, the Colonial Secretary, argued for a more vigorous military policy, and wanted the immediate despatch of reinforcements. The Angora Government, he insisted, should not be allowed to push Britain out of the Zone of the Straits. 'Liberal opinion', he told his colleagues, 'would be a great deal influenced by the recent atrocities and Conservative opinion would not be willing to see the British Flag trampled on.' Churchill suggested that Greece, Serbia and Rumania should each be asked to send troops to the Dardanelles. Austen Chamberlain dissented. He saw no point in preparing to fight 'for something which was not of any great value'. But Lloyd George supported Churchill. Britain, he asserted, must not 'run away before Mustafa Kemal'. It was essential to defend, if necessary by war, Britain's 'supreme interest in the freedom of the Straits'. The Cabinet then authorized Churchill to send a telegram to each of the Dominions, inviting their co-operation 'in the despatch of military reinforcement.'

In the week that followed, British military and naval forces continued to arrive. On September 15 Admiral Brock reached Chanak on board the *Iron Duke*. On September 16 the French sent a company of infantrymen to the town. On September 17 a third British battleship, the *Marlborough*, arrived. The five sea planes of the carrier *Pegasus* carried out daily air reconnaissance. But the Nationalists were not deterred by this growing force, and continued to advance towards Chanak. On September 17 Rumbold reported to Curzon that the Constantinople Government were 'nervous of Kemal', fearing lest he might, having driven the British from Chanak, turn victorious upon Constantinople itself. And yet, nervous though they might be, they were Turkish patriots, and as a result, Rumbold added, were 'rejoicing at success of Kemal' in his triumph over the Greeks.

At the Cabinet meeting of September 15 the British Government had contemplated going to war in order to keep Mustafa Kemal away from

[1] Laming Evans, 1868–1931. Solicitor. Conservative MP from 1910 until his death. Inspector of Administrative Services, War Office, 1914–15. Assumed the prefix surname of Worthington, 1916. Controller, Foreign Trade Department, Foreign Office, 1916. Created Baronet, 1916. Minister of Blockade, 1918; of Pensions, 1919–20. Secretary of State for War, 1921–22 and 1924–29.

the Dardanelles. But no upsurge of approval greeted its decision. The Dominions were unenthusiastic about a second Gallipoli campaign. Only New Zealand agreed to send troops. Australia and Canada refused. South Africa made no reply. The Dominions saw no reason for hostility towards the Turks. But the Kemalist forces, in the moment of their triumph at Smyrna, indulged in atrocities on a massive scale. 'There seems no doubt', Rumbold telegraphed to Curzon on September 17, 'that Turks deliberately massacred many Armenians.' The facts could not be hidden; as soon as they were fully revealed, Rumbold added, 'it will be more difficult for the French to support a nation which commits such barbarities'. That same day Churchill issued a stern communiqué to the Press. 'It would be futile and dangerous', he announced, 'in view of the excited mood and extravagant claims of the Kemalists, to trust simply to diplomatic action. Adequate force must be available to guard the freedom of the Straits and to defend the deep water line between Europe and Asia against a violent and hostile Turkish aggression.' On September 18 the *Daily Mail* insisted 'STOP THIS NEW WAR!'

The French Government was appalled at the thought of war. On September 18 General Pellé left Constantinople, and, without informing Rumbold, entered into direct negotiations with Mustafa Kemal at Smyrna. 'He even enlisted the services of his wife', Rumbold wrote to Oliphant on September 19, 'to suppress the truth about his departure. What can we do with such people?' To Curzon Rumbold wrote that same day:

The crux of the situation remains the extent of Allied unity in the face of the Kemalist menace to Constantinople and the Straits and the extent to which we can rely on the support of our Allies.

I do not think we can count on the Italians for anything at all. My Italian colleague is thoroughly frightened and alarmed at the situation. There are signs that the French are irritated at the prompt action taken by the Cabinet in despatching reinforcements. This irritation may be due to a genuine fear lest the announcement of the despatch of these reinforcements may precipitate matters and induce Mustafa Kemal to forestall us by an advance on Constantinople.

At the present moment Harington and I are in a somewhat difficult position because if Kemal decides to advance along the Ismid Peninsula, we shall be too weak by ourselves to hold the Maltepe line which is just opposite Prinkipo. We might then have to evacuate Constantinople especially if trouble broke out here simultaneously with the advance of the Nationalist forces. . . .

My French colleague's mission to Smyrna was engineered in the secretive fashion. It is quite clear to me that he wished to have several hours' start before we should know anything about his movements. We know that he has seen Mustafa Kemal and I hear that he is expected back to-day. I should not say that he is the man to impress Mustafa Kemal as he is essentially a weak man. He appeared to be straight enough when he came here but he appears to have embarked on a policy of intrigue and is steadily slipping down the slope.

Rumbold did not have faith either in the moral virtues of the Greeks or of the Turks. He had been shaken by the Turkish atrocities of July; but August and September had seen butchery by the Greeks. In his letter to Curzon of September 19 he wrote:

There seems to be unanimity in regard to the way in which the Greeks behaved during their retreat. Sir Harry Lamb states 'that the conduct of the Greeks has been in every way indescribably disgusting'. They went to pieces altogether and there is little to choose between the two races. They have completely smashed up the Smyrna–Aidin Railway, a British concern, and there seems little doubt that in some places they shut up Turks in Mosques and then set the Mosques on fire. The Greek retreat, followed by the scenes at Smyrna form a sickening record of bestiality and barbarity.

Rumbold accepted that Constantinople would soon become part of Nationalist Turkey, as the Constantinople Government had lost all authority. 'I do not believe that the Sultan will be able to stay', he wrote in his letter to Curzon. 'He will no doubt appeal to us for protection. I am very sorry for him for he is a well-meaning man, but he has already burnt his boats as far as the Kemalists are concerned.' By negotiation, or by force, Mustafa Kemal must soon enter the city. Rumbold realized that Britain could not challenge Angora alone. The fact was, he wrote to his stepmother on September 20, 'we *cannot* count on our gallant Allies. The latter are always "playing the dirty" on us . . . if we could reveal some of the things we know about the French . . . the world would be more than astonished.' Allied disunity, characterized by General Pellé's mission to Mustafa Kemal, made his job 'as difficult as it can be, for I have to advise the Government – in conjunction with Harington – and I am hard put to it to know how to advise them for the best. We are literally living on a volcano here and the horrid events at Smyrna have put the wind up all the foreign Colonies at Constantinople, and no wonder.' Rumbold's fears about the Allies were quickly realized; on September 20, he telegraphed to Curzon that the French and Italian Governments had ordered their small forces to leave Chanak at once. If the Turks ignored the British warning to keep out of the neutral zone, and advanced on Chanak, Britain would have to act alone. In a further telegram to Curzon that evening, Rumbold reported Garroni's declaration that public opinion in Italy 'would not tolerate possibility of hostilities with Kemal', and had not only withdrawn her forces from the Dardanelles, but also from the Asiatic shore of the Bosphorus.

On September 20, Curzon, who was in Paris, berated Poincaré for refusing to keep French forces at Chanak. For his part, Poincaré rebuked Curzon for trying, while in Paris, to persuade the Rumanian Foreign Minister[1] to send Rumanian troops to replace those which France had withdrawn. Poincaré was insistent that 'French public opinion would not admit of a shot being fired against a Turk' and that if the Turks wished to do so, 'they could cross to Europe when they pleased'. Curzon was shaken by Poincaré's complete refusal to contemplate military action against the Turks. Bowing to the fact that Britain was now alone, Curzon implored the Cabinet by telegram that evening to 'desist from any action likely to provoke immediate hostilities'. But Harington's instructions remained clear; his force at Chanak must be prepared to fight the Turks if they tried to pierce the town's defences.

In Britain, there was an upsurge of hostility towards Lloyd George's policy. On September 21 the *Daily Mail* demanded: 'GET OUT OF CHANAK'. That morning a deputation of thirty members of the General Council of the Trades Union Congress went to see Lloyd George, and protested strongly against going to war with Turkey.[2] Harington and Rumbold remained calm, despite the agitation around them. 'Horace is well and full of energy', Lady Rumbold wrote to her mother that same day. 'He and the General are a *splendid* pair in an emergency.' Harington himself remained at Constantinople, which he was also under orders to defend. 'If Mustafa is going to fight', he wrote to Rumbold on September 22, 'he is also going to press hard for Constantinople.' That day Rumbold wrote to Frank Lindley, the British Minister in Athens:

I really do not know what is going to happen here. Our gallant Allies have let us down as usual. Having agreed to send detachments to the Asiatic shore of both Straits and to take part in two warnings to Mustafa Kemal not to cross into the neutral zones, they have withdrawn their detachments, thus depriving these two warnings of all value as a mark of Allied solidarity and determination. What can one do with such people? The fact is that the French and Italian Governments are in a most pitiable funk and are ready to buy off Kemal at any price.

The latest accounts are that Kemal will not arrest the movements of his troops and that he will try to come here and turn us out of Chanak also. I think

---

[1] Victor Antonescu, 1871–1946. Rumanian Minister of Justice, 1914–16; of Finance, 1916–17; of Foreign Affairs, 1922; of Justice, 1933 and 1934–35; of Finance, 1935–36; and of Foreign Affairs, 1936–37.

[2] The TUC deputation chose as its three spokesmen J. H. Thomas (General Secretary of the National Union of Railwaymen and later Secretary of State for the Colonies), Ben Tillett (the dockers' leader) and Margaret Bondfield (National Union of General and Municipal Workers, and in 1929 the first woman Cabinet Minister).

it will not be all plain sailing for him but we are very weak, especially at Constantinople. I am expecting at any moment to get instructions to invite both sets of Turks to the conference which, according to a Havas telegram, is to take place in a fortnight. No Turk will ever give a straight answer to a straight question and I foresee what will happen will be that Kemal will make his attendance at the conference subject to certain conditions impossible of acceptance by us. This will lead to delay for which he will blame us and say that he will settle the matter by military means. We may well be in for another war. This will create a very awkward situation for the Government especially as our Trade Unionists are already howling that they will not have war at any price. Altogether Kemal can congratulate himself for having put our Government in a fix.

In Paris, discussions between Curzon and Poincaré continued throughout the afternoon of September 22. During the course of a heated argument Curzon walked out of the conference room. The Italian representative, Count Sforza,[1] acted as a mediating influence. Poincaré apologized for having lost his temper; Curzon agreed to return to the conference table. He then agreed to instruct Harington to enter into direct negotiations with Mustafa Kemal, and to try to fix a line beyond which the Turks could agree not to advance. This proposal, signed by Curzon, Poincaré and Sforza, was telegraphed to Angora on September 23; the Allies added that they 'viewed with favour' the Turkish claim to eastern Thrace and Adrianople, and that, as soon as a peace treaty had been signed, the Allied troops and administators would leave Constantinople.

On the morning of September 23, while the Allied offer was on its way to Angora, a Turkish cavalry detachment of about 200 men crossed into the allied Zone south of Chanak. They were met by a British patrol of thirty troops under Lieutenant Naylor,[2] who asked them to withdraw. The Turks refused, but said they did not wish to fight. Seeing a further 800 Turks riding up, Naylor prudently withdrew. He reported the encounter to Colonel Shuttleworth, who informed Harington: 'The

[1] Count Carlo Sforza, 1873–1952. Entered the Italian Diplomatic Service, 1896; Minister to China, 1911–15; to the Serbian Government in Exile, 1915–18. Italian Representative in Albania and Corfu, 1915–18. Italian High Commissioner, Constantinople, October 1918–June 1919. Minister for Foreign Affairs, June 1920–July 1921. Ambassador to France, February–October 1922. In October 1922 he refused an offer to join Mussolini's Government. Leader of the Democratic Opposition in the Italian Parliament, 1922–26, when Mussolini suppressed all opposition Parties. Minister without Portfolio in Marshal Badoglio's Government, 1944. President of the Consultative Assembly, 1945–46. Minister for Foreign Affairs, 1947–51.

[2] Hugh Maxwell Naylor, 1894–1966. 2nd Lieutenant, 3rd Hussars, August 15, 1914; Lieutenant, 1916. Retired from the Army in 1924. Captain, Reserve of Officers (employed), 1939. After the war he settled in Uganda, where he became Director of the Toro Tea Company. In 1951 he was awarded the OBE for public services in Uganda.

situation was quite unanticipated. Peaceful penetration by armed men who did not wish to fight, and yet refused either to withdraw or to halt, had not been foreseen. . . .' On the morning of September 24 Harington telegraphed to Shuttleworth from Constantinople that he must avoid any unnecessary engagement with Turkish forces. On September 25 a further thousand British troops, the 1st Battalion, King's Own Scottish Borderers, arrived from Egypt, and took up their position to the north of Chanak, from where they could see the Turkish cavalry on the hills to their front. Further troops were on their way from England. The Cabinet were still determined to hold Chanak by force. Late in the evening of September 26, Major-General Marden[1] arrived at the town from Constantinople, on board the destroyer *Montrose*. He at once took over the command from Colonel Shuttleworth, and reorganized the British force into two Brigades, each of three battalions. The 4th Battle Squadron, commanded by Rear-Admiral Kelly,[2] trained its guns on to the hills, confident that it could keep the Turks from Chanak by a ring of fire. But Marden's orders, which he had received from Harington earlier that day, were 'not to fight if he could possibly help it'. That same day, at Rumbold's suggestion, Vice-Admiral Brock instructed Kelly to detain any Greek troopships which tried to go through the Dardanelles on their way to the Sea of Marmora. The aim, Rumbold explained to Curzon in a telegram that evening, was to prevent any Greek troops landing in Thrace and giving the Kemalists an excuse 'for violating neutral zone'.

The British authorities in Constantinople were under no illusions about the strength of the Turkish position, morally as well as materially. On September 26 Rumbold wrote to Oliphant:

Brock, Harington and I have throughout had in mind the absolute necessity of avoiding any action which might lead to war. We feel the last thing our country wants is to have another war and that the average man does not care a straw whether Eastern Thrace and Adrianople belong to the Greeks or Turks. In my view both are absolute barbarians and have recently proved it. We imagine our country *would* fight for the freedom of the Straits, but for nothing else. We have been badly let down by our gallant Allies on the spot and feel very sore about it.

[1] Thomas Owen Marden, 1866–1951. Entered Army, 1886. Commanded the 114th Infantry Brigade, 1915–17; the 6th Division, 1917–19. Major-General Commanding the British Troops in Constantinople, 1920–23. Colonel of the Welch Regiment, 1920–41. Commanded the Welsh Division, 1923–27.

[2] John Donald Kelly, 1871–1936. Entered the Navy, as a cadet, 1884. Commanded HMS *Dublin* at the Dardanelles, 1915. Rear-Admiral, 4th Battle Squadron, Mediterranean, 1922–23. Fourth Sea Lord, 1924–27. Vice-Admiral Commanding 1st Battle Squadron, 1927–29. Knighted, 1929. Admiral, 1930. Commander-in-Chief Atlantic Fleet, 1931–32; Home Fleet, 1932–33; Portsmouth, 1934–36. Admiral of the Fleet, 1936.

It was inevitable, Rumbold added, that in the existing circumstances Eastern Thrace and Adrianople should be restored to Turkey.

On September 26 Sir Harry Lamb, who had arrived on the previous night from Smyrna, gave Rumbold a harrowing account of the violence there. Later that day Rumbold sent George V an account of what Lamb had told him, and of his own reflections on the crises:

He told me that he had noticed a spirit animating the Nationalists when they entered Smyrna which he had never noticed before in a Turk. This spirit may be expressed in the phrase Asia versus Europe. Its outward manifestation is the destruction of European property. He attributes the development of this spirit to the proceedings of the Greeks whilst in occupation of large tracts of Anatolia, and in particular to the atrocities committed by certain elements amongst the Greek troops in their recent retirement to the coast. Armenians, Circassians and native Christians attached to the Greek forces committed every kind of excess. The Greek regular soldier was less to blame but even he indulged in acts of barbarism. The thought that Kemalist forces, animated by such a spirit, may and probably will eventually come to Constantinople is not a pleasing one, and fully justifies the anxiety which prevails here at the present moment amongst the Greek, Armenian, and foreign communities. . . .

The state of extreme tension will continue until the Nationalists have actually accepted to come to a conference and to hold a meeting with the Allied Generals at Mudania or Ismid. Until this happens we are at the mercy of incidents which might end in hostilities. . . .

The firm attitude of the Government in deciding to hold the Neutral Zones and sending out reinforcements for that purpose, cannot fail to impress the Turk, who is only influenced by force and who will contrast the French and Italian attitude unfavourably with ours. To that extent we have maintained our prestige.

The situation is an anxious one. This huge town is full of bad and disorderly elements which need watching. The present British force is quite inadequate to hold the Asiatic approaches to Constantinople and to maintain order in the British sector of the town. I shall therefore be glad when reinforcements reach this place. Meanwhile General Harington's task is an unenviable one.

Harington was anxious to find a peaceful solution. 'Losing a lot of lives in hanging on', he telegraphed to the Chief of the Imperial General Staff, Lord Cavan,[1] on September 26, 'is what I want to guard against. . . . Why not start at once and give Turkey Constantinople and Maritza, having offered them to them, and so end it all. . . . Remember Turks are

---

[1] Frederick Rudolph Lambart, 1856–1946. Entered Army, 1885. 10th Earl of Cavan, 1900. Major-General commanding the 4th (Guards) Brigade, September 1914–June 1915. Commanded the Guards Division, August 1915–January 1916. Commanded the 14th Corps in France and Italy, January 1916–18. Commander-in-Chief, Aldershot, 1920–22. Chief of the Imperial General Staff, 1922–26. Field-Marshal, 1932.

within sight of their goal and are naturally elated. No one is more anxious to avoid a war than I am, but it is the very way to get dragged into one.'

At three in the afternoon of September 27 a group of Cabinet Ministers and service chiefs met in London to discuss the crisis, and to consider Harington's advice.[1] Austen Chamberlain insisted that Britain could not withdraw from Chanak 'with credit to ourselves'; he would consider such a withdrawal 'an humiliation to the British Empire'. The *Daily Mail* had been urging: 'GET OUT OF CHANAK': Cabinet Ministers, however, regarded the need to hold Chanak as of even more importance than the retention of Constantinople. On September 28 the Cabinet telegraphed to Harington that 'in order to reinforce Chanak, you may, if necessary, evacuate Constantinople. . . . Our policy is to hold Gallipoli at all costs and to hold on to Chanak as long as this can be done without undue military risk.'

On September 29 the Cabinet decided that Mustafa Kemal had had long enough to reply to the offer of talks made by the Allies six days before. Churchill was confident that the troops at Chanak could hold their positions. Lloyd George was determined not to give way to Turkish military pressure. The Cabinet asked Rumbold to inform General Pellé that the British would in no circumstances withdraw from Chanak while the Turks were still within the neutral zone. It was up to the French and Italian naval forces at Constantinople, the Cabinet added, to take the necessary action to prevent the Turks from crossing the Bosphorus into Europe. Britain would concentrate all its strength at Chanak. Harington was ordered to inform the Turks that unless they withdrew at once from the neutral zone around Chanak 'all the forces at your disposal – naval, military, aerial – will open fire'. The time limit for this ultimatum, Harington was told 'should be short'. Curzon opposed the despatch of the ultimatum, pleading with the Cabinet to wait another twenty-four hours for Mustafa Kemal's reply; but he was overruled.

As soon as he received the Cabinet ultimatum, Harington consulted Rumbold. Neither of them favoured so drastic a course. Both believed that negotiations were still possible, given time. Rumbold felt that Harington ought to enter into negotiations with Mustafa Kemal on the basis, not of the Paris note of September 23, but without any conditions. He also wanted the Greek forces gathering in eastern Thrace to be ordered

---

[1] The Ministers were Austen Chamberlain (Lord Privy Seal), Churchill (Secretary of State for the Colonies), Lord Lee of Fareham (First Lord of the Admiralty) and Worthington-Evans (Secretary of State for War). The three Service Chiefs were Lords Cavan (Chief of the Imperial General Staff), Trenchard (Chief of the Air Staff) and Beatty (First Sea Lord).

back across the Maritza, leaving eastern Thrace unoccupied as proof that Britain did not intend to keep the Turks out of it.

When the Cabinet met at 10 Downing Street on September 30, it learned that Harington had not delivered its ultimatum, and that Rumbold had insisted that a solution could be negotiated between Britain and the Kemalists once the Greeks could be persuaded to evacuate eastern Thrace. There was much anger that, as the minutes recorded, 'Sir Horace Rumbold and General Harington should apparently contemplate a meeting between the General and Mustapha Kemal at Mudania while the Turkish Nationalists, in defiance of several remonstrances and warnings, were still actively violating the essential condition laid down in the Paris note . . .'; that is, their entry into the neutral zone surrounding Chanak. Rumbold and Harington did not seem to realize, the Cabinet minutes continued, 'the danger to peace' which their attitude 'seemed to involve'.

Rumbold and Harington judged otherwise. It seemed to them that to deliver the Cabinet's ultimatum would constitute a more serious danger to peace than trying to get talks started at Mudania. They therefore decided to continue to hold the ultimatum back, and to proceed with their own negotiations with Mustafa Kemal's agent in Constantinople, Hamid Bey, with whom they were in daily contact, and who had assured them that the Angora Government intended to reply to the Paris note of September 23 within a few days. In his reply to the Cabinet's instruction, Harington therefore maintained his position, insisting that 'it seems very inadvisable just at the moment when within reach of distance of meeting between Allied Generals and Kemal . . . that I should launch an avalanche of fire which will put a match to mine here and everywhere else and from which there will be no drawing back. . . . To suppose my not having fired so far at Chanak has been interpreted as signs of weakness is quite wrong because I have been very careful to warn Hamid that I have full powers of Allied Government behind me and that I shall not hesitate to use it if time comes.' Harington informed the Cabinet that in his opinion Mustafa Kemal 'does not intend to attack Chanak seriously', and added that both Rumbold and Admiral Brock agreed with him. On October 1, before the Cabinet could order Harington to do as he had been told, Mustafa Kemal agreed to meet the Allied generals at Mudania.

The British troops at Chanak remained in place, awaiting the outcome of the Mudania meeting. The Cabinet, after a special meeting on the morning of Sunday, October 1, telegraphed to Rumbold the instructions which Harington was to follow in his discussions with Mustafa Kemal. Angered by Harington's action in not delivering the ultimatum, the Cabinet warned that: 'We cannot contemplate Mudania meeting being spun out from day to day, in order to enable Mustapha Kemal to strengthen his position at Ismid with a view to invading Europe.'

On October 2 Harington left Constantinople for Mudania on board the *Iron Duke*. Rumbold remained in the city. 'It seems to me', he wrote to Oliphant on October 3, 'that I ought to have some guidance as to what I should do in the unfortunate event of our having to fight Kemal. I deal with the Central Government with which we should not be at war. On the other hand if Kemal came here we could not very well remain. Should matters seem hectic by the time you get this letter, you might have a telegram sent to me for my guidance.'

Negotiations at Mudania began on October 3. To the annoyance of the British Cabinet, Mustafa Kemal declined to go himself, sending his victorious general, Ismet Pasha as his representative. The discussion continued for four days. Ismet agreed to accept the Paris note of September 23, and at Chanak the Turkish forces withdrew a thousand yards from the British line. But on October 6 Harington telegraphed to Rumbold that the Turks had crossed into the neutral zone west of Ismid, and Ismet informed him that unless eastern Thrace were handed over to Turkey immediately, the Turks would march across the Ismid Peninsula to the Bosphorus and from there to Europe.

Rumbold was entirely opposed to accepting this demand. But the French intermediary, Franklin-Bouillon,[1] who had arrived at Mudania, told Ismet that France would agree to it. This, Rumbold telegraphed to Curzon on October 6, was a 'treacherous surrender' on the part of an Ally. He believed that a solution was still possible, which would not entail submission to the Nationalist demands. Eleven days earlier, on September 28, he had proposed, in a telegram to Curzon, that one means of lessening the tension in eastern Thrace, and convincing the Turks that Britain wanted a negotiated settlement rather than war, would be to send inter-allied Commissions to the area, with power to halt the Greek attacks on Turkish civilians which had so incensed the Nationalist leaders. Such allied action, Rumbold telegraphed, 'might have a transquillising effect on population of those districts and give Nationalists proof of our good intentions'. Curzon had accepted this scheme. When, at Mudania, Ismet demanded the right to occupy eastern Thrace immediately, Rumbold at once suggested that the inter-allied Commissions which he had proposed

---

[1] 'The ubiquitous M. Franklin-Bouillon', Rumbold wrote to Curzon on October 9, 'though not actually present in the conference room, sought to play the role of mediator between the Allied generals and the Turks. As this personage appears to be devoted to the Turkish cause, his proceedings were a source of embarrassment . . . for there is no doubt that he encouraged the Turks to believe that the Allies were prepared to go further in the way of concessions than is really the case.'

be used as a buffer force until such time as the peace treaty was signed. The Greeks, Rumbold telegraphed to Curzon on October 6, should be made to evacuate eastern Thrace at once, 'on condition that effective allied control be maintained until conclusions of peace'. Curzon accepted Rumbold's suggestion. But the French and Italians rejected it; they wanted the Nationalists to be allowed to occupy eastern Thrace immediately. Rumbold believed that if this happened, the Turks would feel that they could obtain all their demands by the threat of force, and that a peaceful settlement would then be impossible.

Throughout October 6 Rumbold and his fellow High Commissioners discussed the Turkish demands. Both Pellé and Garroni, he telegraphed to Curzon, 'argued strongly in favour of yielding to Turks', and for the restoration of eastern Thrace to Turkey before any peace treaty, and without guarantees for the minorities. Garroni insisted that 'if war resulted', the world 'would attribute it to unwillingness of allied High Commissioners and generals to take responsibility for concessions which were of small account'. Rumbold disagreed. 'I replied', he told Curzon, 'that world would attribute it to intractability of Turks, that the more we yielded to Turks the more demands they would make and that the next might well be evacuation of Constantinople, that General Harington, Admiral Brock and I had done our utmost to avoid war, that there were limits to forbearance of His Majesty's Government and that I must now report facts to my Government and leave it to them to appreciate whether in refusing these demands they were prepared to contemplate war.'

Curzon approved Rumbold's decision not to moderate the British proposals to the point where the Turks would abandon all restraint. That evening he crossed over to Paris, and in the early hours of October 7 persuaded Poincaré to give his support to the British demands. The Italians accepted the French decision without delay. Curzon telegraphed to Rumbold that the Allies could at last present a unified front. Harington, who had returned to Constantinople on the night of October 5, fully expecting that he would have to prepare the city to resist a Nationalist attack, discussed with Rumbold the final points of detail, before returning to Mudania on October 8.

On October 7, the day after the breakdown of the Mudania Conference, a letter was printed in *The Times* and the *Daily Express* from Bonar Law,[1] the leader of the Conservative Party, and until recently

[1] Andrew Bonar Law, 1858–1923. Conservative MP, 1900–10; 1911–23. Leader of the Conservatives in the House of Commons, 1911. Secretary of State for the Colonies, May 1915–December 1916. Chancellor of the Exchequer, 1916–19. Lord Privy Seal, 1919–21, when he resigned because of ill health. Prime Minister, 1922–23.

a senior member of Lloyd George's Cabinet. Britain, he declared, could only keep the Turks from Constantinople and Thrace if the allied powers, including America, agreed to join in such action. It would be wrong for Britain alone, the leading Mohamedan power,[1] 'to show any hostility or unfairness to the Turks'. Without French support, military action must be avoided. 'We cannot alone act', Bonar Law declared, 'as the policeman of the world.'

Bonar Law's letter represented the mounting anger in Britain against what appeared to be a reckless adventure, likely to lead to war. But his fears were not borne out; Curzon had secured French support for Britain's demands and Rumbold had put forward a compromise acceptable to the Turks.

On October 8, after Harington had returned to Mudania, but before he had reopened negotiations, Rumbold took an initiative which helped to reduce the tensions which threatened to precipitate military action. That morning Admiral Brock decided to clear the Bosphorus of all Turkish vessels. Only by drastic naval action, he asserted, could Turkish troops be forestalled in their attempt to cross from Asia to Europe. Reports of Turkish troops violating the neutral zone near Ismid seemed proof that the Admiral must act without delay. But Rumbold deprecated premature action, and instructed the Admiral to wait. 'I have pointed out', he telegraphed to Curzon in defence of his action, 'that Nationalist troops who have crossed the neutral zone yesterday may have been genuinely unaware of its limits.' Curzon at once approved Rumbold's restraining advice.

Harington reopened the Mudania negotiations on the evening of October 8. Ismet, who had no desire for a direct military confrontation with the Greeks in eastern Thrace, accepted as a practical solution Rumbold's proposal for an inter-allied Commission to replace the Greeks in Thrace.

He also accepted Rumbold's assurance that Britain did not seek to embroil the Turks in a new conflict with Greece by bringing their two forces into direct contact, and in circumstances where the Greeks, with direct road and rail communications with Athens, would have many advantages.

On October 8, Lady Rumbold sent her mother an account of the crisis as seen from Constantinople. 'The place is full of war-correspondents', she wrote,

---

[1] There were over 70 million Muslims in India in 1922 and a further 10 million in Egypt. The total Turkish population (Muslim and non-Muslim) in 1922 did not exceed 14 million.

and everyone is strung up. Horace looks very tired this morning and has now got all the High Coms. etc. in his room. He says that never even in 1914, has he worked at such high pressure and for such a length of time. I daren't yet do anything in the way of packing or putting by as it would create an even worse panic. The French are beneath contempt, and the Times and Daily Mail make one sick the way they go on. If *only* they knew! But the Govt. is tied and can't shew them up. Our one bright spot is the Navy, which is *quite* magnificent, four huge ships and lots of smaller. Admiral Tyrwhitt has just been having tea, and told us that last night *one* destroyer out in the Black Sea had held up 4,000 Nationalists, and told them politely to remove themselves from the Neutral Zone, which they did! But I believe they are back again.

Throughout October 9 and 10, the Mudania negotiations continued. Agreement was finally reached, after an all-night session, at 7.15 on the morning of October 11. A Convention was signed to come into force at midnight on October 14. Allied troops were to occupy eastern Thrace for thirty days. As Rumbold had proposed, three Military Commissions headed by a French, a British and an Italian officer, were to take over from October 16 the civil administration of eastern Thrace and the Greek authorities would return to Greece. At Chanak, the Turks were to withdraw 15 kilometres from the coast, and not increase the number of their troops. On the Ismid peninsula the Turks were likewise to withdraw behind the neutral zone. The Allies were to remain in occupation of Constantinople, Ismid, Chanak, and the Gallipoli Peninsula until a formal peace treaty had been negotiated between them and Turkey. Until a peace treaty was signed, the Turks would neither transport troops into eastern Thrace, or raise an army from the Turkish population there.

'Signature of convention', Rumbold telegraphed to Curzon on the afternoon of October 11, 'is largely due to patience, tact and spirit of conciliation shewn by General Harington. Factors which probably determined Turks to sign were knowledge of arrival of British reinforcements, presence of British warships, and fact that these would be used in last resort. Policy of His Majesty's Government has in fact been fully justified.' Three days later, on October 14, Rumbold, with the approval of Brock and Harington, pressed Curzon to prevent any reduction in British military, naval or air strength at Constantinople and the Dardanelles. These forces, he insisted, must be maintained until a peace treaty was signed. 'Ultimate factor which brought Turks to reason at Mudania', he reiterated, 'was our display of force and their knowledge that we would use it in the last resort.' As, in his opinion, neither France nor Italy could be trusted to support Britain during the peace negotiation, Britain's 'chief, if not the only card' in the months to come would be 'the presence of British forces of occupation'. Any withdrawal would be construed as weakness.

Four days after the Mudania Convention came into force, on October 19, Conservative MPs, meeting at the Carlton Club in London, decided to withdraw their support from Lloyd George's Coalition. The Chanak crisis had confirmed them in their distrust of his policies and fear of his methods. Unable to maintain his majority without Conservative support, Lloyd George resigned that same day. Bonar Law became Prime Minister. Curzon, Lloyd George's severest critic during the Chanak crisis, retained his position as Foreign Secretary in Bonar Law's Government. Lord Birkenhead,[1] Austen Chamberlain and Churchill, Lloyd George's principal supporters, were not asked to serve in the new Administration.

The knowledge of Rumbold's achievements during the Chanak crisis brought him a spate of congratulations. 'The credit entirely belongs to you', Harington wrote to him on October 12. That same day Alice Keppel[2] wrote enthusiastically:

You must let me write you a line of the deepest congratulations on the way you and General Harington have managed this most complicated and difficult state of affairs with Kemal. The papers say, you are a 'Monument of discretion'. I think 'Monument' the wrong word but 'the discretion' no one doubts. The fighting 'bloods' at home, have been straining at the leash. Winston longing to drop the paint brush for his sword and L.G. murmuring at every meal, We will fight *to the end*!

On October 13 Nevile Henderson wrote: 'Your own attitude at moments when others were inclined to waver added lustre to the prestige of the High Commission'; and Lord Stamfordham wrote from Buckingham Palace: 'Now that the immediate danger is past, His Majesty wishes me to congratulate you upon the able skill, diplomacy and firmness with which you have conducted the difficult, complicated and delicate negotiations; in such complete harmony with General Harington and Admiral Brock.'

Rumbold gave his own assessment of what he had achieved in a letter to Findlay on October 30. 'Harington and I', he wrote, 'certainly had a rather trying time and if either he or Brock had obeyed their instructions without question, the fat would have been in the fire. During the crisis we constituted ourselves into a kind of war committee and

---

[1] Frederick Edwin Smith, 1872–1930. Known as 'F.E.'. Conservative MP, 1906–16. Head of the Press Bureau, August–October 1914; Solicitor-General, May 1915. Knighted, 1915. Attorney-General, November 1915–19. Created Baron Birkenhead, 1919. Lord Chancellor, 1920–22. Created Viscount, 1921. Created Earl, 1922. Secretary of State for India, 1924–28.

[2] Alice Frederica Edmonstone, 1869–1947. Daughter of Admiral Sir William Edmonstone. In 1891 she married the Hon George Keppel. She first met Edward VII in 1898; they remained close friends until the King's death in 1910.

worked in complete co-operation. This impressed the Government at home and made it easier for us to put the drag on from time to time. We realised of course that there was a war party in the Cabinet headed by LG, with the support of Winston Churchill and Birkenhead.'

Rumbold's actions had helped to avert war; and yet, by the first week in October, he had been convinced that had negotiations failed, Britain could have fought, and defeated, the Turks. 'At Chanak', he wrote to Oliphant on October 17, 'the Turks would have had to attack the most perfect trenches, held by stout fellows and supported by tremendous artillery fire from the ships. On the Ismid Peninsula the two roads along the sea could have been denied to the Turks by our ships, whilst the road down the centre of the Peninsula passes mostly over a bare plain and troops and transports moving along it would have offered a magnificent target for our airmen. There are many here including the British community who would have been pleased to have seen the Turks get a real knock at the beginning, even if we had had difficulties later. I believe if the Turks had tried to take us on and had got a bad knock at the start, the chances were even that they would have thrown up the sponge.'

Rumbold remained at Constantinople until November 15, a month after the signing of the Mudania Convention. In view of his work during the Chanak crisis, and his two-year experience of Turkish affairs, he was asked by Lord Curzon to accompany him to the Lausanne Peace Conference. While waiting for the Conference to begin he reflected on the crisis, and wondered whether the Turks would really keep the peace. As he pointed out to Lord Stamfordham on October 23, the advanced guard of the victorious Turkish army, 'very much elated by its victory . . . is only 25 miles from the capital. No doubt the soldiers, who have not been paid for a very long time, are looking forward to looting this place just as their comrades, or even they themselves, did at Smyrna. It may therefore be difficult for the Kemalist leaders to hold back their troops if the meeting of the Peace Conference is unduly delayed. The Kemalists are quite capable of taking advantage of any excuse for violating the Mudania Convention.' Rumbold had few good words to say about the Turks. 'The fact is', he wrote to Stamfordham, 'that a wave of blind chauvinism is passing over the Turks, who are under the illusion that they can run their country without foreign help. There is only one thing at which they are any good and that is fighting, and from that point of view I am afraid that the trouble we have averted now is only trouble deferred, for the Turk, once back in Europe, may well be the author of another Balkan war in two or three years' time. He will begin by trying to get western Thrace'. To Oliphant on October 28 Rumbold set out his fears in detail:

The public in England, including a certain section of the press, seem to think that with the signature of the Mudania Agreement, all is over bar the shouting. Nothing is further from the truth. The situation here is critical and will remain so throughout the Peace Conference. The latter may even break down. I only suggest to you one or two points on which it may break down. Shall we for instance tamely give the Nationalists Mosul[1] if they ask for it? Are we going to admit that there will be no further guarantees for foreigners and that the latter are to be amenable to pure and unadulterated Turkish justice? If the conference breaks down a very serious situation will immediately arise. It may mean war with us. The Kemalists will march on Constantinople and this again brings me to the question as to what I am to do.

In a month from now our military position here will be worse than it is at present. The Kemalists will be installed in Thrace, they have a strong army round about Ismid and could no doubt engineer a very serious rising in this town. Harington would have to move his troops to Chanak and I should get rid of the British colony. The Constantinople Government would disappear. Is it suggested that I should remain on if we are driven into war with the Kemalists? I venture to think that your best plan would be to allow me full discretion in the circumstances.

You will remember that I am rather an old hand at evacuation. I was at Berlin when the war broke out when we left at 36 hours' notice. I was at Warsaw when the Bolsheviks came to within 10 miles of that place and had to clear out at 5 hours' notice. I did not ask for instructions on that occasion but exercised my discretion. I think I should be allowed to exercise my discretion in the contingency of the withdrawal of the Allied forces, including the British forces, from Constantinople under the pressure of Kemalist troops. It is just as well to be prepared beforehand.

Rumbold's pessimistic attitude arose from his belief that the 'Kemalist Turk', as he wrote to Findlay, his colleague of Cairo days, on October 13, was 'inspired by blind chauvinism, hates all foreigners and thinks that he can run his country himself without any foreign intervention'. To Curzon, on October 31, Rumbold wrote that the spirit which animated the Kemalist Turk 'may be summed up in the expression Asia versus Europe'.

On November 1 the Angora National Assembly formally 'abolished' the Sultanate. Mehmed remained in Constantinople, but his position was precarious. No Turks were prepared to fight to maintain Ottoman rule; those who were most committed to the Sultan prepared, instead, to go into exile.

A week before he left Constantinople Rumbold was caught up in what looked like another war crisis. A series of incidents exacerbated relations

[1] Atatürk wanted the town and vilayet of Mosul to remain in Turkey. But Britain insisted that they were a part of the newly created kingdom of Iraq, which was under British protection. France supported Turkey, but the British view prevailed.

with the Nationalists. A British soldier was shot by two Turks while walking in a Constantinople street, and one Irish Guardsman wounded with a knife. Harington approached Ismet Pasha, who could give no guarantees for the safety of British troops; Constantinople he pointed out, was still under British occupation. The Nationalists had agreed to stay out of the city until the peace treaty was signed. In eastern Thrace, contrary to the Mudania Convention, the Nationalists began to recruit troops. Again Harington protested. 'I have tried to show them the utter folly of their action', he wrote to Rumbold on November 7. Harington told the Turks that they must answer 'yes or no'. Rumbold was emphatic that Britain could not allow the Mudania Convention to be flouted. His disillusionment with the Nationalists was deep. He no longer believed that they had any intention of keeping the peace. 'I think it will be perfectly deplorable', Harington wrote to Rumbold in his letter of November 7, 'if we are plunged into war, especially at this moment, but I am in entire agreement that the Allied Powers cannot stand this insult; a new war now, however, will receive only half-baked support at home.' Rumbold replied to Harington that same day that 'in the event of a rupture, i.e. war with the Turks, our Government will be in a better position now than it was a month ago. For one thing we have got a really united front at last; for another the public at home I think has confidence in you and me here, for it knows how we have struggled to preserve peace and will conclude that if a rupture comes it will be because the Turks have made the situation impossible'.

The Nationalists soon agreed to give up their recruiting in European Turkey. They could not afford to jeopardize the peace conference, even if they did try to give the impression that they were willing to face war with Britain. Nor did Rumbold relish the thought of a new war, however justified he believed it might be. His anger of November 7 had modified a week later, on the eve of his departure. 'It is very galling to have to swallow the numerous breaches of the Mudania Convention', he wrote to Lord Stamfordham on November 13, '. . . and yet if we took a strong line and proclaimed a state of siege we risk bringing the whole Kemalist army to the Bosphorus.' In such an event he had been told by both Harington and Brock, 'there would have to be a forced evacuation of Constantinople under the most trying conditions. I really shudder to think what would happen if we had to leave here in a hurry and abandon the Christian population to its fate.' Rumbold wanted to leave Constantinople for good. 'A swollen-headed Turk is a dreadful person to deal with', he told Stamfordham, 'and I have no wish to stay here under the Kemalist regime. My colleagues and I are agreed in thinking that our

Governments would be wise to transfer us elsewhere after the signature of the Peace Treaty. We are too identified with the Armistice regime, under which we practically ruled this place, to be able to adjust ourselves to new conditions. I shall certainly impress this fact on Lord Curzon when I see him at Lausanne.'

Rumbold was bitter about the attitude of the Press, which had so readily supported the Nationalist cause. 'The Morning Post', he had written to his stepmother on October 22, 'shuts its eyes to the bestialities of the Turks and slobbers over the French who don't deserve it. As for the Daily Mail it is beneath contempt.' Of the French Press he wrote scathingly on November 13, in a letter to Oliphant, that it 'seems to be in the grip of the International financier or Jew who only cares for French financial interests and nothing else. At present the Kemalists have hit the French harder than anybody else and this is likely to continue unless and until the French show their teeth. If only Reuter were able to telegraph one single sentence to the effect that the Allied Governments were prepared to send reinforcements to Turkey, this crisis would be settled and the Nationalists would collapse. But that is just what none of our Governments seem able to do, so we are making bricks without straw, a more than usually difficult process in an oriental country.'

In a letter to her mother on November 6, Lady Rumbold described the atmosphere in Constantinople on the eve of her husband's departure. 'The situation is most unpleasant', she wrote, 'and everyone is strung up and nervy. All except H who is a perfect *marvel* of strength and calm. Everybody looks to him for advice and support, from the General and High Coms. right away down to wretched Greeks, etc. Every day they have meetings and conferences as the situation changes from day to day. . . . Thank goodness it is raining which I hope will damp a little the horrible Nationalists who process about the town.' On the previous day Rumbold, accompanied by Andrew Ryan, had held his final audience with the Sultan. It had lasted for over three hours. 'He said it was a most painful and difficult interview', Lady Rumbold wrote:

On arrival at Yildiz, he and the Dragoman, were met by *one* old chamberlain, instead of the usual rows. And it was pathetic the way this old man tried to pretend it was all right, and to explain that the other chamberlains had been delayed in returning to the Palace. Of course they had all left like rats. The Sultan was very dignified. He is awaiting events, and is guarded by the Grenadiers. He will be looked after I trust and got away if necessary. He was very loathe to let H leave, and talked without ceasing for three and a half hours.

Poor H got back just in time for a conference here which lasted till quarter to nine. He was then up to past twelve sending off telegrams. He slept badly poor dear, and was up again by seven. But luckily he is well and looks all right. Last night we had 150 *Turks* taking refuge here. They were in a hut in the garden, and some in the house. I went down to see them and through an inter-preter 'hoped they would have happier days', what could I say, poor people?

They were most respectable looking people, priests, lawyers, teachers, corres-pondents, etc., also several of high degree, three pashas for instance. They were all terrified of being arrested. One horrible case happened two days ago, an ex-minister was kidnapped. However this little lot have been got away under a strong guard, and put on a ship.

The ship of Turkish exiles sailed safely to Malta. That night a telegram arrived to say that Rumbold was definitely to go to Lausanne.

On November 15 Rumbold and his wife left Constantinople. Two days later the Sultan himself left the city on board the British battleship *Malaya*. At his audience on November 5, Rumbold had promised to give the Sultan any help he required while going into exile, and had arranged for many of the royal financial assets to be transferred to Switzerland. The Sultan never returned to his country or to his capital.

Lady Rumbold was as pleased as her husband to be leaving Turkey. Three days after their departure she wrote to her mother:

I was so anxious about H all these last weeks. The atmosphere was intensely unpleasant, the town full of Kemalists and Bolshevists, and a regular reign of terror going on. People were getting out as fast as they could. I can't tell you all the tragic things that were happening all around. I myself received any number of letters and appeals from people whose husbands were arrested or disappeared, Armenians, Greeks, Turks even. And as for the White Russians, they were in a great panic, coming for advice or to get help for visas, etc.

It was horrid to leave our weeping household, all so frightened poor dears. The little Armenian housemaid whose husband has already been killed by the Turks was particularly upset but I told her she was to bring her children and mother into the Embassy if in danger. We had a terrific send-off, everyone at the station. We were photoed, and cinema-ed, etc., and as we went out Gen. Harington led the cheering.

I really think those remaining behind were depressed to see the stalwart Horace depart, he has been such a *rock* through all these troublous times.

14

Lausanne

1922–1923

The Conference of Lausanne was unique among the post-war conferences. Alone of those who had surrendered in 1918, Turkey had, by the time of her peace negotiations, turned defeat into victory. The driving of the Greeks from the Sakaria river to the Aegean Sea had given her all the psychological advantages, and some of the physical strength, of a victorious power. Her principal negotiator was Ismet Pasha, the General who had secured the victory. By contrast, the representatives of the Allied powers came direct from the humiliation of the Chanak crisis. They were divided among themselves, and were reluctant to use the military force needed to impose a settlement. Germany, Austria-Hungary and Bulgaria had each submitted in 1918 to dictated terms and territorial losses; by the end of 1922 Turkey was in physical possession of almost all the territory she wished to retain. Accepting the loss of her Arab lands – Syria, Palestine, Mesopotamia and Arabia – and willing to allow the Greeks possession of the Aegean Islands, Turkey stood firm for demands which could be justified on ethnographic grounds. The Turkish terms were clear: Turkey must retain Constantinople; her European border must be the Maritza river; the territorial integrity of Anatolia must be secure; no international regime must control the Straits; no Ottoman debts must endanger the economy of the new state; the privileged status of foreigners in Turkey must cease.

The Conference opened on 20 November, 1922. Nine countries were represented: Turkey, the British Empire, France, Italy, Japan, Greece, Rumania, the United States of America and the newly created Kingdom of the Serbs, Croats and Slovenes. Each country was represented by two delegates. Curzon and Rumbold represented the British Empire. Italy was represented by its new leader, Benito Mussolini,[1] who was, Lady

[1] Benito Mussolini, 1883–1945. Socialist journalist and agitator before 1914; editor of *Avanti*. Founded the patriotic *Il Popolo d'Italia*, 1914. Served on the Austrian front, 1917. Founded the Fascist Party at the end of the war. President of the Council of Ministers, 1922–26. Minister for Foreign Affairs, 1924–29 and 1932–36. Head of State and Prime Minister, 1926–43. Minister of War, 1926–29 and 1933–43. Fled from Rome, 1943. Head of the German-controlled Government of Northern Italy, 1944–45. Murdered by Italian anti-Fascists, April 28, 1945.

Rumbold wrote to her mother on November 22, 'most impressive and Napoleonic'. The negotiations continued until 4 February, 1923, with a three-week break over the Christmas and New Year. When disagreements threatened the success of the Conference, Rumbold did not take them over seriously. He had seen 'over and over again', he wrote to Nevile Henderson on 2 January, 1923, situations 'from which one would think that there was no escape except a conflict, and yet in the end a formula has been found which averts the impending catastrophe.'

The Turkish delegates at Lausanne had one great advantage, which Rumbold saw from the outset. 'In the last resort', he explained in his letter to Henderson, 'the Turks I am convinced will not shrink from the use of force, whilst the mere thought of hostilities is repugnant to Bonar Law's mind.' Henderson himself favoured a bold policy whenever difficulties arose. 'I fear trouble', he wrote to Rumbold, also on January 2, 'unless we make it quite clear to the Turks that we are going to make war if they won't give in. Can't we make it clear; send 10,000 men to Malta or something. I think it will be economy in the end.' Harington shared Henderson's belief; but he saw the difficulties more clearly. 'Whilst the Turk has produced an Army in being', he wrote to Rumbold from Constantinople on January 7, 'the late Government got rid of ours, and, at the same time, held on to all these commitments'. 'The nation wants peace so badly', Henderson admitted ruefully in a second letter to Rumbold on January 8, 'that neither it nor Bonar Law want to take even the slight risk of war which the preparation for war would entail. . . . If only we could convince the Turk in some unmistakable manner that we were really prepared to fight, I think he would see his way to give in. . . .'

Rumbold's method throughout the negotiations was, when difficulties threatened, to talk direct to Ismet. 'We came to an apparent deadlock about the Capitulations on Saturday last', he wrote to Henderson on January 9, 'but Ismet came to see me yesterday evening. . . . He got no change from me and I pointed out that there was a deadlock and that the Turks had slammed the door. I spoke very straight to him. . . .' To Lord Stamfordham two days later Rumbold expressed his conviction that, after seven and a half weeks of negotiations, 'I am inclined to think that we shall solve the still outstanding difficulties in some sort of a fashion.' Curzon had persuaded Ismet to agree to allow the Patriarchate to remain at Constantinople – 'a personal triumph' Rumbold told Stamfordham – even though it would lose all political influence, and have no special administrative privileges. The Turks, Rumbold added, had made 'heavy demands on our patience and good temper'. Ismet was not difficult to deal with, but the second Turkish delegate, Riza Nour,[1] 'has no pretensions to being a gentleman and easily loses his temper'.

On January 16 Rumbold wrote to Henderson of a 'great humiliation' that was about to take place. The British delegation had been invited to dine with the Turks. Rumbold explained the reasons for his distress:

I told Lord Curzon early in the Conference that I had never asked a Turk inside my house whilst I was at Constantinople. But the French have let us down. They and the Turks share the same hotel and began by asking the Turks to dinner. The Italians followed suit, with the result that Lord Curzon had to ask the Turks to the big dinner he gave last Saturday. This he did without consulting me, with the result that he is extremely vexed at having to dine with the Turks on Thursday, but there is no alternative, and thus we have the ridiculous spectacle of an exchange of hospitality with people with whom we are trying to make peace and with whom a rupture is possible. It is repugnant to me to think my wife may be taken in to dinner by a man like Riza Nour. It is very disgusting.

Henderson replied, on January 23, that he hoped 'that the food was good even if the humiliation was great'.

By the last week in January the Treaty was practically drafted. Rumbold was bitter at the repeated acceptance of Turkish demands by the French. 'It is a question with them', he wrote to Henderson on January 23, 'of peace at any price . . . a direct result of their idiotic venture in the Ruhr.'[2]

By January 28 the Treaty of Lausanne was completed. The allied powers planned to present it to the Turks on the following day. 'I do not believe that the Turks will sign', Rumbold wrote to his stepmother. If they did not sign, the conference would adjourn 'indefinitely'. He doubted whether anything more serious would happen. 'They can hardly want to go to war with the Allies', he added; and the Allies in their disunion, were certainly not going to make war on Turkey. The French were discontented with the Treaty, believing that it gave Britain what she wanted, but did not give France the economic benefits for which she had hoped, either in the form of Turkish compensation for pre-war bond holders, or

[1] Riza Nour. Born in Sinope in 1879. A doctor. Active in the Young Turk Revolution, 1908; exiled to Albania by the Sultan. Minister of Public Instruction in the Angora Government, 1920; he drafted the laws purifying the Turkish language, ending religious control of education, and abolishing the Sultanate. Negotiated the Soviet–Turkish Treaty of 1921. Minister of Foreign Affairs, 1923.

[2] In December 1922 Germany was declared in default of certain reparations payments (timber deliveries). On January 11, 1923, French troops, tanks and armoured cars occupied Essen; three days later they extended their occupation to the rest of the Ruhr. The Germans resisted by a General Strike. Over a hundred German civilians were killed by French troops, and 140,000 deported from the Ruhr. The French only withdrew in August 1925.

in the form of benefits for French firms with pre-war concessions or French schools and private institutions inside Turkey. On January 30, two days after the Treaty was completed to the satisfaction of both Curzon and Ismet, the French issued a statement to the Press, declaring that the Treaty as it stood formed only 'a basis of discussion' and no more. Ismet, angered by this disclaimer, broke off the negotiations, and returned to Turkey. Rumbold had little sympathy for the Turkish action. 'I have never run up against such a lot of pig-headed, stupid and irritating people in my life', he wrote to Henderson on January 30.

The failure of the Lausanne negotiators to reach agreement on the Treaty raised the question of Britain's future position at Constantinople. 'In our opinion', Rumbold wrote to Henderson on January 30, 'it would be political disaster to leave Constantinople under Turkish pressure.' There must be no bowing to threats; British soldiers must be protected and Britain's position kept secure. 'We would welcome a little display of energy', Rumbold added. In a telegram a few days earlier, dealing with the murder of two British soldiers, Harington had 'foreshadowed drastic action'. But, Rumbold commented to Henderson, 'all he appears to have done was to raid a café and disarm three Turks and an Armenian. This did not strike us as a very far-reaching measure.' Rumbold expressed his fear that both General Harington and Admiral Brock 'had got cold feet'. This, he added, was also Curzon's opinion.

Nevile Henderson still advocated a serious show of force. 'The quickest way to get peace', he wrote to Rumbold on January 30 from Constantinople, 'is to show the Turks that we really are ready to go to war. Arguments and reasoning mean nothing to them, but the certainty that England, however reluctantly, is prepared to fight them again would convince them they must sign.' But not all the British officials felt likewise. Admiral Brock, Henderson continued was 'one of the most convinced advocates of the "Clear-out-of-Constantinople" party. Even Harington believed that as soon as the Lausanne Conference failed, all British forces should leave the city, and take up a defensive position at Gallipoli. Rumbold was shaken by Harington's suggestion, and in a telegram to Henderson deplored any such weakness. Henderson hastened to defend the General. 'He has been inspecting, during the past three weeks, every unit of the force here', Henderson wrote on February 2, 'and is much more convinced than he was that if an emergency arises it will give a very good account of itself'; but on military grounds the British position was 'an unsound one', which, in Henderson's view, was made even less sound by 'the fact that one could not count upon the French in such an emergency'. Harington's aim in withdrawing all British troops to

Gallipoli was, Henderson explained, 'that by going to Gallipoli he would have room to take his coat off for serious business and get the elbow room which is lacking here'.

Rumbold returned to England. After ten weeks of negotiation, he welcomed the two months' leave that was now due to him, and made plans to go as soon as possible to the South of France. On his first weekend back in England he went to Westgate-on-Sea with his wife and children. But on February 10 his holiday was interrupted. Sir Eyre Crowe telegraphed to him from the Foreign Office: 'Telegrams of disquieting character have come from Henderson, and Curzon is not happy about situation at C. He thinks it may be necessary to ask you to return to your post at once for duration of present crisis and will be obliged if you will come up first thing on Monday morning.' The Nationalists, anxious to control the City, seemed unwilling to wait until the Lausanne Conference reconvened.

Rumbold returned to London. Henderson's telegrams left little doubt that the Turks might try to seize Constantinople. After only six days in England, Rumbold set off once more for Turkey, which he had hoped never to see again. 'It's an awful bore having to go back to Constantinople', he wrote to his daughter Constantia on February 13, 'but it can't be helped and we must hope that we shan't have to be away for long for these wretched Turks must make up their minds in the next few weeks whether they want peace or war.' Rumbold reached Constantinople on February 19. 'There is a deserted looking appearance about this place', he wrote to his daughter the following day. 'It seems more squalid than ever.' The political crisis seemed to have passed. The new Nationalist Representative in the city, Adnan Bey,[1] waited for Rumbold to call on him. But Rumbold decided that the Kemalist ought to come to the British Embassy first. 'So I sat tight', he wrote to Curzon on February 27, 'and he came to heel in due course.' 'These matters,' he explained, 'count for a lot in this part of the world.' Unfortunately, Rumbold added, both Pellé and Maissa[2], Garroni's deputy, had 'compromised the position' of the Allies by

---

[1] Abdulhak Adnan Bey, 1882–1955. Born in Gallipoli; studied medicine at Constantinople and Berlin. Member of the Medical Faculty, Constantinople University, 1908–18. Member of the Ottoman Parliament, 1918. Joined Mustafa Kemal in Anatolia, 1919. Minister of National Health and Social Welfare in the first National Assembly at Angora, 1920. Minister of the Interior, 1920–21. Kemalist Representative, Constantinople, 1922. Lived in England and France, 1926–39. While abroad he translated (1935) Bertrand Russell's *The Outline of Philosophy*, and published *La Science chez les Turcs Ottomans* (Paris, 1939). Returned to Turkey in 1940, after Atatürk's death. Took the surname 'Adivar'. He published *Science and Religion Through History* (1944) and *Stop and Think* (1950).

[2] Felice Maissa, born 1850. Entered the Italian Consular Service, 1871. Consul-General, Teheran, 1896–1905. Served in Constantinople as Acting High Commissioner, 1920–21.

going to see Adnan before he had called on them. 'Maissa', Rumbold complained, 'is likely to be even more accommodating to the Turks than Garroni.' The future was uncertain, as Rumbold wrote to Lord Newton on February 27:

It is impossible to say what the fanatics and wildmen at Angora will do. They have got a wonderful treaty and if they were wise they would accept it at once, but the Turk is an extraordinary fool and often seems incapable of seeing which way his bread is buttered. I fancy a great struggle is going on at Angora at the present moment. No authentic news comes through and we are dependent on reports in the local press and on the telegrams which the French Agent in Angora, who is the most gullible person in existence, sends to Pellé.

I cannot think that the Turks will go to war and I suppose they are weighing in the balance the advantage or disadvantage between agreeing to the few financial and economic concessions asked of them or losing the whole treaty and risking complete ruin by going to war. I am fairly optimistic myself and am not worried, but I am rather fed up with Turks and Greeks and should not be sorry to have a change of air and scene.

Rumbold believed that Mustafa Kemal – 'who is a real statesman' he wrote to Sir Reginald Wingate on February 27 – would influence the Grand National Assembly in favour of moderation, and that the negotiations at Lausanne would be resumed. 'But the Turk', he added, 'is a past-master on the art of spinning out matters, and it may be several weeks, or even two months, before the final settlement is reached, even supposing we get a settlement.'

On February 27 Rumbold was received in audience by Abdul Mejid, the former Crown Prince who, after the abdication of the Sultan had been accepted as Caliph by the Nationalists. As Caliph he was the religious head of Turkey's Muslims; but the political authority of the Sultanate had passed to Angora. Kemal's representative in Constantinople, Adnan, was present throughout the audience. Abdul Mejid made a poor impression on Rumbold. 'His boots were deplorable', he wrote to his daughter on the following day, 'and his tie showed the collar stud.' Rumbold described his conversation with the Caliph in a letter to Curzon on March 1:

The Caliph received me cordially. He had grown a beard since I last saw him, the luxuriance of which testified to the efficacy of the prayers which I understand have been offered up in the mosques for its growth. His Majesty no longer had the smart and dapper appearance which characterised him when he was Crown Prince. His dress was somewhat slovenly and his boots were deplorable. An awkward silence reigned for several minutes, which I was eventually driven to break by enquiring after His Majesty's health. We then passed to banal topics, such as the weather and the view over the Bosphorus from the palace windows. I had to bear in mind that all allusion to political subjects must be strictly avoided, and it was evident to me that the Caliph was nervous lest any forbidden topic should be broached. The result was trying and even ludicrous. The brunt of the conversation fell on myself, and ranged over every conceivable subject except politics.

I enquired whether His Majesty had moved into the big palace, to which he replied in the affirmative, stating, however, that it was badly in need of repair. I asked whether His Majesty had composed any more music of late. The Caliph is devoted to music, and has written various compositions which have had more of a *succès d'estime* than a *succès de mérite*. He replied that he had not been able to devote much time to music lately, as he had been too busy. He made the same remark with regard to painting, for he has produced several large canvases in the past. I cannot believe that His Majesty's time is occupied with affairs of State, since he is now a figure-head, and so I could not help wondering whether the Nationalist Government discourages his artistic activities. His Majesty said that he still read a good deal and was in fact at this moment reading Mr. Morgenthau's[1] book.

We then spoke about the reconstruction of Stamboul and of the opportunity which the burnt-out quarters offered of building a really fine town. The Caliph seemed to think that the present capacities of the port would not suffice for the future development of commerce, to which he looked forward. I then asked him what was the state of the health of the town, where there has recently been an epidemic of smallpox. The Caliph replied that he thought matters were better. As far as he was himself concerned, he stated that his doctor had forced him to be vaccinated twice running, though His Majesty declared, with a burst of frankness, 'Je me fiche pas mal de ces choses-là.'

The question of vaccination led us somewhat naturally to the consideration of inoculation against various diseases, which enabled Adnan Bey, who till then had preserved an attitude of respectful humility, to take some part in the conversation in his capacity as a doctor. By an easy process we passed to the subject of Tut-ankh Amen's tomb and to the discussion as to whether it was justifiable to remove the mummy of the Pharaoh and exhibit it in a museum. The Caliph had no very definite ideas on this subject, but Adnan Bey informed us that there were mummies to be found in Asia Minor, as the practice of embalming was prevalent under the Seljucide dynasty. On hearing this the Caliph immediately said that specimens of these mummies ought to be brought to the Constantinople Museum.

[1] Henry Morgenthau, 1856–1946. Born in Germany. Emigrated to the United States, 1865. President, Central Realty Bond & Trust Company, 1899–1905. President, Henry Morgenthau Company, 1905–13. Chairman, Finance Committee of the Democratic National Committee, 1912 and 1916. United States Ambassador, Constantinople, 1913–16; in charge of the interests of Britain, France, Russia, Belgium, Serbia and other belligerents, 1914–16. Honorary knighthood, 1920. Chairman, League of Nations Commission for the Settlement of Greek Refugees, 1923. He published *Secrets of the Bosphorus* in 1918.

After another lengthy pause I enquired whether the Angora Government meant to introduce summer time this year. This matter has hitherto been decided by the High Commissioners, who feel now, however, that it is an internal concern of the Turkish Government. The Caliph at once said that he hoped that his Government would not introduce summer time, which he described as 'cette heure hypocrite'. In using the expression 'his Government', the Caliph made his first slip, and was afterwards careful to refer to 'the Government'.

I said that I was surprised that the Turkish Government, which seemed to wish to march in the vanguard of civilisation, as it had introduced the dry régime, should not also introduce summer time. With regard to the dry régime, I said that I had noticed that subjects of dry States seemed to me to drink more than anybody else when outside their States. The Caliph said that the introduction of prohibition was very necessary in the interest of the Anatolian peasant, who was addicted to drinking the vile spirits provided by the Greeks. This was the nearest approach His Majesty got to making a remark of an international character. As an afterthought, he observed, somewhat unctuously, that the drinking of wine was prohibited by the Moslem religion.

The audience had now lasted nearly an hour, and I felt that I had completely exhausted my powers of conversation. I waited patiently and in silence for some time for the Caliph to terminate the audience, but as he did not do so I took the initiative by saying that I asked to be excused from detaining His Majesty any longer.

The audience left a somewhat depressing impression on my mind. As Crown Prince the Caliph had struck me as an intelligent and versatile man deeply interested in politics, although his ideas were perhaps a little wild. He is now debarred from any intervention in the affairs of State. He cannot be regarded as a Pope; he is, in fact, a mere puppet, whose acts are carefully watched by the Nationalist Government. The side-tracking of an intelligent man and the shabby ceremonial of which he is the centre cannot fail to impress the observer somewhat painfully.

Throughout the first week of March the Grand National Assembly continued its discussion about the draft Treaty. 'All the ignorant gas-bags at Angora are having a run for their money', Rumbold wrote to Lancelot Oliphant on March 5. 'When you come to think of it, it does seem ridiculous that a small nation of seven millions or so inhabitants should be keeping the whole world on tenterhooks.' Four days later the Turks produced their proposals for a revised Treaty. Rumbold at once telegraphed the details to London. 'I am in hopes', he wrote to Oliphant on March 12, 'that the further discussions, which are inevitable, will begin by the end of the month, either here or at Lausanne.' A town in Italy or France, he warned, should be avoided.

The speed with which the Angora Assembly had produced its revisions impressed Rumbold, despite his earlier scathing remarks. Writing to Lord Stamfordham on March 13 he commented formally on both their speed and 'business-like form'. He no longer anticipated even the 'risk of war'; the Turkish Treaty could now be finalized, he believed, in a month or so of discussion. 'I am naturally keen to complete the work I did at Lausanne', he wrote to his stepmother on March 15, 'and to superintend the negotiations for the British Empire – if Curzon cannot superintend them himself.' Once the Treaty were signed he intended to 'go away and wash my hands of Turks, Greeks et hoc genus omne'. In the third week of March it was decided that the Conference would sit, as before, at Lausanne. Rumbold was chosen to head the British Empire delegation.

During his last month in Constantinople, Rumbold spent the time 'working off the Colleagues at a succession of meals', as he wrote to his daughter on March 28. He was appalled at the attitude which many of these 'Colleagues' adopted towards the Nationalist representative in the city. 'The way some of the foreign representatives fawn on Adnan is sickening', he wrote to Oliphant on March 26. 'The other day the Swedish Minister,[1] an oily and thoroughly untrustworthy person, gave a dinner in Adnan's honour. Our old friend Bristol was present and was sent in after Adnan. This did not however prevent him from competing with his host in licking Adnan's boots.' Such flattery, he was convinced, 'is very bad for the Turks', particularly when coming from Admiral Bristol. 'The Americans make one sick', he wrote to Oliphant on April 2. 'They talk big to one's face and pretend to help one and then go behind one's back. At the Conference they once or twice tried to get us to adopt certain suggestions of their own with regard to Minorities and the Armenian National Home. When I asked if they were prepared to press their suggestions themselves, they replied in the negative. As they had no standing on the green I refused to be their instrument.'

Rumbold prepared to leave Constantinople for the last time. He decided to travel by the Orient Express, on any day not chosen by the Turkish delegation. 'I have no intention', he wrote to Eyre Crowe on April 3, 'to travel with Ismet and his phalanx of wild men from Angora.' Among those who sent him advice before he left was one of the senior English administrators in Turkey, Sir Adam Block, who was convinced, as he wrote to Rumbold that same day, that the Turks 'realize they cannot now go to war. We have only to stand firm.'

Rumbold set off for Lausanne on April 19. 'We must really try and fix

[1] Gustav Oscar Wallenberg, 1863–1937. Captain, Swedish Naval Reserve, 1892. Entered Swedish Diplomatic Service, 1896. Minister to Tokyo, 1906–18; to Constantinople and Sofia, 1920–30.

up peace this time . . .', he wrote to Sir Percy Loraine[1] three days earlier, 'but the Nationalist Turk is a difficult man to deal with and the Turkish Delegation consists entirely of backwoodsmen who have no pretensions to being gentlemen and are entirely devoid of the courteous manner of the old-fashioned Turk.' The self-confidence of the Nationalists did not please him. 'An uppish oriental', he told Loraine, 'is an unpleasant animal.'

The reconvened Lausanne Conference opened on April 23. That morning, at Rumbold's suggestion, three Committees were set up. The first, over which he presided, dealt with all territorial and judicial questions. The second, presided over by General Pellé, dealt with financial and sanitary matters. The third, under the principal Italian negotiator, Montagna,[2] dealt with economic questions. Although Ismet accepted this procedure, within twenty-four hours Rumbold was telegraphing to Curzon about Ismet's 'obtuseness and obstinacy'. But forty-eight hours later, Ismet's attitude appeared to have changed. It had become, Rumbold informed Curzon on April 26, 'one of appeal rather than of intransigence', reflecting Turkey's 'extreme need for peace'. Within a week some progress seemed to have been made. The territorial points in dispute were reduced to two: the Italian insistence upon the island of Castellorizo, and the Turkish demand for the Thalweg of the Maritza river. 'I should like to give the Turks the Thalweg', Rumbold wrote to Curzon on April 28, 'in return for their consent to drop their demand for Castellorizo.' He believed that a Treaty acceptable to all would emerge within a few weeks. 'Of course the Turks are finicking and often very stupid, but they seem really keen to get a settlement this time. . . . Their army is no longer what it was, they are stony broke and in urgent need of peace.' Three days later Rumbold wrote to Henderson that 'Ismet is frightfully keen to get peace – and an early peace'. Ismet's keenness, he wrote to Lord Stamfordham on May 5, was 'the best guarantee of our success'.

The outstanding questions, Rumbold believed, were all capable of amicable settlement. These were, he telegraphed to Curzon on May 5, the judicial privileges for foreigners in Turkey, the sovereignty of Castellorizo, the currency in which the foreign bondholders were to be

---

[1] Percy Lyham Loraine, 1880–1961. Served as a 2nd Lieutenant in the South African War, 1900–1. Entered the Diplomatic Service as an Attaché at Constantinople, 1904. 12th Baronet, 1917. 1st Secretary, Warsaw, October 1919. Minister to Teheran, 1921–26; to Athens, 1926–29. High Commissioner for Egypt and the Sudan, 1929–33. Ambassador in Ankara, 1933–39; in Rome, 1939–40.

[2] Giulio Cesare Montagna, born 1874. Italian diplomat. Served in Madrid, London, Washington and Mexico. Worked in the Italian Foreign Ministry, with the rank of Minister, 1008–27. Italian delegate to the Lausanne Conference, 1923–24.

paid, and the liquidation of all allied acts in Turkey between 1918 and 1922. But each of the 160 Articles had to be argued out again, and, as before, the wishes, not only of France and Italy, but also of Serbia, Greece, Rumania, Bulgaria and Yugoslavia, taken into consideration. During the negotiations Rumbold found Ismet, as he told Curzon, 'intractable', 'impervious to all arguments', 'unbending'. Above all, Ismet was unwilling to make any special legal concessions to foreigners inside Turkey. The old privileged positions, such as those of foreign schools, would have to go. Rumbold understood the Turkish position, telegraphing to Curzon on May 17:

We are asking for extremely little, but the Turks do not want to commit themselves even to that little because their attitude towards foreign institutions, and especially schools, is based on extreme nationalism, and they view with implacable hostility the activity of schools which give a foreign or semi-foreign education to large numbers of native children.

During the following week Rumbold proposed a series of compromises, whereby the Turks would guarantee not to take punitive action against foreign schools, in return for the Allies agreeing not to start any new institutions. He also accepted the Turkish demand that foreigners inside Turkey should no longer have customs privileges. 'Only the French and Italians', he informed Curzon in his telegram of May 17, 'attached any importance to these immunities.'

Rumbold's work was made easier throughout the negotiations because British intelligence had succeeded in intercepting Ismet's instructions from Angora. He therefore knew at which point the Turkish delegation was instructed to break off negotiations. On July 18, when the Conference had ended, he explained to Oliphant that 'the information we obtained at the psychological moments from secret sources was invaluable to us, and put us in a position of a man who is playing Bridge and knows the cards in his adversary's hand'. Unfortunately, the complexity of the issues threatened, despite this advantage, to prolong the Conference into June, and the early hopes of a swift negotiation faded away. 'I have been doing my best all this time to hustle the Turks and my colleagues', Rumbold wrote to Curzon on May 19, 'and can honestly say that I am not responsible for what the "Times" of May 18th in its second leading article calls "Successful Procrastination". That article is both ill-informed and unfair.'

On May 21 Rumbold explained to Sir Adam Block in Constantinople that the delays, though vexatious, were no longer serious. 'The Committees of Experts', he wrote, 'to whom we refer articles or sections of the Treaty, after they have been thoroughly thrashed out in Committees, return in agreed texts, and have succeeded in turning some of the most awkward corners.' French and Italian 'obstinacy', he believed, was the main difficulty. Ismet was proving much more amenable, particularly as the Allies had persuaded the Greeks to allow Turkey to keep the Kara-gatch suburb of Adrianople, on the western bank of the Maritza river. 'It will give him something to take back with him', Rumbold explained to Henderson on May 22. This optimistic assertion was premature: 'I am doing everything in my power to get a move on', Rumbold telegraphed to Curzon on May 24, 'but causes of delay are beyond my control especially as I suspect that my French and Italian colleagues have not that authority with their governments which is necessary to make latter realize need for great expedition. In spite of my constant pressure coupled with his own efforts it took General Pellé several days even to get economic expert sent out. . . .' Montagna, he added, was in 'mortal terror' of Mussolini. Rumbold was not impressed by the Italian representative. 'The lack of dignity with which Signor Montagna conducted the proceedings', he telegraphed to Curzon on May 10, 'and which verged at times on buffoonery, produced a very unfavourable impression on General Pellé and myself.'

The question of legal safeguards for foreigners could not be resolved. 'Ismet was too irritating and tiresome for words this morning', Rumbold wrote to Henderson on May 29. 'He is afflicted with a dreadful cough and his deafness, added to his limited intelligence, makes it a work of almost superhuman difficulty to get him to understand any argument at all. . . . True to type, the Turks tried to go back yesterday on what they had agreed to on Saturday. There are times when I wish I could plunge the whole Turkish Delegation into the lake and have done with it.'

Ismet was worried about the genuineness of Britain's intention to remove all her forces from Turkish soil. On May 28 Nevile Henderson telegraphed to Curzon from Constantinople of 'a recrudescence here in press and generally, of theory that Great Britain means to retain her hold on Gallipoli and Straits.' Curzon sent Rumbold the text of this telegram, and at once assured Ismet that Britain intended to evacuate without delay once the Treaty were signed. But Turkish suspicions were deep; Britain had, after all, been the occupying power at Constantinople for over four and a half years. Rumbold advised Curzon to show generosity towards the Turks on the question of early evacuation. He had already warned him, on May 27, of what he believed was 'the danger of mad intransigence at Angora overriding Ismet's strong desire for peace'. When, on May 28, Ismet asked for a decision on the return of Turkish naval and military property, Rumbold at once sought Curzon's authority to offer to return 'anything now in occupied territory', arms, ammunition, ships and installations. Curzon agreed, and Ismet was appeased. But each day brought further problems, as much of personality as of policy. Rumbold was continually assuring Ismet, as he told Curzon in his telegram of May 28, 'that Turks had no grounds for depression or anxiety'. But the Turks were convinced that Britain would not give up the Gallipoli Peninsula, and Rumbold did not always find it easy to remain patient in the face of fears which he had insisted were unfounded. 'At a private meeting with the Turks last Saturday', he wrote to Henderson on June 5, 'I let off steam and unburdened myself of some home truths which I had long contemplated telling the Turks.' Too often he told them, 'their methods were "those of the bazaar".'

But Rumbold understood Ismet's difficulties. 'He is between the hammer and the anvil', he explained to General Harington on June 5, 'and it must be dreadful to have to serve such an ignorant crowd as those at Angora. Although Ismet is the pick of a very moderate bunch of Turks, he is always trying it on himself and one sometimes has great difficulty in keeping one's temper with him.' At one private meeting Rumbold told Ismet that it was 'quite obvious to us that he was being hunted by his own Government', and suggested that he should tell the authorities at Angora 'to keep quiet'. On another occasion, having, as he explained to Henderson on June 12, 'put the wind up the Turks', he noticed that Ismet's hand 'was quite damp'. 'The whole Turkish delegation', he added, 'are afraid of the noose whichever way matters go here. The real villains of the peace are at Angora. . . .'

A week later deadlock was reached. 'There is no work going on at all . . .', Rumbold wrote to Sir Eyre Crowe on June 19. 'We have for the moment exhausted our power of negotiation.' The problem was that of the Turkish Debt to the foreign bondholders. The French wanted the Turks to pay the bondholders in gold. The Turks declined. 'A war on behalf of bondholders', Rumbold wrote to Henderson that day, 'is not a very attractive proposition', particularly as the majority of the bond-holders were French. 'Both French and Turks are quite intransigent on the subject', he added, 'and I have exhausted my energy and ingenuity in trying to effect a compromise between the two. The French seem almost ready to push the matter to the point of presenting an ultimatum to the Turks. . . .' Rumbold wanted the French to accept francs instead of gold. 'I know it is humiliating to give way to the Turks', he wrote in his letter to Crowe, 'but if we are not going to use force, we must make the best bargain we can.' He ended his letter to Crowe on a personal note. 'I hope you do not imagine', he wrote, 'that we are enjoying ourselves here.

Everybody is sick to death of the Conference. I have naturally rather a good temper and plenty of patience, but both will be ruined shortly if this goes on much longer.'

The Debt question lingered on. 'We are very despondent here', Rumbold wrote to Sir Harry Lamb on June 20. 'Both sides have dug themselves in . . . and the Conference has reached the state of trench warfare. . . . I have not been able to extract anything from the Foreign Office for four or five days and I am getting very restive. The Marquess[1] complicates the situation by going away for week-ends.' Even during the week Curzon, in London, was unable to give Lausanne his full attention, for the Ruhr crisis took up most of the Cabinet's time. 'I feel very aggrieved', Rumbold told Lamb, 'and think we are not getting the attention we deserve; and yet it cannot be in anybody's interests that this wretched Conference should be prolonged a day longer than necessary.' The Debt question could not be resolved. 'I dream of bondholders nowadays', he wrote to Sir Adam Block on June 26. 'The other night I dreamt that I had succeeded in getting an enormous dividend for them, but as dreams go by contraries this means that they will get nothing at all.' The Turks, he believed, had put up 'a good fight', but would accept some compromise with the French, rather than risk a new war.

Rumbold was able to make progress towards agreement at a private meeting with Ismet, on the evening of June 22. The two men discussed the Treaty clause by clause. Rumbold insisted that there could be no discussion of the evacuation of allied troops until all other questions had been settled, but he assured Ismet that the Turks 'had no reason to doubt the intentions of the allied Governments'. The question of evacuation, Rumbold declared, 'would be settled in accordance with the Turkish point of view'. Thus put at his ease, Ismet agreed to make substantial concessions on several other disputed points. In order to secure a final settlement of the Graeco-Turkish boundary in Thrace, Rumbold proposed that, in addition to the Maritza river being made the frontier between Greece and Turkey, there should also be a zone of 30 kilometres on both sides of it, in which neither side would place troops or fortifications. This proposal convinced Ismet that the frontier would be secure against sudden Greek attack. He also accepted Rumbold's proposal for an International Commission to delineate the demilitarized zone.[2] But during the next five days Turkish intransigence again threatened to bring the negotiations to a halt. The Turks were reluctant to recognize either the pre-war debts owed to

---

[1] One of Curzon's Foreign Office nicknames; he was also known as 'Pomposo Furioso'.

[2] The International Commission included by Colonel Cornwall, who spent two years, from 1923 to 1925, demarcating the frontiers.

foreign companies, or the special concessions demanded by foreign firms trading or working in Turkey. At a second private meeting, held late on the evening of June 29, Rumbold was blunt in his criticisms of the Turkish attitude, telegraphing to Curzon, at nearly two in the morning, that he had told Ismet:

Delay was entirely due to Turkish government. I did not blame him so much as I did his government.

Ismet of course protested against this but I said that situation was as I had described it. I impressed on him that debt and concession questions were linked together and that we must insist on solution of both. I asked him whether if a solution were found for debt question he was empowered to settle concession question here. He replied categorically in the affirmative.

When, four days later, the Turks issued a public statement deploring the delay in reaching a decision on outstanding questions, Rumbold was incensed. At a further private meeting with Ismet on the evening of July 3, he spoke his mind without restraint, telegraphing to Curzon that night:

I protested vehemently against his action. I said that I had spared no effort to accelerate the settlement of outstanding questions and that it was intolerable that we should be accused of dilatoriness on the ground that we had not accepted, lying down, Turkish view of how they should be settled. Angora government showed clearly that they had no idea of compromise. He himself had transformed jurists formula into something totally inacceptable. Even at earlier stage I had warned him that in discussing it I had gone beyond instructions of His Majesty's Government and could not pledge them to it. It was not until a few days ago that he had told me that he could discuss concessions questions at all. As for evacuation I had always told him, and I now repeated, that while ready to discuss this at same sitting as the other two questions, it must come last in order. I said that his action in publishing note without previous reference to allied delegates was incorrect and would compel us to reply at once showing up its inaccuracies. My observations to him were of the most forcible description.

But the stumbling-block in the first week of July was not Turkish demands, but the French insistence on receiving gold payments for the Turkish pre-war debt. The Turks threatened to return to Angora if the Allies insisted on gold. Rumbold urged Curzon not to support the French in their policy, which might well lead, he telegraphed on July 4, to a renewed Turkish attack against the allied forces in Constantinople and at Chanak. In his telegram, Rumbold warned of the dangers of giving way to the French:

Monsieur Poincaré dismisses possibility of Turkish resistance so lightly or appreciates its consequences so imperfectly that when asked whether he will in

certain eventualities send reinforcements to Constantinople he says that this is
the last thing anyone wishes. This amounts to saying that if above consequences
ensue he expects British to bear almost the entire brunt of the danger at
Constantinople and Chanak. Bulk of allied forces in that area are ours, we alone,
thanks to the French attitude in the past, have any forces at all on the Asiatic
side of the Straits. In these circumstances I cannot see how French can ask us to
pull chestnuts out of the fire for bond-holders, majority of whom are French
citizens and who would themselves gain nothing unless and until we had in-
flicted fresh and crushing defeat on Turkey. I cannot see either, though this is
a question for you rather than for me, how we could justify to British public
opinion rupture of Conference involving so much uncertainty and danger.

Rumbold suggested to Curzon that if Poincaré could be persuaded to
accept payment in francs instead of gold, Ismet would accept. Curzon
accepted Rumbold's suggestion, and began direct negotiations with
Paris.

'I don't want to be an optimist', Rumbold had written to Henderson on
June 26, 'as the Turk has a habit of going back on his assurances, but the
Conference cannot drag on much longer . . .' To his daughter he wrote the
following day: 'I am making desperate efforts to finish these tiresome
negotiations.'

At the beginning of July Curzon agreed to press Poincaré to accept
Rumbold's proposed compromise about the Debt. 'The French are
isolated in this question', Rumbold wrote to Henderson on July 3, 'and the
sense of the Conference is against them and with us.' A further dispute
with France arose over the question of evacuation. Poincaré instructed
Pellé to refuse to evacuate allied troops until the Treaty had been ratified
by the Grand National Assembly at Angora. Rumbold supported Ismet's
appeal that evacuation should begin as soon as the Treaty were signed.
French policy, he had explained in his telegram to Curzon on July 4, was
'both dangerous and unpractical'. If the French insisted on this proposal,
he added, it 'might even wreck conference'. Montagna supported Rumbold in his protest, and the French gave way. Two days later, on July 6,
they also agreed not to insist on their Debt payments being in gold. The
Turks were delighted; 'more arrogant', Rumbold wrote to Henderson,
two days later, 'than I have ever seen them. Their attitude in fact was that
of victors talking to the vanquished.' This new attitude made Rumbold
more appreciative of the French position. 'I banged on the table', he told
Henderson, 'and told the Turks that their attitude disgusted me.' 'There
was a regular row', he explained to his daughter, 'which cleared the air, for
Ismet & Co. were like lambs yesterday.' 'It is too soon to say peace is
assured', Rumbold telegraphed to Curzon on July 9, 'but I no longer have

any serious anxiety about it.' On Sunday, July 10, Rumbold decided to take advantage of the more conciliatory atmosphere. 'I insisted upon continuing the discussions at 11 at night', he wrote to Curzon three days later, 'and when we separated at a little past 1 on Monday morning, it was pretty clear that peace was at last in sight.'

The last dispute had concerned British oil claims in southern Anatolia. Rumbold wanted the Turks to pay compensation for mining rights which had been granted to a private British company before 1914. For nearly two weeks Ismet had refused to confirm the company's rights, Rumbold, having argued with him in vain, finally agreed to let the Turks deal with the British company however they wished. On July 17, he telegraphed to Curzon that, this concession having been made, the Treaty would now be signed. Curzon was furious, informing Rumbold that he had made a quite unnecessary and shameful surrender. On July 19, in a 120-line telegram, Rumbold defended what he had done. The Turks, he told Curzon, had received secret instructions from Angora 'to break rather than yield'. Had he allowed a break to take place, not only France and Italy, but, he added, a considerable section of world opinion 'would have accused His Majesty's Government of destroying certainty of peace for the sake of British oil interests'. Surely, Rumbold protested, nothing could have been further from Curzon's interests 'than that rupture should take place on an exclusively British question' which was certainly of 'secondary importance'. The issue had been made more complex, he explained, by rival American claims to prospect for oil, and the United States delegation, led by Joseph Grew, had sided with the Turks against the British. To have brought the negotiations to a halt, Rumbold insisted, would have committed the British Government 'to open and unpleasant dispute with United States Government', which Curzon, surely, could not wish. 'Before resigning myself to this failure', Rumbold went on, 'I sought for ten days by pressure and persuasion to make Turkish representative yield but every day up to the end his attitude had been hardening owing to receipt of increasingly stringent instructions from Angora. . . . I deeply regret that after three months' arduous negotiations in the course of which you have more than once been good enough to express appreciation of my proceedings, I should have failed to obtain your approval on the last remaining question which stood in the way of peace.'

The final bargaining took place on July 16. From five in the afternoon until two the following morning the remaining details in dispute were successively settled. 'Ismet seemed incapable of understanding the simplest point', Rumbold wrote to Henderson on July 17, 'and the extraction of a concession from him was like pulling out an old molar.'

In a 341-line telegram to Curzon sent after the all-night session was over, Rumbold informed Curzon that a 'spirit of conciliatoriness' had characterized the proceedings. The Debt and evacuation questions no longer contained any disputed points of principle. 'It was agreed', Rumbold telegraphed, 'that the jurists should busy themselves with such drafting amendments as are necessary in the various texts' and that meetings of the three committees should be arranged at once 'to record the final agreements on all points remaining to be settled finally in the conference before the treaty can be printed for signature.' His telegram concluded:

These proceedings closed at 1.30 a.m. this morning. We had been working at high pressure since an early hour on Saturday afternoon, and most of the delegates were reduced to a state of extreme physical exhaustion. This was all the greater as our labours were conducted in an atmosphere of stifling heat. It so happened that the two days also coincided with an annual regatta and fair which were held under the windows of the building in which we meet. To some it appeared that the Near Eastern Peace Conference had assumed the position of one of the gloomier side-shows to the fair. From our own point of view it was extremely trying to have to carry on conversations so laborious and important to the accompaniment in our immediate neighbourhood of merry-go-rounds, dancing, shooting practice and the clash of varied music.

Nearly four months of complex negotiations were over. 'None of us pretend that the Treaty is a glorious instrument', Rumbold told Henderson in his letter of July 10. 'It is nothing of the kind, but as we had to make bricks without straw it has been the best we could do.' 'We ought to have gone for the Turks at the time of the Chanak business', he wrote in exasperation on July 23 to his friend John Baird,[1] 'and bombed Angora with all its gasbags.'

The Treaty of Lausanne was signed on July 24. 'It is a great achievement to have overcome at last the Turkish mistrust and obstructiveness', Nevile Henderson wrote from Yenikeui that day. 'Even if the Peace of Lausanne is not a perfect peace it is at least a stage of which this part of the world stood in sore need. . . . The great relief that peace affords is quite likely to give the mentality of the Turks a new turn. Many of their acts hitherto have been inspired by a mistrust which during the past three years has had time to grow deep roots.'

Rumbold set off for London. 'Not only as Prime Minister', wrote

[1] John Lawrence Baird, 1874–1941. Attaché, Cairo, 1898. Served in the Public Works Department, Egypt, 1900–2. Conservative MP, 1910–25. Succeeded his father as 2nd Baronet, 1920. Minister of Transport, 1922–24. Created Baron Stonehaven, 1925. Governor-General of Australia, 1925–30. Chairman of the Conservative Party Organization, 1931–36. Created Viscount, 1938.

Stanley Baldwin[1] on July 25, 'but also as an old schoolfellow at Hawtrey's I send you a line of welcome on your return home, to express my warm appreciation of the infinite patience you have shewn and the great skill you have displayed in an impossible position.' Even Curzon was mollified by the final result: 'You have indeed earned all our gratitude', he wrote that same day, 'by your patience, good temper, perseverance and unfailing resource.'

[1] Stanley Baldwin, 1867–1947. Conservative MP, 1908–37. Chancellor of the Exchequer, 1922–23. Three times Prime Minister: 1923–24, 1924–29 and 1935–37. Created Earl, 1937.

15

Madrid

1924–1928

Britain's first Labour Government was formed on 22 January 1924, with Ramsay MacDonald as both Prime Minister and Foreign Secretary. Eleven days later, on February 2, he wrote to Rumbold to inform him that he had been appointed Ambassador to Spain, with a salary of £2,500 a year, and an allowance of £3,500. The decision to send Rumbold to Madrid had come from Lord Curzon, who had written on January 22 of how he would watch Rumbold's career 'with an almost paternal interest' and to whom that winter, Rumbold had confided his hopes of being sent to Spain. During his leave he had visited his tea estate in Ceylon; it was six months since he had left Lausanne. 'I should think it would be a very gratifying change', Joseph Grew wrote from Washington, where he had just become Assistant Secretary of State, on April 30, 'after your strenuous experiences with the Turks, both in Constantinople and Lausanne, and all of us, no matter how keen we may be for the fray, must welcome an occasional interlude.'

The Spain to which Rumbold returned, after sixteen years, had undergone great changes. Although King Alfonso and his Court maintained all the trappings of their pre-war elegance, the post-war years had seen a series of political crises, which had turned many Spaniards against democratic government. The attempt to establish full administrative control in the Spanish Zone of Morocco had resulted, since 1909, in a growing military expenditure, continual loss of life, and, since 1918, increasing international disapproval. In September 1923 democracy had been overthrown, and Primo de Rivera,[1] who was both a General and a Marquis, had seized effective power, ruling through a Military Directorate and controlling both Parliament and the King.

[1] Miguel Primo de Rivera, Marquis de Estella, 1870–1930. Lieutenant of Infantry, 1893; served in Morocco, 1893–95, Cuba, 1895–96 and the Philippines, 1897. Governor of Cadiz, 1915; relieved of his office for advocating the acquisition of Gibraltar in return for a Spanish port in North Africa. General, 1916. Senator for Cadiz, 1921. Captain-General of Catalonia, 1923. Seized power on September 12, 1923, when he suspended the constitution and established a Directorate of army and navy officers. Dissolved the Directorate, December 3, 1925, and became Prime Minister. Resigned, January 1930; died in Paris, March 1930.

Rumbold was not greatly impressed by Primo de Rivera's regime. 'Spain', he wrote to his successor at Constantinople, Ronald Lindsay,[1] 'reminds me of someone in a passage in "Alice in Wonderland" which says that there was jam yesterday and there will be jam tomorrow, especially tomorrow, but never any jam today.' The social life of the Embassy reflected that of the Court: 'A lot of Spaniards', Rumbold wrote to his daughter on March 2, 'mostly Dukes, have called. . . .' At the end of March when both Austen Chamberlain and Princess Beatrice,[2] made private visits to Madrid, he was entertaining continually. 'I had the Princess on my hands', he wrote to his daughter on March 23, 'from 10.50 am till nearly 3 pm.' At lunch, fortunately, 'everything – table, servants etc – awfully smart & food & drink A.1'. There was one aspect of Spanish life in which Rumbold could not join. George V had forbidden any British Ambassador in Madrid to attend a bullfight. As a result, Lady Rumbold and Constantia went without him, as the guests of Primo de Rivera.

During Austen Chamberlain's visit, King Alfonso had expressed his belief that the members of the Directorate 'were not very competent as Ministers' and that within six months power would revert to the Assembly, whose loyalty to the Crown would be undiminished. Alfonso insisted that Spain was 'booming', and was, he put it, 'a good horse to back'. Rumbold reported these optimistic assertions to Ramsay MacDonald on March 27. 'As for the work', he had written to Nevile Henderson a month earlier, on February 29, 'it is a flea-bite and much of it commercial'. 'My work here is 80% commercial', he reiterated to Admiral de Robeck on April 4, 'and I do not pretend that it interests me to anything like the extent that it did at any of my previous posts.' To Joseph Grew he wrote three days later that the Madrid embassy was 'in some ways rather a cul-de-sac and there are practically no high politics to deal with'. But, he added, 'perhaps this is just as well as one needs an easy time occasionally'. Rumbold's friends shared this last belief. 'You really wanted a quieter post', Mrs Barton wrote from Geneva on April 29, 'after all the strenuous overwork of the others. Your nerves couldn't have stood another onslaught . . .' On

---

[1] Ronald Charles Lindsay, 1877–1945. 5th son of the 26th Earl of Crawford. Entered Diplomatic Service, 1898. Knighted, 1925. Ambassador, Constantinople, 1925–26; Berlin, 1926–28. Permanent Under-Secretary of State, Foreign Office, 1928–30. Ambassador, Washington, 1930–39.

[2] Princess Beatrice, 1857–1944. Youngest daughter of Queen Victoria, and wife of Henry, Prince of Battenberg; their daughter Ena married King Alfonso XIII in 1906. Rumbold's brother William wrote to him on March 28, 1924: 'I expect old Princess Beatrice was a bit heavy in the hand before you managed to spill some of your best wine down her throat.'

Easter Sunday Mrs Barton had been in Berne. 'I wandered in faithful thought to the grave of your child', she wrote, '& stretched out across much distance a hand to you. . . .'

Rumbold's daughter Constantia was with him in Madrid on her eighteenth birthday. 'I gave her a pearl necklace', he wrote to his stepmother on May 2, 'as I look on her 18th birthday as a sort of coming of age.' 'I hope you will get to know plenty of British Pepitos etc so that you should have a good time when you go about', Rumbold wrote to her on June 14, when she was back in England; 'You are quite the nicest lamb that ever was. . . .' Rumbold's son Tony was in England, at Hawtrey's, preparing for the Eton scholarship exam. 'He will have to put his shoulder to the wheel', Rumbold had written to his stepmother on May 2. 'I shall not be disappointed if he doesn't get it, though being a very ambitious boy he would feel failure acutely, having so far succeeded in everything he set out to do.' In June, Rumbold's son won his scholarship; 'a success', Rumbold wrote to his stepmother on June 17, 'that wildly exceeded our wildest hopes. It shows that the boy is remarkably intelligent, with a capacity for expressing his intelligence. . . . At the bottom of his heart was the determination to play up for his school and to be a credit to the family.'

During June, Rumbold received two private letters from the British Consul-General in Barcelona, Philip Sarell,[1] warning of the dangers of Primo de Rivera's policy towards the Catalans. 'The Directorate seem quite unable to understand', Sarell wrote on June 13, 'that, in these days, people easily suffer from nerves; and that sentimental considerations have an overwhelming importance in politics.' The Catalan clergy and lawyers against whose freedom of speech Primo de Rivera had struck were, Sarell commented, 'two classes who, of all others, are dangerous to disturb'. If only the Directorate would make allowance 'for local sentiment', he added, 'the whole of the tension could be relaxed'. Separatism needed to be humoured, not crushed; but he feared that the Civil Governor, General Lossada,[2] had ' "separatismo" on the brain; and, instead of trying to relieve the strain by making minor concessions . . . he thinks he can carry through a kind of policy of "Thorough".' In his second letter, sent from Barcelona a week later, Sarrell stressed that General Lossada 'has really got the Catalan on the brain'. The Directorate's severity had

---

[1] Philip Charles Sarell, 1866–1942. Entered Consular Service, 1883. British Consul at Dunkirk, 1908–18. Consul-General, Tunis, 1920–23; Barcelona, 1923–26.

[2] Don Carlos de Lossada y Canterac, born 1871. General de Division. Military Historian. Civil Governor of Catalonia, September 1923–October 1924. Military Governor of Algeciras, 1925.

created an 'undercurrent of resentment', which it would not be easy to erase.[1]

Rumbold returned to England at the end of June, delighted to be with his children at the height of summer. In July he went to Eton, to unveil the War Memorial in the Chapel to the eighty boys killed during the war, among them his relative by marriage, Jack Wingfield.[2] During the holiday they visited the British Empire Exhibition at Wembley, where they examined the mock-up of the British naval attack on Zeebrugge of 1918, and visited the Amusement Park. 'I had to go down the giant racer', Rumbold wrote to his stepmother on August 15, 'an hair-raising experience which I don't want to repeat, as well as "Over the Falls" a process in which one loses all vestiges of dignity.' In August he returned to Spain, motoring with his son through Rouen, Tours, Angoulême and Biarritz. 'We saw a lot of Cathedrals', he told his stepmother, 'sampled many hotels and generally enjoyed ourselves.' On the journey he was angered to read in the newspapers that Ramsay MacDonald had resumed trade relations with Soviet Russia. 'It is exasperating', he wrote to his stepmother, 'to think that those disgusting Bolsheviks should have even the appearance of having got the better of us.'

During the autumn the Spanish military situation in Morocco grew steadily worse. 'Owing to the censorship', Rumbold wrote to his stepmother on September 9, 'it is difficult to know what the public think of it all. One thing, however, is certain and that is that the Spaniards are bewildered by the unending stream of communiques and proclamations issued by the Directorate. They infer that things must be far from well to necessitate such frequent pronouncements.'

Throughout the late summer and early autumn Rumbold was at Zarauz, a small village on the Bay of Biscay, sixteen miles west of San Sebastian. There was much golf, tennis and bathing. Three times a week he went into San Sebastian, where the British Embassy had its offices. 'Work is very light', he wrote to Nevile Henderson on September 18, 'what more can one want?' But on September 25, his son's first day at Eton, he wrote to his stepmother that without his son the house was dull, and that a 'mournful wind is whistling round the house as I write'.

---

[1] In September 1924 Primo de Rivera replaced General Lossada by a seventy-year-old General of Catalan origin, General Milans del Bosch. This change, Sarell wrote to Rumbold on September 24, 'must point to a general modification of policy'. But throughout 1926 the Minister of the Interior, General Martinez Anido, enhanced his reputation as the 'strong man' of Primo de Rivera's Cabinet by his drastic measures to suppress terrorism in Barcelona; Rumbold reported this development to King George V on December 16, 1926.

[2] Cecil John Talbot Rhys Wingfield, 1881–1915. Captain, King's Royal Rifle Corps. Died of wounds received in action, April 29, 1915. His brother Charles Wingfield had married Lady Rumbold's sister in 1905.

22   Rumbold with Lord Curzon, Lausanne, 1923.

23 Lord Curzon and his wife at Lausanne.

24 A caricature
of Rumbold
drawn during
the Lausanne
Conference by
Kelen.

25 Rumbold with General
Primo de Rivera in
Madrid, after
Rumbold had
presented his
credentials as
Ambassador to
Spain, 1924.

26   Rumbold in Berlin, 1933.

27   Rumbold and his wife on board his launch on the Wannsee, Berlin.

28   Rumbold takes the Duke and Duchess of York to visit Potsdam, 1928.

29   Adolf Hitler, orator. A sequence of six photographs, sold in Berlin as postcards, 1933. This is Rumbold's daughter's set.

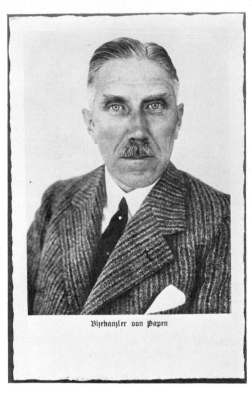

Vizekanzler von Papen

Reichsminister
Dr. Josef Goebbels

30   Von Papen, in 1933
Vice-Chancellor in Hitler's
Cabinet. A contemporary postcard.

31   Dr Goebbels, Minister of
Enlightenment and Propaganda
in Hitler's Cabinet, 1933.

32   Herman Göring, Minister for Air in Hitler's Cabinet, 1933.

Reichsminister
Hermann Göring

On November 3, 1924, Ramsay MacDonald resigned, and on the following day Stanley Baldwin formed his second Conservative Administration. Austen Chamberlain became Foreign Secretary. Rumbold rejoiced at the change, for one of Baldwin's first acts was to refuse to ratify MacDonald's Anglo-Russian trade treaty. 'The Government', Rumbold wrote to his stepmother on November 25, 'seem to me to have handled the Russian question well. The Bolos can whistle for our money.' On December 2 Rumbold saw King Alfonso, who expressed his pleasure at the change in Government in England. The situation in Spain was an uneasy one; a distinguished Spanish writer, Blasco Ibañez,[1] had written a book about the King which was, Rumbold wrote to Austen Chamberlain on December 2, 'a most scurrilous production'. Equally serious, Rumbold had noticed 'a certain amount of uneasiness in business and other circles here. . . . Whilst it is true that rich Spaniards always tend to invest a portion of their savings abroad – at the present moment mostly in dollar securities – there has of late been an increase in such investments.'

Throughout November and December the Spanish position in Morocco had worsened. Primo de Rivera decided upon a policy of gradual withdrawal from the interior. Over 4,000 Spanish troops were killed in two months. Only strict Press censorship kept the extent of the losses from the public 'The Moroccan question', Rumbold wrote to his stepmother on November 20, 'is like a cancer in the life of the country.' On December 6 Rumbold wrote to George V that King Alfonso had 'taken the Moroccan campaign very much to heart. He goes nowhere nor does he allow the Queen to go even to the theatre.' Lord Stamfordham replied on December 30 that in England 'it would not be an exaggeration to say that there is an uneasy apprehension as to the political future of Spain'. But Rumbold was not prepared to forecast any sudden worsening of the situation. 'I have noticed', he replied to Stamfordham a month later, on 30 January 1925, 'certain similarities between this post and my last post in Constantinople. At both posts I have over and over again been told that a crisis is boiling up and that things cannot go on much longer without a crash. But nothing happens and life goes on just as it did before. I have therefore become quite sceptical of crises and do not believe more than five per cent of what I hear.' Rumbold wrote to Philip Sarell on February 10 that he believed Primo de Rivera would bring, 'a certain measure of stability' to Spain; but Lord Stamfordham, writing from Buckingham Palace on February 16,

[1] Vincente Blasco Ibañez, 1867–1928. Novelist and publicist. Founded a republican ournal, *El Pueblo* at Valencia, 1891. Exiled for supporting the Cuban nationalists, 1896. Elected to the Cortes, 1901. His novel, *The Four Horsemen of the Apocalypse*, was made into a film with Rudolph Valentino in 1916. Published several attacks on the monarchy between 1918 and 1923. Exiled by Primo de Rivera, 1923. He died at Menton, in the south of France.

told Rumbold of a conversation with 'a fairly senior member of our Diplomatic Corps' who, he wrote, 'knows Spain and the Spaniards and, in his opinion, political catastrophe was sooner or later inevitable!' This was also Sarell's opinion. On March 31 he warned Rumbold of 'an under-current of Republicanism' in Barcelona which, 'however negligible at the moment, cannot safely be altogether ignored'.

Early in February King Alfonso had suggested to Rumbold that Primo de Rivera, Mussolini and Baldwin ought to call an anti-Bolshevik con-ference. Rumbold was convinced that such a conference could only stimulate anti-monarchist feeling, and, on his own initiative, he deprecated Alfonso's plan. 'I am very glad you choked off the King's suggestion', Austen Chamberlain wrote on February 18. 'It is just the kind of thing which would make a great stir without achieving any useful result.'

Three months later Primo de Rivera appealed to Rumbold for the return of Gibraltar to Spain. He was prepared, he said, to give Britain the Moroccan port of Ceuta in exchange. In a private letter to Austen Chamberlain on May 22, Rumbold outlined Primo de Rivera's arguments:

He said that Gibraltar had an immense sentimental value for the Spaniards, in that it formed part of their peninsula. It was out-of-date as a fortress as it was commanded from the mainland. We had difficulty in supplying it adequately with water. He recognised, of course, that we had spent many millions of money there but we should find Ceuta a far more satisfactory place from every point of view. He pointed out what a wonderful effect the proposed exchange would have on Anglo-Spanish relations. Foreign powers would have nothing to say. Germany was out of action, Italy would be favourable to such an exchange and, as for France, he could not see why she should mix herself up in an arrangement come to between our two countries.

Rumbold pointed out that in May 1924 Ramsay MacDonald had refused to contemplate any bargain over Gibraltar. 'I said', he wrote to Austen Chamberlain in his letter of May 22, 'that I did not think that any British Government would or could give up Gibraltar. It had a great sentimental value for us also but, apart from that, I could not conceive any British Government embarking on the fresh responsibilities which the acquisition of Ceuta would involve.' Primo de Rivera was insistent. He was, he said, quite prepared to go to London to discuss the problem per-sonally with Austen Chamberlain. 'I told him', Rumbold explained, 'that, in my opinion, there was not the slightest chance of your entertaining this proposal.' Chamberlain approved of Rumbold's initiative, and asked Rumbold to inform Primo de Rivera – which he did on June 2 – that 'no British Government at the present time could take this proposed exchange into consideration as a matter of practical politics'.

The British rejection of any bargain over Gibraltar did not prevent Austen Chamberlain from sending Primo de Rivera a friendly message of sympathy for the Spanish difficulties in Morocco. Rumbold welcomed this move, writing to Chamberlain on June 6 that for this renewed Moroccan campaign Primo de Rivera 'has had to overcome a reluctance to sacrifice lives and money'. The Gibraltar rebuff was unfortunate. 'The General has a profound streak of vanity in his composition', Rumbold added, 'and I should not wonder if he has at times cherished the ambition or illusion of going down to history as the man who restored Gibraltar to Spain.' Primo de Rivera did not give up hope. On June 12 he wrote to Rumbold that if 'one day' Britain was willing to discuss the Gibraltar question, Spain herself would be willing to 'prepare opinion in England by means of a big Press campaign, which would not be difficult as I am sure that it would be favourably received'. Primo de Rivera also sent Rumbold 'some old notes of mine' about Gibraltar, in which he declared that for Spain 'the recovery of Gibraltar by friendly methods is essential to her spiritual life', whereas 'very few millions of pounds would make of Ceuta and its surrounding country one of England's most powerful and commodious possessions'.[1]

During the spring and summer of 1925 the Catalans grew restless at Primo de Rivera's failure to grant them the smallest measure of autonomy. In June the police discovered a plot by Catalan separatists to blow up the train in which King Alfonso and Queen Ena would be travelling to Barcelona. Rumbold sent an account of the plot to George V on June 18. Queen Ena, he wrote, had commented 'somewhat bitterly' that it looked to her 'as if She and the King might have had to pay for General Primo de Rivera's policy towards Cataluña'. Philip Sarell, who had been present during the royal visit to Barcelona, had already written pessimistically to Rumbold about the situation, on June 3. King Alfonso, he wrote, was 'very correct and gracious' during the visit, 'but his usual debonnair manner, and smiles, were quite absent'. During the various official ceremonies Sarell thought that Alfonso was 'listless, not to say discouraged; and out of sympathy with the whole proceedings'.

Early in July Rumbold returned to England on leave. In August he went to Marienbad, in Czechoslovakia, his wife and daughter being 'much run down by the London season', as he wrote to his stepmother on August 21. The cure at Marienbad was effective. 'I have taken off about a stone', he

[1] Primo de Rivera was not alone in wanting to annex Gibraltar. In August 1926 King Alfonso told the British Military Attaché in Spain, Major Torr, that very considerable oilfields would soon be discovered in Spain, and that when this happened he would consider 'offering these to the British Admiralty in return for Gibraltar'. Rumbold informed Austen Chamberlain of this royal proposal in a 'Private & Personal' letter on September 10, 1926.

wrote, 'and feel uncommonly light and empty.' The former Austro-Hungarian spa had lost only a little of its social magnetism despite the war, and its incorporation in the new Czechoslovak state. 'Lord Glanely[1] – the racing man – arrived 10 day's ago. . . . Sir Alfred Mond[2] & his wife came about a week ago. I just know them. He is very intelligent but is an awful Jew to look at. As such he fits into the picture here. . . . Albert Mensdorff is staying at Konigswart.' From Marienbad, Rumbold went for ten days to the Dolomites and for a further ten days to the Lido at Venice. On October 13, after his return to Madrid, he wrote to Lord Newton: 'Life on the Lido was a true picture of decadence, and it is not too much to say that seventy to eighty per cent of the people of different nationalities, whom I knew personally or by reputation, had tarnished pasts, irregular presents, and certainly doubtful futures.' Two years later, in a letter to his son, he recalled that Venice had been 'an unhealthy snipemarsh with plenty of rotten birds sheltering in it'.

During September, a series of victories in Morocco strengthened Primo de Rivera's political and military position. 'There is nothing to prevent the Directorate remaining in power for years', Rumbold wrote to his step-mother on October 14, 'for they have the army behind them and there is little, if any, public opinion in Spain.' He believed there was a marked contrast between the suppression of democracy in Spain, and Fascist action in Italy, where, he wrote, 'Mussolini appears to be exceeding all bounds'. He and the Fascists, he added, 'are surely laying up trouble for themselves as every tyranny whether it is Fascismo or Bolshevism inevitably leads to a reaction which is greater or less according to the degree of the tyranny'.

On the frontier between Greece and Bulgaria, 1,500 miles east of Madrid, an outbreak of violence in October threatened to precipitate a Graeco-Bulgarian war. Following the shooting of a Greek sentry by a

---

[1] William James Tatem, 1868–1942. Went to sea as a boy. Later took a job in a shipping office. Shipowner. Chairman of several shipping companies, including the Atlantic Shipping & Trading Company and the Tatem Steam Navigation Company. A Director of the Great Western Railway Co. and Anglo-Ecuadorian Oilfields. One of the wealthiest men in Wales. Created Baronet, 1916; Baron Glanely, 1918. His racing interests were extensive; he won the Derby in 1919, the St Leger in 1930 and 1937, the Oaks in 1930 and the Two Thousand Guineas in 1934. In 1937 he gave £30,000 to charity. He was killed in an air raid.

[2] Alfred Moritz Mond, 1868–1930. Industrialist. Liberal MP, 1906–28. Created Baronet, 1910. First Commissioner of Works, 1916–21. Minister of Health, 1921–22. Chairman, Imperial Chemical Industries, and many other industrial companies. Chairman of the Economic Board for Palestine. Created Baron Melchett, 1928. He married Violet Goetze in 1894 (in 1920 she was created a Dame of the British Empire).

Bulgarian frontier guard, Greek troops had crossed the Bulgarian border and occupied a number of Bulgarian villages. Twelve Bulgarians were killed. Five days later the Greeks withdrew; but the atmosphere on the frontier remained one of suspicion and recrimination. At the League of Nations headquarters in Geneva the possibility of a new Balkan war created an immediate alarm. 'Frontier incidents', Austen Chamberlain told the League Council in Paris on October 27, 'might mean war.' The Council decided to send a special commission of inquiry to the Balkans to fix the responsibility for the incident, to assess what reparations or indemnities might be exacted, and to make suggestions for averting similar incidents in the future. On October 28 Austen Chamberlain telegraphed to Rumbold to ask if he would be willing to be Chairman of the Commission. Rumbold accepted at once. If the dispute could be settled without war, Miles Lampson[1] wrote to him from the Foreign Office on October 31, 'it will be a good step forward in enhancing the prestige of the League and be an effective warning to the Balkans not to embark in future on offensive operations so light-heartedly'. In his letter Lampson stressed that what Austen Chamberlain hoped for most was not so much 'the fixing of responsibility for what is now past', but rather the setting up of 'permanent measures of prevention'.

Rumbold left Madrid on November 5. On the following day, in Geneva, he took the Chair at the first meeting of the Commission.[2] On November 9 the Commissioners went to Belgrade, where the Yugoslav Foreign Minister, Ninčić,[3] assured them that Yugoslavia 'had adopted an attitude of complete impartiality with regard to the matter', and would not try to gain any territorial advantages as a result of the Graeco-Bulgarian tensions. Ninčić also pointed out that in the recurrent violence in Macedonia more deaths were being caused by Bulgarian Nationalists against their fellow Bulgarians, than against Serbs or Greeks.

From Belgrade the Commissioners proceeded to the village of Demir-

---

[1] Miles Wedderburn Lampson, 1880–1964. Entered Foreign Office, 1903. 2nd Secretary, Tokyo, 1908–10. High Commissioner in Siberia, 1920. Minister to China, 1926–33. Knighted, 1927. High Commissioner for Egypt and the Sudan, 1934–36; Ambassador in Cairo, 1936–46. Created Baron Killearn, 1943. Special Commissioner, South-East Asia, 1946–48.

[2] Rumbold's fellow Commissioners were General Ferrario (of Italy), General Serrigny (of France), Pieter Fortuyn (Burgomaster of Rotterdam) and Axel Adlercreutz (Swedish Minister at The Hague, and earlier the Swedish Observer at the Lausanne Conference).

[3] Momčilo Ninčić, 1876–1949. A Radical deputy in the Serb Parliament, 1912. Minister of Finance, 1915–19. Foreign Minister of Yugoslavia, 1922–26; he successfully improved relations with Italy. An opponent of the royal dictatorship set up in 1929. Recalled as Foreign Minister in 1941, in a vain attempt to avert an Italian invasion. Foreign Minister of the Yugoslav Government in Exile, London, 1941–43. In disagreement with Tito, he stayed in exile after the war, and died in Lausanne.

Hissar, on the Graeco-Bulgarian frontier, where the Greek sentry had been shot. For five days, from November 11 to 15, they talked to Greeks and Bulgarians in villages on both sides of the border. They then spent four days in Athens, followed by four days in Sofia, talking to senior ministers and army officers. 'I gained the impression', Rumbold wrote to Austen Chamberlain on December 1, 'that the Greeks are afraid of the Bulgarians.' The Bulgarians seemed delighted to find, only seven years after their defeat, that the League of Nations was not going to treat them as an 'enemy' power, but as a fully independent state. After talking at length to King Boris[1] of Bulgaria, Rumbold formed the impression, as he wrote to Chamberlain, that 'the Bulgarian Government now feel that they have one friend and that they have emerged from their isolation'.

The Commissioners returned to Belgrade on November 26, where, for two days, they worked on their Report. On November 28 it was ready. The frontier situation was a chaotic one, they reported, with sentry duty done by 'very young soldiers' who had received 'only a rudimentary military training'. Frontier duty being so unpopular, it was often entrusted to 'individuals of doubtful character'. The Bulgarian soldier who had killed the Greek sentry had been sent to the post 'as a result of an incident in which he had been involved at another post' six weeks before. After the shooting both sides had shown 'a desire to enter into pourparlers with a view to terminating the incident'. For several hours both the Bulgarian and Greek commanders in the field made 'every effort to stop the affray'. Unfortunately, one of the telegrams sent from the frontier zone to Athens had been altered in transmission. One sentence had read originally: 'Bulgarian forces *amount to* one battalion.' This became: 'The Bulgarians have *attacked with* one battalion.' The Greek High Command acted accordingly, ordering an immediate advance into Bulgaria.

The Bulgarians claimed damages of £79,000 for the period of the Greek occupation, during which time five soldiers and seven civilians had been killed. The Greeks counter-claimed for £142,000, to compensate the families of the Greeks who had been killed or wounded, and to pay for the costs of the transport and feeding of their troops. The Commissioners rejected the Greek claim, stating that Greece 'should make reparation to Bulgaria', and suggesting a sum of £16,000. But, they added, there was 'no question of premeditations on either side', nor did the Greeks have any intention to follow up the operation by any further intrusion into Bulgarian territory. The Commissioners refused to apportion blame. The

---

[1] Boris, 1894–1943. Succeeded his father as King of Bulgaria, October 1918. He authorized his Government to declare war on Britain, December 1941, but refused all German demands to declare war on Russia. He died shortly after a stormy interview with Hitler.

population of the area, Greek and Bulgar alike, had, they wrote, been worked upon for fifty years by 'contradictory propaganda' which had led them 'to distrust one another and to seek to do each other injury'. The sufferings of over two decades of war had, the Commissioners wrote, 'implanted feelings of hatred which cannot be expected to disappear quickly, in view of the fact that the means at the disposal of those at the head of the two countries are unfortunately too limited to allow them to devise and execute measures of relief and remedies on the large scale required'.

The Commissioners made several recommendations which they hoped would avert further incidents. Frontier duty, they believed, 'should be carried out by a special body made up of picked men recruited and trained for this work'. The signalling systems should be improved. At a political level, facilities should be improved to enable minority groups and refugees from past wars to return to their homelands, and to give them compensation for the value of the property which they could not take with them.

On November 28, in Belgrade, Rumbold and his fellow Commissioners presented their Report to representatives of the Greek and Bulgarian Governments. They then returned to Geneva to await developments. Nine days later, on December 7, the League of Nations Council met to consider the report. Rumbold represented his Commissioners during the discussions. The Greeks tried to reject the Report. The Bulgarians set out a detailed justification for their original reparation figure. On December 11 a special committee of the League Council met to discuss these differences, with Austen Chamberlain in the chair. Rumbold was again present at the discussions and spoke against paying Bulgaria more than half her claim. But when the Greek delegate on the committee, Constantinos Rentis,[1] challenged even the smaller figure, Rumbold spoke of what he had seen on the spot of Greek depredations. 'In one district which I visited', he insisted, 'all the pigs had been seized; there was not a single one left.' But Austen Chamberlain pointed out that the culprits need not necessarily have been Greeks, but might have been local thieves, or robber bands, with which the area was infested. Rumbold persisted with his assertion, on more general grounds, that the Greek arguments against paying repar-

---

[1] Constantinos Rentis, born 1884. Entered the Greek Diplomatic Service, 1910. Director of Political Affairs with the Greek Delegation to the Paris Peace Conference, 1919. Minister of Justice and Foreign Affairs, 1922–23. Minister of Foreign Affairs, 1924–25. Represented Greece at the League of Nations Assembly, 1925–26. Imprisoned by the Metaxas administration, 1938; escaped, 1944. Minister of the Interior and Justice, 1945–46. Minister of Foreign Affairs, 1946. Minister of Public Order, 1947. Minister of the Army, 1948. Minister of National Defence, 1950. Minister of the Interior, 1951.

ations could not be justified. The League Council met again on December 14. Austen Chamberlain spoke of the 'great thoroughness' with which Rumbold's Commission had done its work, and accepted its decision that Greece ought to pay Bulgaria a reparation of £16,000, but no more. All its other conclusions were likewise approved.

Rumbold returned to Spain, reaching Madrid on December 17. On the following day he sent his stepmother an account of the Geneva discussions. 'Everything went like clockwork', he wrote, 'and my Commission had, I believe, the unique experience of being publicly thanked at two public sittings of the Council of the League. The whole affair has been a great success for the League, whose officials were more than pleased with me.' As a result of what had been achieved, 'I left Geneva in the odour of sanctity'. The work had been tiring; 'I spent fifteen nights of thirty in November in the train', he wrote to Lord Newton on December 21. 'Moreover we had to work in the train and were fully stretched out in the Balkan capitals.' On December 18 he wrote to his stepmother from Madrid: 'I am now suffering from a reaction and find this place flat, stale and unprofitable.' Spanish politics, he added, seem 'very small beer after what I have been doing, and Spanish politicians are very uninteresting after the great ones of the earth with whom I have been consorting at Geneva. However, I suppose one will settle down again to the usual humdrum existence. The place is quiet enough at the best of times but it is now as dead as the traditional mutton.'

At the beginning of 1926, to the annoyance of many of his Conservative supporters, Primo de Rivera issued several decrees whereby landowners would have their estates revalued, and businesses would be obliged to declare the exact extent of their turnover and profits. On January 13 he explained to Rumbold the purpose of his measures. 'Our friends the grandees etc', Rumbold reported to Sir Maurice de Bunsen on February 8, 'are up in arms at the idea of being mulcted.' One of them, he reported, had declared to him with bitterness: 'We have not been through a Great War, so why should we be taxed like you in England? Moreover, if a Dictatorship – which may be considered Conservative in character – proposes to get increased taxation out of us, what will happen when a Radical Government comes in?' Rumbold was sceptical about Primo de Rivera's chances of gathering the new taxes. 'There is still plenty of corruption', he told de Bunsen, 'and people who ought to know better still do things which would make the average Englishman's hair stand on end.' Rumbold gave as an example one of the richest men in Spain, the

Count of Romanones,[1] who, he explained, 'recently imported a Rolls-Royce on which he managed to pay duty as on a Ford'. But Primo de Rivera did not intend to give in easily, being, Rumbold added, 'a genial person, always brimming over with optimism and with a great belief in his lucky star'. In his reply de Bunsen was sceptical about the future. 'Can we be sure', he wrote on February 18, 'that the Spanish people will not, some day, claim to be heard, & that they would not then seek a scapegoat whom they will regard as responsible for what must be a very heavy bill of costs? That would be a bad setback for the monarchical principal in Europe, if the King were made the scapegoat.'

Writing to George V on February 11, Rumbold outlined what he considered to be the most significant aspects of Primo de Rivera's rule. Although Press Censorship had been maintained, the General 'has not tried to stamp out the whole Opposition Press as has apparently been the case in Italy'. Moreover, the financial policy of the Directorate 'is likely to antagonize the wealthy classes and especially the great landowners'. Spain itself remained, he wrote, a 'pre-war society' which had 'maintained its purity of stock in a really remarkable manner – marriages with Americans and foreigners are very few and far between'.

The anti-monarchical feeling feared by de Bunsen was so strong in Catalonia that, as Rumbold wrote to Lord Stamfordham on April 9, King Alfonso would 'run a decided risk' if he visited Barcelona again. In an attempt to improve Alfonso's status in Spanish eyes, the Spanish Ambassador in London, Merry del Val,[2] had several times suggested a Spanish royal visit to England. Alfonso himself was anxious to receive in person an Honorary Degree which had just been conferred on him by Oxford University. But George V deprecated such a visit, principally because it would involve a return visit by himself to Spain. 'The King has a horror of these foreign visits', Austen Chamberlain wrote to Rumbold on April 23, 'and always replies to one that his Father made them and what was the result? His Father thought that they served the cause of peace; they had at any rate been followed by the Great War.' Chamberlain decided that King Alfonso should be invited to England on condition that the visit would be a private one which King George did not have to return. The reason given to Alfonso, which Rumbold had suggested, was that

---

[1] Alvaro de Figueroa y de Torres, Count of Romanones, 1863–1950. Three times Prime Minister of Spain, 1915, 1917 and 1918–19. Minister of Foreign Affairs in the last Cabinet under the Monarchy, February–April 1931. President of the Academy of Fine Arts.

[2] Alfonso de Merry del Val, 1864–1943. Entered the Spanish Diplomatic Service, 1882. Tutor in English to King Alfonso XIII, 1898–1902. Minister in Brussels, 1911–13. Ambassador to London, 1913–31. Awarded the Grand Cross of the Royal Victorian Order, 1918. Created Marquis, 1925.

George V could not leave England while the industrial situation was so tense, for at the end of April the coal-miners had gone on strike. 'I hear from the Conservatives', Rumbold wrote to his stepmother on May 2, 'that the owners are a stupid and stiff-necked body of men'; but the miners, he believed, would have to realize 'that industries which are not flourishing cannot pay uneconomic wages'. Workers in every industry supported the miners, and a general strike was threatened. 'Where', Rumbold asked, 'is the traditional commonsense and genius for compromise of our countrymen?' He feared that the British Communists would exploit the strike. 'If a few were shot', he added, 'it might clear the air.' The strike was eventually settled without bloodshed. In July King Alfonso's visit took place with little publicity and George V stayed in England as he had wished.

At the end of August Rumbold had an interview with Primo de Rivera in Madrid. The Dictator was worried by international opposition to his demand for the inclusion of Tangier–a Free City–within the Spanish Zone of Morocco. Britain had refused to support any extension of Spanish rule. Without British support, the chance of a peaceful annexation of Tangier was slight, for both Italy and France were determined to resist any change in the status of Tangier. Rumbold stressed these factors in his discussion. Primo de Rivera pleaded with him to try to enlist Austen Chamberlain's support. Such support, Rumbold insisted, was impossible. In a letter to Austen Chamberlain on August 26, he drew a direct parallel between Primo de Rivera's blatant demands for the incorporation of Tangier into Spain, and his increasingly dictatorial methods within Spain. 'Primo is a cunning rather than a clever man', Rumbold wrote in his letter to Chamberlain. 'I think that a man of real ability would not have treated his political opponents as he has been treating them but he is very persistent, and becomes more autocratic the longer his regime lasts.' Primo de Rivera had insisted upon an immediate decision over Tangier; failing such a decision, he declared, Spain would leave the League of Nations. This was an 'indecent manner' of conducting negotiations, Rumbold told Chamberlain, which in his opinion would not succeed in international affairs, any more than in domestic policy.

In a letter to Rumbold on August 30, Austen Chamberlain agreed that Primo de Rivera's diplomacy was 'about as bad as can be'; it was, he added, 'an ill return for our friendship and for the efforts we have made to help them, efforts which would have had a greater chance of success had Primo treated the delicate matters in question with more discretion and a greater reserve'. In his reply on September 10, Rumbold pointed out that Primo de Rivera's threat to withdraw from the League had been first suggested by King Alfonso. It was the King who had 'first started the game of blackmail' as early as March 1926. 'Whilst I am very sorry that the Spaniards have now definitely decided to leave the League', Rumbold added, 'I cannot help feeling rather glad that the Spanish blackmail did not succeed.'

King Alfonso's visit to Barcelona took place in October, and lasted for eleven days. In his Annual Report for 1926, sent to Austen Chamberlain on 9 March 1927, Rumbold recorded that the visit 'aroused no enthusiasm among the Catalans, and the public reception afforded to their Majesties seemed colder than on previous similar occasions'. There was a mood of violence growing in Spain. 'General Primo de Rivera', he wrote to George V on 16 December 1926, 'had been insulted again and again by adherents of the former regime in the hope that he might be goaded into fighting a duel.' Members of the British Embassy had been approached by leading Spaniards and told 'in a most open manner . . . of the necessity of eliminating General Primo de Rivera, even by violent means if necessary.' Political assassination, Rumbold noted, was a feature of Spanish political life, however amazing it might appear 'to the average Englishman'. On 13 January 1927, in a letter to Lord Stamfordham, Rumbold pointed out that in the previous year, within a period of ten weeks, 'there was an abortive conspiracy hatched at Valencia against the Government, insubordination in the Artillery Corps, a plot to fire on the train conveying the King and Queen of Spain to Paris and a futile attempt on Primo de Rivera's life at Barcelona'.

Other than recounting the most recent plot or scandal, there was little work to be done. On February 5, 1927, Rumbold reached his fifty-eighth birthday. On the following day he wrote to his stepmother: 'I am beginning to realise that I am no longer as young as I was. The golf course tells me that. It is 2000 feet above sea level and there is much walking up and down hill with the result that I feel jaded after the 14th hole and play badly.' But, he added proudly, 'I am the only man of my age who does the 18 holes regularly'. Several times in his letters from Spain he had written of the pleasures of retirement. When Philip Sarell retired from the Diplomatic Service Rumbold wrote to him, on 31 May 1926: 'I find that, as time goes on, there are more and more occasions on which I would like to be an entirely free agent without any master.' There was speculation about whether Rumbold would receive another Ambassadorial posting. In 1924, after the Lausanne Conference, there had been talk at the Foreign Office of sending him to Berlin as Lord D'Abernon's successor. Curzon had actually offered him the post, but after a few days the offer had been withdrawn. In 1926 the rumours of Berlin were renewed. But Rumbold felt that the Foreign Office would never agree to sending him to Germany, both because he had been Chargé d'Affaires there on the eve of war, and because of his having had to expose German ill-treatment of British prisoners of war in 1915 and 1916. In an undated letter of early 1927, Rumbold confided to his stepmother that he was disappointed at not going to Berlin when D'Abernon had retired in the previous October. 'Madrid', he wrote, 'is not very interesting politically and the work is small beer in comparison with what I have done in the past.' After four years in Spain, he felt, 'we should have completely exhausted society and the place'. Lord Hardinge had told a mutual friend that Rumbold might be sent to Paris, but, as Rumbold wrote, 'he can't know'.[1]

There was little sense of crisis in Madrid. 'It was all very gentle', Rumbold's First Secretary, Herbert Brooks,[2] later recalled. 'Everything was so slow. It was always "tomorrow". Many of the notes we sent in to the Spanish Foreign Ministry went unanswered. We were always trying to chase them up.' In the summer when the Embassy moved to San Sebastian, 'nothing ever happened. We used to go over to Biarritz to play golf. We had very little contact with Spaniards; they lived hugger-mugger and didn't much invite us into their homes. Since the Spaniards didn't entertain, they didn't get invited to the Embassy. Most of our entertainment was between diplomats.'

Throughout the autumn and winter of 1927 Rumbold watched to see how Primo de Rivera's dictatorship would develop. Early in October he sent Austen Chamberlain details of another revolutionary plot that had been foiled. At the end of October he protested about the Government's financial measures which, he wrote to Austen Chamberlain on October 21, seemed the result of Primo de Rivera's 'slapdash and amateurish' economic policies. 'His Government issue decrees without thinking of the economic consequences of their application', he wrote, 'and the result is that I receive more and more complaints from British Firms and Companies. . . .' In November Rumbold visited both the Free City of Tangier and the Spanish Zone of Morocco, together with his wife and daughter. 'I was much impressed with the type of Spanish military officers we met in the Zone', he wrote to Hugh Gurney on November 14. 'They were real live wires.' To Lord Stamfordham four days later he described his journey from Tetuan to the interior. He had been driven the fifty miles to

---

[1] Hardinge had retired from the Foreign Office in December 1922. He received no further public appointment. Lord Crewe was succeeded as Ambassador in Paris by Lord Tyrrell.
[2] Herbert William Brooks, 1890–   . Second son of the 2nd Baron Crawshaw. Entered the Diplomatic Service, 1913. Attaché, St Petersburg, 1913–18. 1st Secretary, Madrid, 1926–28. Resigned from the Diplomatic Service, 1928. Justice of the Peace, 1942–57. One of his three sons was killed in action in 1944.

Sheshuan – 'one of the most picturesque places I have ever seen' – and during the three and a half hour drive had come to realize, he wrote, the difficult nature of the terrain in which the Spanish Army had been fighting for nearly twenty years. 'There is something really sinister and hostile about the country', he explained, 'which is a tangle of mountains, and I consider it a real triumph for the Spaniards to have been able to pacify it. Not a shot has been fired in the Zone since July 11th....' To Austen Chamberlain, on the same day, he described the successful pacification of the Moroccan tribes as 'a personal triumph for Primo'.

During the first weeks of 1928 Rumbold and his staff prepared the Annual Report on the events in Spain during the previous year. In fifty-five printed pages, the Report touched on every aspect of Spanish official policy. In the political section, which he had written himself, Rumbold pointed out that there was no 'league' of Mediterranean dictatorships, and that Primo de Rivera's dictatorship, thorough though it was, did not meet with the approval of his fellow-dictator, Mussolini, who was constantly complaining that the Spanish Press censorship was too lax, and that Italy was being criticized too often. Primo de Rivera, Rumbold noted, had 'never fully trusted the Italians' and that for as long as he remained in power 'it would be impossible for Spain to base her policy upon an accord or alliance with Italy'. Originally Primo de Rivera had intended to hand over power, after a year or so, to a parliamentary system. But the pacification of Morocco had taken longer than he had envisaged, and the transfer of power had never taken place. 'There is no reason', Rumbold wrote, 'why the present Government should not continue indefinitely in office and thus establish a record for stability.' Primo de Rivera's administration had already lasted longer than that of any Spanish Government since 1885. The General himself, Rumbold wrote, was 'quite remarkable for a Spaniard, for procrastination seems abhorrent to him, and he has a driving power which is seldom found in this country.... One source of his strength is that he has always played up to the Church, and has neglected no opportunity of extolling the women of Spain. He knows his own countrymen very thoroughly, and does not trust them very far.' Rumbold had been impressed by the Dictator's energy. 'In spite of nearly four and a half years strenuous activity', he wrote, 'his capacity for work seems undiminished. He is very strong constitutionally and can do with little sleep.' Although King Alfonso had 'felt irritation ... at having his hand forced in matters where his judgement was opposed to that of his Prime Minister', he had nevertheless, Rumbold reported, recognized 'the services which his Prime Minister has rendered to Spain, and makes the best of the dictatorial regime'.

It was Primo de Rivera's policy towards Catalonia that would be the test, Rumbold believed, of the success or failure of his regime. The separatist movement was not based, in Rumbold's opinion, on real grievances. Only 'small bodies of extremists', he wrote, aimed at complete separation from Spain; they were 'insignificant in numbers and composed of Communists, anarchists and other social ruffians who would always be enemies of society under any regime'. Rumbold saw Primo de Rivera's Government as a guarantee of peace in Catalonia. 'If, however, the present Government fell from office', he wrote in the Annual Report, 'or the reins of power passed into the hands of a weak Government, the Catalan problem might very easily be revived in an acute form.'

Rumbold sent his Annual Report to London on February 17; it reached the Foreign Office a week later, on February 24. While it was in transit, Austen Chamberlain was making arrangements for a comprehensive movement of Ambassadors, to follow Lord Crewe's[1] departure from Paris. Rumbold hoped to be chosen as Crewe's successor, but his hopes were disappointed. The post went instead to his old enemy, Tyrrell, the Permanent Under-Secretary of State for Foreign Affairs. Rumbold and his wife accepted this news, he wrote to his stepmother on February 24, 'with as much philosophy as we can'. Of the senior Embassies, Washington and Berlin remained to be filled. 'We should hate the former', he wrote; which left only Berlin as a possible posting. On February 25 Austen Chamberlain telegraphed, offering him the Berlin Embassy. 'I welcome the opportunity of being in the scrum once more', Rumbold wrote to Sir Ronald Lindsay, his predecessor in Berlin, on March 24, 'for this post – very pleasant as it is in many ways – is rather a backwater'. He was also glad to be leaving Madrid for financial reasons. 'I recently saw official statistics', he told Lindsay, 'showing that Madrid was the next most expensive town after Philadelphia. . . . This place has cost me about £2000 a year over and above salary and allowances.' To Sir Maurice de Bunsen he wrote on the same day: 'Of course we should have preferred Paris to Berlin from almost every point of view, but the latter post is bound to be very interesting and to become more so as time goes on, what with Reparations and the increasingly insistent demands for the evacuation of the Rhineland. . . .' Rumbold's friends and colleagues all realized the importance of Berlin, and congratulated him on his appointment. On April 16 Lord Stamfordham wrote from Windsor Castle: 'Berlin will be

---

[1] Robert Offley Ashburton Crew-Milnes, 1858–1945. Lord-Lieutenant of Ireland, 1892–95. Secretary of State for India, 19010–15. Created Marquess of Crewe, 1911. Lord President of the Council, 1915–16. President of the Board of Education, 1916. Ambassador to Paris, 1922–28. Secretary of State for War, 1931.

of absorbing interest and more especially now that the recuperation of Germany is proceeding with such rapidity.'

Rumbold's final three months in Madrid were crowded with official functions and farewells. 'We have had 3 dinner parties running', he wrote to his stepmother on April 11. His son and daughter were both in Madrid for these 'hectic days' mixing, as Rumbold wrote, 'with the great ones of the earth'.[1] Towards the end of April Rumbold, his wife and children went to French Morocco, driving 1,500 miles and visiting Rabat, Casablanca, Mazagan, Marrakesh, Meknes and Fez. 'Marrakesh', he wrote to his stepmother on April 30, 'would make an ideal spot for an honeymoon'. The only unpleasant incident in the whole trip, he wrote, was on the road between Fez and Tangier 'where we were given tripe to eat. Not knowing what it was and being hungry, we tackled it, only to push away our plates in disgust.'

During May Rumbold made his final preparations for moving to Berlin. 'I shall miss the sun here . . .', he wrote in reply to a letter of congratulation from Frank Savery in Warsaw, 'as also our various friends. Society at Berlin will be very different – in fact, somebody advised me the other day to learn Yiddish.'

---

[1] Among the guests at the Embassy had been Sir Roger Keyes (the hero of the Zeebrugge raid of 1918), Rudyard Kipling, and Primo de Rivera himself.

16

Berlin

1928–1933

As soon as Rumbold's transfer to Berlin was known he received a large number of congratulatory letters. However much he had wanted to go to Paris, his friends believed he would find his greatest challenge in Berlin. David Chapman,[1] who had been Director of the Egyptian Ministry of the Interior thirty years earlier, when Rumbold was in Cairo, wrote on March 1: 'Of course a Republic does not produce such pleasant society as an old established monarchy and I should personally prefer to rub shoulders with the Spaniard than with the Hun – but for your job what an interesting milieu & moment!'

On his arrival in Berlin on August 3, Rumbold was met by the Counsellor of Embassy, Harold Nicolson, who, on the following day, sent a description of the event to his wife.[2] 'The train came in', wrote Nicolson, '& old Rumby bundled out rather embarrassed with an attaché case in one hand & in the other a novel by John Galsworthy.[3] I introduced him to the German Representatives & to the Staff while the crowd gaped & gaped & the policemen stood at the salute. . . . Rumby was confused. "Never", he said, "have I felt so odd." You see, last time the poor man was in Berlin was exactly fourteen years to the day almost – i.e. August 4 1914 – when he was Counsellor & crept out of Berlin under cavalry escort & amid the booings of a crowd. It is odd thus to return.' Nicolson's conclusion, that evening, was: 'He is a nice old bumble bee.' On September 18 Nicolson sent his wife some further impressions of the Rumbolds. 'They are really so appallingly English that it is almost funny . . . as English as eggs and bacon.' Lady Rumbold, he wrote, 'is a handsome woman, & looks dis-

---

[1] David Phelips Chapman, 1855–1939. Entered Army, 1874; retired with the rank of Major, 1891. Director-General, Repression of Slave Trade, Egypt, 1892–1900. Director, Ministry of the Interior, Egypt, 1900–2, when he retired. Inspector of Recruiting, War Office, 1914–15, with the rank of Colonel. His only son was killed in action in 1916.

[2] Vita Sackville-West, 1892–1962. Novelist and poetess. Daughter of the 3rd Baron Sackville. She married Harold Nicolson in 1913. Companion of Honour, 1948.

[3] John Galsworthy, 1867–1933. Novelist and playwright. He published his first novel in 1898; the *Forsyte Saga* in 1922. He was awarded the Order of Merit in 1929 and the Nobel Prize for Literature in 1932. 'We had Galsworthy to lunch a few days' ago', Rumbold wrote to his son on June 23, 1930. 'A nice man with no frills on him. I am told that he is not read as much as he used to be either in England or Germany.'

tinguished in a sort of county family way'. His conclusion, after six weeks, was: 'One can't help liking them. But from a distance. And rather coldly.'

Rumbold found the German democracy easier to work with than the Spanish dictatorship, and was soon on friendly terms with Gustav Stresemann,[1] whose successful attempts to have Germany's grievance taken seriously by her former enemies had done much to reduce the tensions and suspicions of the post-war decade. By 1928 Germany's reparations payments had been much reduced. The allied occupation of the Rhineland was clearly going to be ended within a few years. The Weimar Republic had achieved a respectability and stability which had seemed impossible at the time of the Kaiser's abdication and the social upheavals of the year of defeat. But there were many problems and prejudices waiting to be exploited. One was the dominance of Jews in many professions, and their prominence in the city. 'I am appalled', Rumbold wrote to Sir Ronald Lindsay on October 3, 'by the number of Jews in this place. One cannot get away from them. I am thinking of having a ham-bone amulet made "to keep off the evil nose", but I am afraid that even that would not be a deterrent.' There were 172,672 Jews in Berlin at the census of 1925, out of a total population of 4,024,165. Rumbold could not shake this fact out of his mind. 'We have settled down here and are quite happy', he wrote to Victor Cavendish-Bentinck on November 30, 1928. 'The only fly in the ointment is the number of Jews in the place. One cannot get away from them.'

For her husband's sake Lady Rumbold was delighted at the change from Madrid. 'H is up to his eyes in work', she wrote to her mother on September 23. 'He is like a War-horse on the ramp, and quite in his element again.' When he had been in Berlin for nearly two months, Rumbold sent George V an account of his impressions. On the afternoon after his arrival, he wrote, 'I took a walk through those parts of the town where, in pre-war days, militarism had been most in evidence. . . . One might have been in a totally different town. . . . In the course of my walk I literally only saw half a dozen soldiers. . . . They struck me as undersized and rather unhealthy-looking.' During his first week in Berlin he had visited several restaurants to 'study the crowd'. Again he had been amazed by the contrast with 1914. 'The noisy self-assertiveness and bumptiousness of the

---

[1] Gustav Stresemann, 1878–1929. Born in Berlin, Secretary to the Dresden League of Industrialists, 1903; founder of the German–American Economic Association, 1913. A Reichstag Deputy from 1907 and leader of the National Liberal Party; throughout the First World War he was a leading advocate of the policy of territorial annexation. Founded the German People's Party, 1919. Chancellor of the Reich and Foreign Minister, August–November 1923. Foreign Minister from November 1923 until his death.

pre-war German', he informed the King, 'had completely disappeared. The people seemed quiet and even silent and it was quite clear that they had been thoroughly chastened.' But Rumbold was reluctant to deduce from his observations that there had been any 'change of heart'. Although, he wrote, 'the bulk of Germans have no use for militarism', because it had failed, he felt that they were 'far too great a nation to be content with a subordinate position in Europe and, unless I am mistaken, they mean to have, and will attain, the leading place in Europe, though by economic means'.

The political situation seemed conducive to social reform and the consolidation of democracy. The central Government was a 'Grand Coalition' made up of Ministers from the Social Democrat, Centre, Democratic and Peoples' Parties. The Chancellor, Hermann Müller,[1] was a Social Democrat, once an opponent of heavy naval expenditure, and one of the two German signatories of the Versailles Treaty. 'Herr Müller', Rumbold told the King in his letter of October 24, 'makes a good impression. He is simple and quite ready to talk on political subjects.' The pomp and arrogance of pre-war Germany had, he felt, disappeared. 'One or two Germans of the old regime . . . have called on us', he informed the King, 'but the bulk of the Germans of that category appear to live on their estates in the country and only occasionally come to Berlin for a day or so.'

On October 14 Ramsay MacDonald, who had known Müller for over thirty years, visited Berlin. On October 15 he addressed the Reichstag, the first foreign statesman ever to do so and spoke of the need to build a lasting peace. That evening he dined at the British Embassy. Among the German guests Rumbold had invited Albert Einstein;[2] among the English, Oswald Mosley.[3] Lady Rumbold wrote to her mother on October 16, 'Ramsay

---

[1] Hermann Müller, 1876–1931. Editor of the Socialist Newspaper *Görlitzer Volkszeitung*, 1899–1906. Member of the Council of the German Social Democratic Party from 1906. Member of the Reichstag from 1916 until his death. Minister for Foreign Affairs, June 1919–March 1920. Chairman of the Social Democrat Party in the Reichstag from 1921. Chancellor of the Reich, March–June 1921 and May 1928–March 1930.

[2] Albert Einstein, 1879–1955. Born in Württemberg. Became a Swiss citizen, 1901. Discoverer and exponent of the Theory of Relativity, 1905. Professor of Physics, University of Berlin, 1914–15. Became a German citizen, 1914. Awarded the Nobel Prize for Physics, 1921. Renounced his German citizenship, 1933. Emigrated to the United States, 1933.

[3] Oswald Ernald Mosley, 1896–   . Served with 16th Lancers and the Royal Flying Corps on the Western Front, 1916–18. Conservative Unionist MP, 1918–22; Independent MP, 1922–24. Labour MP, 1924 and 1926–31. Succeeded his father as 2nd Baronet, 1928. Chancellor of the Duchy of Lancaster in the second Labour Government, 1929–30. Founded the newspaper *Action*, 1932. Formed his own Party, the British Union of Fascists (Blackshirts), 1933. Imprisoned under Regulation 18B, 1940. After 1945, took up residence in France. In 1920 he married Lord Curzon's daughter, Lady Cynthia Curzon.

MacDonald himself is a most attractive individual, so good-looking and "distingué".'

On November 6 Rumbold was 'at home' to the diplomatic corps. Over six hundred guests had been invited to the Embassy. 'Lots of gold plate', Lady Rumbold wrote to her mother on the following day, 'and bright pink carnations, and *delicious* buffet of elegant cakes, and canapes. . . .' The guests were met outside the dining-room by 'an impressive being in cocked-hat, black and silver livery, great silver chain and huge "baton", who stood facing the entrance and striking the floor loudly whenever someone arrived.' On November 8, when he was himself the guest at a reception in the Siamese Embassy, Rumbold was delighted to find that the Siamese Ambassador[1] was an Old Etonian. During his first months in Berlin, he had to call on forty-two Ambassadors and Ministers. 'Poor H', Lady Rumbold wrote to her mother on November 9, 'who really has much work of importance, is *frantic* at having to call by appointment on all these folk.'

'The Germans', Rumbold wrote to Lord Stamfordham on November 15, 'were remarkably friendly to Englishmen both official and unofficial. We are asked to go places to which Frenchmen would certainly not be asked'. At the beginning of November he had spent two hours with Gustav Stresemann, who had made himself 'more pleasant than words can say'. But Rumbold warned Lord Stamfordham that Stresemann seemed 'a very bad colour', and was quite exhausted. 'It would be a disaster', Rumbold added, if Stresemann broke down. Germany, he believed, 'needs two men, i.e. Hindenburg and Stresemann, for the next four or five years, by which time the reparations problem will presumably have been settled, the Rhineland evacuated, and Germany have definitely turned the corner.'

Rumbold believed that diplomacy could solve these questions before the grievances they created led to an increase of militarism. But he was under no illusions about the possible growth of the German Army, despite the restrictions laid down in the Versailles Treaty. On 3 January 1929, he informed the Foreign Office, in a 'secret' letter to Lindsay, that according to the Military Attaché, Colonel Cornwall, the existing German Army 'contained the nucleus of a very formidable fighting organization'. Rumbold doubted that there had been any 'flagrant' breach of the Versailles Treaty, but he went on to list several 'definite infractions' of the Treaty

---

[1] His Serene Highness Prince Vipulya Svativongs Svatikul, 1885–1940. Educated at the Princes' School, Bangkok; St Andrew's Preparatory School, Tunbridge Wells; Eton College and University College, Oxford. Joined the Siamese Foreign Ministry, 1909. Minister at Copenhagen, 1924–28. Minister at Berlin, June 1928–October 1929.

which Cornwall had reported after having been present at the autumn
manoeuvres in Lower Silesia. 'In defiance of Article 160 of the Treaty',
Rumbold told Lindsay, 'subsidiary formations such as cavalry brigades and
cyclist battalions were freely employed at manoeuvres'.

Colonel Cornwall had reported specific violations of the Treaty of
Versailles; but the overall ability of the German troops had not made an
entirely favourable impression on him. 'Their tactical methods and
standard of training', he wrote in his Report on the manoeuvres, 'seemed
to me elementary and backward. I am at a loss to explain this, it is not
what I expected. Undoubtedly the German army will lose very heavily
in the first battle of their next war as they did in their last one.' However,
he concluded: 'This does not detract from the fact that the Reichswehr
contains the nucleus of a very formidable fighting organization.' When
Rumbold had discussed the German Army with Stresemann himself on
28 December 1928, the Foreign Minister had protested vigorously that it
could not conceivably be regarded as 'a formidable instrument of war'.
But Cornwall was persistent in his quest for hidden military facts. At
manoeuvres he had seen a motor truck with canvas screens around it,
designed to simulate a tank. With this machine were conducted 'tank'
practice, and 'tank' operations. While visiting Stockholm – for he was
also Military Attaché to Sweden – he found German engineers working
at the leading munitions factory. Scrutinizing the German Press, he found
obituary notices of German pilots and tank officers accidentally killed in
Russia; although their names had been removed from the German Army
list, it was obvious that they had not been mere tourists, for no such
tourism existed. In addition to his own enquiries, he obtained further
information from the American and Swedish Military Attachés, Major
Berggren[1] and Colonel Carpenter,[2] both of whom were alarmed at
the skilful deployment of the small, but potentially strong, German
forces.

During the first four months of 1929 the British and French Governments tried to find an acceptable figure for a final German reparations
payment. Their efforts were made more difficult by Stresemann's continuing illness, and by Hermann Müller's increasing political isolation. On
March 11, Rumbold wrote to the Embassy's Financial Adviser, Ernest

[1] Gustaf Berggren, born 1884. Entered the Swedish Army, 1904; Major, 1926. Military
Attaché in Berlin and Moscow, 1928–33. Lieutenant-Colonel, 1930. Colonel, General
Staff, 1935. In 1944 he published, under the pseudonym Sven Herman Kjellberg, *Ryssland
i krig* (Russia at War).

[2] Edward Carpenter, 1872–1936. Entered the US Cavalry, 1898; Lieutenant-Colonel,
Field Artillery, 1917. Served on the western front, 1918. Colonel, 1918. Military Attaché,
Berlin, June 1928–April 1932.

Rowe-Dutton[1] that, in Berlin, there was 'a hardening of opinion . . . against the settlement of reparations on the basis of a large annuity'. Rumbold feared that if the British and French Governments were to settle on the figure he had heard mentioned – 2 million marks – 'there may be a pretty good row over here leading perhaps to the holding of fresh elections'. In such an event, Alfred Hugenberg's[2] Nationalist Party, whose policy was to 'attack any proposal or any solution', might well win substantial support.

The social life at the Berlin Embassy was varied and time-consuming. When Rumbold's former chief, Sir Maurice de Bunsen, stayed in Berlin, he wrote to his wife, on April 21: 'Horace says swarms of people come to Berlin now – for the good music, plays & general attractions.'[3]

Each summer Rumbold rented a villa on the Wannsee. He bought a motor-boat, and flew the Union Jack at the stern. Every morning he worked; in the afternoon he relaxed. Three afternoons a week he played golf. He still enjoyed tennis; among those who invited him to play on his private court was a wine salesman, from whom he bought his claret, Joachim von Ribbentrop.[4] Evenings were given over to concerts, the theatre and entertainment.

During April 1929 Stresemann's health improved, and Müller surmounted the political uncertainties of the previous months. 'For the moment', Rumbold wrote to Rowe-Dutton on May 22, 'a complete, if perhaps unhealthy, calm reigns here, and I have not had so little to do for years.' But on the day after Rumbold wrote those words, the

[1] Ernest Rowe-Dutton, 1891–1965. Entered the Civil Service, Inland Revenue, 1914; transferred to Treasury, 1919. Financial Adviser to HM Embassy, Berlin, 1928–32; to HM Embassy, Paris, 1934–39. 3rd Secretary, Treasury, 1947. Knighted, 1949. United Kingdom Director of the International Bank for Reconstruction and Development, 1949–51.

[2] Alfred Hugenberg, 1865–1951. Prussian Civil Servant. Violently anti-Polish. An active member of the Pan-German League before 1914. Joined the board of Krupps during the First World War. Entered the Reichstag, 1920. Controlled several publicity firms, and established a virtual monopoly over all German advertising by 1928. President of the Nationalist Party, 1928. Minister of Agriculture and Economics in Hitler's Cabinet, January 1933. Forced to resign, July 1933, when the Nationalist Party was dissolved. Remained in retirement until arrested by British forces, October 1946. Exonerated by the De-Nazification court, 1950.

[3] Among those who dined at the Embassy while Rumbold was in Berlin were Nancy Astor and George Bernard Shaw (on their way to Russia), Charlie Chaplin, General Smuts, Amy Johnson (on a solo flight from England to Japan), Austen Chamberlain's wife Ivy, the Duke and Duchess of York, and H. G. Wells.

[4] Joachim von Ribbentrop, 1893–1946. Champagne salesman in Canada, 1910–14. Lieutenant, Western Front, 1914–18, when he was wounded, and won the Iron Cross, first class. Aide-de-Camp to the German peace delegation in Paris, 1919. Head of a wine import–export business in Berlin, 1920–33. A National Socialist Deputy in the Reichstag, 1933. Ambassador to London, 1936–38. SS-Gruppenführer, 1936. Foreign Minister, 1938–45. Sentenced to death by the Allied Military Tribunal, Nuremberg, and hanged.

calm was disrupted. Harold Nicolson described what happened in a letter to his wife on May 23. Lord Tyrrell, in Paris, had spoken to the former German Secretary of State for Foreign Affairs, Richard von Kühlmann,[1] and had urged Kühlmann 'to put up a scheme whereby the Germans would get their colonies'. Kühlmann hesitated to do so. But Tyrrell was persistent, proposing, if Kühlmann would draw up a memorandum about the return of Germany's lost colonies, that he himself would 'submit it to Baldwin & *not* to Chamberlain', the latter being known to be unsympathetic to such a drastic revision of the Versailles Treaty as would be involved if Germany's colonies – which had been divided among the victors – were to be returned. Kühlmann did as Tyrrell suggested. But a copy of the memorandum reached the Foreign Office, who 'saw red'. The outcome of Tyrrell's initiative was, Nicolson wrote, that 'Rumbie was instructed to make an official complaint to Stresemann about Kühlmann's "interference". This he did. Now Kühlmann is furious & says that he would not have dreamt of interfering if W. Tyrrell had not begged him to do so. Rumbie is puzzled & distressed, & splutters something about W. Tyrrell being "a dirty little tike".'

On June 5 Ramsay MacDonald replaced Baldwin as Prime Minister, and formed his second Labour Government. Two days later Arthur Henderson[2] was appointed Foreign Secretary. To Rumbold's surprise, Henderson asked him, on June 22, to go to Geneva as the British Representative to the Red Cross Conference. The Government had originally selected Lord Robert Cecil as its delegate, but Cecil had declined on the grounds that, being a man of peace, he could not associate himself with any work that was based upon the existence of war. Rumbold accepted with reluctance, and set off for Switzerland. 'I do hope you are not really bored to death at Geneva', Harold Nicolson wrote from Berlin on July 9. 'I cannot conceive what was in the minds of the Foreign Office when they appointed you for this purpose. How angry I should be were I in your place!' Rumbold worked in Geneva for nearly two months, helping to draw up a Prisoners of War Convention the aim of which was to provide a broader

---

[1] Richard von Kühlmann, 1873–1949. Entered the Berlin Foreign Office, 1893. Counsellor of the German Embassy in London, 1908–14. On missions to Turkey and Scandinavia, 1915–17. Secretary of State for Foreign Affairs, 1917–18. An advocate of a negotiated peace, he tried to arrange for negotiations with Sir William Tyrrell in Holland in the summer of 1918, and was dismissed by the Kaiser.

[2] Arthur Henderson, 1863–1935. Foundry worker and trade-unionist; a Wesleyan and an abstainer. Labour MP, 1903–18; 1919–22; 1923; and 1924–31. Chairman of the Parliamentary Labour Party, 1908–10 and 1914–17. President of the Board of Education, 1915–16. Member of the War Cabinet, 1916–18. Home Secretary, 1924. Secretary of State for Foreign Affairs, June 1929–August 1931. President of the World Disarmament Conference, 1932–33. Awarded the Nobel Peace Prize, 1934. His eldest son was killed in action in 1916.

international basis for the treatment of prisoners of war than had existed hitherto. The Convention laid down that prisoners of war were to be removed from the combat zone, and thereafter to be humanely treated without loss of their original citizenship or legal status. It was ratified by Britain, Germany, France and the United States, but not by Japan or the Soviet Union. Unfortunately Rumbold's absence from Berlin coincided with a new crisis in Anglo-German relations. The French were baulking at the idea of reduced German reparations payments, as proposed by the Committee of Experts set up to determine the future payments. The British wanted a lenient policy towards Germany, but were unwilling to put sufficient pressure on the French to swing the balance in Germany's favour. The Germans were disturbed by Britain's attitude. 'It was difficult to explain to the officials at the German Foreign Office', Nicolson wrote to his wife from Berlin on June 27, 'why, at the first crisis in Anglo-German–French relations which has arisen for two years, you should quite gratuitously pack your Ambassador off to Geneva to attend a shoddy red cross conference. Our ways are mysterious in the extreme and I don't wonder that these people here are puzzled.'

Rumbold returned to Berlin on September 1. Harold Nicolson was there to meet him, writing to his wife on the following day: 'Rumbie, Mrs Rumbie, Miss Rumbie, & Master Rumbie *nebst* Valet[1] Rumbie all got out of the train in a row, & each one clasping a novel by John Galsworthy. I never saw anything look so English & solid & decent.' The next few months were seldom disturbed. 'The peace we were enjoying has been broken', Rumbold wrote to his stepmother on September 23, 'though I hope only temporarily, by a most boring inter-Parliamentary Commercial congress which opens today. . . . 25 British MP's as well as Delegates from all the Dominions have arrived for it, some accompanied by their wives and daughters and we are having a lunch of 52 tomorrow. There are entertainments, dinners etc for them every night and I have to go to all these functions.' One of the MPs, Malcolm Bullock,[2] was staying at the Embassy; so too was one of Asquith's daughters, Princess Bibesco.[3] But

[1] Rumbold's first valet in Berlin was called Cumbridge; on several occasions he impersonated Rumbold publicly. Once he went to a party dressed up as the Ambassador and wearing Rumbold's medals. He was soon asked to find other employment.

[2] Harold Malcolm Bullock, 1890–1966. Captain, Scots Guards, 1914–21. In 1919 he married a daughter of the 17th Earl of Derby. Military Secretary, British Embassy, Paris, 1918–20. Conservative MP, 1923–53. On the Committee of the Anglo-German Association, 1923–33. Secretary of the United Associations of Great Britain and France, 1925–50. Created Baronet, 1954. He published *Austria 1918–1938, A Study in Failure* in 1939.

[3] Elizabeth Charlotte Lucy Asquith, 1897–1945. Seventh and youngest child of H. H. Asquith. She married, in 1919, Prince Antoine Bibesco, Rumanian Minister to Madrid.

Rumbold, his wife and daughter had decided to 'go off to Dresden for two nights and get rid of our guests'.

Throughout the autumn of 1929 the two vexed questions of reparations and the allied occupation of the Rhineland, were reaching a solution. Following a conference at The Hague, the 'Occupying Powers' agreed to withdraw their troops from German soil if, for their part, the Germans would agree to a final reparation figure. The Hague Agreements were signed on August 20. Almost immediately British troops began to withdraw. In a letter to Ramsay MacDonald on September 25, Rumbold commented on the increase in British popularity in Germany, and on the enthusiastic reception given to the British delegates to the Inter-Parliamentary Commercial Congress. In his opening speech the leader of the British delegation, Sir Assheton Pownall,[1] had, Rumbold reported, 'dwelt on recent German achievements on land, in the air and at sea. . . . His speech was the "star turn" of the proceedings, and he received twice as much applause as anybody else.'

On October 2 Gustav Stresemann died. An opponent of the Nationalist and right-wing parties, his death was the prelude of a period of uncertainty and confusion in German affairs, made more acute because the Chancellor, Müller, was himself seriously ill and unable to attend to government business. It was Stresemann who had persuaded Müller to take office, and during Stresemann's ascendancy the extremist parties had been unable to make headway in their efforts to discredit the Weimar Republic. Yet Stresemann's achievement had helped to strengthen nationalistic emotions. 'The Germans feel', Rumbold wrote to the King on October 9, 'that Germany is once more looked upon as a great Power, the equal of other great Powers. . . . If German self-confidence stops at this point all will be well.' But, Rumbold added, 'there is always the danger that it may develop into arrogance.' Hugenberg's Nationalist Party had, since August, been vehement in its denunciation of The Hague Agreements, and in demanding that the Reichstag refuse to ratify them. But, Rumbold told the King, 'even here Dr Stresemann has rendered a service to his country, for his death has had a sobering effect on many people hitherto holding wild and impracticable ideas'. Writing to his friend Lord Stonehaven on the following day, Rumbold was less hopeful. 'Stresemann's death is really rather a disaster', he wrote. 'Two props have sustained Germany in recent difficult years, i.e. Hindenburg and Stresemann. Now one is gone and the

---

[1] Assheton Pownall, 1877–1953. Conservative MP, 1918–45. Knighted, 1926. London District Welfare Officer, 1939. Chairman, Public Accounts Committee, House of Commons, 1943–45.

other, although still very vigorous, is an old man of 82 who cannot, in the nature of things, last many years more.' The German, Rumbold believed, 'is not, as a rule, gifted with political instinct, and that was a gift which Stresemann had in a very high degree. His policy will be carried on, but by men of inferior calibre to himself.'

On November 1 the Berlin 'season' began. Rumbold had explained to his stepmother on October 12 the 'dodge' which he had devised to avoid it. He had decided to take three weeks' leave and go with his wife and daughter to Palermo. 'By going away about November 15', he wrote, 'I calculate that we shall escape all dinners etc until January.' Before leaving, he would give a single dinner for fifty people, 'and try & work off all the "duds" at one go'. This he did, and left for Sicily, as he had planned on November 15. While he was away, Harold Nicolson was Chargé d'Affaires. 'I hope you are all absorbing sufficient violet rays', Nicolson wrote on November 27, 'to carry you through what I feel will be a dark and extremly social winter.'

Rumbold returned to Berlin in mid-December. On December 27 he received a secret memorandum from his Air Attaché, Group Captain Christie,[1] with ominous news. The Junkers Aircraft Company, Christie reported, 'are offering aircraft to foreign governments which are readily convertible into military machines.' Under the Versailles Treaty, Germany was not allowed a military air force; yet Christie's information made it obvious that they could build one up if they chose. But by itself, the convertability did not constitute a violation of the Versailles Treaty, and Rumbold could take no official action.

At the end of December, Harold Nicolson left the Berlin Embassy, having decided to give up diplomacy for journalism.[2] Rumbold kept him informed of events in Berlin. 'We had our ball last night', he wrote on January 18, 'to which four or five hundred people came.' There were several German officers, in uniform for the first time since the war. 'Every conceivable person came to the ball', Rumbold noted, 'including bankers,

---

[1] Malcolm Grahame Christie, 1881–1971. An engineer; and graduate of Aachen University. General Manager of the Otto Cokeoven Company of Leeds and President of the Otto Coking Corporation of New York. Served in the Royal Flying Corps, 1914–18, and in the Royal Air Force, 1919–30. Air Attaché, Washington, 1922–26; Berlin, 1927–30. A friend of Göring's, he worked closely with Sir Robert Vansittart in obtaining information about the German air force, and German military plans.

[2] Nicolson joined the staff of Lord Beaverbrook's *Evening Standard* on January 1, 1930. He was joint editor (with Robert Bruce Lockhart) of the 'Londoner's Diary' gossip column. He also wrote weekly book-reviews for the *Daily Express*, and broadcast a series of talks on the BBC called 'People and Things'. During 1930 he published a biography of his father, *Lord Carnock*, which he had completed during his last months in Berlin.

journalists, actresses, tennis stars etc.' Only one invited guest had refused
to come, General Heye,[1] who, Rumbold wrote, 'had decided not to go
to parties during the present distressful condition of Germany'. Rumbold's
comment was: 'a typical example of sickly sentimentality'.

In October 1929 the New York Stock Exchange suffered an unparalleled
collapse, and in the wake of the disaster, the German economy suffered
severely. By the end of December over one and a half million German
workers were unemployed. On December 31, in defiance of the attempts
to solve the economic problem by multi-national agreements, the President of the Reichsbank, Hjalmar Schacht,[2] announced that the Reichsbank
would refuse to participate in any international financial business unless
The Hague Agreements on reparations were cancelled, and all sanctions to
which the Allies were entitled under the Versailles Treaty were abolished.
Confronted by this threat, the American banks concerned broke off negotiations. Schacht was quickly overruled by the German Government, but
his extremist actions encouraged the Nationalist Party to persevere in its
denunciation of all agreements 'based on' or derived from, the Versailles
Treaty. By the end of January 1930 a further million workers had lost
their jobs, bringing the total unemployed to over two and a half million.
'The present parliamentary situation', Rumbold wrote to Orme Sargent[3]
on February 28, 'is too confused to enable an observer to predict what the
outcome is likely to be. Obviously if the Nationalists got control of the
Government, they might be expected to take up the Polish question at no
distant date and with considerable vigour. But Hugenberg is discredited
and I think that the chances are that the government of Germany will, for
the next few years, be based on a combination of moderate parties.' Rumbold saw the eastern question as a major problem for the future. 'I have
not met a single German of any authority', he told Sargent, 'who is content
to accept Germany's present eastern frontiers as definitive.'

On March 12 the Reichstag finally ratified The Hague Agreements.

---

[1] Wilhelm Heye, 1868–1946. Served on the German General Staff, 1914–18. Chief of
Staff of the Army of the North, 1918. Army Commander-in-Chief, 1926–30.

[2] Hjalmar Horace Greely Schacht, 1877–1970. Economist and banker. Assistant Manager,
Dresdner Bank, 1908–15. Managing Partner, National Bank of Germany, 1915–22. Senior
Partner, Schacht & Co., Bankers, of Düsseldorff. Reich Currency Commissioner, 1923.
President of the Reichsbank, 1924–30; reappointed by Hitler, March 1933. Minister of
Economics, 1934–37. Tried by the Nuremberg War Crimes Tribunal, 1946, but acquitted.
He published *76 Jahre Meines Lebens* in 1953 and *1933: Wie eine Demokratie stirbt* in 1968.

[3] Orme Garton Sargent, 1884–1962. Entered Foreign Office, 1906. Second Secretary,
Berne, 1917; 1st Secretary, 1919. At the Paris Peace Conference, 1919. Counsellor, Foreign
Office, 1926. Head of the Central Department of the Foreign Office, 1928–33. Assistant
Under-Secretary of State for Foreign Affairs, 1933. Knighted, 1937. Deputy Under-
Secretary of State, 1939; Permanent Under-Secretary, 1946–49.

Those Germans who had hoped that reparations would have disappeared altogether now that nearly twelve years had passed since Germany's defeat, resented their Government's signature. The fact that Müller, the Chancellor, had also been a signatory of the Versailles Treaty, added a further insult to Nationalist fervour. During the debate, Dr Brüning,[1] the spokesman of the Centre Party, the second strongest party in Müller's coalition, said bitterly to the Reichstag: 'The Young Plan is no contract between equal parties; it is a unilateral *Diktat*, and it is to this *Diktat* that we now bow.'

The third and fourth weeks of March were marked by growing dissent within the coalition. On March 27 Rumbold was due to dine with the Minister of Defence, General Groener.[2] On his arrival at dinner, Groener greeted him with the news that Müller's government was no longer in office; he and all other ministers having resigned half an hour before. Rumbold asked who was likely to become Chancellor. Groener 'stated quite definitely' – Rumbold wrote to Arthur Henderson on March 28 – that Brüning would be asked to form the next government. It was likely to be a coalition 'more to the Right'. But Rumbold doubted that it would be very stable. 'There does not appear', he wrote, 'to be a single, strong and dominant personality in any of the political parties.'

On March 30 Brüning formed his coalition government. Rumbold saw no one in the new Cabinet likely to provide the necessary strong leadership for a cohesive policy. On the fringes of politics, but gaining more support with the growing unemployment, the National Socialist, or Nazi, movement led by Adolf Hitler,[3] threatened to disrupt even further the political life of Germany. By the spring of 1930 its membership had reached more than a quarter of a million, even though it had only twelve

[1] Heinrich Brüning, 1885–1970. Fought in the First World War, winning the Iron Cross second and first class. Served in the Prussian Ministry of Health, 1919–21. Adviser to the German Christian Trade Union Movement, 1922–29. Centre Party Member of the Reichstag, 1924–33. Chancellor of the Reich, 1930–32. Emigrated to the United States, 1934. Lecturer in Government, Harvard University, 1937–39; Professor, 1939–52. Returned to Germany as Professor of Political Science, University of Cologne, 1951–55.

[2] Wilhelm Groener, 1867–1939. Entered the German Army, 1885. Chief of Field-Railway Transport, 1914–16. In charge of the economic intensification of war production, 1916–17. First Quarter-Master General to the Kaiser, October 1918. The leading Military supporter of the Weimar Republic. Minister of Transport, November 1918. Minister of Defence, January 1928–May 1932; in October 1931 he was also appointed Minister of the Interior.

[3] Adolf Hitler, 1889–1945. Born in Austria-Hungary. Served on the Western Front as a Corporal in the German Army, 1914–18; wounded and gassed. Assumed the Leadership of the Nationalist Socialist Workers Party, July 1921. Staged an unsuccessful putsch in Munich, November 8, 1923. Imprisoned in the Landsberg Fortress, January–December 1924. Published *Mein Kampf*, 1925. Chancellor of the German Reich from January 30, 1933, until his death. Chief of State, August 2, 1934. Committed suicide in Berlin, April 30, 1945.

deputies in the Reichstag, elected in 1928, when it had received 800,000 votes. Early in May Colonel Marshall-Cornwall[1] dined with a senior official in the Army Ministry, Colonel Kühlenthal.[2] On May 8 he sent Rumbold a note about the National Socialists, based on what Kühlenthal had told him:

> The National-Socialist movement is a real danger, and far more of a menace to the present constitution than is Communism. The trouble about the 'Brown Shirts' is that their principles and theories are entirely *destructive*. They wish to destroy the present fabric of the State, but have no constructive programme with which to replace it, except a form of mad-dog dictatorship. The movement is, therefore, in the long run far more akin to Bolshevism than to Fascism. Unfortunately the general discontent with the late Government, the Young Plan, etc. had turned the heads of a number of young officers towards the National Socialist movement as a means of escape from Germany's financial and political troubles.
>
> Another serious feature of the movement is the ascendancy which its leader, Adolf Hitler, has the power of exerting. He is a marvellous orator, and possesses an extraordinary gift for hypnotizing his audience and gaining adherents. Even though his policy is a negative one, his personal magnetism is such as to win over quite reasonable people to his standard, and it is this which constitutes the chief danger of the movement.

Rumbold sent Marshall-Cornwall's note to the Foreign Office on May 13. During June and July unemployment rose to almost three million. National Socialist membership rose almost as dramatically, to almost two million. At the beginning of July the last allied troops were evacuated from the Rhineland. In Berlin, Rumbold reported to Arthur Henderson on July 3, there were 'bonfires, bell-ringing and torchlight processions'. But there was no praise for Britain and France. Instead, Hindenburg issued a manifesto, countersigned by the whole Brüning Cabinet, pointing out that although the Rhineland was now freed from foreign troops, 'our brothers on the Saar still await the day of their return to the mother country'. In his letter to the Foreign Secretary, Rumbold commented on this new demand: 'It is an unattractive feature of the German character to display little gratitude for favours received, but when the receipt of favours is followed up by fresh demands, there are grounds for feeling impatient.' That same day Rumbold spoke about the Rhineland

---

[1] Colonel Cornwall had changed his name to Marshall-Cornwall in 1929.

[2] Erich Kühlenthal, 1880–1958. Served in the First World War with the 23rd Artillery Regiment and the 20th Infantry Division. Major, 1923. Colonel Commanding the 3rd (Prussian) Artillery Regiment, Potsdam, 1927. Head of the Intelligence Department of the General Staff, 1928–31. Major-General, 1932. Military Attaché, Paris, Madrid and Lisbon, May 1933–November 1938.

evacuation to Stresemann's successor as Foreign Minister, Dr Curtius,[1] who stressed that for the German people the evacuation was 'a right long overdue', and that while the question of the Saar remained to be settled, there was little cause for German rejoicing. Curtius also told Rumbold 'that Germany could not rest content with her present frontier in the East'.

Far from satisfying grievances, the evacuation of the Rhineland stimulated them. On July 3 Rumbold wrote to Lord Stamfordham that 'the manner in which, having obtained satisfaction on one question, i.e. the evacuation of the Rhineland, the Germans immediately, and on the same day, clamoured for the retrocession of the Saar, was rather blatant and only furnished one more proof that the Germans will always be "Oliver Twists".' When Brüning announced that there would be a General Election on September 14, the agitation for frontier revision grew stronger. On August 10, the leader of the People's Conservative Party, Gottfried Treviranus,[2] a member of Brüning's Cabinet, declared outside the Reichstag to a large crowd that the evacuation of the Rhineland was but the first step on Germany's path to true independence. 'Now', he said, 'the east demands the unification of all German people. In the depths of our souls we are thinking of the Vistula lands, of the unhealed wounds in the eastern flank, that withered lung of the Reich. We think of the iniquitous insistence of Wilson on the un-natural cutting-off of East Prussia and of the half-breed condition to which Danzig was condemned.' Rumbold sent the text of Treviranus's speech to Arthur Henderson on August 12, noting that throughout the German Press it was pointed out that although the speech had created anger and alarm outside Germany, and particularly in Paris and Warsaw, it contained 'nothing that has not often been said before', and that Treviranus had only expressed 'what all Germans feel'.

On the evening of August 12 Treviranus defended, and expanded, his remarks in a wireless interview. 'Germany', he said, 'had an incomparably greater mission in Europe than ever before. It was Germany's task to find and establish the principles of justice, which were essential before the nations of Europe could live together in prosperity.' Justice meant the revision of frontiers; Germany's 'national will to live' could not be repressed

---

[1] Julius Curtius, 1877–1948. Lawyer. Elected to the Reichstag as a deputy of the German People's Party, 1920. Minister for Economic Affairs, 1926–29. Foreign Minister, 1929–32.

[2] Gottfried Reinhold Treviranus, 1891–1971. Served in the Imperial German Navy, 1909–18; commanded a destroyer during the First World War. Retired with the rank of Lieutenant-Commander, 1918. Farmer, 1919–21; Director of the Lippe Agricultural Board, 1921–28. Nationalist Member of the Reichstag, 1924–33; Leader of the People's Conservative Party, 1929–34. Minister of Communications, and Minister without Portfolio, in the Brüning Cabinet, 1930–32. He evaded his Nazi would-be executioners, June 1934, and escaped to England. Deprived of his German citizenship, 1938. Emigrated to Canada, 1939. Returned to Germany, 1948. Living in Switzerland, 1964.

for ever. Once again, the French and Polish Governments protested at these sentiments. On August 15 Rumbold went to see the Secretary of State at the Foreign Office, Bernhard von Bülow,[1] to ask whether Treviranus's speech had been approved by the German Foreign Office. Bülow said that it had not; but, Rumbold wrote to Arthur Henderson on August 18, Bülow went on to point out that in demanding a revision of the eastern frontiers Treviranus 'had only given expression to the view held by every German'. Rumbold reminded Henderson that three months earlier, on May 1, the recently appointed Permanent Under-Secretary of State at the Foreign Office, Robert Vansittart,[2] had written a memorandum in which he warned that the objectives of German policy had in no way been satisfied, either by the allied evacuation of the Rhineland, or by the reparations settlement agreed to at The Hague. Vansittart had outlined four further German aims: the acquisition of colonies, union with Austria, rearmament and a 'drastic modification' of the German–Polish frontier. Each of these demands was contrary to the Versailles Treaty; each, Vansittart believed, was inevitable. Rumbold had not previously shared Vansittart's pessimism, any more than he had accepted Colonel Marshall-Cornwall's fears of a rapid revival of German military strength. He had expected at least 'a pause' in Germany's external activities while the German Government devoted its energies to internal affairs, and until the 'political constellation in Europe' was more favourable to Germany's foreign aspirations.

Remarks such as those of Treviranus, and the wide approval given to them, caused Rumbold to think again. But in a letter to Orme Sargent on August 22, and in a further letter to Arthur Henderson a week later, he showed that he was still uncertain about how to interpret the mounting agitation. To Sargent he expressed the belief that the elections might well 'show some strengthening of the Right, i.e. of the National Socialists', but that there might be 'a return to the Grand Coalition, which would then be composed of the Social-Democrats, Centre and moderate Left parties'. To Henderson he wrote, on August 29, that the appeal for the revision of all aspects of the Versailles Treaty did not come from any one party, or group

[1] Bernhard Wilhelm von Bülow, 1885–1936. German diplomat. Author of several books which defended Germany's pre-1914 policy, and attacked the Versailles Treaty. Secretary of State for Foreign Affairs from 1930 until his death.

[2] Robert Gilbert Vansittart, 1881–1957. Entered the Diplomatic Service, 1902. Assistant Clerk, Foreign Office, 1914; 1st Secretary, 1918; Counsellor, 1920. Secretary to Lord Curzon, 1920–24. Principal Private Secretary to Ramsay MacDonald, 1928–30. Knighted, 1929. Permanent Under-Secretary of State for Foreign Affairs, 1930–38. Chief Diplomatic Adviser to the Foreign Secretary, 1938–41. Created Baron, 1941. His autobiography, *The Mist Procession*, was published posthumously, in 1958.

of parties, and that it was certainly not restricted to the extremists. A revision of the reparations settlement had been demanded, he wrote, by 'the National Socialists, the Nationalists, the People's Conservatives, the People's Party, the State Party and the Communists'. The Centre Party chairman, Dr Kaas,[1] had likewise declared: 'We realise that no German accepts the Young Plan, and the idea of revision is before our eyes.' Only the Social Democrats, he wrote, considered the 'clamour' for revision to be 'undesirable and premature'; but even they made no secret of their hostility to reparations payments.

On September 5, a week before the election, Rumbold sent the Foreign Office a lengthy report of the electoral campaign. Its two outstanding features, he wrote, were 'the apathy of the general public and the pronounced activity of the National Socialists'. Hitler's party was only one of twenty-four parties competing for electoral support. With only twelve members in the Reichstag, it was politically insignificant. But the Nazis claimed, Rumbold reported, to represent, not merely a political party, but a national movement. 'The movement', he wrote, 'is a new and vigorous one and obviously appeals to youth; and now, during the electoral campaign, its youthfulness and vigour are obviously appealing to all those in Germany who are feeling dissatisfied.'[2] Some people believed the Nazis might win fifty or sixty seats; 'this number seems somewhat high', Rumbold commented. But he went on to point out that the varied electoral techniques of the Nazis, and in particular their success in distributing pamphlets, leaflets and placards, was likely to enable them to gain seats 'out of proportion to their real strength'. Rumbold reported much rowdyism, 'often resulting in bloodshed', in the Nazi election campaign. But he could not gauge what effect the violence would have 'upon that nebulous group of dissatisfied people who have hitherto been attracted by the freshness and vigour of the movement'.

On September 9 Rumbold wrote to Lord D'Abernon that the Nazis were 'daily perpetrating outrages which must tend in the long run, to

---

[1] Ludwig Kaas, 1881–1952. A Catholic priest and theologian, the Pope had granted him the honorary title of Papal Domestic Prelate. Professor of Church Law at Trier, 1918. A Centre Party Representative in the Reichstag, 1919–33. Member of the German Delegation to the League of Nations, 1926. Elected Chairman of the Centre Party, December 1928. Asked by Hindenburg to try to form a Government in late November 1932; he was unable to do so, both Hitler and Hugenburg refusing to enter into discussion with him. In 1933 he helped negotiate Hitler's Concordat with the Vatican. Thereafter he remained in Rome, where he became Procurator and Secretary to the College of Cardinals, and supervised the archaeological excavations beneath St Peter's.

[2] Most of the leaders of the Nazi Party were themselves under 40. At the time of the election of 1930, Hitler was aged 41, Göring and Rosenberg 37, Goebbels 33, Himmler, Hans Frank and Robert Ley 30. Hitler's Nationalist rival, Hugenberg, was 65.

disgust the moderate and order-loving German'. The Nazi movement drew its strength, he wrote, 'from the small shop-keeper class' and consisted largely 'of young men and women who often succeed in winning over their parents'. On the same day he wrote to Vansittart that 'not a day passes' without the Nazis 'perpetrating some outrage'.

To the confusion of all forecasters, when the results of the election were announced on September 15 it was discovered that the Nazis had polled 6,500,000 votes. This made them the second largest party in the Reichstag, entitling them to 107 seats. The Social Democrats, the largest party, won two million more votes than the Nazis, giving them 143 seats. The Communists polled two million votes less than the Nazis, gaining 76 seats. Brüning's Centre Party won 69 seats. The former guardians of the right-wing parties, the Hugenberg Nationalists, had only 41. Treviranus's party was reduced to five seats.

On September 18 Rumbold asked the Prussian Secretary of State, Robert Weismann,[1] where the Nazis had got the money necessary to conduct so vigorous an electoral campaign. Weismann replied 'that these funds must come from Russia'. Rumbold doubted that this could be so. Later Weismann added: 'A few Jews might have contributed, in spite of the fact that the National Socialists are very hostile to that race.' Rumbold reported these speculations to Arthur Henderson on the same day.

On September 25 Rumbold wrote to Arthur Henderson: 'I have it on the best authority that one of the most prominent Jewish bankers in Berlin received an assurance of personal safety from Herr Goebbels, the leader of the National Socialists in the Reichstag. Another Jewish banker is stated to have subscribed to the funds of the National Socialists from disgust with, or apprehension at, Social Democratic finance.' On 5 November 1930, Rumbold asked Dr Curtius and General Groener where Nazi funds came from. 'Both Ministers replied', he wrote to Henderson that day, 'that all persons who attended the Nationalist Socialist meetings had to pay an entrance fee of 25 pfg or more'; sometimes seats sold for as much as 25 marks.[2]

On September 25, Hitler made his first important public appearance since the election, at the trial in Leipzig of two young Army officers charged with fomenting a Nazi conspiracy in the Army. At the trial, Hitler said bluntly, as Rumbold reported to the Foreign Office, 'that if his party came into power it would break down the Treaty of Versailles and

---

[1] Robert Weismann, 1869–1942. Born in Frankfurt-am-Main. Lawyer. Secretary of State, Prussia, 1923–32. Emigrated to France in 1933. Died in Nice.

[2] In September 1930 25 pfennigs were worth 3d., and 25 marks were worth £1 5s.

all that flowed from it'. But, he insisted, he would come to power only by legal means. 'He had been a soldier too long', he told the court, 'to believe that it was possible to fight with illegal organizations against an army or a police force.' His party's Storm Troopers were intended solely 'to protect the movement against the left'; they would never be used 'against the State'. But once the Nazis came to power, he declared, 'I can assure you . . . there will be a National Socialist Court of Justice, and there will be atonement for November 1918 and heads will roll in the dust'. Hitler, Rumbold commented in his despatch, had clearly outmanoeuvred the authorities who had brought the two young officers to trial, 'and he may even succeed in making himself a popular hero'[1].

As soon as the Leipzig trial was over, Marshall-Cornwall reported to Rumbold on the political tendencies in the German Army. His report was pessimistic. 'The waves of the older and new patriotism are bound soon to coalesce', he wrote. 'For the moment they are being held in check by the sound common sense of the President and by his Reichswehr Minister [General Groener], whom I regard as the greatest and perhaps only political genius in Germany today. When the time comes for these two pillars of the constitution to be removed, I anticipate serious trouble.' A week later, on October 16, Marshall-Cornwall reported on the tendency for German officers 'to express their patriotic feelings with rather less reticence than previously', giving as an example a senior officer, Colonel Hoepner,[2] who, at the anniversary dinner of the 1st Battalion of the 17th Infantry Regiment, declared: 'The times are about to change, and Germany will again obtain an army such as her people deserve. We Germans are not going to sit still forever as convicts in the foreigners' penal settlement.'

Despite Hitler's electoral success, Brüning remained Chancellor, supported by a coalition of parties which included Hitler's numerical superiors, the Social Democrats. Hitler and the Nazis remained outside the Government, vociferous and uncompromising. Although the Rhineland

---

[1] The two officers, Scheringer and Ludin, were sentenced to 18 months' fortress detention. In 1931 Scheringer became a communist and publicly denounced the Nazis; he escaped liquidation in the purge of 30 June 1934, and survived the war. Ludin entered the Reichstag as a Nazi deputy in 1932, rose to the rank of Major-General, and was Minister to Slovakia, 1940–45; he was executed by Slovak patriots at the end of the war.

[2] Erich Hoepner, 1886–1944. Entered the German Army, 1905. Chief of the General Staff, Wehrkreis I, Königsberg, 1933. After 1933 he became disillusioned with the Nazi movement. In the summer of 1938, while a Lieutenant-General commanding an armoured division in Thuringia, he offered to seize the Munich SS if the Army conspirators were to seize Berlin. He commanded an armoured column which, in October 1941, reached within seventy miles of Moscow. As a result of the failure to capture Moscow, he was dismissed from the Army by Hitler without even a Court Martial. He took an active part in the July Plot against Hitler in 1944, when the conspirators proposed to make him Commander-in-Chief of the German Army. He was executed on August 8, 1944.

had been evacuated by allied troops, no German troops were allowed to enter the province. The Nazis demanded the right to remilitarize the Rhineland, as well as to administer it. Orme Sargent wrote to Rumbold on October 14, to express his fears that the German Government would be forced, under pressure from its extremists, to adopt a 'forward' foreign policy. But in his reply two days later, Rumbold doubted whether the Brüning Government would want to raise the question. Its instinct, he stressed, was to remain on good terms with Britain. When the British airship, the R 101, crashed near Beauvais, while on its inaugural flight to India, Rumbold was impressed at the German reaction. 'The Germans have been most sympathetic', he wrote to his son on October 8, 'indeed I never remember such sympathy before in the relations between the two Countries.'[1]

Rumbold himself was not hostile to German territorial demands, believing that some readjustment of Germany's eastern border was necessary to redress the grievances created by the Versailles frontier-line. The stumbling-block to revision, he felt, was France not Britain. 'Are there', he wrote to Owen O'Malley[2] at the Foreign Office on October 10, 'sufficient Frenchmen in authority broadminded enough to realise that some sacrifice may and will be necessary to remove this cause of unrest.' But, he added, if there were such Frenchmen, 'will they not tend to have the feeling that no sooner is one question settled in Germany's favour than the Germans at once open up another?'

On October 13 the Reichstag met for the first time since the election. Rumbold was present, having gone there, he wrote to his son on the following day, 'to see whether there would be any rows'. In his letter he described the scene:

The house was crammed. When all the other deputies were in their place the Nazi deputies – over 100 strong – dressed in Khaki shirts and breeches and wearing the Swastika badge made a calculated and theatrical entry. The Communists hooted and jeered and most people laughed. The Nazis then gave their leader the Fascist salute but it was quite clear that they are really novices at the game. The whole proceeding was childish and undignified. Throughout the sitting – which only lasted $1\frac{1}{4}$ hours and which was devoted to a roll call of the members Nazis and Communists exchanged insults. At one moment when

---

[1] The R 101 crashed near Beauvais on October 5, 1930. Of the fifty-four passengers and crew, forty-eight lost their lives, including Lord Thomson (Secretary of State for Air) and Sir Sefton Brancker (Director of Civil Aviation).

[2] Owen St Clair O'Malley, 1887–   . Entered Foreign Office, 1911. Counsellor, Peking, 1925. Counsellor, Foreign Office, 1933–37. Minister to Mexico, 1937–38. In charge of the British Embassy to Spain (at St Jean de Luz), 1938–39. Minister to Hungary, 1939–41. Ambassador to Poland, 1942–45; to Portugal, 1945–47. Knighted, 1943.

the Nazi leader in Parliament, Frick,[1] was speaking the Communists crowded up to him shouting 'Lumpenknecht' the nearest translation of which appears to be 'rag and bone merchant'. It might be freely translated, however, as 'dirty dog'. Frick remained calm.

That afternoon, Rumbold told his son, 'groups of hooligans masquerading as young Nazis' milled through the main streets of Berlin breaking the windows of shops 'which they thought belonged to Jews'. The only way to deal with such 'ruffians', he believed, was to 'hurt them severely with rubber truncheons'. The police, who were mobilized to deal with the disturbance, made fifty arrests. But the anti-Semitic violence continued. To maintain his position in the Reichstag, Brüning obtained a majority which enabled him to rule by emergency decree, thus freeing him from dependence upon Nazi votes and stratagems. Rumbold was impressed by Brüning's action, writing to his stepmother on October 19: 'He is a statesman, and the Germans are beginning to be impressed by his firmness.' Four days later he wrote to the King, commenting on the 'patriotism' of the Social Democrats, led by Hermann Müller, in accepting Brüning's policies. The Germans, he wrote, 'respect a leader and they have got one now'. That same day, in a despatch to the Foreign Office, he noted that many Social Democrats reproached Müller for supporting the Brüning decrees, and that 'as time goes on, the Social Democrats leaders may find it increasingly difficult to control their followers'. But he did not think that the Nazis would benefit by this division in the ranks of their main opponents. 'The grotesque points' in the Nazi programme, he wrote in his despatch, 'namely, those advocating the confiscation of the fortunes of Jews and war profiteers, tend, however, to discredit the party, which has not so far put forward a single constructive proposal'.

Rumbold found that many leading Germans did not share his view that the Nazis would discredit themselves by their anti-Semitism and extremism. On October 24 he sent the Foreign Office an account of an interview between Rowe-Dutton and the President of the Reichsbank, Dr Luther.[2] According to Luther, the Nazis were in the process of

[1] Wilhelm Frick, 1877–1946. Lawyer. Chief Assistant, Bavarian Ministry of Justice, 1923, when he helped prevent Hitler being charged with conspiracy. Tried with Hitler, for his part in the Munich putsch, 1924. Joined the Nazi Party, 1925. Nazi Minister of the Interior and of Education, Thuringia, January 1930–April 1931. Reich Minister of the Interior, January 1933–August 1943. Protector of Bohemia and Moravia, August 1943–May 1945. Tried by the International Military Tribunal at Nuremberg and hanged, October 1946.

[2] Hans Luther, 1879–1962. Assistant Burgomaster, Magdeburg, 1907–12. Chairman of the German Municipalities' Congress, 1913–18. Chief Burgomaster of Essen, 1918. Minister for Food and Agriculture, 1922; Finance Minister, 1923–25. Chancellor, 1925–26. Governor of the Reichsbank, March 1930–March 1933. Ambassador to Washington, 1933–37. A High School teacher, Munich, 1952–58. He published his memoirs Politiker ohne Partei in 1960.

becoming respectable Parliamentarians: 'Hitler had orated in the Leipzig treason trial like a demagogue', with that Luther agreed, but, he added, 'the important words of his speech were "legal means", not "rolling heads".' In a note of the conversation Rowe-Dutton commented that Luther was clearly trying to 'educate foreign opinion into regarding Herr Hitler and his followers as responsible people, whose enormous energy only requires to be harnessed to creative work to be of real benefit to Germany'. Dr Luther's attitude to Hitler was shared by Dr Curtius, the Foreign Minister. On October 27 Curtius agreed with Rumbold that Nazi street tactics 'such as the smashing of street windows', had disgusted a great many reasonably-minded Germans; but, he added, 'let there be no mistake, the movement, as an expression of present-day discontent in Germany and a desire for better things, had come to stay. It had stirred the nation up and could not be left out of account. 'Moreover', Curtius added, 'Hitler seemed to be becoming quite reasonable. . . .'

Rumbold was sceptical about this comforting advice. He had been studying the Nazi Party's programme, as laid down in the 'Twenty-Five Points' of 1922, and as elaborated in a commentary drawn up by a leading Nazi 'ideologist', Alfred Rosenberg.[1] This commentary had first appeared in 1922. It was reissued on 30 September 1930, two weeks after the election. On October 31 Rumbold sent a copy to the Foreign Office, and on the same day summarized, in a lengthy despatch to Arthur Henderson, the basic tenets of the Nazi creed. All Germans must be consolidated into 'one great German state'; the Treaty of Versailles must be abolished; colonies and 'living space' were needed 'to feed the nation and absorb the surplus population'; no Jew would be allowed to remain a German citizen, but could continue to live in Germany only 'under laws applying to foreigners'; no Jew could be the editor or correspondent of a German newspaper; all Jews who had entered Germany as refugees since August 1914 were to be deported; all war profits would be confiscated; all industrial trusts and department stores would be nationalized; all land speculation would be halted; all those found guilty of usury and profiteering 'are to be punished with death'; exceptionally gifted children would be educated free by the State; the physical fitness of the nation's youth would be encouraged by compulsory gymnastics and sport; pornographic literature would be abolished. Rumbold was impressed by some of the

[1] Alfred Rosenberg, 1893–1946. Editor of the Nazi Party Newspaper, *Völkischer Beobachter*, 1921–38. Elected a Member of the Reichstag, 1930. The leading Nazi authority on Russian and Baltic questions; Director of the National Socialist Party Foreign Bureau. Supervisor of Youth Education, 1940–41. Minister for the Occupied Eastern Territory, 1941–45. Tried at Nuremberg by the Allied War Crimes Tribunal, and hanged, October 16, 1946. His book, *Der Mythos des 20 Jahrhunderts*, first published in 1930, was a textbook of racial superiority.

programme, which was, he believed, Nationalist in a good sense, 'in all its striving for a greater, better, cleaner and less corrupt Germany. That is the healthy side. . . .' But he was appalled by both its anti-Semitic, and in parts 'almost Communist' aspects. Some people, he reported, felt that the contradictions in the programme would lead the party to split; but from all he had heard, Hitler himself 'was still able, apparently whenever he wished, to exercise a remarkable influence over the whole party'. Whether the Nazis split, or held together, he was convinced that 'the revival of nationalism has come to stay' and that 'it must result in the prosecution of a more forward foreign policy by Germany in the future'.

On October 31 Rumbold completed ten years' service as an Ambassador. He was nearly sixty-two. He had hoped to take two months' leave that winter, and go to Ceylon; but the developments in Berlin made that impossible. Instead, he and his wife went to Italy for three weeks, spending a few days in Naples, Sorrento and Florence, and from there they went to Paris for six days. Although, as he wrote to Lord Stamfordham on December 12, after his return to Berlin, 'I went away in search of sun and warmth to curtail the long German winter', he had also spent several hours with Sir Ronald Graham and William Tyrrell, the Ambassadors in Rome and Paris, discussing the German problem. Tyrrell insisted that British policy ought to be closely linked to that of France; Graham believed that the French 'obsession' with a German attack was unjustified. Rumbold tended to support Graham, believing, as he wrote to him on his return to Berlin, on December 19, 'that French fears of an "attaque brusquée" on the part of Germany merely made us here smile. How on earth could the German army engage in such a venture without heavy guns, tanks, aeroplanes and the other indispensable paraphernalia of war which they are not allowed to have by treaty.'

Rumbold spent the Christmas of 1930 and the New Year of 1931 with his wife and son in the Bavarian Alps. On his return to Berlin, he found that the growing economic distress had led the Brüning Government to give up most of its official banquets. Unemployment had reached four million. The strength of the Nazis was still increasing, and was much in evidence. The Nazi Party, Rumbold wrote to Arthur Henderson on January 5, 'has quite recently spurned in the coarsest and most offensive terms the suggestion of collaboration with any other party in the State.' In deference to Nazi 'street clamour', Brüning had agreed to ban the antiwar film *All Quiet on the Western Front*.[1] The Nazis, he wrote to

---

[1] Rumbold saw *All Quiet on the Western Front* on March 4, 1931, at a private showing. 'It is the most powerful and gripping film I have ever seen', he wrote to his son later in the day, 'and I, for one, am still under its impression.'

Henderson on January 16, 'are an irresponsible party and cannot be entrusted with the Government.'

The gaiety of Berlin was fast disappearing. 'The rich Jewish bankers', Rumbold wrote to his son on January 19, 'most of whom have lost money, are lying very low not wishing to attract attention from the Nazis. There is a policeman on duty outside our home. I don't know why, but I believe that several of the Foreign Missions are being guarded in this manner.'

Within the British Foreign Office the meaning of the Nazi movement and the reasons for its success were much discussed. Robert Vansittart believed that Nazism was a resurgence of the 'Old Adam' in Germany; an amoral, primitive spirit which could not easily be satisfied, and must certainly not be ignored. Orme Sargent echoed this view when he wrote to Rumbold on January 13 that Hitler's success pointed to 'a belief in force as opposed to cooperation in the solution of European problems'. In his reply to Sargent on January 23 Rumbold wrote: 'In the eyes of the Nazis, Germany is like Prometheus bound and Hitler, or the Nazi movement, is cast for the part of Hercules. This aspiration for freedom and for equality has come to stay and is an element which every German Government must take with account. It is bound, in my opinion, to exercise an influence on the conduct of Germany's foreign policy and has begun to exercise such an influence.' The 'Hitler movement', Rumbold added, had not entirely harmed Germany; it had caused both Europe and the world, 'to take far more account of this efficient and industrious nation of sixty-four million inhabitants, placed in the centre of Europe, and to ask "Quo vadis Germania?" ' The question was an urgent one. 'The unemployment tide is rising steadily'; Rumbold wrote to Sargent a week later, on January 30 'it passed the 4·7 million mark a few days ago'. Sargent had asked Rumbold to forecast future developments. This Rumbold did not feel able to do. 'The situation in Germany is constantly changing', he wrote. 'The Chancellor's Government is a precarious one. It has no definite majority in the Reichstag. It is an emergency Government dealing with an abnormal situation at a time when a variety of vital political and economic factors in Germany are in flux. All I can do, therefore, is to give you, from time to time and to the best of my ability, an appreciation of the situation.'

Through February Rumbold watched the progress of German politics. Unemployment approached five million. Trade and industry made no recovery. The Nazi rank and file were pressing Hitler not to co-operate with the other political parties, but to return to the streets, and extend their support by violence and intimidation. On February 26 Rumbold sent

Arthur Henderson a long, pessimistic despatch. The Germans wanted an end to reparations. They were eager to rearm. They dreamed of the return of their lost territories in the east. 'A war against Poland to rectify the eastern frontiers', Rumbold noted, 'would be in the nature of a crusade.' The Nazis, he added, 'as well as the other parties of the Right, include conscription in their programme as a matter of course'. The ban on conscription was yet another restriction laid down in the Versailles Treaty, and denounced by every Nazi speaker on every public platform. On March 4 Rumbold wrote to Henderson again. Britain's only chance of averting a Nazi triumph, he argued, was to support Brüning. The only way of supporting Brüning was to give Germany some economic help, to come to an arrangement, possibly a moratorium, on reparations, or to organize some international credit operation on Germany's behalf. The least that could be done, Rumbold added in a further letter to Henderson two days later, was for Ramsay MacDonald to testify publicly 'to the statesmanlike and energetic manner with which Brüning is grappling with difficulties which are common to practically all the great countries of the world'. Some gesture should be made to make Brüning feel that the British were willing to help him; even an invitation to London would help to lessen German fears of isolation.

MacDonald agreed to Rumbold's suggestion that Brüning should be invited to London. But before the visit could be arranged, the international situation again worsened. On February 26 the French Minister of War, André Maginot,[1] in a debate on the army estimates in the French Chamber, stated that the countries 'which were the aggressors' in 1914 would have to accept a limitation of armaments 'more severe' than that of the nations 'which committed no aggression and which refuse to commit one'. Maginot was insistent that there could 'be no question of going back on the military clauses of the Versailles Treaty'. The Germans were incensed by these remarks. General Groener, in a statement to the Reichstag on March 9, insisted that 'the Versailles thesis for Germany's sole responsibility' for the war had been refuted. Dr Curtius told Rumbold that Maginot's remarks on March 18 had 'poisoned the atmosphere' between France and Germany. The Germans, he said, would never accept that they had been responsible for the war. They rejected absolutely the war guilt charge.

Brüning's government did not intend to submit to the restrictions of the

---

[1] André Maginot, 1877–1932. Socialist deputy, 1910. Under-Secretary of State for War, 1913–14. Served on the Western Front, 1914–16, when he was wounded. Minister of Colonies, 1917; of Pensions, 1920–24; of War, 1924; of Colonies, 1928–29; of War (for the second time), 1929–32. He piloted through Parliament the Law of January 4, 1930, establishing the line of fortifications in eastern France, known as the 'Maginot Line'.

Versailles Treaty if it could find a way around them. Secret rearmament and military training continued without pause. Work on tank manufacture, forbidden by the Versailles Treaty, was being carried out secretly, both in Sweden and the Soviet Union by German experts. During the winter Colonel Marshall-Cornwall had collected a certain amount of evidence of infringements of the military restrictions. He estimated that there were about 7,000 soldiers in excess of those allowed by Treaty, undergoing training in military depots. He had been shown photographs of an armoured motor-cycle combination, fitted with a machine-gun, which had actually been constructed in Germany.

In March 1931 Brüning took a sudden initiative in foreign policy which aroused immediate antagonism in France, and deep suspicion in England. Shortly after Dr Curtius returned from a visit to Vienna, it was announced that Germany and Austria intended to form a Customs Union. On March 21, Robert Vansittart warned the Austrian Minister to London, George Franckenstein,[1] that such a Union might be a direct breach of Article 88 of the Treaty of Saint-Germain, whereby Austria agreed not to commit any act 'which might directly or indirectly or by any means whatever compromise her independence'. On March 23 Rumbold saw Dr Curtius, who insisted that the agreement had no political significance, but should be regarded as the first step in the creation of a free trade area, which other nations were welcome to join. 'The greater the number of States participating in such a Customs Union', Curtius told Rumbold, 'the larger would be free trade area between these States'. Neither Rumbold nor the Foreign Office were much impressed by this line of argument. If the German aim was a wider economic plan, they asked, why had it not been mentioned to some of the other nations who might be asked to participate in it?

On March 25, at Arthur Henderson's request, Rumbold warned Brüning of the 'great concern' in both Britain and France that the Germans should show an 'apparent disregard' of their Treaty obligation. Rumbold pointed out that even in Germany there were misgivings about the proposal, and stressed that 'it was surely not in Germany's interest' that the French should be angered at the very moment when the Disarmament Conference was about to meet, and the French Foreign Minister, Briand,[2]

---

[1] George Franckenstein, 1878–1953. Before 1914, served in the Austro-Hungarian embassies in Washington, St Petersburg, Rome, Tokyo and London. Member of the Austrian Peace Delegation, Paris, 1919. Austrian Minister to London, 1920–38. Knight Grand Cross of the Royal Victorian Order, 1937. Became a British subject, 1938. He published *Facts and Features of My Life* in 1939.

[2] Aristide Briand, 1862–1932. Secretary-General of the French Socialist Party, 1901. Elected Deputy in 1902, he was appointed to Ministerial Office twenty-three times before

was sympathetic towards the German desire for equality of armaments. Brüning assured Rumbold that his government 'had not had any political considerations at the back of their minds when negotiating agreement with Austria'. But, he added, 'Germany had few rights and if she was going to be checked at every turn the position of his Government would become impossible'. He believed there would be an 'explosion' in Germany if France insisted on blocking Germany's legitimate aspirations. Rumbold made no comment, but in a telegram to Arthur Henderson on the following day he deprecated too much British protest or pressure. The plan for a Customs Union, he believed, did not foreshadow a closer political link. There would be serious repercussions if Britain opposed the Customs Union. 'Any outside interference', Rumbold stated, 'which is not based on legal and convincing grounds is liable to be represented as an attempt to bully Germany, and to be exploited to detriment of ex-allies'. In a letter to Henderson on March 27 Rumbold reported that Brüning's attitude throughout their interview had been 'absolutely firm, and I could not shake him in the least'; the Chancellor, he added, 'was imposing considerable restraint on himself, and his language was that of suppressed bitterness'. Rumbold had rebuked Brüning for 'exploding a bomb' by the suddenness of the announcement of the Customs Union. The German method of diplomacy seemed calculated to offend Britain and to frighten France; but, Rumbold told Henderson, this method had psychological importance for the Germans, which Brüning understood, and would not abandon. 'This was the first time since the war', he wrote, 'that Germany has asserted herself in an important matter. We must expect, under this Chancellor, to see Germany affirming with increasing emphasis any rights to which she thinks she is entitled.'

Rumbold wanted the British Government to make every effort to mediate between France and Germany, for he believed that Briand and Brüning were capable of an agreement on disarmament, and must not be allowed to drift apart. If Brüning fell from power, he doubted that a new Chancellor could be found who would be either willing, or able, to negotiate with France. 'It is vital', he wrote to the King on April 3, 'that the Disarmament Conference should lead to a real and substantial reduction of armaments in Europe.' Briand, he believed, would agree to this; and France's 'satellites', Poland and Czechoslovakia, would then follow suit. If disarmament made no progress, opinion in Germany would

his death. Foreign Minister 1915–17, 1921–22, April–November 1925 and 1926–32. A strong supporter of the League of Nations, in August 1928 he obtained the signature of sixty nations (including Britain and Germany) to the Briand–Kellogg Pact, which outlawed war between states. He was awarded the Nobel Peace Prize in 1926.

soon harden. 'It cannot be too much realised abroad', Rumbold told the King, 'that the Germans are becoming increasingly impatient of anything which seems to have the appearance of unequal treatment.' He did not feel that the hostile, almost hysterical British and French reaction to the proposed Customs Union was justified. 'I do not believe that the "Anschluss" question played a part in the projected customs union', he wrote to Orme Sargent on May 9. 'The Germans', he believed, 'were really anxious to do something to relieve the economic situation, and were not merely aiming at a success in the domain of foreign policy.' Had Brüning abandoned the scheme 'at the first sign of foreign opposition', he added, 'he would have lost so much prestige that he might have fallen'. Rumbold warned Sargent that if foreign pressure succeeded in frustrating what Germany regarded as her legitimate plans and policies, it would 'create a bitter sense of grievance and a feeling that Germany cannot expect justice so long as she remains disarmed'.

The theme of Rumbold's despatches during the spring of 1931 was that Brüning must be trusted, and supported, by Britain. It was not, he believed, a question only of support on specific problems, whether French disarmament, the Austro-German customs union, or the removal of reparations, but also of the need to raise German morale. Rumbold had been surprised, and shaken, by what he described to Vansittart on May 29 as a 'wave of depression, even hopelessness, which has swept over the German people'. The German public was losing confidence in its leaders, seeing 'no end to the sacrifices it is called upon to endure'. The morale of the Germans had almost collapsed. 'They seem to themselves', Rumbold wrote, 'to have nothing to lose and nothing to hope for.' They could not rearm; they could not try to form an economic bloc without international protest; the number of unemployed had reached five million; trade was stagnant; industry almost at a standstill. 'It is the lack of hope', Rumbold wrote, 'which makes the situation seem to them so depressing, and makes it difficult for Brüning to keep them in hand.'

The only person who would gain an advantage by Brüning's collapse was Hitler; this Rumbold reiterated in his letters to the Foreign Office. On May 29 he informed Arthur Henderson that at a recent public meeting in Berlin Hitler had spoken 'no word of politics', but having devoted much of his speech to 'self-discipline, self-control, self-sacrifice', had then 'thundered against materialism, slack manners and morals. Like an American revivalist, he worked 10,000 young people up to indescribable ecstasies of excitement.' Hitler's appeal was that he offered more than political solutions; his was the party which promised moral regeneration. Nor was Nazi extremism a barrier to Hitler's success. 'His watchword for the moment is "Moderation" ', Rumbold wrote. Brüning himself told Rumbold, at a luncheon on May 28, that Hitler 'was not unreasonable', even though the Nazi Party was, in the Chancellor's view, 'quite unfitted for responsibility', and most of its deputies in the Reichstag 'young and unbalanced'.

At the beginning of June, following Rumbold's suggestion, Brüning and Curtius were invited to Chequers as Ramsay MacDonald's guests. The visit was appreciated by the German Ministers, who were able, in a relaxed atmosphere, to explain their problems. They made it clear that Germany could not go on paying reparations even on the reduced scale laid down in June 1929. 'The people were in despair', Brüning told MacDonald, 'and the growing power of the Nazis and the Communists was a menace.' Bruning's sense of urgency impressed MacDonald, and led to positive British action on Germany's behalf. The American President, Herbert Hoover,[1] had been hostile to German appeals for economic leniency; but on June 29, having studied the contents of the Chequers discussions, he proposed a twelve-month suspension of reparations payment, and of inter-allied debts.

During June Rumbold returned to England on leave. In London he met Harold Nicolson, who told him that he had joined Oswald Mosley's movement, and intended to stand for Parliament.[2] On July 16, in the midst of a severe German economic crisis, he returned to Berlin. The whole German banking system was on the verge of collapse. 'The atmosphere', he wrote to his son three days later, 'rather reminds me of that which prevailed just before war broke out.'

Writing to the King's new Private Secretary, Sir Clive Wigram,[3] on July 22, Rumbold reiterated his view that it was up to the French Government to make concessions to the Germans over reparations, if European confidence, and calm, were to be restored. In 1914, he wrote, 'Germany was the villain of the piece'; but now, he felt, 'France is the Power which has to be persuaded to be reasonable'. He almost wished that France had suffered more by the world economic depression. 'Misfortunes', he wrote,

---

[1] Herbert Clark Hoover, 1874–1964. Mining engineer. In charge of International Food Relief for Belgium, 1914; for Europe, 1916; for Russia, 1921. Thirty-first President of the United States, 1928–32.

[2] From 1930 to 1932 Nicolson was associated with Oswald Mosley in the formation of the New Party. He edited Mosley's paper, *Action*, and, as a New Party candidate in the election of October 1931, came fifth in a poll of five. In 1935 he was elected to Parliament as National Government M.P. (with a majority over the Labour candidate of only 87).

[3] Clive Wigram, 1873–1960. Served in the Indian Army, 1897–99. Aide-de-Camp to Lord Curzon (then Viceroy of India), 1899–1904. Assistant Private Secretary to King George V, 1910–31; Private Secretary, 1931–35. Knighted, 1928. Created Baron, 1935. His second son was killed in action in 1943.

'make the world akin. France will certainly not escape eventually . . . but she would be more inclined to be helpful if she were herself feeling the pinch.' But the French Government was reluctant to give Germany an economic breathing space by agreeing to abandon reparations. The effect of the economic crisis in Berlin, Rumbold told Wigram, was visual and immediate. 'Large and luxurious cars disappeared off the streets, traffic diminished and many Germans stayed at home. . . . The Golf Club, which on Saturday afternoons is generally crowded, especially with Hebrews, was almost deserted.'

The economic crisis was advantageous to Hitler; on July 24 Rumbold sent Arthur Henderson the comment of a British Consul, Francis Shepherd,[1] that in Hamburg the serious economic situation 'is considered to be too serious for indulging in communism, and the tendency of business men to lean towards the National Socialists has, if anything, increased.'

On July 27 Ramsay MacDonald and Arthur Henderson visited Berlin, 'not merely to return the German visit to Chequers', MacDonald told Brüning in a speech that evening, 'but to show the world that despite the difficulties of the present situation our confidence in Germany continues unimpaired'. Throughout July 28 the British and German leaders discussed the economic crisis. Brüning asked the British to use their influence with France to resolve the reparations problem. MacDonald assured him that Britain 'could not support the French idea of a long credit' the only effect of which would be 'to pile up further commitments for Germany'. At a Press Conference that afternoon MacDonald warned of the dangers 'if the young generation should be brought up in a narrow ultra-Nationalist spirit, or in a spirit of enmity and suspicion'. Rumbold was impressed by the way in which MacDonald convinced the Germans that Britain would not automatically follow the French lead, but would look with sympathy upon Germany's economic difficulties. Writing to his wife on July 30, of MacDonald's reception by the Berlin crowd, Rumbold wrote: 'The Prime Minister was heartily cheered. I noticed with interest quite a number of Nazis in the crowd who gave him the Fascist salute', Rumbold himself had been given a rousing cheer. 'I must say', he added, 'I never expected to be cheered by a German crowd.'[2]

[1] Francis Michie Shepherd, 1893–1962. Served as an artillery officer, 1915–20. Entered the Consular Service, 1920. Acting Consul-General in Hamburg, 1928–32. Minister Resident, Port-au-Prince (Haiti), 1935–38; Consul, Dresden, 1936. Consul-General in Danzig, 1939; in Reykjavik (Iceland), 1940; Leopoldville (Congo), 1942; Batavia (Indonesia), 1947. Knighted, 1948. Ambassador in Teheran, 1948–50; in Warsaw, 1952–54.

[2] Rumbold had one grievance in the aftermath of MacDonald's visit, writing, on February 24, 1932, to Sir Francis Lindley, the British Ambassador in Tokyo, that 'when the PM and Henderson returned the visit of the German Ministers in the summer I had every-

During the summer the rigours of the economic crisis spread to Britain, where unemployment reached 3,000,000 in July. The most discussed solution was a reduction of wages, and the cutting down of the dole. 'What we require', Clive Wigram wrote to Rumbold on August 3, 'is a National Emergency Government, but no two men I meet can agree how this can be found. Neither Ramsay MacDonald nor Baldwin will agree to serve under the other. . . . A neutral head of proved ability who would command the confidence of the Nation is hard to find. I have heard Derby mentioned, but I doubt whether his health would stand too much strain.'

At a Cabinet meeting on August 23 MacDonald insisted on the need to reduce unemployment in the interests of economy. Ministers were divided and, agreement proving impossible, MacDonald resigned. The King asked MacDonald to remain at the head of an all-Party 'National' Government. MacDonald accepted, to a storm of protest from the majority of the Labour Party. Contrary to what Wigram had reported, Baldwin agreed to serve under MacDonald, and was appointed Lord President of the Council. MacDonald formed his new Cabinet on August 25. Four posts, including his own, went to his newly created National Labour Party. The Conservatives received four posts, the Liberals two. Lord Reading,[1] a Liberal, succeeded Arthur Henderson as Foreign Secretary.

Rumbold was pleased by Lord Reading's appointment. 'The Liberals are a first rate team', he wrote to his stepmother on August 16. 'Though I neither like or trust LG, I shouldn't mind seeing the country governed by Liberals if we could get rid of LG.' With the exception of the Minister of Health, Neville Chamberlain,[2] the new Conservative Ministers did not impress him. 'The Party has some younger men of ability', he wrote, 'but Baldwin (himself no flyer) never seems to give them a chance.' Rumbold approved of MacDonald's courage in abandoning the majority of his Labour followers, and in agreeing to lead an all-Party Government. Above all, he admired Baldwin for agreeing to serve under MacDonald. 'That he

---

thing ready on the appointed day, but the visit was postponed at the very last minute and took place a fortnight later. This gave an awful lot of trouble, but I never had a line of thanks either from the PM or from Henderson for all my trouble and hospitality.'

[1] Rufus Daniel Isaacs, 1860–1935. Liberal MP, 1904–13. Knighted, 1910. Solicitor-General, 1910. Attorney-General, 1910–13. Entered Cabinet, 1912. Lord Chief Justice, 1913–21. Created Baron Reading, 1914; Viscount, 1916; Earl, 1917. Special Ambassador to the USA, 1918. Viceroy of India, 1921–26. Created Marquess, 1926. Secretary of State for Foreign Affairs, August 25–November 4, 1931.

[2] Arthur Neville Chamberlain, 1869–1940. Lord Mayor of Birmingham, 1915–16. Director-General of National Service, 1916–17. Conservative MP, 1918–40. Minister of Health, 1923, 1924–39 and August–November 1931. Chancellor of the Exchequer, 1923–24 and 1931–37. Prime Minister, 1937–40. Lord President of the Council from May 1940 until his death six months later.

has done so', he told his stepmother, 'is a proof of his patriotism.'

On October 17, as a result of the economy measures brought in by the National Government, Rumbold's salary of £2,500 a year was reduced by £250. 'In addition to the above', he wrote to his son on the following day, 'come the increase of 6d. in the income tax as well as an increase in the super-tax – result, total income diminished by roughly a quarter. But I don't complain.'

During the autumn the German economic crisis lessened. Unemployment, while still just below four million, had begun to fall slightly. But the political crisis continued. There were more than three-quarters of a million registered members of the Nazi Party, and no slackening off of applications to join. In local elections in Hamburg, both Nazis and Communists increased their vote. 'We are living not by the hour', Dr Curtius told Rumbold at the end of September, 'but by the minute hand of the clock.' Brüning continued to rule by emergency decrees. 'Their number and complexity', Rumbold wrote to Lord Reading on October 7, 'are bewildering to the officials who have to give effect to them.' Salaries and wages were both reduced by Government order. But prices did not fall as Brüning had hoped. The French Ambassador to Berlin, André François-Poncet,[1] told Rumbold 'that the cost of living in Berlin is two to three times as much again as that in France'. Most serious of all, Rumbold himself believed, was Brüning's own sudden loss of popularity. 'Chancellor has lost 80 per cent of his prestige at home . . .', Rumbold telegraphed to Lord Reading on October 9, 'his best friends are deserting him. He takes nobody into his counsel and his prestige abroad is only factor which makes for his retention in office.' The political situation, Rumbold added, 'is both obscure and disquieting'. Among the Emergency Decrees of Brüning's Government were several which adversely affected British residents in Germany. On 4 April 1932, Rumbold sent the Foreign Office a despatch about the hardship which these Decrees had entailed. The Decree of 30 August 1931, he explained, required all foreign residents in Germany to surrender their gold to the Reichsbank before September 6, and, if the Reichsbank demanded it, to sell all such gold to the Reichsbank in exchange for German marks. A further Decree of October 2 ordered foreign residents to exchange all their foreign currency into Marks. Rumbold wrote:

---

[1] André François-Poncet, 1887–   . A student in Germany before 1914. Served as an infantry officer on the Western Front, 1914–16, and awarded the Croix de Guerre. Republican Deputy, 1924–31. Under-Secretary of State for Foreign Affairs, 1928–31. Ambassador to Berlin, 1931–38; to Rome, 1938–40. Imprisoned by the Gestapo, 1943–45. Published *Souvenirs d'une Ambassade à Berlin* in 1946 and *De Versailles à Potsdam* in 1948. French High Commissioner in Germany, 1949–55; Ambassador to Bonn, 1955.

For example, a British subject in Germany, according to the present German law, cannot make a donation to the hospital of his native town, is forbidden to pay his life insurance premium, is precluded from buying a house or a motor car and presumably is debarred from disposing of his ready cash by will without previous permission. A British chartered accountant resident in Berlin has been informed by the Reichsbank that he had no right to pay his annual life insurance premium in England without the written permission of the Reichsbank. This is not only an absurd and anomalous position, but is an unprecedented interference with the rights of British subjects in their own property within His Majesty's dominions, and it is considered dangerous that such a law should be allowed to form a precedent for Germany, or any other country.

On October 9 Brüning reconstructed his Cabinet. General Groener, the Minister of Defence, was also given the post of Minister of the Interior. 'He thus controls both army and police', Rumbold telegraphed to Lord Reading on October 9. Brüning himself took over the Foreign Ministry from Curtius. The reshuffle made it clear, Rumbold telegraphed to Reading on October 10, that Brüning had 'failed to secure the support of leading persons, notably in industry, and the new Cabinet is generally considered to be weaker than the last'.

On October 10, together with Captain Göring,[1] Hitler was received in audience by Hindenburg, and explained to the President the aims of the Nazi movement. On the following day, at the mountain resort of Bad Harzburg, Hitler, Göring and Goebbels[2] met the leaders of the other nationalist parties in order to show the existence of a 'National opposition'. On October 14 Rumbold sent Lord Reading a full account of the Harzburg meeting. Hitler had declared that in order to save Germany from Bolshevism, the Nazis 'were ready to accept responsibility and take over the government'; they would join hands with anyone who was prepared 'to fight the international spirit of Marxism'.

[1] Hermann Göring, 1893–1946. Served as a Lieutenant in the German Infantry, 1914. Commander of the Richthofen Fighter Squadron, 1918. A follower of Hitler, 1923. Wounded during the unsuccessful Munich putsch of November 1923, after which he escaped to Austria, Italy and Sweden. Air Adviser in Denmark and Sweden, 1924–28. Returned to Germany, and elected to the Reichstag, 1928. President of the Reichstag, 1932–33. Prime Minister of Prussia, 1933. Commander-in-Chief of the German Air Force, 1933–45. Air Chief Marshal, 1935. Commissioner for the Four-Year Plan, 1936. Field-Marshal, 1938. President of the General Council for the War Economy, 1940. Sentenced to death at Nuremberg, October 1946, but committed suicide the night before his intended execution.

[2] Joseph Goebbels, 1897–1945. Rejected for military service because of a deformed foot. Doctor of Philosophy at Heidelberg, 1921. Unsuccessful playwright. Joined the Hitler movement in 1922. Appointed by Hitler to be Gauleiter of Berlin, 1926. Founder of *Der Angriff* ('The Attack'), a Berlin Nazi newspaper, 1927. Elected to the Reichstag, 1929. Propaganda Leader of the Nazi Party, 1929. Minister of Enlightenment and Propaganda, 1933–45. Committed suicide in Berlin, after murdering his six children, May 1, 1945.

On October 16, Brüning succeeded in gaining a vote of confidence in the Reichstag, with a majority of twenty-five. But the Nazi efforts were unabated. On October 23 Rumbold sent Lord Reading an account of a rally at Brunswick on the previous weekend. 'Over 70,000 Nazis', he wrote, 'conveyed by 38 special trains and 5,000 motor lorries, entered Brunswick on the Saturday and remained over Sunday. The programme included numerous parades, a torchlight tattoo, a march past and, of course, several speeches by the leader of the movement, Adolf Hitler himself.' During the 'celebrations', two people were killed and several injured. 'It is quite possible', Rumbold wrote, 'that the incidents were largely due to Communist provocation.'

On October 30, before going to Italy for a month's leave, Rumbold saw Brüning, and asked him about Germany's future. Later that day he sent Lord Reading an account of their conversation. Brüning had stressed that the steady increase in support for the Nazis 'was a manifestation of despair at and discontent with the disappointment of the past and present conditions. It was a movement of youth.' On November 15, while Rumbold was in Italy, the Nazis received the largest number of votes in the Federal elections in the State of Hesse. The Social Democrats, who had previously been the leading party, received only 168,000 votes, compared with the Nazi total of 291,000. Brüning's Centre Party came third, with 112,000 votes.

In Britain, at a General Election on October 27, the National Government won 473 seats, as against Labour's 52. The National Labour Party, led by MacDonald, won only 13 seats. MacDonald remained Prime Minister, at the head of a predominantly Conservative Government. Sir John Simon,[1] a Liberal National, succeeded Lord Reading as Foreign Secretary on November 5. Neville Chamberlain became Chancellor of the Exchequer. 'I think we now have a strong Government composed of some very able men', Rumbold wrote to his son from Rapallo on November 10. 'Now that America has, for the moment, withdrawn into her shell, it is more than ever necessary that our country should play its part in world affairs. Otherwise Europe will be left at the mercy of the French.'

Rumbold believed that if France were prepared to be more flexible in its policies towards Germany, Brüning's position could be improved and the Nazi appeal considerably weakened. In late September he had read a des-

---

[1] John Allsebrook Simon, 1873–1954. Liberal MP, 1906–18; 1922–31. Solicitor-General, 1910–13. Knighted, 1911. Attorney-General, with a seat in the Cabinet, 1913–15. Home Secretary, May 1915–January 1916, when he resigned in opposition to conscription. Major, Royal Air Force, serving in France, 1917–18. Liberal National MP, 1931–40. Secretary of State for Foreign Affairs, 1931–35. Home Secretary, 1935–37. Chancellor of the Exchequer, 1937–40. Created Viscount, 1940. Lord Chancellor, 1940–45.

patch from Lord Tyrrell to the Foreign Office, in which Tyrrell maintained that French policy would be more sympathetic to Germany if the Germans would be willing to accept the Treaty of Versailles. 'No German Government', Rumbold had written to Orme Sargent on September 25, 'could give such an undertaking.' Taking the example of Germany's eastern frontier, Rumbold expressed sympathy with German aspirations. The German–Polish frontier had 'absurd' features, he wrote, which he 'as an Englishman and a parent' would be sorry to see defended by British troops. Nor, he wrote, was it fair to impute, as Tyrrell had done, a consistently militaristic tone to German policy and the German people. 'The dream of a German hegemony in Europe', Rumbold believed, had been dissipated, 'certainly for a long time', by the defeat of 1918. German militarism was bankrupt. Even if the Nazis spoke in militaristic tones, 'it would not be fair', Rumbold wrote in his letter to Sargent, 'to tar the bulk of the German population with the Nazi brush'. But if the French continued to refuse both to disarm and to abandon their demand for reparations, there would be, as Rumbold wrote to his son on December 13, a 'Dämmerung of this world'.

Rumbold had returned to Berlin on December 2. While he had been on leave, Hitler had made strenuous efforts to impress on all who met him that the Nazis were capable of responsible government. Rumbold did not believe this to be so, and did not wish to give Hitler a chance to try to impress him. 'A friend of Hitler's', he wrote to Orme Sargent on December 4, 'was lunching with Cornwall, the Military Attaché, yesterday and said that he might bring Hitler to lunch. . . . But I have told Cornwall that he must certainly not entertain any such suggestion.'[1]

Throughout the winter Hitler was being spoken of as the next Chancellor. On December 15 Rumbold wrote to Rowe-Dutton that 'the sedulously propagated idea that Hitler is Brüning's inevitable successor and the "man of tomorrow" is as much the result of mass suggestion and of a psychological state as anything else. One tends to forget that Hitler has serious difficulties of his own, not the least of which is the wretched quality of his so-called lieutenants.' The following year, he told Rowe-Dutton, might see the Nazi Party 'break into half'. But three days later, in a long and detailed letter to the new Secretary of State, Sir John Simon, he warned against attaching too much importance to the discrepancies between Hitler's increasingly moderate statements, and the continuing

---

[1] The friend was 'Putzi' Hanfstaengel, who had sheltered Hitler after the abortive Munich putsch of 1925. Marshall-Cornwall later recalled how Rumbold had said to him, over the telephone: 'I won't see Hitler, and I won't let any member of my staff see Hitler.' This peremptory order made Marshall-Cornwall 'very indignant'; but in retrospect he felt that Rumbold had been wise not to meet Hitler while he was in opposition.

extremism of his supporters. 'For the moment', Rumbold wrote, 'the Nazi movement holds its followers in a grip resembling that of a religious revival. . . . Whatever his followers may say and do, the Nazi leader has only to issue a command to insure instant obedience. He does not hesitate to contradict his lieutenants or reduce them to ridicule without in any way seeming to undermine party loyalty.'

The possibility of a Hitler Government, Rumbold believed, need not cause too much alarm. 'There is a German proverb', he told Simon in his letter of December 18, 'which says that the soup is not eaten as hot as it is cooked.' A coalition of the Right, including the Nazis, might, he explained, 'prove more amenable in matters of foreign policy than the outer world suspects, and it would probably contain some of the ablest men and best brains in the country'. But Rumbold did not disregard the dangers. On December 12 he had sent Simon a report by Colonel Marshall-Cornwall which showed that it was not the Nazi Party alone that posed a threat to the future stability of Europe, but also the German Army. Marshall-Cornwall gave evidence of several flagrant violations of the Versailles Treaty. Stocks of weapons were being accumulated. In many technical branches the German Army was 'in advance of other countries'. Cavalry regiments were being transformed into machine-gun regiments. Artillery companies were being mechanized. Research was being done into the construction of military aircraft. Each of these developments infringed the limitations of the Versailles Treaty. Another ominous development, Marshall-Cornwall reported, was that 'most of the younger officers sympathize with Nazi ideals'.[1] There was, he added, an 'innate Germanic urge to be marshalled in mass and to march at the sound of a drum'. Marshall-Cornwall declared that, after four years' observation, he did not regard the German Army 'as a present danger to any neighbouring Power'; but he ended on a warning note:

There are evident signs, though, that a change of system is not only meditated but is being actively prepared. New weapons are being tested and their manufacture organised; reserve stocks of ammunition are being accumulated and new methods of transport and communication developed. So far it has proved impossible to do much in the way of training illegal reserves of man-power, but the patriotic associations have successfully upheld the military tradition and fostered the fighting spirit. The danger is not imminent, but it is throwing its shadow ahead. Infractions of the treaty restrictions have lately become more

[1] Forty years later Marshall-Cornwall recalled that many of the young officers whom he met were convinced 'that the only way to restore their national integrity was to join the Nazi Party'; on one occasion Colonel Fischer, the head of the Intelligence Department of the German Army, had said to him: 'You can't expect us to look to Britain while you go on treating us like a nigger state.'

frequent and less concealed; one wonders whether this does not denote the thin end of the wedge which will split the whole fabric of the treaty. The next few months may see a new and more active political orientation in Germany, and the movement for liberation once launched will be difficult to arrest. It seems advisable to reflect whether we can continue to suppress Germany's potential military power by methods which ultimately rest on the deployment of superior strength.

For Germany, 1932 promised to be a year of amelioration. The British Government were prepared to sponsor two conferences, one to bring about the disarmament of Germany's neighbours, the other to reduce, or even bring to an end, the reparations owed by Germany to the victorious powers of 1918. The reparations conference was the first to be arranged. It was to take place at Lausanne, beginning on January 18. The German Press, Rumbold wrote to Sir John Simon on the last day of 1931, were giving credit to the British Government 'for their energy in hastening the date of the conference'. On January 5 Rumbold sent Simon a nine-page private letter, in which he set out his personal assessment of the state of German public opinion. The two principal moderate parties, the Centre and the Social Democrats, had taken up the Nationalist view of reparations; that they must be abolished. No scheme of long-term payments, or deferred payments, would satisfy them. The Centre Party spokesman, Dr Kaas, had declared, in a newspaper article, that 'German payments in any shape or form are out of the question'. But it was the Nazis who had made the greatest political capital by their total unqualified hostility to reparations, and by their demands that Germany should be militarily as strong as her neighbour. 'The Hitler slogan', Rumbold added, 'was "Germany awake", which implied the words "and assert thyself". That was the spirit in which the Germans were going into the reparations and disarmament conferences. There must be no mistake about that.' Brüning's emergency decrees had 'cut deeply into the life of every German'. But reduced wages, and severe economic restrictions, meant that 'in their hearts the German people were determined that the sacrifices which they had been called on to bear should not be in vain, and that they should have some recompense in the shape of complete relief from reparations'.

On January 8, at an interview with Rumbold, Brüning made it clear that his Government would not accept any solution about reparations other than that they should be cancelled altogether. 'Germany', he told Rumbold, 'was not in a position to pay reparations either now or at any time in the foreseeable future.' Rumbold argued that once Germany returned to prosperity, there would be money enough to pay reparations; for example, once the German railways were making a profit, surplus railway revenue could be paid over to the allied powers. Brüning replied that such a scheme was 'an entire illusion'; the railways would always be in debt to the various municipalities which subsidized them. Rumbold persisted in his argument, but, as he telegraphed to Simon immediately after the interview: 'Chancellor then said that he was forced to take the psychology of the German nation into account. He could not indefinitely call on it to make sacrifices without a prospect of a final relief from the reparations burden. A moratorium for two, three, or even four years would merely prolong the uncertainty and increase the feeling of hopelessness in the nation.'

Somehow the gist of this interview was leaked to the Press. The result was an outburst of fury from the French. In the resulting crisis, the opening of the Lausanne Conference, due later that month, was postponed until June. On January 20, when a further postponement, until October, was suggested, Rumbold telegraphed to Simon: 'If matters are allowed to drift there is a real risk that the Brüning Government may be swept away long before October and replaced by a National Socialist combination which will flatly reject emergency plan and refuse all further reparations payments.' Finally it was agreed to hold the conference in June.

Rumbold wrote to Sir George Grahame[1] on January 18 that the Press leak 'succeeded in poisoning the international atmosphere for at least ten days'. To his stepmother, on the previous day, he had written: 'If there is one thing I hate it is figuring in the press. . . .' The resulting crisis was evidence, he told his stepmother, 'that European nerves are in such a deplorable state that they can't stand any shock at all. And all this 14 years after the war! It is really rather tragic.'

One outcome of the leak was an immediate increase in Brüning's popularity inside Germany. The Chancellor had said 'no' to reparations. When Harold Nicolson arrived in Berlin on a private visit on January 22 he found that Brüning's position had been strengthened; Hitler's correspondingly weakened. 'Arrive Berlin in a misty dawn', he wrote in his diary. 'Go to see Rumbold. He tells me that he thinks the Hitlerites have missed the boat and are losing ground every day.' After two days in Berlin, Nicolson felt able to confirm Rumbold's impressions. 'The unintellectual people', he wrote in his diary on January 24, 'are beginning to feel that Brüning and not Hitler represents the soul of Germany.' 'Rumbold', Nicolson wrote in his diary, 'feels that anything may happen and that the only thing certain is uncertainty.'

On January 18 Rumbold received a disturbing document from Colonel

---

[1] George Dixon Grahame, 1873–1940. Entered Diplomatic Service, 1896; knighted, 1918. Ambassador at Brussels, 1920–28; Madrid, 1928–35.

Marshall-Cornwall. It was an account of the internal organization of the Nazi Party, and its highly military nature. Not only had fourteen Sturm-Abteilung (SA) groups been formed, of over 30,000 men each, but an officers' training school had been set up at Munich which had already trained nearly 500 'leaders'. A smaller organization, the Schutzstaffel (SS), was providing 'a corps d'élite or guards corps of specially selected men'. Motor drivers and mechanics, and schoolboys and girls, were also being organized in special units. It was difficult to decide, Marshall-Cornwall wrote, how much all this was 'political buffoonery'; he himself feared that the nature of the organization pointed 'to more dangerous ideals of expansion, and the resuscitation of former military traditions'. In forwarding this despatch to Sir John Simon on January 19, Rumbold commented that the 'somewhat flamboyant plan' of the Nazi organization had been worked out largely to make political propaganda, and that 'the actual training done by the storm detachments is at the most of a very sketchy nature'. But he went on to draw Simon's attention to Hitler's own description of his 'ideal', which Marshall-Cornwall had quoted. The Nazi aim, Hitler had written in *Mein Kampf*, was 'not to set up a more or less well trained army, but to convert a whole nation into the spiritual frame of unconditional willingness and preparedness to fight in self-defence. This demand has nothing to do with weapons and military organization, but is a question of the inner consolidation of a national body. . . .'

While waiting for the reparations conference to meet, several leading German politicians began to press for a return to Germany of some of her lost colonies. On January 31 Rumbold was invited to dine with Trevi-ranus, Dr Luther and Duke Adolf of Mecklenburg,[1] a former Governor of Togoland.[2] Before setting off, Rumbold wrote to his son that he imagined that the guests 'will propagand me in favour of the return of one or two of the former German colonies, but there is nothing doing in that direction'. On February 2 Rumbold sent Orme Sargent a full account of the dinner conversation. 'They one and all pointed out', he wrote, 'that Germany needed an outlet and that it was not sufficient for Germans to settle in the colonies of other countries.' Luther warned that unless the youth of Germany had a colonial outlet they might be 'drawn by despair into the ranks of the extreme Right or the extreme Left. . . . If Germany had an outlet in the shape of a colony or colonies in Africa the attentions at all events of some of these young men would be directed to those settle-

[1] Duke Adolf Friedrich von Mecklenburg, 1873–1969. Governor of Togoland, 1912–14. Member of the International Olympic Committee, 1926. President German Olympic Committee, 1949–51. Author of *Ins Innerste Afrika* (1909) and *Vom Kongo zum Niger und Nil* (1912).

[2] The British had captured Togoland on August 26, 1914, after three weeks' fighting. In 1919 it became a League of Nations Mandate, and was divided between Britain and France.

ments.' The Germans also insisted that the return of their colonies 'would cement the friendship between England and Germany'. They asked if Rumbold would be willing to bring about meetings between prominent Englishmen and Germans to discuss the Colonial question. 'I told him quite plainly', Rumbold informed Sargent, 'that I could do nothing of the sort and that I would not even touch the matter.'

At the beginning of February the Germans began to protest over alleged Lithuanian ill-treatment of the German-speaking inhabitants of Memel, a Baltic port which had been German until 1918[1]. On February 2 Rumbold wrote to the British Minister to Lithuania, Hughe Knatchbull-Hugesson,[2] of 'the cussedness which is peculiar to this race'. To his son, on February 7, he wrote bitterly: 'It is intolerable that such a rotten little affair should absorb so much time and money (in telegrams) and if our man in Riga goes on telegraphing at the present rate he will upset the equilibrium of the budget and we shall have to put another penny on the income tax. . . . 7 telegrams came in yesterday and 3 this morning.' The Memel crisis prompted him to reflect, in his letter to his son: 'Every foreigner in his heart of hearts relies finally on us, in the long run. We are the linch-pin of the world's political structure, and, as was said of the Austro-Hungarian Empire before the war, if we didn't exist we should have to be invented.' This, he added, would be said 'with more truth about us than about Austria-Hungary. And so, with these patriotic reflections, I will end. . . .'

Throughout the spring Rumbold continued to collect as much information as he could about German domestic politics, and to send it to the Foreign Office, and to the King. He attended several sessions of the Reichstag, he dined with leading German politicians, soldiers and businessmen, he followed carefully the German Press, and noted assiduously the utterances of the principal contenders for power. At the end of February he was present at the Reichstag meeting when Brüning won a further vote of confidence. But he was much struck, he wrote to Clive Wigram on February 27, 'by the unmannerly behaviour of the Nazis. They are like a lot of ill-bred schoolboys, who, to our ideas, behave like cads. The thought that the destinies of the country might be entrusted to such people is rather depressing.' But, he added, 'we are far from that yet'. The possibility of a Nazi success was a daily theme of Rumbold's correspondence. 'Is a Hitler Govt coming?' Nevile Henderson had written from Belgrade

---

[1] Memel was reincorporated in Germany on March 22, 1939.

[2] Hughe Montgomery Knatchbull-Hugesson, 1886–1971. Entered Foreign Office, 1908. Counsellor, Brussels, 1926–30. British Minister to the Baltic States (Latvia, Lithuania and Estonia), 1930–34; to Teheran, 1934–36. Knighted, 1936. Ambassador in Peking, 1936–38; in Ankara, 1939–44; in Brussels, 1944–47. He published *Diplomat in Peace and War* in 1949.

on February 17; 'It appears to me that it must in the end – though I can't see much good resulting therefrom. The German Minister here[1] is an ardent Hitlerite.' There were, of course, 'decent elements in the Nazi party', Rumbold wrote to his son on February 28, 'but their parliamentary representatives are deplorable and their leaders beneath contempt. Goebbels is a wretched little creature.'

At the end of February Rumbold met General von Hammerstein,[2] one of the most influential officers in the German Army, at dinner, and on March 1 sent Sir John Simon an account of their conversation. When Rumbold mentioned the crude behaviour of the Nazi deputies in the Reichstag, Hammerstein replied that 'it would not be altogether fair to judge the Nazi party by the conduct of its representatives in Parliament, as it also contained good elements. Its leaders were, of course, deplorable.' The German nation, he said, 'would not stand a dictatorship'. Hitler, he added, was 'a very mediocre personality', and could not be compared with Mussolini.

Hitler continued to advance his power within the democratic framework. In March 1932 he challenged Hindenburg for the German Presidency. The challenge was unsuccessful. In the first ballot, on March 13, Hindenburg polled over eighteen and a half million votes, Hitler just under eleven and a half. The Communist candidate, Ernst Thaelmann[3] received five million. Because Hindenburg failed to win an absolute majority, a second ballot was fixed for April 10.

Although the first ballot had not brought Hitler victory, it had secured him five million votes more than the Nazis had won in the General Election of 1931. In a letter to Simon on March 16, Rumbold commented on the remarkable organization of the Nazis: 'Every village and hamlet in the remotest parts of the country was canvassed diligently.' But Hitler's

---

[1] Christian Albrecht Ulrich von Hassell, 1881–1944. A member of the Hanoverian nobility and a son-in-law of Admiral Tirpitz. Entered the German Diplomatic Service, 1919. Minister in Copenhagen, 1926–30; Belgrade, 1930–32. Ambassador to the Vatican, 1932–38. He became an early member of the German opposition to Hitler, and a candidate for the post of Foreign Minister should Hitler be overthrown. He was sentenced to death for his part in the July Plot, and hanged by the Nazis on September 8, 1944.

[2] Kurt von Hammerstein-Equord, 1878–1943. Entered the German Army, 1898; Captain, General Staff, 1913; Major, 1914; General, 1930. Chief of Staff of the German Army, 1930–34. Commanded Army Group A, based on Cologne, 1939. An outspoken opponent of the Nazis, from 1938 until his death he was a leading member of the anti-Hitler circle; in September 1939 he had hoped to entice Hitler to Cologne in order to arrest him. After his death his widow and daughter were confined in Buchenwald Concentration Camp.

[3] Ernst Thaelmann, 1886–1944. Dockworker. A Social Democrat before 1914. Communist Member of the Reichstag, 1924–33, and Leader of the Communist Party. Imprisoned without trial on the Nazi accession to power, he died in Buchenwald Concentration Camp on August 28, 1944.

'raucous campaign against the Jews', he added, had done the Nazis much harm, and had driven the Jews to support Hindenburg. The 'traditional' Jewish weapons against oppression, Rumbold wrote, 'their intelligence and their wealth, was employed against the Nationalist Socialist, and their friends abroad, and especially in America, came generously to their help'. Nevertheless, he wrote to his son on March 18, Hitler's hopes were not totally extinguished: 'all the youth of the country – or much of it – is on his side', a good reason, Rumbold added, for raising the voting age to twenty-five – 'Youths and maidens of 20 aren't really mature.'

The second ballot took place on April 10. Hindenburg received over nineteen million votes and was re-elected President. Hitler received nearly thirteen and a half million votes, almost 40 per cent of the votes. The result showed, Rumbold wrote to his stepmother on April 13, that 'the Hitler movement is stronger than ever'. Hitler, he went on, 'has the gift of appealing to the discontented and youthful elements of the population, though when one tries to analyse the substance of his speeches one finds that they mainly consist of windy phrases. He may be compared to a re-vivalist preacher with the appearance of a greengrocer wearing an air-force moustache.'

Rumbold had been impressed by Hitler's energy during the campaign for the second poll. Although Brüning had campaigned vigorously for Hindenburg, Hitler had been undeterred, even spurred on to greater efforts, making, as Rumbold reported to Simon on April 13, 'a whirlwind tour of the country, travelling by aeroplane, often at great risk in stormy weather, and giving proof of extraordinary resolution'. He had also altered the tone of his propaganda. 'His posters and pamphlets', Rumbold wrote, 'showed him in a paternal guise, stooping over perambulators and accepting bouquets. His party was, he declared, not at all a reactionary party. His followers were fathers and mothers of families similar in all respects to Socialist fathers and mothers.' The Presidential election was a setback for Hitler, but not a serious one. On April 13 Robert Weismann, the Prussian Secretary of State, told Rumbold that both Hindenburg and Brüning had been much displeased by the second ballot, because it had made it clear that the Nazi movement 'was still making progress'. Two days earlier General Groener had told him that he had formed the impression 'that Hitler was a visionary, but quite a decent sort of man'.

On April 24 there were elections for the Prussian Landtag. The Nazi Party made extraordinary gains, increasing their number of seats from 9 to 162, and forming the largest group, though not a majority, in the pro-vincial assembly. Even in the Army the Nazis were winning support.

When, eleven days before the Prussian elections, the Nazi storm troops (SA) and defence squads (SS) had been banned, there was 'marked disapproval' within the Army at such action, as the new Military Attaché, Colonel Thorne,[1] reported to Rumbold on April 19. 'The officers as a whole', wrote Thorne, 'feel that the Nazi movement is the best available means of disciplining the youth of the country, for whom no service in the army is possible, and that it keeps them out of the Communist ranks; in addition it is an attractive method to the Germans as a whole of expressing their devotion to their country.'

The Foreign Office asked Rumbold's opinion of the two election results. 'Hitlerites do not constitute a majority of the German people', he wrote to Orme Sargent on May 3, 'nor do I think they will do so, unless the Disarmament and Reparation Conferences are a washout, and other unpleasant things happen to Germany.'

In May Rumbold took two weeks' leave. He went to see the King and spent nearly an hour with him, discussing German affairs. He also lunched with the editor of the *Observer*, J. L. Garvin,[2] who informed him that England was unlikely to agree to cancel reparations, as such a move would lead the Americans to say that if Britain could afford to give up the money owed her by Germany, she was surely rich enough to pay the war debts she owed to America at a more substantial rate. On May 26 Garvin wrote to Rumbold, setting out what he thought the Germans, and Brüning, ought to do:

I think Germany will have to take the bull by the horns and that a German Catholic Chancellor will have to repeat Martin Luther: 'Hier steh Ich; Ich kann kein anders; Gott helfe mir; Amen'. That is:—'It is impossible for us to pay; God help us: whether it ever will be possible for us to pay only God knows!' Then there will be sympathy; which there never is with us; in spite of the grinding pressure on ourselves we look too quiet and carry our heads too high! Sympathy with Germany, if Catholic Brüning spoke like Luther at Worms, would be followed by action on America's part (German volk there!)

---

[1] Augustus Francis Andrew Nicol Thorne, 1885–1970. Joined Grenadier Guards, 1904. Commanded the 3rd battalion, Grenadier Guards, 1916–18. Assistant Military Attaché, Washington, 1919–20. Military Attaché, Berlin, 1932–35. Major-General Commanding the Brigade of Guards, 1938–39. Commanded the 48th Division, BEF, 1939–40. Commanded Scottish Command, 1941–45. Knighted, 1942. President of the Old Etonian Association, 1949–50. Served in the Norwegian Ministry of Defence, 1950–51. In 1972 Thorne's son commented: 'My father learnt German before the War, when he was in Freiburg-im-Breisgau in 1910–11. The Germans respected that; and also the fact that he had lost three brothers, and his wife had lost two brothers, during the War.'

[2] James Louis Garvin, 1868–1947. Editor, the *Observer*, 1908–42. Editor, the *Pall Mall Gazette*, 1912–15. Editor-in-Chief, the *Encyclopaedia Britannica*, 1926–29. His only son, Roland, had been killed in action on the Western Front in 1916.

But it was too late for Brüning to speak out. On May 30, as a result of an intrigue led by General Kurt von Schleicher,[1] Hindenburg dismissed Brüning, and invited Count von Papen[2] to become Chancellor of Germany. General Schleicher became Minister of Defence.

Seven of the nine members of von Papen's Cabinet were from noble families; for the first time since the establishment of the Weimar Republic in 1919 there was no representative of organized Labour. Nor was any National Socialist asked to participate. 'I didn't think it possible', Rumbold wrote to his son on May 31, while still in London, 'that the President and the intriguers who must have been getting at him would bring about Brüning's resignation just at this moment and throw away their greatest asset and best trump card; the Teuton is an incredible being – he is the reverse of a political animal.'

On June 4, two days after his return to Berlin, Rumbold sent Sir John Simon information which he had gleaned about Brüning's fall. 'Berlin intriguers', he telegraphed, 'aimed not so much at Brüning's dismissal as at establishment of a strong government at home with right-tendencies in order to stave off Hitler and his anti-capitalist programme. Schleicher in particular is said to have been prepared if necessary to suspend the Constitution rather than entrust defence forces to an inexperienced demagogue'. On June 6 Rumbold asked Bülow, the Secretary of State, what Hitler's relations with the new government would be. Bülow believed, Rumbold reported to Simon on June 9, that Papen's Government 'seemed to be fairly confident that Hitler would support them and they expected to stay in office for a considerable time – perhaps four years'. But he feared that the change of Government was for the worst; it had, he wrote to Vansittart on June 14, 'caused the Nationalist and jingo elements in the Foreign Office to throw off the mask'.

The Lausanne Conference on reparations opened on June 16, and continued for more than three weeks, until July 9. Sixteen countries were present. Ramsay MacDonald represented Britain; von Papen represented

---

[1] Kurt von Schleicher, 1882–1934. Entered the Imperial German Army, 1900. Appointed to the General Staff, May 1914. Served under Groener, and then Ludendorff, 1914–18. Organized the military measures against the Communist uprisings in Saxony and Thuringia, 1923. Colonel, 1926; Major-General, 1929. Defence Minister June–December 1932. Chancellor, December 1932–January 1933. Murdered by the Nazi SS, June 30, 1934.

[2] Franz von Papen, 1879–1969. Cavalry officer, and member of the Westphalian aristocracy. Military Attaché, Washington, 1914–16; expelled from the United States on a charge of sabotage. A leading shareholder in the Centre Party newspaper, *Germania*. Never elected to the Reichstag. Chancellor, June–November 1932. A member of Hitler's Cabinet, 1933–34. Ambassador to Vienna, 1934–38. Tried at Nuremberg, and acquitted, 1946.

Germany, and Edouard Herriot[1] represented France. Simultaneously, at Geneva, the world disarmament talks continued to make little progress. 'The Prime Minister and our other Cabinet Ministers', Clive Wigram wrote to Rumbold on June 29, 'are working like niggers at Lausanne and Geneva, but if anything will come out of it, heaven only knows!' On June 16, the day of the opening of the Lausanne Conference, von Papen had rescinded Brüning's order forbidding the Nazi storm troops from parading or wearing uniforms. The result of this, Rumbold wrote to Wigram a week later, was 'the revival of daily brawls, which always end in the death or wounding of some of the participants . . . one cannot wonder that the French may be chary of agreeing to an appreciable reduction in their army when they see the illicit armies tolerated by the German Government'.

Hitler's electoral successes continued. On June 19, in the provincial election in Hesse, the Nazi vote had increased from 37 per cent to 44 per cent of the total vote cast, the Nazis thereby maintaining their position as the largest single party, though still without an overall majority. The Social Democrats came second, with 21 per cent, the Centre Party third with 14 per cent, the Communists fourth with $13\frac{1}{2}$ per cent.

The street violence continued throughout July, and there were several deaths each week. 'The victims', Rumbold wrote to Simon on July 16, 'are not always necessarily members of the Hitler storm troops or Communists, but are often inoffensive women and young boys.' Amid these brutalities, the ending of the Lausanne Conference passed almost unnoticed inside Germany. Yet the Conference had achieved just what the Germans had wanted; reparations were no more. On July 9 Sir Maurice Hankey wrote to Rumbold from Lausanne of 'this rather notable day in European history, when we have just signed the ending of reparations'; but it was a day which contemporaries were soon to forget. Violence mounted in Germany as July progressed. A General Election was due to be held on the last day of the month. The German triumph at Lausanne marked a major success of the policy which Stresemann had begun and Brüning continued; but such comment as there was in the German Press was hostile to the settlement. It must be borne in mind, Rumbold wrote to Hankey on July 15, 'that it is a German characteristic never to admit that any arrangement is entirely satisfactory from the German point of

---

[1] Edouard Herriot, 1872–1957. Mayor of Lyon, 1905–40. Senator, 1912–19. Minister of Public Works, 1916–17. President of the Radical Party, 1919–40; of the Socialist–Radical Party, 1945–57. Deputy 1919–40. Prime Minister, June 1924–April 1925 and July 1926. Held numerous Ministerial posts, 1926–36. President of the Chamber, 1936–40. Interned in Germany, 1944–45. President of the National Assembly, 1947–54. Among his many publications were *La Russie Nouvelle* (1922) and a biography of *Beethoven* (1932).

view'. Rumbold's comments were supported in the Foreign Office. Two
months later Orme Sargent minuted: 'It must be remembered that for the
last 13 years every one of the demands which Germany has put forward
has received sympathetic encouragement from this country.'

The General Election of July 31 was indecisive. The Nazis had more
than doubled their vote since the previous General Election of September
1930, but still did not have an overall majority. With over thirteen and
a half million votes, they were the largest party in the State, receiving
230 seats. The Social Democrats polled nearly eight million votes, receiving 133 seats. The Communists, with just over five million votes, had
78 seats, and the Centre Party four and a half million votes, 69 seats. The
Nazis achieved over 37 per cent of the total poll, but Hitler's impetus
appeared to be on the wane. 'So far from achieving the 51% which
his followers hoped', Rumbold wrote to Simon on August 3, 'Hitler
seems now to have exhausted his reserves.'

Despite his election success, Hitler was not invited to join von Papen's
Cabinet. 'The Nazis', Rumbold reiterated in a letter to Simon on August 4
'are now in a difficult position. It would appear that they have shot their
bolt.' Their immediate reaction was to increase the terror in the streets.
Writing to Simon on August 10, Rumbold described how, in Königsberg,
'prominent Socialists and Communists were surprised at night and
murdered in their beds or shot down at the doors of their houses. The
windows of shops owned by Jews were smashed and their contents
looted. Petrol stations were set on fire, whilst attacks with high explosives
were directed against the offices of Democratic newspapers.' For ten days,
in every part of Germany, there was 'shooting, stabbing, arson and the use
of high explosives'. On August 9, in an attempt to halt the violence, von
Papen issued an emergency decree, imposing the death penalty for attacking a political opponent. Four days later, in the presence of von Papen,
Hindenburg asked Hitler if he would be willing to join von Papen's
Government. Hitler declined; demanding instead that he himself should be
invited to become Chancellor, and be given complete control of the State.

The position in the Reichstag was unprecedented. The Nazis, with 230
of the 602 seats, held no places in the Cabinet. Von Papen's Government,
as Rumbold had telegraphed to Simon on July 29, 'represents no party, its
members . . . taking no part in the election'. The Ministers were chosen,
not by any mandate from the electorate for the parties to which they
belonged, but by von Papen's personal decision. At a celebration in the
Reichstag on August 11, to mark the anniversary of the establishment of
the Weimar Republic, both the Nazi and Social Democratic deputies
stayed away.

On August 22 Rumbold was received by von Papen, with whom he had a lengthy conversation which he reported to Simon later in the day. The Reichstag would meet on August 30, von Papen told him, and would be presided over by the Communist revolutionary, Klara Zetkin,[1] who, as the senior member of the Reichstag, was entitled to that ceremonial honour. 'What a comment', von Papen exclaimed, 'on the results of the parliamentary system.' Klara Zetkin, he added, would be coming specially from Moscow for the ceremony. Von Papen also told Rumbold that Hindenburg would not be prepared to entrust Hitler with the Chancellor-ship, 'even should the latter be able to assure the President that he had formed a coalition with a working majority'.

On August 29 von Papen offered Hitler the post of Vice-Chancellor within his Cabinet. 'Hitler however', Rumbold telegraphed to Simon on the following day, 'maintained his demand to be entrusted with full power, namely the formation of government.' The Reichstag met on August 30. Rumbold, who was present, wrote to Simon that same day of how all the 230 Nazi deputies were in their 'brown shirt' uniform, 'looking smart and well-groomed'. As Klara Zetkin took the chair the other 88 Communist deputies rose and gave three 'Red front' cheers. 'In a silence so complete as to be almost uncanny', Rumbold continued, 'Klara Zetkin, though ill and struggling for breath, made a speech of a propagandist order, in which she referred to the collapse of capitalism, the coming revolution, and abused the Papen Government.' The Nazi deputies, he added, 'displayed complete unconcern'.

Von Papen had planned to introduce a Decree in the Reichstag to enable industrialists to lower wages. But on September 12 the Com-munists insisted on bringing a motion of no confidence. Von Papen at once tried to dissolve the Reichstag, but Göring, the President of the Session, refused to read, or indeed to pick up, the dissolution paper which von Papen produced, and the Communist vote of censure was passed, with full Nazi support, by 512 votes to 42. Von Papen promptly dissolved the Reichstag, and a new General Election, the second of the year, was fixed for November 6. 'The Nazis and the Centre will, I think, lose ground', Rumbold wrote to his son on September 18, 'and the Communists will gain.' But, as he informed Simon three days later, the Nazis would 'so far as can be foreseen, still remain the strongest party in the State'.

On September 28 Rumbold had a long conversation with Hindenburg's

---

[1] Klara Zetkin, 1857–1934. Schoolteacher. Editor of the Women's Social Democratic Party newspaper, *Gleichheit*, 1891–1916. A member of the German Communist Party from its foundation in 1919, and one of the Party's leading orators. Communist Deputy in the Reichstag, 1920–33. She died at Archangel, in the Soviet Union.

Secretary of State, Otto Meissner.[1] 'I asked Dr Meissner what impressions he had formed of Hitler', Rumbold wrote to Simon later that day. 'He replied that when one could get him alone he was quite reasonable and moderate, but he was apt to go into a kind of trance, when he talked wildly and had to be brought down to earth again. His habits were ascetic, for he drank nothing and did not smoke. It would be a mistake to suppose that he was not still the directing force of his movement. He was the real leader.'

On September 29 Colonel Thorne sent Rumbold his report on the German Army manoeuvres near Frankfurt. The general public, he wrote, 'who flocked to the manoeuvres from near and far, showed such marked interest in the work of the troops that on several occasions machine gun posts etc were entirely hidden by a circle of interested spectators'. The manoeuvres themselves had been far more efficient than those which Marshall-Cornwall had watched in 1928. 'I have to acknowledge', Colonel Thorne concluded, 'being immensely impressed by the obvious efficiency of the German troops and the high standard of training to which they have been brought.'

Rumbold spent October on leave, driving in his Rolls-Royce through Nuremberg and Innsbruck to Lake Garda, and then, after a week in Italy, going on to Cap d'Antibes, in the South of France. 'I was very sorry to leave Italy', he wrote to his son from Cap d'Antibes on October 16, 'and came away greatly impressed by the driving force of Mussolini. The roads everywhere are just as good as any we have in England and they have numerous auto-stradas which we haven't.' It would be a good idea, Rumbold wrote, if Mussolini were to go on a mission to Russia to 'clear up the mess there. He would soon put a stop to the gangsters and racketeers just as he ended the Mafia.' On November 1 Rumbold returned to England. While he was still on leave, the German General Election took place. The Nazis retained their position as the largest single party, although the percentage of their vote dropped from 37 to 33. The Social Democrats remained the second largest party, with 20 per cent of the vote. The Communist percentage rose from just over 14 to almost 17.

Rumbold returned to Berlin in the second week of November. Von Papen was struggling to form a new Government. Hitler declared that he would never accept any position except that of Chancellor. The Centre Party also refused to enter Papen's Cabinet. Hindenburg insisted that the

[1] Otto Meissner, 1880–1953. A Prussian Civil Servant, his career before 1914 was spent in the railway administration of Alsace-Lorraine. State Secretary to successive Presidents of the Republic, 1920–37. Promoted Minister of State, 1937. Tried as a War Criminal at Nuremberg, 1947; acquitted of all charges, 1949. He published his memoirs, *Staatssekretär unter Ebert, Hindenburg, und Hitler* in 1950.

new Government should be a national one, based on the principal political parties. This having proved impossible, on November 17 von Papen resigned. 'Tomorrow', Rumbold wrote to his son on November 18, 'the old President is to receive Hitler and much will turn on that interview. If they came to terms there will be the possibility of a Coalition, but if they don't, then there may be a renewal of the experiment of Presidential Gov. . . . Meanwhile we have to keep our eyes skinned and are spending quite a deal of public money on telegrams.'

Hitler saw Hindenburg on November 19. He told the President that he would only place his movement at the disposal of a Government of which he himself was the head. Negotiations continued for several days, but Hitler would not modify his demands. By November 30 it was becoming likely that General Schleicher might form a Government; on that day he offered Hitler the post of Vice-Chancellor, together with a number of Ministries for his supporters. But Hitler declined; he must have full powers, he insisted, or remain in opposition.

On December 2 General Schleicher became Chancellor. 'His aim', Rumbold wrote to Simon on December 7, 'is to tame, without destroying, the valuable national movement which he feels is hidden somewhere in Hitlerism.' On December 21 Rumbold had his first audience with the new Chancellor, asking him how he viewed his future relations with the Nazis. 'He replied', Rumbold wrote to Simon after the audience, that he had some hopes that the Nazi Party 'would come to heel and would support his Government'. Some Nazis, said Schleicher, were prepared to do this, but Hitler himself 'was an incalculable personality and nobody could forecast his line of action'. Nevertheless, Schleicher informed Rumbold, his aim was to 'harness' the Nazi movement 'in the service of the State'. Ten days later, when Schleicher spoke to Reuter's agent in Berlin, Victor Bodker,[1] he spoke 'in contemptuous terms' about Hitler, whom he described as 'a mystic and impractical person'. Bodker passed on this scathing comment to Rumbold, who sent it to the Foreign Office on 4 January 1933, in a confidential letter to Orme Sargent.

Hitler's strength continued to grow; on January 15, in provincial elections at Lippe, the Nazi vote was increased by 20 per cent over the previous November. Hitler's support was already being sought by Schleicher's enemies; on January 4 von Papen had met Hitler at Cologne, and proposed that they work together towards the establishment of a new Government, in which they would have equal powers. Hitler reiterated his demand that unless he were given full powers, he wanted no part in any administration.

---

[1] Victor Bodker, 1890–   . Entered Reuter's Agency, 1920. Served for several years in India. Posted to Berlin, 1923–34. Left Reuters, 1934. Editor, *Cyprus Mail*, 1935–46.

On January 18, two weeks before the Reichstag was due to meet, Rumbold informed Simon that a 'complete state of uncertainty prevails in the political world here, and nobody knows whether the Reichstag *will* meet. . . .' On January 27 he dined with Meissner, who told him that 'a proposal was on foot to constitute what he called a majority government embracing all parties', with Hitler as Chancellor and Papen as Vice-Chancellor. The Nazis, said Meissner, would have 'one or two other portfolios'. He saw no danger in a Hitler Government, telling Rumbold that 'Hitler had shown signs of late of being more moderate and had realised that his policy of negation was leading nowhere'. The Centre Party, he said, 'felt it would anyhow be necessary some time or other to saddle Hitler with the responsibility and let him show the country what he could do. There was also a general feeling that a government under Hitler which included a proportion of ministers who were not National Socialists would be unable to embark on dangerous experiments.'

From his talk with Meissner on January 27, Rumbold drew the conclusion 'that Schleicher is finished'. This was indeed so; on the following day Schleicher resigned. Hindenburg had refused to give him permission to dissolve the Reichstag immediately it met on January 31. Schleicher had been Chancellor for only fifty-four days.

On January 30, two days after Schleicher's resignation, Hindenburg followed the constitutional procedure of entrusting the Chancellorship to the leader of the strongest party in the Reichstag. In this way, Hitler achieved his ambition. But although he had become Chancellor, only a minority of his Cabinet were members of the Nazi Party. Non-Nazis held some of the more important posts: von Papen became Vice-Chancellor, von Neurath[1] remained Foreign Minister, Hugenberg, the Nationalist leader, became Minister of Commerce and of Food. Hindenburg intended these non-Nazis to act as a moderating influence on Hitler. But the Nazis realized that their victory was complete. That night the watchers from the British Embassy witnessed the Nazi triumph: 'From 8 p.m. till past midnight', Lady Rumbold wrote to her mother two days later,

a continuous procession went past the Embassy, of Nazis in uniform and their admirers, bands, flags, torches, over 4 hours of it! The old President watched from his window, and a little further down the street the new Chancellor Hitler

---

[1] Freiherr Constantin von Neurath, 1873–1956. Entered the German Diplomatic Service as a Vice-Consul, London, 1903. Served in Constantinople and Copenhagen. Ambassador to Rome, 1922; in London, 1930–32. Minister for Foreign Affairs (first under von Papen, then under Hitler), 1932–38. Reich Protector for Bohemia and Moravia (resident in Prague), 1939–41. Senior SS Group Leader, 1943. Sentenced to fifteen years' imprisonment by the International Military Tribunal, October 1946; released November 1954.

and his supporters stood on a balcony, and had a stupendous ovation. On *our* steps, and perched up on the ledge with the columns stood wild enthusiasts, singing all the old German hymns! Every now and then there were shouts of 'Germany awake', 'Down with the Jews', 'Heil Hitler'! It seemed as tho' the whole of Berlin was processing along the Wilhelm Str.

Rumbold himself had watched with his wife, but, after a few minutes, retreated in disgust to an inner room. Lady Rumbold sensed, as clearly as her husband, what was to come. Her letter continued:

I think it is the result of 14 years of suppression and acute suffering and misery. They also suffered from an 'inferiority complex' and quite rightly too. Now the numbed feeling is wearing off and they again feel their immense strength. You can't keep them down, and I have never thought it was a wise thing to attempt. The reaction was bound to come. One can only hope that Hitler and his crowd won't force the pace. They are sure to start in before long on the Revision of the Versailles Treaty, but no one breathes it yet. And they will want their Colonies back. So there is plenty of trouble ahead. At the moment they are wildly nationalistic.

On February 4 Rumbold discussed the change of Government with von Neurath. 'The Hitler experiment', Neurath remarked, 'had to be tried some time or other', Rumbold echoed Neurath's remarks in a letter to his son on the following day, when he declared: 'The Hitler experiment had to be made sometime or other, and we shall now see what it will bring forth.'

Within a week of Hitler being invited to become Chancellor, it became obvious that he was not going to observe any of the normal procedures or decencies of political life. The hope that he would be held in check by the non-Nazi members of his Cabinet, or that the responsibilities of power would modify his behaviour proved illusory. 'It looks as if the present Government are going to rule the country with a high hand', Rumbold wrote to Sir Clive Wigram on February 7. 'They yesterday published a press law, entitled "The Law for the Protection of the German People", which is about as Draconian as you could get.... If the press law is rigorously applied it might easily stifle the opposition press.' The political situation, he added, was 'really extraordinary, and one wonders sometimes whether the protagonists are normal'. In a despatch to Sir John Simon that same day, Rumbold cast doubt on von Papen's belief 'that he has definitely roped in the Nazi movement and harnessed it to the chariot of the Right'. Hitler, he pointed out, had been, since January 31, 'invested with all the dignity of the Chancellorship', and had asserted his powers to the full, if not beyond. Within a week of coming to power Hitler had set aside a verdict in the Supreme Court whereby the Reich Government could not overrule the powers of the Prussian State Government; he had dismissed the Prussian Prime Minister, Otto Braun;[1] he had taken over full control of the national broadcasting company; he had given himself the right to suppress any newspaper or book; and he had persuaded Hindenburg to dissolve the Reichstag, and to order new elections for March 5.

On February 8 Rumbold dined with Hindenburg at the annual Presidential dinner for the heads of diplomatic missions. Hitler was present, and Rumbold had a brief conversation with him. 'We spoke about Berchtesgaden, Bavaria and Munich', Rumbold wrote to his son five days later. 'On my observing that Munich was pretty dead as compared with the time when I was in charge there in 1909 since Berlin seemed to attract everything to itself, Hitler said that the Federal States and municipalities were themselves to blame for this state of things.'

On February 10 Rumbold heard Hitler speak at the opening of the International Motor Show. 'He certainly has the gift of appealing to the mob', Rumbold wrote to his son, 'though not to the critical faculty.' At the show, Rumbold introduced his daughter to Hitler. Five days later he sent Simon an account of the impressions which Hitler had made on him. At the Hindenburg dinner 'he was quite simple and unaffected . . . his behaviour was somewhat different from that of Mussolini when the latter first became Dictator'. Unlike Mussolini, Hitler appeared 'quite at his ease. He never touches wine nor does he eat meat, explaining that if he did he would lose some of his magnetism'. At the Motor Show the Chancellor had 'got carried away' making a speech. 'I had never heard him before', Rumbold told Simon, 'and realised that his oratory is more calculated to appeal to the mob than the critical faculty. He was very civil to myself and I hear that he and his movement are anxious to stand well with us.'

On February 16 the new Air Attaché, Wing-Commander Herring,[2] sent Rumbold a memorandum in which he gave details of the Nazi

---

[1] Otto Braun, 1872–1955. A printer and journalist. Elected to the Prussian Diet, 1913, and to the Prussian National Assembly, 1919. Prussian Minister of Agriculture, 1919. Prime Minister of Prussia, 1920–21, 1922 and 1925–33. A Social Democrat member of the Reichstag, 1920–33. In exile in Switzerland from March 1933, until his death. He published, in 1940, *Von Weimar zu Hitler*.

[2] Justin Howard Herring, 1889–   . A tea planter in Ceylon, 1912–14. Joined the Royal Flying Corps, 1915. Served on the Western Front, Mesopotamia and Salonika, 1915–18; awarded the MC (1916) and DSO (1917). Commanded No. 4 School of Navigation and Bomb Dropping, 1918–19. Commanded the Aerial Committee of Control, Munich, 1919–21, and the Guarantee Committee, Berlin, 1922–26. Wing-Commander, 1923. Commanded No. 2 Flying Training Command, 1927–29. Air Attaché, Berlin, 1931–34. Acting Group Captain, 1932; Group Captain, 1935. Invented the 'Harwell Box' to give wireless operators ground training in Wireless Telegraphy, 1939. Training air crews for heavy bombers, 1940. President of the Aviation Candidate Selection Board, Air Ministry, 1942.

establishment of an independent Air Commissariat and of the ascendancy of Captain Göring over this embryo Air Force. He also reported at length two speeches which Göring had made on becoming head of the new air department. On February 1, in a speech at the German Aero Club, Göring had announced that the Nazi Cabinet at its very first meeting, 'were unanimous in the policy of granting the necessary additional funds for aviation so as to enable it to obtain the status required for the security of the German people as a whole'. Three days later, at the formal transfer of the air section of the Ministry of Transport to a separate department under Göring's control, he had declared that for years he had worked abroad with the object of freeing Germany of the present restrictions. At last his life's wish had been satisfied by his being appointed Commissar for Aviation. Even now the way was not free, and all existing restrictions must be rescinded.[1]

On February 22, after three weeks of Nazi rule, Rumbold sent Simon a full account of the changes that had taken place. Germany, he wrote, was divided 'in an almost unprecedented fashion'. Hindenburg's 'arbitrary decision' to invite Hitler to be Chancellor had placed a minority 'in supreme control'. Against this minority were ranged 'the entire intelligentsia of the country, its scientists, writers, artists, the Bar, the Church, the Universities . . . the Federation of German industies, the Hansa League, representing the great shipping and export industries, the trades unions, the Episcopal and Catholic Churches. . . .' The Nazi supporters, Rumbold explained, were mostly 'millions of immature young men and women on whose ignorance unscrupulous demagogues have successfully played'.

The election campaign was violent and vituperative. The Nazis blamed their opponents for Germany's defeat in 1918, claiming that they alone had the will to revive Germany's old military spirit. In his despatch to Sir John Simon of February 22 Rumbold commented:

Hitler may be no statesman, but he is an uncommonly clever and audacious demagogue and fully alive to every popular instinct. By the simple process of iteration and reiteration he has convinced the youth of this country that the present unemployment is the work of successive Governments of the Left. Germany, he says, is a heap of ruins. The elementary truth is that Germany was a heap of ruins in 1918, and that the German parties of the Left, meeting with a certain amount of sympathy even at Versailles, salved the structure of the Reich, maintained its unity and ultimately rebuilt it.

[1] A month later, on March 16, 1933, Rumbold telegraphed to Sir John Simon: 'Göring is a megalomanic and is said to be a drug addict. His speeches are doing a great deal of harm and are impossible.'

On the night of February 27 the Reichstag building was set on fire, apparently by a single fanatic, a Dutch Communist, van der Lubbe.[1] The Nazis at once used the fire as an excuse to clamp down on all Communist electoral activity. Hundreds of Communists were seized by the police and detained, and Göring issued orders for the arrest of all Communist deputies. On March 1 Rumbold telegraphed to Simon that 'police measures and especially Nazi auxiliaries have cowed population'. At the same time, news of political clashes and arrests was hard to obtain, 'as censorship is now very severe'. A new decree was issued last night, he added, 'suspending such rights as personal freedom, secrecy of posts and telegraphs, free speech, and inviolability of domicile and property'. Brüning was refused permission to make an electoral address on behalf of the Centre Party. The election campaign itself was being used to destroy democracy. 'Various Ministers', Rumbold had written to his son on February 26, 'have already announced that the Government will stay in office no matter what the verdict of the country will be.'

During the first five days of March the Nazi terror campaign continued. 'A number of prominent adherents of the Left', Rumbold telegraphed to Simon on March 2, 'have fled for refuge to places on or beyond the frontier.' The situation in Berlin was 'hysterical and unpleasant'. The 'final round' of the election campaign, Rumbold wrote to Simon on March 7, had been repeated hints 'that a massacre of the Jews and the leading Marxist politicians would take place on the night before the poll'. But when Rumbold protested to Neurath about the rumours of anti-Jewish action, the Foreign Secretary assured him that he did not think the Jews of Germany 'had anything to fear'.

The first, and last, General Election of Hitler's Chancellorship was held on March 5. Although the Nazi vote increased to over seventeen million, it was still not an absolute majority in a total of nearly forty million electors. The next largest parties were the Social Democrats, with seven million votes, the Communists, with just under five million, and the Centre Party, with nearly four and a half million. The Nazis had obtained 44 per cent of the total poll, and 288 of the 647 seats in the Reichstag. Hitler, although disappointed by the results, was not deterred. On March 7 Rumbold reported to Simon that when the Reichstag met 'the Chancellor

---

[1] Marius van der Lubbe, 1910–34. A Dutch brick-mason. After an accident at work he lost most of his sight. Thereupon he worked as a waiter, potato merchant, sand scooper and market-gardener's man. Member of the youth organization of the Dutch Communist Party. Imprisoned for two weeks in Leyden (Holland) for breaking the windows of the Office of Public Assistance. After Hitler's advent to power in January 1933 he believed it was his mission to awake the world conscience to the Nazi danger. Convicted of high treason for his part in the Reichstag fire, February 27, 1933; guillotined at Leipzig, January 10, 1934.

will ask it to give him an Enabling Bill and will then dispense with Parliament for a considerable time to come'. Hitler lost no time in asserting his total control over the police, the Press, and the Federal States. 'Country is in a very nervous condition', Rumbold telegraphed to Vansittart on March 10, 'and outrages are still reported from all quarters.' Hitler had appointed commissioners for Saxony and Baden, with the result that their two elected governments had resigned. 'Bavarian Government', Rumbold added, 'while remaining in office have only nominal authority.' Throughout Germany, individual Social Democrat and Centre Party leaders had been beaten up by Nazi thugs.

A pretence of legality was still maintained. When Rumbold protested to the German Foreign Office about an incident in which two Indians had been molested by Nazis, he was told, as he telegraphed to Lord Tyrrell on March 10, that 'Hitler himself had been told of the attack', and 'was inclined to view that these incidents had been caused by *agents provocateurs* i.e. Communists dressed in Nazi uniform'. If, Hitler declared, it could be proved that any Nazi had been involved, 'he would have him put up against a wall and shot'.[1]

The Nazi consolidation of power proceeded without respite. Sometimes the measures seemed trivial. 'Suppression of nudism and jazz', Godfrey Thomas wrote to Rumbold on March 11 'are not very effective as a cure for unemployment.' But every day brought major changes, each one of which, in calmer times, would have led to prolonged debate and serious protest. A Propaganda Ministry was established, with Joseph Goebbels at its head, to supervise all broadcasting and publications. The eighty-one Communist deputies elected on March 5 were informed that they were not to be invited to the opening of the Reichstag. All municipal administrations were taken over by Nazi nominees. The Nazis, Rumbold telegraphed to Simon on March 14, had succeeded, for the moment at least, 'in bringing to the surface the worst traits in German character, i.e. a mean spirit of revenge, a tendency to brutality, and a noisy and irresponsible jingoism'. This boded ill for Germany's neighbours. 'I am for force', Hitler had said in a speech on March 11, 'because in force I see strength, and in strength the eternal mother of rights, and in rights the root of life itself.'

In the second week of March Hitler decided to impose his authority on Bavaria, whose Government had tried throughout to resist Nazi intimidation. On March 9 he dismissed the Minister of the Interior, Karl

---

[1] The two Indians, Mr Naidu and Mr Nambiar, were detained for eight and twenty-six days respectively, without any charge being brought against them. Following Rumbold's protests, they were released. Their attackers were never caught.

Stützel,[1] and appointed a veteran Bavarian Nazi, General von Epp,[2] to take charge of 'law and order' in the State. Rumbold described the sequel in a letter to Vansittart on March 15:

The new officials proceeded at once to carry out the repressive measures which are now being enforced in all parts of Germany, on the model laid down by Captain Göring in Prussia, against those whose political activities, ideals or religious opinions are not considered to be sufficiently national. The papers of the Left were suppressed and their offices broken into and wrecked; the head-quarters of trade unions and Jewish organisations were occupied and ransacked; eminent members of the late Government, such as Herr Stützel, the Minister of the Interior, were dragged from their beds in the middle of the night . . . .

In the same despatch, Rumbold described a similar Nazi seizure of power in Baden, where, on March 9, Nazi Ministers were appointed to replace the existing Cabinet of Social Democrat and Centre Party members. In Württemberg, despite a protest from the State Government direct to Hindenburg, a Nazi, Wilhelm Murr,[3] was appointed Prime Minister on March 11, an appointment which the Provincial Diet was forced to confirm three days later. On March 12 a similar process was completed in Hesse, where another Nazi, Dr Ferdinand Werner,[4] was appointed Prime Minister, and the Diet dissolved for six months. The three Hansa towns of Hamburg, Bremen and Lübeck had each suffered, Rumbold wrote, 'a similar fate'. By threats of violence, by the use of the Emergency powers granted to him by Hindenburg, and by swift, crude, bludgeoning action, Hitler had established his power throughout Germany. 'With the establishment of this impressive uniformity between Reich and States', Rumbold concluded, 'and with the removal of the majority of all "unsympathetic functionaries" from their posts, the final stage in the national

[1] Karl Stützel, 1872–1944. Lawyer. Served as a Captain on the Western Front, 1914–16; awarded the Iron Cross. A senior Civil Servant in the Bavarian Ministry of the Interior from 1918; Bavarian Minister of the Interior, 1924–33. He left office on March 17, 1933.

[2] Franz Xaver Ritter von Epp, 1868–1947. Entered the Army, 1887. Served in the Allied Expeditionary Force to China, 1901–2; in the campaign against the Hereros in German South-West Africa, 1904–7, and in the First World War. A Free Corps leader; he commanded the troops which defeated the Soviet Republic of Bavaria, 1919, and helped to suppress labour unrest in the Ruhr, 1920. Military Commander of Munich, 1921. An early financer of the Nazi Party, and Chief of the Nazi Party's Department for Colonial Policy. In 1938 he was one of the senior veterans who doubted Germany's ability to emerge victorious from a major war.

[3] Wilhelm Murr, 1888–1945. Merchant. Nazi Party Deputy in the Reichstag, September 1930–May 1932. Prime Minister of Württemberg, March 1933. Nazi Representative in Württemberg, November 1933–May 1945. Committed suicide, May 14, 1945.

[4] Ferdinand Friedrich Karl Werner, 1876–1961. A Member of the Reichstag, 1911–18 and 1924–28. A leading Hesse Nazi and noted anti-Semite. Speaker of the Hesse Parliament, 1932–33. Prime Minister of Hesse, 1933.

revolution has been concluded, and the ground has been cleared for "constructive" work.'

Hitler's 'constructive' work, which Rumbold reported in great detail, totally destroyed the democracy established in 1918. Law and order, he wrote in a letter to Vansittart on March 15, had 'practically been suspended in most towns. Communists having gone to ground, reprisals were visited in most cases on Social Democrats, Democrats, Jews and members of the Centre Party. Even Dr Brüning himself thought it wiser to change his quarters when he learned that a man resembling him had been attacked in the streets . . . out of about 200 Social Democratic papers only five still appear.' Flying squads of 'irresponsible young men' had been busy destroying printing presses, horse-whipping journalists and lawyers, and causing such fear for the future that a massive exodus had begun, not only of Jews, but of all those liberal-minded men threatened by the new intolerance. 'The departure from Germany of so many writers, artists, musicians and political leaders', Rumbold added, 'has created for the moment a kind of vacuum, for whatever may have been the shortcomings of the Democratic parties, they numbered among their following the intellectual life of the capital and nearly all that was original and stimulating in the world of art and letters'.

On March 21 Rumbold informed Simon of how the Jews had been singled out for ill-treatment and abuse. Bruno Walter,[1] the conductor, had been prevented from conducting a concert at Leipzig.[2] Einstein's house had been searched for explosives. All over Germany Jewish musicians were dismissed from orchestras, Jewish actors driven off the stage, and Jewish judges refused entry into court. 'Dreadful things happen all the time', Lady Rumbold wrote to her mother on March 22, 'and as the press is muzzled are never heard by the public. All sorts of terrorising of Jews and Socialists, and 40,000 are supposed to be in prison . . . endless writers and professors, etc., are persecuted, whilst old government officials are ruthlessly turned out, often without pensions. It is hateful and uncivilized!'

[1] Bruno Walter Schlesinger, 1876–1962. Born in Berlin. Assistant conductor, under Gustav Mahler, at the Municipal Theatre in Hamburg, 1894. General Director of the Munich Opera, 1917–22. Conducted orchestras in Berlin and Leipzig, 1922–32. Guest conductor, New York, 1932. Lost all his German engagements, 1933. Conducted in New York, under Toscanini, 1933–36. Musical Director of the Vienna Opera, 1936; moved to France when the Germans annexed Austria, 1938; moved to the United States on the outbreak of war in Europe, 1939. Conductor and Musical Adviser, New York Philharmonic, 1947–49.

[2] Another distinguished conductor, Furtwängler, had been asked to take Bruno Walter's place, but had, Rumbold reported, 'indignantly refused'. On March 21, 1933, Furtwängler conducted the *Meistersinger* at the Opera, on the occasion of the opening of the Reichstag, in the presence of Hitler and his Cabinet.

On March 21 Rumbold was present at the ceremonial opening of the Reichstag, which took place at the Garrison Church in Potsdam. For the first time since Germany's defeat in 1918, a political ceremony was given military trappings. 'The entire gallery on one side of the church', Rumbold wrote to Simon later that day, 'was filled with marshals, generals, and admirals of the Imperial regime, headed by Field-Marshal Mackensen,[1] wearing the uniform of the Death's Head Hussars. The other officers were also in their pre-war uniforms. . . . The spirit of Weimar had yielded to the spirit of Potsdam, and I had the feeling that I was assisting at the demise of the republic. . . .' Hindenburg spoke briefly, appealing for 'a proud and free Germany, united in herself'. Hitler spoke next; after promising that he would 'cherish the great traditions of the German people', he declared that Germany had neither been responsible for the war, nor had lost it. On the following day he announced that he had prepared an 'Enabling Bill' which would suspend the Weimar Constitution, and give the Government power to pass any legislation it chose without a parliamentary majority. This Bill, which needed a two-thirds majority to become law, was submitted to the Reichstag on March 23. The Social Democrat Party Chairman, Otto Wels,[2] opposed it, but the Centre Party leader, Dr Kaas, gave it his party's support. The Bill was put to the vote, and passed by 441 votes to 94. The Centre Party's 73 votes had given Hitler the two-thirds majority needed; the Weimar Constitution was at an end. 'I understand that the reason why the Centre Party passed Enabling Bill', Rumbold telegraphed to Simon on March 31, 'was because they knew their leaders would also be persecuted and sent to concentration camps on the slightest pretext.'

The first changes which Hitler instituted after the Enabling Bill was passed were against the half million Jews of Germany. On March 28 Rumbold sent Simon a report of the 'gross injustice' to which the Jews were being subjected. 'Throughout the public services', he wrote, 'they are being systematically removed from their posts.' On March 30 he sent Simon details of a Manifesto which had just been issued by the Nazis, in

---

[1] August von Mackensen, 1849–1945. Joined the Death's Head Hussars, 1869; served as a regimental officer in the Franco-Prussian War, 1870–71. Accompanied the Kaiser on his visit to Palestine, 1898. Commanded the 9th Army on the Eastern Front, 1914–15, defeating the Russians at Kutno and Lodz. Commanded the German–Austrian 11th Army in Galicia, April 1915, achieving the German breakthrough at Gorlice and Tarnow. Field-Marshal, June 1915. Defeated the Russians at Pinsk, September 1915; overran the Serbians, November 1915 and the Rumanians, 1916–17. Interned by the French, November 1918–December 1919. He retired from the Army in 1920.

[2] Otto Wels, 1873–1939. Social Democrat member of the Reichstag, 1912–18 and 1920–33. Commandant of Berlin, 1918. Chairman of Social Democrat Party, 1931–33. In exile in Prague, 1933–38; in Paris from 1938 until his death.

which local organizations throughout Germany were instructed 'to carry on anti-Jewish propaganda among the people'. Typical of the daily anti-semitic actions, Rumbold reported, Lion Feuchtwanger,[1] the distinguished Jewish writer, had had all his literary manuscripts seized.

On April 1, despite a private protest from Hindenburg, Hitler declared a boycott of all Jewish shops, business houses, lawyers and doctors. Lady Rumbold sent an account of the boycott to her mother on April 2:

In the morning we sallied out in the car to explore, Tony and I and Lady Ovey[2] (just arrived from Moscow). I said I *fully* intended to go into a shop to buy something even if it was picketed by Nazis. We tried Wertheimer, a dense crowd was standing at each entrance and in front of the doors 2 or 3 Nazis aggressively blocking the way. We saw that it was impossible without making a scene to push past. We then went down the Kurfurstendam. Nearly every other shop is Jew there. We walked along with the crowds. The shops were mostly open, but in front of each Jew shop were 2 or 3 stalwart Nazis standing blocking the door. Tony asked one if the shop was open and the man answered yes, but as he stood *plum* in the middle of the doorway you would have had to push him on one side to get through. *Obviously* no one felt inclined to make a scene or provoke an incident. So the crowds just processed along, and the Nazis just terrorized and dominated! On every Jew shop was plastered a large notice warning the public not to buy in Jewish shops. In many cases special notices were put up saying that sweated labour was employed in that particular shop, and often you saw caricatures of Jewish noses. It was utterly cruel and Hunnish the whole thing, just doing down a heap of defenceless people. Also any number of cafés were placarded, and of course quite empty. Then on the address plates at the entrances of blocks of flats of Jewish doctors, lawyers, or businessmen were plastered the same kind of warning, so the whole of Berlin was speckled with these placards.

Three days later she added: 'To see people pilloried in this fashion, a very large number of them quite harmless, hardworking people, was altogether revolting, and it left a very nasty taste in the mouth. I shall never forget it.'

On April 5 Rumbold sent Simon two full accounts of the ill treatment of the Jews. 'Large concentration camps', he wrote, 'are being established in various parts of the country, one camp near Munich being sufficiently large to hold 5,000 prisoners.'[3] On April 10 he informed Margot

[1] Lion Feuchtwanger, 1884–1958. Born in Munich. German dramatist and novelist. Among his novels were *Jew Süss* (1925) and *Josephus* (1932). Emigrated to France, 1933. Deprived of German citizenship, 1934. Imprisoned by the French Vichy Government at Aix-en-Provence, 1940. Escaped to the United States, 1940. Died in Los Angeles.

[2] Madame Marie-Armande de Barrios, daughter of Georges René Vignet. Born in Peru; lived most of her life in Mexico. In 1930 she married, as his second wife, Sir Esmond Ovey (British Ambassador to Moscow, 1929–33). She died in 1954.

[3] This was Dachau concentration camp, ten miles north-west of Munich.

Asquith[1] of the camps, which, he wrote, included 'thousands of so-called Marxists and pacifists'. Writing to the President of the Saar Commission, Geoffrey Knox,[2] on the following day, Rumbold described how, in Berlin, 'nobody feels himself safe or able to talk or walk freely. One might almost be in Russia, but although the Bolsheviks have tried to harry their political opponents almost to extinction, I do not remember that either they or Mussolini formed concentration camps.'

Rumbold was depressed by Hitler's success in cowing all opposition. 'During a large part of my term of office here', he wrote to J. L. Garvin on April 12, 'Germany was under-dog, and I contributed to the best of power to help Brüning in his difficult task. I now have the feeling that my efforts and those of others have been a wash-out, and that we are rapidly getting back to the 1913–14 atmosphere.' A day later Rumbold had further cause for despair. Yet another law came into force, aimed principally at driving out all Jews from public service, national, local and municipal. Under the new law, only 'Aryans' could retain their jobs as civil servants. 'The stipulation in regard to Aryan descent', Rumbold wrote to Simon on April 13, 'will, it is understood, be interpreted as debarring civil servants of whom even one grandparent was Jewish.'

On April 23 Rumbold wrote to his son of how the Nazis had 'installed a Commissar in the Golf Club to make sure that the Committee is purged of Jews'. Two days earlier, he and his daughter had gone to a concert at the Philharmonic Hall in aid of the victims of a mining disaster in the Saar. The concert was under Hindenburg's patronage, with Furtwängler[3] conducting. 'We sat in the third row', Rumbold wrote to his son. 'In the front row close to us sat Kühlmann with an elderly lady and next to him was a big man looking rather like a prize-fighter. After the audience had settled down to listen to the last item on the programme two policemen entered the hall, tapped the big man on the shoulder and invited him to accompany them. He objected whereupon they took him by the arm and marched him out of the hall. A whole posse of police was waiting a few yards off. None of the spectators dared to show any reaction to this arrest though Kühlmann looked considerably astonished. This sort of thing is probably going on all over the place in this land of the free.'

¹ Emma Alice Margaret Tennant, 1864–1945. Known as Margot. Asquith's second wife; they were married in 1894.

² Geoffrey George Knox, 1884–1958. Entered the Diplomatic Service as a Student Interpreter, Levant, 1906. Served in the war, on the Western Front, 1917–18. Chairman of the Saar Governing Commission, 1932–35. Knighted, 1935. Minister to Budapest, 1935–39; to Rio de Janeiro, 1939–41.

³ Wilhelm Furtwängler, 1886–1954. Born in Berlin; educated in Munich. Conductor of the Berlin Philharmonic Orchestra, 1922–34; of the Berlin State Opera, 1933–34. Conducted at the Bayreuth Festival, 1931, 1936, 1937, and the Salzburg and Luzern Music Festivals.

On April 25 Colonel Thorne gave Rumbold a detailed account of the semi-military training received by German youth. In it he pointed out that on April 3 Hitler had transferred control of all youth clubs from private hands to the Ministry of Labour. The clubs themselves, Thorne added, had been organized on a semi-military basis before the Nazi seizure of power, encouraged to do so by General Groener and General Schleicher. Thorne warned that these youth activities went far beyond 'Boy Scouts' instruction; they included pack marches of sixteen miles with over fifty pounds of equipment and 'exercises involving scouting, attack and defence, withdrawal and pursuit, surprise and ambuscades, the enemy as a rule being designated either smuggler bands or Communists'. Even groups which were intended to give athletic and religious training to younger boys of twelve to sixteen had begun to train in this para-military fashion. Thorne gave Rumbold full lists of the camps set up, the equipment provided, and the courses that took place. 'The cumulative effect of these measures', he wrote, 'will be to produce a very large reserve of personnel who will require little further training to take their places in the armed forces of the country on the outbreak of war.'

After three months of Nazi rule, Rumbold was convinced that Hitler would not be overthrown. 'The parliamentary regime', he wrote to Simon in a five-thousand word despatch on April 26, 'has been replaced by a regime of brute force. . . . Parliament has ceased to have any *raison d'être*. The Nazi leader has only to express a wish to have it fulfilled by his followers.' Even the Army, he wrote, could not remain 'immune from Hitlerism' for long. 'Sooner or later, especially if the President dies, the Reichswehr may be expected to throw in their lot with the present regime.'[1]

There was no need, Rumbold believed, for anyone to remain in ignorance about Hitler's aims and beliefs. Hitler's own book, *Mein Kampf*, made clear beyond doubt, he wrote to Simon in his despatch of April 26, 'the principles which have guided him during the last fourteen years'. Rumbold sent Simon an outline of Hitler's thesis:

He starts with the assertions that man is a fighting animal; therefore the nation is, he concludes, a fighting unit, being a community of fighters. Any living organism which ceases to fight for its existence is, he asserts, doomed to extinction. A country or a race which ceases to fight is equally doomed. The

---

[1] Rumbold's forecast was correct. Hindenburg died on August 1, 1934. On the following day the armed forces swore an oath of loyalty to Hitler as their Commander-in-Chief. The oath became Law within three weeks. It read: 'I swear before God to give my unconditional obedience to Adolf Hitler, *Führer* of the Reich and of the German People, Supreme Commander of the *Wehrmacht*, and I pledge my word as a brave soldier to observe this oath always, even at peril of my life.'

fighting capacity of a race depends on its purity. Hence the necessity for ridding it of foreign impurities. The Jewish race, owing to its universality, is of necessity pacifist and internationalist. Pacifism is the deadliest sin, for pacifism means the surrender of the race in the fight for existence. The first duty of every country is, therefore, to nationalise the masses; intelligence is of secondary importance in the case of the individual; will and determination are of higher importance. The individual who is born to command is more valuable than countless thousands of subordinate natures. Only brute force can ensure the survival of the race. Hence the necessity for military forms. The race must fight; a race that rests must rust and perish. The German race, had it been united in time, would now be master of the globe today. The new Reich must gather within its fold all the scattered German elements in Europe. A race which has suffered defeat can be rescued by restoring its self-confidence. Above all things, the army must be taught to believe in its own invincibility. To restore the German nation again 'it is only necessary to convince the people that the recovery of freedom by force of arms is a possibility'.

Hitler describes at great length in his turgid style the task which the new Germany must therefore set itself. Intellectualism is undesirable. The ultimate aim of education is to produce a German who can be converted with the minimum of training into a soldier. The idea that there is something reprehensible in chauvinism is entirely mistaken. 'Indeed, the greatest upheavals in history would have been unthinkable had it not been for the driving force of fanatical and hysterical passions. Nothing could have been effected by the *bourgeois* virtues of peace and order. The world is now moving towards such an upheaval, and the new (German) State must see to it that the race is ready for the last and greatest decisions on this earth' (p. 475, 17th edition of 'Mein Kampf'). Again and again he proclaims that fanatical conviction and uncompromising resolution are indispensable qualities in a leader.

The climax of education is military service (p. 476). A man may be a living lexicon, but unless he is a soldier he will fail in the great crises of life.

Rumbold insisted that these crude beliefs were not mere verbiage on Hitler's part. 'I fear,' he wrote, 'that it would be misleading to base any hope for a return to sanity or a serious modification of the views of the Chancellor or his entourage.' Hitler was a man of 'extraordinary obstinacy'. He was also a person of 'sufficient native cunning' to realize the need for 'camouflage'. Great efforts would be made, had already been made, to conceal jingoism and militarism 'in harmless language'. Whenever foreign statesmen took alarm, they would be answered, Rumbold believed, by 'protestations of peace' from Hitler. Rumbold concluded his despatch:

The German people today no longer feel humiliated or oppressed. The Hitler Government have had the courage to revolt against Versailles, to challenge France and the other signatories of the treaty without any serious consequences. For a defeated country this represents an immense moral advance. For its leader,

Hitler, it represents overwhelming prestige and popularity. Someone has aptly said that nationalism is the illegitimate offspring of patriotism by inferiority complex. Germany has been suffering from such a complex for over a decade. Hitlerism has eradicated it, but only at the cost of burdening Europe with a new outbreak of nationalism.

Within the Foreign Office this despatch was known as the 'Mein Kampf' despatch. It was read by Ramsay MacDonald, and circulated to the Cabinet, in which Neville Chamberlain was Chancellor of the Exchequer. One friend who understood the implications of what Rumbold was reporting was J. L. Garvin, to whom he had sent several accounts of Nazi methods and intentions. The Germans, Garvin wrote to Rumbold on May 1, who were 'definitely superior in personal industry and in so many aptitudes for combination, seem as definitely inferior in political wisdom. There is no sign of psychological intelligence with regard to any other nation whatever.' The British mistake, Garvin wrote, 'was not to have crossed the Rhine in full massiveness in 1919; not to have dictated at Berlin itself a more impressive and competent peace. They would have understood then what indisputable Defeat means. They don't now. The psychological infatuation of their hereditary militarism was not thoroughly broken.'

Rumbold never deflected from his view that Nazism was evil. 'I am a convinced believer in the liberty of the subject', he wrote to his son on May 7. 'This may not necessarily make for a very efficient state but we have got along very well all these centuries and should be very rash to attempt any new experiments. . . . We shall judge this system by its fruits and I very much doubt whether the latter will either be abundant or refreshing.' Rumbold's distaste for the Nazi regime was paralleled by worries about its future intentions abroad. He wrote to Vansittart on May 10, that Hitler wanted to avoid war 'for some time to come' while consolidating his internal power; but, Rumbold added, 'I should not like to bank on his desire for peace four or five years hence'. Many who read his 'Mein Kampf' despatch shared his anxieties.[1]

On May 11 Rumbold had his first formal meeting with Hitler. On the previous evening he had received a telegram from Simon instructing him to make clear to Hitler that his 'oppressive policy' towards the Jews had lost Germany the sympathy gained in England over the previous ten years. When the meeting began, Hitler launched at once into a criticism of Germany's eastern frontier. It was drawn too far west, and would have

---

[1] The President of the Saar Commission, Geoffrey Knox, wrote to Rumbold on May 10: 'I am ending a flying visit to London, where I have had the undiluted joy of reading your recent despatch on Nazi policy. The Office are enthusiastic about it.' On September 14 Harold Laski, the socialist political theorist and writer, asked Rumbold if Dodd, the new American Ambassador to Berlin could have a copy.

to be revised. Then he praised the peacefulness of 'the recent revolution in Germany', it had, he insisted, been accompanied by 'the minimum of violence and bloodshed . . . not even a pane of glass had been broken in Berlin'. His mission, he went on, was to fight and destroy Communism and Marxism. Rumbold then raised the question of the treatment of the Jews by the new regime, a topic which caused Hitler to work himself up, as Rumbold informed Simon, 'into a state of great excitement'. There were not enough jobs in Germany for 'pure-bred' Germans, Hitler shouted, as if addressing an open air meeting; 'the Jews must suffer with the rest'. Rumbold listened for a while as Hitler spoke 'with great ferocity' against Jewish influence, and the need to root it out. Then he retaliated; public opinion in England, he said, had been shocked to see that 'prominent men in every department of cultural life had either been deprived of their posts or compelled to leave the country because of their racial origin'. He gave the example of Einstein. Hitler replied that Einstein 'had attacked his Government violently from American soil' and told Rumbold that if a corresponding English scientist were to attack the British Government's policies he would likewise risk being molested. 'I disagreed entirely with this view', Rumbold reported to Simon. Finally Hitler informed Rumbold that he believed it was essential for Germany 'to be on good terms with England'. Rumbold replied by pointing out that Hitler's policy towards Jews and political opponents had 'forfeited' British sympathy for Germany. After an hour, the meeting came to an end. Rumbold summed up his impressions in the final paragraph of his despatch to Simon:

My comment on the foregoing is that Herr Hitler is himself responsible for the anti-Jewish policy of the German Government and that it would be a mistake to believe that it is the policy of his wilder men whom he has difficulty in controlling. Anybody who had had the opportunity of listening to his remarks on the subject of Jews could not have failed, like myself, to realise that he is a fanatic on the subject. He is also convinced of his mission to fight Communism and destroy Marxism, which term embraces all his political adversaries. Speaking generally, my experience has been that it is difficult, if not impossible, to argue with convinced Nazis about any of their principal tenets.

Towards the end of the interview Hitler had asked Rumbold to give a copy of his remarks about the Jews to the Foreign Minister, von Neurath. Rumbold had done so. Six days later, when Hitler spoke in the Reichstag, he spoke in a conciliatory mood that surprised all those present. Apparently von Neurath had been so impressed by the strength of the British protest that he had, as Rumbold reported to Simon on May 17, urged Hitler to talk 'in moderate tones' and had persuaded Hitler to have the words 'leise und langsam' (softly and slowly) written in large letters on a sheet of paper in front of him. Hitler had demanded a revision of the Versailles Treaty; but he had gone on to declare that a new war 'could only lead to the collapse of the present order of society', and to insist that he wanted treaty revision by peaceful means. He wanted Europe's wounds to be closed and healed. He had no designs on any nation's independence. Both France and Poland had a right to exist: 'We regard the European nations around us as an established fact.' The German Government wanted to discuss all outstanding questions 'peacefully and reasonably'. Military action in Europe, he declared, even if accompanied by 'complete success', would involve sacrifices 'out of all proportion to any ultimate goal'.

Hitler had discovered a formula for respectability. For the next five years he was to repeat it, successfully, many times. Protestations of peace, coupled with specific demands; reiterated demands for fair treatment, followed by expressions of concern about the horrors of war.

During his Reichstag speech of May 17, Hitler had refrained from blaming the Jews for Germany's defeat in 1918, or for her subsequent ills. He had heeded Rumbold's warning. But Rumbold was not impressed; he still believed that the extremism of 1925, as expressed in *Mein Kampf*, the street violence and terror of 1932, and the swift, total extinction of democracy in 1933 were the true pointers to Hitler's future behaviour. 'The stronger Hitler becomes at home', he wrote to Vansittart on May 30, 'the more he can afford to be conciliatory abroad. Intervention by foreign countries is his greatest danger. His speech of the 17 May showed how much he was alive to that danger. His first concern is to remain in power in Germany, and I doubt if he will risk complications with the outer world for a long time to come.' But, Rumbold stressed, Hitler 'will not shrink from downright brutality in his efforts to stay in power', and he would want to use his power for more than domestic triumphs. A 'great deal of water' would have to flow under the bridge before Germany would be able to contemplate war 'with any prospect of success', but, Rumbold warned:

That Hitlerism will ultimately lead to war is a contingency which cannot be ruled out, unless in the meanwhile mankind can devise some air-tight scheme for settling disputes and keeping the peace. In this country of abounding energy and stamina the present revival of nationalism is definitely disquieting. The educational system is being recast and the new history books will, I understand, make it clear to the children that the German soldier is invincible unless Marxist treachery stabs him in the back. Pacifism is now ranked with Communism as the lowest crime in the Statute Book. The glorification of militarism, the incessant celebration of anniversaries, the return to the heroic ideal, all point in one direction.

In Berlin itself Rumbold had a receptive listener in the Berlin correspondent of *The Times*, Norman Ebbutt.[1] Ebbutt's deputy in Berlin, Douglas Reed,[2] later wrote of how Rumbold established 'a relationship of confidence' with Ebbutt, so much so that he was the source 'of Ebbutt's remarkable prognostication, published in *The Times* during the early months of Hitlerism, that its coming meant war in about five years'.

Rumbold was to leave Berlin on July 1. His diplomatic career was at an end; he was sixty-four. 'There is no question whatever of a prolongation for me', he had written to his son on May 28. 'Various English colleagues of mine have written to me from other posts to express astonishment that the powers that be should swop horses whilst crossing the stream and the Germans are equally puzzled. But there it is.' To Sir Eric Phipps,[3] who was to be his successor, he wrote of how he had tried since 1928 to build up 'a certain sympathy for Germany and an understanding of her difficulties'. Hitler and the Nazis, he added, 'managed to scrap all this within a fortnight . . . it is as well that the new situation should be handled by a new man.' Rumbold's staff were disappointed he was to leave them. Throughout his five years in Berlin he had won their loyalty and admiration. Many of those who had served under him in Berlin later recalled the strong impression that he had made upon them. 'He was entirely unpretentious', James Bowker[4] recalled; 'he never tried to impress anyone. At the same time he was most receptive of anything one put to him'; and Timothy Breen[5] wrote: 'He was a genial chief. When one worked with him he would emit a gentle sniff from time to time. This was as far as he got in signifying blame or praise or any human emotion.

[1] Norman Ebbutt, 1894–1968. Correspondent of the *Morning Leader* in Paris, 1911; Russia, 1912. Lieutenant, Royal Naval Volunteer Reserve, 1914–19. Chief Correspondent of *The Times* in Berlin from 1927 until expelled from Berlin by the Nazis, August 21, 1937.

[2] Douglas Reed, 1895–   . A publisher's office boy, 1908; a bank clerk, 1914. Served in the infantry and air force, 1915–18, when he was twice wounded. Newspaper clerk, 1921. Joined the staff of *The Times*, 1924. Assistant Berlin Correspondent of *The Times*, 1929–35; Central European Correspondent, 1935–38. War Correspondent, Normandy, 1944. Among his many published works are *The Burning of the Reichstag* (1934), *Insanity Fair* (1938) and *Disgrace Abounding* (1939).

[3] Eric Clare Edmund Phipps, 1875–1945. Entered Diplomatic Service, 1899. Knighted, 1927. Minister to Vienna, 1928–33. Ambassador to Berlin, 1933–37; to Paris, 1937–39.

[4] Reginald James Bowker, 1901–   . Entered the Diplomatic Service, 1925. 3rd Secretary, Berlin, November 1928–September 1930. Minister in Cairo, 1945–47; High Commissioner to Burma, 1948–50. Assistant Under-Secretary of State at the Foreign Office, 1950–54. Knighted, 1952. Ambassador at Ankara, 1954–58; at Vienna, 1956–61. Member of the London Committee of the Ottoman Bank since 1961.

[5] Timothy Florence Breen, 1885–1966. Served in the European War, 1914–18, and awarded the Military Cross. Major, British Military Mission, Berlin, 1919–21. Press Attaché (First Secretary), British Embassy, Berlin, 1921–37.

His voice was invariably low and I do not remember to have seen him in a temper until his first interview with Hitler. He came back with a very red face. . . .' Thirty years later his French colleague, François-Poncet, recalled of Rumbold: 'Il m'avait inspiré, d'ailleurs, la plus grande estime par sa franchise, son courage et son horreur du Nazisme. C'était un Anglais de bonne souche. Nous étions toujours d'accord, lui et moi. Il adorait les truffes, le foie gras et le champagne. . . .'[1]

Rumbold's final month in Berlin confirmed his belief that the regime would not change its methods. He was amazed, when lunching privately with Brüning on June 13, to discover that the former Chancellor 'was prepared to support Hitler if the latter pursued a moderate policy'. This was particularly striking, he wrote to Simon the following day, because on June 10 a meeting of Catholic artisans at Munich had been broken up by Nazi storm troops with much violence, the police having 'declined to interfere'. But Brüning insisted that 'it would be a mistake to believe that the continual marching, counter-marching and flag-wagging indicated a real revival of militarism in Germany'; he himself looked forward to the restoration of the monarchy, which he told Rumbold, 'would make for stability and would be a guarantee against foreign adventures'. Such thoughts seemed to Rumbold to be unrealistic in the extreme.[2] The terror could not be minimized, nor Hitler's ultimate intentions ignored. Many of his own friends, he wrote to Harold Nicolson on June 21, 'have disappeared from the scene and have either left the country or may even be behind barbed wire'. He saw no evidence for the belief that Nazism would modify and become respectable. 'One hears almost daily of excesses committed by brown-shirted bravos and hooligans. It is quite clear that the unruly elements are getting out of hand. That is one of Hitler's dangers. . . . I never expected to go through a real revolution before I left Germany. But that is what it has been.' On June 28 he wrote to Sir Clive Wigram: 'Many of us here feel as if we were living in a lunatic asylum.'

In the last week of June Hitler, who had already outlawed the Communist Party, took steps to destroy both the Social Democrat and German National parties. The Social Democrat Party funds were expropriated and Hugenberg was removed from the Cabinet. Pressure was put on both the

---

[1] It was François-Poncet who said of Rumbold 'Malgré sa mine idiote, c'est un homme intelligent.'

[2] Throughout his period in Berlin Rumbold had been careful not to encourage those who supported a return of the monarchy. Peter Thorne, the son of the Military Attaché, later recalled how Crown Prince William had often been seen 'hanging about' the Wannsee Golf Club, but that Rumbold had consistently declined to enter into any political conversations with him.

Evangelical and Catholic Churches. Nor were military preparations neglected. On June 27, Rumbold sent the Foreign Office a memorandum by
the Air Attaché, Group Captain Herring. This memorandum made it
clear, Rumbold wrote to Simon that day, 'that Germany is building
military aircraft', and that since Hitler had come to power the German air
authorities saw no need to hide the fact, although it was a violation of the
Versailles Treaty. On June 20 Herring had sent Rumbold an example of
one such violation:

During an Air Display at Tempelhof on 18.6.33, I met for the first time the
wife of an important German aeronautical official who has been intimately
connected with aviation in this country for many years. This lady did not appear
to be very interested in the proceedings and in an attempt at relieving the tedium
I pointed to the new Heinkel and Junkers express postal aircraft and said 'Those
are two of the newest types in Germany'. She turned slowly to her husband and
still slightly bored said 'Oh, those will be two of the new single seater fighters
I suppose'.

In his memorandum, Herring pointed out that Nazi policy was 'to unify
all German air interests under the direction of the Air Ministry, to guide
the activities of each club, school, air line or factory along the route
decided by the Air Ministry so that German aviation shall be a force with
which other nations possessing fighting air services will be forced to
reckon'. He noted that all those taking part in aviation were being encouraged to wear a uniform, 'since the discipline of a man in uniform has
been found in Germany to be much superior to that of a man in civilian
clothes'. Herring concluded:

There is no doubt that the Nazi regime has placed German aviation on an
altogether different and better footing from the Nazi point of view; a process
of mobilisation is in progress and when the attendant disorganisation is over it
may be anticipated with confidence that all German aviation will remain a
Government controlled branch of the public life so long as the Nazi regime
lasts. The appearance of a military air service would be unlikely to alter the
character of the organisation now coming into being, for it is difficult to
visualise Germany as content with the size of any of her fighting services and
she may therefore be counted on to retain the machinery she has been at such
pains to perfect for establishing a supply of pilots, other personnel and aircraft
against times of emergency.[1]

In his final despatch, on June 30, Rumbold reflected on what was
happening in Germany, and on its implications. It was 'only fair', he

[1] Rumbold was disturbed by Group Captain Herring's reports; but Herring later recalled
that when he returned to England in 1934 he found the Secretary of State for Air, Lord
Londonderry, reluctant to accept the implications of what he had discovered, or to listen
to what he had to say about the pace and nature of German air development.

wrote, to recognize 'the good points in the Hitler ideology'. These, he believed, were its attempt to develop 'a spirit of comradeship and of unselfish devotion to the State. . . . Class warfare is to cease and labour to be ennobled.' But the mission of the Hitler creed was to make Germany the 'moral leader of Europe', and by its example and initiative 'to regenerate nations which have been corrupted by democracy and by association with the Jews'. Hitler himself was regarded by his followers as having 'an almost divine mission', and was often compared with Mahomet. 'More than one paper', Rumbold noted, 'has accepted the comparison.'

None of the Nazi leaders, wrote Rumbold, were men 'of real worth'. The leader of the Labour Front, Dr Ley,[1] was a man 'with all the aggressive and brutal characteristics of a low-class Prussian. He is a drunkard.' Wilhelm Frick in Prussia, Hans Frank[2] in Bavaria, were typical of the type of Nazi official 'who will not hesitate to adopt the most ruthless methods and outlandish ideas'. At the summit of the system, Hitler, Göring and Goebbels, were each 'notoriously pathological cases', the first two as a result of 'wounds and hardship' in the war, the last 'as a result of a physical defect[3] and neglect in childhood'. The regime had lost contact with legality in all internal matters, and was teaching the nation to despise legality in international affairs. Rumbold's despatch continued:

The average German does not appear to possess a true sense of proportion. Hitlerism *inter alia* is a reaction from what are alleged to be the criminal shortcomings and international outlook of all German Governments since 1919. It has, therefore, gone to the other extreme and produced an aggressive nationalism which is accompanied by a seemingly profound contempt for and disregard of foreign opinion. Soviet methods are being used, as exemplified by the arrest of prominent personalities, such as Dr Löbe,[4] without any indication of the reasons

[1] Robert Ley, 1890–1945. A leading Nazi organizer; Gauleiter for Cologne-Aachen, 1928–33. Leader of the German Labour Front, 1933–45, which replaced the Trade Union Movement during the Nazi era. Committed suicide at Nuremberg, October 26, 1945, shortly before the opening of the War Crimes trial.

[2] Hans Frank, 1900–46. Barrister. Joined the Nazi Party, September 1923; took part in the unsuccessful putsch of November 1923. Legal adviser and defence counsel to the Nazi Party, 1923–33. A National Socialist Deputy in the Reichstag, 1931. Bavarian Minister of Justice, 1933. Reich Minister without Portfolio, 1933. In his *Guiding Principles for German Judges* (1936) he declared: 'The judge has no right of review over the decisions of the Führer as embodied in a law or decree.' Governor-General of Poland, 1939–45. Sentenced to death by the International Military Tribunal at Nuremberg, and hanged October 16, 1946.

[3] Goebbels had a club foot; it was often made fun of by anti-Nazi cartoonists.

[4] Paul Löbe, 1875–1967. Editor of the Breslau *Volkswacht*, 1899–1919. President of the Reichstag from 1920 to 1932, when he was replaced by Göring. Imprisoned by the Nazis, 1933–44. Co-publisher of the Berlin *Telegraf*, 1945–48. Member of the Bundestag, 1949–53. In 1954 he became President of the Committee for German Unity.

for those arrests, confiscation of the funds and property of the parties in opposition to the present regime and, generally, the continued execution of measures
which are in direct conflict with the existence of what may be termed a
'Rechtsstaat'.

The 'Rechtsstaat', or state based upon a legal framework, had disappeared. Hitler, Rumbold concluded, had 'firmly riveted his hold on
the country'. In his despatch Rumbold pointed out that when he had said
his farewell to Hindenburg on June 29, it was clear that Dr Meissner, the
President's Secretary of State, had received a 'strong hint' from the Nazis
not to give Hindenburg too much information about 'the distressing
incidents which had occurred as a result of the anti-Jewish policy of the
present regime'. It was therefore not surprising when Rumbold found that
Hindenburg did not appear 'to be concerned at recent events'. Yet
Rumbold himself had been shaken by the facts which he had learned about
the cruelty of the regime, giving Simon details of how several prominent
politicians, Provincial Governors and Mayors among them, had been
marched through the streets to concentration camps and hard labour.
'Unpleasant incidents and excesses', Rumbold wrote, 'are bound to occur
during a revolution, but the deliberate ruthlessness and brutality which
have been practised during the last five months seem both excessive and
unnecessary.' There was no doubt, he concluded, 'that the persons directing the policy of the Hitler Government are not normal'.

17

Retirement

1933–1936

Rumbold's pessimistic assessment of the Nazi regime did not meet with an entirely favourable response in England. On July 8, a week after Rumbold's final warning despatch, Hitler signed his first important treaty with a foreign government, the Concordat with the Vatican. The treaty was ratified on July 20, providing respectability for a regime which Rumbold was convinced was evil. On the day that the Condordat was ratified, The Times declared in an editorial:

> Herr Hitler is certainly not devoid of ideals. . . . He undoubtedly desires to re-inculcate the old German virtues of loyalty, self-discipline, and service to the State. Some of the grosser forms of post-war demoralization have been checked under the new regime; and Herr Hitler will win support which may be very valuable to him if he will genuinely devote himself to the moral and economic resurrection of his country.

Rumbold left Berlin in the last week of July, and set off in his Rolls-Royce on a 5,000-mile motor trip in search of relaxation and amusement. On August 1, when he was at Bayreuth, he wrote to his son of how life was, 'very strenuous, what with the heat, bad food and very long operas'. Hitler was present at every performance which Rumbold attended. 'We sat at a table quite close to him', Lady Rumbold wrote to her mother on July 31:

> and he came to shake us warmly by the hand. He was tremendously guarded, but the people were allowed to pass his table and say 'Heil'. . . . There is something rather pathetic about him, he is so small and his white face with untidy lock of hair looks strained. At the same time when he is pleased it lights up with a very human smile. It is extraordinary how they adore that man, the old women, the children, and the young men just standing round and gazing at him in a rapt almost foolish adoration. I think it is largely the courage of the little fellow that appeals, and the knowledge of the huge weight of responsibility that weighs on him. They all feel they want to protect him and help him on his difficult way.

From Bayreuth, Rumbold and his wife went to Marienbad for three weeks, where they entertained ex-King Alfonso to lunch.[1] From Marienbad he drove to the Bavarian Alps for a further three weeks, tried to lose weight, and played golf almost every day. From Bavaria he drove to Italy, where he spent a few days on Lake Como, at a hotel where, as he wrote to his son on September 18 'snobs abound & try to scrape acquaintance. Knowing me as you do you will realize that this is very distasteful to me and I try to keep clear of most people.'

Rumbold regretted having had to leave Berlin, and was disappointed not to have been offered some non-diplomatic post on his retirement. 'I really believe', he wrote to his brother William from Bavaria on September 7, 'that I have done more work and taken greater risks than any of my colleagues of equal rank.' At the end of September he returned to London. The Foreign Office gave him an allowance of £5,280, and an annual pension of £1,500. He invested most of the allowance, which brought him a further income of £220 a year.

In mid-October Germany left the League of Nations. 'The fatherland is making the world hum', Rumbold wrote to his son on October 15, 'and I don't see the outcome.' He felt, he added, 'like an old war horse scenting the fray, and as I have pretty well always been in the scrum hitherto rather regret that I am not in it now'. Another retired 'war horse' was Austen Chamberlain,[2] with whom Rumbold sometimes dined, and who wrote, with a certain optimism, on November 13: 'I prefer Hitler as I see him to von Papen on the one side or Goebbels and Göring on the other, and the bigger he is and the more dominating the more chance there seems of his gradually becoming more reasonable.'

On November 16 Rumbold left England with his wife and daughter for a six-month visit to Ceylon. They sailed from Toulon two days later, on board the Orient Line steamship *Oriana*, reaching Colombo on December 2. Rumbold went at once to his tea estate, where for several days he was busy making plans for rebuilding and extending the main bungalows, and watching the process of tea picking. 'The factory is very smart', he wrote to his son on December 10, 'and everything seemed to be in excellent order.' While in Ceylon he received a telegram from Ramsay MacDonald, offering him the Grand Cross of the Order of the Bath. He had hoped for a peerage, and contemplated refusing the GCB. But refusal, he wrote to his son from Colombo on December 16 'would have

---

[1] King Alfonso had gone into exile on April 14, 1931, following a Republican victory in municipal elections throughout Spain. A Republican regime (the second in Spain's history) had been established without bloodshed, but in July 1936 civil war broke out following a military uprising.

[2] Chamberlain's last Cabinet appointment had been as First Lord of the Admiralty in the National Government, from August to October 1931. He died in March 1937.

almost been an insult and have put me out of court. But it means that you will not eventually adorn the Upper House unless you get there by your own exertions. I shall now be thrown back on myself for occupation in the future.' He was disappointed in not having the chance to sit, and speak, in the House of Lords. 'I can't help feeling', he added, 'that the way in which this honour has been offered to me is rather curious and looks as if the powers that be were not altogether sure of themselves. But, being so far away, I can do nothing about the matter.'

From Ceylon, Rumbold went to Madras, the scene of Sir Thomas Rumbold's activities over a hundred and fifty years before. After visiting the temples at Madura, Trichinopoly and Tanjore he came to the conclusion, as he wrote to his son on December 23, 'that the Hindu religion is somewhat bestial'. But Indian village life fascinated him. 'Our family has had so many connections with India in the past', he wrote on December 29, 'that I can't help feeling that there is something like a call of the blood'. In January he was in Hyderabad, where he found the grave of his grandfather, Sir William Rumbold, in a small cemetery in the Residency garden. From Hyderabad he went to Calcutta, where his father had been born a hundred and five years earlier. At Darjeeling he was in an earthquake which killed several people. He was in the bathroom at the time. 'Another minute of it', he wrote to his son on January 16, 'and you would have been the sole representative of the senior branch of the family. My first concern was to adjust my costume so as to present, at all events, a decent appearance. . . .'

In February Rumbold stayed with the Viceroy, Lord Willingdon,[1] in New Delhi. In the Viceroy's house, he wrote to his stepmother on February 4, 'the greatest luxury prevails'. 'Except when one is staying with a Governor or Viceroy', he wrote to his son on February 5, 'one wakes up to the accompaniment of expectorations, clearing of throats and other noises suggestive of retching or sea-sickness which are perfectly disgusting. The natives all over India have these unpleasant habits.'

Even in India Rumbold could not escape from worrying about Europe. In mid-February his son and some friends were assaulted by the SS in Munich. 'The whole incident is typical of Germans', Rumbold wrote to his son on February 24. 'Their innate brutality comes out. . . . It is not surprising you didn't get any satisfaction. Unless the victims are diplomats, the SS get away with their brutalities every time. . . . You were

---

[1] Freeman Freeman-Thomas, 1866–1941. Liberal MP 1900–6 and 1906–10. Junior Lord of the Treasury, 1905–12. Created Baron Willingdon, 1910. Governor of Bombay, 1913–19 and of Madras, 1919–24. Created Viscount, 1924. Governor-General of Canada, 1926–31. Created Earl, 1931. Viceroy of India, 1931–36. Created Marquess, 1936.

lucky to escape with a black eye as you might well have been hammered by one of those flexible coils of wire with a knob at the end with which the SS used to delight in beating up Jews.'[1]

Early in March the Labour Party, which had suffered so severe a defeat in the General Election of 1931, began to make progress in the local elections in London. Rumbold was not pleased by Labour's success. A large proportion of the British electors, he wrote to his son from Bombay on March 10, 'is a cussed beast who never seems to realize when he is well off. He takes benefits for granted. If I hadn't such a violent dislike for Nazi or Fascist methods, including suppression of free speech and the liberty of the press I shouldn't at all mind seeing the Cripps's,[2] Maxtons[3] et hoc genus omne behind barbed wire for a bit.'

From Berlin, the news was of an apparent reconciliation between the Nazis and the British; a reconciliation which Rumbold found distasteful, and whose permanence he doubted. 'Eden's[4] visit here was a distinct success', Basil Newton[5] wrote from Berlin on March 26. 'He liked Hitler and we hear on good authority that Hitler liked him, and they were both impressed by each other's sincerity and good intentions.' Newton reported that he himself had dined with Brüning, who said that if the extremists in the Nazi movement were removed he would be willing to work with Hitler, for whom, Newton added, 'he evidently entertains sympathy and respect'. Rumbold received Newton's letter on his return to England at the beginning of April. He did not believe that Hitler was at variance with the extremists; he saw no difference between them. He was convinced that Hitler would continue to direct the policy of the Nazi Party according to his own plans and philosophy, of which virulent anti-Semitism was one. The regime, he wrote to his son on April 8, was 'as strong as ever'. In June Brüning came to London, and Rumbold spoke to him at length on June 7,

---

[1] Among Anthony Rumbold's friends who were involved in the incident was a French student, Jacques Caron de la Rue de Beaumarchais, who in 1972 became French Ambassador in London.

[2] Richard Stafford Cripps, 1889–1952. Labour MP, 1931–50. Solicitor-General, 1930–31. Knighted, 1930. Ambassador to Moscow, 1940–42. Minister of Aircraft Production, 1942–45. President of the Board of Trade, 1945. Chancellor of the Exchequer, 1947–50.

[3] James Maxton, 1885–1946. Labour MP, 1922–46. Chairman of the Independent Labour Party, 1926–31 and 1934–39. Biographer of Lenin.

[4] Robert Anthony Eden, 1897–   . Served on the Western Front, 1915–18, when he was awarded the Military Cross. Conservative MP, 1923–57. Parliamentary Under-Secretary, Foreign Office, 1931–33. Lord Privy Seal, 1934–35. Minister for League of Nations Affairs, 1935. Foreign Secretary, 1935–38, 1940–45 and 1951–55. Knight of the Garter, 1954. Prime Minister, 1955–57. Created Earl of Avon, 1961. His elder son was killed in action in 1945.

[5] Basil Cochrane Newton, 1889–1965. Entered Foreign Office, 1912. Acting Counsellor, Peking, 1927–29. Counsellor, Berlin, 1930–35; Minister, 1935–37. Minister to Prague, 1937–39. Knighted, 1939. Ambassador to Baghdad, 1939–41.

sending a report of their conversation to Orme Sargent at the Foreign Office. The hopes which Brüning had expressed to Newton three months earlier had disappeared. Rumbold found the former Chancellor 'much depressed and perturbed by the future outlook for his country'. Those Social Democrat leaders who remained in Germany, Brüning said, 'were men broken in health and spirit'. Once Hindenburg died, Hitler 'would undoubtedly either succeed him, or put in some nominee subservient to himself. In either case Hitler would then be in control of the Army.' Brüning told Rumbold that he blamed much of the success of the Nazis to the evil effects of the British blockade of the war. The young men who supported Hitler were 'not normal: their nerves have gone as a result of the privations to which they and their mothers were exposed during the war, and they are unduly emotional'. Only when the next generation reached maturity would there be 'a saner view of affairs'.

On June 28 Rumbold learned more of Brüning's opinions, this time from Harold Nicolson. The only hope of returning to normal government, Brüning told Nicolson, was 'by way of a restoration of the monarchy'. General Weygand had expressed the same opinion to Nicolson a few days earlier. The difficult question was, who should become Kaiser. 'Personally', Nicolson wrote to Rumbold, 'I should like to see the Emperor restored, and designating his own successor.'

During the summer Rumbold leased a London house, 4 Grosvenor Crescent, and settled down to retirement. His household consisted of a butler, a footman, a cook, two housemaids and a chauffeur. During Ascot week he played golf with the Aga Khan.[1] Later he wrote to his brother, William, about the Aga Khan: 'He is a d–d sight too prosperous and the idea that his prosperity depends on the small but numerous contributions of his sect many of whom are frightfully poor rather revolts me.'

In July and August Rumbold returned to Marienbad. Among those taking the cure was a former German Chancellor, Dr Wirth,[2] who had been warned, as Rumbold wrote to his daughter on August 15, 'to stay out of Germany as otherwise he would be shot'. A few weeks later, when

[1] Aga Sultan Mahomed Shah, 1877–1957. Head of the Ismaili Muslims. Knighted, 1898. Founded the Muslim University, Aligarh, 1910. Member of the Viceroy's Council. Head of the Indian Delegation to the League of Nations Assembly, 1932–37. Privy Councillor, 1934. President of the League of Nations Assembly, Geneva, 1937. His horses won the Derby five times, in 1930, 1935, 1936, 1948 and 1952.

[2] Karl Joseph Wirth, 1879–1956. Professor of Natural Science at Freiburg Technical College, 1908. Minister of Finance for Baden, 1918. German Minister of Finance, March 1920–February 1922. Chancellor, May 1921–November 1922. Minister in charge of German interests of the occupied areas (Rhineland, Saar, etc.) in Müller's Cabinet, 1929. Minister of the Interior in Brüning's Cabinet, 1931. In exile from 1933 in Britain, Switzerland, and the United States; he returned to Germany after the war.

back in England, Rumbold was prompted by an article in the *Daily Mail* to write to his son, on September 8: 'I wonder whether we shall have to fight the Germans again some day.[1] It is an unpleasant speculation.' J. L. Garvin, the editor of the *Observer*, was convinced that war would come. 'The worst is', he wrote to Rumbold on 29 January 1935, 'that the danger is still much less visible than the naval menace was early in the century; and that when realities are clear, say in 1937, it will be hard indeed to make up leeway. Brooding forces one to think that plain British strength means peace; our weakness, war in the end!'

In February Rumbold went to Rome with his wife and daughter. 'Mussolini has done an enormous amount of tidying up since we were last here', he wrote to his son on February 4. 'He has cleared away any number of mean houses which were clustered round old monuments and laid the sites out as gardens. Cars no longer hoot, Italians no longer spit nor accost women and even the fleas have gone. He is a great man and the outer eye is impressed. One need not go deeper, at least I don't want to.' While in Rome, Rumbold, his wife and daughter had an audience of the new Pope, whom Rumbold had known in Warsaw. 'He kept us for $\frac{1}{2}$ an hour', Rumbold wrote to his son on February 20, 'which is considered a long audience, and was most "affable" – a description which the late Curzon was wont to apply to what he called the "average British Admiral".'

Rumbold did a certain amount of voluntary work. He was a Vice-President of the British Olympic Association, and a member of the Board of Conciliation between Denmark and Sweden. He served on the Baronetage Committee of the Privy Council. He also agreed to become a Civil Service Commissioner, examining candidates for Foreign Office entrance.[2] But his mind remained focused on Germany, and German affairs continued to dominate international affairs. On March 15, a week after the French Cabinet had approved an extended period of national service from eighteen months to two years, Hitler introduced compulsory military service to Germany. German disarmament, insisted upon in the

[1] On September 8, 1934, the *Daily Mail* published an article by George Ward Price, who described how the Germans 'are undertaking a systematic transformation of their national character. Individual ambition is to give place to the idea of being a unit in a mighty state.' The six million boys and girls in the Hitler Youth Movement were imbued, he wrote, with an intense patriotism which would make them 'a most formidable people'. 'Those who think of the Nazi regime as a passing political phenomenon', he concluded, 'have not reckoned with the permanence of the impression which it is making on the responsible mind of German youth.'

[2] In the Foreign Office examination of 1936, Rumbold gave his highest marks in the Viva Voce to Archibald Ross and Con O'Neill. Ross was later Ambassador to Portugal (1961–66) and Sweden (1966–70), O'Neill to Finland (1961–63) and to the European Communities in Brussels (1963–65).

Versailles Treaty, was at an end. On March 23 Rumbold wrote to his son:

It is only a melancholy satisfaction to have been a true prophet of the course of events in Germany. It is a good thing no doubt that all camouflage has disappeared and that we know where we are with the Germans. But Germany is setting out to be the strongest Power on the Continent and when she thinks she is strong enough she will no doubt try to settle the Memel and Austrian questions by having recourse to Machtpolitik. I haven't much faith in any arrangements to which she may subscribe now for if and when she signs any agreement she will make mental reservations. I also foresee that she will end by repudiating all loans made to her – municipal and others. Her adverse balance of trade seems to get worse and she will need a lot of money for her projected armaments. All this is very pessimistic but I feel pessimistic. I hope I may prove a false prophet in this case; that wouldn't matter as I am no longer advising the Government. My feeling is that the Germans have an unlimited capacity for slimness and deceit. Only a short time ago they proclaimed that they were defenceless against air attacks. Look at their air force now. They are fathers of hypocrisy.

From Venice, on April 5, Rumbold sent his daughter his thoughts on Anglo-German relations, and on Sir John Simon's visit to Hitler at the end of March. 'It is as well', he wrote, 'that Simon – a congenital pacifist – should have seen the Führer with his own eyes and have been brought to a sense of realities.' Britain was bound, he believed, 'to disappoint both sides', if she tried to mediate between Germany and her neighbours. 'We are in the following difficulty', he explained to his daughter:

We English don't apparently want to be a party to anything having the appearance of a combination against Germany so as to avoid the pre-war system of alliances etc. . . . On the other hand it is quite certain that if we let matters drift and take *no* precautions Germany will, in 2 years' time be absolutely top dog and able to do what she likes. . . . That is how I see it. . . . She is literally the only Power likely to break the peace and some way must be found of letting her – not necessarily by name – know that any Power breaking the peace will be brought to book by all the others.

When Rumbold returned to England at the end of June, his opinion was sought by many of those who were worried about Germany's growing military and air strength. During July he spoke on this subject to the Foreign Affairs Committee of the House of Commons, and also to the Secretary of State for War, Lord Halifax.[1] His message was the same:

---

[1] Edward Frederick Lindley Wood, 1881–1959. Conservative MP, 1910–25. President of the Board of Education, 1922–24 and 1932–35. Created Baron Irwin, 1925. Viceroy of India, 1926–31. Succeeded his father as 3rd Viscount Halifax, 1934. Secretary of State for

Hitler wanted to establish a German military hegemony over Europe, and would do so by whatever means he believed would be most effective, overt or secret, crude or subtle. When he was approached by Philip Conwell-Evans,[1] and asked to join the newly created Anglo-German Fellowship, he declined.[2] He did not believe that British goodwill could modify German policy, nor could he accept the argument put forward by many members of the Fellowship that the dangers of communism were so great that the Nazis must be welcomed as allies in a crusade against Soviet Russia.

In October Anthony Eden asked Rumbold to serve on a League of Nations Committee on the Refugees Question. Rumbold accepted, and in November attended the first meeting of the Committee at Geneva.

On November 8, just before leaving for Geneva, Rumbold broadcast for twenty minutes on the BBC on Lord Cromer. In his broadcast, which was reprinted in *The Listener* on November 13, Rumbold described Cromer as 'by temperament inclined to be autocratic'; but he also reminded his listeners of more leisured days. 'In the afternoon he played lawn tennis as often as he could . . . his regular evening occupations were playing patience or translating Homer aloud. . . .' The broadcast brought him much correspondence from those who had known Cromer, reviving memories of the distant past.

During the last week of November and the first two weeks of December, Rumbold was at Geneva, examining the problem of refugees, and trying to work out what part the League of Nations should play in resettlement and relief. He and his fellow Committee members,[3] in their Report of

---

War, June to November 1935. Lord Privy Seal, 1935–37. Lord President of the Council, 1937–38. Secretary of State for Foreign Affairs, 1938–40. Ambassador at Washington, 1941–46. Created Earl, 1944. He published his memoirs, *Fulness of Days* in 1957. One of his two sons was killed in action in 1942.

[1] Philip Conwell-Evans, 1891–1968. Lecturer in history at Königsberg University, East Prussia, 1932–34. Joint Secretary of the Anglo-German Fellowship, 1934–39. Instrumental in arranging the visits of Lord Lothian and Lloyd George to Hitler (in the latter visit acting as interpreter). A friend of Ribbentrop's, he was alerted to the dangers of Nazi foreign policy in the summer of 1938, and worked subsequently for Sir Robert Vansittart, collecting information about German intentions.

[2] The Anglo-German Fellowship was founded in March 1935, to replace the Anglo-German Association, which had disapproved of Nazi methods. The Fellowship had its own magazine, the *Anglo-German Review*, and was initially supported by several large business firms, including Unilever, Dunlop Rubber, Shell Mex and BP, and Guinness.

[3] The other members of the Committee were a Norwegian, Michael Hansson (a Member of the Permanent Court of Arbitration at The Hague); an Italian, De Michelis (formerly Commissioner-General of Emigration); a Czech, Stefan Osúsky (Czech Minister in Paris); and a Frenchman, P. Roland-Marcel (a Councillor of State and former Prefect of Bas-Rhin).

3 January 1936, urged all Governments to act in unison to deal with the exodus of refugees from Germany, which had already reached 100,000, and could only increase. They saw also a need for refugees to be protected in the countries to which they had fled, and hoped that the refugees themselves would 'encourage among their children the idea that they should become citizens of the country in which they had settled. The second generation will thus be spared the hardships of exile.'

During the early months of 1936, Rumbold went first to the South of France, and then to Algeria, in search of sun and relaxation. While he was in France, the murder of the Japanese statesman, Viscount Saito, whom he had known in Japan before 1914, led him to exclaim to his son on March 1: 'What a curse militarism is and how lucky we are not to have it in our country.' At Monte Carlo he met the former Prussian Secretary of State, Robert Weismann, who was now in exile, and told Rumbold that 'you cannot indefinitely drill and regiment a whole population without having an explosion at the end'. In Weismann's view 'Germany was getting back to 1914'. On March 7, while Rumbold was in Algeria, Hitler took a step which seemed to confirm this view. He decided, contrary to the freely negotiated Locarno Treaty of 1925, to remilitarize the Rhineland. Within twenty-four hours 35,000 German troops had entered the province. British reactions were mixed. *The Times* declared that Hitler's action was not to be condemned, but provided a 'chance to rebuild'. The violation of Locarno should be seen as opening an avenue of peace, not war. Lord Lothian – the former Philip Kerr – believed that the Germans were 'only going into their own back garden', and that Britain should now seek closer relations with Germany. Rumbold was sceptical of the possibility of preserving peace by pursuing an appeasement policy. On March 15 he wrote to his son that, within the Cabinet, Lord Halifax represented 'the policy of accommodation with the Germans'. How was it possible, he added, 'to trust the latter? They only keep a treaty as long as it suits them.'

Hitler declared that, with the remilitarization of the Rhineland, Germany had no further territorial ambitions. British opinion was confused as well as divided. 'Personally I would not trust the present rulers of Germany round the corner', the editor of *The Times*, Geoffrey Dawson,[1] wrote to Rumbold on June 14. 'But I would unhesitatingly try to come to an understanding with them, *while keeping my eyes wide open*. After all, as Winston said the other day, we cannot afford to be the enemy of every

---

[1] Geoffrey Robinson, 1874–1944. Private Secretary to Lord Milner, South Africa, 1901–5. Editor of *The Times*, 1912–19 and 1925–41. He assumed the surname of Dawson in 1917.

nation at once, and for the time being I would far rather have Germany on my side than Italy.' Rumbold saw no future in either Anglo-German or Anglo-Italian co-operation. In August, while he was again at Marien-bad, he was told by ex-King Alfonso that the outbreak of civil war in Spain made it imperative that Britain, Germany and Italy should 'get together and police Europe'. But, Rumbold wrote to his son on August 4, 'I told him that we hated Fascists a little less than we did the Communists.'

During 1936 Rumbold had tried to warn those who believed that Hitler's demands were reasonable, and that statesmanship consisted in meeting them. On April 21 he had written to a leading exponent of Anglo-German co-operation, Lord Lothian:

I wonder whether our people sufficiently realise how unscrupulous the two principal dictators in Europe today are. I have carefully studied Hitler and his past. He and Mussolini hold what they call 'das Leben des Volkes' as the supreme interest, superior to the observance of any treaty or engagement. If such a treaty is a bar to what they think is or should be the development of their respective countries they will scrap it without compunction. I have no confidence in either of these two men and am a convinced partisan of the principle of collective security properly applied. It is, indeed, our only safeguard.

But other influences weighed more with Lothian. He visited Hitler twice, and was impressed by Hitler's protestations of friendship and moderation. Geoffrey Dawson shared Lothian's opinions, writing to him on 23 May 1937:

I should like to get going with the Germans. I simply cannot understand why they should apparently be so much annoyed with *The Times* at this moment. I spend my nights in taking out anything which I think will hurt their suscepti-bilities and in dropping in little things which are intended to soothe them.

Rumbold found Dawson's editorial policy distasteful, and said so, writing to him with firmness:

I have rather come to the conclusion that the average Englishman – whilst full of common-sense as regards internal affairs – is often muddle-headed, sloppy and gullible when he considers foreign affairs. One often hears such phrases as 'the Germans are so like us'. Nothing is more untrue. I could quote many points of difference. For one thing Germans have a streak of brutality which is quite absent in the ordinary Englishman. And Germans like to put up with things which are repugnant to the average man of this country. My point is, therefore, that we should know the people with whom we propose to deal.

Now Hitler has quite consistently applied the principles of *Mein Kampf* in Germany herself. He has now got to apply them in his foreign policy and that's where the trouble is coming. The value to us of an understanding with Germany is not only that it may bring peace and stability in Western Europe but that it may act as a drag on Hitler's adventures in Central and Eastern Europe. Once he embarks on any adventure in those regions war is, to my mind, a dead certainty. The ordinary Englishman does not realise that the German is an inexorable Oliver Twist. Give him something and it is a jumping-off ground for asking for something else.

18

Palestine

1936–1937

Rumbold had not expected further official employment. He was 67 years old. But in 1936 the Government asked him to go to Palestine.

Since the defeat of Turkey in 1918, the British Government had administered Palestine, first as the occupying power, then as ruler under a League of Nations Mandate. The administration had been made difficult on account of the conflicting claims and aspirations of the Arabs and Jews. The Balfour Declaration of 2 November 1917 had promised British support for a Jewish 'national home' in Palestine; but the Declaration had also laid down 'that nothing shall be done which may prejudice the civil and religious rights of existing non-Jewish communities in Palestine'. This dual obligation was reiterated on 24 July 1922, when Britain's Mandate over Palestine was formally approved by the League of Nations. In 1918 there had been less than 100,000 Jews in Palestine, and over half a million Arabs. The Arabs saw no danger in such a ratio. But with the influx of Jewish immigrants and refugees – 25,000 Jews fled from Russia between 1920 and 1923 – Arab resentment grew, and there were frequent violent clashes. In August 1929 more than a hundred Jewish men, women and children were killed by Arabs at Hebron and Safed. The Jews acted vigorously in their own defence, and reprisals followed. British troops tried, unsuccessfully, to keep the peace; each week brought a death or wounding, an ambush or an explosion.

When Hitler came to power in Germany the number of Jews reaching Palestine rose considerably. In order to lessen Arab fears of being outnumbered, the British tried to limit immigration. In reply, the Jews organized illegal landings. By 1936 there were 400,000 Jewish settlers in Palestine, nearly 25 per cent. of the total population. In the spring of 1936 Arab riots broke out in Jaffa, and spread rapidly throughout the territory of the Mandate. Once more, the Jews retaliated in self-defence, and violence continued for the rest of the year. The British garrison of 20,000 men could not keep the peace. The violence took many forms. During the year the Arabs cut down nearly 150,000 Jewish owned fruit trees and over 60,000 forest trees which had been planted in the previous decade

33 Rumbold with his daughter, wife and son, Berlin, 1933.

34 Rumbold relaxes in
Bavaria, while
Ambassador to
Germany.

35 Sir Thomas Beecham, Rumbold, and Wilhelm Furtwängler in Berlin.

36 'Heil Hitler', 1933. A contemporary postcard, bought in Berlin by Rumbold's daughter.

37 Rumbold says farewell to Hindenburg, May 1933. Otto Meissner is on Rumbold's right; Basil Newton is between Hindenburg and Lady Rumbold.

38 Rumbold on the verandah of his tea estate bungalow, Ceylon, December 1933.

39 Rumbold visits a temple in southern India, January 1934.

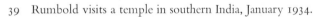

40   Rumbold with his nephew Alistair in Palestine, 1936.

41 The Peel Commission arrives in Palestine, 11 November 1936. John Martin on Rumbold's right: Lord Peel far right.

42 Members of the Peel Commission at Tiberias, 21 November 1936. *Left to right:* Sir Harold Morris, Rumbold, Peel and Coupland.

43 Lord Peel and Rumbold at the King David Hotel, Jerusalem.

44 The Peel Commission hears Chaim Weizmann's evidence, 25 November 1936. Rumbold and Lord Peel are on the left; Weizmann (in dark jacket) has his back to the camera.

Horace Rumbold

45   Rumbold's portrait, drawn for Grillons' Club by F. A. de B. Footner,
and signed by Rumbold himself.

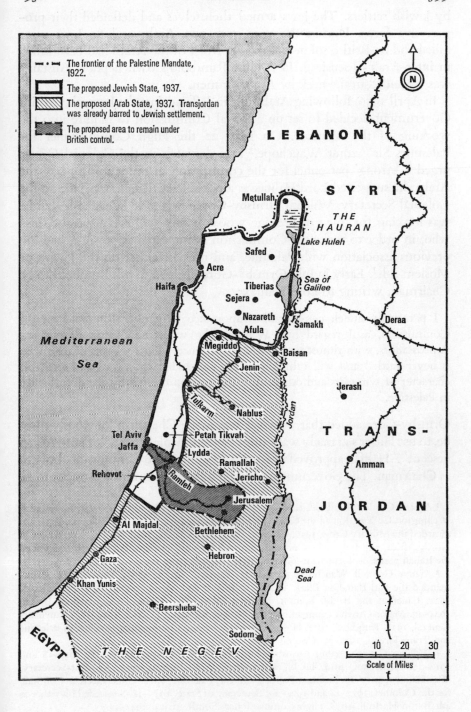

The frontier of the Palestine Mandate, 1922.

The proposed Jewish State, 1937.

The proposed Arab State, 1937. Transjordan was already barred to Jewish settlement.

The proposed area to remain under British control.

by Jewish settlers. The Jews armed themselves and defended their property by force. During the year over 200 Arabs and 81 Jews were killed and 21 British soldiers also died. Most of the Arabs had been killed in inter-Arab dissensions. In August Rumbold's own nephew Alistair,[1] was wounded in the neck by Arab gunmen.

In April 1936, following Arab riots in Jaffa against the Jews, the British Government decided to set up a Royal Commission to inquire into the working of the Mandate. On May 22 the High Commissioner for Palestine, Sir Arthur Wauchope,[2] in a despatch to the Colonial Office, urged a 'strong' personnel for the commission in order to 'impress' the Arabs; he suggested Lord Halifax as a possible chairman. On June 10 the Colonial Secretary, William Ormsby-Gore,[3] wrote to Wauchope that he was looking for 'men of prestige whose names will carry weight', and who, in order to make the Commission as impartial as possible, had 'no previous association with Palestine, and no past either on the Jewish or Moslem side'. Early in July Ormsby-Gore decided to ask Rumbold to be Chairman, writing to Lord Halifax:

I personally attach considerable importance to getting Rumbold on the Commission, as I regard him as much the wisest and sanest of our ex-Ambassadors, with almost world-wide experience. In fact the sort of man who is never rattled and will calm down the somewhat emotional and excitable character of witnesses and others after the tension created by the disturbances in Palestine.

Ormsby-Gore added that whoever was made Chairman 'obviously must be, to use Hitler's in many ways most objectionable phrase, "of pure Aryan descent".' Halifax approved of Rumbold joining the Commission, but not as Chairman. The Government felt that a Royal Commission ought to be

---

[1] Alistair Gordon Rumbold, 1914–   . Son of Rumbold's brother William. Educated at Wellington College. Joined the Cameron Highlanders, 1934. Served in Palestine, 1936–39; awarded the Military Cross, 1936. Captain, 1939; Staff Officer, 1940. Major, 1942; served in North Africa, and Italy, where he was captured by the Germans, but escaped and joined the Italian partisans. Lieutenant-Colonel, 1951. Retired from the Army, 1959.

[2] Arthur Grenfell Wauchope, 1874–1947. Entered Army, 1893; Major, 1914. Commanded the 2nd Battalion Black Watch, in France and Mesopotamia, 1914–18. Colonel, 1922. Chief of the British Section, Military Inter-Allied Control Commission, Berlin, 1924–27. Major-General commanding the Northern Ireland District, 1929–31. Lieutenant-General, 1931. Knighted, 1931. High Commissioner and Commander-in-Chief in Palestine and Trans-Jordan, 1931–38. General, 1936.

[3] William George Arthur Ormsby-Gore, 1885–1964. Conservative MP, 1910–18 and 1918–38. Lieutenant, 1914; Intelligence Officer, Arab Bureau, 1916. Assistant-Secretary, War Cabinet, 1917–18. Assistant Political Officer, Palestine, 1918. Under-Secretary of State for the Colonies, 1922–24 and 1924–29; Secretary of State, 1936–38. Succeeded his father as 4th Baron Harlech, 1938. High Commissioner, South Africa, 1941–44.

ENGLAND-PALESTINE
COMPARISON

(omitting the desert area of the Negeb to
the South of Palestine.)

headed by a Peer. On July 14 the Chairmanship was offered to Lord Peel,[1] a former Secretary of State for India. Rumbold was then invited to serve as Peel's deputy. He accepted on July 16, writing to Ormsby-Gore: 'I am under no illusion as to the difficulty of the task confronting the Commission but the work is bound to be most interesting.' Four days later Ormsby-Gore wrote to Wauchope that Rumbold had agreed to join the Commission on the condition that he 'has time to do his "annual cure"!' On July 22 Rumbold and Peel met John Martin,[2] whom Ormsby-Gore had chosen as Secretary to the Commission. The other members were chosen within the week.[3] In the House of Commons, Josiah Wedgwood[4] protested: 'Why is the House of Lords contributing as Chairman one whose whole record and convictions are so strikingly pro-Moslem'.

Rumbold decided to take his wife and daughter with him to Palestine, an unusual procedure, and John Martin made the necessary arrangements for them to stay in the King David Hotel in Jerusalem. The Treasury baulked at the idea of paying for Rumbold's servant, being worried, as a Treasury official, H. R. Foyle,[5] wrote to John Martin, 'that this might really be a servant for Lady Rumbold'. Martin was able to impress on the Treasury that Rumbold did not resort to such stratagems. He also dealt with the correspondence that began to descend upon the Commissioners,

[1] William Robert Wellesley Peel, 1867–1937. Conservative MP, 1900–6 and 1909–12. Succeeded his father as Viscount Peel, 1912. Chairman of the London County Council, 1914. Chairman of the Committee on the Detention of Neutral Vessels, 1916. Under-Secretary of State for War, 1919–21. Chancellor of the Duchy of Lancaster and Minister of Transport, 1921–22. Secretary of State for India, 1922–24 and 1928–29. Created Earl, 1929. Lord Privy Seal, 1931. Member of the Indian Round Table Conference, 1930–31. Chairman, Burma Round Table Conference, 1931–32; the Palestine Royal Commission, 1936–37.

[2] John Miller Martin, 1904–   . Entered the Dominions Office, 1927. Seconded to the Malayan Civil Service, 1931–34. Secretary, Palestine Royal Commission, 1936–37. Private Secretary to the Prime Minister (Winston Churchill), 1940–41; Principal Private Secretary, 1941–45. Assistant Under-Secretary of State, Colonial Office, 1945–56. Deputy Under-Secretary of State, 1956–65. Knighted, 1952. High Commissioner, Malta, 1965–67.

[3] There were four other Commissioners: Sir Laurie Hammond (former Governor of Assam); Sir Morris Carter (former President of the Court of Appeal for Eastern Africa); Sir Harold Morris (President of the Industrial Court); and Reginald Coupland (Professor of Colonial History at Oxford).

[4] Josiah Clement Wedgwood, 1872–1943. Naval architect, 1896–1900. Liberal MP, 1906–18; Labour MP, 1918–42. Commander, Royal Naval Air Service, 1914–15; severely wounded at Gallipoli while in command of a unit of armoured cars, 1915. Assistant Director of Trench Warfare, 1917. Colonel, 1918. Vice-Chairman of the Labour Party, 1921–24. Chancellor of the Duchy of Lancaster in the first Labour Government, 1924. Created Baron, 1942. Among his published works were Memoirs of a Fighting Life (1940) and Testament to Democracy, (1942); he was an ardent supporter of the Zionist cause.

[5] Herbert Reginald Foyle, 1885–1965. Entered Civil Service, Board of Education, 1904; General Post Office, 1906. Inland Revenue, 1907. Principal, Treasury, 1920–41. War Damage Commission, 1941–46.

particularly from the Jews. On August 19 Arthur Lourie[1] wrote on behalf of the Jewish Agency,[2] asking that the evidence should be given in public. But Sir Arthur Wauchope wanted all the meetings to be in secret. Peel tried to argue against Wauchope, writing to Martin on August 25 that closed sessions 'would create an atmosphere of secrecy and suspicion which I am most anxious to avoid', and three days later Rumbold wrote to Martin, endorsing Peel's argument. On October 6 the Commissioners held their first meeting, in London, to decide on procedure.[3] It was eventually resolved that some evidence would have to be heard in secret. During October, while waiting to set off, the Commissioners studied a large number of memoranda prepared by the Government of Palestine. These included comprehensive statistics on population, immigration, land use, industrial development, the 're-settlement of displaced Arab culti-vators', and the organization of the Jewish population. The memoranda filled 207 closely printed foolscap pages[4]. Two further sets of papers from the Palestine Government, one marked secret, the other confidential, were also printed, but never made public. These dealt in detail with the recent Arab–Jewish disturbances, with the financial activities of the Jewish Agency and with the military problems of the Mandate. In addition to this material from British officials in Jerusalem, John Martin also prepared for the Commissioners a set of eighteen White Papers and other docu-ments on Palestine, issued by the British Government between 1917 and 1937, together with a series of maps; and each member of the Commission was given these official materials in a bulky bound volume.

On November 6 the Commissioners left London for Palestine. John Martin wrote to his mother four days later that at Victoria Station 'the press photographers were there in full force and we were blinded with flashes when Constantia Rumbold put her head out of the window as the train moved off.'

During the Commissioners' journey the Arabs announced that they

[1] Arthur Lourie, 1903–   . Born in Johannesburg. Lectured in Law at Witwatersrand University. Political Secretary of the Jewish Agency in London, 1933–40. Director of the Jewish Agency United Nations Affairs Office, New York, 1946–48. Israel Consul-General, New York, 1948–53. Ambassador in Ottawa, 1957–59; in London, 1960–65.

[2] The Jewish Agency had been set up in 1929, with the task of 'advising and co-operating with the Government' on all matters relating to the Jewish National Home. The role of the Agency was laid down in Article 4 of the Mandate. Among its work, it undertook to house new immigrants, to carry out agricultural research, to organize an educational system, and to use the money collected from world Jewry for agricultural settlement and social welfare.

[3] The minutes of this meeting were originally in the Colonial Office, reference 733/320. But a note in the box states that they were 'destroyed under statute'.

[4] These memoranda were published in 1937 by the Stationery Office as Colonial No 133, *Palestine Royal Commission: Memoranda Prepared by the Government of Palestine.*

would boycott the Commission. Rumbold was much angered by this, writing to his son from Port Said on November 10: 'I, for one, consider their action a piece of gross insolence, and I think this view is shared by the others. We shall proceed without them. The Arabs are fools and have played straight into the hands of the Jews who must be chortling.' But the Arab action did not prejudice him against the Arab case. The 'irritating behaviour or characteristics of *each* party' he told his son, 'act as a check on any bias one might have in favour of Arabs or Jews'.

The Commissioners reached Palestine on November 11, Armistice Day, and attended a ceremony at the British War Cemetery on Mount Scopus, overlooking Jerusalem. 'No one in the circumstances', the *Report* declared:

. . . could help reflecting that the Peace which followed the Armistice of 1918 had been an even less real peace in Palestine than in Europe. Something like another war, however minute in scale, had recently been waged, and something like another armistice had been concluded. The more we saw and the more we heard in the days that followed, the clearer it became that this armistice was only a suspension of hostilities not a preliminary to peace. The Arab leaders had refused to co-operate with us in our search for a means of settling the dispute. It was believed in many quarters that another outbreak might occur at any moment. Several isolated murders or assaults occurred during our stay, and at one time acts of brigandage were reported almost every day. It was impossible not to feel the sense of tension at Jerusalem, and of pessimism. In neutral circles the task we had undertaken was regarded as well-nigh impossible.

On November 12 Sir Arthur Wauchope welcomed the Commissioners officially at Government House, pointing out in his speech that a Royal Commission was 'the highest form of inquiry known in the British Empire . . . impartial, independent and uncontrolled by the Government of the day'. Peel, in his reply, spoke of the Arab decision to boycott the inquiry. 'It would be most unfortunate', he said, 'if without their advice and assistance we were compelled to arrive at conclusions and to make decisions.' But the Arabs insisted on staying away, refusing to participate in any discussions that might consolidate the Jewish national home.

For two days the Commissioners made an extended tour, visiting Ramallah, Jaffa, Tel Aviv and Petah Tikva on November 13, and Bethlehem, Hebron, Beersheba and Rehovot on November 14. John Martin later recalled an incident which had, he believed, made a considerable emotional impact on Rumbold and his colleagues. While visiting a Jewish agricultural settlement the Commissioners had seen a man living in a rough hut, but with a piano, and musical scores. Rumbold thought he had met the man before. On asking his name, it appeared that he was a well-known German musician, from Leipzig, who had once played at the

Berlin Embassy. 'We all felt uncomfortable about his plight', Martin later recalled. Rumbold began to commiserate with the man. 'This is a terrible change for you', he said, condoling. But the musician replied, to Rumbold's surprise: 'It *is* a change, from Hell to Heaven'. The Jewish need of a haven was obvious, not from this chance encounter alone, but from all that the Commissioners saw and heard. It was equally obvious that this haven had now become a reality, and that Palestine, even under the Mandate, offered persecuted Jewry its main objection, a Jewish National Home.

The Commissioners held their first official sessions in Jerusalem on November 16 and 17. Both sessions were secret.[1] Sir Arthur Wauchope was the witness on both days. On November 18, at the Commission's first public session, an official of the Government of Palestine, Eric Mills,[2] was examined about Jewish immigration. He informed them that on his estimate there were, in mid-1936, 940,000 Arab and 370,000 Jews living in Palestine, and that 134,000 of the Jews had arrived since Hitler had come to power in Germany three and a half years before. Rumbold pressed Mills to tell him how effective was the work of the British Passport Control Officers, who scrutinized potential Jewish immigrants in Warsaw and Berlin; Mills answered that it was as effective as it need be. Later in the session Colonel Heron[3] informed them of the great influx of Jewish doctors, 600 in 1936 alone, mostly from Germany, Poland and Czechoslovakia. 'There is rather a struggle to get patients' he told the Commissioners, 'which does not improve matters.' A total of 2000 Jewish doctors had reached Palestine since 1933; many could not find work as doctors and had been 'absorbed in other jobs'. There was, Colonel Heron believed, too much immigration of doctors, dentists and scientists.

On November 19, after taking more evidence from Eric Mills, the Commissioners drove to northern Palestine, visiting the Arab towns of Nablus and Afula, and the Jewish settlement at Sejera. That night they

[1] The Colonial Office copy of the secret evidence was destroyed by statute (see p. 403, n. 3). All the evidence given in the public sessions, and the cross-examination, was published by the Stationery Office in 1937, as *Palestine Royal Commission: Minutes of Evidence Heard at Public Sessions* (Colonial No. 134). Despite both Peel and Rumbold's reluctance to hold too many secret sessions, only 31 of the Commission's 66 meetings were held in public.

[2] Eric Mills, 1892–1961. Served with the Government of Palestine, 1917–48; in 1936 he was Commissioner for Migration and Statistics, and also Director of the Department of Immigration. On special duties in Jamaica, 1949; Fiji, 1950; the Anglo-Egyptian Sudan, 1950–51 and British Guiana, 1952–56. In 1931 wrote he the *Report of the Census of Palestine*.

[3] George Wykeham Heron, 1880–1963. House physician, Westminster Hospital, 1904. Joined Royal Army Medical Corps, 1905. Served in the Egyptian Expeditionary Force 1914–18. Colonel, 1918. Director of Medical Services, Government of Palestine, 1920–44. Controller of Medical Supplies, Palestine, 1939–45. Knighted, 1944.

stayed at Tiberias, driving on the following day to Nazareth and Haifa, and returning in the evening to Tiberias. On November 21 they went to Safed and Acre, again returning to Tiberias for the night. Throughout their travels they questioned British officials, and Jews and Arabs. On November 22 they visited the Huleh swamp and the northern border town of Metullah. On the following day they returned to Jerusalem through Baisan and Jenin.

The public meetings of the Commission reopened on November 24, when several British officials were questioned about land policy. Lewis Andrews,[1] the acting Director of the Department of Development for the Galilee District, told the Commissioners that although he and his officials had made every effort to collect evidence of the Arab charge that Arab farmers had been displaced by Jews, little evidence had been forthcoming. The Arabs had been invited, and encouraged to complain, but few had done so. 'The only answer I can give', Andrews told Lord Peel, 'is that there were not so many people displaced as we imagined.' He put the total figure at no more than two thousand, many of whom had found employment 'in other agricultural industries or in orange groves . . .'.

November 25 was given over to the evidence and cross examination of Dr Chaim Weizmann,[2] the Zionist leader whose efforts in 1917 had been instrumental in the evolution of the Balfour Declaration. In a moving speech, Weizmann outlined the history and aims of Zionism. The Jewish problem, he said, was 'a problem of the homelessness of a people . . . almost everything to the east of the Rhine is today in a position politically and economically, which is, if I may say so – and I am not given I think to exaggeration – something which is neither life nor death. . . .' It was not only a German problem, he insisted. 'The German tragedy . . .' he continued, 'is in size much smaller than the Polish; it is of manageable proportions and, moreover, the German Jews are stronger, economically

[1] Lewis Yelland Andrews, 1896–1937. Born in Australia. On active service in Palestine, 1917–18. Demobilized with the rank of Captain, 1919. District Officer, Haifa, 1921–25. Assistant District Commissioner of the Northern District (Galilee), 1925–29. Acting Director, Department of Development, 1932–36. Member of the General Agricultural Council, 1935. District Commissioner, Galilee District, 1936–37. While the Peel Commissioners were in Palestine, he acted as their Liaison Officer, supervising and arranging details of their travels through Palestine. Murdered at Nazareth by Arabs. His widow's pension was calculated as if he had been a Major-General killed in action.

[2] Chaim Weizmann, 1874–1952. Born in Russia. Educated in Germany. Reader in Biochemistry, University of Manchester, 1906. Naturalized as a British subject, 1910. Director Admiralty Laboratories, 1916–19. President of the World Zionist Organization, and of the Jewish Agency for Palestine, 1921–31 and 1935–46. Chairman, Board of Governors, Hebrew University of Jerusalem, 1932–50. Adviser to the Ministry of Supply, London, 1939–45. First President of the State of Israel from 1949 until his death. His eldest son, Flight-Lieutenant, Michael Weizmann, RAF, was killed in action in 1942.

stronger; they can resist the onslaught much better than the Polish Jews, who have been ground down now for almost a century. . . .' Weizmann went on to explain the appeal of Palestine to the Jews:

We are a stiff-necked people and a people of long memory. We never forget. Whether it is our misfortune or whether it is our good fortune, we have never forgotten Palestine, and this steadfastness, which has preserved the Jew through the ages and through a career which is almost one long chain of inhuman suffering, is primarily due to some physiological or pathological attachment to Palestine. We have never forgotten it; we have never given it up. We have survived the Babylonian destruction. We have survived the Roman destruction. The Jews put up a fairly severe fight and the Roman invasion, which destroyed half of the civilized world, did not destroy small Judaea; and whenever they once got a chance, the slightest chance, there they returned, there they created their literature, their colonies, towns and communities, and if the Commission would take the trouble to study the post-Roman period of the Jews, and the life of the Jews in Palestine, they would find that there was not a single century in the nineteen centuries which have passed since the destruction of Palestine as a Jewish political entity, not one single century in which the Jews did not attempt to come back. It is a fallacy, if I may submit it, to think that those 1900 years were, so to say, a desert of time; they were not. When the material props of the Jewish commonwealth were destroyed, the Jews carried Palestine in their hearts and in their heads wherever they went.

Weizmann went on to explain to the Commissioners his concept of what the Jews had already achieved in Palestine, and how Palestine could prosper. In 1920, he said, there had been 'no Treasury, no funds, no experience, a broken up people, no training, a people which for centuries had been divorced from agricultural pursuits. . . .' After only sixteen years 'we stand before an achievement on which I think we can look with a certain amount of respect and on which, I will not hide from you, we look with a certain amount of pride'. The Jewish owned land in Palestine amounted to only 400,000 acres, but into that land had been sunk 'the sweat and blood of our pioneers'.

On November 26 Weizmann again appeared before the Commissioners, to give evidence about the April disturbances; the session was not open to the public, and is not referred to in the evidence of the Palestine Royal Commission.[1] But Weizmann's wife Vera,[2] in a diary which she kept throughout the sittings of the Peel Commission, wrote:

[1] There is a note of the secret session in the *Palestine Post* (27 Nov 1936), which stated that Weizmann gave evidence on November 26 from 10.30 to 1.15.
[2] Vera Khatzman, 1881–1961. Born in Rostov-on-Don. Medical student at Geneva, 1900–06. Married Weizmann in 1906. Medical Officer, Manchester Corporation, 1913–16. One of the founders of the Women's International Zionist Organization, 1918.

Ch. gave his evidence in camera for $2\frac{3}{4}$ hours. What a difference to his feelings on his return. He looked pale, sad & worn out. His first words were: I feel the c's mind is made up; we shall have to make concessions. They are convinced that our case is a good one, but the Imperial interests are of the first consideration; they can't afford to quarrel with the Arabs. We have come to an impasse. The British can't afford to enforce peace by force; the public opinion would not tolerate it. If they were sure of European peace for the next three years, they might [have] acted differently. Therefore for the next few years they will have to go slowly & see to the future more remote. Ch. is afraid least should they crystallise the N.H. and enforce the immigration not exceeding the Arab natural increase, which will mean a permanent jewish minority. Such were Ch's general impressions. Lord Peel asked: 'can you & we take upon us the responsibility of bringing thousands of jews in without giving them a proper protection?' Ch. – 'we think in different categories, my lord. The Jews protected in Poland would prefer to live unprotected in Palestine.' At these words Hammond[1] had tears in his eyes.

They all were most kind and understanding with the exception of Rumbold. He asked 'When will the J.N.H. be finished?' 'Never' said Chaim, 'England is never finished. . . .'

Ch. could give only his impressions to his colleagues, who all flocked in to our flat. Great gloom spread over them & I had to shake them all up. We must not give the impression either to the Jews, administration or Arabs, that we have any misgivings.

The public sessions continued on November 27; as Lord Peel was unwell, Rumbold presided. The principal witness was the Director of Education, H. E. Bowman,[2] whom Rumbold had known slightly in Cairo, and who had been in Palestine since the beginning of the Mandate. He explained to the Commissioners why the educational system, which he had tried to develop in such a way as to promote Arab–Jewish understanding, had failed to do so. The language barrier, the religious barrier, and political tensions were too great. The school system had to be kept separate because, in a mixed school, 'you at once reduce your working week to four days, or, have no Moslems present on Fridays, no Jews on Saturday, no

---

[1] Egbert Laurie Lucas Hammond, 1873–1939. Entered the Indian Civil Service, 1893. An expert on Indian electoral law. Chief Secretary, Government of Bihar and Orissa, 1924–27. Knighted, 1927. Governor of Assam, 1927–32. Member, Royal Commission on Palestine, 1936–37.

[2] Humphrey Ernest Bowman, 1879–1965. Entered the Education Department of the Egyptian Government, 1903. Seconded to the Sudan Education Service, 1911–13. Director, Egyptian Students in England, 1913–14. Served in the army on the western front and in Mesopotamia, 1914–18. In charge of the Department of Education, Iraq, 1918–20. Returned to Egypt, 1920. Seconded to the Palestine Government to organize its Department of Education, 1920. Remained in the Palestine Government Service until 1936. He published *Middle East Window* in 1942.

Christians[1] on Sunday . . .'. It was as a result of this evidence that Professor Coupland,[2] who did most of the questioning of Bowman, began to evolve the idea of partition as an alternative to Arab–Jewish co-existence.

On November 28, a Saturday, the Commission rested, and Rumbold visited the old city of Jerusalem. On the Sunday he remained at his hotel. On November 30 the Commission met again. 'The work for H and the Commission', Lady Rumbold wrote to her mother, 'is *unbelievably* difficult. . . . These 6 just, upright men trying to do the right thing, and yet there seems to be *no* solution.' That morning the Commission examined Moshe Shertok,[3] head of the Political Department of the Jewish Agency. Rumbold asked Shertok if the town of Tel Aviv was being built up deliberately as 'a sort of artificial creation with a view to getting more and more immigrants in and creating a sort of snowball process'. Shertok replied: 'you might call the whole process of the settlement of Palestine a snowball process. Naturally every wave of immigrants creates possibilities of salvation not only for themselves but for those coming after them. There is a succession of immigration waves into this country'. Rumbold questioned Shertok about how far the Jewish Agency policy of granting labour certificates to European Jews took into account 'the economic absorptive capacity' of Palestine. Shertok claimed that it did. When Rumbold pointed out that the granting of certificates to German Jews since 1933 'really had nothing to do with the absorptive capacity of the country' Shertok replied tersely: 'We are never oblivious of the conditions under which our people live in the Diaspora'. In his statement five days before, Chaim Weizmann had dealt with this same question.

[1] According to the Census of 1931, there were 91,000 Christians, 284,000 Jews and 759,000 Muslims in Palestine. The largest number of Christians were at Jerusalem (20,000) and Bethlehem (10,000).

[2] Reginald Coupland, 1884–1952. Lecturer in Ancient History, Oxford, 1907–14; Lecturer in Colonial History, 1913–18. Editor of the *Round Table* 1917–19 and 1939–41. Fellow of All Souls College, 1920–48. Beit Professor of the History of the British Empire, Oxford, 1920–48. Adviser, Burma Round Table Conference, 1931. Member of the Palestine Royal Commission, 1936–37. Member of the Cripps' Mission to India, 1942. Author of many books on Indian and colonial history. Knighted, 1944.

[3] Moshe Shertok, 1894–1965. Born in the Ukraine. Settled in Palestine with his parents, 1906. Moved to Jaffa, 1908. One of the founders of Tel Aviv, 1909. Studied law in Constantinople, 1912–14. Enlisted in the Turkish Army, 1914. Served as an interpreter on the Staff of the Commander of the German Army in Turkey, 1914–17. Studied at the London School of Economics, 1920–24. Deputy editor of the Palestine labour daily newspaper, *Davar*, 1925–31. Secretary of the Jewish Agency's political department, 1931; head of the political department, 1933. A leader of the movement for Jewish recruitment in the British army, 1939. Led the struggle at the United National General Assembly for the approval of the United Nations Palestine Partition Plan, 1947. On Israel's independence he took the surname of Sharett. Foreign Minister of the State of Israel, 1947–54; Prime Minister, Jan 1954–Nov 1955. Foreign Minister, 1955–60. Chairman of the Jewish Agency, 1960.

'Belgium may be overpopulated', he had told the Commissioners, 'but when a Belgian comes from exile back home he is not asked at the frontier whether he falls within the absorptive capacity of Belgium.'

Moshe Shertok's evidence continued for two more days. Palestine, he told the Commissioners on December 2, offered 'a promise of a future for large numbers of young people from abroad'; the Jewish Agency had 365 training centres in 24 countries, whose aim was 'to prepare those people for the career of a manual labourer in Palestine' and to see them once they had emigrated, 'in all occupations from the very roughest'. They were being taught Hebrew, agriculture and hard labour. In all, there were 6,500 'pioneers' in training. Shertok was confident that all who

‫„ ‫י‬ ‫ב‬ ‫ד״‬ ‫תוספת‬ ‫ערב‬

A Jewish view of the Peel Commissioners at work

wished to go to Palestine would find work. Rumbold, who was worried about the influx of Bolshevik Jews, asked Shertok whether such 'undesirables' could come in under the labour schedule. Shertok tried to put Rumbold's mind at rest, assuring him that 'We exercise very considerable control over this and we go to great lengths to prevent the entrance of communists in this country'. Rumbold was still dubious. 'You do not think that there are any number of Bolshevik Jews in the country?' he asked; but Shertok reiterated that 'in the selection of our immigrants we take the greatest possible care to prevent people already holding communist views coming here . . .'. Finally Rumbold asked him if Communists could 'slip in' as illegal immigrants, to which Shertok answered that they might. But he insisted that the number of Jews in Palestine who had turned Communist since their arrival 'must be very low'.

On December 3 Shertok was joined by another senior member of the

Jewish Agency, Eliahu Epstein,[1] who told the Commissioners about Arab immigration, and the danger of a 'deterioration of the standards of life in Palestine' if Syrian Arabs from the Hauran continued to cross the border, as they had done in large numbers, since the establishment of the Mandate, particularly in time of drought. As many as 8,000, Epstein calculated, had entered illegally, and remained in Palestine, in the previous five years. On December 8 Epstein and Shertok elaborated these complaints. Arab immigration from neighbouring countries, Epstein asserted, 'is causing a number of social and economic evils'. Shertok added that there were cases 'where an Arab peasant takes on a Haurani as a farm hand, leaving him in charge of the farm, while he himself goes to a Jewish colony to be employed by a Jewish orange grower, in view of the difference between the wage he gets from the Jewish orange grower and the wage paid to the Haurani. Shertok added that even the Government, through contractors, made use of this cheap, illegal labour. The Hauranis, Epstein declared, were a simple minded people, who 'lay themselves open to incitement by agitators'; nor did any Arab equivalent of the Jewish Agency exist to help them. They lived, Epstein asserted, 'in very unhygienic and insanitary conditions, often on the beach. As many as 10,000 illegal Arab immigrants, some from the Hauran, some from Trans-Jordan, were being employed by the Government in the port of Haifa. Rumbold was eager to examine the conclusions of this argument. 'If you debar various people from Trans-Jordan and Hauranis from coming in to work in the port', he asked, 'your contention is that the Government would then be able to employ Jews, it would give more opportunity to Jewish labour? Is that your contention?' Epstein was equally blunt in his reply. 'Yes', he said ' . . . our main contention is that, so far as there is an absorptive capacity in Palestine for immigrants from outside, that should be primarily used to allow Jews to come in and get that employment.'

The Jewish Agency had already taken over many of the functions of Government in relation to the Jewish immigrants. The Commissioners soon found that in its assertiveness, its competence, and its ambition, it was quite prepared to take over the full responsibilities of Government. On December 8 Dr Ruppin,[2] head of the Institute of Economic Research at the

[1] Eliahu Epstein, 1903–   . Born in Russia. Active in the Zionist movement in Russia as a student. Imprisoned in Kiev, 1922. Settled in Palestine 1925. During his first ten years in Palestine he made a special study of the Bedouin. Director of the Middle East section of the Jewish Agency's Political Department, 1934–45. In 1948 he changed his surname to 'Elath'. Israeli Ambassador in Washington, 1949–50; in London, 1950–59. President of the Hebrew University, 1962–68. He published *Ha-Bedu'im* in 1933, a biography of the Mufti of Jerusalem (in Hebrew) in 1968, *British Roots to India* (1971) and *San Francisco Diary* (1972).

[2] Arthur Ruppin, 1876–1943. Born in the Posen district of Prussia. Studied law and economics at Berlin and Halle universities, 1899–1902. Director of the Berlin Bureau for

Jewish Agency, explained some of the work which it had done. Cows had been imported from Holland, poultry from the United States, banana trees from Africa. Co-operative settlements had been established 'in which the people did not feel that they were administrated to by the administrator, but in which they had a feeling that they were creating something by their own force'. Swamps had been drained, deserts irrigated, citrus groves established. Schools and farms had been established, financed largely by the Women's International Zionist Organisation, WIZO, to train girls in agriculture, so that the wife of the farmer could be a farmer herself.[1] In the towns, the Jewish Agency had opened infant welfare centres, and by its own exertions, and funds, had reduced the level of infant mortality, both Jewish and Arab. In the countryside as well, Ruppin asserted on December 9, his second day of giving evidence, Arabs gained by Jewish enterprise. They had found in the Jews an expanding and profitable market for their produce, they had learnt from the Jews innumerable techniques of building and irrigation. Ruppin urged the Mandatory authorities to act with greater vigour, to spend more on education, to assist farmers by cheap loans, to develop their own irrigation schemes, and to realize that even the water supply could be greatly increased if the Government were prepared to make the effort. 'The mountains of Palestine must not remain barren' he urged. 'They can be made green and fertile'.

Rumbold was angered by Ruppin's attack. In demanding a dynamic policy, he declared, Ruppin and his colleagues in the Jewish Agency were 'inferring that the Government has been behindhand in developing the natural resources of the country. . . . Have you ever reflected that the Government have been administering this country under the Mandate only for 14 years'. To which Dr Ruppin replied: 'Yes'. Rumbold persisted in his questioning. 'You seem to think' he went on, 'the Government has got an inexhaustible purse which is to be put at your disposal, but that is not so.' Ruppin replied that Jewish immigration had brought much wealth to Palestine; and the Government had a budget surplus of six

---

Jewish Statistics and Demography, 1903–07. First visited Palestine, 1907. Head of the Palestine Office of the Zionist Executive, 1908; a pioneer of Jewish agricultural settlement and land purchase. Instrumental in the purchase of land in Haifa, Jerusalem and Tel Aviv. Forced by the Turks to leave Palestine, 1916, he settled in Constantinople, 1916–20. Member of the Zionist Executive, 1921–27 and 1929–31. Head of the Brit Shalom organization which sought to reconcile Arabs and Jews and establish a bi-national state in Palestine, 1925–29. Head of the Jewish Agency Department for the Settlement of German Immigrants, 1933–35. Director of the Institute of Economic Research, established by the Jewish Agency, 1935.

[1] WIZO was founded in June 1920 on the initiative of several prominent Jewish women, including Weizmann's wife Vera. The organization's headquarters were in London until 1949, when they moved to Israel, WIZO's original aim was to train the farmer's wife as 'an effective partner in the redemption of the land through self-labour', and to safeguard the family 'through hygiene and proper nutrition'.

million pounds, and that if it undertook large scale drainage and irrigation works the cost would be spread 'over a long series of years'. He continued:

It may be that we are impatient, but we are being pressed very much by Jews who would like to settle here and who cannot settle here if the development activities are not carried out in rather quick tempo. I understand all the difficulties, and I am far from accusing the Government. I am concerned here not so much with the past; I am concerned with the future, and I believe quite a lot of things could and should be done now.

On December 14 Rumbold clashed again with a member of the Jewish Agency, Dr Maurice Hexter,[1] whom he pressed about the limit of Jewish settlement. If the Jews were given all the land which Dr Ruppin had estimated as irrigable – $1\frac{1}{2}$ million dunams – 'would you admit', Rumbold asked, 'that that was the last possibility of settlement for Jews and that there was nothing more. . . .' 'Would you admit', he repeated, 'that that finished the possibilities of the settlement of Jews on the land.' Hexter replied that it would depend on 'what possibilities existed and would turn out to be available later'. To this Rumbold replied: 'I see. It is an unending process, an unending vista of possibilities.' To predict 'the end of the race', Hexter retorted, 'is a very hazardous thing'.

Rumbold continued to press the Jewish witnesses, anxious to learn the full extent of their pretensions, often suspicious of their statistics, sometimes caustic about their aspirations. He strongly resented any criticism they made of the British administration; and he was alert to any apparent lack of concern towards Arab rights. But the Jews were never at a loss to answer him. The representatives of the Jewish Agency were well-informed, practical men, who had for over five years been conducting their own comprehensive administration, duplicating, and even going beyond, what the Government were doing. They were confident of their powers to take responsibility, and eager to extend the area under their virtual jurisdiction. It was clear that their aim was eventual sovereignty. Rumbold was quick to challenge any such claims. When, on December 16, Samuel Tolkowsky,[2] the General Manager of the Jaffa Citrus Exchange, used the

---

[1] Maurice B. Hexter, 1891– . Born in Cincinnati, Ohio. Member of the Executive of the Jewish Agency, 1929–38. Head of the Colonisation Department of the Jewish Agency. Member of the General Agricultural Council of the Government of Palestine. President of the American Jewish Joint Agricultural Corporation. Resident in New York since 1945.

[2] Samuel Tolkowsky, 1886–1965. Born in Antwerp. Settled in Israel, 1911. Served under Weizmann on the Zionist Political Committee in London, 1916–18. Secretary of the Zionist delegation to the Paris Peace Conference, 1918–19. Active in various economic and public fields in Jaffa and Tel Aviv between the wars. Israeli Consul-General (later Minister) in Berne, 1949–56. Among his books were *The Gateway to Palestine – History of Jaffa* (1924) and *A History of the Culture and Use of Citrus Fruits* (1938). His son Dan, a Flight-Lieutenant in the Royal Air Force, 1940–45, commanded the Israeli Air Force, 1953–58.

word 'territory' in reference to the Jewish area of Jaffa, Rumbold commented that the word 'Territory' was generally associated with a State, and in this context 'might give rise to misrepresentation'. Tolkowsky explained that he had 'meant to convey the idea of land within a Jewish administrative area'; he then went on to criticise the actions of the Mandate Government, which, he insisted, 'has not tried to find a way out of the present difficulties, has not tried with enough energy, and has not tried with enough belief and faith in the development of the country'.

A young Jewish journalist, Joshua Iusman,[1] who had been present at each of the public sessions of the Commission, later recalled the feelings of his fellow listeners:

The atmosphere here towards the Commission was at first hostile. People said: 'After all, it is a British commission'; and in most people's minds a British Commission meant the British Government. People could not believe in the possibility of a British Commission producing a report contrary to the views of the Palestine Government. But we took it very seriously, and the sessions were very solemn. I remember how, while Weizmann was speaking, the British policeman wept.

Peel sat there as if napping. But suddenly he would ask a question which showed that he had understood exactly what was being said. He had an extremely penetrating mind and we were amazed at how he grasped the internal Jewish problems of Palestine.

We were quite worried during the first sessions, fearing that the Commission was not really friendly. But after the first few sessions we realised that they really wanted to know about what was going on and that they were probing the Palestine Government as rigorously as they probed the Jewish Agency. We soon realised that we could not fool them, that we had to speak as we felt.

Rumbold, red-faced, looked extremely British, like an old guard Conservative Empire builder. Everybody was concerned about whether he would be fair. While Peel would be brief, Rumbold always went into the argument. His questions gave the impression that he was not very fair. He became our main worry. We saw him as a negative feature.

After the first three or four sessions our attitude towards the Commission changed. It became clear that they were not merely going through the motions of a report, but were going to be extremely thorough. But we were very touchy. Each question that sounded a little unfriendly was immediately blown

[1] Joshua Iusman. Born in Warsaw, 1914. Went to Palestine as the correspondent of the Warsaw Yiddish daily, 'Haynt', 1934. Deputy Director of the Telegraphic News Agency 'Palcor', 1935–39. Served in the Political Department of the Jewish Agency, 1936–47; in the British Army, 1940–46. Member of the Israel delegation to the United Nations, 1953–56. Appointed Jerusalem editor of the Hebrew daily 'Maariv', 1956.

up as proof of their hostility. Their ability to sift the conflicting evidence was amazing. At first everyone prepared their statements with great confidence, but soon all those who were scheduled to appear became frightened; after the first experiences of Peel and Rumbold they became jittery.

The Commissioners worked at full stretch. On December 4 the *Palestine Post* gave an account of their day. They rose at 6.30 each morning. After breakfast they reviewed the material which was to form the basis of the evidence of the next witness. Witnesses were then examined from 10.30 until shortly after 1 o'clock. In the afternoon the Commissioners met again, to discuss the evidence which had been presented. 'The strain is great', wrote the *Palestine Post*, 'and rumour has it that one or two of the Commissioners are beginning to feel the effects of such continuous and arduous work'. On January 15 Rumbold wrote to his son: 'Peel and I are finding some of our colleagues rather difficult to manage. They complain that we have been driving them too hard but as we ourselves are always prepared to work they really have no case.' There was another reason for haste, which Rumbold did not mention. Peel was 'determined to get back to England as soon as he can', John Martin wrote to his mother on December 20, as he was anxious to attend to his business commitments.

Between sessions, and at weekends, Rumbold continued to see something of Palestine. On December 1 he had visited an Arab horticultural centre near Hebron; on the afternoon of December 5 he went to Jaffa; on December 7 he visited the Jewish Agency's Agricultural Experimental Station at Rehovot. He was glad to get away from Jerusalem. The climate was beginning to give him rather severe headaches, and he found, as Lady Rumbold wrote to her mother on December 14, 'a mass of intrigue' to disentangle. Lord Peel had already complained to Ormsby-Gore on December 1 that Jerusalem was 'very noisy, and we are constantly beset by visitors, callers, officials and go-betweens. . . . Some of my colleagues find the air here very trying and cannot sleep at all well'.

Christmas offered a break from the accumulated strains of cross-examination and analysis. On December 26 Rumbold was in Jericho, and on December 27 he and Peel went to Damascus, while Professor Coupland went to Rehovot to see Dr Weizmann. Coupland had begun to see a means of reconciling Arab and Jewish aspirations. He believed that part of Palestine could be given to the Jews, and part to the Arabs; a partition not only of land, but of sovereignty. The Jews would have their State, albeit in a much truncated form; the Arabs would be free, in the areas allotted to them, from any Jewish settlement or expansion. In a similar way, Trans-Jordan had been entirely closed to Jewish settlers since its establishment, by Britain, in 1922. Coupland's historical research had convinced him that two peoples, each with a separate sense of national identity, could not live together as equal partners in a single state. This argument was strongly challenged by the Government of Palestine. The Chief Secretary, John Hall,[1] had told the Commissioners in secret session on December 4, that he was convinced that Jews and Arabs could be ruled effectively under a British administration, 'joint government rather than territorial division – joint government with balances'. Later Hall repeated these views to Rumbold at a private dinner, and Rumbold, he later recalled, seemed to accept them. Coupland was impressed by the Jewish Agency's activities, and believed that the Jews could govern themselves; Rumbold and Peel had faith in the efficacy of British rule.

The Commission resumed its sessions on December 28. Two leading Jewish pioneers in the field of social services, Henrietta Szold[2] and Dr Katznelson,[3] protested that the Government had neglected its public health duties, particularly towards mental diseases. Once more, Rumbold was angered by their criticisms. 'Are you aware', he asked Miss Szold, 'that the Government have provided funds and have a site for a hospital at Bethlehem for 240 cases?' But Miss Szold replied that the promise to build the hospital had been made in 1929, that it was to have been opened in 1932, 'and it is now 1936', with still no hospital. Surely, Rumbold went on, the seventeen years of British rule had not been enough to do all the Jews believe ought to have been done. 'Do you consider', he asked Miss Szold, 'in that time the Government could produce the complete apparatus of a thoroughly up-to-date country?'; to which Miss Szold replied:

[1] John Hathorn Hall, 1894– . Served in the First World War, winning the Military Cross. Joined the Egyptian Civil Service, 1919; the Colonial Office, 1921. Chief Secretary, Palestine, 1933–37. British Resident, Zanzibar, 1937–40. Governor of Aden, 1940–44. Knighted, 1941. Governor of Uganda, 1944–51. A Director of the Midland Bank Ltd.

[2] Henrietta Szold, 1860–1945. Born in Baltimore, Maryland; her parents had emigrated from Hungary to the United States a year before her birth. Teacher. Organized a night school for Russian immigrants, 1888. Joined the Zionist Association of Baltimore, 1899. Editor of the *American Jewish Year Book*, 1904–08. First visited Palestine, 1909. Secretary, Federation of American Zionists, 1910. Founded the American Women's Zionist Organization, 1912. Organized the American Zionist Medical Unit, which she went with to Palestine in 1920. Member of the World Zionist Organization, 1927. Director of the Youth Aliyah, set up by the Jewish Agency to train German children for transfer to Palestine, 1933; by 1935 over 1,000 children were settled in twenty-three colonies in Palestine (30,000 children had arrived by 1948). At the Zionist Congress of 1937 (in Zurich) she argued in favour of a bi-national Arab–Jewish state.

[3] Nissan Avraham Katznelson, 1888–1956. Born in Russia. Studied at St Petersburg and Moscow Universities; served as a physician with the Russian Army, 1914–18. Director of the Constantinople Office of the Zionist Executive, 1919–20. Settled in Palestine, 1924. Director of the Health Department of the Zionist Executive, 1925–39. Director-General of the Israeli Ministry of Health, 1948. Member of the Provisional Council of State, 1948. Israel Minister to the Scandinavian Countries, 1950–56.

'In the health services, yes.' When Rumbold pointed out that the increased Jewish immigration had brought much greater demands for health services among the Jews, she replied that the Jews had 'also brought a great deal of capital into the country'. Dr Katznelson pointed out that from the moment the immigrant landed at Haifa, and paid two shillings for his first two inoculations, 'he is paying more than the Government actually spends . . . it perhaps cost Government not 2 shillings but a few pennies and the immigrant pays for all the services provided for his needs'. In addition, the Jewish Agency paid the full cost of school hygiene, infant welfare, adult hospitalisation and all dispensary services. All the Jews were asking for, Katznelson went on, was for Government support 'to a very modest extent'. The Jewish Agency had already paid £290,000 towards their medical services, while the Government grant was only £60,000. 'We are not requesting a complete system of health services on a European standard', Katznelson insisted. 'We are requesting the minimum which in our opinion is quite practicable within the limits of the Government resources.' When Rumbold tried to claim that the Government could not be expected to give special benefit to the richer – that was, Jewish – section of the population Katznelson pointed out that the Jewish community was composed of the poor as well as the rich, and the poorer Jews had themselves organised a medical service costing nearly £200,000 'by means of health insurance and the membership dues of the workers'. Rumbold said no more.

On December 30 the Commissioners examined several representatives of the General Federation of Jewish Labour, or Histadrut. Goldie Meyerson[1] pointed out that as the Government had no Unemployment Insurance Scheme, the Histadrut had set up its own scheme; yet it had been unable to secure Government assistance. For education, she added, the Government paid only £7,000 towards the total cost of £53,000; this created a serious burden because 'our people are such that they consider education is a primary need for the family . . .'. Goldie Meyerson's colleague on the Histadrut, Berl Katznelson,[2] told the Commission, through

---

[1] Goldie Mabovitch, 1898–   . Born in Kiev. Emigrated with her parents to the United States, 1906, and settled in Milwaukee. Married Morris Meyerson, with whom she emigrated to Palestine in 1921. Joined the Executive Committee of the Histadrut, 1934. Acting head of the Political Department of the Jewish Agency, 1946–48. Took the name Golda Meir, 1948. Israel Minister to Moscow, 1948–49. Minister of Labour, 1949–56; an advocate of unrestricted immigration. Foreign Minister, 1956–65. Prime Minister, 1969–   .

[2] Berl Katznelson, 1887–1944. Born in Russia. Emigrated to Palestine at the age of twenty-one. Secretary of the Council of Judean Farm Workers, 1911. A leader of organized labour, in 1919 he advocated the establishment of a Jewish State in Palestine, and encouraged illegal immigration. 'From now on', he said in 1939, 'not the pioneer but the refugee will lead us.'

an interpreter, that the fundamental Jewish grievance was 'want of sympathy on the part of the Administration towards their work; they all too often have to regard themselves as step-children of the State'. To another Labour representative, Dov Hos,[1] Rumbold put the question: 'Would it be correct to say all these numerous institutions you have founded here and which are, many of them, very admirable, would it be correct to say you expect the Government to supplement with funds various organisations which you have founded here and that if they do not do so that constitutes a grievance?' To which Hos replied that the Jewish institutions to which Rumbold had referred 'as a rule, perform duties which in other countries the Government is performing, and in our opinion the Government should perform here'. Where the Jews established hospitals or schools, he added, 'that is relieving Government from the responsibility and expense connected with them'. Rumbold's patience was at an end. 'Now let me tell you this', he expostulated. 'Lord Cromer was in Egypt for twenty-five years and he took over a country which was in a very bad way indeed. It took him nearly twenty-five years to restore that country to prosperity. . . . My impression is that the task here is more difficult than that Lord Cromer had, because not only was this country completely derelict when the Mandatory Power took over, but the Mandatory has had to develop the country having regard to the unique experiment, the injection of an alien race into the body politic of this native race. . . .'

The Jews were outraged to be called an 'alien race'. Dov Hos replied that the Jews would not describe themselves as an alien race, but as 'children returning to their country, to the country where they lived or to a country where they are going to have their home'. Jewish immigration, he added, carried with it not only 'enthusiasm and devotion to the work, but the actual possibilities of development which were not inherent in this country, which did not exist here before the arrival of the Jews'. Rumbold's use of the phrase 'alien race' was much criticized. 'Perhaps nothing will so have depressed the Jews of this country and abroad', declared the *Palestine Post* on 1 January 1937, 'as the epithet which fell from the lips of Sir Horace. He really leaves the Arab Committee little to say'. At the Commissioner's next public session, on January 5, Rumbold explained

[1] Dov Hos, 1894–1940. Born in Russia. Emigrated to Palestine with his parents when he was twelve. Joined the labour movement (under the influence of Berl Katznelson), 1913. Volunteered for the Turkish Army, 1914. Because he defended Jewish settlements against Arab marauders while holding a commission in the Turkish army he was sentenced to death. He escaped, and joined the Jewish Legion of the British Army, 1918. A pioneer of aviation in Palestine. Acted as liaison officer between the British and Jewish labour movements. Founded the Public Works Office of General Federation of Jewish Labour. Deputy Mayor of Tel Aviv, 1935–40. Together with his wife and daughter he was killed in a road accident.

that what he meant by 'alien race' was 'a race having different characteristics from the Arab race. That seems to me quite the obvious interpretation. . . .'

Rumbold's remark about the 'alien race' had one unfortunate personal repercussion. On New Year's Eve the King David Hotel held a dance for 500 Jews. That night, while Rumbold was asleep, a young woman burst into his room, carrying a small trumpet, which she blew until he woke up. She then declared, as John Martin reported to his mother on January 3, that Rumbold 'was the ugliest member of the Commission, and told him various other home truths while he cowered helpless beneath the counterpane'. Sir John Hathorn Hall later recalled that the woman had thrust a petition into Rumbold's hands and had urged him to read it, but that as he could not find his glasses, he was 'unable to read anything, and the lady was soon removed'.

Rumbold had been surprised by the extent of Jewish criticism, and by the obvious determination of the Jewish community to expand and flourish. The rapid growth of Tel Aviv seemed to him a deliberate attempt to encourage continual Jewish immigration.[1] On January 5 he closely cross-examined the Mayor of Tel Aviv, Israel Rokach,[2] about plans for the growth of his city. Once more, it became clear that the Jews had no intention of curbing their expansion. At the same time, they resented the attitude of the Mandatory Power in not contributing more than six per cent towards the city's annual budget. With more 'goodwill and understanding' Rokach asserted, the Government could do much to help improve the town's facilities. When Rumbold asked why the municipality paid a higher wage to its police force than was paid by the Government to its police, Rokach declared that 'there is a standard of living in Tel Aviv which lays it down that a minimum amount must be paid to a man, especially a family man'. When Lord Peel commented that Tel Aviv's growth reminded him of a large American town, Rokach mentioned that he hoped Tel Aviv would grow as large as Los Angeles. Rumbold commented sarcastically: 'With the cinema business and all?'; to which Rokach replied: 'No, without the cinema business. We want culture, but

---

[1] Tel Aviv was founded in 1909, in an area of sand dunes a few miles south of Jaffa, by Jews who wished to live in a European style town. It remained a suburb of Jaffa until 1921, when it was granted a charter giving it the right to levy taxes and establish a municipal court. In 1934 its population reached 100,000; a further 50,000 inhabitants had settled between then and the end of 1936.

[2] Israel Rokach, 1896–1959. Born in Jaffa. Graduated from Lausanne as an electrical engineer. Elected to the first Tel Aviv Municipal Council, 1922. Deputy Mayor of Tel Aviv, 1929–36; Mayor, 1936–53. Detained by the British for having aided underground activity against the Mandatory Government, 1947. Israeli Minister of the Interior, 1953–55. Deputy speaker of the Knesset, 1957–59.

not the cinema.'[1] Lady Rumbold was less scathing of the influx of Jews to Tel Aviv, writing to her mother on 6 January 1937, 'Ugly as it really is, that mushroom town, we were impressed by the happy, cheerful, & *very* busy people running about in it. They feel it is their *own*, & that they are free, not looked down on & despised & constantly being harried (& worse). So tho' they are a strangely unpleasing race, one admires this effort of theirs. . . .'

On January 7 the Commission held its last public session with a Jewish witness, David Ben-Gurion.[2] In answer to a question from Rumbold, he declared that the aim of the Jewish Agency, of whose Executive he was the Chairman, was 'to make the Jewish people master of its own destiny, not subject to the will and mercy of others – to make it like any other free people'. But, he insisted, it was no part of the Jewish aim 'to dominate anybody else'. The Arabs, he added, 'have a right not to be at the mercy of the Jews'. He went on:

For the solution of the Jewish problem, for our free national future, it is not necessary that Palestine should constitute a separate State and we should be only too glad if in the future, when the Jewish National Home is fully established, Palestine shall be eternally and completely free, but that it should be a member of a greater unit, that is the British Commonwealth of Nations. There is a third reason why we do not use the formula of a Jewish State. There are Holy Places in Palestine which are holy to the whole civilised world and we are unwilling and it is not in our interest that we should be made responsible for them. We recognise that they should be placed under a higher supervision, under some international control or a mandatory or some other international body, as is laid down in the Mandate.

Ben-Gurion ended his evidence by a discussion of Arab–Jewish relations. He applauded the fact that the people of Egypt, Iraq, and Syria had achieved independence, and declared that there was 'no conflict of interest between the Jewish people as a whole and the Arab people as a whole. . . . We need each other. We can benefit each other. . . . It is our belief that a great Jewish community, a free Jewish nation, in Palestine, with a large

---

[1] One of the contemporary complaints against Jews was that they monopolized the cinema business (in Germany before 1933, in Hollywood since), and produced films which were superficial and corrupting.

[2] David Green, 1886–   . Born in Russia. Emigrated to Israel, 1906. Agricultural worker and watchman in various agricultural settlements. A leading advocate of Hebrew as the sole language of Jewish public life. Took the name 'Ben-Gurion' in 1910, while on the editorial staff of *Ahdut* ('Unity') in Jerusalem. Studied law in Salonika, 1912–14, and Constantinople, 1915. Accused by the Turks of conspiring to create a Jewish state, and exiled to Egypt, 1915. Served in the Jewish Legion (39th Battalion, Royal Fusiliers), 1918. Secretary-General of the Histadrut, 1921. Member of the Jewish Agency Executive, 1933; Chairman, 1935–48. Proclaimed the State of Israel, May 14, 1948. Prime Minister of Israel, 1948–53, and 1955–63.

scope for its activities, will be of great benefit to our Arab neighbours, and from the recognition of this fact will come a lasting peace and lasting co-operation between the two peoples.' Five days later, when the Commission began to examine the Arabs, who had belatedly agreed to attend, it became apparent that the possibility of such co-operation was remote. Reginald Coupland had already come to such a conclusion, and at a secret session on January 8 asked Dr Weizmann direct whether he would agree to the partition of Palestine into two separate political units, one Jewish, the other Arab. Writing of the incident twelve years later, Coupland recalled that Weizmann had said 'he would think it over'. A week later, on January 16, Coupland went privately to see Weizmann near Haifa, at the Jewish colony of Nahalal. Coupland recalled that although they only spoke together for 'less than an hour', Weizmann had told him 'that personally and provisionally, and provided the frontiers were drawn to his satisfaction, he favoured the idea of Partition'.

The first Arab witness was the Mufti of Jerusalem,[1] who came before the Commission with nine other members of the Arab Higher Committee. The proceedings were conducted through an interpreter. The Balfour Declaration, he declared, was 'extremely prejudicial to the interests of the Arabs. . . . The Jews were enabled to acquire large areas in the most fertile of Arab lands. . . . Every hope which the Arabs had of attaining independence was frustrated'. The Jews, he went on, had as their 'ultimate aim' the reconstruction of the Temple of Solomon on the ruins of the Moslem holy places in Jerusalem. The Jews, he believed, 'had various means of securing their aims . . . wide means of propaganda . . . their relations with British statesmen and others. . . . What can Arabs do? Who could prevent the Jews from making such claims to Moslem shrines'. When Rumbold asked the Mufti if he thought the Jews would be able 'to remove the Mandatory Power', the Mufti replied: 'What I can see, and my experience up to now, shows that the Jews can do anything as far as Palestine is concerned. . . . I know that the Jews have great influence in England.'

[1] Haj Amin el-Husseini. Born 1897. Left Palestine after the Arab riots of 1920; sentenced to fifteen years' imprisonment *in absentia* for his part in arousing the Arabs against the Jews. Appointed Mufti of Jerusalem (by Herbert Samuel), March 1921, in succession to his half-brother. A senior member of the Executive Committee of the Supreme Moslem Council, and leader of the anti-Jewish movement among the Arabs of Palestine. Fled Palestine in disguise after the murder of Lewis Andrews in 1937. In exile in Baghdad in 1941, he helped to direct a pro-German uprising. Broadcast from Berlin, 1942; while in Berlin he protested to Hitler when some small exceptions were made to Jewish children being sent to Concentration Camps. Imprisoned in France, 1945–46. Went to Cairo, 1946; there the Arab League Council transferred to him all funds for Palestinian purposes. In 1948 he urged the total expulsion of all Jews from Palestine. Living in Beirut (1972).

Rumbold had been vexed by Jewish self-confidence; he was equally vexed by the exaggerated language of the Arabs. The Mufti wanted the Balfour Declaration annulled, and Palestine made over to a sovereign Arab body. When Rumbold asked him whether Palestine could 'assimilate and digest' the 400,000 Jews already there, the Mufti replied in a single word: 'No'. When Rumbold asked him if he would have preferred Turkey as the Mandatory Power, the Mufti answered that the Arabs would prefer 'complete independence.' Lord Peel then asked if the Turks had been 'less under the influence of the Jews' than the British; to which the Mufti replied: 'Yes'.

The Arabs continued to give evidence for five more days. Rumbold derided their assertion that British Jews could assert an undue influence over Government policy. One senior Arab representative, Awni Bey,[1] declared that British officers in Palestine 'fear the loss of office because of the influence of the Jews.' When Rumbold questioned him further he asserted again that British officers 'showed partiality to the Jews because they feared the Jews'. Later, in answer to a question from Rumbold on January 13, Awni Bey declared: 'Every Arab in Palestine will do everything possible in his power to crush down that Zionism, because Zionism and Arabism can never be united together.' He rejected the idea of Arab–Jewish co-operation within a single state: 'What we say is that we want a National Palestine Government . . . we object to the existence of 400,000 Jews in this country.' On January 14 Rumbold was stirred to remark: 'Arabs and Jews seem to be agreed about the shortcomings of the Government. I suppose it is their only point of agreement.' The last Arab witness, George Antonius,[2] who was called on January 18, made a moving and reasoned appeal, in which he declared that it was not antisemitism, but a desire for national independence, which motivated the Arabs in their refusal to compromise with the Jews. 'There are certain things you cannot compromise', he said, 'and one of them is national independence.'

Lady Rumbold looked sympathetically on the Arab claims. On 6 January

[1] Awni Bey Abdelhadi. One of the founders, in 1910, of Al-Fatat, a secret Arab society whose aim was to prepare for a revolt against the Turks. A Delegate of the Hedjaz at the Paris Peace Conference, he was a signatory of the Treaty of Versailles. Secretary of the Higher Arab Committee, 1936. Arrested after the murder of Lewis Andrews, 1937. Leader of the 'Independence' Party, Gaza, 1948. Died in Cairo in 1970.

[2] George Antonius, 1891–1942. A Christian Arab, born in the Lebanon. Educated at Alexandria and Cambridge. Entered the Palestine Civil Service as Chief Inspector in the Department of Education, 1921. Transferred to the Government Secretariat, and served there as Assistant Secretary until 1930. Published The Arab Awakening, 1938. Secretary-General of the Arab Delegation to the St James Palace Conference, London, 1939. Because he was a member of a minority group (the Christian Arabs), he was often treated with suspicion by the Palestine Arabs whose cause he served so well.

1937, she had written to her mother of 'the awful problem' in Palestine, where the Jews, with 'all their brain & money backing' were 'pitted against the poor backward Arab'. Six days later she wrote again: 'I think Balfour is much to blame for letting the Jews in here. They are so clever & pushing that of course they are a menace to the poor Arabs.' But Rumbold had been disturbed by the Arab attitude to the Jews, and after hearing the Arabs give evidence to the Commission, Lady Rumbold saw what he meant, writing to her mother on January 14, that they had 'no spirit of compromise in them'.

The Arabs and Jews had revealed apparently irreconcilable positions. The Jews were devoting much energy and money to building up their own administrative activities, and to creating, through the Jewish Agency, a virtual state within a state. The Arabs saw this activity as a threat to their existence, and as proof of a wider Zionist 'conspiracy' to drive them out of Palestine altogether. The Government of Palestine believed that it could hold the ring, by firm rule, by constant scrutiny of all land sales and urban expansion, and above all by restricting Jewish immigration. The Arabs rejected the idea of such a 'balance'; the Jews rejected any limit on immigration. Rumbold and Peel were willing to give the Mandatory authority a chance. But Professor Coupland felt that Arab–Jewish co-operation was impossible, and argued in favour of two separate national states, one Arab and one Jewish, with Britain retaining control only over Jerusalem and the Holy Places.

Unknown to Rumbold or his fellow Commissioners, their private deliberations had not been as private as they believed. From the day of their first, secret, discussions on November 16, the Jewish Agency had succeeded in fixing a listening device in the room in which the Commissioners discussed the evidence they had taken. It seemed to the clandestine listeners of the Jewish Agency that the Peel Commissioners did not regard the Government of Palestine as an effective governing instrument, for in their private discussions they would often comment scathingly on the Government's lack of real control, and on its lack of accurate information. The apparent inability of the British officials to carry out the needs of the Mandate seemed a persistent theme of these discussions. This, coupled with the clear determination of the Arabs, and of the Mufti in particular, to refuse to accept any form of cooperation with the Jews, made the Jewish Agency suspect that partition might seem, to the Commissioners, a preferable alternative to the continuation of British rule.

The Commissioners decided to carry on their private discussions in Egypt, and left Palestine on January 20. 'Their departure was rather hurried', commented the *Palestine Post*. Rumbold was glad to leave Jerusalem, but unhappy about Coupland's proposals. Before leaving he dined again with the Chief Secretary, John Hall, and told him that the Commission was likely to recommend a continuation of British rule. But once the Commissioners reached Cairo, Coupland's arguments began to prevail.

During February, after the Commissioners had returned to London, a dispute arose about the expenses of their journey from Jerusalem to Cairo, and their stay in Cairo. Rumbold's expenses were particularly challenged, as he had stayed in Egypt for an extra week with his family. John Martin was asked by the Commissioners to deal with these complaints, which emanated from the same Treasury official, H. R. Foyle, who had challenged Rumbold's right to take a servant with him to Palestine. Why, he asked on February 11, had three cars been hired to take Rumbold and Peel from Jerusalem to Cairo; surely the train was adequate. Martin replied on February 13 that the train journey from Lydda to Kantara was 'a very uncomfortable one', and that the total cost of thirty-six pounds for three cars, was not excessive. The journey itself had not been a success. 'In fact', Martin explained to Foyle, 'one of the cars fell down a 15 foot embankment and landed on its head'. Of the visit to Cairo, Martin explained that although it was 'not strictly official', the Commissioners had been uncomfortable in Jerusalem as 'most of them found it trying to their health'. Rumbold, Martin added, had paid for his extra week himself. The Treasury was placated.

When the Commissioners reached London their work continued. There were several memoranda on economic subjects, sent in to them by the Jewish Agency, which had to be digested. On January 19 they received a long letter from Dr Weizmann, who had also returned to London, setting out his answers to the various questions which he had been asked at secret sessions held on November 26, December 16 and December 23. In answer to Rumbold's question about when the Jewish National Home would be completed, Weizmann declared: 'The Jewish National Home is no home unless its doors remain open to as many Jews desirous of entering Palestine as the country can economically absorb . . . the Mandate cannot be terminated until after the League of Nations had satisfied itself that the Jewish National Home has developed to such a stage that its further free growth is assured by its own strength, or that such constitutional and other safeguards have been provided in the place of the Mandate as would effectively guarantee a continued growth of the National Home unhampered by any political limitations'.

In answer to the suggestion that there should be a halt to Jewish immigration, Weizmann replied that such a move 'would be encouraging in the Arabs the belief that disturbances bring their rewards . . .'.

On February 11 the Commissioners examined Josiah Wedgwood, in a room in the House of Lords. Wedgwood spoke strongly about the anti-Jewish attitude of the Government of Palestine. As one example, he cited the Government's failure to help the Jews in developing Tel Aviv. 'Have you taken into account', Rumbold asked him, 'the rapidity with which Tel Aviv has grown?' To which Wedgwood replied: 'I do not think the rapidity of the growth of a town is any bar to the putting up of public offices.'

During March Lloyd George was questioned by the Commissioners, and gave them an account of what had been in his mind at the time of the Balfour Declaration in 1917. 'The idea was . . .', he told them, 'that a Jewish State was not to be set up immediately by the Peace Treaty without reference to the wishes of the majority of the inhabitants. On the other hand, it was contemplated that when the time arrived for according representative institutions to Palestine, if the Jews had meanwhile responded to the opportunity afforded them by the idea of a national home and had become a definite majority of the inhabitants, then Palestine would become a Jewish Commonwealth'.

On March 12 Winston Churchill was called before the Commissioners. As Colonial Secretary in 1922, he had been responsible for the original administration of the Mandate, and was questioned about his intentions. In answer to a question from Lord Peel, he declared that the Jewish right to immigration ought not to be curtailed by the 'economic absorptive capacity' of Palestine, and spoke of 'the good faith of England to the Jews'. This arose, he said, 'because we gained great advantages in the War. We did not adopt Zionism entirely out of altruistic love of starting a Zionist colony: it was a matter of great importance to this country. It was a potent factor on public opinion in America and we are bound by honour, and I think upon the merits, to push this thing as far as we can. . . .' The British Government had certainly committed itself, he went on, 'to the idea that some day, somehow, far off in the future, subject to justice and economic convenience, there might well be a great Jewish State there, numbered by millions, far exceeding the present inhabitants of the country. . . . We never committed ourselves to making Palestine a Jewish State . . . but if more and more Jews gather to that Home and all is worked from age to age, from generation to generation, with justice and fair consideration to those displaced and so forth, certainly it was contemplated and intended that they might in the course of time become an overwhelmingly Jewish State'.

Rumbold took up the questioning. Was there not, he asked, 'harsh injustice' to the Arabs if Palestine attracted too many Jews from outside?

Churchill replied that even when the Jewish Home 'will become all Palestine', and it eventually would, there was no injustice. 'Why', he asked, 'is there harsh injustice done if people come in and make a livelihood for more, and make the desert into palm groves and orange groves? Why is it injustice because there is more work and wealth for everybody? There is no injustice. The injustice is when those who live in the country leave it to be desert for thousands of years'.

When Rumbold pointed out the danger to British troops of the 'periodical disturbances' in Palestine, Churchill replied that the idea of creating a National Home for the Jews was 'the prime and dominating pledge upon which Britain must act'. If Britain became weak, 'somebody else might have to take it on', but while Britain remained in Palestine 'that is what we are undoubtedly pledged to'. He opposed Partition. British rule must continue, and a Jewish majority be accepted as the ultimate result. Rumbold spoke up for the Arabs, who were, he said, 'the indigenous population', subjected in 1918 'to the invasion of a foreign race'. Churchill objected to the phrase 'foreign race'. The Arabs, he said, had come in after the Jews. It was the 'great hordes of Islam' who 'smashed' Palestine up. 'You have seen the terraces on the hills which used to be cultivated', he told Rumbold, 'which under Arab rule have remained a desert.' Rumbold insisted that the backwardness had come under Turkish rule, but Churchill insisted that 'where the Arab goes it is often desert'. When Rumbold spoke of the Arab civilisation in Spain, Churchill retorted: 'I am glad they were thrown out.' It was 'for the good of the world', he told Lord Peel a few moments later, 'that the place should be cultivated, and it never will be cultivated by the Arabs.' When Rumbold answered that 'the Jews can pour money into Palestine. I think they have already poured in £80,000,000.' The Arabs have no money', Churchill made no reply.

Towards the end of the session, Rumbold asked Churchill when he would consider the Jewish Home to be established, and Britain's undertaking fulfilled. 'At what point?' Rumbold asked; to which Churchill replied: 'when it was quite clear the Jewish preponderance in Palestine was very marked, decisive, and when we were satisfied that we had no further duties to discharge to the Arab population, the Arab minority'.

None of Churchill's evidence was included in the Commission's Report. He was even reluctant to have it printed secretly. 'There are a few references to nationalities', he wrote to Lord Peel on March 16, 'which would not be suited to appear in a permanent record.'

From the moment the Commissioners had returned to England, John Martin had been preparing an outline of their Report. But the major part was prepared by Reginald Coupland, who ensured that in the redrafting, his own influence would predominate. On February 2 he wrote to Martin: 'I deeply appreciate your letting me see an advance copy of your scheme. . . . I have marked with red pencil the parts I should like to draft. They are large and important parts! In fact, the most important!!' Coupland was determined that Partition should be recommended without ambiguity or compromise. 'I think the Chairman may find himself in difficulties', he wrote in his letter to Martin, 'if he leaves the drafting problem open. HR may say at a meeting, "I should like to draft that" . . . and it would be a trifle difficult to turn him down.' Coupland proposed a procedure whereby, as he explained, 'while apparently summing up discussions, we should actually be drafting the Report'. Although Rumbold accepted this procedure, Martin later recalled how, nevertheless, he 'was very unhappy about Partition all the time at the end. He seemed to be overborne by Coupland. He got flustered, he didn't argue. He should have written a minority report, but he didn't seem to be willing to face that'. In July 1937 the Royal Commission on Palestine published its Report; Rumbold signed it with the others.

The overwhelming Arab fear, the Report stated, was that the Arabs of Palestine would be 'overwhelmed and therefore dominated by Jewish immigrants'. Even if Jewish immigration were restricted to 30,000 a year – the number for 1936 – Jews would outnumber the Arabs by 1960. If immigration remained at the 1935 figure of 60,000, Jews would outnumber Arabs by 1947. To avoid an immediate exacerbation of Arab fears, the Commissioners recommended an annual limit to Jewish immigration of 12,000, for a period of five years. But they warned that this would be only a palliative, not a solution. The Arabs would continue to want the Jews out of Palestine, in order to have for themselves 'the same national status as that attained, or soon to be attained, by all the other Arabs of Asia'.

As it was impossible to devise any form of government for Palestine which would satisfy both Arabs and Jews, the Report concluded that Partition 'seems to offer at least a chance of ultimate peace. We can see none in any other plan'. Under Partition, it added, neither Arab nor Jew would get all they wanted, but without it, civil war would continue, and both sides would lose. Partition would mean 'that the Arabs must acquiesce in the exclusion from their sovereignty of a piece of territory, long occupied and once ruled by them'. For their part, 'the Jews must be content with less than the Land of Israel they once ruled and have hoped to rule again'. But if Partition were accepted, Arabs and Jews could both live in peace, in separate communities. The Commissioners realized that for the Arabs, the acceptance of a Jewish territory, however narrowly drawn, involved a sacrifice. But, they added, if the Arabs were willing to make that sacrifice, 'they would earn the gratitude not of the Jews alone but of all the Western World'.

In Parliament there was little enthusiasm for the Peel Commission Report, and Sir Archibald Sinclair,[1] the leader of the Liberal Party in the House of Commons, attacked the Partition scheme with vigour, insisting that the Jews would never be content with so small a State as the Report proposed, but that 'established along an indefensible coastal strip, congested, opulent, behind them the pressure of impoverished and persecuted World Jewry' they would 'be fired by the urge to reach by force or by contrivance the goal of Mount Zion and the Jordan Valley'. In August 1937, at the Twentieth Zionist Congress, held in Zurich, Partition itself was accepted, but the scheme of Partition suggested in the Report was voted to be 'unacceptable'. A month later, in Damascus, four hundred Arabs, representing all the Arab States as well as Palestine itself, resolved that Palestine was 'an integral part of the Arabian homeland', and insisted that Britain had to chose 'between our friendship and the Jews'. By the end of the year violence had broken out again; in October a group of Arabs murdered Lewis Andrews, the District Commissioner for Galilee, who had been responsible for arranging the Peel Commissioners' travels through Palestine.

The continuing atrocities against the Jews hardened Rumbold's heart against the Arabs. On December 10 he wrote to John Martin: 'I wish that our military and police could round up and hang a few more Arabs "pour décourager les autres".' On 13 January 1938 he wrote to his son: 'My own dislike of the Palestinian Arab increases daily.'

Rumbold had returned to England from his cure at Marienbad at the end of September 1937. On October 12 he spoke to the Royal Empire Society about Palestine. He had been much impressed, he said, by the efforts of the Jews who had 'literally turned the desert into cultivable land', and who, by draining the swamps, had not only gained new cultivable land for themselves, but had improved the health of the Arabs in the former swamp lands. The Jewish hospitals, schools, and research laboratories, he added, likewise 'command admiration'. Yet Jewish enterprise and settlement had alienated the Arabs, and made a joint Arab Jewish State, under British rule, impossible. Partition, Rumbold argued, would

---

[1] Archibald Henry MacDonald Sinclair, 1890–1970. Entered Army, 1910. Succeeded his father as 4th Baronet, 1912. Served on the western front, 1914–18. Private Secretary to the Secretary of State for War, 1919–21; to the Secretary of State for Colonies, 1921–22. Liberal MP, 1922–45. Secretary of State for Scotland, 1931–32; for Air, 1940–45. Created Viscount Thurso, 1952.

enable the Jews, for the first time in nearly two thousand years, to cease living 'a minority life', and would give the Arabs of Palestine a national status, free from the fear of eventual Jewish control.

A lively discussion followed Rumbold's speech. Two distinguished Jews, Norman Bentwich,[1] and Herbert Samuel,[2] rejected the contention of the Peel Commission that Arab and Jews could not live together in peace. Bentwich declared that there was a real possibility of 'peace and understanding in an undivided Palestine'. Samuel, to Rumbold's surprise, mocked at the ability of 'these little States' to survive, and preferred 'a proper devolution of powers' within a single State.

Dr Weizmann was among those present at the discussion. Unlike Bentwich and Samuel, he said he would 'heartily support' the Partition plan. 'It was not an ideal solution', he added, 'but there was no ideal solution to any problem in the world.' Of course Samuel was right to stress how small the State would be; but that was no reason, in Weizmann's mind, to dismiss the idea. The Jews wanted a State. However small, the Partition scheme enabled them to fulfil this aspiration. 'No one would be happier than the Jews', he said, 'if for once they would have an opportunity of carrying, themselves, the burden of defending their own homes.' But two months later, faced by the mounting violence, the British Cabinet decided that progress towards Partition was not practicable, and that the Mandate must remain; in December 1937 the Government announced that they did not consider themselves bound by Lord Peel's recommendations.

Rumbold was disillusioned by the way in which the efforts of the Peel Commission seemed to have been in vain, despite the enormous amount of evidence that had been collected, and the effort which had been expended. 'By the light of what has happened', he wrote to his son on 26 November 1938, 'I have to admit that we all of us wasted 10 months of our time. Well, there it is and I will never undertake Government work again'.

[1] Norman Bentwich, 1883–1971. Called to the Bar, 1908. Co-editor (with Harry Sacher) of the *Jewish Review*, 1910–13 and 1932–34. Employed in the Ministry of Justice, Cairo, 1912–15. Major, Camel Transport, 1916–18. Attorney-General, Government of Palestine, 1920–31. Professor of International Relations, Jerusalem, 1932–51. Author of over 30 works, including *Palestine* (1934), *The Refugees from Germany* (1936) and *My 77 years* (1962).

[2] Herbert Louis Samuel, 1870–1963. Liberal MP, 1902–18; 1929–35. Chancellor of the Duchy of Lancaster, 1909–10. Postmaster-General, 1910–14. President of the Local Government Board, 1914–15. Home Secretary, Jan–Dec 1916. High Commissioner for Palestine, 1920–25. Knighted, 1920. Home Secretary, 1931–32. Created Viscount, 1937.

19

Retirement

1937–1941

At the end of 1936, while Rumbold was still in Palestine, he was angered to learn that several prominent Englishmen wanted to give Hitler some proof of Britain's friendly and constructive intentions. Geoffrey Dawson in *The Times*, and J. L. Garvin in the *Observer*, both tried to mould public opinion in this direction. Writing in the *Observer* on 12 December 1936, Garvin commented sympathetically on Hitler's desire 'to restore vigorous enterprise in the colonial field' and believed that such a policy was 'no menace to any of the Dominions'. If Germany were denied a colonial empire it would lead, he wrote, to 'the sure catastrophe of another general war'. Garvin went on to approve Hitler's aim of 'The making of Greater Germany by union or closer union with the Austrian and Bohemian Families of the common race.' 'Garvin has gone completely off the rails', Rumbold wrote to his son on Christmas Day, 1936. 'Last Sunday he advocated handing Germany back all her Colonies. . . .'

In July 1937 Rumbold went for his annual cure in Marienbad, where once again he took the waters, played golf and watched his fellow guests. The Spanish situation was uppermost in his mind.[1] In August Lord Newton arrived, eager, Rumbold wrote to his daughter on August 11, 'to go to Spain to investigate Franco's[2] position with a view to making propaganda in his favour. I am trying to choke him off. He is always meddling in things which don't concern him.' On his way from Marienbad to Austria, Rumbold drove through Germany. Near Regensburg, he was shocked to see, at the entrance to a village, a large placard with the words: 'Jews are not wanted here.'

Neville Chamberlain had succeeded Baldwin as Prime Minister in May, and during the summer he decided on a more active Government policy

[1] By July 1937, after a year of civil war, the Spanish Republican forces were being driven back towards Madrid by the Nationalist forces advancing from the south, the west and the north. Madrid was not occupied by the Nationalists until March 1939.

[2] Francisco Franco Bahamonde, 1892–   . Entered the Spanish Army, 1907. Second-in-Command of the Spanish Foreign Legion, 1920. During the Republican regime he served abroad, in the Balearic Islands, Morocco and the Canary Islands. One of the leaders of the Nationalist revolt, July 1936. Head of the State, 1939. Sent Spanish volunteers to fight with Germany against Russia, June 1941.

towards Nazi Germany, hoping to inaugurate a period of improved Anglo-German relations. In November 1937, as part of this new policy of positive appeasement, Lord Halifax went to Germany to see Hitler. 'I doubt whether anything much will come of the visit', Rumbold wrote to his son on November 19, 'but it is as well – in order to satisfy the public – to leave no stone unturned to try to come to some arrangement with Germany.' Before Halifax left London, Rumbold sent him a copy of a book called *The House That Hitler Built*, written by an Australian Professor, Stephen Roberts.[1] 'It contains an admirable character sketch of Hitler', Rumbold told his son. 'I thought it just as well that Halifax should realize the sort of man he was dealing with.' 'It is the most extraordinary comment on human evolution', Roberts had written, 'that, in this age of science and progress, the fate of mankind rests on the whimsy of an abnormal mind, infinitely more so than in the days of the old despots whom we criticize so much.'

In January 1938, Rumbold and his wife left England for a two-month holiday in Egypt. On January 21, he wrote to his son of his 'disgust at the action of Franco's aeroplanes in dropping powerful bombs on Barcelona (not a military objective) when the streets were crowded'. Over 200 people had been killed and 400 wounded. Such an 'exhibition of frightfulness', he added, would not increase sympathy for Franco, despite his growing military successes against the Republicans.[2]

The Egyptians were not pleased to see Rumbold, even though he came as a tourist. The Peel Commission's Report had been considered a betrayal of the Arab cause. The fact that the Commissioners had actually worked on their Report in Cairo added to the Egyptians' anger. One paper headlined the news of his arrival: 'A Dog Returns to His Vomit'. When asked by journalists if he could justify giving the Jews a national home, he replied that he stood by the Report.

After a week in Cairo, Rumbold and his wife took a Nile steamer to Wady Halfa. On board the steamer, Rumbold celebrated his sixty-ninth birthday. In the Press, he followed carefully developments in Germany. The removal of von Neurath, and his replacement by Ribbentrop as Foreign Secretary, he deplored. Equally deplorable, he felt, was the friend-

---

[1] Stephen Henry Roberts, 1901–71. Born in Australia. Research Fellow, Melbourne University, 1920–25. Researched in France, 1925–29 and in Germany, 1935–37. He published *The House That Hitler Built* in 1937. Vice-Chancellor and Principal, University of Sydney, 1947–67. Knighted, 1965.

[2] In April 1938, Rumbold lunched with Queen Ena in London. 'She was', he wrote to his daughter on April 10, 'very elated over Franco's successes and advances into Catalonia, but I found it difficult to echo this elation. It is, of course, better that Franco should win but I confess that I am not very easy as to what will happen once he *has* won.'

ship between Nevile Henderson, who had just been appointed Ambassador to Berlin, and Göring. On February 10 the wrote to his son: 'Henderson is rather stupid in identifying himself with Göring, from whom he can get nothing and whom he can't influence.'

While Rumbold was in Egypt the Foreign Secretary, Anthony Eden, resigned in protest against Neville Chamberlain's pro-Italian policy. Rumbold wrote at once to Eden 'as an average Englishman', to applaud his action. To his son he wrote on March 2, from Luxor: 'I don't think that Chamberlain knows the technique of dealing with Dictators who are necessarily bullies. The more you truckle to them the more arrogant they become.' The only result of Halifax's visit to Hitler, he wrote, had been a speech by Hitler containing 'contemptuous references to Eden' and 'offensive' language about Britain. The best way of dealing with 'the gangsters at present in power in Europe', Rumbold added, was 'to keep a stiff upper lip and let them go to smash as quickly as possible. I don't see that Nevile Henderson achieved much by sucking up to Göring.' The extent to which Chamberlain was grovelling before Hitler and Mussolini was, Rumbold wrote, 'the fly in the ointment as regards our delightful trip'. Two days later, on March 4, he wrote to his daughter that it was essential for the Government to be 're-arming hard the whole time'.

On March 12 German troops crossed the Austrian frontier, and within twenty-four hours Austria was annexed to Germany. 'I felt as if I would like to see 20 strokes of the cat administered to Hitler and his principal colleagues', Rumbold wrote to his daughter from Cairo on March 14. 'Adolf has got away with it again all along the line. . . . Our pro-Germans in London must look pretty fools today and I more than ever congratulate myself on never having joined the Anglo-German fellowship or gone to one of their entertainments.' To his son, that same day, Rumbold wrote: 'The British people may register disapproval and protest but they will not fight for Austrian independence.' The democracies, he added, must be 'sufficiently armed', in order to be able to say to Hitler and to Mussolini, 'this far and no further'. His conclusion was a pessimistic one: 'they are going to get away with a lot more before they are stopped, if, indeed, we ever have the guts to stop them'. Whatever happened, Britain should not waste its energies in quarrelling with the United States 'over some rotten Antarctic islands'.[1]

---

[1] Not Antarctic, but Pacific Islands. By an Order-in-Council of March 18, 1937, the British Government annexed Canton and Enderbury Islands, which were incorporated for administrative purposes into the Gilbert and Ellice Colony. Simultaneously, President Roosevelt declared United States sovereignty over the islands and filed the Proclamation with the National Archives in Washington. After a lengthy dispute, it was agreed, in April 1939, to establish a joint Anglo-American Condominium for 50 years, until 1989.

Rumbold returned to London at the end of March. The German annexation of Austria dominated his thoughts. 'I blew up when I heard the news', he wrote to his son on March 29, 'and couldn't sleep for 2 nights.' The British public, he discovered, 'flatter themselves that the Nazis will not do anything more for the moment and that they will be good boys for a time'. This, he told his son, was 'a dangerous assumption . . . they want to get away with as much as they can before the democracies can make a stand'. One of those who did not have illusions about Hitler's intentions was Sir Maurice Hankey, who wrote to Chamberlain's close adviser, Sir Horace Wilson[1] on 15 March 1938: 'I think you will find it worth your while, as I did, to glance through the attached prophetic despatch by Rumbold of five years ago. It shows, in the light of other events, how closely Hitler has adhered to *Mein Kampf* and provides some guide to the future.' Rumbold feared German intrigue in the Sudeten German districts of Czechoslovakia. But public opinion was such, he found, that even had he wanted to, Chamberlain could not have given the Czechs 'a firm guarantee of support if they were attacked'. Sir Horace Wilson was among those who wanted, instead, to see British pressure put on the Czechs to make territorial concessions to Germany.

In view of the annexation of Austria, Rumbold decided that he would have to give up his plans to go to Marienbad. 'Knowing how anti-Nazi I am', he wrote to his son, 'the Germans might easily pick me out of the train and make things unpleasant for me.' Threats against individuals had always been a part of the Nazi technique, and continued unabated. The Austrian Minister to London, George Franckenstein, who had been ordered by Ribbentrop to return to Vienna, refused, choosing instead to become an exile.

The continual talk about Hitler, and pro-German feeling in England, made Rumbold angry. 'Whenever 2 or 3 people are gathered together', he wrote to his son on April 10, 'the talk is of the "house painter" and his fellow gangsters. Besides being an objectionable personality in himself he adds to his offence by becoming a bore.' On Good Friday he sat next to Lord Peel's sister[2] at dinner. 'She got my goat', he wrote to his son on Easter Day, 'by talking in the way I am afraid so many or quite a number

[1] Horace John Wilson, 1882–1972. Entered the Civil Service, 1900; Permanent Secretary, Ministry of Labour, 1921–30. Knighted, 1924. Chief Industrial Adviser to the Government, 1930–39. Seconded to the Treasury for special service with Stanley Baldwin, 1935–37, and with Neville Chamberlain, 1937–40 (when he had a room at 10 Downing Street). Permanent Secretary of the Treasury and Head of the Civil Service, 1939–42.

[2] Julia Beatrice Peel, 1864–1949. Daughter of the 1st Viscount Peel and granddaughter of Sir Robert Peel. She married, in 1895, James Rochfort Maguire, a close collaborator of Cecil Rhodes and later a Conservative MP, who died in 1925. She was a Vice-President of St Mary's Hospital, Paddington.

of people in her class of society talk. Thus, the annexation of Austria was a good thing, it would be a bad day for England if Hitler got bumped off – the only thing that really mattered was our trade. I replied bluntly that a good many people over here were lamentably ignorant about Germany and the Nazis and talked a lot of foolishness. She saw I was roused and looked rather frightened.'

Rumbold was angered still further when the former Secretary of State for Air, Lord Londonderry,[1] published a book, *Ourselves and Germany*, at the end of March. Londonderry argued that it was still possible to reach a lasting agreement with Hitler. On April 12 Rumbold wrote to protest. The annexation of Austria, he declared, 'seems to me to make it difficult for us to resume conversations with the Germans. . . . Germany wants her Colonies back and is not prepared to make any bargain about the Colonies. On what basis, therefore, are we going to have discussions with her?' He saw the general situation as 'a race between the two dictatorships and the two big democracies in the sense that the former mean to get away with as much as they could before the latter were so fully armed as to be able to call a halt'. It might be possible, he added, to come to some agreement with Mussolini, and to detach him from Hitler, but such an agreement would have to be rigidly adhered to, 'and with dictators, circumstances alter cases'. Rumbold pointed out that the real opportunity to appease Germany had been before Hitler had come to power, when, under the Chancellorship of Müller or Brüning, goodwill could have been translated into practical politics. Some good feeling had been built up, belatedly, while Brüning was Chancellor, but, Rumbold added, the French had not given British efforts sufficient support, and everything that had been achieved 'was scrapped in ten days when the Nazi régime came in'. Londonderry was impressed by Rumbold's letter, which he sent to Lord Halifax on April 26 with a covering note: 'I agree with most of what he says and, moreover, I feel that he speaks with authority by reason of his experience.' In his draft reply Halifax wrote: 'I have always thought that it was unfortunate that H. Rumbold had to be moved, when he was, from Berlin, and can't help feeling that this must be added to the larger mistakes to which he refers and at which we have missed opportunities.'

In sending Rumbold's letter to Halifax, Lord Londonderry had omitted two sentences about Nevile Henderson which read: 'He made the mistake of rushing his fences when he first took up his post. An unofficial, but very

---

[1] Charles Stewart Henry Vane-Tempest-Stewart, 1878–1949. Conservative MP, 1906–15. Served on the Western Front, Royal Horse Guards, 1915. Succeeded his father as 7th Marquess of Londonderry, 1915. Under-Secretary of State for Air, 1920–21. Secretary of State for Air, 1931–35. Chief Commissioner, Civil Air Guard, 1938–45.

well-known personality, just back from Berlin and Austria tells me that Henderson is almost a danger in the sense that he is all for letting the Germans take all they want'.

Halifax had begun to question the merits of an appeasement policy, but Neville Chamberlain was determined to reach a satisfactory, and if possible a lasting agreement with Germany. He was even prepared to see Britain taking the initiative in persuading the Czechs to make concessions to Germany. Rumbold deprecated such a policy. 'Let Hitler come to Chamberlain', he wrote to his son on April 20, but there must be no 'smug complacency' on Britain's part, and no lapsing into the belief 'that Hitler is not hatching any further mischief'. But on April 28, in a letter to Lord Londonderry, Rumbold wrote: '. . . the Czechs are partly to blame for not sooner agreeing with their adversary – or at all events trying to do so'.

The mischief that Rumbold feared soon began. In May, German pressure mounted against Czechoslovakia. It seemed that Hitler would be satisfied with nothing less than the annexation of the German-speaking areas of Czechoslovakia. These areas had never belonged to Germany; before 1918 they had been part of Austria-Hungary. But this did not deter those Englishmen who wanted a 'fair deal' for Germany from saying that Hitler's demands were justified. Halifax sent Ribbentrop a message on May 22, to say that if Britain and Germany allowed the Czech crisis to 'get out of hand', the only ones to profit 'would be the communists'. The more explicit Hitler's demands grew, the more the British Government seemed anxious to satisfy them. Nevile Henderson wanted Britain to put pressure on the Czechs to make the maximum concessions to Germany. Chamberlain hoped that if Britain helped Germany over the Czech crisis, Hitler would be willing to discuss more constructive measures of appeasement in the economic and colonial sphere. Rumbold deprecated these hopes. He was dismayed by the British desire for an agreement with Hitler, whether based on hope or fear, writing to his son on July 22:

There are quite a number of people here who bleat about an understanding with Germany which, in my view, and until we are immensely strong, is a Will-o'-the-wisp. The people in question are actuated by funk and nothing else. There is a lot of obscurantism in the press and amongst the public who hate to call a spade a spade and wilfully shut their eyes to facts. The fact is that many people will not or cannot recognise that we are up against unscrupulous gangsters in the shape of Hitler, Himmler[1] & Co.

[1] Heinrich Himmler, 1900–45. Born in Munich. Served as a naval ensign, 1918. A standard-bearer at Hitler's November putsch of 1923. Chicken farmer, 1923–29. Head of the SS, 1929–45; and of the Federal German Police Force, 1936–45. A leading figure in the Nazi

At the end of July Rumbold dined with Chamberlain and, contrary to what he had expected, was impressed. 'Chamberlain', he wrote to his son on July 31, 'appeared to have had his eyes properly opened by the rape of Austria and won't allow the wool to be pulled over his eyes a second time. I think he now knows the Huns for what they are.' But the events of the following two months did not bear out Rumbold's analysis. Chamberlain believed that it was possible to reach a binding agreement with Hitler, and, in September, as the German pressure against the Czechs grew, he decided to go to see Hitler, and speak to him personally about a settlement.

The result was not as Rumbold had hoped. On September 24 Chamberlain told his Inner Cabinet that he thought he had 'established some degree of personal influence over Herr Hitler'; later, that same day, to the full Cabinet, he said that Hitler was 'extremely anxious to secure the friendship of Great Britain'. It would be a 'great tragedy', Chamberlain told his colleagues, 'if we lost an opportunity of reaching an understanding with Germany. He thought he had now established an influence over Herr Hitler and that the latter trusted him and was willing to work with him.'

The majority of Englishmen knew nothing of Chamberlain's conviction that Hitler trusted him, and that the Czech crisis could result, not only in peace, but in improved Anglo-German relations. Rumbold was convinced that if Hitler were given what he was demanding, he would soon demand more. 'The next victims', he wrote to his brother William on September 21, 'will be the Lithuanians (Memel) and then the Poles. . . . In fact we shall never have peace until the Nazi regime crashes, either as a result of an unsuccessful war for Germany, or an internal revolution in that country.' Rumbold was disgusted by Chamberlain's decision to put pressure on Czechoslovakia to surrender its borderlands to Germany. There was no parallel, he wrote to his son on September 22 to 'calling on an independent Sovereign Power to agree within 36 hours to give up a large slice of its territory containing valuable economic resources and its defence line. All the friends with whom I have spoken feel profoundly humiliated and depressed and I really believe that if Chamberlain were to go to the country now he would risk defeat.' If Chamberlain did get peace, Rumbold added, 'it will be a bad and only temporary peace'.

---

policy of mass murder and exterminations during the Second World War. Minister of the Interior, 1943–45. Appointed Commander-in-Chief of the Home Army after the attempt on Hitler's life of July 20, 1944. Entered into secret negotiation with the World Jewish Congress, April 1945. Hoped to become Head of State and to negotiate with the Allies, May 1945. Committed suicide while being searched by British troops May 23, 1945.

Rumbold was deeply sceptical of the Prime Minister's policy. 'I doubt whether Chamberlain or the Government yet realise the nature of the man with whom they are dealing, or his ultimate ambitions', he wrote to his son in his letter of September 22. 'Hitler is devoid of all honour and scruples. He has no regard for pledges, conventions or life. He is, in fact, evil.'

On September 26 Hitler put forward his further territorial demands. These constituted, Rumbold wrote to his brother on the following day, 'a brutal ultimatum to the Czechs'. But Chamberlain was prepared to accept them, telegraphing to Hitler on September 27: 'I feel certain that you can get all essentials without war and without delay.' He was prepared, he said, to fly to see Hitler again, his third visit in fourteen days. Rumbold, caught up in the popular excitement at the possibility that peace would be preserved, wrote to his son on September 18:

The PM has been marvellous. One can't imagine the lethargic Baldwin or old 'wait and see' (Asquith) doing what Chamberlain has done. And now, at the eleventh hour, when it was 3 to 1 on war comes the news of the meeting between Hitler, Mussolini, Chamberlain and Daladier[1] at Munich to-morrow. Again Chamberlain's idea. The first posters only mentioned Hitler, Mussolini and our PM and I thought there would be 2 brigands against one honest man. They may yet save the peace and everybody is much bucked. Long before you get this you will know whether it is peace or war.

One of the principal villains of the piece has been Ribbentrop – a contemptible and disastrous cad if ever there was one. This wine-tout has always been an aggravating element and still seems to have lots of influence.

On September 29 Chamberlain flew to Munich; in the early hours of October 1 he and Hitler signed their agreement, whereby Germany annexed the German-speaking areas of Czechoslovakia. Chamberlain returned to London, and to a hero's welcome: at the airport he read out a declaration, signed by Hitler and himself, describing the Munich agreement as 'symbolic of the desire of our two people never to go to war with one another'.

Throughout England there was widespread relief that war had been avoided; but Rumbold did not share in it. 'One has gone through a variety of emotions', Lady Rumbold wrote to their son on October 2, 'but one predominates, in *this* family at least, of profound disgust that Hitler has got away with it yet again. . . . If five years ago more real

---

[1] Edouard Daladier, 1884–1970. Mayor of Carpentras, 1912–58. Member of the Chamber of Deputies, 1919. Minister of Colonies, 1924. Minister of War, 1933. Minister of Foreign Affairs, 1934. Minister of Defence, 1936. President of the Council, 1938–40; also Minister of War and Defence. For his part in the Munich Conference he received the Grand Cross of the Order of St Michael and St George (GCMG).

attention had been paid to daddy's warning last despatch from Berlin, they would have been more prepared with armaments. He feels it quite dreadfully, and is in a very despondent mood.' Harold Nicolson had lunched with them two days before. He had been, Lady Rumbold continued, 'very distraught & disgusted. He will be a bit violent in the House tomorrow, I expect.'[1] On October 5 Rumbold wrote to his son:

The crisis is over and we have a respite but not, in my view, more than that. London was a curious sight last week as war drew nearer and nearer. The people were calm and quiet and ready to accept what was coming to them, and a good deal was coming. Our air defences and precautions are by no means ready or perfect and there would have been great destruction and loss of life. Perhaps I am a fatalist but I have made up my mind that this house and everybody in it might have been destroyed this week. I am by no means a brave man and confess that, had it come to a war I should have been filled with trepidation at the blast of the first siren. Well, we have been spared that. The nation really behaved magnificently.

There was bound to be a wave of mass hysteria born from a sense of great relief and balanced judgment was impossible for the first 48 hours. But now many people are beginning to doubt whether Chamberlain really has brought back 'peace with honour'. Incidentally the phrase is '*peace without dishonour*' – a difference. Very many people feel that we have somehow been humiliated. The British sporting instinct resents the mutilation of a small State by a big bully and hates having given way before a Nazi dictator. These are twin reactions. I have talked with a policeman, our chauffeur, a liftman and a hairdresser. They all felt that there was something wrong. They felt humiliated and every one of them firmly believed that we should sooner or later have to have show-down with Hitler. . . . I don't think anybody here – except a few dyed in the wool old buffers – attaches the slightest value to Hitler's statement that he has no further territorial claims in Europe. As for the declarations Chamberlain brought back, when we were at the cinema a few nights ago and the screen showed his arrival at Heston and waving the declaration a man sitting behind us said in a loud voice 'another scrap of paper' and there was no dissent.

I feel pretty miserable about it all and so do many of my friends. All we can do now is to speed up armaments and make ourselves immensely strong. We shall then be able to talk with the enemy in the gate.

[1] Speaking in the House of Commons on October 5, 1938, Nicolson declared: 'I know that in these days of realism principles are considered as rather eccentric and ideals are identified with hysteria. I know that those of us who believe in the traditions of our policy, who believe in the precepts which we have inherited from our ancestors, who believe that one great function of this country is to maintain moral standards in Europe, to maintain a settled pattern of international relations, not to make friends with people who are demonstrably evil, not to go out of our way to make friends with them but to set up some sort of standard by which the smaller powers can test what is good in international conduct and what is not – I know that those who hold such beliefs are accused of possessing the Foreign Office mind. I thank God that I possess the Foreign Office mind.'

In mid-October Rumbold and his wife sailed on the *Queen Mary* to the United States, where their son, who had entered the Diplomatic Service three years before, was Third Secretary in the British Embassy. Rumbold was excited by the skyline and skyscrapers of New York, which, he wrote to his daughter on October 21, far surpassed anything he had imagined. He went up the Empire State Building – 'about 4 times the height of the Pyramids'. In Washington he met several Americans whom he had known during his career, including Irwin Laughlin, who took him to see the Supreme Court, and his old enemy, Admiral Bristol, who took him to the Horse Show. After a week in Washington he went for a weekend to Virginia. After a further ten days in Washington, he and his wife sailed from New York in the *Normandie* on November 12.

On his return to England Rumbold found, as he wrote to his son on November 18, that there was still much criticism of Chamberlain's foreign policy. 'The fact that some 200 MPs have expressed confidence in Chamberlain', he wrote, 'is in itself a proof, to my mind, that his position was shaken and needed fortifying.' At each dinner, in every club 'passions are running high' he added, 'and I feel as if I should like to inflict personal castigation on the prominent pro-Germans in this country'. On November 26 he sent his son a fuller account of opinion as he had found it:

There is much uneasiness amongst supporters of the Government and mis-giving that the latter do not really mean business as regards the speed and volume of rearmament. Hardly anybody has any use for or belief in the policy of appeasement and many point to the pogroms in Germany as a commentary on the character of Chamberlain's new friend Hitler.[1] Reference to appeasement in the country have no reaction or only provoke sarcasm. Moreover people just back from Germany report that there is much abuse by the Nazis of Chamber-lain. The Germans are profoundly irritated by our expressed intention to re-arm to the limit as well as by our attitude on the question of the German Colonies.

There is, of course, general disgust with the treatment of the Jews in Germany. Nobody has a good word for the Nazis and Ribbentrop is especially singled out for abuse – being constantly referred to as a 'swine'. But I don't notice that violent hatred of the Germans such as obtains in the States. In fact there is a de-featist element in the business world and amongst the so-called upper classes. These people would be ready to give Hitler anything for the sake of peace.

[1] On November 8, 1938, a Jewish refugee from Germany shot Ernst vom Rath, the third Counsellor at the German Embassy in Paris. On November 9, within twenty-four hours of the shooting, a massive official pogrom took place throughout Germany. Over a hundred synagogues were burned down, and 7,500 Jewish shops ransacked. Thirty-five Jews were killed; many thousands were sent to concentration camps. On November 12, at a secret meeting of Nazi leaders, Göring declared: 'I would have preferred it if you had killed 200 Jews instead of destroying so much valuable property.' As a 'punishment' for vom Rath's murder, the Jews of Germany were fined one milliard marks.

They don't want anything to interfere with their business or with the even tenor of their lives. The country as a whole is absolutely sound – in fact the proletariat is almost pugnacious. The result of the Bridgwater election was a real shock to the Government and this has been followed by Lewisham where the Conservative majority was more than halved.[1] The Government can't ignore these warnings. I think they have been doing their best in Paris to get the French to pull themselves together and to concert measures of defence. When I talk of the Government I mean Chamberlain. He is described as a man running in blinkers and unwilling to see anything which is likely to interfere with his policy.

A minority of Englishmen still denied that Nazism was wholly evil. 'One Lord Brocket',[2] Rumbold wrote to his son in his letter of November 26, 'who must be the most gullible of asses, has just returned to England from shooting with Göring, who told him that neither he, Göring, nor Hitler had had any knowledge of the recent Nazi action against the Jews.' On December 7 Rumbold sent his son a survey of the various speculations. Some feared a German attack on Italy, and the annexation of the Trentino and Trieste. Others thought Hitler might mount a propaganda campaign in the spring for the return of some of Germany's former colonial possessions. There was talk of Hitler supporting Mussolini in an attempt to force France to surrender Corsica to Italy. Colonel Christie, Rumbold's former Air Attaché in Berlin, was certain that some German military action in the East was most likely, and told Rumbold that 'an adventure towards Memel or even the Ukraine' was the common talk among military circles inside Germany. 'But what then', Rumbold asked his son, 'about the Poles?'

On December 15 Rumbold wrote to his son of the 'increasing disgust with Germany' among all groups of English society, and of 'a growing conviction that there is nothing to be done with the Nazis. Even the pro-Germans like Londonderry are turning against them.' There was no doubt in Rumbold's mind that 1939 would see further aggressive action by Hitler. 'The Germans will threaten us'; he wrote to his brother William on January 24, 'in fact, this year, 1939 is their last chance of doing so with

[1] The Government had suffered a setback in three by-elections in November 1938. On November 7, Mrs J. L. Adamson (Labour) won Dartford from Godfrey Mitchell (Conservative) with a majority of 5,648. On November 18, at Bridgwater, Vernon Bartlett (Independent) defeated P. G. Heathcoat-Amory (Conservative) by 2,332 votes. On November 24, Henry Brooke (Conservative) held West Lewisham from Arthur Skeffington (Labour), but with a much reduced majority.

[2] Arthur Ronald Nall Nall-Cain, 1904–67. Conservative MP, 1931–34. Succeeded his father as 2nd Baron Brocket, 1934. A leading member of the Anglo-German Fellowship, 1934–39. Chairman, Brocket Estates Ltd; Vice-Chairman, Allied Breweries. President of the National Sheep Breeders' Association, 1945–47. President of the Association of Land and Property Owners from 1960 until his death.

any success'. There was a general feeling of uneasiness, he wrote to his son that same day, that Chamberlain and his colleagues 'are not really and effectively getting on with their armament plans. . . . They are trying to carry through rearmament whilst not departing from a peace economy.' In Rumbold's opinion, Chamberlain did not seem to recognize 'that we are not in a state of peace but rather in a state of armistice'. Nor did the possibility of war turn everyone into patriots. 'Defeatism', he wrote to his brother on January 31, 'can be traced mainly to the Stock exchange. I know that it is unpleasant not to be able to do business, but people in the City oughtn't to go about whining, which they do. They haven't any guts at all. There is also a small clique in Mayfair which is rotten from that point of view.'

On February 5 Rumbold celebrated his seventieth birthday. Among the letters of congratulation was one from the German Ambassador in London, von Dirksen,[1] who sent him 'in remembrance of your stay in Germany . . . some bottles of Rhine Wine'. Harold Nicolson sent a copy of his most recent book, *Diplomacy*, which Rumbold found, to his astonishment, had been dedicated to himself as 'the ideal diplomat'. He spent the morning of his birthday playing golf near Ascot, went to Eton for tea, and dined in London with the Dilettanti Society. He was convinced that if war were to come, it would begin in 1939. 'I feel that it would be suicidal for the Dictators to attack France and ourselves after 1939', he wrote to his son on February 9. But he refused to be rattled. 'I can't help feeling a certain contempt', he wrote to his son, 'for the jittery disposition of the Government, or some members thereof.'

On March 15 German troops entered Prague. 'Even Chamberlain's eyes must now be opened', Rumbold wrote to his son that afternoon, 'to the fact that Hitler's statements and assurances are not worth the breath with which they are uttered. . . . I confess that I have never in my life felt so disheartened as I do now. Add to this the cowardice and folly of the Government in the Palestine question[2] and the cup is full.' Rumbold was

[1] Herbert von Dirksen, 1882–1955. Secretary, Prussian Minister of Commerce, 1904. Served on the Western Front as a Captain, 1914–18. Consul-General, Danzig, 1923. Ambassador, Moscow, 1928–33; Tokyo, 1933–38; London, May 1938–September 1939.

[2] On February 8, 1939, the British Government had convened a conference at St James's Palace in London of Arab and Jewish leaders, and sought to annul the recommendations of the Peel Commission. But the Jews said that the Peel proposals were as far as they were prepared to go, and that they could accept no less in the way of territory. For their part, the Arabs demanded a total halt to Jewish immigration and land purchase. The Conference broke down on March 15. Two months later, on May 17, 1939, the Government issued a White Paper declaring that there would be no partition of Palestine, and that Jewish immigration should be restricted to 10,000 a year 'unless the Arabs of Palestine are prepared to acquiesce in it'.

bitter that his own warnings of six years before had been ignored, and angry that Chamberlain should have been misled about Hitler's intentions. That night Rumbold dined at Grillions Club. Among those at dinner was Winston Churchill, to whom Rumbold wrote on the following morning:

You asked me last night what I thought of the present situation and I replied that I was profoundly disheartened. This was an understatement. I have had several difficult and depressing situations to deal with in the course of my career and I have, on the whole, been inclined to optimism. But I have never felt so depressed or so nauseated as I feel now and this because it seems to me that our Government have for a year or more, failed to look ahead or to understand the character of the man with whom they are dealing.

In April 1933 I warned the Government of the nature of the beast and of the system which had arisen in Germany. My despatch was largely an analysis of the more salient passages in 'Mein Kampf' and was, I am told, called 'the Mein Kampf despatch'. That is my only consolation but a poor one for, as I see it, we have reached the position of speculating gloomily which country is going to be involved in the next act of brigandage knowing perfectly well – except, perhaps, in the case of Switzerland or Holland – that we shall do nothing about it. At the utmost our PM will utter a bleat in the House. Having now read his statement or speech of yesterday I consider that it was anything but a la hauteur, whilst his conception of a breach of faith is not that of the average Englishman.

I am inclined to think that the northern gangster may go for Memel next and that his fellow brigand in the south will try for Albania. I only hope that it will not enter into the PM's head to pay Hitler another visit. The season ticket he took to Canossa last autumn is more than sufficient and there is no doubt that what the Arabs would call the 'father of appeasement' was outwitted and fooled by the 'father of lies or treachery' i.e. Hitler at Munich.

The seizure of the Czech aeroplanes and gold etc is such an accession of strength to Hitler that I don't put it past him to challenge us now in a most direct manner. . . . I do not think it consistent with our dignity – if we have any left – to keep on our Ambassador at Berlin who ought to be recalled on indefinite leave. As you know, the Americans have done this in the case of their Ambassador.[1] They are, it is true, 4,000 miles away. But my gorge rises at the thought that the King should be personally represented at the Capital of a bandit Government.

This requires no answer. It was some relief to my feelings to pour out some of my bitterness to you for I know you feel much the same as I do.

To this Churchill replied on March 19: 'it seems to me that Hitler will not stop short of the Black Sea unless arrested by the threat of a general

---

[1] Hugh Robert Wilson, 1885–1946. Entered the United States Diplomatic Service, 1911. Minister in Berne, 1927–37. Assistant Secretary of State, 1937. Ambassador to Berlin, 1938–39. He published *Education of a Diplomat* (1938) and *Diplomat Between Wars* (1941).

war, or by actual hostilities'. Rumbold's letter had contained two accurate forecasts. The Germans seized Memel on March 23; the Italians invaded Albania on April 7. Chamberlain reacted with a vigour which surprised his critics, giving Poland, whom many thought would be Hitler's next victim, a British guarantee against aggression. On several occasions in late March and early April, Lord Halifax asked Rumbold for his opinion on the crisis, and Rumbold reiterated his conviction that Hitler would be unable, either by the demands of his philosophy or by the momentum of his movement, to call a halt to territorial expansion in the East. In a letter to Halifax on March 28 Rumbold stated that in his view 'the Nazi system cannot be static and must be dynamic'. But, he warned, if 'a league against aggression by Germany were formed and which, in his view, would imply the crystallisation of the Reich on its present basis Hitler might – taking into account his increasing financial and economic difficulties coupled with an assumption or calculation that neither the French nor we are yet completely rearmed – well risk a gambler's throw and provoke a general war.' Hitler, he concluded, 'is an unpleasant mixture of mysticism and cunning. . . . far more dangerous than Napoleon for he has an unrivalled and unscrupulous propaganda machine at his command, to say nothing of the wireless which enables him to act very quickly. And then there is air power.' On April 6 Rumbold wrote to his son, summarizing the advice which he had given to the Foreign Secretary. To stand by Poland, he had said, '*did* entail a risk of war if (a) Hitler thought that our new policy would have the effect of stabilising, or rather crystallising, the Reich on its present basis, (b) Germany's increasing economic difficulties became very grave, (c) Hitler felt that neither France nor ourselves would be fully prepared until next year.' A combination of these three factors, he believed, 'might make Hitler go off the deep end'.

During the spring and summer the speculation and tension mounted. 'Hitler is not only public enemy No 1', Rumbold wrote to his son on April 20, 'but public bore No 1.' Everybody in England, he wrote a week later, 'is absolutely fed up by the prolonged tension which is becoming intolerable and which surely can't last without an explosion'. On May 11 he wrote again to his son, reiterating what he had told Halifax, that 'National Socialism is not a static movement. If it is obliged to remain static, i.e. if Hitler can no longer pay dividends in the shape of bloodless foreign adventures, the movement will begin to disintegrate from internal difficulties. The risk then is that Hitler may go off the deep end and plunge into a war which would be a desperate gamble. So I look to the autumn for events.'

On June 30 Lord Halifax, speaking at Chatham House, warned Hitler that further aggression by Germany would be met by force. On July 1 Rumbold wrote to congratulate him on saying 'what was required to be said in no uncertain language'. But, he went on: 'To my mind Hitler has now got himself into a situation from which he has no retreat without loss of face unless he starts a war, in which case his regime will also crash in the long run.' Rumbold was doubtful as to whether Halifax's warning could possibly influence Hitler. The time for such warnings was long past. 'Hitler and Ribbentrop', he wrote, 'are like deaf adders. They do not want to hear the truth and their campaign of hate against us is being deliberately worked up for some definite object.'

During the summer of 1939 Rumbold agreed to serve as Chairman of the Co-ordinating Foundation, a new organization whose aim was to help resettle the Jews who emigrated from Germany. The Foundation wanted to encourage Jewish settlement in British Guiana, and to persuade the British Government to give its approval to this plan. It hoped, by pressure and persuasion, to improve the conditions of Jews inside Germany, and to encourage and organize Jewish emigration from Germany. The Foundation held its first full meeting on August 1. President Roosevelt[1] gave it his approval. A week later, on August 8, Rumbold persuaded the Belgian statesman, Paul van Zeeland,[2] to become its Director. During August the Germans themselves appeared willing to discuss the Foundation's plan for accelerated emigration out of Germany.[3]

The main hope for peace, Rumbold wrote to his brother William on April 15, was a strong 'anti-aggression front' which it would be 'folly for the Axis to take on'. When Chamberlain opened negotiations with Russia, Rumbold believed that the non-aggression front could soon be a reality. But, he wrote to his son on June 1, 'the Russians having been cold-shouldered for so long and being semi-Orientals are very suspicious. . . . The Germans, of course, would do anything to prevent our getting together with the Muscovites.' The Russian negotiations dragged on through the summer. Rumbold's confidence in their outcome waned. 'I have a sort of feeling', he wrote to his son on August 21, 'that the Russians may double-cross us. They are most unreliable.'

[1] Franklin Delano Roosevelt, 1882–1945. Lawyer. Assistant Secretary of the Navy, 1913–20. Governor of New York State, 1929–33. President of the United States, 1933–45.

[2] Paul van Zeeland, 1893–   . A Director of the Belgian National Bank, 1926; Deputy Governor, 1934. Prime Minister of Belgium, 1935–37 (when he devalued the franc by 28 per cent). President of the Co-ordinating Foundation for Refugees, 1939. In exile in England, 1940. Minister of Foreign Affairs, 1949–54.

[3] Several prominent British Jews joined the foundation and gave it their financial backing. These included Lord Bearsted (a Director of Lloyds Bank), Lionel de Rothschild (a partner of N. M. Rothschild & Sons, bankers) and Simon Marks (Managing Director of Marks and Spencer Ltd).

On August 23, while the British negotiators were still in Moscow, Ribbentrop flew to Moscow and signed a Russo-German non-aggression pact, by which neither power would join any combination against the other. In a secret clause, eastern Poland and the Baltic States were to come within Russia's sphere of influence in the event of Poland's 'disintegration' as a State.

As soon as the Russo-German pact was signed, Hitler began to abuse the Poles, and to demand territorial concessions. On August 25, in reaction to Hitler's threats, Britain signed a formal Treaty of Alliance with Poland. Three days later, on August 28 Rumbold wrote to his son: 'My own belief now is that war is inevitable. It is impossible to reason with Hitler who repeats the parrot cry that he must have Danzig and now the Corridor. . . . We are up against men who are the incarnation of evil. I hope they may have a bloody fate.' If only, he added, the German generals 'were sensible and showed real concern for their country they would now arrest Hitler and the leading Nazi chiefs. But they haven't got the guts for this.' Four days later, on September 1, Hitler invaded Poland. In accordance with their Alliance, Britain and France declared war on Germany on September 3.

Rumbold saw little hope for the Poles. 'They are out-numbered, out-gunned and overwhelmed in the air', he wrote to his son on September 9. He hoped that in the west the French might try 'to break through the Siegfried line', but realized that such a move 'would be a costly business', and was not surprised when the French decided not to attack. British aeroplanes had been busy in the first week of the war dropping leaflets over Germany. 'They might as well have dropped bombs instead of leaflets', Rumbold commented. On September 16, in accordance with the secret clause in the Russo-German pact, Soviet forces moved into eastern Poland. 'I am almost beginning to believe', Rumbold wrote to his brother the following day, 'that the world has been delivered over to the evil one and I shouldn't be in the least surprised to see a combination of the 3 Dictators, Stalin, Hitler and Mussolini against the Democracies. Japan might join in and I wouldn't bank too strongly on Turkey.'[1] Amid all the gloom, there was only one 'comforting reflection', he wrote, 'i.e. that many Germans are being killed with every day that passes. If we could kill a million or two there might be a revolution in Germany.'

Shortly before war was declared Rumbold had been asked to act as an adviser to the Ministry of Economic Warfare. He was appointed Chairman

---

[1] Italy declared war on Britain and France on June 10, 1940. Japan attacked British, Dutch and United States territory in the Far East on December 7, 1941. But Turkey remained neutral until February 23, 1945, when she declared war on both Germany and Japan.

of the 'Black List Committee', which issued a list of 278 firms whose trade was to be boycotted, as being of benefit to Germany. Rumbold's Committee had held its first meeting on September 4, the day after war was declared. Thenceforth it met regularly two or three times a week. Evidence was submitted by various Government departments about the trading activities of firms based in neutral countries. Rumbold and his Committee had to decide whether these firms were helping the German war effort in any way, or being used for undercover activities. Three legal experts were appointed to advise on all questions of law,[1] and the work of the Committee was co-ordinated by a civil servant in the Department of Overseas Trade, Joseph Reading.[2] For the first four months of the war the Committee met in a room at the London School of Economics, which had been requisitioned by the Government. Later it moved, with the Ministry of Economic Warfare, to Berkeley Square House. Reading later wrote of Rumbold's chairmanship: 'I would have said that his judgement was superb, his attention to detail considerable and he would certainly not accept a poorly documented case. . . . As to the man, I found him an excellent master, considerate and extremely courteous, as one would expect. Once he found his staff to be competent he largely left the secretariat to carry on using their own initiative. His one insistence was, however, that the minutes of each meeting should be circulated to members within 24 hours. As some of the meetings continued until 7 p.m. this could lead to the burning of the midnight oil.' Rumbold never allowed his anger to prejudice his work. 'I well recall', Joseph Reading wrote more than thirty years later, 'that on the fall of France and the entry of Italy into the war at the height of the blitz, most of the members of the Committee became somewhat belligerent. "Take it out of the swine" they thought; "make the Statutory List as long as possible". "Not so", said Sir Horace. He continued to keep a calm control of the Committee's corporate action by demanding real evidence before making the recommendations.'

'It is a great satisfaction', Rumbold wrote to his son on September 24, 'to be actively helping to ruin German trade.' Despite the rapid German advance through Poland in the first and second weeks of September, he was confident of the outcome. 'You need not fear', he had written to his

[1] The legal experts were Lionel (later Lord) Cohen; J. B. Linden, QC; and Gerald Fitzmaurice (later Senior Judge of the International Court of Justice at The Hague).

[2] Joseph Lewis Reading, 1907– . Entered the Civil Service, in the Department of Overseas Trade, 1932. 3rd Secretary, British Embassy, Washington, 1939. Industrial Intelligence Centre, Department of Overseas Trade, 1939–42. Principal, Ministry of Economic Warfare, 1939–44. Assistant Secretary, Ministry of Production, 1944–45; Board of Trade, 1945. Director of the British Industries Fair, 1952–55. Senior British Trade Commissioner in New Zealand, 1963–67. Secretary, Movement of Exports, National Economic Development Office, 1972.

son on September 18, 'that there will be any weakening in the resolve to finish and destroy the villainous crew now ruling Germany. The unanimity in this country is quite remarkable. But the news is bad.' He did not fear a German attack in the West. 'If the Germans try to turn the Maginot line through Holland', he wrote to his brother William on September 24, 'they will be up against the Dutch and Belgian armies to say nothing of the French and ourselves and I should then hope to see the German right wing massacred to the last man.' These were optimistic expectations of a victory on the Western Front. Rumbold, however, made an accurate assessment of what would occur in the East. 'I predict', he wrote to his son on September 28, 'that the Russians will eventually – sooner rather than later – seize or proclaim a protectorate over the Baltic States and take Bessarabia from Roumania.'[1]

As well as his work at the Ministry of Economic Warfare, Rumbold was a member of a small committee whose aim, he wrote to his son on October 8, was 'to get in touch with the most influential German political refugees with a view to upsetting the present regime in Germany and showing the Germans that an alternate regime is possible'.[2] There were two drawbacks in the work as far as Rumbold was concerned. The first, he wrote to his son, was that 'our Secretary is a refugee German Jew who is well off and who has not made a good impression on me. He has all the Jewish unpleasant characteristics and I don't like discussing confidential matters in front of him'. The second drawback was that in order to persuade German refugees to speak against Hitler, it was necessary to give them an idea of what sort of peace the Allies would agree to once Hitler was overthrown. But the refugees, as Rumbold noted, were all 'patriotic Germans', and wanted as good a settlement as possible. This Rumbold could not guarantee. The peace terms, he wrote to his son, would be determined by 'the duration of the war' and by 'the degree of frightfulness employed by the Germans'. Merely 'to sweep away Hitler and his gang' after the war would not, he believed, be sufficient. 'We shall have', he wrote to his son, 'at great cost to the French and ourselves, to kill hundreds of thousands of young Nazis and SS troops in the German army.'

Rumbold's outspokenly hostile attitude to the Nazis did not commend itself to everybody. In mid-October both he and Harold Nicolson had been suggested to the BBC as people who ought to broadcast on Germany.

---

[1] Russia annexed Bessarabia on June 28, 1940. Of the three Baltic States, Lithuania was incorporated into the Soviet Union on August 3, 1940; Estonia and Latvia two days later.

[2] The other members of the committee were Alfred Duff Cooper (the only Cabinet Minister who resigned at the time of Munich), the journalist Wickham Steed, the historian R. W. Seton-Watson, and Harold Nicolson.

'We were both promptly rejected', Rumbold wrote to his son on October 21, 'on the ground that we were too anti-Nazi.'

During the late autumn and winter Hitler consolidated his position in Poland. Throughout the conquered territory intellectuals, priests, political leaders, prominent Jews were arrested and shot. 'I confess that I hate the Germans more and more', Rumbold wrote to his brother William on November 19, 'and can only wonder how I managed to live among them for 5 years.'

Although no German bombs fell on London, and no French attack took place against the Siegfried Line, Rumbold was not lulled by the 'phoney war' into complacency. 'We must make up our minds to a terrific onslaught in every element early this spring – say in March', he wrote to his son on 13 January 1940. The German attack on the Western Front, he believed, would be 'even more terrific than the attack on 18 March 1918 which all but succeeded'. During January there was talk of a negotiated peace, and the Dutch Foreign Minister, van Kleffens,[1] proposed the opening of negotiations as soon as possible. 'Can he not see that peace *now* would amount to a German victory?' Rumbold wrote to his son on January 28. 'Some of these neutrals don't seem to be able to look beyond their noses.' Even American neutrality angered him. 'I don't think my temper would stand a sojourn in the USA just now', he added.

On March 21, when Rumbold dined at Grillions Club, Churchill and Lord Trenchard[2] were among the members present. 'Trenchard developed his favourite theme', Rumbold wrote to his son three days later, 'i.e. that we ought to have bombed north-west Germany thoroughly as soon as war broke out. Our not having done so had enabled German propaganda to put out that we had been afraid to attack Germany. Churchill, much quieter than usual, was rather reserved but implied that we were not yet quite strong enough in the air.'

At the end of March Nevile Henderson sent Rumbold a copy of his book *Failure of a Mission*, describing his two years as Ambassador in Berlin from

---

[1] Eelco Nicolaas van Kleffens, 1894–　　. Secretary to the Directors of the Royal Dutch Petroleum Company, 1921–22. Deputy Chief, Legal Section of the Dutch Foreign Ministry, 1922–27; Chief of the Diplomatic Section, 1929–39. Minister to Switzerland, 1939. Foreign Minister, 1939–46; in exile in London, 1940–45. Dutch Delegate to the United Nations, 1946. Ambassador to Washington, 1947–50. Minister to Portugal, 1950–56. President of the 9th Session of the United Nations General Assembly, 1954. Resident in Portugal since 1956.

[2] Hugh Montague Trenchard, 1873–1956. Entered Army, 1893. Dangerously wounded during the South African War, 1901. Commanded the Royal Flying Corps on the Western Front, 1915–17. Major-General, 1916. Knighted, 1918. Chief of the Air Staff, 1918–29. Created Baron, 1930. Commissioner, Metropolitan Police, 1931–35. Order of Merit, 1951. His elder son was killed in action in 1943.

1937 to 1939. On April 15 Rumbold wrote to Henderson to thank him, and went on:

You have described your book as 'the failure of a mission' but, for 2 reasons, nobody could have succeeded at Berlin. Those reasons are a) the nature and character of the beast with which any British Representative would have had to deal and b) the fatuous belief of Chamberlain and, presumably, of his Government that, in 1937, it was possible to achieve anything by a policy of appeasement of Germany. Incidentally Germans are incurable Oliver Twists.

At the luncheon at the Dorchester last Wednesday Halifax put the matter in its proper light by saying that we were up against 'evil'. Hitler is an evil man and his regime and philosophy are evil. You cannot compromise with evil. The institution of labour camps and 'strength through joy organisations' weigh as nothing against the main tenets of Hitler's philosophy. It is quite easy to wipe out unemployment if you resort to conscription on a vast scale and put a lot of people into labour camps. . . .

Just seven years ago I sent home a despatch in which I summarised all the sinister passages of 'Mein Kampf' and drew attention to the revival of militarism which could only have one end i.e. war. And that was the concern of all who were threatened. This despatch which was called the Mein Kampf despatch made a considerable sensation but was pigeon-holed in due course. Neither MacDonald nor Baldwin would face facts. The former is dead – the latter completely discredited. Blame attaches to several of the present Ministers. The safety of the Empire is more important than balanced budgets or disarmament aspirations. Baldwin & Co. literally gambled with the safety of the Empire and this was unpardonable. Our Government should have started to rearm intensively after the reoccupation of the Rhineland which showed what Hitler thought of international obligations. You may say that the country would not have stood for re-armament. What then is the rôle of a government? Should it be to keep itself and its party in power at all costs or, if necessary, to tell the country unpalatable truths. If Baldwin had resigned on the question of rearmament the resignation of a Government with such an overwhelming majority would have produced an immense effect.

What then – failing earlier re-armament – ought our policy to have been? It ought, in my view, and as I wrote to Eden to have been one of polite reserve towards Germany. Given the German character such an attitude would have had a far greater effect on the Germans than a policy of appeasement which, to use a French expression, 'pêchait par la base'. No expeditions to Nuremberg etc. Watchful waiting, however. I have always thanked my stars that I left Berlin before having to establish social intercourse with the ruffians surrounding Hitler. The Germans certainly did not want to fight us and the French yellow book reveals that they have had a respect for our air-force. The Germans tend to lie and boast and it was a mistake, in my view, to take their statements about their armaments too literally. However, that is all past and it is no use crying over spilt milk. What about the future.

Speculations as to the nature of the peace settlement are quite premature mainly for 3 considerations:—

a) We do not know what Europe may be like after the war. The struggle may and probably will extend to other countries.
b) We do not know in what manner the Germans are going to continue to fight the war. They may even use fouler methods than those they have hitherto employed thereby creating a psychological atmosphere or state of mind inimical to any moderate peace settlement.
c) Nor do we know – and that is more important than anything – what the French view of the peace settlement may be.

I anticipate, however, that the peace terms will be severe – as they ought to be. Inter alia there will have to be reparations for Poland, Czecho-Slovakia, Norway etc. I have no sympathy for the Germans millions of whom stand behind Hitler. They deserve what, I hope, is coming to them. But I admit that we have to kill the beast first.

In April the British took an initiative to break the 'phoney war'. Under Churchill's direction, the Admiralty sought to prevent the Germans from carrying Swedish iron-ore down the coast of Norway. But the British action came too late; within a few days the Germans had counter-attacked, and succeeded in occupying all of southern Norway. Rumbold was confident that the Germans would be unable to drive the British from the bases which they had established on the Norwegian Coast. 'By the time you get this', he wrote to his son on April 13, 'I hope we shall have chased the Germans from Norway or killed or interned their troops there.' But within three weeks it was the Germans who had driven the British out of Norway, and in Britain there was growing discontent at a Government which could allow the Germans to win so considerable an advantage. On May 4 Rumbold wrote to his son of a widespread feeling that 'given the nature of our enemy and his methods, the Allies are *over scrupulous* and are always allowing themselves to be taken by surprise. . . . I shouldn't mind betting that if things go on as they are doing now there may be a very great change in the Government of this country before very long. . . . The trouble is that nobody sees where the thrusters are to be found.' On May 7 and 8 the House of Commons debated the Norwegian failure. Chamberlain resented the strong criticisms, not only of policy, but of himself. 'We should do better', he said, 'to occupy ourselves with increasing our war effort than disputing about the form of Government.' In the Division on May 8 Chamberlain had a majority of eighty-one, but thirty Conservatives had voted against him. The Labour opposition, fortified by this rebellion, demanded a Coalition, and insisted that Chamberlain should not lead it.

On May 10 Hitler invaded Holland, Belgium and France. That afternoon Chamberlain resigned, and Churchill became Prime Minister, at the head of a Coalition Government. Within a week the Germans had broken through the French and Belgian defences. 'We are living in anxious times', Rumbold wrote to his son on May 18, 'and the battle now going on is like a sword of Damocles suspended over one's head.' The Churchill Government met with his approval. 'Thank God he has side-tracked Simon',[1] he wrote. For three weeks the German advance continued. Holland was overrun and Belgium surrendered. At the beginning of June the British Expeditionary Force had to be evacuated from the beaches of Dunkirk, and brought back to Britain. This sequence of disasters did not break the British morale; rather, it strengthened it. 'This nation can afford to be told the truth', Rumbold wrote to his brother on June 5, 'and is all the better for it. We have at last got a Government of thrusters and energetic men. We could not have gone on with the old gang who never understood Germany.'

On June 16 General Pétain[2] became Prime Minister of France, and at once sought an armistice with Germany; Britain was alone. 'We are still amazed by the subservience of the Pétain Government', Rumbold wrote to his son on July 7. 'Never has a great country sunk so low. . . . The reaction in this country to the French collapse was practically unanimous: 'Thank God that we are now quit of foreigners and doubtful allies and are on our own.' Everybody felt that we had been let down by one nation after another and had lost valuable lives in the process. I have become definitely anti-foreign. . . .'

Throughout July the British awaited a German invasion. Rumbold was confident that, if invasion came, Hitler would have to fight for every mile. 'It is annoying that he should still have the initiative', he wrote to his son on July 23, 'the day will come, however, when we shall have numerical superiority in the air and that day will come sooner than many think. What I hope will then happen is that we shall systematically blot out one town after the other in Western Germany, extending our operations eastwards. If I know anything about German psychology, the

---

[1] On May 12, 1940, Sir John Simon, the Chancellor of the Exchequer, was appointed Lord Chancellor, an office which Churchill excluded from the War Cabinet.

[2] Henri Philippe Benoni Omer Joseph Pétain, 1856–1951. Commanded an Infantry Regiment, August 1914; an Army Corps, October 1914; the 2nd Army, June 1915. In charge at the siege of Verdun, 1916. Chief of the General Staff, April 1917. Commander-in-Chief, May 1917–November 1918. Vice-President of the Supreme War Council, 1920–30. War Minister, 1934. Ambassador to Madrid, 1939 40. Prime Minister, June 16, 1940; he negotiated the armistice with Germany, June 22, 1940. Chief of State, 1940–44. Condemned to death after the liberation of France, August 14, 1945; the sentence was commuted to life imprisonment.

Germans will then cry for mercy. They killed some 30,000 people in Rotterdam.[1] Let us give them a taste of their own medicine. Do not let us be mealy-mouthed.'

Since the outbreak of war Rumbold had been at work on a volume of reminiscences. Several publishers had asked him to write an account of his whole career, but he decided to write instead of his experiences in Berlin in 1914. His detailed notes of the crisis, which he had written down in the first month of the war, provided the book with its outline and its chronology. Rumbold consulted the published British, German and Austrian documents, and the memoirs which had appeared between the wars. The result was a volume of 373 pages, *The War Crisis in Berlin July–August 1914*. The book was widely reviewed and well-received, showing, according to Harold Nicolson,[2] 'by what gradations of ill-intention, weakness and misunderstanding great wars arise'. In the August issue of *The Nineteenth Century and After*, Philip Conwell-Evans, once a strong supporter of Nazi Germany, praised Rumbold's 'flair for perceiving and countering the wiles of his opponent' and, in the course of his review recalled how, when he himself had been in Berlin in 1933, 'it was rumoured that the Chancellor, Hitler, shrinking before Rumbold's vigorous protests against the persecution of the Jews, took refuge in hysterical bawling with his hair falling over his eyebrows – behaviour hardly likely to impress the Ambassador who, for all his vitality and energy, has always insisted on preserving the decencies and conventions of social life.'

At the end of July Rumbold fell ill, and had to go to Harrogate to recuperate. 'I was, and still am, very much out of condition', he wrote to his brother on August 15, 'and felt extremely tired.' At the beginning of September he returned to London. The German blitz had begun. 'We all sleep in the basement . . .', he wrote to his brother on September 15, 'I sleep on a sort of trestle bed under the arch of a passage leading to the area. The basement is really as good as a shelter. A direct hit would, of course, do us in.'

Early in September Rumbold had been asked by the Foreign Office to go on a special diplomatic mission to South America. Passages were found on board ship for himself, his wife and his daughter. 'We three are not keen to go', he wrote to his brother in his letter of September 15. 'We feel that we shall be cut off from news at a moment of supreme

---

[1] On May 14 the Germans had bombed the centre of Rotterdam, killing 940 people. Two hours later the city surrendered. At the time the figure of 30,000 dead was believed to be true. Only after the war did more accurate figures emerge.

[2] In his introduction to the second (1944) edition of Rumbold's book.

importance to the country. However, one must play up during a war.' But within two weeks the mission was cancelled. German submarines torpedoed the *City of Benares* in the mid-Atlantic, and 600 refugee children were drowned. Rumbold decided that he could not risk the lives of his wife and daughter. 'As Ethel absolutely refused to let me go alone', he explained to his brother on September 28, 'I chucked the whole thing. . . . I was never very keen on the job and the only thing I regret is the prospect of a warm winter and seeing Chile again. So we remain here to face the bombs.'

The bombing of London continued without respite throughout October. 'Our neighbourhood is now getting very lively', Rumbold wrote to his brother on October 9, 'but a miss is as good as a mile.' And on October 20 he wrote again: 'Clubland has suffered severely what with the Carlton, Reform and several other Clubs. Whitehall has also got it in the neck. The Treasury is a sight. The majority of the FO windows are no more. Leicester Square is bad. St James' Church in Piccadilly has been ruined, likewise two houses immediately opposite it. There is much damage in Lowndes Street. . . .' Philip Conwell-Evans later recalled: 'During the blitz, I took courage from Rumbold. He was sitting by the window of the Travellers' Club as the bombs were falling in Piccadilly Circus. He didn't budge from the window.'

His one hope, Rumbold wrote to his brother in his letter of October 20, was that 'we shall soon get busy with Berlin and destroy the centre of the town'. On November 15, after the centre of Coventry had been destroyed, and the Cathedral gutted by a German raid, he wrote to his brother: 'I would like to see the whole of the available RAF bombing force sent to raid Nuremberg and destroy that town completely.' But for the time being it was Britain alone that suffered. 'The new underground station in Sloane Square was demolished by an aerial torpedo', he wrote to his brother on the following day. 'As there were two trains in the station at the time some 30 people were killed. A little further afield the Naval & Military Club has been wrecked by a direct hit. . . . Some underground lavatories at the corner of Green Park, Piccadilly and the Ritz have also been destroyed, with considerable loss of life.' But Rumbold still saw a chance of victory. If Hitler could not break Britain's spirit by the spring, he wrote to his son on December 7, 'he never will'.

On December 12, Lord Lothian, whom Chamberlain had sent to Washington as Ambassador, died. There was much speculation about his successor. Churchill thought first of sending Vansittart; then, to the Foreign Office's alarm, he proposed Lloyd George. A dozen other names were suggested, including Rumbold's. 'Oh, dear Horace', Lady

Desborough[1] wrote on December 16, 'how profoundly we all wish that you would go as Ambassador to Washington. You would be so far better than anyone.' But on December 22 Churchill offered the post to Lord Halifax; indeed, forced it upon him, much to his annoyance, and Anthony Eden replaced Halifax as Foreign Secretary.

At the beginning of 1941 Rumbold was taken seriously ill with heart trouble. In April he had to give up his Chairmanship of the 'Black List Committee', and go to a nursing home near Maidenhead. He looked forward to the end of the war, and to the chance, as soon as it was over, of a long cruise in the sun. But it was not to be. On May 24 he died.

In the aftermath of Rumbold's death, his widow received several hundred letters of condolence. 'I have always deplored', wrote Anthony Eden, 'and always shall, the decision that moved Sir Horace from Berlin, when he was doing such wonderful service. No one ever had a clearer perspective of the dangers, & his dispassionate but far-seeing analysis of things to come should have earned the reward of a fuller understanding at home.' He represented, wrote Harold Nicolson, 'a standard of integrity, intelligence and fair-mindedness and courage which was higher than that of most people. . . . What a great & good man he was.' No man, wrote Lord Hardinge, 'ever did his duty more loyally and unselfishly than Horace'. Colonel Christie, the former Air Attaché in Berlin, wrote to Constantia Rumbold of how her father had done his job 'without seeking power positions, limelight, bauble & lucre'. On June 3 Brüning wrote to Lady Rumbold, from his exile at Harvard, that had Rumbold been allowed to remain in Berlin after 1933 'the whole trend of politics would have been very different and many of the terrible events through which the world is passing could have been avoided'. He added: 'I have not hesitated to express this opinion very frankly whenever I have been in England during the years of my exile.'

Rumbold had served in the Diplomatic Service for forty-two years. His Englishness was complete to the point of caricature. His political opinions were stoutly conservative, his attitude to foreigners detached and sceptical. He disliked dictatorship wherever he found it, despite his own extreme opinions on many issues. He was a precise and cautious person, not given to exaggeration or panic. In moments of crisis he was invariably calm. He

[1] Ethel Anne Priscilla Fane, 1867–1952. Co-heiress to the Barony of Butler. She married William Henry Grenfell (later 1st Baron Desborough) in 1887. Two of their three sons were killed in the First World War, their third son in a motor-car accident in 1926. A distant relative of Lady Rumbold, the Rumbolds were often guests at her home in Hertfordshire.

formed his judgments with deliberation, and defended them without excitement. His reports were always detailed, factual and terse. In negotiation, he was thorough and firm. To foreigners he gave the impression of passivity, even stupidity. But those who worked with him realized the extent of his understanding, and of his feelings. He did not muffle his opinions, or accept uncritically the policy prevailing in London. To a succession of Foreign Secretaries, including Sir Edward Grey, Lord Curzon, Ramsay MacDonald, Austen Chamberlain and Sir John Simon, he sent the information and sounded the alarms which he believed to be necessary. He had devoted his life to interpreting events in foreign countries, and had become accepted as a master of his profession.

List of Sources

List of sources quoted verbatim in this volume, other than those in the Rumbold papers:

page
72   Rumbold to Grey, 15 Feb 1909. Foreign Office papers 371/670
72   Rumbold to Grey, 12 Jan 1909. FO 371/671
77   Rumbold to Grey, 30 May 1909. FO 371/689: No 148
77   Rumbold to Grey, 31 May 1909. FO 371/690: No 150
78   Information enclosed with Rumbold's despatch of 3 June 1909. FO 371/796: No 154
87   Rumbold to Cromer, 17 Dec 1910. Cromer papers, FO 633/14
92   Rumbold to Grey, 17 July 1911. FO 371/1140: No 209
97   Rumbold to Grey, 20 Feb 1913 (received in London 2½ weeks later). FO 371/1663: No 46
135   Lord Newton's diary, 5 May 1916. Newton papers
135   Lord Newton's diary, 10 Aug 1916. Newton papers
140   Rumbold to Balfour, 1 Feb 1917. FO 371/2939: No 78
140   Rumbold to Balfour, 3 Feb 1917. FO 371/2939: No 73
140   Rumbold to Balfour, 6 Feb 1917. FO 371/2939: No 94
140   Rumbold to Balfour, 10 Feb 1917. FO 371/2939: No 109
141   Rumbold to the Foreign Office, 13 Feb 1917. FO 371/2939: No 115
141   Rumbold to the Foreign Office, 23 Feb 1917. FO 371/2939: No 154
142   Rumbold to the Foreign Office, 14 March 1917. FO 371/2939: No 215
143   Rumbold to Balfour, 24 May 1918. FO 371/3278: No 414
143   Rumbold to Balfour, 30 July 1918. FO 371/3278: No 581
148   Rumbold to the Foreign Office, 3 April 1917. FO 371/3009: No 278
148   Rumbold to the Foreign Office, 13 April 1917. FO 371/3009: No 289
159   Rumbold to Balfour, 5 April 1917, FO 371/2863: unnumbered
160   Rumbold to Balfour, 29 Oct 1917. FO 371/3007: No 135
161   Rumbold to the Foreign Office, 12 May 1917. FO 371/3050: No 309
161   Rumbold to Lord Robert Cecil, 7 June 1917. FO 371/3050: No 378
162   Rumbold to the Foreign Office, 15 June 1917. FO 371/3057: No 497
162   Rumbold to Balfour, 30 June 1917. FO 371/3057: No 542
162   Lord Robert Cecil, Minute of 8 July 1917. FO 371/3057
162   Rumbold to Balfour, 24 July 1917. FO 371/3057: unnumbered
163   Rumbold to the Foreign Office, 17 Nov 1917. FO 371/3057: No 1103
166   Rumbold to the Foreign Office, 27 Nov 1917. FO 371/2864: Nos 1157 and 1158
175   Rumbold to Balfour, 14 Aug 1918. FO 371/3133: No 615
176   Derby diary, 19 Oct 1918. Copy, Balfour papers
186   V. Cavendish-Bentinck: letter to the author, 10 Oct 1972
186   Rumbold to Balfour, 21 Jan 1917. FO 371/3007 (footnote)

191	Rumbold to Curzon, 19 Jan 1920. FO 688/3 : No 41 (draft)
193	Rumbold to Curzon, 17 Feb 1920. FO 688/3 : No 78 (draft)
196	Rumbold to Curzon, 12 May 1920. FO 688/3 : No 323 (draft)
213	Rumbold to Curzon, 28 Aug 1920. FO 688/2 : No 547 (draft)
217	Sir Henry Wilson diary, 27 Oct 1920: Wilson papers
218	Sir Anthony Rumbold: conversation with the author, 21 Feb 1972
231	Sir Henry Mack: letter to the author, 18 April 1972
231	Rumbold to Curzon, 4 Jan 1921. FO 371/6556 (footnote)
240	Rumbold to Oliphant, 6 June 1921. Oliphant papers, FO 800/253
244	Rumbold to Curzon, 9 Nov 1921. FO 371/6476
245	Rumbold to Curzon, 10 Nov 1921. FO 371/6536: No 718
245	Rumbold to Curzon, 11 Dec 1921. FO 371/6480: unnumbered
251	Rumbold to Curzon, 21 Nov 1921. FO 371/6535: No 738
251	Rumbold to Curzon, 24 Nov 1921. FO 371/6536: No 749
251	Rumbold to the Foreign Office, 22 Feb 1922. FO 371/7656: No 113
251	Rumbold to the Foreign Office, 27 Feb 1922. FO 371/7856: No 121
258	Rumbold to Curzon, 2 Sept 1922. FO 371/9887: No 780
260	Rumbold to Curzon, 12 Sept 1922. FO 371/7889: No 801
260	Rumbold to Curzon, 12 Sept 1922. FO 371/7889: No 806
260	Rumbold to Curzon, 19 Sept 1922. FO 371/7888: No 415
261	Rumbold to Curzon, 17 Sept 1922. FO 371/7888: No 425
263	Rumbold to Curzon, 20 Sept 1922. FO 371/7891: No 440
270	Rumbold to Curzon, 28 Sept 1922. FO 371/7894: No 465
270	Rumbold to Curzon, 9 Oct 1922. FO 371/7903: No 882 (footnote)
270	Rumbold to Curzon, 6 Oct 1922. FO 371/7899: No 524
273	Rumbold to Curzon, 11 Oct 1922. FO 371/7902: No 554
273	Rumbold to Curzon, 14 Oct 1922. FO 371/7903: No 564
289	Rumbold to Curzon, 24 April 1923. FO 371/9075: No 6
289	Rumbold to Curzon, 26 April 1923. FO 371/9075
289	Rumbold to Curzon, 5 May 1923. FO 371/9076: No 35
290	Rumbold to Curzon, 17 May 1923. FO 371/9077: No 67
291	Rumbold to Curzon, 24 May 1923. FO 371/9078: No 96
291	Nevile Henderson to Curzon, 28 May 1923. FO 371/9097: No 318
293	Rumbold to Curzon, 28 May 1923. FO 371/9097: unnumbered
294	Rumbold to Curzon, 20 (30) June 1923. FO 371/9084: No 236
294	Rumbold to Curzon, 3 July 1923. FO 371/9085: No 245
294	Rumbold to Curzon, 4 July 1923. FO 371/9085: No 249
295	Rumbold to Curzon, 9 July 1923. FO 371/9086: No 263
296	Rumbold to Curzon, 13 July 1923. FO 371/9086: No 268
296	Curzon to Rumbold, 19 July 1923. FO 371/9088: No 297
314	The Hon. Herbert Brooks: conversation with the author, 5 May 1972
318	Harold Nicolson to his wife, 4 Aug 1928. Nicolson papers
319	Harold Nicolson to his wife, 18 Sept 1928. Nicolson papers
322	Rumbold to the Foreign Office, 28 Sept 1928. FO 371/12889 (enclosing Col. Cornwall's Report)

323 De Bunsen to his wife, 21 April 1929. De Bunsen papers
324 Harold Nicolson to his wife, 23 May 1929. Nicolson papers
325 Harold Nicolson to his wife, 27 June 1929. Nicolson papers
325 Harold Nicolson to his wife, 2 Sept 1929. Nicolson papers
327 Christie to Rumbold, 27 Dec 1929. FO 371/13635: 202–204
335 Rumbold to Arthur Henderson, 9 Oct 1930. FO 371/14372 (enclosing Marshall-Cornwall's Report)
335 Marshall-Cornwall's Report of 16 Oct 1930. FO 371/14372: No 386
348 Rumbold to Simon, 4 April 1932. FO 371/15942: No 232
351 Sir James Marshall-Cornwall: conversation with the author, 19 April 1972 (footnote)
352 *ibid.*
355 Marshall-Cornwall to Rumbold, 18 Jan 1932. FO 371/15942: No 729
355 Rumbold to Simon, 19 Jan 1932. FO 371/15942: No 729
359 Colonel Peter Thorne: conversation with the author, 11 May 1972 (footnote)
362 Orme Sargent minute, 14 Sept 1932. FO 371/15950
364 Thorne to Rumbold, 29 Sept 1932. FO 371/15950: No 743
369 Herring to Rumbold, 16 Feb 1933. FO 371/16732
369 Rumbold to Simon, 16 March 1933. FO 371/16732: No 51 (footnote)
377 Thorne to Rumbold, 25 April 1933. FO 371/16707
382 Douglas Reed: letter to the author, 26 March 1964
382 Sir James Bowker: conversation with the author, 19 May 1972
382 Timothy Breen: letter to the author, 21 March 1963
383 André François-Poncet: letter to the author, 25 Feb 1964
383 Colonel Peter Thorne: conversation with the author, 11 May 1972 (footnote)
384 Rumbold to Simon, 27 June 1933. FO 371/16733
384 Herring to Rumbold, 20 June 1933. FO 371/16733
384 Herring's Memorandum of 21 June 1933. FO 371/16733
384 Group-Captain Herring: conversation with the author, 30 June 1972
396 Rumbold to Lothian, 21 April 1936. Lothian papers
396 Dawson to Lothian, 23 April 1937. Lothian papers
396 Rumbold to Dawson, undated. Geoffrey Dawson papers
400 Wauchope to the Colonial Office, 22 May 1936. Colonial Office papers 733/318
400 Ormsby-Gore to Wauchope, 10 June 1936. CO 733/318
400 Ormsby-Gore to Halifax, (early) July 1936. CO 733/319
402 Rumbold to Ormsby-Gore, 16 July 1936. CO 733/319
402 Ormsby-Gore to Wauchope, 20 July 1936. CO 733/319
402 H. R. Foyle to John Martin, 12 Aug 1936. CO 733/319
403 Lourie to Martin, 19 Aug 1936. CO 733/318
403 Lord Peel to John Martin, 25 Aug 1936. CO 733/318
403 John Martin to his mother, 10 Nov 1936. Martin papers
407 Vera Weizmann diary, 26 Nov 1936. Weizmann papers
414 J. Iusman: conversation with the author, 19 Oct 1972
415 Lord Peel to Ormsby-Gore, 1 Dec 1936. CO 733/319
415 John Martin to his mother, 20 Dec 1936. Martin papers
416 Sir John Hathorn Hall: conversation with the author, 11 May 1972

419   John Martin to his mother, 3 Jan 1937. Martin papers

419   Sir John Hall; conversation with the author, 11 May 1972

424   John Martin to H. A. Foyle, 13 Feb 1937. CO 733/342

424   Weizmann to the Peel Commission, 19 Jan 1937. CO 733/342

425   Wedgewood evidence, 11 Feb 1937. CO 733/342

425   Lloyd George evidence, March 1937. CO 733/342

425   Churchill evidence, 12 March 1937. Copy, Churchill papers 2/317

426   Churchill to Peel, 16 March 1937. Copy, Churchill papers 2/317

433   Sir M. Hankey to Sir H. Wilson, 15 March 1938. Cabinet papers 21/540

434   Rumbold to Londonderry, 12 April 1938. Copy, Halifax papers: FO 800/316

434   Londonderry to Halifax, 26 April 1938. Halifax papers: FO 800/316

434   Halifax to Londonderry, (27) April 1938. Halifax papers: FO 800/316 (draft)

434   Rumbold to Londonderry, 12 April 1938. Montgomery Hyde papers

435   Rumbold to Londonderry, 28 April 1938. Montgomery Hyde papers

443   Rumbold to Halifax, 28 March 1939. Halifax papers: FO 800/315

444   Rumbold to Halifax, 1 July 1939. Halifax papers: FO 800/316

446   J. L. Reading: letter to the author, 20 March 1972

449   Rumbold to Nevile Henderson, 15 April 1940. Henderson papers: FO 800/270

Index

Compiled by the author